Facebook® Marketing ALL-IN-ONE

FOR DUMMIES®

A Wiley Brand

3rd Edition

by Andrea Vahl
John Haydon
Jan Zimmerman

FOR DUMMIES®
A Wiley Brand

Facebook® Marketing All-in-One For Dummies®, 3rd Edition

Published by
John Wiley & Sons, Inc.
111 River Street
Hoboken, NJ 07030-5774
www.wiley.com

Copyright © 2014 by John Wiley & Sons, Inc., Hoboken, New Jersey

Published by John Wiley & Sons, Inc., Hoboken, New Jersey

Published simultaneously in Canada

Table of Contents

Introduction *1*

    About This Book 1

    Foolish Assumptions.. 2

    Icons Used in This Book 2

    How This Book is Organized 3

        Book I: Joining the Facebook Marketing Revolution 3

        Book II: Claiming Your Presence on Facebook.................. 3

        Book III: Adding the Basics to Your Facebook Page 4

        Book IV: Building, Engaging, Retaining, and Selling
           to Your Community 4

        Book V: Understanding Facebook Applications.................. 4

        Book VI: Making Facebook Come Alive with Events
           and Contests 4

        Book VII: Facebook Advertising 4

        Book VIII: Advanced Facebook Marketing Tactics 5

        Book IX: Measuring, Monitoring, and Analyzing................ 5

    Beyond the Book 5

    Where to Go from Here... 6

Book I: Joining the Facebook Marketing Revolution *7*

Chapter 1: Exploring Facebook Marketing 9

    Seeing the Business Potential of Facebook........................... 9

        Asking yourself what you're after 10

        Using Facebook to your advantage 10

        Reaping the benefits for business-to-consumer companies........... 11

        Reaping the benefits for business-to-business companies............. 14

        Developing genuine relationships with customers
           and prospects 15

        Creating one-to-one customer engagement...................... 15

        Providing prompt customer service 16

        Creating a shopping portal 18

    Using Facebook with the Global Market.............................. 19

    Understanding Facebook Marketing Basics 20

        Marketing on your Page and your Profile........................... 20

        Developing your Page to be a hub of activity 21

        Understanding privacy options 22

        Keeping things professional but personal.......................... 25

Chapter 2: Creating Your Facebook Marketing Plan 27

Defining Your Ideal Audience on Facebook 27
    Identifying the demographics of your ideal audience 28
    Understanding the psychographics of your ideal audience 28
Finding Your Ideal Audience inside Facebook 29
    Filtering Facebook Search results 31
    Using Facebook Ads to research your ideal audience 32
Identifying Your Facebook Marketing Plan's Core Goals 35
    Defining your Facebook marketing goals 35
    Deciding on a social media budget 36
    Deciding whether a Facebook Ads campaign is right for you 36
Rules for Successful Facebook Pages 37
    Rule #1: Be deliberate, and manage expectations 37
    Rule #2: Focus on smart branding 38
    Rule #3: Create fresh content 39
    Rule #4: Give your Page a human touch 40
    Rule #5: Cultivate engagement with two-way dialog 42
    Rule #6: Encourage fan-to-fan conversations 42
    Rule #7: Make word-of-mouth advocacy easy 43
    Rule #8: Create consistent calls to action 43
    Rule #9: Monitor, measure, and track 44
    Summing up the nine rules 44
Setting Up Resources and Manpower for Your Plan 45
    Identifying your existing resources and manpower 45
    Deciding on in-house or outsourced marketing 46
Defining Your Admin Team 48
    Filling the five admin roles 49
    Adding an admin 49
    Deleting an admin 51
    Choosing the right Page manager 51
    Considering a social media manager 52
    Coordinating admin posts and strategies 53
Measuring Your Return on Investment 54
    Defining success 54
    Measuring brand ROI 55
    Measuring financial ROI 55

Book II: Claiming Your Presence on Facebook 57

Chapter 1: Understanding Facebook Pages and Personal Accounts 59

Reviewing Facebook Pages and Account Types 60
Navigating Your Personal Profile Timeline and the Follow Button 60
    Creating a personal Profile 61
    Turning on the Follow button 63
    Talking about the Ticker 65

Getting Down to Business..66
Making a Places Page 68
Creating a Facebook Group..71
Setting Up an Interest Page 72

Chapter 2: Creating Your Business Page.....................77

Considering a Few Things before You Start.............................77
    Choosing the right name for your business Page...........78
    Choosing the right type of business Page 79
Setting Up Your New Business Page 81
    Creating a business Page 81
    Opening your page...83
    Unpublish your Page 85
Completing, Publishing, and Promoting Your Page....................86
    Getting your Facebook images right 87
    Completing the Info Page 91
    Adding Facebook-built apps.....................................93
    Adding custom apps...94
    Posting status updates..96
    Publishing your Page..97
    Editing and adding milestones..................................97
    Inviting your Facebook Friends..................................99
    Inviting e-mail contacts 100
    Sharing your Page..102
    Promoting this Page on your website 104
    Setting up your mobile phone..................................105
Claiming a Facebook Place..106
Merging a Facebook Place with Your Page 108
Managing Missteps...110
    Creating personal Profiles with a business name..........110
    Sorting out or deleting a personal Profile set up as a business........110
    Changing your business Page type or name 113

Chapter 3: Administering Your Facebook Business Page 115

Viewing Facebook as Your Page...115
    Liking other Pages as your Page...............................118
    Changing voice preferences 119
    Touring the Admin panel..119
Understanding How Other People See Your Page.....................123
    Cover photo..124
    Featured apps...125
    Profile image..126
    Friends (Mutual connections)..................................126
    About section 126
    The numbers 127
    The likes..129
    Message button...130
    Drop-down menus on Pages.....................................130

Editing Your Page 132
Edit Settings 135
Admin Roles 138
Apps 140
Audience Suggestions 140
Featured 140
Mobile 142
Use Activity Log 143
See Banned Users 143
Build Audience 144
See Insights 144
Help 144

Chapter 4: Arranging What Your Visitors See................... 145

Finding Your Page 145
Understanding How Apps Act as Navigation Links 147
Adding Facebook Apps to Your Page 148
Events app 149
Photos app 150
Notes app 152
Video app 154
Changing the Order of Apps on Your Page 155
Using the Hover Card as an Ad 156

Chapter 5: Using Your Personal Profile to Support Your Business . . . 159

Determining Whether the Follow Button Is Right for You 159
Turning On Your Follow Button 162
Editing the Follow Settings 164
Seeing How to Post Publicly 165
Marketing Basics with a Personal Profile 167
Understanding Friend Followers and Public Followers 169
Adding Public Life Events to Your Personal Profile 171
Adjusting Your Timeline for Public Viewing 172
Uploading a Cover Photo that Supports Your Business 174

Book III: Adding the Basics to Your Facebook Page 175

Chapter 1: Posting to Your Page 177

Posting Updates to Your Timeline via the Publisher 177
How long to make your post 178
How often to post an update 179
What types of material to include 179
Including Attachments 180
Updating status and posting links 181
Attaching photos 183

Attaching video 186
Scheduling posts 188
Adding events 189
Adding milestones 189
Using Facebook Offers 191
Targeting Your Updates by Location and Language 192
Boosting posts 194
Pinning and highlighting posts 194

Chapter 2: Facebook Apps 101 197

Defining Apps and Understanding Facebook Installed Apps 197
Adding an App to Your Page 201
Rearranging the Positions of Your Apps 203
Deleting an App from Your Page 204
Customizing the App Title and App Photo 204
Finding Apps in Your Page Dashboard 205

Chapter 3: Importing Your Blog Posts into Your Facebook Page 207

Getting the Address of Your RSS Feed 207
On Internet Explorer 208
On Firefox 208
In HTML code 209
Introducing the Facebook Blog-Import Applications 210
Using the NetworkedBlogs Application 210
Registering your blog on NetworkedBlogs 211
Verifying ownership of your blog 213
Setting up syndication 215
Reposting a blog post with NetworkedBlogs 216
Adding the NetworkedBlogs tab to your Facebook Page 217
Installing Social RSS 218
Using Social RSS 220
Deciding when to upgrade to paid service 221
Using RSS Graffiti 221
Using the dlvr.it Tool 224

Chapter 4: Connecting Your Page to Twitter 229

To Connect or Not to Connect 229
Connecting Facebook and Twitter 230
Linking your Facebook Page to Twitter 230
Seeing what happens to too-long tweets 233
Using HootSuite to Update Facebook 234
Using Other Posting Applications 237
SocialOomph 238
Buffer 238
Sprout Social 239
Adding a Twitter Tab to Your Facebook Page 240

Chapter 5: The Fine Print: Legal and Other Considerations **243**

Digesting Legal Considerations 243
Understanding U.S. Regulations on Testimonials and Reviews 245
Meeting Content Compliance for Certain Industries 248

Book IV: Building, Engaging, Retaining, and Selling to Your Community 251

Chapter 1: Building Visibility for Your Page **253**

Inviting Your Existing Customers and Connections to Your Page 254
    Changing your hold message 254
    Adding your Page address to your e-mail signature 255
    Including your new Facebook address on hard
      copy mailings 258
    Updating your letterhead and stationery 259
    Including a Facebook icon on your web page 259
    Linking to your Page from your Profile 260
    Inviting your other social networks to visit your Page 262
    Growing your Page manually or buying automatic fans 263
Sharing Your Page with Your Friends on Facebook 263
    Inviting Facebook Friends to your Page 264
    Sharing your Page 265
    Sending requests to promote your Page 268
    Finding and thanking your key enthusiasts 269
Adding Photos to Attract People to Your Page 269
    Creating a marketing strategy with your Cover photo 270
    Creating a marketing strategy with photo albums 270
    Uploading photos to your Facebook Page 271
    Sharing your albums and photos 273
    Sharing with people other than your personal Friends
      on Facebook 275

Chapter 2: Engaging and Retaining Your Community **277**

Creating Posts and Updates That Engage Your Readers 278
    Asking questions 279
    Giving away something 279
    Promoting your fans and enthusiasts 280
    Tagging key players in updates 280
    Using public posts to thank people 282
    Creating a posting schedule 283
    Targeting your posts to be seen 284
    Understanding the News Feed Algorithm 285
    Using News Feed optimization strategies 286

Creating and Participating in Conversations with Your Audience 287
    Optimize the settings for posts to your Timeline 287
    Understanding the different views people see on your Page 288
    Being responsive and allowing conversation 289
Keeping the Conversation Civil 290
    Reporting a poster 290
    Remembering that users can block your posts too 292

Chapter 3: Using Like Links and Buttons 295

Comparing the Like Button and Like Link 295
Answering Common Questions 296
Placing the Like Button Code 302
Generating the Code for a Like Button 303

Chapter 4: Expanding Your E-Commerce Products and Services 307

Understanding Facebook e-Commerce 308
Using the Featured Apps Space for Your Store 308
    Posting product images 309
    Posting off-Facebook URLs 310
    Posting an offer 310
Using PayPal to Accept Payment 310
Finding e-Commerce Apps That Fit Your Needs 311
    Storenvy 311
    Ecwid 312
    ShopTab 313
    Etsy 313
Installing a Facebook e-Commerce App 314
Creating a Link to Your Website Store on Your Page 315
Using Other Apps to Create a Custom Link for Your Storefront 315
    ShortStack 315
    TabSite 316
    Heyo 316
    BandPage 316
Posting Facebook Offers 317

Chapter 5: Building Visibility for Your Timeline 319

Inviting People to Follow Instead of Friend 320
Connecting Your Timeline to Your Offline World 320
Creating a Cover Photo Strategy 321
Making Photo Albums Public 322
    Making a new Public album 323
    Making an existing album Public 324
Using Life Events to Support Your Business 325
Adjusting and Adding Apps 326
    Moving apps 326
    Choosing apps 326

Book V: Understanding Facebook Applications 329

Chapter 1: Customizing Your Page with Facebook Apps 331

Understanding How Facebook Users Make Use of Apps 331
Introducing Apps Developed by Facebook 332
Finding and Adding Apps to Your Page 335
Deleting Apps from Your Page 337
Using Apps for Marketing 337
    Contact forms and e-mail forms 338
    Discussion board apps 338
    Video apps 339
    Pinterest apps 340
    Google+ 340
    Social RSS 340
    Other apps 341
    Facebook mobile app 342

Chapter 2: Using iFrame Apps to Create Custom Tabs 343

Looking at Tabs 344
Defining iFrames 345
Outlining the Options 346
    Building an iFrame application 346
    Hiring someone to build the application for you 347
    Using a third-party application 348
Exploring the Facebook Developers Site 348
Becoming a Verified Facebook Developer 349
    Verifying with a mobile phone number 350
    Verifying with a credit card 351
Creating an iFrame Application 351
    Making the iFrame app 352
    Installing the iFrame application on your Facebook Page 355
Using Third-Party Applications 356
    Heyo 357
    Static HTML for Pages 358
    ShortStack 360
    Static HTML: iFrame Tabs 361
    TabSite 363
    FanPageEngine 364

Book VI: Making Facebook Come Alive with Events and Contests 365

Chapter 1: Creating Facebook Events 367

Getting Started with Facebook Events 367
Showing Your Facebook Events in Different Places 369

Adding the Events app to your Page 372
Entering the event details..375
Synching events with your personal calendar 378
Editing your event...378
Canceling your event 380
Uncovering Limitations of Facebook Events.........................380
Promoting an Event...381
Inviting your community to your event 381
Encouraging interaction within your Facebook Event.................386
Sharing your Facebook Event outside Facebook..........387

Chapter 2: Building Excitement with a Contest 389
Thinking about Running a Contest?..389
Deciding What You Want from a Contest...............................391
Choosing a Contest Type...393
Understanding Facebook and Legal Restrictions.................397
Defining Success 398
Setting targets 398
Setting your plan..399

Chapter 3: Running a Timeline Contest 401
Preparing for Your Timeline Contest.....................................401
Understanding the rules 402
Assembling the parts...403
Administering Your Timeline Contest 408
Editing your post 408
Sharing your contest 408
Promoting Your Timeline Contest...411
Selecting a Lucky Winner 412
Exporting data with Contest Capture............................412
Using Woobox to pick a winner 414

Chapter 4: Using Third-Party Contest Applications 417
Finding a Contest Application..417
Comparing Contest Applications on the Web.......................418
Getting to Know the Contest Applications 420
Exploring TabSite...420
Looking at Heyo 421
Investigating Woobox...421
Understanding Offerpop 422
Delivering the Prizes 422
Budgeting for an App 422
Designing Your Contest with the TabSite Application 423
Signing up for TabSite 423
Creating a sweepstakes with TabSite.............................424
Using the Heyo Application for Your Sweepstakes.............431

Using the Woobox Sweepstakes Application...433
Signing up for Woobox...434
Adding a sweepstakes..434
Customize your sweepstakes...436
Choosing a payment plan...437
Adding the sweepstakes to your Page...438
Using the Offerpop Application..439
Signing up for Offerpop..439
Publishing a sweepstakes...440
Adjusting the App's Photo...443
Editing the position of the app..443
Editing the cover photo and title of an app.................................444

Chapter 5: Promoting Your Contest and Analyzing the Results.....447

Setting Up a Blog Tour..447
Promoting Your Contest on Your Blog or Website..............................449
Using Facebook Open Graph to Allow Entries Anywhere
on the Web...451
Using Social Media to Promote Your Contest......................................452
Twitter..453
LinkedIn..454
YouTube...454
Using Facebook to Promote an External Contest................................455
Analyzing Your Contest Results...456
Using analytics within third-party contest applications..............456
Monitoring community growth and tracking
Facebook Insights..458
Adjusting Your Strategy Based on Analytics..459
Planning Future Contests...461
Mapping out your contests for the year.......................................461
Watching for successful contest ideas..462

Book VII: Facebook Advertising................................... 467

Chapter 1: Advertising in Facebook............................469

Introducing Facebook Advertising...469
Understanding auction bidding...470
Setting a flat fee to promote a post..471
Paying a premium price..471
Targeting your ads strategically..471
Grasping the Anatomy of Facebook Ads...475
Advertising by objective...476
Promoting posts...477
Advertising on Facebook versus other platforms........................477
Comparing CTR and conversion rates..478

Defining Types of Ads 479
        Looking at Promoted posts in more detail 480
        Structuring ad campaigns strategically 482
        Knowing what you can't advertise 483
    Identifying Your Goals 484
        Gaining connections 484
        Acquiring leads 488
        Reconnecting with your community 489
    Making Your Initial Decisions 490
        Allocating a budget 490
        Rotating your ad 490
        Setting a time frame 490

Chapter 2: Creating a Facebook Ad. 493
    Getting Started with the Ads Create Tool 493
    Identifying Your Internal or External Ad Objectives 496
        Building your internal market 496
        Building your outside market 499
    Making an Ad Work 502
        Selecting images 502
        Editing text and links 504
    Targeting Your Audience 508
        Locations 508
        Demographics 508
        Interests 512
        Behaviors 513
        More Categories 514
        Connections 514
    Setting Up Your Account and Campaign Page 514
        Filling Out the Account and Campaign section 514
        Completing the Bidding and Pricing section 517
    Crossing the Finish Line 518
        Placing your order 518
        Getting your ads approved 519

Chapter 3: Exploring Power Editor 521
    Deciding Whether Power Editor Is for You 521
    Enabling Power Editor 522
    Navigating Power Editor 524
    Campaigning in Power Editor 526
        Creating and importing a campaign from Excel 527
        Creating ad sets in Power Editor 528
        Creating an ad in Power Editor 530
        Modifying existing campaigns, ad sets, or ads 532
        Editing Campaigns, Ad Sets, and Ads with Excel 532
        Managing multiple items with the Manage Ads drop-down 533

Using Power Editor to Create and Promote Posts 534
    Creating a post in Power Editor...535
    Promoting a post from Power Editor 537
Pinpointing Your Ideal Audience...538
    Reaching your ideal audience with Facebook
        and Partner Categories...538
    Reaching existing customers and prospects with
        Custom Audiences 540
Optimizing Ad Bids in Power Editor 547
    Setting up manual bids...548
Optimizing Ads for Ideal Placement...549
Tracking Conversions 550

Chapter 4: Testing, Measuring, and Modifying Your Ad 553

Understanding the Ads Manager 553
    Notifications and Daily Spend 555
    Menus 556
    Categories 556
    Left sidebar 558
Adding a User to Your Facebook Ads Account................................559
Changing Your Attack Plan...562
Trying Out Split-Testing...562
    Split-testing your ad title and text 563
    Split-testing your ad images 564
    Split-testing your targeting 565
    Testing your landing page 567
Viewing Facebook Reports 567
    Setting up your report...568
    Decoding column headings for General Metrics....................571
    Customizing your report with Columns and Filters 572
    Adding filters 576
    Viewing Old Reports...578

Book VIII: Advanced Facebook Marketing Tactics 581

Chapter 1: An Introduction to Advanced Facebook Marketing 583

Remembering the Nine Core Facebook Marketing Rules 584
Creating a Facebook Experience 585
    Planning the experience...586
    Optimizing the experience...586
Building Social Proof with Facebook Ads...587
Experimenting with Custom Apps...588
Targeting Your Audience with Custom Lists 589
    Creating your custom lists...590
    Adding custom lists to your Favorites 591

Creating Interests Lists to Focus on the People Who
    Matter Most to Your Business...592
Using Facebook Offers for Your Local or Online Business 595
    Creating and promoting a Facebook offer 596
Expanding Your Page's Exposure...601
Engaging with Likes..601
Getting Viral Exposure..602
    Reaching a new audience with hashtags 602
    Watching the future: Autoplay video ads in News Feeds 603
    Follow your prospects through third-party
        retargeting services 604

Chapter 2: Marketing with Facebook Social Plug-ins 607
Understanding Facebook's Social Plug-ins.....................................607
    Explaining how plug-ins work 608
    Maximizing the value of Facebook plug-ins.........................609
Choosing the Right Facebook Plug-ins for Your Business 610
    Increasing site traffic with the Like Button plug-in........................611
    Using a Like Box plug-in to grow your Facebook base.................615
    Sharing selectively with the Share Button plug-in......................617
    Finding out more about your visitors with the Login tool 618
    Using a Recommendations Feed plug-in for social proof 620
    Offering smart suggestions with the Recommendations
        Bar plug-in 621
    Spotlighting your latest website content with the
        Activity Feed plug-in 622
    Optimizing the Comments plug-in 623
    Embedding Facebook posts on your website 625
    Attracting a larger audience with the Follow Button plug-in 625
    Sharing super-selectively with the Send Button plug-in..............627
    Optimizing your connections with Facepile............................627
Finding and Installing Open Source Facebook Plug-ins.........................629
    Installing a WordPress plug-in 629
    Using Share buttons for multiple social networks 630

Chapter 3: Discovering Live Video on Facebook 633
Understanding the Benefits of Live Video.......................................633
    Attracting viewers with chat 634
    Getting closer to customers 635
    Supplementing traditional advertising.................................635
Choosing Your Streaming Application...635
Streaming from Your Facebook Page with the Livestream
    Application...637
    Creating a Livestream account 637
    Creating an event in Livestream 639
    Installing the Livestream app on your Facebook Page 640

Streaming with Google Hangouts on Air with 22Social 644
Creating a Google Hangout on Air 644
Installing the 22Social app on your Page 644
Creating Buzz about Your Live Video..647
Posting to your Facebook Page in advance............................647
Sharing during your event 648
Sharing viewer comments with other social media 649
Partnering with other events and organizers 650

Chapter 4: Using Facebook for Mobile Marketing 653

Understanding the Rapid Growth of the Mobile World..........................653
Optimizing Your Facebook Presence for Users on the Move 656
Adjusting your Facebook posts for mobile users..........................656
Adjusting your Facebook Page for mobile madness 658
Getting your Facebook Page found in a mobile search..............660
Using Facebook Nearby 661
Taking Advantage of Facebook Mobile Ads 662
Displaying Facebook Ads in mobile News Feeds 662
Displaying Facebook Offers, Likes, and more in
mobile News Feeds 664
Setting up a mobile ad campaign in Facebook............................665
Measuring Your Mobile Success..668
Using Google Analytics to track mobile traffic............................669
Using Facebook's Ads Manager to measure ad results.................670

Book IX: Measuring, Monitoring, and Analyzing 673

Chapter 1: Setting Realistic Targets to Identify Success 675

Exploring Social Monitoring and Measuring...675
Knowing the Importance of Social Media Monitoring 676
Seeing why monitoring online conversations is important..........677
Understanding the importance of real-time engagement.............678
Monitoring the right way 680
Identifying your monitoring outcomes 681
Knowing the Importance of Social Media Measuring..............................682
Seeing why measuring online activity is important 682
Using Google Keyword Planner..683
Determining what you should measure for your ROI 684
Turning social activity into key metric indicators 686

Chapter 2: Exploring Facebook Insights 693

Getting Started with Insights..693
Accessing Insights data..694
Understanding the Overview display...695

Delving into Insights Details: Categories 697
  Tracking your Like activity 697
  Reach-ing for the Facebook stars 699
  Visiting the Visits tab 701
  Perusing the Posts tab 702
  Profiling your People 704
  Making sense of the numbers 705
Making Greater Use of Insights 706
  Exporting the data 706
  Evaluating the impact of your content 708
Evaluating Activity outside Facebook 710
Making Changes Based on Insights 711

**Chapter 3: Using Third-Party Monitoring Tools and
Analyzing Results. 715**

Choosing the Best Tool for Your Business 715
  User flexibility 716
  Ease of setup 716
  Ease of use 716
  Ease of reporting 716
  Cost 716
  Training and support 717
Choosing Monitoring Tools: Your Third-Party Options 717
  Bitly 717
  Mention 718
  Google Analytics 719
  HootSuite 722
  Social Mention 722
  Crowdbooster 723
  AgoraPulse 724
  Hyper Alerts 725
  Sprout Social 725
  Topsy 727
  Klout 727
Finding the Biggest Payoff with Your Monitoring Efforts 728
Analyzing Results and Taking Action 729
  Building a tracking guide 729
  Allocating manpower and resources from analysis 731
  Identifying the time-wasters 731
  Making adjustments on the fly 732
  Building on your success 732

Index **733**

Introduction

*O*ne thing we know for sure from writing this book is that Facebook loves change. The folks at Facebook love to change things up — tweak the platform; upgrade programs; and above all, innovate each chance they get. This is great for everyone who's looking to use Facebook to grow a business but not so great for anyone who's writing a "how things work" book about Facebook marketing. On Facebook, how things work one day may not be how things work the next day! The good news is that we were able to stay on top of all the changes and pack this book with the latest and greatest Facebook marketing strategies.

That said, Facebook's unwavering dedication to innovation is exactly why it is the social networking powerhouse that it is today. With Facebook's constant growth and massive influence, it's obvious that Facebook isn't just a flash-in-the-pan phenomenon. These days, you can't surf the web, listen to the radio, watch TV, or even flip through a magazine without hearing or seeing something about Facebook.

Facebook represents a huge opportunity for your business. If you're in a business of any kind, you absolutely should consider Facebook to be a key player in your marketing strategy. With Facebook having over 1 billion active users, your ideal audience is highly likely to be spending time there. You have a huge opportunity to capture the attention of, and build relationships with, the people who could potentially be your most loyal customers. When you fully leverage the power of Facebook, you can build an engaging Facebook presence, attract and engage quality customers, and quickly grow your business.

About This Book

Whether you're a complete newbie on Facebook or a veteran who's looking to take Facebook marketing to a new level, this book is for you. You can play many roles on Facebook, and this book gives you the tools to decide how Facebook fits into your overall marketing plan.

You may decide that you want to use Facebook as a mini hub — an extension of your own website where your fans first go to get to know, like, and trust you. After you create a solid relationship with your fans, you can encourage them to visit your website to find out more about what you have to offer. Or you may want to use Facebook as a robust customer-service portal: a place where you answer client questions, help troubleshoot product challenges, and become the go-to source for all your clients' needs. Or you may want to use it to advertise your product or service and use Facebook's robust targeting to find your perfect client.

Your opportunities are endless, and this book helps you understand which opportunities are right for your business.

Foolish Assumptions

To get real results from the strategies and tips in this book, you don't need any special skills. As long as you have basic computer skills and can navigate the Internet with ease, you will be able to apply the strategies described throughout with little or no stress. Having some knowledge of how to change image sizes can be helpful to optimize your posts or Facebook ads.

This book is ideal for anyone who is looking to market a local business, an online business, or a brand on Facebook, but it can also be helpful for anyone who has a solid business idea and wants to learn how to launch a new business endeavor on Facebook.

Specifically, this book is for anyone who

✦ Is fairly new to Facebook marketing and is looking for a way to grow their online exposure

✦ Doesn't have a Facebook Page but is interested in the right way to start one on Facebook

✦ Is already on Facebook and has a Page, and is looking to take that Page to the next level

The good news is that you don't have to be an online marketing pro to take advantage of all the strategies outlined in this book!

Icons Used in This Book

All through the book, special icons appear in the margin to draw your attention to particular bits and pieces of information. The following descriptions demystify these graphics:

Pay especially close attention on the rare occasions when you see this icon.

When you see this icon, try to hang on to what we tell you; it's important to keep in mind.

This icon signifies a trick or another bit of helpful information that you may find especially useful.

We use this icon sparingly; it indicates information that's safe to skip but that you might find interesting.

How This Book is Organized

Facebook Marketing All-in-One For Dummies, 3rd Edition, is divided into nine minibooks that take you from understanding why Facebook is important for your business marketing strategy all the way through studying advanced marketing tactics and measurement.

Each minibook is designed to be a complete, stand-alone guide to help you master the subject covered within. You can read this book cover to cover, or choose the areas that interest you and dive right in. The following sections describe all nine minibooks so that you can determine which ones will help you the most.

Book I: Joining the Facebook Marketing Revolution

You may wonder how Facebook can benefit your business. How do you get started — and, more important, why? This minibook helps you understand the potential that Facebook holds for any business and how to reap the rewards of a well-crafted Facebook marketing plan.

We lead you through the basics of searching for and finding your audience on Facebook, defining your goals, and putting in place the measurement tools you need to monitor your return on investment.

Book II: Claiming Your Presence on Facebook

Plant your flag and set up your Facebook Page in this minibook. Book II walks you through the setup process, including selecting a Page type and naming your Page, so that your business can start connecting with potential customers all over the world. You also get a complete tour so that you know how to navigate the Admin panel and editing dashboard.

Book III: Adding the Basics to Your Facebook Page

Find out all the different ways to post content to your Page, including videos, links, and photos. You also discover how to customize your tabs so that your Facebook Page is branded and stands out.

If you have a blog, you can automatically import the blog posts to save time. Connect your Page to your Twitter accounts to create a richer experience for your community members and also to save time.

Book IV: Building, Engaging, Retaining, and Selling to Your Community

Start by building visibility to your Page through your existing customers and then find creative ways to connect to new Facebook users. This minibook gives you plenty of ways to engage your customers and basic rules for participating in the conversation in a meaningful way. You also find out how to expand your e-commerce by bringing it to your Facebook Page with apps via an online Facebook store.

Book V: Understanding Facebook Applications

Explore the world of Facebook applications in this minibook; find out how applications can integrate with your Page to make it a better place for your community. Look at the best existing applications to add, and find out about custom iFrame applications that help you create any type of tab you can imagine.

Book VI: Making Facebook Come Alive with Events and Contests

In this minibook, you discover the ins and outs of creating and marketing your Event. If your Facebook Page needs a little fun, consider holding a contest to engage and grow your community. Book VI covers the different types of contests, how to follow Facebook's contest rules, and what applications can help you run your contest. Make sure that you're getting the most out of your contest efforts with promotional strategies and results analysis.

Book VII: Facebook Advertising

Advertising on Facebook is a world unto itself. In the first chapter, we introduce you to the basics of advertising and how to make strategic business and financial decisions. The second chapter is a how-to chapter on using the Ads Create tool; it covers everything from the basics of creating an ad to establishing parameters for advertising campaigns. For more advanced users, the third chapter provides how-to advice on using the Power Editor. The last chapter in this minibook shows you how to assess the performance of your ads using the Ads Manager tool.

Book VIII: Advanced Facebook Marketing Tactics

This minibook looks at specific marketing tactics for sophisticated Facebook users. Once you have mastered the basics, you'll be ready to explore some of these challenges. The overview in the first chapter explores tools for highly targeted marketing, making Facebook offers, and using new Facebook features to increase viral marketing exposure. The second chapter explains how to use social plug-ins to integrate Facebook with your website. In Chapter 3, you'll learn how to take advantage of live video on Facebook. And, finally in Chapter 4, you'll see how to exploit the growing power of Facebook in mobile environments for both posting and advertising.

Book IX: Measuring, Monitoring, and Analyzing

The final minibook returns to business principals with three chapters on important measurement tools you can use to assess the performance of all your Facebook activity. The first chapter emphasizes the importance of measuring and monitoring social media-specific performance indicators and of calculating the return on your investment in time and money. In the second chapter you learn how to use Facebook Insights to assess internal performance, while the third and final chapter discusses how to select third-party monitoring tools that enable you to compare and contrast Facebook with other online marketing efforts.

Beyond the Book

We put some information online, as well:

+ **Cheat Sheet:** Find handy Facebook marketing tips and advice to reference quickly and easily when you don't have the book handy. This book's Cheat Sheet can be found here:

    www.dummies.com/cheatsheet/facebookmarketingaio

+ **Dummies.com online articles:** Each parts page has a link to an additional Facebook marketing article at Dummies.com. Check out this book's articles at:

    www.dummies.com/extras/facebookmarketingaio

+ **Updates:** Occasionally, we have updates to our technology books. If this book does have technical updates, they'll be posted here:

    www.dummies.com/extras/facebookmarketingaio

Where to Go from Here

This book can be read in any order you choose. Each chapter stands on its own and can help you tackle specific tasks. If you've just started thinking about marketing yourself on Facebook but don't know where to begin, head to Book I. If you already have a Facebook Page and a basic understanding of how Facebook works, you can optimize your Page by starting with Book II. Your first stop may be the table of contents, where you can look up sections that you need any time.

Book I
Joining the Facebook Marketing Revolution

getting started with

Facebook Marketing

Contents at a Glance

Chapter 1: Exploring Facebook Marketing 9

Seeing the Business Potential of Facebook...9
Using Facebook with the Global Market...19
Understanding Facebook Marketing Basics..20

Chapter 2: Creating Your Facebook Marketing Plan 27

Defining Your Ideal Audience on Facebook..27
Finding Your Ideal Audience inside Facebook......................................29
Identifying Your Facebook Marketing Plan's Core Goals.....................35
Rules for Successful Facebook Pages...37
Setting Up Resources and Manpower for Your Plan.............................45
Defining Your Admin Team 48
Measuring Your Return on Investment 54

Chapter 1: Exploring Facebook Marketing

In This Chapter

✔ Discovering Facebook's marketing potential

✔ Looking at four key Facebook marketing strategies

✔ Mastering the art of Facebook engagement

✔ Examining Facebook's global market opportunities

✔ Understanding the basics of Facebook marketing

✔ Seeing the benefits of selling from the Facebook platform

Facebook is the most powerful social network on the planet. With more than one billion active users, Facebook presents a unique opportunity to connect with and educate your ideal audience in a way that your website and your blog can't even come close to matching.

The reach of the Facebook platform has grown exponentially in the past few years and will only continue to get bigger. In fact, the number of Facebook Pages created by brands was over 50 million in February of 2013. Today, almost anyone or any company can find a following on Facebook, from big brands such as Starbucks to small mom-and-pop shops. Facebook's platform can turn a business into a living, breathing, one-to-one online marketing machine. Facebook has changed the game, and there's no better time than the present to jump on board.

In this chapter, we cover why Facebook should become a key marketing tool to help you grow your business. Specifically, we look at Facebook's massive marketing potential, its expansive capability to reach your ideal audience, and the core strategies you can implement today to seamlessly add Facebook to your marketing program.

Seeing the Business Potential of Facebook

We have good news and bad news for you when it comes to Facebook marketing.

✦ *The bad news first:* Facebook marketing isn't free. Sure, it doesn't cost actual dollars to get set up with a presence on Facebook, but it will cost you time and effort — two hot commodities that most business owners have very little of these days. You have to account for the time and energy it takes to plan your strategy, set it up, train yourself, execute your plan, build your relationships, and take care of your new customers after you start seeing your efforts pay off. And although you don't need to be tied to Facebook 24/7 to see results, dedicated time and effort are essential when creating a successful Facebook marketing plan, and your time and effort are anything but free.

✦ *And for the good news:* This book and our collective experience can help you streamline your Facebook marketing efforts and eliminate the guesswork that often goes into figuring out anything that's new and somewhat complex.

Remember this very important fact: You are *not* in the business of Facebook marketing. Your job is not to become an expert or a master of Facebook. As you navigate this book, remember that your job is to be an expert at your business — and Facebook is a tool that you will use to do that. Take the pressure off yourself to master Facebook marketing. This will make all the difference as you master the strategies outlined throughout these pages.

Facebook can help you create exposure and awareness for your business, increase sales, collect market data, enhance your customers' experience, and increase your position as an authority in your field. However, before you can start to see real results, you must determine why you're on Facebook.

Asking yourself what you're after

If you take the time to ponder the following questions, you'll gradually begin to create a road map to Facebook marketing success:

✦ **Why do you want to use Facebook to market your business?** More specifically, what do you hope to gain from your use of Facebook, and how will it help your business?

✦ **Who is your ideal audience?** Get specific here. Who are you talking to? What are the demographics, needs, wants, and challenges of the folks who will buy your products, programs, or services?

✦ **What do you want your ideal audience to do via your efforts on Facebook?** In other words, what feelings, actions, or behaviors do you want your audience to experience?

✦ **How can you be useful?** Finally, remember that Facebook is a friend network where brands are relatively unwelcome. How can you use Facebook to be useful to your customers?

Using Facebook to your advantage

When you're clear about *why* you're on Facebook, you're better able to design a strategy that best fits your business needs. We explore many potential strategies through the course of this book.

For now, though, in the name of helping you better understand how you can use Facebook to market your business, here's a list of just a few ideas you can implement when you embrace Facebook marketing:

✦ **Set up special promotions inside Facebook, and offer special deals exclusively to your Facebook community.** You could create a coupon that your visitors can print and bring into your store for a special discount, for example.

✦ **Offer Q&A sessions in real time.** Your visitors can post questions about your niche, product, or service; then you and your team can offer great advice and information to your Facebook community.

✦ **Highlight your Facebook fans by offering a Member of the Month award.** You could choose and highlight one fan who shows exemplary participation in your Facebook community. People love to be acknowledged, and Facebook is a fantastic platform for recognizing your best clients and prospects.

✦ **Highlight your own employees with an Employee of the Month feature on your Facebook Page.** Profile someone who's making a difference at the company. You can include photos and video to make it even more entertaining and interesting to your audience.

✦ **Sell your products and services directly inside Facebook.** Include a button that links your fans to an electronic shopping cart to enable them to buy in the moment. You have many opportunities to promote and sell your products and services on Facebook.

The preceding list is just a glimpse of what you can do inside Facebook's powerful walls. Many more opportunities await you, as we explain in later minibooks.

Reaping the benefits for business-to-consumer companies

When it comes to business-to-consumer (B2C) companies, one of the greatest advantages of Facebook marketing is the ability to engage one-on-one with your ideal clients. By asking questions, encouraging conversations, and creating personal engagement with your customers and prospects, you can build relationships in a way that wasn't possible before social networking took the marketing world by storm.

Although we all know that consumer brands with big marketing budgets can attract millions of followers on Facebook, there's still room for the little guys.

Here's a thought experiment: Rather than feel frustrated because your company can't compete with big-brand giants on Facebook, turn the success of those companies into an opportunity for you to model the best and learn from them.

Here are four key strategies that the big B2C companies have adopted in their Facebook marketing strategies to help them stand out from the rest:

✦ **Acknowledge your fans.** The B2C giants on Facebook do a fantastic job of spotlighting their fans. When fans feel appreciated, they continue to engage with your Page.

One great example of this strategy comes from Oreo, which knows a thing or two about standing out. Oreo created a campaign to spotlight what fans think about Oreos. Fans share their videos, photos, and stories via a Facebook app, providing Oreo with limitless content and customer loyalty. Oreo's Facebook Page has millions of fans, so those folks must be doing something right! See Figure 1-1.

Figure 1-1: Oreo can wow its audience by creating unique experiences.

✦ **Know your audience.** When you're clear about who you're communicating with on Facebook, you can create experiences around your audience's interest and likes. An example of a B2C company that's in tune with its audience is Red Bull, as evidenced by that Page's custom apps and unique content.

The team behind Red Bull's Facebook Page knows what its audience will respond to best and then delivers. A series of online games and apps for fans, for example, is geared toward sports and high-impact competitions, as shown in Figure 1-2.

✦ **Mix up your media.** Facebook strategies that infuse a variety of media, including photos and video, often draw a bigger crowd. One example is JetBlue's airline terminal live music shows.

JetBlue knows that many of their customers appreciate culture. Working with local and independent artists, they presented live music concerts at several of their locations, as shown in Figure 1-3. So not only are they using videos, but they're also providing rich cultural experiences in addition to affordable and enjoyable air travel! Very smart, JetBlue!

✦ **Have fun.** Face it, most people log on to Facebook to have fun and connect with friends. Interacting with businesses is a distant consideration. That doesn't mean, however, that these users aren't a captive audience! The key is to infuse fun into your Facebook activity when appropriate.

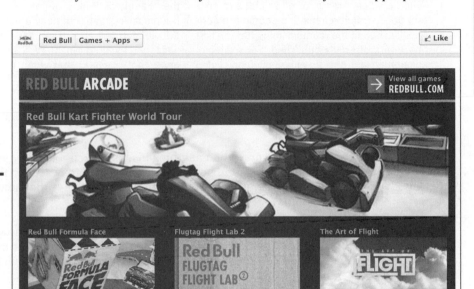

Figure 1-2:
Red Bull keeps it fun with its Red Bull Arcade on Facebook.

Figure 1-3:
JetBlue shares performing artist info with their fans.

Going viral

When a video, article, or other piece of content goes *viral*, it means that people are continually sharing that content long after the first few hours after it's published. For example, someone might post an amazingly funny video on YouTube. People start to pass it along to their friends by e-mailing the link, posting it on their Facebook Pages, and tweeting about it. If a massive number of people begin to share the video, it will appear on major news websites, and even late night TV. When that happens, the virality of that video can increase exponentially!

Photos are viewed more than anything else on Facebook. They go viral quickly because when a fan posts a photo, that photo is sent to the News Feeds of all their friends. Hundreds of thousands of potential new fans will see these photos.

When reviewing these four strategies illustrated by some well-known B2C companies, remember that you, too, can create these experiences for little or no cost. Again, model the best that's out there, and make the strategies work for your own business.

Reaping the benefits for business-to-business companies

We know that Facebook marketing works well for B2C businesses, but if you're a business-to-business (B2B) company, you may be wondering whether Facebook makes sense. In short, the answer is yes! In fact, according to the 2013 State of Inbound Marketing Research Report from HubSpot, 41 percent of B2B companies have reported acquiring a customer through Facebook.

Not only can B2B companies incorporate the four key strategies mentioned in the preceding section, but B2B companies also have a unique advantage over B2C when it comes to Facebook marketing: Facebook's platform is designed to support exactly what B2B companies need to be successful in attracting clients and securing sales.

To better explain this idea, here are three factors that make B2B a perfect fit for Facebook marketing:

✦ **B2B has a smaller potential customer base.** B2B companies don't have to constantly focus on growing their numbers of followers to hundreds of thousands; instead, they can put the majority of their focus on nurturing the relationships they already have. Facebook is a platform that thrives on one-to-one relationships.

✦ **Buying decisions in B2B rely heavily on word of mouth and reputation.** Businesses that are looking to make a huge buying decision often want to know what their peers are doing and how they feel about a product or service. Facebook's open network allows people to see who their peers are interacting with and what they're talking about at any given time, therefore making it easy to find out what others think about a product or service.

✦ **B2B generally has a higher average price point than B2C.** When the price of the product or service is considered to be high, the client is likely to seek out information and content to support buying decisions. On Facebook, content is king. The more high-value content a company can generate, the more likely it will be to attract the ideal client base and become a Facebook success story.

For B2B companies, connection, knowledge sharing, and reputation management are key ingredients of success. Facebook's unique platform can help optimize these key strategies.

Developing genuine relationships with customers and prospects

No matter whether your business is B2B or B2C, it really comes down to one person talking to another. No one wants to interact with a faceless brand, business, or logo. We all want to buy from a friend — someone we trust and feel comfortable engaging with regularly.

Facebook allows us to move beyond the obstacles of traditional marketing (very one-sided) and instead communicate with our clients and prospects on a one-on-one level by putting a face with a name, making the entire exchange more human.

Creating one-to-one customer engagement

Engagement is crucial in mastering Facebook marketing. If you build rapport and can get your Facebook community talking, your efforts will go a long way.

It's one thing to broadcast a special promotion on Facebook, but it's an entirely different experience to ask your fans a question related to your products and services and receive 50 responses from people telling you exactly how they feel about what you're selling. In many cases, this real-time engagement can be priceless. In Figure 1-4, the popular online shoe and clothing retailer Zappos.com asks its female fans about "girls night" preferences for fingernail polish color preferences.

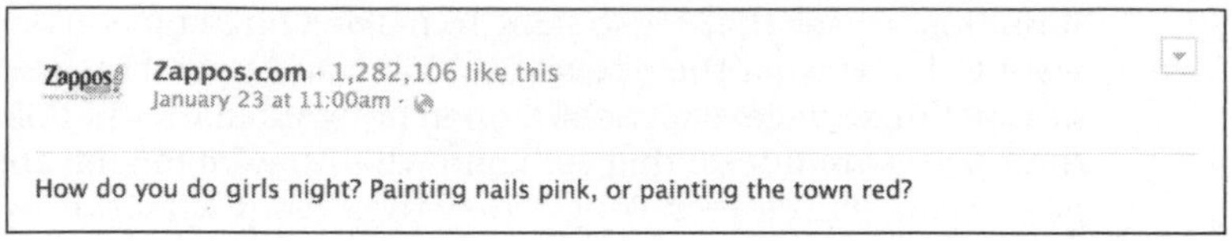

Figure 1-4:
Ask (a question), and ye shall receive.

Zappos.com · 1,282,106 like this
January 23 at 11:00am ·

How do you do girls night? Painting nails pink, or painting the town red?

One very successful Facebook marketing strategy is to ask your followers interesting questions. It's human nature to enjoy talking about likes and interests; therefore, encourage sharing by asking your fans to express their thoughts about their likes and interests. It's a great way to increase fan engagement.

Providing prompt customer service

Before the days of social networking, phone calls, e-mails, and handwritten letters were just about your only options when it came to reaching out to your clients. Today, you can send a tweet or make a Facebook post to inform your customers of new features, benefits, or changes to your products or services. Social media allows you to get the word out quickly, making it easier for you to keep your customers informed and satisfied.

If you optimize your Facebook marketing experience, you can provide your customers a superior customer experience — a much richer experience than you've ever been able to offer before. Not only can you create a social media experience in which you're keeping your customers informed, but you can also give them an opportunity to reach out to you.

Imagine this: You sell shoes. A client orders a pair of your shoes online and receives them in the mail. When the shoes arrive, they're the wrong pair. That client logs on to Facebook and posts this message:

> I just received my much anticipated pair of red stilettos in the mail today . . . too bad the company messed up and sent me sneakers instead! I'm frustrated!

At first glance, you may think that a post like that would hurt your business. On social sites like Facebook and Twitter, however, you can turn a potentially bad post into an opportunity to gain a customer for life.

Imagine that you respond within just five minutes with this post:

> Julie, we are so sorry that you received the wrong pair of shoes! We are shipping your red stilettos overnight, and make sure to look for the 50% off coupon we included in your box as well. Two pairs of shoes are always better than one!

Here's what's great: The opportunity for real-time problem solving is powerful. You not only just saved a sale and made Julie a happy customer, but you also showed anyone watching on Facebook that you care about your clients and will go above and beyond the call of duty to make them happy. This type of experience wasn't possible before social media came on the scene.

You can find out more about online tools that will help you monitor who's talking about you online in Book IX, Chapter 3. These tools will help you stay in the know and in tune with your customers. They will also save you precious time and effort when managing your Facebook activity.

In addition to proactively monitoring Facebook for customer service issues, you can use many robust tools to create a virtual service desk directly inside Facebook. Livescribe, for example, has incorporated a support desk directly into its Facebook Page. As you can see in Figure 1-5, you can ask the folks at Livescribe a question, share an idea, report a problem, or even give praise directly from that Facebook Page.

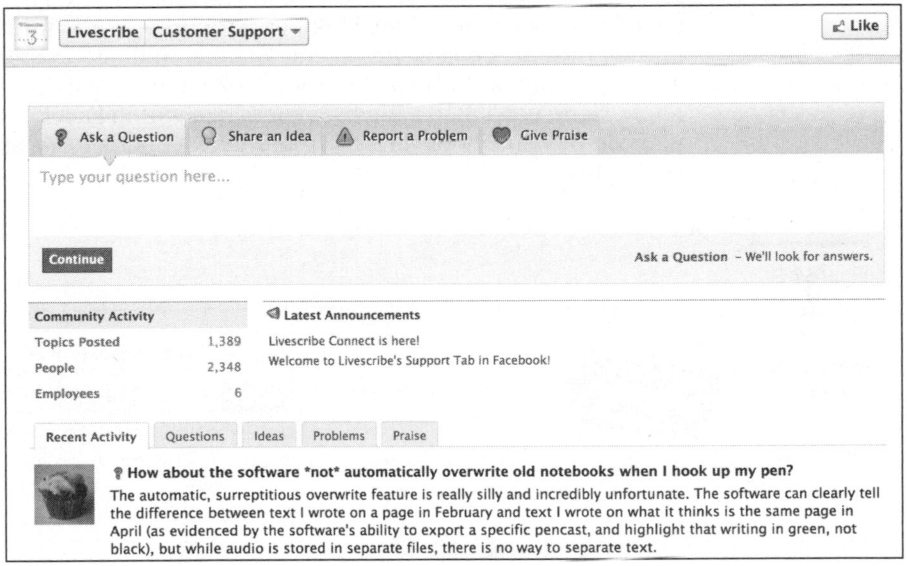

Livescribe Customer Support ▾	👍 **Like**

💡 Ask a Question	💡 Share an Idea	⚠ Report a Problem	💜 Give Praise

Type your question here...

Continue   Ask a Question – We'll look for answers.

Community Activity		◁ **Latest Announcements**
Topics Posted	1,389	Livescribe Connect is here!
People	2,348	Welcome to Livescribe's Support Tab in Facebook!
Employees	6	

Recent Activity | Questions | Ideas | Problems | Praise

💡 **How about the software *not* automatically overwrite old notebooks when I hook up my pen?**
The automatic, surreptitious overwrite feature is really silly and incredibly unfortunate. The software can clearly tell the difference between text I wrote on a page in February and text I wrote on what it thinks is the same page in April (as evidenced by the software's ability to export a specific pencast, and highlight that writing in green, not black), but while audio is stored in separate files, there is no way to separate text.

Figure 1-5:
Check out the Livescribe Facebook support desk.

Customers commonly use social media sites to post questions or complaints. If you provide a designated place for support, you're likely to keep your customers happy and turn them into repeat buyers!

What's even more important is that others can see these posts. Then fans and potential buyers can go to this custom app to get answers or see what others are saying about the products. It's another great way to educate fans about your products and services. In addition, this tool can cut down service calls when it's executed correctly, saving your company time and money.

Creating a shopping portal

Facebook's expansion into the e-commerce sector might forever change the way we shop. In the past, creating an e-commerce website took a lot of money and even more time. Today, Facebook's platform — interwoven with third-party apps — has allowed millions of businesses to showcase their products and services and to sell them online. (To find out more about how third-party apps can be part of your Facebook marketing strategy, check out Book V.)

When it comes to the kinds of shopping interfaces you can create on Facebook, you have two options:

✦ **A storefront:** Here's where potential buyers come to browse products. When users want to buy, they click the Buy button and are then taken to a separate, e-commerce website to finalize the purchase. Currently, this type of shopping interface is the most popular, but we'll likely see the second interface option (see next bullet) catch up soon.

✦ **A fully functioning store:** Your second interface option involves creating a full-blown store where shoppers can browse and purchase without leaving the Facebook environment. You can find one example of such a fully functioning store on the Facebook Page for the Grandma Mary Show. Here, you'll find a buying experience within Facebook where you can buy an e-book directly from that Facebook Page, as shown in Figure 1-6.

Figure 1-6:
The Grandma Mary Show allows e-book purchases from directly inside the Facebook e-commerce platform.

When Facebook users post about products they love, the users' friends naturally want to know more. This curiosity creates viral exposure for your products and services.

Facebook offers an extremely valuable opportunity to showcase your products and services and to create a new portal where you can sell your goods.

Using Facebook with the Global Market

Few people would deny that the social media phenomenon — and Facebook, specifically — is growing at a staggering pace. Online users in Australia, Japan, and Italy all show even stronger adoption of social media than Americans do, and those in China, Denmark, and Sweden are said to be adopting social media at the same rates as Americans.

With more than 80 percent of Facebook users located outside the United States, it's essential to understand Facebook's place in the global market.

Facebook breaks down barriers and makes introducing your products and services to international audiences easier. Here are some opportunities you can explore to extend your brand's footprint in the global market:

✦ **Use Facebook advertising to reach international audiences.** You can target 25 countries with one Facebook Ad, or you can target one country at a time and drill down into specific cities within the country. You can also create multiple ads and target numerous cities in the countries you want to target with your ads. The more localized you make your ads, the better chance you have of reaching your ideal audience.

Going international

To give you a glimpse of the magnitude of Facebook's global reach, here are some statistics provided by Facebook as of April 2014:

✔ More than 1.3 billion active users.

✔ More than 60% of Facebook's active users log on to Facebook in any given day.

✔ More than 945 million active users access Facebook through their mobile devices monthly, and people who use Facebook on their mobile devices are twice as active on Facebook as nonmobile users.

✔ Young adults continue to be the heaviest Facebook users, but the most rapid growth is among those 50 years old and older. This group is the fastest-growing demographic on Facebook today.

✔ Although the United States is the largest country on Facebook, the UK is Facebook's second-largest market, with more than 23 million users. Brazil and Indonesia are in the third and fourth spots.

✦ **Translate your content.** With the rise of international markets on Facebook today, consider translating your content on Facebook. In fact, English accounts for only 31 percent of language use online. Facebook has its own crowdsourced translation product: Facebook Translation app.

In many countries, the majority of people do not have access to computers with Internet access. Mobile devices are making it possible for Facebook to reach more people, however.

Understanding Facebook Marketing Basics

Facebook can supercharge your existing marketing efforts by giving you a platform to grow your audience, create deeper connections, and create new experiences to foster loyal client relationships. Facebook's unique platforms that let you market and promote your brand online are your Profile and your Facebook Page.

The Subscribe button, which is optional, allows Facebook users who aren't your Friends on Facebook to subscribe to your updates, meaning that they can see your public posts in their News Feeds.

Subscribing to someone's personal account is a lot like following someone on Twitter. In other words, you don't have to be Friends with someone on Facebook to see their Public posts. If you're marketing a personal brand, the Profile with a Subscribe button may be perfect for your marketing outcomes. There are some strategic marketing reasons to have a personal account with the Subscribe button. We cover the complete marketing strategy for activating your Subscribe button in Book II, Chapter 1.

The other way to market on Facebook is via a Facebook Page. Pages are like digital storefronts, or places where your prospects can take a digital walk around your business to learn more about your brand and what you have to offer. Here you can highlight your best programs, products, and services to interact with an interested audience.

A large portion of this book is dedicated to creating and optimizing your Facebook Page. Before we get into the how-to's and strategies, though, we point out a few of the most important details you need to know to get off on the right foot.

Marketing on your Page and your Profile

Although you'll soon find out all you'll ever need to know about the differences between a Profile and a Page, for the purposes of starting things off, here's a quick rundown:

✦ **When you sign up for Facebook, you create a Facebook Profile.**

A Profile is meant to be all about you. It has been referred to as a living scrapbook of your life. It highlights who you are and gives details about your life experiences over time. With the addition of the Subscribe button, you now have the option to make some of your posts public and other posts private. The opportunity to select who sees your posts gives you a unique advantage by allowing you to be selective and use your Profile to connect with family members and friends, as well as to post information about your business.

✦ **Promoting your business or brand for monetary gain via a Profile goes against Facebook's terms of service.**

It isn't against the rules, however, to mention your business and keep your relatives, friends, and those subscribed to your Profile informed about new happenings with your business.

✦ **A Facebook Page is designed specifically to highlight your business, and its purpose is to allow businesses to communicate with their customers and fans.**

Those who follow your Facebook Page expect to see promotions and conversations about your programs and services, so it's perfectly acceptable to promote your business on a Facebook Page.

For a more comprehensive understanding of Profiles and Pages, check out Book II, Chapter 1.

Developing your Page to be a hub of activity

Your Facebook Page can serve as a meeting place for people who have similar interests and values. Involve your customers in your conversations by asking them questions and encouraging them to share their thoughts.

One way you can create a hub of activity is to encourage your fans to use your Facebook community as a platform where they can connect with other like-minded individuals.

You can become the go-to source in your industry, for example, making your Page the hub of your industry's latest news and happenings. By delivering valuable content via your Facebook Page, you're setting up your company as the authority — a trusted advisor.

One great example of a company using Facebook to position itself as the go-to source for an industry is HubSpot, a major player in the marketing automation software space (see Figure 1-7).

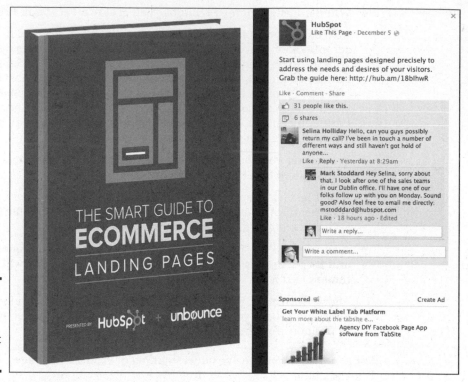

Figure 1-7:
HubSpot
Facebook
engagement
activity.

During the course of this book, you'll have the opportunity to familiarize yourself with many strategies that can help you create a unique hub of activity, including a bunch of strategies we show you in Book VII.

Understanding privacy options

After you set up your Facebook Profile, you have several privacy options to choose among to determine just how much or how little of your Facebook self you want to share. These options become even more important if you decide to activate the Subscribe button, making your Profile more accessible.

First, Facebook has what it calls an "inline audience selector," which is a drop-down menu that lets you decide which group of people sees your post (see Figure 1-8).

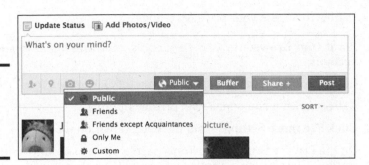

Figure 1-8:
The inline
audience
selector
options.

With the inline audience selector, you can choose to display your post to five groups:

✦ **Public:** All your Facebook Friends and anyone who has subscribed to your Profile Timeline can see your post.

✦ **Friends:** All your Facebook Friends can see your post.

✦ **Friends Except Acquaintances:** All your Facebook Friends whom you manually selected as Close Friends can see your post. This group is pulled from a custom list that you set up manually. We discuss the strategy behind custom lists in Book VII, Chapter 1.

✦ **Only Me:** You can post something that only you will see on Facebook, but we realize that this seems a bit silly to do! This is a good option if, for example, you don't want people to see old photos you have uploaded but you don't want to outright delete them.

✦ **Custom:** You can manually choose the individual Friends who see your post.

You can not only select an audience when you post, but also change your selection at any time. To do this, hover on your posts' globe icon, as shown in Figure 1-9, and then choose your audience preference from the drop-down menu.

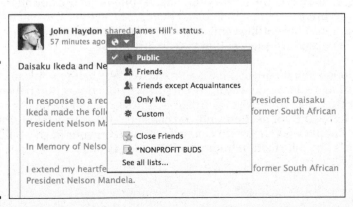

Figure 1-9:
The audi-
ence selec-
tor allows
you to
change who
sees your
post.

Here's how to access your privacy settings:

1. **Point your browser to** www.facebook.com, **and log in to your account.**

2. **In the top-right corner of your screen, click the lock icon.**

   A drop-down menu opens with privacy options.

3. **Click See more Settings from the drop-down menu.**

   On the Privacy Settings and Tools page, you can see all your options for setting your privacy controls on Facebook, as shown in Figure 1-10.

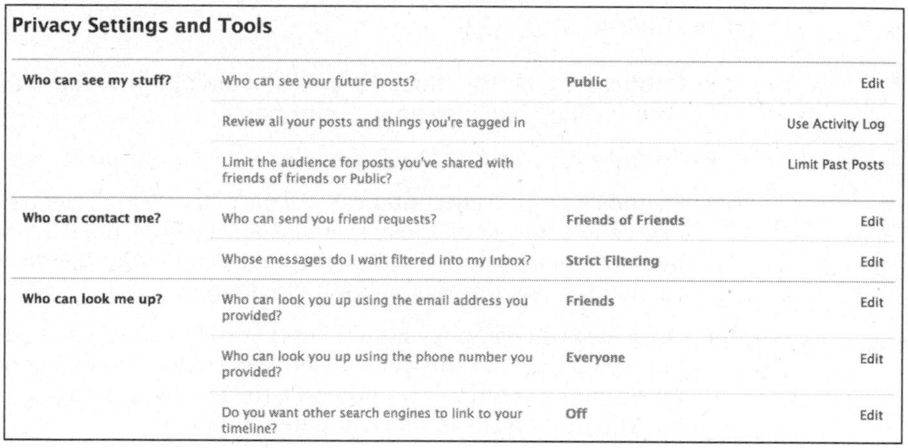

Privacy Settings and Tools

Who can see my stuff?	Who can see your future posts?	Public	Edit
	Review all your posts and things you're tagged in		Use Activity Log
	Limit the audience for posts you've shared with friends of friends or Public?		Limit Past Posts
Who can contact me?	Who can send you friend requests?	Friends of Friends	Edit
	Whose messages do I want filtered into my inbox?	Strict Filtering	Edit
Who can look me up?	Who can look you up using the email address you provided?	Friends	Edit
	Who can look you up using the phone number you provided?	Everyone	Edit
	Do you want other search engines to link to your timeline?	Off	Edit

Figure 1-10: Privacy Settings page on Facebook.

Facebook's privacy settings allow you to control exactly who sees what within your Facebook Profile. The challenge is that the privacy settings are extremely detailed, and Facebook changes or upgrades them often. But don't worry: When Facebook does make changes, it always notifies users, thereby keeping everyone informed.

Also included on the privacy options dashboard is the option to set your default privacy setting to Public, Friends, or Custom. You can also dive deeper into the settings and customize specific sections of your Profile Timeline, and we suggest that you do just that.

Although you do need to have a Profile in place before you can create a business Page, there's no way for others to see the connection between your new Page and your existing Profile — unless you tell them, of course. Only you know the connection, and you can keep it that way for eternity, if you like. People who choose to connect with you on your Page won't be able to access any information from your Facebook Profile.

Keeping things professional but personal

Facebook gives you the opportunity to give a face and personality to your company. Sure, many of us use Facebook in our day-to-day business (as we mention earlier in this chapter), but the vast majority of Facebookers are there to engage with their friends and have fun. And no matter how serious your product or service may be, you always have room for a little levity.

People want to know *you,* not your brand. Be careful about using jargon in your posts and coming across as too "corporate" because this is often seen as inauthentic on social networking sites. Talk to your Facebook community as though the people in it are your friends, not potential clients. The more real you are on Facebook, the more your fans will want to engage with you and your business.

Chapter 2: Creating Your Facebook Marketing Plan

In This Chapter

✔ **Researching and targeting your ideal audience on Facebook**

✔ **Finding new connections using Facebook's Graph Search**

✔ **Understanding the core rules for a successful Facebook Page**

✔ **Creating a Facebook team that will help grow your community**

✔ **Measuring the success of your Facebook investment**

*F*acebook has changed the game of marketing for everyone. In the past, people who were interested in your products or services would read a brochure, visit your bricks-and-mortar shop, or maybe watch a commercial to find out the information they needed before making a buying decision. Today, people go to Google or search popular social networks for answers to their questions instead. That's why you need an online presence, in real time, to answer their questions when they seek you out. After all, if you make customers wait, they can be knocking on a competitor's virtual door with a click of a button. With that in mind, it's essential that you create a solid, well thought-out Facebook marketing plan that defines your goals and maps your online strategies.

By the end of this chapter, you'll be able to start putting your Facebook marketing plan to work. Begin by defining your target audience and finding that audience inside the virtual walls of Facebook.

Defining Your Ideal Audience on Facebook

Facebook has more than one billion active users as of this writing, so more likely than not, your brand will find an audience on Facebook. The key here is finding out where they are and what they do while they're inside this thriving social network.

The first step in creating a Facebook marketing plan involves articulating your *brand*. You want to determine who you are and who your customers are.

Ask yourself what's unique about your product or service, and what about your product or service attracts buyers. Are you a life coach who teaches people how to find a career aligned with their true passion? Are you a yoga teacher who lives a green lifestyle and sells organic specialty soaps online? In a nutshell, who are you, and what do you do? After you get clear about your brand, you can identify your ideal audience.

Identifying the demographics of your ideal audience

Before you begin marketing on Facebook, you want to compile all the information you already have regarding the demographics of your ideal audience. Commonly used demographics include gender, race, age, location, income, and education.

If you haven't done this research, one way to approach finding your target demographic is to survey your existing customers. Ask them questions to find out their specific demographics to help you understand who is buying your products or services.

To help survey your audience, you can use inexpensive (and often free) online tools to make the process easy and anonymous for your audience. Two great sites to explore are Polldaddy (www.polldaddy.com) and SurveyMonkey (www.surveymonkey.com).

With your audience demographic information in hand, using the tips and techniques we highlight in this chapter, you can research similar Facebook users to find potential customers to target inside Facebook. The more information you collect before you start to market on Facebook, the more success you'll have finding potential clients. As you dig deeper into Facebook marketing in this chapter, we show you precisely how to use your existing information to find your ideal audience on Facebook.

Understanding the psychographics of your ideal audience

The more you understand your target audience, the better equipped you are to keep the attention of your existing audience and attract new clients as well.

Psychographics are attributes often related to personality, values, attitudes, or interests. Figuring out what a person likes or dislikes, or even favorite hobbies, can be priceless information as you market your products or services because the more you know about your ideal audience, the better you can create marketing messages that will grab their attention and encourage them to take action. You have different ways to figure out the psychographics of your ideal audience:

✦ **Ask them.** Use your social media networks to post engaging, thought-provoking questions to learn more about your audience. Ask them about their interests, hobbies, and needs. People love to talk about themselves, and if they trust you, they'll often reveal even more than you initially asked.

✦ **Try online surveys.** As we mention earlier in this chapter, offering prizes or giveaways in exchange for information is a great strategy to get people to participate in your surveys. **Remember:** The more you know, the smarter you can be in your overall marketing activity.

✦ **Figure out what your customers want to know from you.** What information do you have that they want? If you cast too wide of a net, you're likely to come up short in the end. Make sure to stay focused on the people who matter most to your business's success.

✦ **Find out where your audience spends time while on Facebook.** What Facebook Pages do they interact with often? Who do they follow? What do they post in their own personal Facebook Profiles? This information will tell you a lot about your Facebook audience. (In Book IX, we walk you through how to use the Facebook tracking tool, Insights, as well as third-party monitoring tools. Understanding these tools will help you monitor your ideal audience's activity and interactions on Facebook.)

After you know what your business is about, what you're selling, and who your audience is, you want to spend a little time on your tone. In other words, you want to talk to your Facebook audience in a manner that they're familiar with.

Always stay conversational, but try to use words and phrases that they use in their everyday conversations. If your audience is 14-year-old boys who love to skateboard, for example, you'll talk to them much differently than you would to an audience of new moms looking to connect with other moms. When you know your audience's lingo and style of communication, you can quickly become part of the community.

Finding Your Ideal Audience inside Facebook

One of the biggest benefits of marketing on Facebook is that you have access to the information that Facebook users add to their personal Profiles. Depending on users' Profile privacy settings, you may be able to see their date of birth, marital status, hometown, current location, political views, religious views, employment details, hobbies, interests, and bios. In the past, with traditional marketing, people would pay big bucks for this type of information, but now it's free to you — and at your fingertips.

Facebook's Graph Search is a great tool you can use to research your audience on Facebook. Enter keywords in the search field, and the people, groups, and Pages related to your keyword(s) will show up in the search results.

Facebook's Graph Search is also powerful way to get to know your Facebook fans. When you do a search using Graph Search, you are not limited to keyword searches. You can gain insight into your Facebook Page fanbase.

For example, you see other pages liked by women who like your Facebook Page (as shown in Figure 2-1). This information not only can give you insight into your fans' personalities, but it can also help you discover partnerships that you didn't know existed. For example, based on the information you've received about your business, you might want to reach out to one of these other pages to see if there's a mutually beneficial relationship to explore. This tool is a very powerful one, to say the least.

Here's how to use Facebook Search:

1. **Log in to your Facebook account, and locate the search query field at the top of the page.**

2. **Enter the keyword or phrase you want to search for.**

Facebook displays top results a variety of ways to filter your search.

3. **Select the search query you like to view: Groups, Pages, Hashtags, Apps, Posts, and Web Results.**

To check out an example of a Facebook Search query, see Figure 2-1.

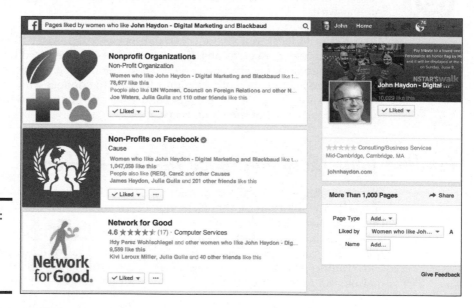

Figure 2-1: The Facebook Search page.

You can search for the following types of content depending upon the search phrase you use:

✦ Pages

✦ Places

✦ Groups

✦ Apps

✦ Events

✦ Music

✦ Web Results

✦ Posts by Friends

✦ Public Posts

✦ Posts in Groups

You can also conduct more complex searches using Graph Search. For example, Figure 2-1 displays pages liked by women who also like John Haydon, digital marketing, and Blackbaud.

Here are several search queries to get you started:

✦ Favorite interests of people who like [*name of your page*]

✦ Favorite interests of people who like [*name of your page*] and Susan G. Komen

✦ Groups of people who like [*name of your page*]

✦ Pages liked by people who like [*name of your page*]

✦ Pages liked by women who like [*name of your page*]

✦ Pages liked by men who like [*name of your page*]

✦ Fans of [*your page*] and [*name of your page*]

✦ Restaurants in [*your city*] visited by people who like [*name of your page*]

✦ Pages like by people who live in [*your city*] and like [*name of your page*]

After you click a specific category or query, the search results for that keyword show up in one stream. Figure 2-2 shows an example search for the word *sushi* in the category Places.

Filtering Facebook Search results

After you complete your search inquiry, what do you do with all that info? Here are a few strategies for putting that info to use in going after your ideal audience on Facebook:

✦ **Send a Friend request.** Identify the Facebook users you want to target, and Friend them on Facebook. If the Facebook user has enabled messaging, you may be able to send him a personal e-mail via Facebook. Sending a personal note is smart, but make sure they are really a friend! Otherwise, you run the risk of offending a potential customer.

Be mindful when sending personal messages to people you do not yet personally know. Be careful to not come across as "spammy" or too pushy. Keep the tone friendly, casual, and to the point.

Figure 2-2:
Click the
category
of your
choice to
see results
for your
keyword.

✦ **Ask them to join your Page.** Invite your targeted users to like your Page by sending them an e-mail inside Facebook, including the link to your Facebook Page, and requesting that they check out your Page and click the Like button to join your community. In the e-mail, briefly tell them why it's a good idea to join your Page.

✦ **Join the groups that count the most.** The best strategy is to join active Facebook groups related to your brand or niche and become part of that community. After joining, consistently post helpful tips that will eventually connect people to your Facebook Page, as shown in Figure 2-3.

Using Facebook Ads to research your ideal audience

Even if you don't plan to use Facebook Ads as part of your overall Facebook marketing plan, you can still benefit from the Facebook Ads platform to find out to what degree your target audience is on Facebook.

Here's how you can access this valuable information:

1. **Log in to your Facebook account, and click the drop-down menu next to the word *Home* in the top-right corner of your page.**

2. **From the drop-down menu, choose Create Ads.**

   You're taken to the Ads dashboard. "What kind of results do you want for your ads?" appears at the top of the page with several choices.

3. **Select Page Likes on the left and then choose your Page on the right.**

Figure 2-3:
Post com-
ments to a
Facebook
group
devoted to
your niche.

4. **On the next screen, below Audience, type a country name.**

   You can get more specific by choosing states, provinces, cities, and zip codes. You can enter multiple states, cities, and zip codes in the same location field. However, if you enter two or more countries in the country field, you will lose the option to list states, cities, and zip codes. You want to drill down as much as possible to get a good representation of your ideal client on Facebook.

5. **(Optional) Indicate a specific age or an age range, or specify gender.**

6. **In the Interests section, enter a keyword that describes your audience.**

   After you type in a keyword, a drop-down menu appears, as shown in Figure 2-4.

7. **Choose keywords that Facebook identifies as best choices based on your initial keyword.**

8. **Press Enter/Return.**

   Then you can be even more specific by selecting subcategories.

To better understand the physical location of your fans, take a look at the demographics data in your Insights dashboard (the area where you will find metrics details for your Facebook Page). You can find out more about Insights in Book IX, Chapter 2.

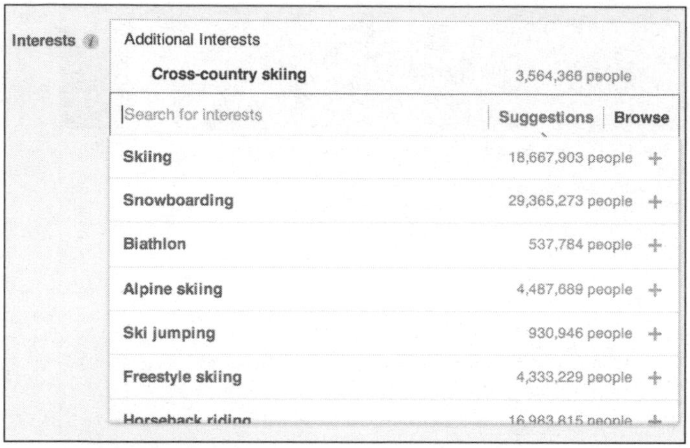

Figure 2-4:
Targeting
Facebook
users by
interests.

Suppose that you choose *cross-country skiing* as your keyword because
you know that your target audience consists of avid cyclists who will likely
mention cycling in their personal Profiles. After you choose this keyword,
you will see other related interests. You can click any of the boxes that also
relate to your target audience and thereby drill-down on your target audience even more, as shown in Figure 2-5.

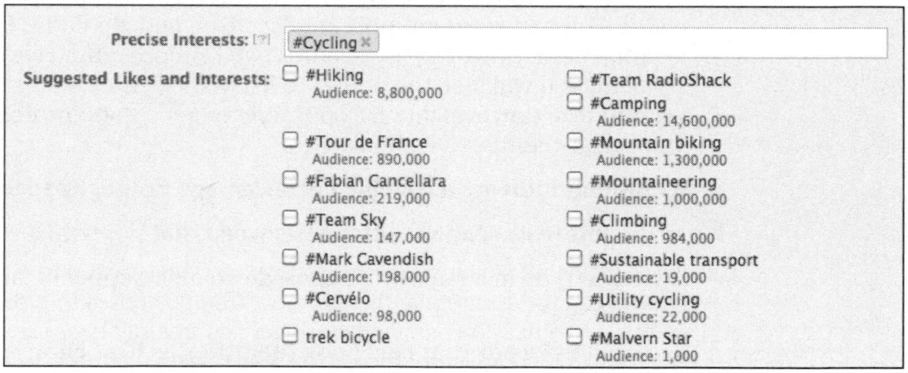

Figure 2-5:
Select addi-
tional inter-
ests that
Facebook
suggests.

After you enter the appropriate information for location, demographics, and
interests, a number on the right side of the screen shows you how many
people on Facebook match your ideal target audience criteria, as shown in
Figure 2-6. If you have that nugget of information, you know whether your
target audience is on Facebook.

10,600 people

✓ **You've defined your audience.**

Continue to the next section once you're happy with your audience.

Your ad targets people:

- Who live in the United States
- Who live within 50 miles of Boston, MA
- exactly between the ages of 25 and 56 inclusive
- Who are female
- Who like Cross-country skiing or Freestyle skiing
- Who are not already connected to Community Music Center of Boston

Figure 2-6:
Check out how many people meet your ideal audience criteria.

Identifying Your Facebook Marketing Plan's Core Goals

With Facebook growing by the minute, there's no question that it must be a part of your marketing mix. These days, however, it's not enough to just sign up for a Facebook account, put up a Facebook Page, and hope that potential readers find you.

Book II is dedicated to showing you everything you need to know about the importance of a Facebook Page and how to strategically set one up. To set up your Facebook marketing foundation, however, it's essential to create a Facebook marketing plan or strategy. Think of your strategy as a road map — the directions you need to create a thriving, active, loyal community on Facebook.

The strategy behind a Facebook marketing plan doesn't need to be complicated, but it does need to be carefully thought out. When it comes to growing a brand on Facebook, business owners and marketers commonly become stuck, often because they overcomplicate things. The goal of this section is to help you create a Facebook marketing plan without going absolutely crazy in the process.

Defining your Facebook marketing goals

As you think about crafting your Facebook marketing plan, understand what Facebook can do for your business.

Consider these Facebook marketing goals as you craft your new plan:

✦ Increasing overall exposure

✦ Building brand awareness

+ Creating a loyal, engaged community
+ Listening to your clients' needs, interests, and feedback
+ Monitoring what people are saying about your brand
+ Driving action (often in the form of sales of your products or services)

These six core goals will help you shape the specific outcomes you want to achieve from your Facebook marketing plan. We explore these core goals throughout the book to ensure you have the tools to create a successful Facebook marketing plan. One of the first steps when creating your marketing plan and determining your goals is to decide on a social media budget.

Deciding on a social media budget

You've likely heard that social media marketing is free. We're sorry to break it to you here, but that's not exactly the case. It can be free, but in some areas, we encourage you to consider spending a little money to take your campaign to a professional level.

Here are three areas where you should consider spending a little money:

+ **Branding:** We suggest that you hire a designer to create a look and feel for all your social media profiles. All your profiles should be consistent across channels and match your branding as much as possible. With everything that you need easily accessible online these days, finding a designer for this task is affordable and quick. Sites like www.freelance.com and www.tweetpages.com are great resources to find designers to create your social media profiles. In Book III, Chapter 2, we show you how to use custom apps to brand your Facebook Page.

+ **Social media consulting:** We often suggest that entrepreneurs and businesses that are new in the social media arena spend a little money educating themselves. Although we don't suggest that you run out and hire someone to take over your social media activity, we do suggest that you consult a social media expert for a review of your social media strategy to gain feedback on and insight into your new plan.

+ **Facebook Ads:** The third area you may want to consider budgeting leads you right into the next section.

Deciding whether a Facebook Ads campaign is right for you

Consider experimenting with Facebook Ads, even if you only plan to test them for a limited time with a small budget. You may be pleasantly surprised by the effectiveness of this advertising channel — Facebook Ads allow you to promote your business, get more likes for your Facebook Page, and drive more leads to build up your sales funnel.

Facebook Ads are so popular because its targeting is like that of no other advertising vehicle available today. You can target by gender, age, race, location, and interests — and even by who is or who isn't a liker of a specific Facebook Page. It's an impressive tool worth checking out, for sure.

We spend an entire minibook (Book VIII, to be exact) exploring Facebook Ads in greater depth.

After you establish your core goals for your Facebook marketing plan, you can focus on creating a successful Facebook Page.

Rules for Successful Facebook Pages

One of the most important questions to ask as you create your Facebook marketing plan is, "What do I want to achieve with my Facebook Page and overall marketing on Facebook?"

To help you sort through the many layers of Facebook marketing, consider nine core rules as you create your Facebook Page:

+ Be deliberate, and manage expectations.
+ Focus on smart branding.
+ Create fresh content.
+ Give your Page a human touch.
+ Cultivate engagement with two-way dialog.
+ Encourage fan-to-fan conversations.
+ Make word-of-mouth advocacy easy.
+ Create consistent calls to action.
+ Monitor, measure, and track.

Dive into the following sections to explore the nine core rules for a successful Facebook Page.

Rule #1: Be deliberate, and manage expectations

Before you do anything else, decide why you want to have a presence on Facebook. What is your overall vision for your Page? Often, your vision for Facebook will be aligned with your overall company vision.

If you own a high-end clothing store for women, for example, your company vision may be to offer the highest fashion and the best-quality clothing in your area to make women feel great about how they look. On Facebook, your vision for your store may be to create a community for women who love high fashion, giving them a place to talk about clothes and share ideas. Your

Facebook Page can become a hub for fashion-minded women (and the best place for you to engage with your ideal audience on Facebook).

Having a clear vision does two things:

✦ Allows you and your team to clearly understand why you're on Facebook. When you understand the why, your actions are deliberate and have purpose.

✦ Helps you communicate your vision to your Facebook fans, who then will know how to interact with your Page.

Your vision is only as strong as the person or team behind it. It's up to you to spread the word. The good news is that after you have a solid fan base, your fans will help spread your message and virally attract new followers. It's up to you to sell your vision to get others to pay attention.

Rule #2: Focus on smart branding

One way to understand the power of a Facebook Page is to look at it as a mini version of your own website. Some of the most successful Facebook Pages act as an extension of the brand and are essentially mini websites inside Facebook. Smart branding allows you to create a bridge from Facebook to your website. The key is to create a Page that sparks familiarity with your brand when your existing customers visit your Page.

Here are two examples of Facebook Pages (one of which is shown in Figure 2-7) that do a great job of mirroring their website branding. Check them out to see branding done right.

Social Media Examiner

Website: www.socialmediaexaminer.com

Facebook Page: www.facebook.com/smexaminer

Best Friends Animal Society

Website: http://bestfriends.org

Facebook Page: www.facebook.com/bestfriendsanimalsociety

You can't expect that consumers on Facebook will find you easily and automatically. Facebook users typically don't search actively for a brand's Facebook Page; instead, most users stumble upon a Page, either through a Friend's Page or from a hub such as your website. Branding your Page allows you to make your Page dynamic (stand out above the rest) and more viral (increasing the number of people who will see it).

Figure 2-7:
Smart
branding via
Best Friends
Animal
Society.

Rule #3: Create fresh content

To get the most reach for your content, do the following:

✦ **Make sure that your content educates, entertains, and empowers your fans.** This will pique their interest and keep them coming back for more.

✦ **Publish everything you have in as many places as possible.** You want to get your content online and seen by as many prospects as possible.

✦ **Monitor what others are publishing.** If you see something that would be valuable to your audience — and isn't in direct competition with your business — publish that content (and make sure to give the content's publisher credit for it!). Third-party publishing is a great way to continue to add value for your fans without having to create all the content yourself.

To help create content consistently, we suggest that you create an editorial calendar. It's a very simple task.

1. **Create a six-month digital calendar.**

Use a word processing program like Microsoft Word, or find a digital calendar online. One of our favorite digital calendar sites is www.calendars thatwork.com. Google calendars is also an excellent tool to use.

2. **Decide how often you want to create content, and in what form.**

Consider creating some of these:

• Blog posts

• Video posts

- Articles
- Reports
- Podcasts

Or create any other form of media you know your audience will like. Mix it up, delivering your content in many formats to attract a wider reach of ideal clients.

3. **Brainstorm content ideas related to your brand or niche.**

   Again, think of what interests your clients most. (*Hint:* Check out your competition's content. This will help you decide what may be best for your audience.)

4. **Create a calendar of content.**

   Choose the specific dates on which you plan to post, and list the topic of the content and the type of delivery. You might add the following in the June 18 box, for example: *Blog post and Facebook update on "How to Create a Facebook Page."* It's as easy as that!

Stay diligent with your content calendar. After you create it, stick with it. The more disciplined you are in sticking to your content calendar, the more traction you will gain with your audience.

Rule #4: Give your Page a human touch

To give your Page a human touch, highlight the team behind it. Your fans don't want to connect with your brand or product; they want to connect with you. As you have likely heard numerous times, social media is about transparency and authenticity. People want to know that they're communicating with the real you; that's why first names and photos are the norm on Facebook.

Brands that allow their Page administrators to have real conversations with their fans are much more likely to have active, engaging Pages. Here are a few key strategies to give your Facebook Page a human touch:

✦ Address your fans by their first names, and craft your posts in the first-person singular voice.

✦ Use a conversational tone in your posts.

✦ Encourage your Page administrators to add their names at the end of their posts, as shown in Figure 2-8.

✦ If you have multiple admins, add your Page administrators' photos and bios on a custom tab. This allows your fans to get to know the people who are representing your Page.

Figure 2-8:
Have Page
admins add
their names
to their
posts, like
melissa l.
did.

Best Friends Animal Society shared a link.
December 4

From stumbling across Best Friends in 2010 by finding our magazine in a waiting room, to attending the No More Homeless Pets Conference and now running a successful rescue that's saved over 224 cats already this year, it's safe to say Kim is on a roll! GET INSPIRED: http://bit.ly/InspiredByBestFriends. –melissa l.

Don't make your Page another static website. Give it a human touch by encouraging your admin team members to be themselves and communicate with your fans as though they were talking to their friends, and give each post that spark of personality (see Figure 2-9).

Figure 2-9:
A Facebook
Page tab
that spot-
lights the
Page admin-
istrators.

Rule #5: Cultivate engagement with two-way dialog

In a nutshell, engagement is about getting your fans to take action, which means posting on your Page, commenting on your posts, clicking the Like button next to your posts, and sharing your content. A well-executed engagement strategy takes time and effort. More than anything, engagement is really about showing up daily and taking a genuine interest in the likes, interests, and opinions of your fans.

An effective engagement plan is about your fans and not about you. Remember that people love to talk about themselves, so craft your posts and questions around them, and you're sure to see some great conversations begin to surface on your Page. Check out Figure 2-10 for an example of a question that's about the user — not about a brand.

Figure 2-10: Make your posts less promotional and more inclined to engage people.

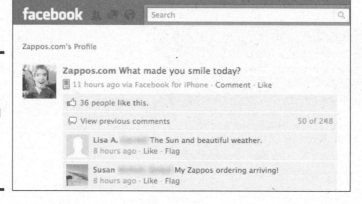

A massive fan base left disengaged is a recipe for disaster! Take action; start talking with your fans regularly.

Rule #6: Encourage fan-to-fan conversations

The key here is to enhance your fans' experience by creating a community that encourages peer-to-peer communication. Here are key strategies you can use to get fans talking to one another:

✦ **Showcase fans.** Create a Member of the Month campaign or an opportunity to spotlight your fans directly on your Facebook Page. When fans are recognized, they tell their Friends, which encourages even more fan-to-fan interaction.

✦ **Recognize top contributors.** When you have someone on your Page who likes to answer questions from fans, or who often offers tips or suggestions, take advantage of that enthusiasm. Ask the fan to be an ambassador for your Page, and encourage him to help out when appropriate.

Give your biggest advocates specific guidelines and responsibilities, and reward them with perks. Their involvement will free up time for you to concentrate on other ways to grow your Page.

Booshaka (`http://booshaka.com`) is a Facebook app that allows you to rank your Facebook fans by engagement, starting with the most engaged at the top of the list.

Rule #7: Make word-of-mouth advocacy easy

It's a fact that customers trust their friends and other customers more than they trust a brand. Think of it this way. If you were going to buy a new pair of running shoes, who would you listen to: your good friend who is an avid runner and who just purchased a pair, or the shoe manufacturer that's posting a promotion about those shoes on its Facebook Page? Gravitating toward the person you have a relationship with is human nature. That's precisely why word-of-mouth advocacy is essential.

To encourage word-of-mouth advocacy, make it easy for your fans to talk about you. Here are a couple of suggestions:

✦ **Ask a fan to like a post or share a post.** When you post a link to a new article on your Facebook Page, add a line at the end of the post that says, "If you like this article, please click the link to share it with your friends!" Keep the tone light and conversational, and your fans will be happy to oblige.

✦ **Do something that encourages self-expression.** People love to talk about themselves and share their thoughts, feelings, and feedback. Create an experience that makes them want to share your content with their friends. This is how the viral experience is created. To do this, you can create a poll on your Page or run a contest that gets your audience excited about engaging with you. We mention testing polls earlier in this chapter. (To find out more about contests on Facebook, check out Book VI, Chapter 2.)

Rule #8: Create consistent calls to action

To move your fans to action, you need to give them a reason to take action. Discounts or specials are great ways to reward your clients. You're saying, "Hey, I really appreciate your being a fan. Thanks for coming on over. I want to do something special for you now."

✦ Give out discount codes.

✦ Create a special custom app for your Page (see Book V, Chapter 2) and allow your fans to print the coupons.

✦ Ask fans to sign up for your online newsletter or a giveaway. This strategy is considered to be an *opt-in strategy,* and with custom apps, you can easily create an opt-in box (see Figure 2-11) to collect the names and e-mail addresses of your fans. Again, check out Book V, Chapter 2 for details about customized apps.

You want to keep your fans happy and get them to take action. Everybody loves a discount or a special, so think of ways you can incorporate these items into your Facebook marketing plan.

Figure 2-11:
Add an
opt-in
box on a
Facebook
Page.

Rule #9: Monitor, measure, and track

Although it may not sound like a fun task, it's essential that you monitor, measure, and track your Facebook activity.

In Book IX, we explore in depth the various ways for you to do this, but for the sake of your Facebook marketing plan, have surefire methods that let you consistently track your Facebook marketing progress.

The great thing about social media marketing is that it's not set in stone. In the past, you would have to print a marketing brochure for thousands (if not hundreds of thousands) of dollars and then cross your fingers, hoping that it worked because if it flopped, you had to wait until that brochure ran out and then spend a handful of money to test something new.

On Facebook and other social sites, most of the time tweaking a marketing campaign is as easy as clicking a button. That's a huge advantage of marketing online.

The key here is being diligent about testing what's working and instantly tweaking what's not. When you get into this habit, you can see progress much faster than you ever did with traditional marketing endeavors.

Summing up the nine rules

There's a lot of noise on the web about the do's and don'ts of social media marketing, and it tends to be overwhelming. This chapter's nine core rules are meant to simplify your process.

If you add a bunch of extra components to the rules, you're less likely to see the results you want — or, worse, you're likely to get overwhelmed and not take action. In short, ignore the chatter, and stick to the plan.

Creating a Facebook Page is fairly simple, but growing its momentum and getting it to thrive takes time, dedication, and some planning. Don't expect to create a Page and then see a massive following instantaneously. Create valuable content, encourage fans to share your Page with their friends, and tell people about it. With time and patience, you'll see your Page grow.

Setting Up Resources and Manpower for Your Plan

After you nail down what goes into your Facebook marketing plan, you'll want to explore what resources and manpower you have at your disposal. If you're an entrepreneur or the owner of a small business, you probably don't have a large team. The good news is that you don't need a large team behind you to attract a captive audience on Facebook. By following the nine core rules of a Facebook Page that we describe in the preceding section — and by keeping your Facebook marketing plan simple — you can grow your Page to the level you need with only a few hands on deck.

The following sections show you how to identify the people and resources you need to put your Facebook marketing plan to work.

Identifying your existing resources and manpower

First, do an internal assessment to identify your resources and manpower. For entrepreneurs and small business owners, the essential players are

✦ **At least two Page administrators.** Assign one admin the Page manager role, and the other person can be a content creator or moderator. We discuss all admin roles in more detail later in this chapter and in Book II, Chapter 3.

✦ **A designer and a programmer to help with your branding.** If you have the funds, we also suggest that you put some money toward a few sessions with a social media strategy consultant who will review your existing plan.

For larger businesses, if you have a marketing team, we suggest integrating your Facebook marketing plan into your existing marketing initiatives. Your Facebook marketing plan shouldn't be a stand-alone Facebook marketing tool; instead, it should be closely integrated into your overall marketing plan. Sit down with your existing marketing team, and go through the six Facebook marketing goals and nine core rules of a successful Facebook Page to see how they align with the programs and initiatives you already have in place.

Integrating your social media strategies

Along with your Facebook marketing plan, you'll likely want to consider other social media initiatives. Perhaps you'll want to include Twitter in your social media mix or create a YouTube channel as part of your social media outreach plan.

To get the most momentum for your social media marketing plan, don't separate your social media marketing efforts. One person, or one solid team, should oversee all social media efforts. It's important to have strong synergy among all social media sites; therefore, you want the person managing your Facebook Page to know firsthand what's taking place on your Twitter account, YouTube channel, and any other social site.

Deciding on in-house or outsourced marketing

After you decide to create a Facebook marketing plan, you have to decide who's going to run it. You have multiple options to consider for your social media management and support.

Option 1: Hire an agency (or consultant) to manage your Facebook Page

Like most things, this option has both pros and cons. We offer both sides for your consideration.

Pros:

✦ **You gain access to social media expertise and knowledge.** This is especially helpful if your knowledge is limited.

✦ **An agency or consultant can save you a tremendous amount of time.** If you're not consistently listening to your fans and interacting with them regularly, they will quickly lose interest in your Page. It might be a smart move for you to hire someone to take on this important task.

✦ **Social media experts tend to be in the know about the latest trends.** Because social media changes quickly, it's important to stay on the cutting edge and be the first to adopt new strategies or tools as they prove to be promising. An agency or consultant can advise you on the latest and greatest in social media marketing to keep you current and ahead of the pack.

✦ **You get expert advice on your social media content strategy.** One of the most important pieces of your Facebook marketing strategy is the content you post on your social networks. An agency or consultant can help you create a content plan to align with your overall marketing plan.

✦ **An agency or expert has access to monitoring and tracking tools and technology that you may not have.** This is important, because an agency can quickly see what is working and what needs tweaking, allowing your campaign to be monitored in real time.

Cons:

✦ **An agency won't know your products or services as well as you do.** If you're not careful, an agency may end up representing you or your brand in ways that don't particularly inspire confidence. Potential customers often ask questions about a product or service via a company's Facebook Page. Ask yourself this question: If an agency or consultant were managing your Page, would that agency or consultant be able to give the prospects accurate information?

Incorrect information could cost you a new client — or, worse, earn you backlash from your Facebook fans. One solution is to make sure that your agency or consultant has direct access to the appropriate people inside your company who can provide real-time support when needed.

✦ **An agency won't understand your brand as well as you do.** Successful brands have a specific voice, and it's critical that this voice be consistent throughout all your marketing initiatives. That said, it's paramount that your agency or consultant understand your brand voice and be clear on your brand personality and positioning. This clarity allows for a seamless transition between your company's communication style and the agency's communication on your behalf.

✦ **An agency won't know your company culture intimately and will be unaware of behind-the-scenes activities.** One of the most important aspects of Facebook marketing is the transparency factor. Your fans want to know your company and brand at an intimate level. That's what makes social media networking so attractive to consumers.

Only you and those who work with you intimately know what your company stands for and what its values are. This is difficult to explain to someone from the outside who isn't experiencing it firsthand. An agency or consultant isn't part of your culture and won't be able to communicate the special benefits of that culture to your fans unless you educate that agency or consultant in advance, which takes some dedication on your part.

Some of the most popular brands on Facebook allow their fans to get a glimpse of their company culture and what goes on behind the scenes. Zappos is a great example; see www.facebook.com/zappos.

✦ **If you (or someone on your team) don't manage your Facebook Page directly, you won't see what's happening on a day-to-day basis.** This situation means you lose a little control of what's taking place on your Page.

One solution is to ask your agency or consultant to report to you on a regular basis, informing you about what's taking place on your Page, and letting you know about any challenges and what was done to take care of them.

If you do decide to hire an agency or consultant, make sure that you discuss what's expected; the procedures you want the agency or consultant to adhere to at all times; and the rules, guidelines, and any specific procedures to follow in case of a crisis on any of your social networking sites.

Option 2: Self-manage your Facebook marketing plan

Most small to midsize businesses manage their Facebook marketing plan in-house. Overall, this strategy has multiple benefits. If you're managing your strategy in-house, you essentially eliminate all the cons discussed in the preceding section.

Option 3: Use the hybrid model

If you're new in the social media arena (as most people are), consider hiring support to some degree.

One solution that we suggest is the hybrid model. In essence, you hire an agency or consultant to help build your social media marketing strategy (including your Facebook marketing plan), and that agency or consultant can also support the launch of the strategy in the early stages. When things are off the ground and running smoothly (which may take about six months to get going), you and your team take over. You not only benefit from the agent's or consultant's expertise and experience, but also work in a certain amount of training so that you and your team are well equipped to take over after the agent's or consultant's contract ends.

Defining Your Admin Team

Among the most important roles on your Facebook Page are the administrator and administration team. You can have just one person manage your Page and oversee the management, monitoring, and content creation, but we suggest that you assign multiple admins to help support your Facebook Page activity. The great news is that you can assign different permissions to specific admin roles, meaning that you don't have to give full access of your Page to all your admins.

Having a few admins is a smart strategy because your admins can divide and conquer. With multiple admins, you can assign roles and responsibilities that are aligned with the admins' skills and strengths, and your Page will be more consistently managed when multiple people watch over day-to-day activity.

Make sure to assign each admin clear tasks to prevent overlap or confusion on your Page. Create a set of rules and guidelines to make sure that everyone is clear of the Page expectations for admins.

Filling the five admin roles

The five admin roles are

✦ **Manager** has full access to your Page. A manager can manage admin roles (meaning that he can add and delete admins and assign admin roles), edit the Page, add apps, create posts, respond to and delete comments, send messages, create Ads, and view Insights.

✦ **Content creator** can edit the Page, add apps, create posts, respond to and delete comments, send messages, create Ads, and view Insights.

✦ **Moderator** can respond to and delete comments, send messages, create Ads, and view Insights.

✦ **Advertiser** can create Ads and view Insights.

✦ **Insights Analyst** can view Insights.

Because you can assign different levels of access to your Page admins, take advantage of this feature by assigning some of your Facebook tasks to different people on your team.

Adding an admin

To add an admin to your Facebook Page, you have to be an admin manager of your Page. Only admin managers can add other admins. Here's how you do it:

1. **Log in to Facebook and go to your Facebook Page.**

2. **Choose Manage Admin Roles from the Edit Page drop-down menu (at the top of your Facebook Page in the Admin Panel).**

   You're taken to your admin page.

   If you already have multiple admins, your current admins' images and names pop up. You also see a field where you can enter the name or e-mail address of a person you want to add as an admin, as shown in Figure 2-12.

3. **Type the name or e-mail address of each person you want to add as an admin.**

   As you type the name, a drop-down menu appears, with possible choices of people you may be searching for.

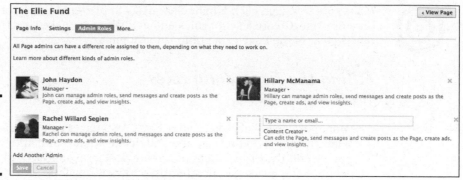

Figure 2-12:
Add a new
admin to
your Page.

4. **Click the correct name and profile image in the drop-down menu.**

   The full name populates instantly.

   Any admin of your Page must be Friends of your personal Profile or must
   have liked your Page. If you want to add someone who doesn't fit either
   description, you can add him as an admin by typing the e-mail address
   he uses to log in to Facebook. When you enter the e-mail address, that
   person receives an e-mail from Facebook, saying that he was made an
   admin of your Page.

5. **(Optional) Add more admins by clicking the Add Another Admin link.**

   The link is above the Save button; see Figure 2-12.

6. **If necessary, change the roles of your existing admins by clicking the
   drop-down menu below a name and choosing a new role, as shown in
   Figure 2-13.**

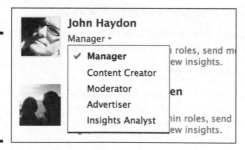

Figure 2-13:
Choose a
specific
admin
role for an
admin.

7. **Click Save.**

   You're prompted to add your Facebook password to secure the changes.

Deleting an admin

To delete an admin, follow these simple instructions:

1. **Log in to Facebook and go to your Facebook Page.**

2. **Choose Manage Admin Roles from the Edit Page drop-down menu (at the top of your Facebook Page in the Admin Panel).**

   You're taken to your admin page. If you already have multiple admins, your current admins' images and names pop up.

3. **Click the X next to the name of the admin you want to delete.**

4. **Click Save.**

   You're prompted to add your Facebook password to secure the changes.

   When you remove an admin, that person is automatically removed from your admin list. She won't receive notification that she's been removed as an admin.

Just as you're able to remove other admins of your Page, you can remove yourself as an admin. We don't recommend doing this, however. If you remove yourself as an admin of your Page, you lose all access to your Page, and you can no longer act as the owner of the Page. This means that you can't edit the Page, you can no longer post on behalf of the Page, and you can't access the Facebook Page dashboard. *Always keep yourself as an admin of your Facebook Page.*

Choosing the right Page manager

The *Page manager* is the admin of your Page who is ultimately responsible for managing the Page and making sure that it runs smoothly. In many ways, this admin manages the other admins who you've assigned to the Page. Additionally, the Page manager should be well aware of your Facebook marketing plan and should execute that plan on a daily basis.

A Page manager interacts with your fans daily, so take the time to choose this person wisely. More often than not, the person you end up choosing is already on your internal team because he knows your brand and your clients better than someone from the outside does. If you do need to hire an outside source, make sure that you train that person well and monitor her activity closely.

Checking out personality traits

When looking for the right manager for your Page, you want to make sure that person's personality is a good fit for your audience. Here are six personality traits of a superstar Page manager:

✦ Natural communicator

✦ Problem solver

+ Person who enjoys people

+ Good listener

+ Professional

+ Positive and enthusiastic

In addition to these traits, consider your ideal audience. Make sure that your Page manager will connect easily with your fans.

Searching for skills

Although personality traits are important for a Page manager, keep in mind that any successful Page manager must also possess these necessary skills:

+ Solid understanding of social networking

+ Social media savvy

+ Strong commitment to helping people in social channels

+ Ability to multitask and think quickly

+ Knowledge and understanding of online marketing

+ Ability to grasp how social media activity aligns with business goals

Making the final choice

To make the right decision, here are some important questions to ask before you decide who will ultimately manage your Facebook Page:

+ Does this person show the ability to be social online?

+ Does this person show a genuine interest in connecting with our clients?

+ Can I trust this person to be professional and respectful at all times?

+ Do people naturally gravitate toward this person?

+ Will this person actively contribute to new ideas to grow the Page and make it better each day?

Considering a social media manager

A *social media manager* differs from a Facebook Page manager in that the social media manager is responsible for all social media channels, as well as the overall social media marketing strategy. In addition, a social media manager must interact regularly with your internal marketing team (if you have one).

The size of your organization, your overall budget, and your access to resources are major factors in deciding whether a social media manager is right for your business.

A social media manager must possess personality traits and skill sets similar to those of Page manager. See "Choosing the right Page manager," earlier in this chapter, to review the necessary traits and skills.

In addition, the social media manager must know your company, brand, products, and services well, and must have a strong background in traditional marketing as well as a strong grasp of new media marketing trends.

In a nutshell, social media manager is a higher-level position than Page manager and has many more responsibilities. Whereas you may be able to add the Page manager role to an existing employee's plate, the social media manager role is more robust and time-consuming, and requires more experience and a higher-level skill set than that of Page manager.

We suggest that you start small:

✦ First, identify and test a dedicated manager for your Facebook Page, and hire a social media consultant or agency for just a few months to get you up and running.

✦ Next, review your activity, and decide whether a social media manager would add value and growth to your overall plan.

✦ Finally, just as you would with a Page manager and admins of your Facebook Page, if you decide to hire a social media manager, make sure to create clear roles, responsibilities, and guidelines for this position.

Coordinating admin posts and strategies

Strive to assign clear guidelines and rules not only for your Page manager but also for your multiple admins. To keep your admins on task without duplicating efforts, give them clear direction. That way, your Page will be updated regularly, your fans will be supported, and your admins won't be confused about their Page responsibilities.

As we mention earlier in this chapter, an editorial calendar can come in handy when coordinating posts and marketing messages. To ensure all your admins are on the same page, encourage each of them to use the same editorial calendar to track activity.

Here are some guidelines to consider as you coordinate posts and strategies:

✦ **Decide how you want your admins to post on your Page.** Here are some questions you want to ask about your status updates and posts on your Timeline:

• How often will you post updates to your Page?

• What will you post about?

• Will you include links in your posts to direct fans to content outside Facebook?

- Will you use third-party content, such as posts from your favorite blog sites and videos from YouTube, to add value?

- Will you mix up the media, using video, audio, and photos?

✦ **Determine a communication strategy.** There's a fine balance between controlling the conversations on your Page and allowing your fans to interact freely with each other without much policing on your part. Decide how your admins should manage this important balance. The goal is to monitor your Page so that it has no inappropriate behavior or content that could damage your reputation, but at the same time, not be too controlling (because you might stop conversations that otherwise would develop freely).

✦ **Assign and document roles.** One admin may be responsible for posting one third-party article a day, and another admin may be assigned the task of uploading company videos throughout the week. Other tasks could include posting questions, uploading company photos to a photo album, monitoring and responding to all fan posts, and posting on fan Pages to increase overall engagement. Whatever the tasks, make sure that your admins are clear on their duties so they're not confused.

✦ **Create internal guidelines.** Every Facebook Page should have a "do's and don'ts" list associated with it, and your internal team should use that list as a guide. Make very clear what you allow and what you won't tolerate on your Page. Include what can and can't be discussed, including company-related content and personal content. Decide how often you'll promote your programs and services, and explain what acceptable promotion looks like. Think about your company, your mission, and your goals, and carefully craft your guidelines around them. The time you spend on this task will spare you a lot of headaches in the future!

Measuring Your Return on Investment

Because we're still in the early days of social media marketing, measuring return on investment (ROI) is, in a word, tough. There's still much debate about what you can and can't measure because in many ways, social media is considered to be a soft marketing vehicle, meaning it's still debatable how we should measure hard metrics like dollars earned and customers acquired.

With that in mind, think about your marketing goals and what you plan to accomplish via your new Facebook marketing plan. If you start from there, you're sure to identify areas that you can measure to track your results.

Defining success

To define success, it's essential to have a solid Facebook marketing plan. You have to know what success looks like before you start. For you, success may include getting people to interact and leave comments on your Facebook

Page, encouraging your Facebook fans to check out your website, and/or selling your products and services on your Facebook Page. It comes down to aligning your social media metrics with the metrics your company is already comfortable with. In Book IX, we drill into the specific areas you'll want to track and analyze to make sure that your Facebook marketing plan is working for you.

Measuring brand ROI

The best way to think about measuring brand ROI is to consider how recognizable your brand is to your target audience. It really comes down to identifying how often your fans are engaging with your Page. The number of likes you have is important, but the frequency at which your fans are responding to your questions or engaging with your posts is even more important. You want to track how many times your fans are clicking your links and responding to your posts with comments.

In addition, you want to consider how well your existing customers can identify with your brand on Facebook. Is your Facebook branding consistent with your website, products, and or services? You want to create a bridge from Facebook to your main hub, and you do this with consistent branding.

Measuring financial ROI

The best way to measure financial ROI for your Facebook marketing plan is to set benchmarks. You want to clearly document what you're working toward in terms of sales and how you can use Facebook as part of this strategy. You also want to decide whether your goal is to sell directly from your Page or to use your Page as a channel to funnel interested prospects to a sales page after you build their trust and offer them immense value. Measuring your financial ROI comes down to your sales strategy for your Page.

If your goal is to sell your products or services from your Facebook Page, you need to identify benchmarks for this process. Look at how many people you manage to attract to your Page daily; track which tabs they click and how long they stay on your Page overall. You can do all this by using Facebook Insights and third-party monitoring tools.

In Book IX, we walk you through how to use Facebook Insights and third-party monitoring tools to help you better understand how to track your financial ROI for your Facebook marketing initiatives.

Book II

Claiming Your Presence on Facebook

For more on how to get started on claiming your presence on Facebook, go to www.dummies.com/extras/facebookmarketingaio.

Contents at a Glance

Chapter 1: Understanding Facebook Pages and Personal Accounts 59

Reviewing Facebook Pages and Account Types 60
Navigating Your Personal Profile Timeline and the Follow Button 60
Getting Down to Business...66
Making a Places Page 68
Creating a Facebook Group 71
Setting Up an Interest Page 72

Chapter 2: Creating Your Business Page 77

Considering a Few Things before You Start 77
Setting Up Your New Business Page 81
Completing, Publishing, and Promoting Your Page 86
Claiming a Facebook Place 106
Merging a Facebook Place with Your Page 108
Managing Missteps..110

Chapter 3: Administering Your Facebook Business Page 115

Viewing Facebook as Your Page 115
Understanding How Other People See Your Page..................................123
Editing Your Page 132
Edit Settings...135

Chapter 4: Arranging What Your Visitors See 145

Finding Your Page 145
Understanding How Apps Act as Navigation Links 147
Adding Facebook Apps to Your Page 148
Changing the Order of Apps on Your Page 155
Using the Hover Card as an Ad 156

Chapter 5: Using Your Personal Profile to Support Your Business 159

Determining Whether the Follow Button Is Right for You 159
Turning On Your Follow Button 162
Editing the Follow Settings 164
Seeing How to Post Publicly...165
Marketing Basics with a Personal Profile 167
Understanding Friend Followers and Public Followers...........................169
Adding Public Life Events to Your Personal Profile 171
Adjusting Your Timeline for Public Viewing...172
Uploading a Cover Photo that Supports Your Business 174

Chapter 1: Understanding Facebook Pages and Personal Accounts

In This Chapter

✔ Familiarizing yourself with Facebook Page and account options

✔ Addressing privacy concerns

✔ Understanding why you need a Profile to have a business Page on Facebook

✔ Knowing when to use Facebook as your personal account or as your Page

✔ Taking the big view of how a Page works and where everything is located

Facebook offers Pages to encourage community and networking. To create the biggest buzz around your product, service, or business, you need to be aware of the Facebook Page and account options and of the pros and cons of each. This chapter explains those options so that you can decide which type of Page best fits your needs.

We cover Profiles, Pages, Places, Groups, Interest Pages, and limited business accounts. Although each choice has merit, it's usually best to create a Page for your product, service, or business (and we explain why in this chapter).

If you already have a Profile on Facebook (a Timeline), you know how easy it is to create an account. You may think it's a snap to set up your own Page for your business, too, and figure that you'll just skip this chapter. We have one word for you: Don't! You need to know some intricacies of crafting a Profile or Page that you might otherwise miss along the way.

One of the most important things we discuss in this chapter is who can and cannot create a certain kind of Page. We go into detail as we discuss each type of Facebook Page, but the gist is this: You must be an authorized representative of an organization to create a Page for it. If you aren't the authorized representative and want to create a space where fans of a certain topic or figure can share their thoughts and opinions, Facebook suggests that you create a Group for them. We discuss Facebook Groups in this chapter, too.

You can also create a Page to express support for a brand, entity, or public figure, provided that it is not likely to be confused with an official page or to violate someone's rights. See the Facebook Page Terms for all the guidelines: `https://www.facebook.com/page_guidelines.php`.

Reviewing Facebook Pages and Account Types

The two ways to establish a presence on Facebook are Profiles for yourself and for business. Here are the two ways to establish a presence on Facebook:

✦ **Profile** (sometimes called "the Timeline" because of its chronological design), allows you to have subscribers (more on that in a moment), but in essence, it's just a "personal profile." This is your "face" on Facebook, but on a more informal level, something that a friend (or your mom, or a Fantasy Football colleague) would see. Compare that with a Page for a business . . . which is the next bullet.

✦ **Pages** also use the Timeline design. You can create a Page for a formal entity — like a business or a band or a celebrity — and some people call these "business Pages."

When we use the word *Timeline* in this chapter, we put either *personal* or *business* in front of it so you don't get confused. (That's a heroic goal on Facebook: not to get confused!) Don't get bogged down in the vocab.

You can also use Facebook Groups to supplement your Facebook marketing efforts. Another thing you may run across on Facebook is an Interest Page. The next few sections offer a brief review of these entities and explain why you should avoid or embrace them. Everyone's needs are a little different, though.

Navigating Your Personal Profile Timeline and the Follow Button

Over 1 billion people use Facebook as a social space to keep up with friends, share photos and links, and share great stuff they find online. It's a space where people can connect after not being in touch for a long time or find people they would like to get to know better. It's a place for social interaction. It's where the social party is right now! It's time to join the party by creating a Profile and using Facebook as a social and commerce environment.

Facebook likes to keep the two uses — social and commerce — separate, but Facebook also has a Follow system as a way for public figures to market themselves in a personal Profile.

Following someone's Profile is a lot like following someone on Twitter. In other words, you don't have to be Friends with someone on Facebook to see that person's Public posts. Whenever you post, you can designate Public, Friends, or a custom list depending on who you want to see the post. A Public post is an open post; anyone who has a Facebook account can see it.

There's a very clear marketing strategy behind activating your Follow button on a Profile. We cover this strategy in just a moment, but here's the gist of it:

✦ If you're branding yourself, consider allowing the Follow button on your Profile and possibly creating a Page for a business. This applies to speakers, artists, authors, or anyone who is the "face" of their business branding.

✦ If you're branding your business, create a Page for that. This applies to corporations, restaurants, or any business that is known by the business name only.

By creating a Profile and activating your Follow button, you can be Friends with friends and relatives and ask your existing customers to follow your Profile. If you also build your business Page on Facebook, you can go back to your followers and invite them, if appropriate. If you don't have this initial personal connection, the only way to invite people to your Page is through things like paid Facebook Ads, marketing materials, Facebook buttons on your website, or e-mail.

A Profile on Facebook is easy to start. One of the fastest-growing demographics joining are people over 35. If you've never enjoyed a social space, it may feel a bit strange at first, but you'll catch on. Then you'll see how easy it is to engage and develop social connections for your business.

Creating a personal Profile

We feel that a Facebook Profile is a vital first step, especially if you're a public figure and plan to use the Follow option.

If you don't already have a Profile set up on Facebook, run (don't walk) to www.facebook.com, and set up an account. Facebook makes it super easy. Right from the home page, enter your

✦ First and last name

✦ E-mail address (and then again as confirmation)

✦ Password

✦ Gender

✦ Birthday

Facebook requires all users to provide their real date of birth to encourage authenticity and provide only age-appropriate access to content. You will be able to hide this information from your personal connections (and people who like your business Page), if you want, and its use is governed by the Facebook Privacy Policy.

After entering the necessary personal information, click the Sign Up button. You now have a Facebook Profile. Figure 1-1 shows what your Timeline looks like before you have added anything and after you add Cover photos and make a few posts.

Figure 1-1:
A Timeline.

Some people worry that visitors will see the connection between their Profile and the business Page they create, so they make a bogus personal Profile before they open their business Page. We don't recommend doing this, either. Besides, Facebook frowns on creating fake accounts. By *frowns on,* we mean that Facebook might delete *all* your Facebook accounts if it discovers that you've been creating fake Profiles. Don't risk the wrath of Facebook by setting up a bogus account!

Be assured that people who choose to connect to your business Page won't be able to see that you're the Page owner or Admin (administrator), or have access to your Profile unless you change your Page settings to list yourself publicly as an Admin of the Page.

It's all very clear from Facebook's side: You may create business Pages only to represent real organizations of which you are an authorized representative. There's no pretending to be someone you're not. In other words, even if you intended all along for the account you created to be just a great joke, Facebook lacks a sense of humor in that regard.

It's against Facebook policy to create a Profile that uses the name of the business — as in, *O'Grady's* for the first name and *Cleaners* for the last name. If you do create a Profile for your business in this fashion, Facebook can (and will) delete all your accounts, and they won't be reinstated. In case you mistakenly create a personal Profile with your business name, we explain how to move it to a Page it in the next chapter.

If you already have a Profile with your real name, with many Friends who are actually business connections, you may want to explore the subscribe option or build a business Page and ask everyone to like it.

If your Profile has been functioning as a business, with a business name (like *O'Grady Cleaners*), you may want to change the account name to your real name and then explore the Subscribe option and/or build a business Page and ask everyone to like it.

Turning on the Follow button

We mention earlier in this chapter that you have good marketing reasons for a Profile with the Follow button activated. If you already have lots of Facebook Friends who are more like potential customers or clients, and you haven't taken the time to create a business Page (and probably won't), this approach is for you! We go over all this more thoroughly in Book II, Chapter 4, and we cover it a bit more in Book IV, Chapter 5. In the meantime, if you're ready to open the Follow button on your Profile, read on.

Here's how to turn on the Follow button on your personal Profile:

1. **Click the down arrow in the upper-right corner of Facebook.**

    A drop-down menu appears.

2. **Select Settings.**

3. **Click Followers on the left sidebar.**

4. **Select Everybody from the drop-down menu next to the Who Can Follow Me section. (See Figure 1-2.)**

5. **Adjust the settings to your liking for Follower Comments and Notifications.**

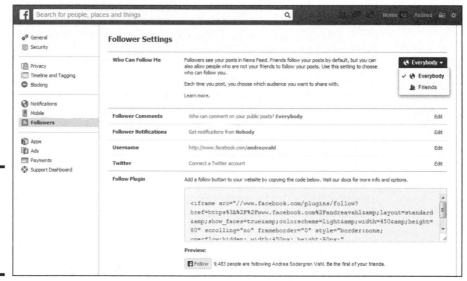

Figure 1-2: Here is where you adjust your Follower settings.

Enabling the Follow button is optional. You can enjoy a Profile and share with only Friends and family; you don't have to turn on the Follow button.

A Profile's follow system offers these highlights:

✦ After someone follows you, that person sees your Public updates in his or her News Feed. People may also discover your Profile through the People to Follow box on the right side of their News Feed or through their Friends' News Feed stories.

✦ Followers can share your Public posts, which broadcasts your post and Profile to a larger audience.

✦ You can have an unlimited number of followers (no more 5,000 Friend limit).

✦ You can block people from being able to follow you by adjusting your Privacy Settings Block List.

✦ You can connect with and promote to people on Facebook who prefer to subscribe to instead of like a business Page.

✦ When your Follow button is open, anyone who requests to be your friend automatically becomes a follower unless you then block them. Now you know they're getting your public updates; you don't have to friend them unless you want to also get their updates.

✦ When you unfriend someone, they remain a Follower unless you block them.

✦ You can unfollow a friend. You are still Friends, but you do not receive their updates in your News Feed.

✦ Personal profiles get more exposure in the News Feed due to Facebook's News Feed algorithm. (See Chapter 2 of Book IV for more information on the News Feed algorithm.) You have a better chance of being seen if you're also using your Personal profile to post about your business.

For more information about the Follow features, see Facebook's Help section at `https://www.facebook.com/help/follow/`.

Talking about the Ticker

Before we move on to the Facebook Page, take a minute to look at the Ticker. The *Ticker* is a column of real-time notifications on the right side of your News Feed page; see Figure 1-3. You see it when you're logged in to your personal Profile. The Ticker has been rumored to be going away but no formal announcement has been made.

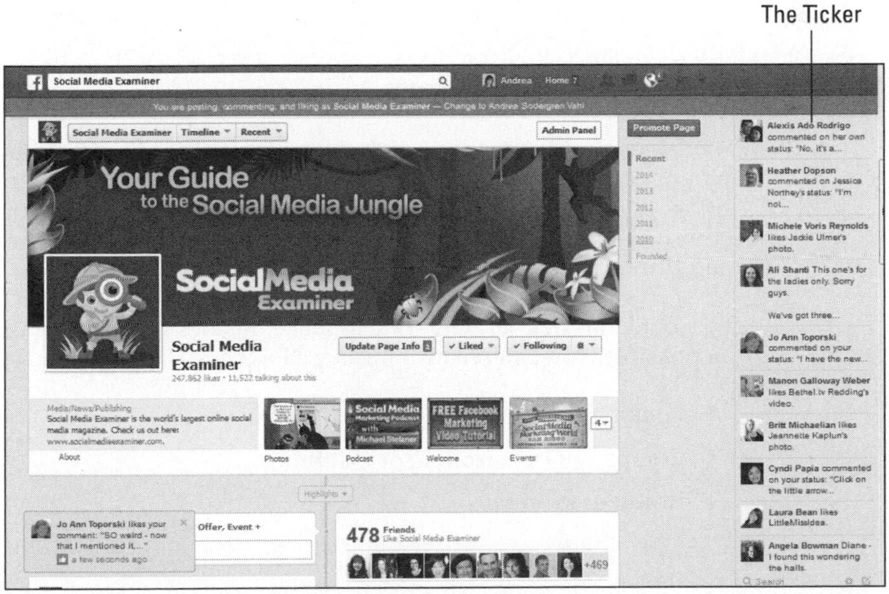

Book II
Chapter 1

Understanding
Facebook Pages and
Personal Accounts

The Ticker

Figure 1-3:
This is the Ticker.

A nice thing about the Ticker when you're using the personal Profile Subscription option is that your Public posts appear in your subscribers' News Feeds. When someone comments on a post, the link and the comment appear in the Ticker; therefore, more people have the opportunity to see it. Notice also that you can see the Ticker when you are logged in as your personal profile even if you are on a Page as shown in Figure 1-3.

When you hover on any item in the Ticker, a pop-up window displays the post and comments, and you can interact with it right there. You can also reply as your Page; more on that topic coming up in Book II, Chapter 3.

Other business advantages of the Ticker include

✦ Comments made on older posts (either as a Public post to your subscribers or as your business Page) are posted to the Ticker, so you can keep getting exposure even after a post is days, weeks, or months old. Encourage new comments and reply to new comments. Each engagement returns it to the Ticker.

✦ When people like your business Page, that action appears in the Ticker. Anyone seeing that notification can hover on it and like your Page, too, right from the pop-up window.

✦ Every time you add a picture to your personal or business Page, a notification appears in the Ticker. When someone hovers on it, she can comment right there. Takeaway? Post a lot of pictures!

After setting up a Profile, having started finding old and new friends on Facebook, and trying out the Follow system with your Public posts, you can explore a business Page.

Getting Down to Business

A business Page provides wonderful opportunities for marketing and promoting your business. It doesn't matter whether you're talking about a bricks-and-mortar business or a virtual consulting firm that you run out of your car. This Page can help your business grow, which we cover in Book I and throughout this entire book.

Facebook has deliberately tried to make business Pages as broad and useful as possible. You can create a business Page for all of the following:

✦ Local Business or Place

✦ Company, Organization, or Institution

✦ Brand or Product

✦ Artist, Band, or Public Figure

✦ Entertainment

✦ Cause or Community

In Book II, Chapter 2, we explain each option in detail and discuss how to choose the one that's right for you. We also give you the steps for creating your business Page on Facebook.

As we note in the section on personal Profiles earlier in this chapter, you can opt to have only a Profile with the Follow button activated and post Public posts. You don't need to create a business Page at all. But creating a personal Profile and then creating a Facebook business Page makes sense for most people because of the features both have. Take a look at some of the things you can do with a Page that you can't do with a Personal profile:

✦ Have multiple Admins.

✦ Access Facebook Insights.

✦ Install custom tabs.

✦ Run a contest.

✦ Advertise your Page.

✦ Target updates by criteria like gender, location, age, and language.

These business Page features are integral parts of the reason why you should use a business Page as your product, service, or company hub on Facebook.

If you're branding yourself and don't need any of the Page apps (you find out about them in Book V) or a detailed analytics system (Book IX), develop the personal Profile with the Follow button. If you're branding your business and need both ads and deep analytics, open a business Page.

Although you may want to keep your Profile private and connect only with certain people, you'll likely want as many people as possible to connect with your business on Facebook. The way to do that is via a Facebook business Page, which has no limits on the number of fans (that is, likes) you can have and lets you install applications as well.

Applications ("apps") are useful to business Pages. You can install apps for contact forms, newsletter signups, live video chats, and much more. Depending on which apps you install, you can use these apps to improve your fans' interaction with your page and to streamline your Facebook administrative duties. We tell you all about Facebook applications and give you our top suggestions for apps in Book V and throughout this book. We give you a little peek at what you can expect your business Page to resemble in Figure 1-4.

Figure 1-4:
An example
of a
Facebook
business
Page.

Making a Places Page

Places — an effort by Facebook to create a community experience with your Facebook Friends while you're out and about — ties the computer Facebook experience to the mobile Facebook experience. Places is Facebook's answer to other geolocation applications, like Foursquare.

Places allows your fans to use their smartphones through http://touch. facebook.com to check in to your bricks-and-mortar store or restaurant when they visit. This check-in shows up in their News Feeds so that their Friends will see it. The average Facebook user has 130 Friends, so that's a lot of extra promotion for you!

Figure 1-5 shows what Places on a mobile phone may look like when someone checks in. Note that this is from an Android device, an iPhone looks slightly different. At the top of the Page is the option of Liking the Page, Reviewing the Page, or Checking in. If you select the More button you can Call, Share, Copy Link, Suggest Edits, or Report. Currently, you don't see any custom apps on the mobile interface.

If you scroll down the mobile Page, you see the friends who have liked the Page or checked in to the Place, photos that have been taken at the Place, and then posts by the Page itself.

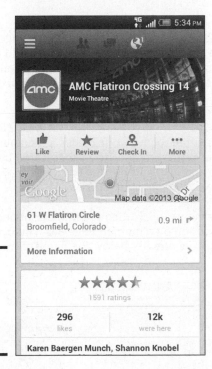

Figure 1-5:
A Places
Check-In
Page on
a mobile
interface.

Places Pages can be created by anyone at any time. When users check in via their smartphones by using `http://touch.facebook.com` or `http://m.facebook.com`, and the place the user is checking in to doesn't have a Places Page, he or she can create one. As a business owner, you can surely see why you'd want to retain control of your Places Page rather than leave that control to the masses. You have two options:

✦ If your business doesn't have a Places Page, you can create one just by indicating that you're a Local Business in the Page category.

✦ If a Places Page is already created for your business, don't worry! You can still claim the Places Page as the official representative and obtain control of the page.

We explain how to figure out whether your business already has a Places Page created in Chapter 2 of this minibook.

After you determine whether you have a Places Page, claim your Facebook Places Page so that you have control of how that Page is administered. When you claim your Places Page, you're just confirming with Facebook that you're the owner of the company or an authorized representative acting on behalf of the company.

After you claim your Places Page, you can merge your Places Page with your business Page on Facebook. If you merge your business Page and Places Page, create your business Page first and then claim or create your Places Page. Merging a business Page and a Places Page keeps everything from your business Page (photos, posts, events, video, and ads).

Including a physical street address when you create a business Page automatically adds the ability for people to give your Places a recommendation. They can give your place a star rating which is then aggregated below your name (as shown in Figure 1-5) and also add a comment if desired. This can contribute to your social proof.

A merged Page looks a lot like Figure 1-6. Notice the number of people who have checked in. The About section on a merged Page has a map, and the Review section star rating displays directly below the name of the Page.

Figure 1-6: This is how a merged Places and business Page looks.

Creating a Facebook Group

A Facebook Group isn't officially a business-type Page that people Like.
A Facebook Group can supplement a business's Page, however, and Groups
deserve a mention when discussing how to market your business on Facebook.
You have three options when it comes to creating a Facebook Group:

✦ **Closed Groups:** This type is the default. The members are *public* (meaning that the Facebook community can see that the group exists), but
the content is private. You see the updates to this type of group in your
News Feed, with an icon. When you hover over it, the text reads `Shared
with: Members of {group name}`.

✦ **Open Groups:** The members and content are public. Anything you post
inside this group will show up on your Groups Timeline, as well as on
your Friends' News Feeds.

✦ **Secret Groups:** The members and content are private. As with the
Closed Group, you see the updates in your News Feed, with an icon.
When you hover over it, the text reads `Shared with: Members of
Group Name`. No one else besides the Group members will see the
updates in any way.

Most group Pages look the same but simply have different privacy settings.
Figure 1-7 shows what a Groups Page looks like to members. This particular
group decided to use an image at the top of the Page, but you can have the
thumbnail images of the members across the top.

**Book II
Chapter 1**

**Understanding
Facebook Pages and
Personal Accounts**

Figure 1-7:
A Facebook
Groups
Page is a
great way to
collaborate
on projects
or discuss
specific
topics.

Although a Groups Page isn't considered to be an official business Page, it can offer some wonderful benefits when it's used in conjunction with your business Page. To see what we mean, consider the following business uses for a group Page:

✦ **You can create a Closed Groups Page for the members of a collaborative project.** The members of this type of group are public as a way to create a bit of mystery or buzz about an upcoming event for those who see the group listing in Facebook Search, but discussions between members are private.

✦ **You can create an Open group for discussion around your niche.** Something that people do is to create a Facebook group about their niche if there are a lot of questions or topics to discuss. You will have to moderate the topics and start discussions as well, but it's a wonderful and innovative way to advertise your expertise! If you do this, be prepared for others to jump in with answers to the questions as well.

✦ **You can create a Secret Groups Page for your staff.** With a Secret Groups Page in place, your staff can post updates, links, videos, events, and documents that only those staff members in the group can see. They can have a group chat, and everyone can type text in the chat box at the same time. A Facebook group chat in the morning, before work starts, would be a fun way to start the day. Here's a great post on using Secret Groups for businesses:

> www.socialmediaexaminer.com/how-to-use-secret-facebook-groups-to-enhance-your-business

See what types of Groups some of your friends have joined by going to www.facebook.com/findgroups.

Setting Up an Interest Page

Interest Pages, formerly known as Community Pages, are Facebook Pages dedicated to a single cause or topic. Facebook automatically generates them from the fields that people fill out in their Profiles. These Pages should not be confused with the Cause or Community business Page options that individuals can create.

This section explains the generic Facebook-generated Interest Page, and we explain the Cause or Community option for a Page in Book II, Chapter 2. We know that the terms are confusing, but these are two separate types of Pages. Figures 1-8 and 1-9 show how these pages differ.

Figure 1-8:
A generic,
Facebook-
generated
Interest
Page.

Figure 1-9:
A Cause or
Community
Page has
all the func-
tions of a
business
Page.

Generic, Facebook-created Interest Pages are commonly disregarded because
they lack the information and functionality of business Pages. They don't
make good business hubs for several reasons:

✦ **No one owns an Interest Page.** You can't administer or impose your business culture on a generic community Page because it doesn't belong to you.

✦ **You can't post regularly to a generic Interest Page.** These pages pull in articles that you or your Friends post about a topic, but no one can contribute information directly to an Interest Page. The only way to have any post show up on an Interest Page is to use the keyword that is the Page's title. Use *yoga* in a post, for example, and it shows up on the Interest Page for yoga. In fact, as you can see in Figure 1-8, Interest Pages don't have a traditional Timeline. Instead, you land on the Info tab, which is really just a landing page; you can't interact with the information.

✦ **You can't install applications on an Interest Page.** As we state earlier in this chapter, applications can be important parts of your marketing strategies because they customize and add function to your business Page.

✦ **Updates to Interest Pages don't appear in the News Feed.** Although an Interest Page has a Like button at the top (just as a business Page does), these pages don't generate News Feed stories, so you won't see anything from an Interest Page showing up in your personal News Feed (and neither will your customers and fans). If you click the Like button, though, that Page shows up in your personal Profile below Likes and Interests on your Info tab.

So how do you know whether you're looking at a generic, Facebook-generated Interest Page? There are several ways (refer to Figure 1-8):

✦ On an Interest Page, there's no large Cover photo, and the information at the top is taken from Wikipedia. Below the Wikipedia entry you see your Friends who like the Interest, Related Pages, and Related Groups, as well as possible other information. There is no traditional Timeline. On the other hand, a community business Page has a large Cover photo and up to four featured app boxes.

✦ Most Interest Pages display a related Wikipedia article if one is available. You may also see posts by your Friends or the global Facebook community that contain the keyword of the Interest Page. (If the Interest Page is for yoga, for example, any articles posted by your Friends that contain the word *yoga* show up here.)

✦ Many Interest Pages display a generic image as the Profile image, whereas others display an image related to the topic. Depending on the type of interest, you may see a gray square with a white silhouette of a specific image (such as a briefcase, a student in a mortarboard, or a molecule); a logo or image from a business, school, or topic; and so on. Sometimes, an image from the Wikipedia article is used in that space, as you see in Figure 1-9.

We encourage you to search your business name to see whether Facebook has created Interest Pages for it. You may find two types of unclaimed Pages. One is a generic Company Page, and another is a Place Page. When you find a Place Page with your business name, you can start the process of claiming it. Look for the Know The Owner? button, and click it. Then enter your e-mail address and start the process to claim the Page (see Figure 1-10).

Click this button to claim the page.

Figure 1-10:
Find any
Place Pages
with your
business
name, and
start the
process of
claiming
them.

The other type of Page that may have your name is a generic Company Page.
These types of Pages are created automatically when someone (and maybe
it was even you!) edits their Works and Education section in their Profile.
If they type your business name without linking it to your Facebook Page,
Facebook creates a generic Company Page. See Figure 1-11.

Figure 1-11:
A generic
Company
Page is cre-
ated when
someone
enters a
business
name as an
employer.

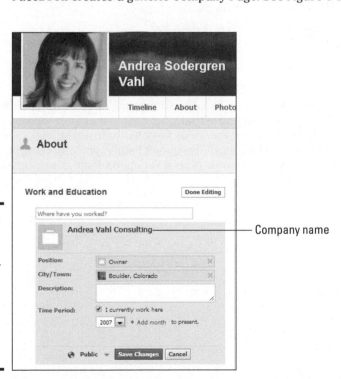

Company name

Unfortunately, there is no way to claim these generic Pages or track down who created them. You can typically tell a generic Company Page by the suitcase photo and the fact that they have no other information about them, as shown in Figure 1-12. Note that people can still Like these Pages — and they may even think that they are Liking your business! However, these generic Pages can't be updated, so it's in your best interest to make sure people are directed to your official Page.

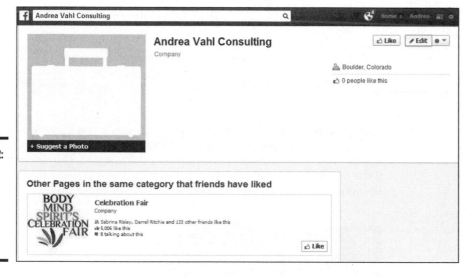

Figure 1-12:
A generic Company Page does not have a way to claim it.

The best thing you can do to make sure your Page is found before these generic Pages is to make sure that your profile and your employee's profiles are linked to your official Facebook Page as their workplace. (See Chapter 5 of this minibook.) The generic Facebook Pages typically disappear from the search results as long as your official Facebook Page is getting more Likes than the generic Page.

Chapter 2: Creating Your Business Page

In This Chapter

✔ Choosing your Page name and type

✔ Modifying Page settings to match your needs

✔ Going through the steps to publish your new business Page

✔ Sharing your business Page with customers

✔ Managing missteps

This chapter is all about creating your business presence on Facebook by opening a Facebook Page. We always think it's a good idea to read the instructions before building something new, and we suggest that here, too. Choosing your Page type and category might be very clear-cut for you — or maybe not. Reading and exploring how it works can be an interesting first step.

In this chapter, we take you through the steps to create your Facebook business Page. Then, we show you how to let people know that your Page is open for business. If you're reading this after you've already created an account or a business Page on Facebook, but you might have done it the wrong way, we address that, too.

 One way that we enjoy exploring what other people have done is by going to www.facebook.com/pages. Check out the names of Pages: You can sort by the types at the top of the Page. Explore by clicking a few Pages. You can learn a lot by seeing how other businesses created their Pages.

Considering a Few Things before You Start

Creating your Facebook business Page is an important process, and we want you to be as awake as possible while going through it. Some of the selections you make will determine many future functions, such as the information fields on your Info Page that you'll surely want to use in your marketing plan. In particular, you want to carefully consider what to name your Page and which type of business Page to create.

You can change the Page type at any time, but making changes will affect the types of informational fields you have available for use, too.

Choosing the right name for your business Page

The name you give to your business Page is extremely important because it becomes the title of your Page. When a customer, fan, or Friend searches for your business Page on Facebook, this name/title will enable her to find you. Because naming your Page is so important, we'd like you to mull over a few things. Here are a few naming do's and don'ts to consider before you create your business Page:

Page names must

+ Use proper, grammatically correct capitalization

+ Have logical, correct punctuation

+ Include your name, if you're branding yourself

+ Include your business keywords, if you're branding your niche or product

Page names can't use the following:

+ Excessive capitalization or all capitals

+ Symbols such as ! or ® or ™ (although you can use a hyphen)

+ Repeated and unnecessary punctuation

+ Abusive terms

+ The word *Facebook* or any variation of it

Facebook wants you to create concise Page names without long tag lines after the name. You can use up to 75 character spaces for your Page name, but we encourage you to keep things short and sweet. All the businesses we know that created long Page names eventually wanted to shorten them. Consider this example of a Page created with a very long tagline: iPhoneLife Magazine & iPhoneLife.com — *User created stories, tips & reviews.* A real mouthful. Facebook approved it, and it was used that way for a year until Facebook gave Pages the capability to change their names — and this company jumped to truncate the name to *iPhone Life magazine.*

Typically, you can't change a Page name after it has more than 200 likes, but this editing door opened for just a few days after a major Facebook update. This option to change a Page name has come and gone two times since we started writing this chapter. We don't know whether it will be around when you create your Page, so think through your name carefully in case you can't change it in the future. Facebook doesn't want you to use superfluous descriptions or unnecessary qualifiers, such as the word *official* in a Page name. Campaign names and regional or demographic qualifiers, though, are acceptable. Nike Football Spain is just fine, for example.

Stay clear of generic terms for your Page name, too. If you name a Page using a generic reference to the category — such as *Jewelry* instead of *Sparkle's Jewelry Store* — you may have your administrative rights removed, and the Page will become an uneditable, Facebook-generated Interest Page.

Choosing the right type of business Page

Facebook offers six types of Facebook Pages so that you can choose the one that best fits with your product, service, brand, or business. When you go to www.facebook.com/pages/create.php, you see the business Page options, as shown in Figure 2-1.

Book II
Chapter 2

Creating Your
Business Page

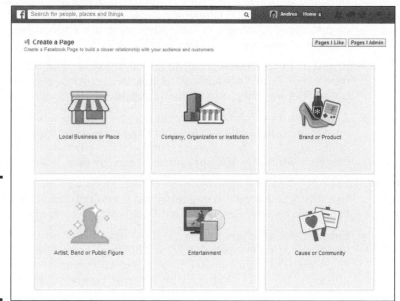

Figure 2-1: Choose one of these six options to create your business Page.

The following list gives you the skinny on what each Page type offers and when you should choose a particular Page type over another:

✦ **Local Business or Place:** This Page type is for bricks-and-mortar businesses. Choose this type only if you truly have a local, open-to-the-public type of business. When you choose this category, a Facebook Place is automatically created for you, as well where people can check in.

Don't list your home office as a Local Business!

The Local Business or Place option offers a drop-down menu with 40 category choices. You can choose one of these categories to create a Page. Or, if none of the categories fits your business, choose the Local Business category and go from there. The Info Profile for this type of business Page is very detailed, with editing fields for hours of operation, parking options, and price ranges.

✦ **Company, Organization, or Institution:** This Page type is for a company that isn't necessarily open to the public the way a local business would be. Many of the categories in this drop-down menu are the same as those for the Local Business or Place type, but the resulting Info Page won't have the same detailed interface to fill in for prices, parking, and so on.

If you have multiple stores in the same city, you need to sit down and decide on a company policy about Facebook Pages. Do you or your store managers want to manage one Page or a Page for each store? Starbucks runs one company Page, for example; Aveda has a custom link that helps you find a local store. Obviously, these are large corporations, but other companies give managers the option to open a Page as long as they adhere to company social media policies.

✦ **Brand or Product:** If you sell an actual physical product, this is the Page type to consider. Facebook offers many categories: cars, clothing, computers, pet supplies, and a generic product/service category.

✦ **Artist, Band or Public Figure:** Obviously, if you're a band or artist, this type is the one to choose, but this Page type also covers politicians, businesspeople, chefs, dancers, and actors. You may think that the actor category would be in Entertainment (see the next bullet), but it isn't! It's here, under the Artist, Band or Public Figure.

Use this type for your band. However, if you're promoting your CD on Facebook, use the Entertainment type with the category Album.

✦ **Entertainment:** If you have a TV show or a magazine, or are creating a Page just for your music CD, select this Page type. There are close to 30 different categories listed here. We're still trying to figure out why Library is listed as a category under Entertainment. Is your library entertaining?

✦ **Cause or Community:** If you've been on Facebook for a while, don't confuse this type of Page with the Causes application. If you're new to Facebook and are creating a Page for a nonprofit or community organization, don't select this Page type — instead, opt for Company, Organization, or Institution, and select the category of Non-Profit.

You must be the official, recognized, and authorized representative of whatever type and category of Page you create on Facebook.

Every Page type has an Info section (also known as the About section). Filling out your Info section completely is important because it's is indexed in Google, and the Short Description gets used when someone shares your Page. Anyone can share your Page by using a Share link, which they can see after clicking the gear icon in the top-right corner of the Page. Most Page categories use the Short Description text to populate the Share invitation. Clicking that Share link autopopulates a post that goes on your personal account Timeline and is visible in the News Feed. Because you're the Page Admin, you can use the Invite Your Friends function. Everyone else can only use the Share option.

You can share to your own Timeline, to someone else's Timeline, to a group, or in a private message. You can add personal text with a share post but not with an Invite Your Friends function. We go into detail on how to do all that in Book IV, Chapter 1.

Don't worry too much about the Page category. You can adjust the Page type and category setting later. The interface is a bit different and can be accessed right from the top of your Page. The steps to change your Page type and category are at the end of this chapter and in Chapter 3 of this minibook.

**Book II
Chapter 2**

**Creating Your
Business Page**

Setting Up Your New Business Page

Goodness. Finally. Time to set up a new business Page on Facebook!

Creating a business Page

Are you ready? Before you create your business Page, first read through these steps. Follow along when you read them again:

1. **Log in to your personal Facebook account.**

2. **Go to** `http://facebook.com/pages/create.php`.

    Doing so brings up a screen showing six Page types.

3. **(Optional) Click each Page type and then click the drop-down category list, as shown in Figure 2-2. Look for a category that matches your business.**

4. **Select the type of Page to create.**

    New options become available for you to fill in.

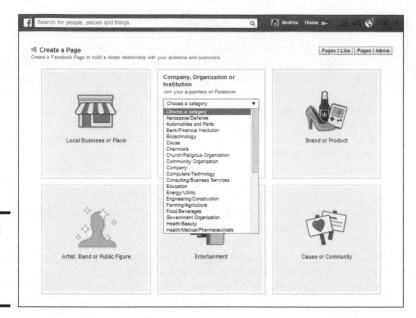

Figure 2-2:
Find a
category
for your
business.

5. **Select the category of Page you want.**

   The category you choose determines the types of Info fields that are available for your Page. All types, except Cause or Community, ask you to select a category for your Page. The reason to find the best category is that the category determines what details are shown on your business Page's Info link. The Book category, for example, displays an Info link with fields for the International Standard Book Number (ISBN); the Café category gives you fields for hours and types of credit cards you take.

   You can change the category later if needed.

6. **Type the requested information.**

   Depending on which business Page type you choose, you see different text fields to fill in. The Name field ends up being the title of the Page. Each of the six types calls the Name field something different: Local Business calls it Business or Place Name; Company calls it Company Name; Brand or Product calls it Brand or Product Name; Artist or Band calls it Name; Entertainment calls it Name; and Cause or Community calls it Cause or Community Name.

   Facebook likes (well, actually insists on) first letters being capitalized for Page names. And you need to fill out all fields to be able to create your Page.

   Take the time to think through this whole naming business. Better yet, read the "Choosing the right name for your business Page" section, earlier in this chapter. You'll be able to change a Page name only until you have 200 people who like your Page. After that point, you're stuck with it unless Facebook opens the link to change it again. So think it through. You can send a request to Facebook to change the name, but it can be challenging to go that route.

7. **Select the I Agree to Facebook Pages Terms check box.**

   You must be the official representative of this person, business, band, or product to create this Page. If you're not, you're in violation of Facebook Terms and Services; Facebook can (and will) remove your Profile and not reinstate it.

8. **Click the Get Started button.**

   You created a Facebook Page!

Opening your page

The first screen you see after clicking the Get Started button looks like Figure 2-3. Facebook takes you through a two- to three-step process (depending on your category) to fill in and open your Page to the public.

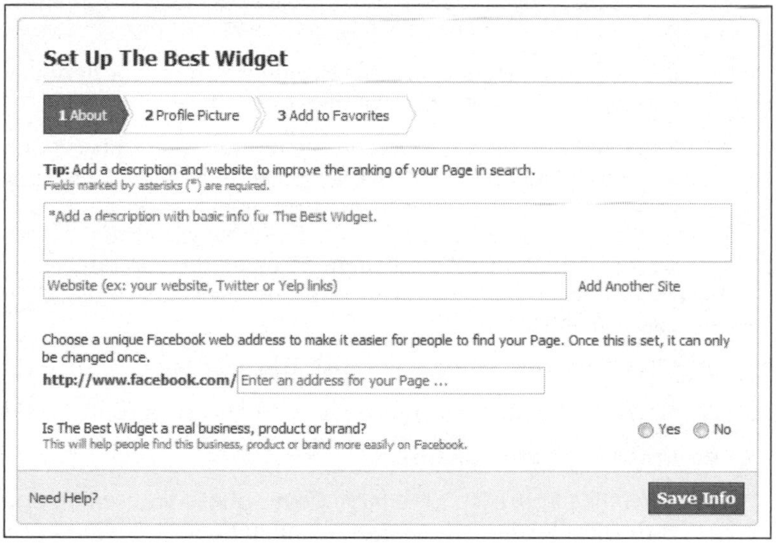

Set Up The Best Widget

1 About   2 Profile Picture   3 Add to Favorites

Tip: Add a description and website to improve the ranking of your Page in search.
Fields marked by asterisks (*) are required.

*Add a description with basic info for The Best Widget.

Website (ex: your website, Twitter or Yelp links)   Add Another Site

Choose a unique Facebook web address to make it easier for people to find your Page. Once this is set, it can only be changed once.

http://www.facebook.com/ Enter an address for your Page ...

Is The Best Widget a real business, product or brand?   ○ Yes ○ No
This will help people find this business, product or brand more easily on Facebook.

Need Help?   **Save Info**

Figure 2-3:
Facebook guides you as you customize your business Page.

1. **Upload your Profile image and click Next.**

2. **Fill in a basic description about your Page.**

   This section is mandatory but can be edited later.

   The basic description appears on your Timeline. You have a 155-character limit to describe your business, so don't get too wordy!

3. **Add your website and any other site links, such as Twitter or LinkedIn.**

   In our testing, we found that you can add as many links as you want.

   Always check the exact URL before entering it so that the links will be hyperlinked correctly.

4. **Choose your unique Facebook web address.**

   We have to state right here that this section comes and goes. Sometimes we see this option available, and sometimes we don't. And this section isn't mandatory, so if you don't want to set it right away, you can always set it later.

   The unique web address is very good to have because you can then easily tell someone how to find your business on Facebook without someone having to use the Search bar which doesn't always yield complete results.

   The unique web address — sometimes called a *vanity URL* — is the part of a Facebook address for your Page:

   ```
   http://facebook.com/TheMissPhyllisCollection
   ```

   Before you get a username, the address might look like this:

   ```
   https://www.facebook.com/pages/The-Miss-Phyllis-
       Collection/139008436119989
   ```

   If you see this step, think this through: In our experience, you can change the URL for the Page only once more.

   You can have capital letters in the unique web address (and the address is not case sensitive). For example, `www.facebook.com/GrandmaMaryShow` works just the same as `www.facebook.com/grandmamaryshow` and is more readable with the first letters of the words capitalized. We recommend using the capital letters for the first letter of each word when appropriate. You cannot use spaces, but you can use underscores.

5. **Click Save Info when you finish this section.**

   Step 2 of the process appears: to upload your profile picture.

6. **Upload a Profile picture.**

   A Profile picture isn't the large Cover photo you see on other Pages. This is the smaller, square image located in the bottom-left corner overlaying the Cover photo. The image can be any shape, but the viewable part is square (180 x 180 pixels; px). In just a moment, you can specify what part of this image becomes the thumbnail that will accompany your posts.

   You can choose to upload a profile picture from your computer or have Facebook find one from your website. Unless you happen to have the perfect sized photo on your website, we recommend uploading one that you have sized beforehand from your computer.

7. **Click Next.**

8. **Click Add to Favorites. (This might not appear depending on your category.)**

   Facebook prompts you to add your new Page to your Favorites that appear on the left sidebar of your personal profile so you can easily access it later.

That's it! You're taken to your new Facebook Page with your Admin panel at the top of the Page.

You can see how that looks in Figure 2-4.

Figure 2-4: The Admin panel is your main interface for working with your new Page.

Unpublish your Page

When you create a new Page, Facebook defaults it as published! Yikes! You may want to unpublish your Page to the public so that you can continue to work on it privately. Just look for the Edit Page button, and follow these steps:

1. **Click the Edit Page button.**

    This button is at the top of your new Page.

2. **Choose Edit Settings from the drop-down menu.**

3. **Click the Edit link on the right side of the Page Visibility setting.**

4. **Select the Unpublish Page check box and click Save Changes, so that only Admins can see this Page.**

    This option, shown in Figure 2-5, effectively unpublishes your new Page, hiding it from everyone except Page Admins.

    Your business Page is now visible only to you and any other Admins. After you deck out your Page with a Cover image, detailed info, photos, and other fun things, you can publish the Page for all to see by coming back to this Page and clearing the Page Visibility check box.

Click here.

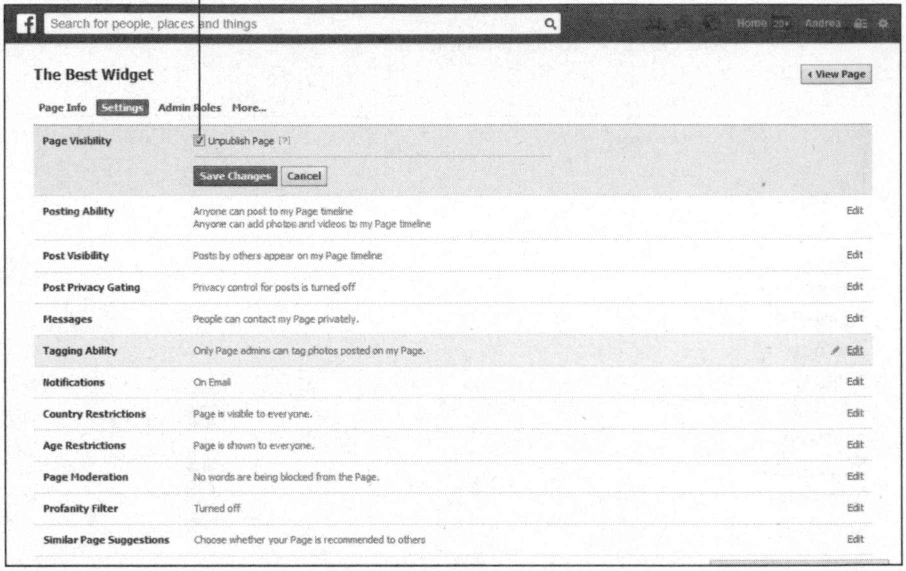

Figure 2-5:
Hide your
Page from
the public.

Completing, Publishing, and Promoting Your Page

Now you need to complete your Page so that you can publish it and promote
it. To see what a finished Local Business Page might look like for a food
establishment, check out the Facebook business Page for Merante Brothers
Market, at www.facebook.com/meranteboys. Figure 2-6 shows the Cover
photo, the custom apps, the Page category, the address, the phone number,
and the hours. This is what you're going for when you go through this section and fill out more info.

Figure 2-6:
This Local
Business
Page is
full of vital
information.

You have several steps to go through, as follows:

1. Adding a Cover photo and adjusting your Profile image thumbnail
2. Completing your About Page
3. Adding Facebook-built apps and custom apps
4. Posting status updates
5. Publishing your Page
6. Adding milestones
7. Promoting this Page on your website
8. Setting up your mobile phone so that you can check your Page on the go

In the following sections, we walk you through each step. Try not to skip ahead because these steps are important for forming your new Page!

Getting your Facebook images right

You know all about a picture saying a thousand words, right? Your Facebook Cover and Profile photos say a lot about you and your business, so be sure to have images for both that convey a positive message. And now that Facebook creates a nice little "hover card" when someone hovers over your Page name in the News Feed, you want to make sure it looks fantastic. This hover card will show the Cover photo, Profile photo, total number of Likes, who likes the Page, and the Page type.

Adding a Cover photo

You need to add a Cover photo to your Page — no ifs, ands, or buts about it.

If you're branding yourself, feature your face in this Cover photo image, to help connect the human element to the rest of the Page that contains text and links. Adding this personal touch can make people feel more connected to you — and to what you're selling.

If you're branding your company, make sure that your logo or product image is on this image. Take care that nothing important in the image appears in the lower-left corner of the image. Your profile picture covers that section of your cover photo.

Whichever way you choose, the image fills the top position on your Page, as shown in Figure 2-7. If you're branding yourself, we highly recommend that you create and use a custom image that contains your logo and your photo.

The image size is 851 x 315 px. The space you get for a Cover photo is quite a bit larger than the space for a Profile picture and can really make a statement on your Page.

Figure 2-7:
Use the
Cover photo
to make an
impression
and connect
with your
audience.

Facebook allows website addresses or any text on a cover photo as long as it isn't deceptive or misleading. Facebook does state that the cover photo space "isn't meant for promotions, coupons, or advertisements," but you can get creative to show what your business is about and have some text or taglines on the photo.

Try to think of this image as what you're trying to brand as the "feeling" of your business. There are great strategies you can use with this image, which we outline in Books IV and IX. In general, think of changing this image with your other promotions so that they support one another.

To upload a cover photo from your hard drive to your Facebook Page, follow these steps:

1. **If this is the first Cover photo you're adding, look for the Add a Cover button, where the Cover image will appear.**

    If you're changing the Cover photo, just hover over the Cover photo and click the Change Cover button.

    A hidden link with a pencil icon comes up, as shown in Figure 2-8.

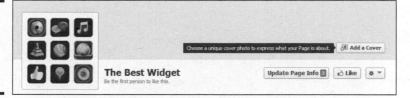

Book II
Chapter 2

Creating Your
Business Page

Figure 2-8:
Start by
uploading a
great cover
image.

2. **Click Add a Cover or the Change Cover button.**

   If this is the first time you're uploading a cover photo, a pop-up box tells you that the cover photo isn't meant for promotions, coupons, or advertisements.

3. **Click the Okay button.**

4. **Click the Upload photo in the Image dialog box that appears and then browse to and select the image on your computer that you want to upload.**

5. **Click Open.**

   Facebook starts the upload process.

   The best size is 851 x 315 px. If you upload a larger image, you can drag it around to get the best placement. If the image is larger than 851 x 315, only a portion of it will appear as the Cover photo for your Page; when clicked, the image opens to the complete size of the photo. If the image is less than 300 px wide, Facebook displays an error message and tells you that the image is too small to use in this space.

6. **Adjust the image as necessary.**

7. **Click Save Changes.**

   After the file is uploaded, you go back to the Page.

8. **Click the image, click Edit, and add a description that includes your best link (back to your website, for example).**

   Adding a description — with a link to your website — for every image needs to be second nature on Facebook. See Figure 2-9 for that interface.

Cover photos are set to Public viewing. You can't change that viewing setting (and why would you?). You see the globe icon that Facebook uses to denote Public when you upload the image.

Figure 2-9: Always add a photo description that includes a link to your website.

Adjusting your Profile thumbnail image

After you have your Cover image just right, you may want to check the thumbnail that Facebook generates for your Profile image. A *thumbnail* is a smaller version of your Profile image. In the world of Facebook, a thumbnail image shows up next to every status update or comment you make as your Page. As you can imagine, your thumbnail is a key component in branding your business Page.

And now that Facebook creates a nice, little "hover card" when someone hovers over your Page name in the News Feed, you want to make sure it looks fantastic. This hover card will show the Cover photo, Profile photo, and the Page type.

The Profile image is 180 x 180 px. If you upload an image larger than that, Facebook gives you a cropping interface to select a square part of the image.

After you have the Profile image uploaded, you may want to adjust the thumbnail image. Follow these steps to adjust the thumbnail image:

1. **Hover over your Profile image.**

   A hidden link with a pencil icon comes up.

2. **Click the Edit Profile Picture link.**

   You see several links: Choose from Photos, Take Photo, Upload Photo, Edit Thumbnail, and Remove.

3. **Click the Edit Thumbnail link.**

   Doing so pulls up the Edit Thumbnail dialog box, as shown in Figure 2-10.

Figure 2-10:
You can
adjust your
thumbnail
to look just
right.

4. **Drag the thumbnail image around until it looks good as a thumbnail.**

5. **Click Save.**

This is an image; therefore, it has a description area where you can add text and hyperlinks. Click the Photos app box (located just under the cover photo); then click the Profile Pictures album and the image itself. Add text and hyperlinks in the top-right corner where you see the words Add a Description.

Book II
Chapter 2

Creating Your
Business Page

Completing the Info Page

The next step is filling in the fields on the Info Page, which is also known as the About Page. Depending on the Page type and category, the fields will be different. The TV Show category has a field called Plot, for example, whereas the Book category has a field for the ISBN.

The following examples use the Company Page type and the Company category. Follow these steps:

1. **At the top of the Admin panel, click the Edit Page button and then click Update Page Info.**

   This step opens the Page dashboard to the Page Info tab as shown in Figure 2-11.

2. **At the top of the Basic Information interface, you can change the name of your Page by clicking Edit on the right side of the Name field.**

   You can change the name of your Page until you have 200 likes. After you have 200 likes, you will have to request a name change from Facebook's Help area, and they aren't always very responsive.

3. **Add your Page Address if you haven't done so in the setup by clicking Enter a Facebook Web Address.**

   If you already set your Page address in the "Setting Up Your New Business Page" section earlier in this chapter, you can don't have to worry about this. If you have set it already, you may be able to change it one time, so use that change wisely.

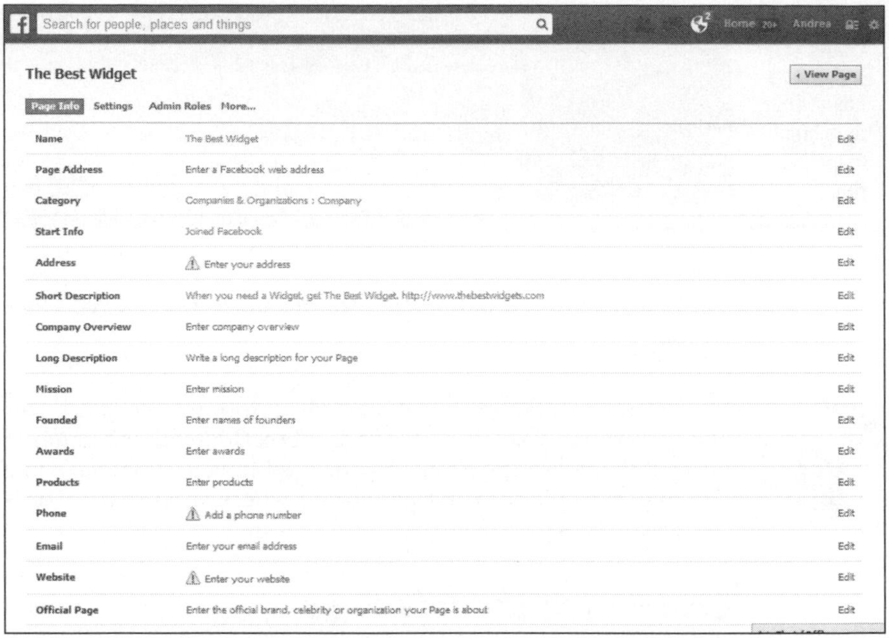

Figure 2-11:
The Page
Info section
of your Page
dashboard.

4. **Select Create a Web Address for This Page.**

   You're taken to a new page where you can check the availability of your custom URL.

5. **If you find one that's available, click Confirm and then navigate back to the Page Info section.**

6. **Change the Category if desired.**

   You can change the category of your Page if you find a better match for your business. The fields you have filled out in the About section are ported over to the new fields of the new category as best as possible. Some Categories also have the option to add Topics or Subcategories.

7. **Modify the Name and Start Info section.**

   You can change the name of your Page in this space. After you have more than 200 likes, you have the option to change the name just one more time.

   The Start Info and date are important to modify. If you use the current day, month, and year, you won't be able to add anything to the Page's Timeline from the past. If you think that you'll have milestones to add with a past date, make the Start date further back than that date. You can also decide whether you want this first date type to be Born, Founded, Started, Open, Created, or Launched. Milestones are explained in Book III of this minibook.

8. **In the Address section, add a physical address. Or not.**

   The Address section is important for local businesses.

   If you add a physical address in this section, your Page is now a Places Page. You have a new function on your Page where anyone can add a public Recommendation. Think this through. It's best to use this address space only if you have actual hours when your place of business is open. You will still have the subcategories you chose at the top of the Page, with a few added functions; people can check in to your business and use the Review function.

9. **In the Short Description field, enter your website URL and promotional or informational text.**

   The About field is vital. This bit of text is right below the Page's Profile image. People will be able to see about 155 characters. Make sure that you have an `http://` link as the very first thing so that you have a hyperlink to your website or products.

**Book II
Chapter 2**

**Creating Your
Business Page**

10. **Fill out the rest of the fields.**

    The next set of fields depends on your Page type. Fill out all the fields. One of them is the text that auto-populates the invitation that's generated when you (or anyone) shares the Page.

    Generally, the Company Overview or Long Description field is used for this sharing invite. You will check this sharing process in the next chapter, and this is where to revisit to edit the text. Add a lot of keywords in these sections because the About Page is indexed in Google.

11. **Add an Official Page (Optional).**

    Fill in this field only if you're creating a Page about a brand, a celebrity, or an organization that you don't officially represent. Don't add any text in this field if this is not the case because Facebook will connect your Page to the Official Page, and it doesn't make sense for your business to be connected to another Page. In most cases, there is no need to type anything here.

    Leave it blank if this doesn't apply to you.

    Now you see the Short Description text below the Profile image and other information, depending on your Page type.

Adding Facebook-built apps

Facebook has a set of apps built for Pages: Photos, Events, Notes, and Video. They may not show up in the featured app space. You need to add them first. (The Photos App is usually added because you've uploaded a profile and cover photos.)

Don't add these apps unless you plan on using them. After all: Why have an Events app showing if there will never be an Event?

Here's how to add the Facebook apps:

1. **On your Facebook Page, click the down arrow on the right side of the Page next to the apps.**

   A second row of blank apps appears.

2. **Click the + symbol in the upper-right corner of any blank app (as shown in Figure 2-12).**

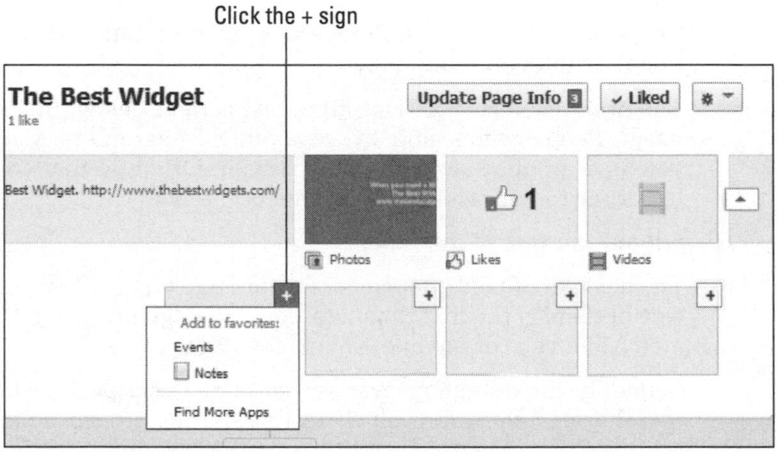

Click the + sign

Figure 2-12: Add the desired Facebook apps to your Page.

An Add to Favorites drop-down menu shows the app names. You can click Find More Apps to go to the Facebook Apps Center (covered in Book V).

3. **Click the name of the app you want to add: Events, Notes, or Videos.**

   The app appears in your Apps area.

Facebook doesn't let you change the image or the hyperlinked text at the bottom of these apps. The image is connected to the last item created with that app. The Photo app shows the latest uploaded or tagged image; the Notes app shows a lined paper image with some of the words on the note; the Video app shows a screen shot of your latest video upload; and the Events app shows the image you've uploaded to the latest event listing.

The hyperlinked text below these boxes is only Photos, Events, Notes, or Video. You can change the image for any custom apps you add, and you can change the hyperlinked text, too.

Adding custom apps

The next most important task in developing your Page is organizing and adding a few custom apps. We talk a lot about adding apps in Book V, Chapter 1, but here's a quick overview.

Right below the Cover photo are four featured apps. One of them is Photos, which is a Facebook app — and because it's a Facebook app, you can't move it, hide it, or change the hyperlinked text. The latest photo you've uploaded or tagged with the Page name is what shows up in this box.

The next three spaces are available to place custom apps. In fact, there are 12 more spaces for custom apps (more on that in a moment), but only a total of four apps show in this featured space. You can edit and modify the hyperlinked text and the image on the app box, and can change their order.

Depending on your business, the type of apps you set here can be different, but most businesses use three main types:

✦ **Email Capture with a Free Gift:** If you already use an e-mail list service (such as MailChimp, iContact, or Constant Contact), check to see whether it has a Facebook integration you can use for this app box. If not, you can always grab the HTML code for your sign-up form and place it in this space, using Heyo's HTML app (`https://heyo.com`) or an HTML app from any other third party (Involver, Woobox, and so on).

✦ **Event Announcement or flyer:** If you have an event coming up or a sales flyer to promote, you don't have to use the Facebook Event app; you can create a nice Page for your event by using any third-party app that allows you to add an image or HTML code.

✦ **Sales Page:** If your sales Page is 850 px wide or less, you can use Thunderpenny's website app to pull the whole web page into Facebook. You can still use this app if your sales Page is wider, but the sales Page will be shrunk down smaller and may not be readable.

Figure 2-13 shows a Page that uses custom apps.

Figure 2-13: Here's a great use of custom apps.

Currently, people can see custom apps only when they view your Page on a computer. The mobile view of a business Page through the Facebook app doesn't show any custom apps. Also, if you create a post with a link to a custom app, and someone taps that link on a mobile app, he or she is just redirected back to the Page's Timeline or taken to the browser interface. We all hope this changes in the future because many custom apps are important to a business on Facebook.

Make sure that you explore Book V to see how to add custom apps to your Page and Book VIII to see how you can use these apps to market effectively on Facebook.

Posting status updates

Posting a few interesting status updates before you publish your Page so as to populate your Timeline encourages people to stick around after they find your business on Facebook. We suggest adding informational posts about the purpose of your Page and its history, and also some introductory posts about you or your business. You should also include one post with a link to either your website or e-commerce site. Another good idea is to add at least one milestone to your Page, which we discuss a bit later in this chapter.

Posting to your Page is so important that we have an entire minibook devoted to that topic! Book III is a complete discussion of how to use this feature, but to get your Page ready to publish, you need at least a few posts.

On your Page, look for the publishing area, as shown in Figure 2-14.

Figure 2-14: Create posts to your Page.

Follow these steps to create a simple post:

1. **Click in the What Have You Been Up To? text field.**

You also see several icons along the bottom of this space for scheduling, targeting, adding a location, and adding a file. Note that the targeting option only is available after you have 5,000 likes on your Page. Again, refer to Book III for more explanation about these icons.

2. **Type something interesting.**

A complete discussion about posting is in Book III.

3. **Click Post.**

This post shows up on the Timeline. No one will see it until you publish the Page. After the Page is published, you need to create more posts so that they go out into the News Feeds of the people who have liked your Page.

If you created a Local Business Page, you also have the ability to create an offer. We talk about offers in Book III.

Publishing your Page

Before you can invite your Friends and promote your business on Facebook, you need to publish your Page. Your Page is already published automatically when you first created it, but if you unpublished it to work on it first, you do need to publish it again. Here's how:

1. **Go to your Page's Admin panel.**

2. **Click the Edit Page button, and choose Edit Settings from the drop-down menu.**

3. **Click Edit on the right side of the Page Visibility section.**

4. **Clear the Unpublish Page check box.**

5. **Click the Save Changes button.**

Now the Page is published. People can find it in a search, and it's open for people to like.

Editing and adding milestones

One of the best posts for a new Page is a milestone. In fact, when you created your Page, Facebook created your first milestone! When you look at your Timeline, you see that the very first post is a milestone. It may read `Founded on` (and then the date you created the Page). The first thing you want to do is edit this milestone. If it stays at this point in time, you won't be able to add any milestones in the past. Therefore, edit the date for this first milestone back before the milestones you want to add later.

Milestones are similar to Life Events on your personal account. They are similar in how they look and are placed on the Timeline structure. Whereas Life Events tell the story of your personal life, milestones help to tell the story of your business.

Creating milestones is fully discussed in Book III, Chapter 1.

Follow these steps to edit the first milestone:

1. **Find the first milestone: When Was This Founded?**

2. **Hover over the top-right corner, and then click the down arrow and the Edit link that appear.**

3. **Adjust the date to be as far back as you want.**

   You can also adjust the Milestone type (Opening, Started, Founded, Launched, Born, or Created).

4. **(Optional) Add the location, story, and upload a photo.**

   We love stories and photos, and Facebook does, too. Add them and make them as personal as possible, and you'll get a better response for the milestone. Ideal image size for a milestone is 843 px x 403 px. Add the location if the milestone happened somewhere in particular.

5. **Click Save.**

   Now you're free to add milestones to any date from this one to the present. You can't add a milestone to a future date.

If you don't see this starting milestone, when you try to create a milestone, Facebook asks you to create the first one first. Got that? Just go through the prompts, and remember to date it as far back as you can so that you can add other milestones that happened in the past.

Here's how to create the next milestone:

1. **On your Page, click inside the publishing area.**

2. **Click Event, Milestone + (or it may be listed as Offer, Event).**

   A menu opens with these choices: Offer, Event, and Milestone.

3. **Click Milestone.**

   See Figure 2-15 for the areas you need to fill in.

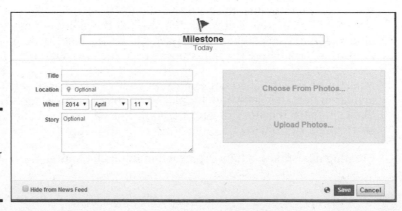

Figure 2-15: These are the fields for creating a milestone.

4. **In the Title field, add a title.**

   This becomes the title of the milestone. The large-font title at the top of this interface changes as you fill in this field. The flag icon doesn't change.

5. **(Optional) Fill in the location if it's important to the milestone.**

6. **Add the date.**

   When you add a specific date, the milestone will attach to the Timeline at that particular date.

7. **Type the story.**

   Adding a story makes the milestone much more interesting.

8. **Upload an image that goes with the milestone.**

   The ideal image size is 843 px x 403 px.

9. **(Optional) To hide this milestone from the News Feed, select the Hide from News Feed check box.**

10. **Click Save.**

Milestones are formatted as highlights on the Timeline, which means that they span the whole Page from left to right.

Inviting your Facebook Friends

The next step is inviting your Friends to like your Page. We suggest customizing your Page as much as possible (with posts, photos, and apps) before inviting and sharing it, but if you feel that your Page is ready, inviting your Facebook Friends is next.

1. **Go to your Page as your Personal profile.**

   Notice that your name is in the upper-right corner of the page.

2. **On the Admin panel of your new Page, click the Build Audience button (at the top).**

   When you click that button, a drop-down menu appears.

3. **Click the Invite Friends link.**

   A new dialog box appears, in which you can select your personal Facebook Friends to invite them to like your Page.

4. **To select a Friend, click the Invite button next to that person's name.**

5. **Continue clicking until you select everyone you want to share your Page with.**

   Notice the Filter drop-down menu. If you have a lot of Friends, you can filter certain selections (by location or shared group, for example) for easier selection, as shown in Figure 2-16. You can also see who you have already invited and who already likes your Page.

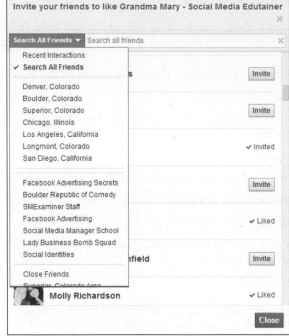

Figure 2-16:
Inviting your Friends is easier if you use the Filter drop-down menu.

6. **Click the Close button.**

   Your Friends get a generic-looking invitation delivered to their Notifications area.

Inviting e-mail contacts

Your contacts outside Facebook may be a gold mine of people who would benefit from your Page. With the help of the Invite Email Contacts dialog box, you can import the contact info for all the folks you know into a space where you can invite them to your Page.

Keep in mind a few things about this process:

✦ Only Admins of Pages with fewer than 5,000 likes can import their e-mail lists and invite people on those lists to like their Page, so invite your e-mail contacts before you reach that number.

✦ Facebook imports your contact file securely. You can suggest your Page to your contacts after that. If you use Gmail, for example, you need to export your contacts in CSV (comma-separated value) format and then upload the .csv file to Facebook.

To import your contacts, go to the Admin panel, and click Build Audience to access the drop-down menu; next, click the Invite Email Contacts link. Doing so brings up the Invite Email Contacts dialog box, as shown in Figure 2-17.

Figure 2-17: You can import your e-mail contacts to tell your Friends and contacts about your new Page.

The idea here is that you can do one of two things:

+ Upload a contacts file you put together yourself.

+ Have Facebook search your Constant Contact, MailChimp, VerticalResponse, Outlook, Hotmail, AOL, and Yahoo! accounts to find people who are already on Facebook. When you click the Invite Contacts link next to any of those services, type your e-mail address and password, and then click the Find Contacts button.

To help you create a contacts file to upload, Facebook has created instructions specific to whichever mail system you use. When you click the Other Email Service link and type a Gmail address, for example, Facebook presents instructions for exporting your Gmail contacts in a file that Facebook can use.

Then you can select the people you want to invite to your Page. The preview shown in Figure 2-18 depicts how the invitation looks to those whose e-mail address matches a personal Facebook account, as you can see at the top; the bottom shows how it would look if it were sent to an e-mail address that isn't associated with a Facebook account.

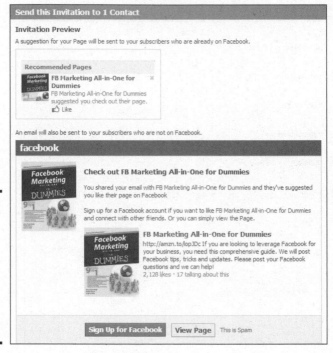

Figure 2-18: Facebook sends a message to your e-mail contacts and invites them to like your Page.

For users already on Facebook, this invitation shows up on the right side of their News Feed as an invitation from your Page. If users don't have a Facebook account, they get an e-mail suggesting that they join Facebook so that they can like your Page.

Facebook puts Page invitations in a fairly obscure place: www.facebook. com/pages. No one knows to go there, but Facebook has a link at the top of this webpage called Invites with all the invitations that have been sent to you. Currently, it's the best place to go to see those invitations. Spread the word.

Sharing your Page

To find the Share Page option, go back to the Build Audience menu on your Admin panel. Keep in mind that you can only see this link if you're viewing the Page as your Profile. The Share Page process looks the same whether or not you're an Admin of the Page, but non-Admins will access the Share link through the gear icon located below the Cover photo to the right.

No matter where the link is found, when you click the link, the Share This Page dialog box (shown in Figure 2-19) appears. In this dialog box, you can create a nice invitation that you can post to your personal account Timeline, to someone else's Timeline, to a group Page, to another Page for which you're an Admin, or to a private Facebook Message.

Book II
Chapter 2

Creating Your
Business Page

Choose where to share this   Add a message   Review the autopopulated text

Figure 2-19: The Share Page dialog box has a few things you need to check before you send out invitations.

Review the image   Choose Public or Custom

Check out a few things before you send invitations:

✦ **Review the autopopulated text.** This text is pulled right off your Info tab — generally, the text in the Company Overview field. If you don't like what's written here, you have to go back to the Info tab and change the text there. Or you can click the text; an editor interface comes up, and you can type whatever text you want.

   Other people will be using this Share function, so you want to enter the text that you want to show up here automatically so they don't have to edit it. Go back to your Info tab to fix the text if needed.

✦ **Review the image.** This image is the Profile image, not the Cover image. If you want something else to show up there, you need to change the Profile image for the Page. It's not editable from this Share interface.

✦ **Add a message.** Make sure that you list the benefits for liking the Page. You can create a nice, little message that's compelling. You can mention that you have contests and free events — whatever is appropriate for your business.

✦ **Decide where to Share.** You can share on your own personal Timeline, on a Friend's Timeline, in a group, on another Page for which you're an Admin, or in a private Facebook Message. Click the drop-down menu to choose which one you want.

✦ **Decide whether your shared update will be Public, Friends, one of your lists, or Custom.** You can change the viewing filter by clicking the Public icon to reveal a drop-down menu and changing it to a Facebook Friends list or a custom list.

After you review the invitation, click Share Page.

The Buffer button (shown in Figure 2-19) appears because of an app called Buffer, which lets you schedule posts for later. Depending on what types of apps work with Facebook, you may see different sharing options.

Promoting this Page on your website

One of the best ways to have people connect with your business on Facebook is to place a *Like Box* (a box that can be placed in your website's sidebar) on your website or blog.

To customize a Facebook Like Box, go to

```
https://developers.facebook.com/docs/reference/plugins/like-box
```

You can tweak the Like Box's design to your heart's content. When you're done tweaking, you receive a code to place on your website or blog.

A complete description and instructions are in Book VII, Chapter 2, where all the Facebook social plug-ins are explained.

To be clear, there are social plug-ins, and there are badges. A *badge* contains a link that takes people back to your Page, whereas a *social plug-in* allows you to click the Like button for a Page without leaving the website on which the box is placed.

You can create four types of badges for your website. Two types work with your Page: the Like badge and the Page badge. You can find the interface to create them at www.facebook.com/badges. We don't recommend using badges, however, they're not helpful in attracting more likes; they don't contain a built-in Like button, as Like *boxes* do.

Setting up your mobile phone

Facebook understands that you aren't always at your desk or computer when you need to post an update to your business Page. If you're on the go and need to share something with your fans, you can use your smartphone, and in this section, we show you how.

1. **Return to your Page's Admin panel.**

2. **Choose Edit Page⇨Update Page Info.**

3. **From the menu across the top, choose More.**

A drop-down menu appears.

4. **Choose Mobile.**

Currently, you have three Mobile options:

**Book II
Chapter 2**

Creating Your
Business Page

✦ **With Mobile Email:** This option gives you the information you need to upload photos or post updates from your mobile e-mail account. Each Page can have its own Facebook e-mail address, which Facebook creates for you automatically. You can use this address to send e-mails that will post on your Page. If you want Facebook to send this e-mail address to you *in* an e-mail, click the Learn More button. This new interface lets you choose to have the e-mail sent to the e-mail address of your choice or to your phone. It also lets you refresh the e-mail to create a new one. You can refresh your e-mail only a few times. See Figure 2-20.

Do not share this e-mail address with anyone because whoever has the e-mail address is posting as your Page from their mobile device. It's almost like giving away Admin privileges to your Page.

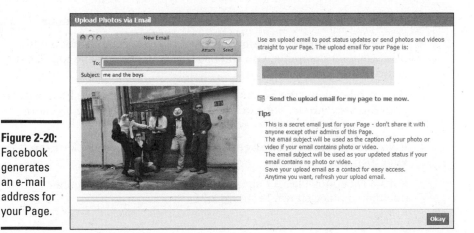

Figure 2-20: Facebook generates an e-mail address for your Page.

When you have the e-mail address in place and want to upload a photo, e-mail the photo to this address, and include a caption in the e-mail's Subject line. To update your status, write in the e-mail Subject line and leave the e-mail body blank.

✦ **With Mobile Web:** This option reminds you how to find your Page when you're using a mobile browser. Having a username set up simplifies this process. We talk about usernames in Chapter 1 of this minibook. You can also use the Pages App for phones.

✦ **With the iPhone:** Facebook continues to update its official app for all iOS devices. If you want to post directly to your Page, it might be better to use the Pages app Facebook developed instead of trying to create a bookmark on your phone, as Facebook suggests in the text currently on this Mobile tab. As with all things Facebook, the text here might change at any moment.

If you have a smartphone with a Facebook app, it's probably easier just to open the app and post a status update inside the app. If you have an administrative team that will be posting to your Page, make sure that the team members get the mobile e-mail address.

Claiming a Facebook Place

If you have a bricks-and-mortar store, you need to claim your Places Page as it shows up in mobile Facebook. Then you can merge your Places information with your official business Page on Facebook. As we mention earlier, anyone can create a Facebook Place with their mobile phone.

To claim your Place, follow these steps:

1. **Go to** www.facebook.com **and search for your business name.**

   You don't need to be on a smartphone to do this, but it's not a bad idea. On your computer, you can use the Search bar at the top of every Facebook screen.

   When you're using the Facebook search bar, you can type **Places named** *yourbusinessname*. The unclaimed places typically have a generic icon next to them rather than a profile photo.

2. **If your business's Place already exists on Facebook, click or tap it to visit its page.**

   If it's a Facebook Places Page that is unclaimed, it looks similar to the unclaimed place shown in Figure 2-21.

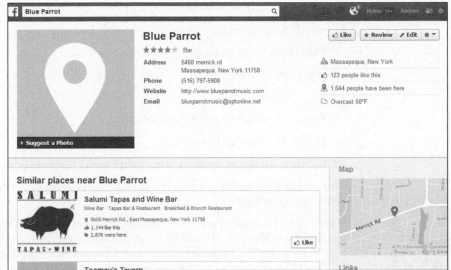

Figure 2-21:
A Places
Page that is
unclaimed.

3. **Click the gear icon in the upper right and choose Is This Your Business?**

   A pop-up window asks you to verify that you're an official representative
   of the physical location.

4. **Select the I Am An Official Representative of** *Your Business Name*
   check box (as shown in Figure 2-22). Then click the Continue button.

   You see a Verify Page Info page.

Figure 2-22:
Claim a
Places
Page.

5. **Enter your business information, and click or tap Continue.**

   Facebook asks you to provide the following information:

   - Official name of business
   - Business address
   - Your job title
   - Business phone number (optional)
   - Business website (optional)

6. **Verify your business by providing additional information.**

   You're asked to verify ownership through an e-mail or a document-verification process.

   Your e-mail address must be a business address (one that has your business name in the domain name). If you choose document verification, you have to provide scanned images of a phone or utility bill that includes the business's name and address.

7. **Click or tap Submit.**

   After your claim is confirmed, you own your Place on Facebook. By claiming your Place (even if you already have the information on your regular business Page Info tab), you can manage your Place's address, contact information, business hours, Profile picture, Admins, and other settings that people see on Facebook mobile.

Merging a Facebook Place with Your Page

After you claim your Place, Facebook may automatically merge the Place with your current Page if they have the same (or similar) Page name and address — but this doesn't always happen.

To merge the Place and the Page, make sure both addresses match. Wait about a week to see whether they get merged automatically. If they don't, you can take steps to request a merge because when you merge a Place and a Page, you keep the information, posts, and photos from just one of them. Decide which one you want to keep before you get started. Then follow these steps while logged in as your Personal profile:

1. **Go to the Page you want to keep. Click Edit Page at the top of the Admin panel.**

2. **Choose Edit Settings from the drop-down menu.**

3. **Select Merge Pages at the bottom of the page.**

   You can click the Learn More link to read more about merging.

4. **Click the Merge Duplicate Pages link.**

   A new page lists the precautions you need to be aware of with merging two pages.

5. **Select the I Have Read and Understand the Above Information check box.**

   You get the option to select the Page you want to keep in the merge.

6. **Choose the appropriate Page from the drop-down menu.**

7. **Select the I Understand These Pages I Merge Must Be About the Same Thing check box.**

   Now you can select the other Page(s) you want to merge with the main Page.

8. **Select a Page from the drop-down menu, as shown in Figure 2-23.**

   You can merge up to five additional Pages with the one main Page, but you have to be Admin of all Pages.

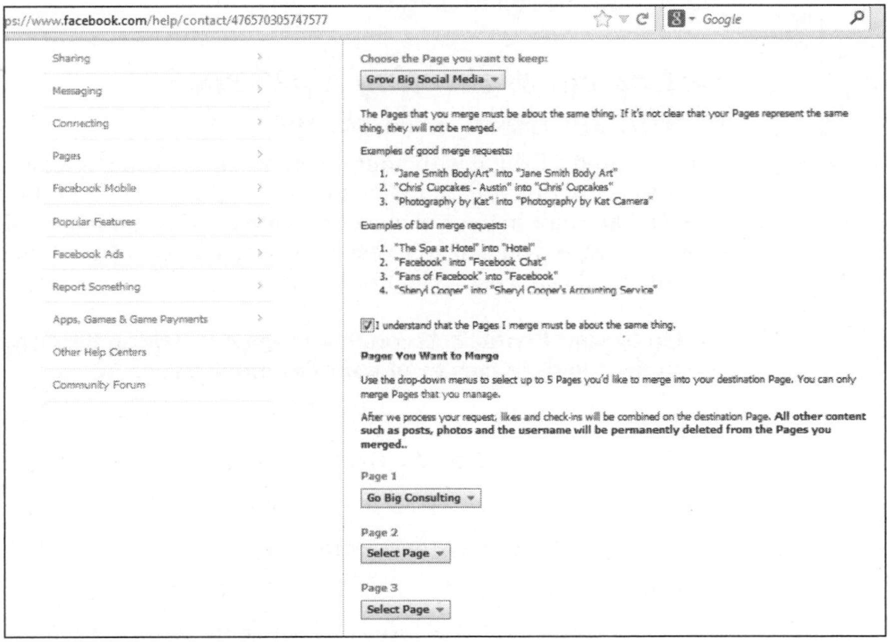

Figure 2-23: Merging a Places Page with your Page.

9. **Click the blue Send button.**

   A dialog box thanks you for your submission and says you'll get an e-mail from Facebook shortly.

Managing Missteps

You may discover that you made a mistake when you created your business Page. Maybe you created your personal Profile for your business instead of a business Page. Maybe you created the wrong kind of business Page and want to change it. Or maybe you created a Profile in your name, but most of your Friends are connected to your Profile because of the business you promote from this account. You can almost always fix your issue — but the sooner you realize and can correct your mistake, the better. It's always easier to change a Page when you have fewer connections.

Creating personal Profiles with a business name

A misconception that users have is that it's perfectly okay to create a Profile using a business name (first name O'Grady's, last name Cleaners, for example). This is completely against Facebook rules. If you committed that misstep, don't worry: It's fixable. If you've developed an extensive group of Friends under this name, you can either ask them to move over and like your new business Page or change the name of this account to your actual name and activate the Follow button.

Sorting out or deleting a personal Profile set up as a business

If you created a Profile with your business name, you can change the name of your account to your actual name, as long as you don't already have a personal account in your name. (If you already have a personal account with your real name, you'll need to ask people to move to your business Page and then delete this account.) Follow these steps:

1. **Go to your Profile's Account Settings by clicking the drop-down arrow in the top-right corner of your Facebook Page.**

   Or go directly to www.facebook.com/settings.

2. **Click the Edit link to the right of Name.**

3. **Change the name to your actual name.**

4. **Enter your Facebook password.**

5. **Click Save Changes.**

Alternatively, build your new, honest-to-goodness official business Page and then add a status message regarding the change to the original personal Profile you created for the business. The new status update should give your Friends the URL to the new business Page and explain that you created a new business Page to conform to Facebook guidelines. Tell them that you hope they'll join you over there and like the Page.

If you created this Profile under the business name and won't be changing the name to your actual name, you can also tell Friends that you'll be deactivating the current Profile Page and explain what they can find at the new business Page (such as coupons, special deals, updates, and so on). You'll likely need to post this status update several times before people migrate over. We suggest setting a deadline for moving to the new business Page so that your connections will know exactly when you'll deactivate the business-name Profile Page.

If you go this route, make sure to designate your *real* personal account an Admin of the business Page before you delete the rogue personal account. Otherwise, you won't be able to get back to the new business Page.

If you created a Profile in your real name but promoted your business from there, you can keep the original personal Profile as your personal account, activate the Follow button (as we describe earlier in this chapter), and post Public updates to subscribers.

Here's a sample of a post that Jane wrote, asking her Friends to move over to her business Page:

> Hi everyone, I have a new Page for my new CD of contemporary lullabies, "Midnight Lullaby." This project has been a long time coming, and I'm hoping you can check it out and click the Like button. Here's the link: www.facebook.com/ladylullabymusic. I plan to add many things to this new Page, but for right now please Like it, and I'll keep you posted from there. This new Page is where I will be spending my time on Facebook, so if you want to connect with me, please do it from there.
>
> Thank you!
>
> Jane (Jane Roman Pitt) www.facebook.com/midnightlullabyCD

She decided to keep her original Profile because it was under her name but moved all her posts about her business to her new Page. She had already created a vanity URL for her personal Profile with her CD's name, which couldn't be modified at the time.

If you set your personal account username to be your business name, you might be able to change it. Go to your Settings, and then General. If you can change it, the interface to do so will be there. If you have already changed it once, you will not be able to change it again.

Migrating your Profile to a Facebook Page

If every one of your friends on your Profile is truly interested in your business, you can migrate your Profile to a Page. All your friends will become fans of the new Page, but that is all. Your posts, photos, and Group memberships will be gone so be careful if you go this route!

To start the process, go to

`https://www.facebook.com/pages/create.php?migrate`

Then continue the Facebook Page setup as outlined in the first part of this Chapter.

Deleting a Personal account

Follow these steps if you decide to delete your personal account with the business name, but remember: You must have a personal account to have a business Page. So if you delete the personal account instead of changing the profile name to your real name, you'll need to open another personal account before you open a Page.

If you already have a personal account, make sure to assign your real account the role of Page Admin *before* you delete the incorrectly created personal account.

Follow these steps:

1. **Log in to Facebook with the e-mail you used to create your business's personal account.**

2. **Click the down arrow in the top-right corner of your Page.**

3. **Choose Settings from the menu.**

4. **On the left menu, choose General.**

   On the bottom of this page you can download a copy of your Facebook data. If you do, click the link and follow the steps to create an archive of this personal account's photos, posts, and messages.

5. **After downloading the data (optional), go back to the left menu under Settings and choose Security.**

   On the bottom of this page, look for the Deactivate Your Account link.

   At this point, if you're sure you won't need this personal account, you can completely delete the account (instead of deactivating) by going to `www.facebook.com/help/delete_account`.

   Otherwise, Deactivating leaves the door open to bring the personal account back at any time by logging in with this account's e-mail and password. Deactivating hides all the data from this account, and keeps it in a drawer in Texas somewhere.

6. **If you Deactivate, click the link on the Security tab and go through the process. Otherwise, go to Step 7.**

7. **If you decide to Delete, go to** `www.facebook.com/help/delete_account`.

8. **After you deactivate or delete your personal account with the business name, sign in to Facebook with your new (or regular) personal account, go to your new official business Page, and start interacting with your connections! Welcome them to your new space, and encourage them to interact with you.**

Changing your business Page type or name

Sometimes, people make a business Page and realize that they've made a mistake. Maybe they chose the wrong type of business Page, or they want to change the name of the Page or the category that's associated with the Page. You can change the category or type of Page at any time, but you can change a business Page's name only if fewer than 200 people like the Page. Sometimes, Facebook allows Pages with more than 200 likes to change their name, but this seems to be a random event.

To make those types of changes, follow these steps:

1. **Log in to Facebook.**

2. **Go to your Page.**

   You can find your Page quickly by looking in the left menu while viewing your personal account news feed.

3. **In the Admin panel, click Edit Page; then click Update Page Info.**

   You arrive at the Basic Information tab, shown in Figure 2-24.

**Book II
Chapter 2**

**Creating Your
Business Page**

Figure 2-24:
Change
or modify
a Page
category or
name here.

You can edit the category, subcategory, and name of your business Page. When you click the Category field, you see two drop-down menus. You can take any of the following actions to make desired changes:

- *To change the category of your business Page:* Click the first drop-down menu, and make your choice.

- *To change the subcategory of your business Page:* Click the second drop-down menu, and make your choice.

- *To change your business Page name:* Click the Name field, delete the existing name, and retype the new name. The new name appears as the title of your Page but won't change your vanity URL (username).

If you have more than 200 likes but must change your business Page name, Facebook sometimes puts a Request a Change link in the Name field where you can go through the process of changing it one time. The only other recourse is to delete the original Page and start from scratch. We sincerely discourage you from doing this because you'll lose all of your likes (connections) and will have to re-create your community from scratch. Also, changing your name after you have more than 200 likes may be confusing for your audience.

If you must delete your Page, however, follow these steps:

1. **Log in to Facebook.**

2. **Find your Page name in the left menu.**

   If you don't see the name of your Page, click the More link to see the list of all your Pages.

3. **Click the Edit Page button.**

4. **Choose Edit Settings from the drop-down menu.**

5. **Click the Remove Page link at the very bottom of the Page.**

   Another link appears: Delete <page name>.

6. **Click the Delete <page name > link.**

   A confirmation dialog box asks whether you really, *really* want to do this. After all, this deletion is permanent.

   Any Admin can delete a Page that he administers. Please delete with caution, though, because you absolutely can't bring back a deleted Page.

7. **Click Delete.**

   Your Page is history.

Chapter 3: Administering Your Facebook Business Page

In This Chapter

✔ Interacting with Facebook as your Profile or as your Page

✔ Understanding what other people see when they visit your Page

✔ Knowing how to use your Page Admin panel and editing dashboard

A fter you become a Page Admin, Facebook grants you an additional permission: You can view Facebook as yourself (that is, through your Profile) or as your Page (that is, through your business Page). This particular administrative perk can be a little confusing at first, but by the end of this chapter, you'll completely understand how and when to use this option.

As Admin of your Facebook business Page, you need to maintain it. An important part of maintenance is simply understanding how your Page looks to visitors and fans, what you can customize and control, and what Page elements are visible only to you when you're acting as the Admin and when you are viewing your Page "as" your Page. This chapter explains the elements of your business Page and then shows you how to use your Admin panel and administrative editing dashboard to control some of those aspects.

Viewing Facebook as Your Page

Now that you have a Facebook business Page, you have two separate Profiles with Facebook: your personal Profile and your Page Profile. Each Profile allows you to view Facebook, post status updates, and comment on other posts. Depending on which Profile you're using, though, you show up as either your Profile (you) or your Page Profile (your business).

In addition, each Profile has its own News Feed:

✦ **Your Profile News Feed:** Based on your Friends' status updates and the business Pages you've liked as your personal Profile

✦ **Your Page Profile News Feed:** Based solely on the Pages you've liked as your Page (which we explain in a minute)

In this section, we explain how and when you may want to use each of your Profile options. Before we do, though, you may find it helpful to see each of these Profile options in action. Start by changing your Profile view from (personal) Profile to Page Profile. To do that, follow these steps:

1. **Log in to Facebook as you normally do.**
2. **Click the wheel in the top-right corner of the page.**
3. **From the drop-down menu, choose the Page link that you want to use.**

   This menu is where you toggle among your personal and Page Profiles. If you're an Admin of several pages, you need to select the correct Page.

After you click the preferred Page link, you're taken directly to that Page. Now you're viewing your Page "as" your Page, not as your personal account with Admin privileges for the Page. This point is an important one to understand, and you may need to switch between your personal Profile and your Page Profile to see the differences.

When you change over to working as your Page, you should see your Page's Admin panel expanded to include these sections: Notifications, Messages, See Likes (with a Promote Page button underneath), Pages to Watch, and Page Tips. See Figure 3-1 for that view.

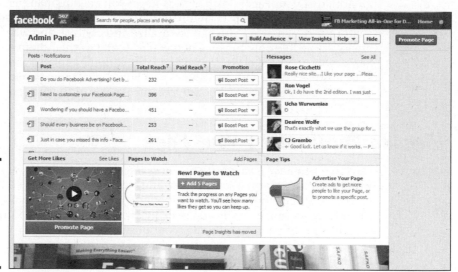

Figure 3-1:
This Admin panel is available for every Page you create.

We go over all those sections later in this chapter. For now, we stick to the two different Profiles you have available and how those views look while you're on your Page.

We're sure that you're used to seeing your personal account News Feed. Well, a business Page can have a News Feed, too! Your Page Profile News Feed is based solely on the Pages you've liked as your Page. To see that

News Feed, click the link in the top-right of the Page called Home. This feed functions just the same as your personal Profile News Feed, except that it's filled with posts from other Facebook Pages that you (as your Page) have liked. If you haven't liked any Pages yet as your Page, you won't have anything in this News Feed. You can't like a personal account as a Page, so this feed shows only Page updates.

How does a Page like another Page? The next section explains how. Right now, to switch back to your personal Profile, follow these steps:

1. **Click the down arrow in the top-right corner of the page.**

2. **From the drop-down menu, choose Use Facebook as** *your personal account name.*

    This menu is where you toggle your personal and Page Profiles.

Book II
Chapter 3

Administering Your
Facebook Business
Page

There's one more little view that you need to understand. When you're on Facebook as yourself, and you go to your Page, you see a notification bar at the top of the page that looks like Figure 3-2. Facebook adds this notification to make it very obvious "who" you are while you're on your Page — your personal account or your Page. We know that this feature has a little Dr. Seuss feeling to it, but the more you test it, the more you'll understand it. If you switch to posting or commenting as your Personal profile, you can comment as yourself on the Page. You may want to do that for a company page, so you can interact personally.

Figure 3-2:
Change who
(your per-
sonal Profile
or business
Page) will
post on the
Page.

Click to change who's posting

Now that you've had a chance to see your Profile options and are comfortable switching between them, we have a few tips for you:

+ If you're viewing Facebook while logged in as your Page, and you go to another business Page for which you're an Admin, you won't be able to do any Admin stuff (editing, posting as that Page, and so on) until you switch back to your personal Profile.

+ You can't post as your Page on anyone's personal Facebook Profile, but you can post as your Page on another Page.

✦ Try not to be too spammy by posting as your Page all the time. Yes, this option is a great way to promote your Page, but remember that Facebook is a social network, not a place to go dropping your business name everywhere!

✦ You can also easily toggle back and forth between your Personal Profile and your Page by going to Edit Page at the top of your Admin Panel and selecting "Use Facebook as *your profile or your Page whichever you need to switch to*" from the drop-down menu.

Liking other Pages as your Page

If you've been on Facebook for a while, maybe you've already liked your favorite business Pages as yourself (that is, your personal Profile). If so, you know that when you like a Page, any status updates or shared content for that Page make their way into your News Feed. Liking a Page is one more way to keep up with the brands you enjoy.

Commenting as your business Page instead of yourself is one way to promote your own business Page and increase its visibility in new communities.

We encourage you to spend some time developing a strategy around which Pages you want to have associated with your own business Page. When you're choosing which Pages to like, it's a good idea to choose Pages that you think will fit with your audience's expectations. Liking the NFL Page, for example, would seem incongruous with your Doll Factory Page and wouldn't mesh well with your established community. On the other hand, that same community may appreciate a link to another business Page about restoring antique dolls.

If you're viewing a Page as your Page, and you prefer to comment as your personal Profile instead, you need to switch back to your Profile (by choosing your Profile from the Account drop-down menu). When you switch back, you're deposited on your Profile News Feed instead of the Page you were just viewing. You need to navigate back to that Page and then leave your comment as your personal Profile.

Follow these steps to like a Page as your business Page:

1. **Switch to your business Page, as noted previously.**

2. **Navigate to a Page you want to like.**

   You can either search for that Page name or type in the Page URL in your browser navigation window.

3. **Click the Like button under the cover photo of the Page.**

   Note that this process is the same one you use when you like a Page as your personal Profile.

4. **(Optional) Post a comment.**

   Pages don't receive notification when a Page likes them, so it's nice to leave a comment as your Page to say hello. The Page owner will, however, be able to see that you've liked his Page as a Page when he looks through his likers and filters for Pages (more on that coming up). When you leave your comment, the posting name and thumbnail image are that of your Page Profile, not your personal Profile.

When one business Page likes another business Page, that like doesn't count toward the total number of likes. Suppose that Blogging Basics 101 has 800 likes. If the Simply Amusing Designs Page decides to like Blogging Basics 101, the total number of likes on Blogging Basics 101 stays at 800 instead of increasing to 801. That way, the likes on a Page aren't artificially inflated by personal and business Profiles owned by the same person.

Using a strategy of liking certain Pages as your Page gives you a curated News Feed for you to view (as your Page). It's a bit like creating a list of the businesses you want to keep up with. The Home News Feed for your Page Profile can be a great place to view what other Pages are doing for marketing on Facebook, too.

Changing voice preferences

By default, your Facebook business Page settings are such that when you're on your own business Page, any post you make appears to be from your Page. (In other words, the Page image thumbnail and name are what people see for those posts.) You can change this setting and post as yourself (your personal Profile) on your own Page, too. Your Page may be for your magazine, for example, but you want to post as yourself — the publisher — for a particular reply or comment to a post. You need to change the voice by clicking the link shown in Figure 3-2, earlier in this chapter. You see this link only if you've gone to the Page as your personal Profile. Businesses have to decide how they want their Admins to post and comment on the Page. Some businesses "sign" their posts with their real names, and some switch between Page Profile and personal Profile, depending on what they're posting on the Page.

How an Admin posts on a Page should be spelled out in a social media policy so that everyone is on the same page (pun intended).

Touring the Admin panel

The general layout of the Admin panel is shown in Figure 3-3. The panel has five sections, and you can expand each section by clicking the blue highlighted link to the right of its name. Also, you can Show or Hide the Admin panel itself by clicking the Show/Hide button in the top-right corner of the Page. In this section, we give you a quick tour of the Admin panel's sections.

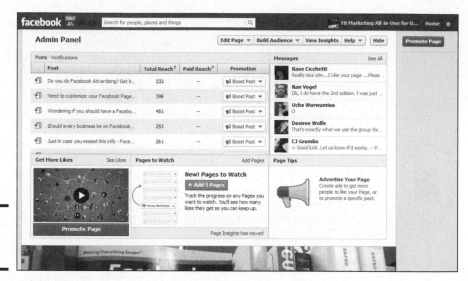

Figure 3-3:
The Admin
panel.

Posts/Notifications

The Posts/Notifications section sits in the top-left corner of the Admin panel. You can toggle between the list of recent posts on your Page and the Notifications for your Page by clicking the highlighted Posts or the highlighted Notifications.

The Posts section shows your five most recent posts with the Total Reach of each post. You also have the option to Boost the Post (pay to push it into the News Feeds) right from this screen. The stars next to your post indicate which ones are performing a little better in terms of engagement; Facebook wants you to consider boosting those further with an ad. Find out more about Boosting Posts in Book VII.

The Notifications section contains a chronological list of actions on your Page: likes, comments, shares, posts to your Timeline, and so on. You can see at a glance the last five or six actions. You also see a red number if there are any notification actions that you haven't viewed yet, and you can click the See All link to open a list of all notifications. When you click any notification, the activity opens. If you click a notification about someone liking an image, for example, when you click the notification, you go right to that image and can view all the comments.

Messages

The Messages section, to the right of the Notifications section, is an inbox containing messages that people have left for your Page to answer. You can turn on the Message feature or turn it off. (In Figure 3-3, earlier in this chapter, the feature is turned on.) You need to make sure that you're aware of this section and either get e-mail notifications when someone leaves a message or check this section often so you can answer messages in a timely manner.

To turn the Message feature on or off, follow these steps:

1. **Click the Edit Page button at the top of your Page.**
2. **Choose Edit Settings from the drop-down menu.**
3. **Click Edit next to the Messages section.**
4. **Select the box next to "Allow people to contact my page privately by showing the Message button."**

   If you don't want the message button showing, uncheck this box.

5. **Click the Save Changes button.**

To read and reply to your messages, go to the Messages section on the Admin Panel and select See All. You can use the search box or click on the magnifying glass as shown in Figure 3-4 to filter by Unread Messages, Archived Messages, Sent Messages, Email only, and Spam.

Messages are private to the Admins of a Page. Posts left on your Page's Timeline are public. These are two different types of notifications you need to address as an Admin of your Page. Later on in this chapter, we have a more detailed explanation of Page Messages.

**Book II
Chapter 3**

Administering Your
Facebook Business
Page

See archived messages   Search messages

Figure 3-4:
The
Messages
interface
lets you
archive or
search for
messages
left for your
Page.

Get More Likes

The Get More Likes section, below the Posts/Notifications section, is mostly an advertisement by Facebook to tell you to promote your Page — but you can click the See Likes link to see a list of all the people who have liked your Page. Note that you can scroll down the list and click See More to get a look at more of the people who have Liked your Page.

Choose Pages That Like This from the drop-down menu that appears if you click People Who Like This (see Figure 3-5) to see the list of Pages who have liked your Page. If you're viewing your Page as your Page, you can click those Page names to go to their Page and like the Page as your Page. If you're viewing your Page as yourself as an Admin, when you click the Page names and go to their Page, clicking the Like button is a personal like. You can also click the X next to a Page or a person and Remove them as a fan.

Notice you can also make someone an Admin from this screen by clicking the gear icon and then selecting Make Admin as shown in Figure 3-5. Be careful you don't accidentally make an unsuspecting fan an Admin.

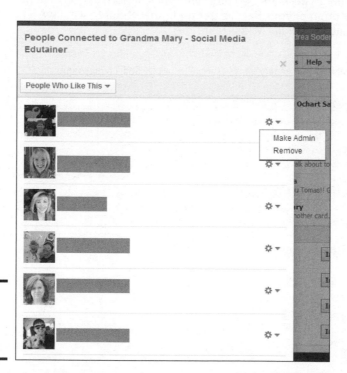

Figure 3-5: See who likes your Page.

Check your new likes on a regular basis, and welcome new people to your Page by posting their first names or by tagging their business Pages. (Find out all about tagging in Book IV, Chapter 2.) Sort the new likes by Page; then like those Pages as your Page and leave comments.

Pages to Watch

The next section inside your Admin panel is Pages to Watch, which is a way to track the progress of other Facebook Pages. You can add up to five Facebook Pages and watch how many new Likes they get over the previous rolling one-week period. Click the blue Add Pages link to search for Pages you want to add.

In theory, you can add any Page but you may want to focus on adding your competition so you can keep tabs on what they are doing on Facebook to get new Likes.

After you add a Page here, the Page Admin gets a notification: Another Page Added *your Page name* as a Page to Watch. They aren't told which Page added them.

After adding the Pages in the Pages to Watch area (remember, this is optional), you can get a snapshot of how many new Likes they have and click over to their Page to see what's been going on.

Page Tips

Currently, the last section of the Admin panel is a space where Facebook can post things it wants you to see. On one day, for example, Facebook offered a promotion for business cards from Moo.com, so you could click the Next link to scroll through the promotions. We can imagine this space being used for all sorts of announcements and promotional offers.

Understanding How Other People See Your Page

We think it's a good idea to give you an overview of some fully functioning Pages so you can see how business Pages look to the public. The best place to start is www.facebook.com/pages (you must be logged in as your profile, not your Page). Click any of the Pages listed, and note these Page features:

✦ Cover photo

✦ Profile photo

✦ Featured apps

✦ Profile image

✦ Friends (mutual connections)

✦ About section

✦ Talking about This (number of people who are interacting with your Page)

✦ Likes (number of personal Profiles that have liked the Page)

✦ Message button (may not be available if the Page has not enabled it)

✦ Latest posts from the Page

Figure 3-6 has callouts for each item on this list so you can see how these elements appear on a business Page. The following sections explain these elements. Also note that you can see additional information by clicking on the Likes, About, Photos, Apps, and More links.

Number of people commenting, posting, and sharing

Profile image   Number of likes   Cover photo

Figure 3-6:
A business
Page as
seen by the
public.

Featured apps   The About section

Cover photo

One of the biggest changes in Facebook Pages recently was the format change to Timeline. Now personal accounts and business Pages have the Timeline structure, and one of the most important components of the Timeline is the Cover photo. This image is 851 pixels (px) x 315 px.

We don't know whether you've noticed, but now when you hover over any account in the News Feed (personal or business Page), a box called the *hover card* pops up, showing you the Profile image, the Cover photo, and some text related to that account. The text that appears for a business Page is the category. New Media Expo does a great job of using a Cover image and a Profile image to create a great effect, as shown in Figure 3-7.

The hover card can be considered a free ad. If done well, like in the New Media Expo example, branding and information can be conveyed beautifully. Notice in the example how you see the date of the event, thumbnails of any Facebook Friends who are attending (social proof), an image of the excitement of attending (the Cover image), and a quick way to like the Page.

Check your Page's hover card by going to your Page and hovering over your own Page's name on a recent post. Does the hover card fully convey the qualities or products and services your business provides?

Figure 3-7:
Here's a great example of why a Cover photo, Profile image, and page category are important.

Featured apps

If you have a brand-new Page and haven't added any Facebook apps or custom apps yet (more on that soon), your visitors see only one or two app boxes below your Cover photo: Photos and Likes (if you or someone else has liked the Page). You want to add apps as you develop your Page, and we show you how to do that in Chapter 2 of this minibook. You may want to add your e-commerce page, newsletter sign-up page, YouTube videos, and many more things.

Your visitors see these Featured apps on your Page and are able to click through all of them. If you have more than three app boxes, visitors to your site can expand or contract the apps by clicking the See all link in the Apps section or by clicking the More link under the cover photo.

Keep two things in mind:

✦ Currently, you can't see any custom apps through the official Facebook mobile app unless the app developers have a mobile-ready link available.

✦ Most people don't know how to click the More link to reveal the other apps.

Three highly functional apps probably are plenty to have in the beginning. As you create contests and other offers, you can add apps that contain that information.

Profile image

The Profile image is important for many reasons; its thumbnail is what accompanies your posts, it's on the hover card (previously mentioned), and you can use promotional text on it.

If you're branding your business logo, the Profile image is a great place to put it. If you're branding yourself, your lovely face needs to be in this position. If you have events, you can use the Profile image to promote the date and location (see the New Media Expo example in Figure 3-7).

Friends (Mutual connections)

Facebook has a section in the top-right corner of personal Profile Timeline that shows friendship connections. If you're viewing Facebook with your personal Profile and go to someone's personal Profile, you can see which Friends you have in common with that person, which photos you and that person tagged have in common, and Pages that both of you liked.

Facebook created a similar space for Pages. When you visit any Facebook Page, you see in the top-left corner (below the Cover photo) a similar space showing which of your personal Profile Friends have liked that Page too. You see this display only if you're viewing Pages as your personal Profile. If you switch over to viewing Facebook as your Page, that section disappears.

About section

Below the Cover photo on the left side is a little section that shows a little bit of text. This area contains some of the words you put in the Short Description on the Page Info section when you started your Page.

To adjust the text that shows up here, follow along:

1. **Click the About area or the word "About."**

   You'll see the Basic Information for your page.

2. **Hover over the top-right corner of About and click the hidden Edit button.**

   The Page Info section opens.

3. **Click Edit next to the field and type your changes.**

4. **Click Save Changes when you're done.**

Any web address you enter in the About field on the Basic Information page (if it contains the `http://` part) will be hyperlinked, so make sure that you type it in full so that people go to the correct page when they click the address.

Book II
Chapter 3

Administering Your
Facebook Business
Page

Notice what's appealing in the About section on other Pages. Some Pages use the space to give viewers a quick explanation of the Page and to list a call to action. You can even put customer testimonials in this section. Here are a few good examples:

✦ **Mari Smith** (`https://www.facebook.com/marismith/info`): This is a great example of using links to products and a complete description of her services. Mari is a must-Like on Facebook — she provides a ton of great information!

✦ **Inbound Zombie** (`https://www.facebook.com/InboundZombie/info`): See how you can use customer testimonials and information about actual results to showcase a business.

✦ **New York Times** (`https://www.facebook.com/nytimes/info`): The *New York Times* uses Milestones effectively on its Facebook Page. The Milestones are listed on the About page.

The numbers

When you click the Likes link below the cover photo, you can see more data about a Page. Two numbers are listed below the name of any business Page. Everyone can see these public numbers:

✦ **Total Page Likes:** The number of people who have clicked the Like button at the top of the Page. This number doesn't include business Pages that have liked the Page — only personal Profiles that have done so.

✦ **People Talking About This:** The "talking about this" number, discussed fully in Book IX, is the number of people who have interacted with your Page in any way, such as liking it, posting to your Timeline, commenting, or sharing one of your posts in a rolling one week period.

✦ **New Page Likes:** You can see how many new Likes the Page has gotten over the past 7 days, and the graph also compares this week's new Likes with last week's Likes as shown in Figure 3-8.

Note: If you have a local business and your Page is a Places Page (see Chapter 1 of this minibook), there's a third number, for check-ins.

Figure 3-8: If you click Likes on any Page, you can see more information.

As you build the number of people who click the Like button, and you follow the suggestions in this book about creating a good community on your Page, you'll naturally find more interaction on your Page. You also have a better chance of getting into the News Feed of your community (more about that in Book IV, Chapter 2) and, we hope, increased revenue or branding awareness — whatever main goal you chose for your Page (see Book I, Chapter 2).

Some Facebook consultants say that a good time to start running contests is when you reach more than 1,000 likes because you should have plenty of entries then. You know your niche better than anyone else, though. When you reach a milestone number, do something special for your Page community. Some Pages celebrate milestones at 100, 500, 1,000, 2,000 likes, and so on. Think up something special for each milestone. If you decide to give away something, make sure that you follow Facebook's guidelines for sweepstakes and contests. You can find all the info in Book VI, Chapter 2.

The likes

Below the Cover photo is the Likes section. If you selected Manage Permissions, Post Visibility check box, there will be a box for Post to Page above the Likes section. In the Likes section, you and your visitors can see other Pages that your business Page has liked, as shown in Figure 3-9. This section shows up to three other Pages. Every time anyone refreshes your Page, the Pages listed are in a different order. Also, you can set your Admin dashboard to display three Featured likes. We show you how to do that a little later in this chapter.

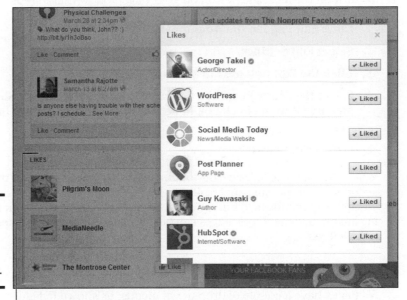

Figure 3-9:
A Page has liked these other business Pages.

The Pages that another Page Likes are visible in the left sidebar

You need to decide whether you want your visitors to see these Pages. Some businesses like to associate themselves with certain Pages to add to their reputations; others don't want to show anything that takes someone off their Page.

These Pages are not the ones that you liked as your personal Profile. Pages that you like as yourself (that is, as your personal Profile) are listed on your personal Profile's Info page.

Message button

You have the option to turn on or off the private Message button on your Page. If the button is turned on, you see it on the Page. If the button is turned off, you won't see it.

This Message button functions just like a Private Message on your personal account. Your Page can receive private messages, too. You can think of Messages as a kind of e-mail inbox. That's the way Facebook wants you to look at Page Messages.

To turn on the Message button on your Page, follow these steps:

1. **Click Edit Page in the Admin panel.**
2. **Select Edit Settings.**
3. **Click the Edit link next to Messages.**
4. **Select the Allow People to Contact My Page Privately By Showing the Message Button check box to activate the Message button on your Page.**
5. **Click Save Changes.**

When you have the Message button turned on, you need to check the Messages section of your Admin panel regularly. Reply to messages just as you reply to e-mails. You cannot send outbound messages as your Page without first receiving an inbound messages. Pages can only Reply to messages, not send them out unsolicited.

Drop-down menus on Pages

All Pages have a couple of drop-down menus, as shown in Figure 3-10. Click the icon to see a variety of links that we'll go through next. What regular visitors see through this gear icon on your Page and what you (and any Admin of any Facebook Page) see will be different. Also, if you're viewing your Page as your Page, you see a different view from the Admin view.

Figure 3-10: Clicting the gear icon drops down a list of handy links.

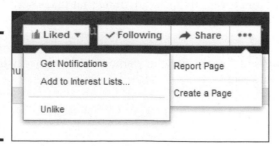

If you haven't Liked the Page yet, you only see the Like button and then once you have Liked it, you have some additional options if you click the Liked drop-down menu:

✦ **Get Notifications:** This option turns on notifications for you for this Page so that any time this Page has a new post, you get a notification on your personal profile. Turn on Notifications for Pages that you really care about so you don't miss anything. But don't turn on Notifications for every Page you Like or you will be overwhelmed.

✦ **Add to Interest Lists:** This option enables you to add the Page to a Facebook Interest List. Using Interest Lists can be a strategy to get your Page seen by a larger audience. Book VIII, Chapter 1 discusses advanced marketing strategies. This Add to Interest link is seen by anyone on any Page.

✦ **Unlike:** You can Unlike the Page with this selection.

Under the drop-down menu shown with the three dots you see a couple of options.

✦ **Report Page (visible on other Pages, not your own):** You can report any Page if you feel that it's breaking Facebook rules, and other people can report your Page if they feel that it's breaking Facebook rules. When you click this link, you bring up a dialog box that takes you through the process of reporting the Page. If you don't see this as a link, you can click the Visit Help Center link and search for Reporting a Page.

✦ **Create a Page:** This is a quick link to go to the interface to create a new Page. Everyone sees this link.

Between the two drop-down menus you see two options.

✦ **Following:** You can unfollow a Page you Like which means that you won't get updates in your News Feed from this Page even though you Like the Page.

✦ **Share:** This option is by far the most important. You want visitors to your Page to choose it! Doing so brings up a post (that you can edit) that appears on their Timelines for all their Friends to see. (We talk about sharing in detail in Book IV, Chapter 1.) Go ahead and choose this option on any Page to see what happens. All the information in the post comes from particular fields on the Info link for the Page you're viewing. If the Page didn't put information in the Company Overview section (or other fields — again, review Book IV, Chapter 1), there will be no text, just the name of the Page hyperlinked back to the Page. You may want to adjust your own Page after seeing how it looks on someone else's Page.

Book II Chapter 3

Administering Your Facebook Business Page

Editing Your Page

Now that you know how other people see your Page, you can see how it looks from the inside! This section explores all the ways you can edit your Page. You see where you add applications (apps), change the information people see about your Page, change your Profile image, and do many other things.

To start, click the Edit Page button at the top of your Admin panel, as shown in Figure 3-11.

You can click Update Page Info, Edit Settings, or Manage Admin Roles. It doesn't matter, because clicking any of these will put you on your Page's editing dashboard. You'll be able to choose the item you want from the top menu. The other two selections — Use Activity Log and See Banned Users — are covered a bit later in this chapter.

Figure 3-11: Click this button to find the interface for editing your Page.

You're looking at your business Page's administrative dashboard, as shown in Figure 3-12. This dashboard is where you edit and modify your Page. Notice the nice collection of navigation links across the top. In the following sections, we walk you through each of these options.

Figure 3-12:
The Page
dashboard
for editing
your Page.

Remember all that work you did to figure out the type and category you wanted when you created your Page? Remember the Info editing? Well, if not, that's okay. You can edit everything on your Page's Info tab by clicking the Update Page Info link on your administrative dashboard. Each section can be edited by clicking the Edit link on the right side of the name of the field.

The fields you find on the Page About tab are specific to the category and Page type you selected when creating your Page. You can change the category and Page type for your Page by choosing new settings from the drop-down menus. The first drop-down menu allows you to choose a new category for your Page; the second drop-down menu allows you to choose a new Page type. Make sure that you click Save Changes before editing the fields, because those fields might change with the category change.

Fill in all the fields, remembering that you don't have to stick to what the fields are asking for. The Founded field, for example, allows you to have up to 260 characters, but you don't have to use that many.

You can also add your Twitter username, website address, LinkedIn profile page, and any number of other things. If you include a web address, make sure to include http:// so that the address will be hyperlinked.

When you create your Page, the URL is long and unwieldy because it contains your Page's ID number. It looks something like this:

```
http://www.facebook.com/pages/The-Social-Classroom-with-Phyllis-
     Khare/123451234512345
```

What you want is a vanity URL (or pretty URL). Facebook also calls it a "username." You want it to look like this:

```
http://facebook.com/TheSocialClassroom
```

When you set up your business Page, or when you've reached the requested 25 likes on your Page, navigate to the Basic Information tab from your administrative dashboard, or go directly to www.facebook.com/username.

You can use the Username page to set your Profile username, too. Make sure that you don't set your business Page name to your personal name! Notice the username page has two sections (see Figure 3-13): one for your personal name and one for your Pages. Your best bet is to set your personal account to your name (such as www.facebook.com/andreavahl) and then set your Page URL.

Click the Check Availability button to check available usernames. A Username Available box comes up, displaying several things to keep in mind about a username, such as making sure that you have the right to use the name you've selected.

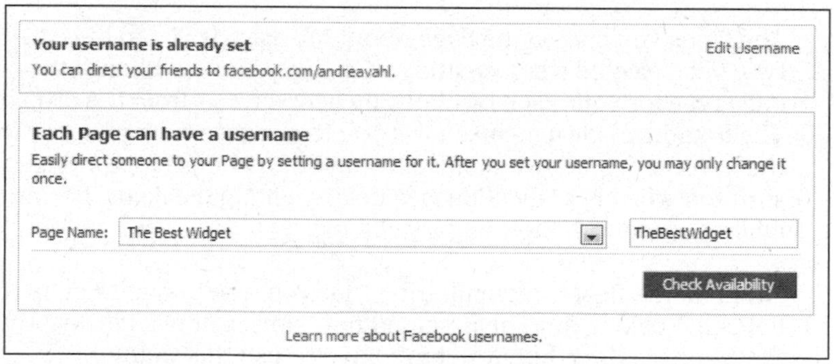

Figure 3-13:
When setting your username for your Page, make sure you are selecting for Pages, not your personal account.

Your username is already set   Edit Username

You can direct your friends to facebook.com/andreavahl.

Each Page can have a username

Easily direct someone to your Page by setting a username for it. After you set your username, you may only change it once.

Page Name: | The Best Widget   ▾ | TheBestWidget

Check Availability

Learn more about Facebook usernames.

When you have something that you like, and it's available, click Confirm. Now you have a nice, neat URL for your Facebook Page. You can use this URL on everything, including letterhead, websites, and e-mail signatures. We go into great detail on how to use this URL in Book IV. In the meantime, put this URL in your next e-mail to your customers so that they can find you easily on Facebook.

Edit Settings

The Settings section gives you options that determine how a person can interact with your Page, as shown in Figure 3-14. We want to explain each option on this page because these options directly affect how first-time and loyal visitors see and network on your Page. Click the Edit link next to the name of each section to open up the options for each section.

Figure 3-14: Change how people can interact with your Page.

✦ **Page Visibility:** We discuss the Page Visibility check box in detail in Chapter 2 of this minibook. Selecting this check box hides your Page from the public until it's ready for viewing.

✦ **Posting Ability:** This section has two check boxes: Everyone Can Post to the Page's Timeline and Everyone Can Add Photos and Videos to the Page's Timeline. Selecting these check boxes allows anyone to create a new post directly on the Page's Timeline. If you prefer to have people only be able to comment on the Page's own posts and not as a new post on the Timeline, then clear these two check boxes. You can read Book IV, Chapter 2, where we discuss this more thoroughly.

Sometimes you want (or don't want) random visitors to be able to post videos or photos on your Page. You can always remove random spam posts, but you can nip spam in the bud by not allowing outside posts.

✦ **Post Visibility:** You can collect all the posts that others make on your Timeline by selecting this check box. Then you can decide whether you want to make these posts visible or hide them from the Page. After reviewing the posts, you can highlight any of them so they show up in the Highlight view.

You can also choose to remove the Recent Posts by Others box by clearing the Highlight Recent Posts by Others in a Box at the Top of My Page Timeline check box. This doesn't prevent people from posting but may make other people's comments less obvious to visitors to your Page. On the other hand, it's nice to show that you're getting interaction on your Page and responding to it.

✦ **Post Targeting and Privacy:** By default, this option is off. Turning it on allows you to select an audience each time you post where you can target by country or language. This is different than the Targeting option on the posts that exists because when you use Post Privacy Gating, the post is actually hidden from your Timeline from everyone except that audience.

✦ **Messages:** When you select this check box, people can message the Page just like they can message a person's personal Profile. We discussed this earlier in this chapter in the section, "Touring the Admin panel."

✦ **Tagging Ability:** Select this check box to allow people to tag photos they take with the name of your Page. Think this one through. If your business sponsors events or has products that are sold in stores, you want your fans to be able to take a photo and tag your Page so those photos end up in your Page's albums. But some people use this feature to get the attention of a Page or to spam the Page. To remove a tag, view the photo, click the Options button at the bottom of the photo, and then select Report/ Remove tag. Then select the radio button to remove the tag.

✦ **Notifications:** You can choose to get notifications On Facebook, which means you get a notification on your personal Profile as well as your Page which works well if you are on Facebook frequently. You can also select Email notifications. Each admin will have their own preferences set up in this section. E-mail notifications work well if you aren't on Facebook that often and want to be notified if someone posts on your Page or comments on a Post.

✦ **Country Restrictions:** When you leave this field blank, anyone can see the Page whether she is logged into Facebook or not. When you type a country's name in this field, you can select the country's name that is autosuggested. Then you have two radio button choices: Only Show This Page to Viewers in These Countries, or Hide This Page from Viewers in These Countries.

Be careful about setting the Country Restrictions or Age Restrictions because these settings will cause your Page not to be visible unless someone is logged in to Facebook. The person needs to be logged into Facebook before Facebook can determine whether they live in the right country or are the right age. These restrictions even affect your Like Box not showing up on your website unless someone is logged into Facebook.

✦ **Age Restrictions:** The default setting allows anyone older than 13 to see your Page. If you need to restrict viewing to people older than 17, 18, 19, or 21, you can set that level by choosing it from the drop-down menu.

If you're promoting a business connected with alcohol, the Alcohol-Related age restriction sets the minimum age based on the location of the user. Only users in Canada and South Korea who are 19 or older, users in Japan and Paraguay who are 20 or older, users in India who are 25 or older, and users elsewhere (including the United States) who are 21 or older can view your Page. Facebook makes the point quite clearly that you are ultimately responsible for who sees your Page, however.

✦ **Page Moderation:** You can add comma-separated keywords that Facebook automatically marks as spam if they show up in a post to your Page or in a comment on a post.

✦ **Profanity Filter:** The drop-down list gives you three choices; None, Medium, and Strong. We know that we should come up with a witty description here, but &*%@# if we can! Seriously, if you think that people might come by your Page and use profanity, choose Medium or Strong.

✦ **Similar Page Suggestions:** Facebook has a feature that when someone Likes a Page, a section appears where Facebook shows similar pages that they can Like if they want. Including your Page in this option means that your Page gets suggested to others but it also means that other Pages (and possibly competitors Pages) are suggested to people when they Like your Page. If you have concerns about that happening, clear the check box to opt out of this feature.

✦ **Replies:** The comment replies allows you to reply to a specific comment, and it will be indented to show that the reply is for that comment alone. Before this option, the comments were in one long thread, and it was hard to tell who was talking to who so you always had to mention the person's name.

✦ **Merge Pages:** This option is for merging duplicate Pages and Places. We cover this in more detail in Chapter 2 of this minibook.

✦ **Remove Page:** This deletes your Page. Keep in mind that you can't undo this action. Deleting a Page deletes everything — photos, posts, and so on. Make sure that you copy everything you want from the Page before you choose this option.

If you delete a Page for which you had already set a vanity URL (and you want to use that particular URL for a new Page), that URL won't be available for at least 14 days after deletion. If it isn't available after that

**Book II
Chapter 3**

**Administering Your
Facebook Business
Page**

period, you need to file an infringement form with Facebook and ask to use it again. It may be easier to just hide the Page by selecting the Page Visibility check box at the top of the Manage Permissions section. Find the infringement form at

www.facebook.com/help/contact/?id=208282075858952

Below the Email Notifications check box, look for the View All Email Settings for Your Pages link. See it? We suggest that you click it. When you do, you're taken to your personal Profile settings that shows all your e-mail notification settings. You may want to go through this page, as we were surprised by how many e-mail notification settings we needed to change, especially for apps.

Admin Roles

Admins are people who can administer your Page. To get to the Admins, click Edit Page and Manage Admin Roles. There are five types of Admin roles, which we describe in this list:

✦ **Manager:** The *Manager* role is what you are when you create the Page. You and anyone else with this designation can edit and delete items on your Page, ban users, post status updates and comments, and send messages to fans. Everything you can do with your Page, Manager Admins can do, too.

✦ **Content Creator:** Anyone with the *Content Creator* Admin status can edit the Page, create a status update, create ads, and view Insights on your Facebook business Page, and it will look as though the Page made the update, not them personally (unless they change the voice, as discussed at the beginning of this chapter). The status update has the Page thumbnail image and the Page name listed. A Content Creator can do everything that a Manager can do except add or remove Admins.

✦ **Moderator:** The *Moderator* Admin status allows someone to reply to comments, ban and block people, send messages, create ads, and view Insights, but not to create a post on the Page.

✦ **Advertiser:** The *Advertiser* Admin status allows someone to view Insights and to create and manage ads on behalf of the Page.

✦ **Insights Analyst:** The *Insights Analyst* Admin status lets someone into the Insights interface and download data from that area.

Here are some quick points about being an Admin of a Page:

✦ You can have as many Admins and Admin types as you want.

✦ Always have at least one other person as your Manager Admin in case you're unavailable to make changes in other Manager roles.

✦ All Admins need to click the Your Settings link on the navigation menu to adjust the e-mail notification settings and must understand the voice process. By default, Facebook selects the e-mail notification check box for all activity on the Page. This setting means that all Admins receive e-mail notification whenever someone posts or comments on the Page unless Admins deselect it. We discuss this topic in the "Your Settings" section, earlier in the chapter.

✦ As a Manager Admin, you can remove your own Admin status or another Admin. Then you view your Page just the way any fan of your Page does. You don't see the Admin panel, and when you post, you post from your personal Profile. You don't receive any e-mail notifications for the Page.

✦ Facebook requires each Page to have at least one Manager Admin. If you try to remove yourself as a Manager Admin before adding someone else, you won't be able to remove yourself.

Here are the steps for adding someone to your Page as any type of Admin:

1. **Go to your Page, and click the Edit Page button.**

2. **Choose Manage Admin Roles from the drop-down choices.**

3. **Type the name or e-mail address of the person you want to add as an Admin.**

   If you start typing the name, Facebook displays suggestions; just click a name to select it. You need to be a Friend of this person to be able to add him as an Admin this way.

   If you aren't the person's Facebook Friend, you can add the e-mail address that he used to open the Facebook account. The person receives a Facebook notification that they have been made an Admin of the Page. If you're having trouble adding the Admin, it can help to have them make sure they like the Page.

4. **Choose the Admin role from the drop-down menu.**

5. **Click the Save Changes button.**

   A security dialog box appears where you have to enter your personal Facebook password.

6. **Enter your Facebook password as a security step and click Confirm.**

   That person is added to the list of Admins for the Page.

Here are the steps for removing someone as an Admin of your Page:

1. **Go to your Page, and click the Edit Page button.**

2. **Choose Manage Admin Roles in the drop-down choices.**

3. **Click the X next to the name of the person you want to remove.**

   If you're removing yourself, click the X next to your name.

   You won't be able to edit your Page or gain access to Insights, ads, notifications, and so on when you remove yourself as an Admin. If you try to remove yourself as an Admin before adding another Manager Admin, you won't be able to remove yourself.

4. **Click Save Changes.**

5. **Enter your Facebook password as a security step and click Confirm.**

Apps

Under the More menu in the Page dashboard, Apps is the first selection. Apps (applications) are developed by third parties, or by Facebook itself, to expand the functions of Facebook. Thousands of apps are available. You can connect an app to your Page to expand what people can do on your Page. Facebook has an App Center that you can explore but the App Center tends to focus more on Facebook games. You can see the Apps here: `https://www.facebook.com/appcenter/`.

When you create a new Page, you need to activate a few apps right away because they create important links that people will be looking for on your Page. These apps, developed by Facebook, are

- ✦ Photos

- ✦ Video

- ✦ Events (if your business will be having them)

Chapter 4 of this minibook explains all the steps for adding applications to your new Page.

Applications are so important to Facebook that we discuss them in all nine minibooks, especially Book V.

Audience Suggestions

The second menu item under the More drop-down menu in the Page dashboard is Audience Suggestions. The audience of your Page can make suggestions to improve your Page's information. You can review and accept or decline the suggestions here.

Featured

The third selection under the More menu on the Page dashboard is Featured. The Featured tab has two parts: Likes and Page Owners. We describe both in the next sections.

Editing Featured Likes

The Likes section lets you feature up to five Facebook Pages in a section of your Timeline. You can specify which Pages you've liked as your Page will be shown there by selecting five of them as Featured. The steps for liking a Page as your

Page and featuring a Page are outlined earlier in this chapter. Click the Edit Featured Likes button and select the check box next to the five Pages you'd like to feature on your Page. Any time you want to feature different Pages, just return to this tab and click the button again and check the five you want.

To have Pages show up in the Likes section of your business Page, follow these steps:

1. **Log in to Facebook as you normally do.**

2. **Click the drop-down arrow in the top-right corner of the page.**

3. **Choose the Page you want to switch to under the "Use Facebook as" prompt.**

This menu is where you toggle between your personal and Page Profiles. If you're an Admin of several Pages, you need to select the correct Page, or you can select your profile name to return back to your personal profile.

4. **Navigate to the Page you want to include in your Like section.**

5. **Click the Like button at the top of that Page.**

When you return to your own business Page, the Page that you liked is listed in the Likes section of your own Page's Timeline. After you like more than three Pages, you need to decide which of these Pages you want to feature.

To adjust which Pages are featured on your Page, follow these steps:

1. **Log in to Facebook as you normally do.**

2. **Go to your Page.**

You can do this next step as an Admin or as your Page.

3. **Click the Edit Page button at the top of the Admin panel and choose Update Page Info.**

This step gives you access to your editing menu.

4. **Click the More link and then choose Featured from the drop-down menu.**

5. **Click the Edit Featured Likes button.**

You see all the Pages that you've liked as your Page.

6. **Select the five Pages that you want to feature.**

If you don't want to feature any Pages, clear all check boxes.

7. **Click Save.**

As we explain at the beginning of this chapter, you can like Pages as your Page now, so if you have been on Facebook for a while and have liked certain business Pages through your personal Profile, you can log in as your Page and like those Pages as your Page.

Editing Featured Page Owners

The second section of the Featured tab — Page Owners — raises the curtain on the Admins of the Page. Some businesses want to keep that information private; others want the world to know. This section is where you get to make that decision. When you Feature any or all of the Admins, the Admins have their personal-account thumbnail images and their names listed on the Page's Timeline.

Mobile

The last selection under the More menu on the Page dashboard is Mobile. When you select the Mobile link, you have the opportunity to create three kinds of mobile connections to your Page:

✦ **With Mobile E-mail:** We discuss your mobile e-mail options in Chapter 1 of this minibook, but to recap, you can send a post or upload a photo to your Page by using an e-mail address created specifically for your Page. Facebook puts your unique e-mail address in this section for easy reference. What you type in the subject line of the e-mail on your mobile phone becomes the update to your Page, or if you're uploading a photo, the subject line becomes the caption. Nothing that you type in the body of the e-mail shows up, so leave it blank.

✦ **With Mobile Web:** You can see how your Page looks on a mobile phone by typing its URL in the phone's browser. It's easier to type in a custom URL on a mobile device, so Facebook put a link for creating a Page username in this part of the dashboard. The link to create a custom URL is `http://facebook.com/username`.

If you type **www.facebook.com/grandmamaryshow** on an Android phone, for example, you're redirected to `http://m.facebook.com/grandmamaryshow` (notice the `m` that precedes `facebook`). It turns out that your phone is so smart, it knows when you're looking at Facebook on a phone, so it directs you to the mobile interface for Facebook. Your Page will look a bit different from how it looks on a computer, so make sure that you check it.

You can also type **http://touch.facebook.com/*yourpagename*** to see how your Page will look to those who view it on a phone.

✦ **With the iPhone:** First, install the Facebook app on your iPhone or iPad; then log in. When you click the menu icon (a box with three horizontal lines), you see the Pages for which you're an Admin in the left navigation menu.

We recommend that you get the Facebook Page Manager app. You can do a search in the App Store for it. It's really handy if you manage several Pages.

For the remainder of the Admin tour, go back to the Admin panel on your main Page.

Use Activity Log

Access the Activity Log by clicking Edit Page and then Use Activity Log from your Admin panel. The Activity Log shows everything that happens on your Page from the time you started it. You can see all the Photos, Comments, Posts by Others, Spam, and more listed chronologically. You can scroll through the posts or skip to a certain time frame by clicking on the date on the right (although that feature doesn't always work that well). You can filter what you are looking at by clicking the selection on the left sidebar, as shown in Figure 3-15.

Click on the selections to filter the Activity Log by this activity

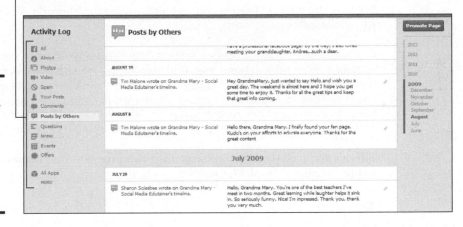

Figure 3-15: The Activity Log allows you to sort by certain types of posts on your Page.

If you have scheduled posts, you also find those posts here so that you can edit them or delete them.

Notice that you can view Spam from the Activity Log. We recommend you regularly check this section to see whether any posts are being "accidentally" marked as Spam that you want to allow on your Page. To unmark a post as spam, click the "circle with the line through it" symbol that appears to the right of the Post. A drop-down menu appears where you can select Unmark as Spam. Now the post appears on your Page, and you can answer it as your Page.

See Banned Users

When you select this option from the Admin panel, a pop-up box appears showing you the banned users and giving the option to unban them. This pop-up box is actually the same one that appears when you click See Likes on the Admin Panel but is just defaulted to showing you the banned users. Hopefully you won't have to ban too many users along your Facebook marketing journey. We find that we mostly ban people for excessive spam, but that doesn't happen too often.

Build Audience

When you click the Build Audience selection, you see different options if you're logged in as your Page (you only get the Promote Page option) or if you're logged in as your personal Profile (you see Invite Friends, Share Page, and Promote Page).

We cover the Invite Friends and Share Page options extensively in Chapter 2 of this minibook and the Promote Page option is for advertising your Page. We cover that much more extensively in Book VII.

See Insights

Clicking the Insights link on your administrative dashboard takes you directly to your Insights dashboard.

Insights is Facebook's analytics system. You can see who uses your Page, as well as see her interactions, age, and gender; where she lives; and her cats' names (well, no, not yet). You can also see very detailed graphs about the users of your Page and their interactions with it. Get acquainted with the Insights dashboard because it can really help you see who your audience is and give you insight into what people respond to most on your Page.

There's so much to this wonderful analytics program that we dedicate an entire chapter — Book IX, Chapter 2 — to it.

Help

This selection has a drop-down menu to get you to various types of help. If you select Visit Help Center, it links directly to the business Pages Help section rather than to some general Facebook help page. The page has many sections with a wealth of information to help you with your Page.

We feel that it's good to go straight to the horse's mouth (what does that mean, anyway?) when we have a question about Facebook. That's why this link to the Help section for Pages is handy to have on the editing menu.

Interactive help from Facebook can also be hard to come by, though, and that's why the Facebook Help Community selection from the drop-down menu can be a good place to go as well. Here you can post questions or search for answers to your particular problem when the Facebook Help Center isn't enough.

Facebook also has a Getting Started section of their Help which can be good for beginners. (But you won't need that because you have this lovely book to help you out!)

The last option from the Help drop-down menu is Send Feedback. You can use this link to provide Feedback to Facebook about something not working on your Page or a suggestion for Pages.

Chapter 4: Arranging What Your Visitors See

In This Chapter

✔ **Finding your new Page**

✔ **Understanding how apps act as navigation links**

✔ **Changing the order of the apps**

✔ **Using the hover card as an ad**

You and your Page Admins need to be very familiar with how your Page looks to visitors on Facebook. In Chapter 3 of this minibook, we discuss how to present yourself when new visitors arrive on your Page. In this chapter, we tell you how to move your apps around and switch up your Cover image for the best impact on the Page and in the News Feed.

Finding Your Page

The first question we get from marketers who are new to Facebook is, "How do I find my Page?" Facebook used to make it hard to find one's own Page, but it created a left-column bookmarks menu with links to everything you need, as shown in Figure 4-1. Click More to see the whole list. ***Note:*** You see this bookmarks menu when you're viewing your Profile's News Feed.

You can find your Page easily by using any of the following options:

✦ **Look for the Page name in the left column of your personal account's News Feed.** Any Page that you created or serve as Admin for will be listed there, below the Pages heading. If you're an Admin for more than four Pages, click the More link that shows up when you hover over the Page names to open a new page with all your Pages listed.

✦ **Click the down arrow in the upper corner and select your Page name from the drop-down menu.** This is the preferred method of navigating to your Page because now you're officially logged in as your Page and acting as your Page on Facebook. The other methods described here result in you still being logged in as your profile while on your Page. That isn't a problem but may be confusing if you try to go to your Page's News Feed.

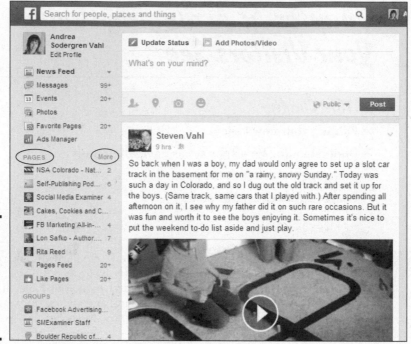

Figure 4-1:
The book-
marks menu
appears to
the left of
your News
Feed.

✦ **Add the Page's username to the browser bar after** www.facebook.
   com. After you get a vanity URL (see Chapter 3 of this minibook for how
   to create one), you can add the username to the Facebook URL in your
   browser bar and then bookmark the URL on your computer for easy
   access. This is how an URL looks after you add the vanity URL: www.
   facebook.com/*yourusername*. For example:

   www.facebook.com/GrandmaMaryShow

✦ **Use the Facebook search bar.** This search bar is at the top of every
   Facebook page. Start typing your Page's username, and Facebook displays it for you to select. If your business Page doesn't come up as you
   type, type the name of the Page completely and then click the See More
   Results link at the bottom of Facebook's suggestions list.

   You may also see the Find All Pages Named choice from the drop-down
   menu, and then your search term. When you click that choice, you have
   a list of Pages with that term in the name.

   This Facebook search function — Graph Search — is pretty powerful.
   You can type things like **Pages liked by** to get a drop-down list of suggestions such as My Friends, Members of a Group, and more. You can use
   the Graph Search to find all kinds of targeted Interests and other Pages.

Understanding How Apps Act as Navigation Links

In Chapter 3 of this minibook, we give you a little tour of a business Page and show you where everything is located. The boxes below your Cover image that you and your visitors see on your Page are actually applications, which are add-ons that provide extra functionality to your Page. We explain them a bit in Chapter 3 of this minibook and more thoroughly in Book V. In this chapter, we show you how to move them around for the best effect.

As we note in Chapter 3 of this minibook, when you create your Page, the public sees only two apps: Photos and Likes (if at least one person has liked the Page). You can add some great apps to the app section right away, such as Events, Notes, and Video. These apps were developed and designed by Facebook, so they're in the queue (so to speak), ready to be added to your Page. In Chapter 3 of this minibook and in all the following minibooks (especially Books IV and V), we describe how to add custom-built links, such as Welcome links, store links, YouTube links, and hundreds of others.

Apps act as gateways. You can set up an app to take people back to

Book II
Chapter 4

Arranging What
Your Visitors See

+ Your website's home page

+ Your product pages (not on Facebook)

+ Your sales pages

+ Your contest pages

Using a simple image and a link, you can create an app space to link anywhere.

You can also create a Facebook ad that goes right back to the app. If you have a webinar sign-up app, for example, you can create an ad that's linked directly to that sign-up interface. You can target the ad to your existing fans or use the app as a "fan gate," requiring a visitor to like your Page to get the webinar info.

If you have a contest, create an ad that links right back to that app on your Page. Design the app so that visitors need to click Like to see the contest rules and enter the contest. This is a fantastic way to garner more likes for your Page and to create buzz and excitement about your contest.

Each app has its own unique URL that you can share anywhere — on Twitter, with your e-mail subscribers, or on your blog. Each app can also be its own mini-website. To get an app's URL address, click the app and look at the address in the browser window. You can copy and share that address on another site or even paste it into the Status of your Facebook Page to direct your Fans to the app.

After their initial visit to your business Page, most people view your Page's updates only via their News Feed and Ticker: They will rarely visit your actual business Page. Facebook has a featured called —the *hover card* — which shows your Cover image, Profile image, and Page category when a reader mouses over your Page name in his News Feed. We go over that topic in a moment. If you want your audience to visit your Page and explore your other apps, you need to provide strong calls to action in your status updates and provide a link directly to the app. Examples of a call to action include a request to like your Page, join an event, or participate in a contest. To develop a stronger sense of community, bringing people back to your Page is an important goal.

Adding Facebook Apps to Your Page

The number of available Facebook-developed apps is getting smaller and smaller. Currently, four Facebook apps are available: Photos, Notes, Video, and Events. When you start your Page, you have only Photos added by default, and you can't remove the Photos app from your Page.

To make sure that your visitors can see the apps you want, follow these steps:

1. **Go to your Page and click the down arrow on the right side of the current installed apps just under your cover photo.**

2. **Go to a blank box with a plus arrow and click the plus symbol.**

It doesn't matter which box you select. Facebook adds the app in the next available space.

3. **Select the app that you want to add from the drop-down menu.**

You now see the app showing in the box.

You can also use your Admin dashboard area to add and remove your installed apps to your Page. The Admin dashboard area is especially helpful if you have installed other apps to your Page and aren't sure how to find them. To see the list of all your apps and add them to your Page through the Admin dashboard, follow these steps:

1. **Go to your Page and click the Edit Page button in the Admin panel.**

2. **Click Update Page Info.**

Your Admin dashboard opens.

3. **Click the More link and then choose Apps from the drop-down menu.**

The Apps tab shows all the apps connected to your Page.

4. **Find the app that you want to add to the Apps section of your Page Timeline, and click the Edit Settings link below the name of the app.**

A dialog box appears. For most applications, the dialog box has only a Profile tab. The Events dialog box has two tabs: Profile and Additional Permissions. The Additional Permissions are needed if you want to allow the Events app to publish the event(s) to your Timeline.

5. **Click the Add Link on the Profile tab.**

What you see next depends on the app you're adding. We note those variations later.

6. **Click Okay.**

The app is listed in your Page's app section for all to see. You may have to adjust the position of the app, as we show you later in this chapter.

You can use these instructions to turn on any of the following Facebook apps.

Events app

If your business has events, you may want to add this link by following the steps in the preceding section. Figure 4-2 shows a convention center's Events page. Notice that the interface has tabs for Upcoming Events and Past Events.

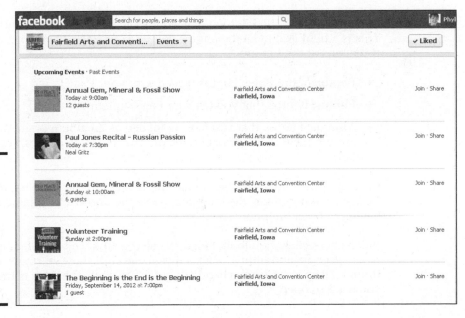

Figure 4-2: The Events application lists the Events that your business wants to showcase.

If you click an Event title, you're taken to that particular event Page. Using Facebook Events for marketing is discussed thoroughly in Book VI, Chapter 1.

Photos app

This application is automatically added in the app section for a new Page. Because Facebook redesigned the whole photo interface (with a grid-style photos stream, and the ability to like and comment on the photo thumbnails), you want to make sure your photos are a great addition to your Page.

Having this app on your Page allows visitors to see the photos you uploaded to your Page and also photos tagged with your Page's name (if you set that option in your Page settings). You can arrange your photos in custom-titled albums, but Facebook keeps your Profile images in one album called Profile Pictures (and you can't change the name of this album).

If you post a photo to the Page Timeline, Facebook puts it in an album called Timeline Photos. You can't change the name of this album, either, but you can delete photos that end up in this album. We discuss photo uploading, arranging, album naming, and the world of images in Book IV, Chapter 1.

As we discuss in Chapter 3 of this minibook, you can prevent a liker from posting photos to your Page by making the appropriate setting in the Posting Ability section after selecting Edit Page and Edit Settings on your administrative dashboard.

People who click the Photo app on your Page see your Page's Photos Stream. This is a tight grid of all the photos you, as your Page, have uploaded. The three tabs at the top are

✦ **Photos of the Page:** Photos tagged with your Page name

✦ **Photos:** Photos that you (as your Page) uploaded

✦ **Albums:** Photos that you have uploaded as an album or are naturally grouped together such as Profile photos, Timeline photos, or Mobile uploads

Clicking the Photo app on your Page takes users to the middle tab — Photos. Notice each photo has the interface to like the photo and comment without having to open the photo to full view.

When users click the Album tab, they see the album as thumbnails. If you hover over an album thumbnail, a five-image slideshow starts inside the thumbnail space, which is handy to quickly see whether this is the album you want to open.

When you click any album, another grid appears with the same setup of seeing the Like and comments interface on the thumbnails of the photos in the album. When you click an individual photo, a lightbox opens. A *lightbox* is a dialog box that shows specific information — in this case, your photos, descriptions, and any comments. The lightbox has arrows on either side so that the visitor can move through the photo album one image at a time. Hidden links show up when a visitor hovers over the bottom of any image: Tag Photo (may not be visible if the Tag option is not enabled by the Page), Options, Share, Send, and Like.

If you're an Admin of the Page, you see several other links below the Options link: Edit Location, Change Date, Rotate Left, Rotate Right, Download, Make Profile Picture, Make Album Cover, Get Link, Move to Other Album, Delete this Photo, and Enter Fullscreen. Your visitors to your photos see only Download, Embed Post, Report, and Enter Fullscreen. Each option is fairly self-explanatory, except for the Embed Post, which we discuss more in Book IX. You can embed any Facebook post into your blog or website.

You can use photos like ads because you can upload an image of your promotional page or text. Then, in the description section, place the hyperlinked URL that people can click to buy a product or sign up for something. Figure 4-3 shows an example of how much information you can put in the description section. We spend some time on the marketing possibilities of photos in Facebook in Book IV, Chapter 1.

Figure 4-3: Notice the full description (on right) that includes links.

Notes app

A *note* is a public post and appears in the News Feed for all fans to see, and anyone tagged in the note receives a notification. The Notes app used to be the only place to publish a really long post, but now you can have an almost unlimited number of characters (currently more than 63,000) in a regular post, too. We like to think of a note as being similar to a blog post. You can title the note, upload a photo with it, and add some formatting (bold, italic, underline, bullets, numbering, and quotations) to it. The people who are tagged receive a notification and can view the note. (They can untag themselves if they don't want to be attached to the note publicly.)

You can create a note and tag people and Pages to view it. You can tag your Friends and any Facebook Page. When you create a note, a notification appears in your Page Timeline and goes out to your likers' News Feeds for everyone to see.

You can consider the Notes apps as a blog, an additional blog, or a larger posting space. You can create a special type of conversation among you and your likers. This conversation space could be for people who are enthusiastic about a particular subject. If you've already added the Notes app to your app section (see the generic instructions in "Adding Facebook Apps to Your Page," earlier in this chapter), follow these steps to create and manage your notes:

1. **Click the Notes app in your Page's app section below the Cover image.**

    If you don't see the app, you need to add it to the app section. (See "Adding Facebook Apps to Your Page," earlier in this chapter.)

2. **Click the +Write a Note button in the top-right corner.**

    This button opens an editing space where you can create a title, type the text of the note, tag people and/or Pages, add a photo, preview, save a draft, and publish.

3. **Enter the title and body of the note.**

    You can use a few formatting tools, such as bold and italic.

    A note can be really long. How long? We don't know exactly, but we've seen up to five pages' worth fit in there. So write away!

4. **Tag people and Pages.**

    To tag a person or a Page, start typing the person's name or the Page name in the Tag field. Facebook displays a list of your Friends and Pages. Click the ones you want to tag (see Figure 4-4).

5. **Click the Add a Photo link, browse to the photo on your computer, and upload it.**

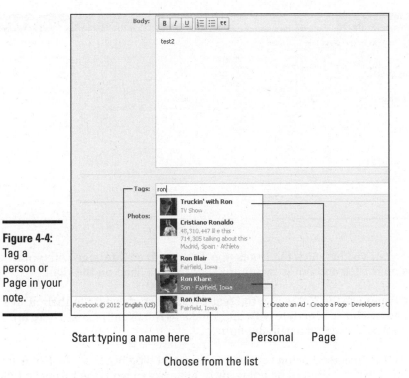

Figure 4-4:
Tag a
person or
Page in your
note.

Start typing a name here   Personal   Page

Choose from the list

Book II
Chapter 4

Arranging What
Your Visitors See

6. **Click Publish, Preview, Save Draft, or Discard.**

You can decide how to proceed with this step:

- *Publish:* Your note is published to the world! The note shows up as a Page status update and appears in likers' News Feeds. Any people or Pages you tagged are notified. Anyone can read and comment on your note.

- *Preview:* When you click Preview, you see exactly how your note will look when viewed. It has two links at the top: Publish and Edit. You can edit the note (click Edit) or go ahead with the publishing process (click Publish).

- *Save Draft:* Click the Save Draft to save draft of this note to work on later. The next time you want to edit the note, look for the Notes app box. When you click that box, a Page Name Drafts link appears next to the Page's name. Click the Drafts link to see a list of all your note drafts (see Figure 4-5). Just click the title you want to start editing. Non-Admins won't see the link to your drafts.

- *Discard:* Discarding a note removes it from your drafts. Discard is a way to delete before something is published.

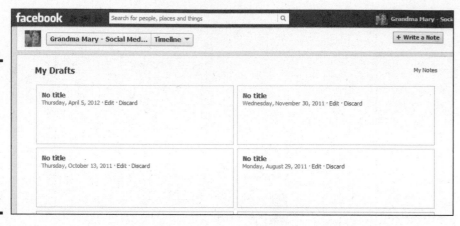

Figure 4-5:
Click the
Notes app
box and
then the
link to your
drafts to
choose the
Note to edit.

When your visitors click the Notes app, they go to an interface with your notes on the left and notes by other Pages they've liked on the right.

Many Pages use the Notes app to create a daily list of events in their stores or a daily webinar schedule with quick links to the Event pages. There are many ways to use this particular app.

We don't recommend using Facebook Notes as a blog because the Notes feature has been rumored to be going away. In any case, you don't want to put anything in the Notes feature without a backup copy somewhere else.

Video app

Here's another app that you may need to think through before you add it to your Page's app section. The Facebook Video app may not be the best app for you to use on your Page. If your business uses a lot of videos, you may want to explore a few third-party apps before making a final decision to add this one. As an alternative, we discuss using YouTube for marketing in Book III, Chapter 1.

Here are a few points about the Facebook-built Video app:

✦ If you post a status update with a YouTube URL, the video won't show up on the Video page. You have to upload or record a video with the Facebook Video app for the video to be listed on the Video page.

✦ Facebook does provide a lightbox interface for videos the way it does for photos.

✦ If people share your Page's video by posting it to their Timelines, users have the option to like your Page by clicking a Like button in the corner.

The Facebook Video app does show up separately on your Page but is actually incorporated as an Album within your Photos. Click the Photos App, and you see a spot to add a Photo or a Video in the upper right.

The video size limit is up to 20 minutes long with a maximum size file of 1,024MB. Facebook supports almost all video file formats, but you may have the best luck with the MP4 format. This page in the Facebook Help section lists all the supported types:

```
https://www.facebook.com/help/218673814818907
```

The easiest way to upload a video is to

1. **Go to your Facebook Page.**
2. **Click the Photo/Video selection.**
3. **Click Upload Photos/Video.**
4. **Add some text about the video.**
5. **Click Choose File to browse your computer for the video you want to upload.**
6. **Click Post to share the video to your Timeline.**

   You can go to the Photos app on your Page and click the Add Video button in the top-right corner of the page. As of this writing, the Photos app offers this option, but not the Video app.

Changing the Order of Apps on Your Page

All apps on your business Page, except Photos, can be rearranged for added exposure. Three apps — *Featured apps* — are visible. When you click the See All link, you see all your Apps that are installed on your Timeline (Favorites), but the visitors to your Page see only the first the first 12 apps. You can add and remove apps from Favorites. Because the only visible apps are the ones in the first three, make sure those are arranged how you want. To rearrange the order of the apps, follow these steps:

1. **Click the down arrow next to your apps to expand all the apps you have available.**
2. **Mouse over the app you want to move.**

   You see a pencil icon in the top-right corner of the app, as shown in Figure 4-6.

Figure 4-6: Hover over an app to reveal the pencil icon, then click the icon to swap the app.

Click to rearrange your apps

3. **Click the pencil icon.**

   A drop-down menu appears.

4. **From the drop-down menu, choose the app to swap.**

5. **Click the arrow next to your apps again to see how the new lineup looks.**

   You may need to repeat this process to get the apps in the positions where you want them.

After clicking the pencil icon, you can also choose Remove from Favorites to make the app box disappear. You can still get to the apps you've removed; see Chapter 2 of this minibook for details.

Using the Hover Card as an Ad

A nice little feature that Facebook has is the hover card (see Figure 4-7). A *hover card* is a little pop-up box that contains a quick view of information about a Page or person (including the Cover photo, Profile image, or Page category) when you hover your cursor over the person's or Page's name in your News Feed.

From a hover card, you can

✦ Like or unlike a Page.

✦ Request to be a Friend or subscriber.

✦ Add to an Interest list or create a custom list for the person or Page.

✦ Message the person or Page.

✦ Get Notifications.

✦ Adjust your Settings (show all updates, most updates, or only important).

Figure 4-7:
Hover cards
give you a
quick view
of informa-
tion about
a person or
Page.

The nice thing about a hover card is the overall impression it gives. See
Figure 4-8 for a well-done Page design with a really nice hover card that
works as an ad without being an ad!

Figure 4-8:
This hover
card for
New Media
Expo looks
like a won-
derful ad
without
being an ad.

To create beautiful hover cards like the one shown in Figure 4-8, do the following:

✦ Make sure your Page's Cover photo is an inviting image that conveys the spirit of your upcoming event.

✦ Create and upload a new Profile image that includes the dates and location of the upcoming event.

✦ Check your Page type under Edit Page, Update Info. Change the category in the fields provided.

After you complete these tasks, hover over your own Page's name in the Timeline to see how your hover card looks.

Chapter 5: Using Your Personal Profile to Support Your Business

In This Chapter

✔ Finding out whether you should turn on your Follow button

✔ Understanding how to post publicly

✔ Posting business milestones on your personal Profile

✔ Changing your Public Timeline to support your business

✔ Using personal Cover photos that support your business

We deliberately crafted the title of this chapter. Notice the word *support* in the title. We're not suggesting that you turn your personal Profile into a straight-up business Page. Please make sure that you understand the difference between a Profile and a business Page by reading all of this book!

What we're saying is that you can use your Profile to support your business in some very specific ways, such as finding out whether the Follow button is right for you, understanding the difference between a Public post and a Friends post, and how you can use photos on your Profile that support your business without breaking any Facebook rules.

Facebook realized that some people in this world are best served by a modified personal Profile instead of a business Page. These people are considered to be public figures. Are you a public figure? Maybe you are but don't realize it!

Determining Whether the Follow Button Is Right for You

The Follow button is something you can turn on inside your Profile so that people can follow your public updates. We describe each of these terms in this list:

✦ **Turn on:** You can switch on this system, and you can switch it off. You need to make a few adjustments when you turn it on.

✦ **Follow:** This is a one-way connection inside Facebook. You can follow someone without being his Friend. You and your Friends are following one another. If you are following someone but he isn't following you, you see his Public posts, but he doesn't see yours. After you turn on your Follow button, anyone, anywhere in the world can follow your Public posts.

✦ **Public updates:** You can post an update designated as Public, which means that anyone can see it, including your Friends and those who have followed you. And as an added bonus, if someone has requested to be your Friend and you haven't responded, he is automatically a follower and will see your Public posts.

The biggest pro for turning on the Follow button is that there's no limit on the number of followers you can have. (In comparison, the Friend limit on Facebook is currently 5,000.) You can go through your Friend list and unfriend people you don't really know, and they will automatically become a Follower. This cleans up your Friends list. The biggest con for turning on the Follow button is having to create Public posts. Public posts are generally different from what you might be used to posting on Facebook. The public is not so interested in your cat, but it might be very interested in your work with the Humane Society. There is a difference in those two kinds of posts, and you'll need to remember to make both.

So now you need to determine whether you are a public figure and whether you should go through the process of turning on your Follow button. Through this process, you also see whether you need to have both a Profile with the Follow button turned on *and* a business Page. Table 5-1 shows the different available features for a personal Timeline with the Follow button and a business Page.

Note: Turning on your Follow button is available only to those over the age of 18.

Table 5-1	Which Facebook Features Do You Need?	
Available Features	*Personal Timeline + Follow Button*	*Business Page*
Use for both Friends and a bigger audience	X	
Quick mobile updating	X	
Timeline applications (personal)	X	
Interest lists/groups/chat	X	
Privacy settings	X	

Available Features	Personal Timeline + Follow Button	Business Page
Timeline layout	X	X
Facebook Insights		X
Multiple people can admin		X
Custom tabs and apps		X
Target updates by location/language		X
Promote with ads and sponsored stories		X

Use these questions to help determine whether the using Follow button is right for you. Keep count of how many questions you answer, "Yes." By the end of the quiz, it will be obvious whether you need to continue reading this chapter.

✦ **Do you consider yourself to be a public figure?**

"Public figure" is a slippery term. According to Facebook, authors, magazine and newspaper writers, politicians, actors, and radio and TV personalities are public figures, but there are other definitions, too.

✦ **Do others consider you to be a public figure?**

When others think of you, do they think "public figure"? You may be a spokesperson for some type of event (local, regional, or national), or you may represent a topic (such as a conversation in your business niche or a nonprofit organization).

✦ **Are you considered to be an expert in your field?**

Do people seek you out when they have a question about your business niche? Do you speak about your business niche at events?

✦ **When people look at you, do they think of your business?**

Most small-business people carry both sides of their lives — business and personal — with them wherever they go. If you're walking down the street, and someone says "Hi," does she also ask you about your family or your business or both?

✦ **Do you like to share things that are business-related?**

Look back at your personal posts on Facebook for the past year. How many of them are related to your business niche? Would you share more of those types of posts if you felt that people wanted to see them?

✦ **Do you have people who want to be your Facebook Friends but are really business contacts?**

Have people who you don't know personally asked to be your Friends? Have you ignored a bunch of people who've asked to be your Friends?

✦ **Are you branding yourself?**

Are you setting yourself up to be a public figure in the future? Do you want to be a public figure?

✦ **Are you and your products the same thing?**

Do you sell information products that feature you as the expert?

✦ **Are you branding your company to include you?**

Apple = Steve Jobs. Is that the kind of relationship you have with your company?

Don't turn on your Follow button if you answered most of the questions, "No."

Do turn on your Follow button if

✦ You answered most of the questions, "Yes."

✦ You're branding yourself.

✦ You're branding your products, and people think of you and your products together.

If you're branding your company, you don't *have* to turn on your Follow button. If you enjoy your business and have a great passion for it, though, consider turning on the Follow button so you can expand your territory of influence.

We show you how to turn on your Follow button in the next section. Anyone can turn on his Follow button (even people who answered "No" to all the previous questions). Give it a whirl: You can turn it on to test it out and then turn it off if it doesn't work for you.

Turning On Your Follow Button

So you decide to turn on your Follow button. Take a minute to understand some important points about the Follow system, which can be very confusing at first.

"Follow" is how Facebook explains a connection. You and your Friends are following one another. You're still called Friends, but the function is "following."

After you turn on your Follow button, you won't be able to see the Follow button on your Timeline. This aspect is the most frustrating part of teaching people how to turn on the button! Just trust us on this one. The button is there; you just can't see it if you're logged in as yourself.

To turn on your Follow button, follow these steps:

1. **Click the down arrow at the top-right of any Facebook page and click Account Settings.**

2. **In the left sidebar, click Followers.**

   Now you are on a page with several sections. The top section is labeled Who Can Follow Me.

3. **Select Everybody from the drop-down menu, as shown in Figure 5-1.**

Book II
Chapter 5

Figure 5-1: Select Everybody to turn on your Follow button.

You also need to continue the process and edit your settings for comments and notifications. We will get to that in the next section. Here are a few interesting points about the Follow button:

✦ The number of Followers for someone incorporates the number of people who clicked the Follow button and the total number of Followers to Interest lists they're featured on. Read more about the Followers through Interest lists later in this chapter.

✦ Only people who allow Followers have a Follow button on their Profiles. If you don't see the button on a person's Timeline, you can't follow his updates without being his Friend. In that case. you see the Add Friend button instead. Sometimes, you see two buttons: Add Friend and Following, as shown in Figure 5-2. When both buttons appear, you know that you've followed this person's Public updates, and you can make a Friend request.

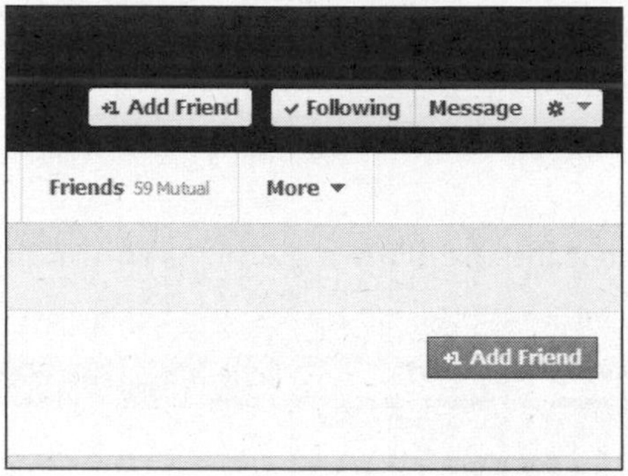

Figure 5-2: Sometimes, you see Add Friend and Following buttons.

How do people follow *your* updates? After you allow followers, a Follow button shows up on your Profile. Someone would need to visit your Timeline to click the Follow button, or click the Follow button if your Profile shows up in the Ticker. Or, if someone hovers over your name somewhere on Facebook (such as a comment in a thread) they have the option of following you right from the hover card that pops up. Facebook might change these ways, or add to them in the future. Facebook has also created a nice interface (`https://www.facebook.com/follow/suggestions`) where you can see all the people who have turned on their Follow button.

Followers can see only the things on your personal Profile that you share publicly. We show you how to see which things are public on your Timeline in the "Adjusting Your Timeline for Public Viewing" section later in this chapter.

Avoid heavy sales-type marketing techniques in your Public posts. Even though the follow system is like having an opt-in newsletter, you still need to remember that Facebook is a social platform.

Editing the Follow Settings

After you turn on your Follow button, you need to adjust the settings for Comments and Notifications. Both settings are important, and we explain them both in this section. You can go back and change these settings at any time, so don't stress about them too much at this point. See how everything goes; you'll know what you need to change over time.

When you select Everybody next to Who Can Follow Me (refer to Figure 5-1) to turn on your Follow button, you see a new dialog box with the following settings to adjust. After you adjust any of these settings, they're automatically saved:

✦ **Follower Comments:** Who can comment on your public updates? The drop-down menu lists Everybody, Friends of Friends, and Friends. Think about your choice. If you create Public posts, you want your Followers to be able to comment on them, so choose Everybody.

✦ **Follower Notifications:** Notifications tell you when new people Follow you, like one of your posts, and so on. You can decide whether you want notifications from Friends of Friends, Everybody, or Nobody. You can choose Everybody and see how things go. You can always come back and adjust these settings. We show you how to do that in a moment.

✦ **Username:** If you haven't set your personal Profile username (a.k.a. vanity URL) yet, you can click the link and go through the process of creating a nice URL.

You can set your personal username and your custom URL for your Pages by going to this address: `https://www.facebook.com/username`.

✦ **Twitter:** You can connect or disconnect your Profile to your Twitter account here. You can also set it at `http://facebook.com/twitter`.

✦ **Follow Plugin:** You can add a Follow button to your website to encourage more followers. This button allows people to Follow you on Facebook without leaving your website and is similar to the Like button or Like Box for Facebook Pages. All you need to do is copy the code provided and add it to your website.

To adjust these settings at a later date, just come back to this Page in your profile's Settings page. Also notice that you can see how your Timeline appears to your Followers by clicking the link at the bottom of this page: Want to Know What Followers Can See? View Your Public Timeline.

Visit this link from time to time to make sure you haven't shared anything publicly that you didn't want to. You can adjust the settings on any post or picture after you've posted them.

Another interesting fact: After you turn on your Follow button, if someone asks to be your Friend, and you ignore her, that person automatically becomes a follower and can see your public posts.

Seeing How to Post Publicly

After you turn on your Follow button, and people are starting to follow you, you need to remember to post publicly the kinds of things that will support your business.

Because this is a post from your Profile, add your personal take, feelings, and experience to the post. The following list offers some examples of types of Public posts:

✦ **Posts of public photos:** If you have a new product coming out, post a picture of yourself holding it. In the description of the photo, talk about your *personal* experience with that product. Did it take a long time to develop? Did development involve some twist of fate? Did you have a personal "A-ha!" moment about it? What was the personal connection?

✦ **Links to articles:** If you're being featured in an article, post the link to the article. Then in the post, talk about what it was like to be interviewed. What did the interviewer leave out? Did you like how the interviewer worked?

✦ **Release of new product:** You developed a new information product. Don't be blatant about it, but don't just post a discount code! Talk about your personal reasons for developing the product. Talk about the process of creating something new. People will click through if your post resonates with them.

Figure 5-3 shows where the posting icon is located. You need to make sure that you select Public (the option with the globe icon).

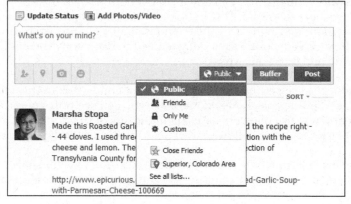

Figure 5-3: Set the posting icon to Public (globe icon).

You can change the icon when you're posting on your Timeline and in the News Feed view. Just remember to check the icon before you post. You can change the icon on your mobile phone with the same process of using the drop-down menu and selecting the globe.

If you need to change the setting from Friends to Public, or vice versa, just click the drop-down arrow on the post, and choose the setting you intend to use.

Sometimes, the way you posted the last time is the default for the next time you post. This situation happens a lot when you post from a mobile device. You can make sure that the default is always Public or always Friends by going to your Privacy Settings (see Figure 5-4) on your computer and setting your preferred default. If you tend to post things from your phone that need to be public, choose Public as the default.

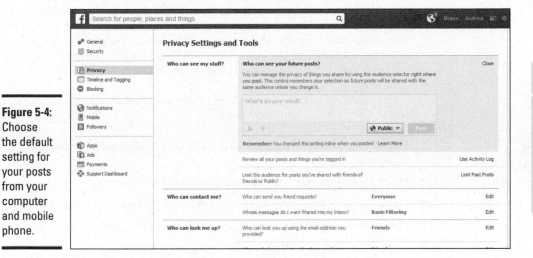

Figure 5-4: Choose the default setting for your posts from your computer and mobile phone.

Marketing Basics with a Personal Profile

This section title might bring up all sorts of comments, such as, "You can't market on a personal account." That's completely true. But you can support your marketing by allowing people into your business world through your personal experience of your business. There's an art to sharing and marketing appropriately through a personal account. As we state at the beginning of this chapter, if you wrap your posts in deeply personal impressions, being human and being transparent, you can open this personal-account door to more potential customers.

As with all social accounts, learning how to be an attraction-based marketer will serve you well. Some of the tenets of attraction-based marketing are

✦ **Giving content freely:** Figure out how much of your business content can be used freely, without links to your blog or as a tease. Give help to those who need it. This technique show two things: You have expert understanding of your niche, and you're a nice person. Both aspects are highly attractive in a business sense.

✦ **Being human:** Some of the most successful people in almost any business are the ones who let you into their thinking, emotions, and experiences. They tell you when they were wrong and when they nailed something. They're accessible and friendly.

✦ **Being hooked up:** Make all the important links back to your products and services easy to find. Make it extremely easy for someone to read your posts and then find your website or product pages. The About section on your personal account needs a really good review to make sure that people can click over to your site from there. If you also have a business Page, you need to make sure that the Work section of your personal account actually links to your Page, not to a phantom Interest Page. Review Book II, Chapter 2 for that discussion.

If you've turned on your Follow button, you can do all the things we suggest in Book II, Chapter 2, including these:

✦ Add your personal Facebook URL to your letterhead and e-mail signatures.

✦ Make an announcement via your other social accounts.

✦ Mention the Follow button in all interviews and promotional materials.

✦ Put your personal account URL on your business card.

✦ Embed the Follow button on your blog or website.

If you get some traction with people following you, you may find yourself on this page:

```
https://www.facebook.com/follow/suggestions
```

Make sure that you visit that page and follow other people in your industry or in a niche that provides you customers. After you follow those updates, comment and enliven conversation like this:

✦ Follow excellent connections in your business niche (especially bloggers and media writers).

✦ Post only excellent comments — not flippant, throwaway comments.

✦ Always reply to comments, both on your Timeline and on the other person's Timeline.

Many people you follow may be "A-list people," in that every time they post, hundreds of people comment. You may notice that some Internet rock stars (including Mari Smith and Robert Scoble) really interact with their followers. Robert responds only to what he would call intelligent questions. The lesson is this: Don't just post "I agree" or "Good post."

Understanding Friend Followers and Public Followers

After you turn on your Follow button, you have three types of followers:

✦ **Public Followers:** These are people who have followed your Public posts. If you ignore a Friend Request, they automatically become a follower and will see your Public posts.

✦ **Friend Followers:** These are your Facebook Friends. You are following each other. When you create a Public post, your Friends will see it, too. When you create a post and change the viewing icon to Friends, only people in this category will see the post.

✦ **Followers via Lists:** Anyone on Facebook can create an *Interest list,* which is a list of people and Pages you collect together. You can put all the TV Show Pages on one list, all the Natural food chefs in another, and so on. Then you can click the name of the List in the left sidebar (on the News Feed view) and see only the posts from the people and Pages on that List.

If someone puts your personal Profile on a list and shares the list, people will be able to follow the list. When that happens, you gain another number in this category. Even though they're following the list, Facebook gives you the added number. You can find Interest lists to follow at www.facebook.com/addlist.

Book II
Chapter 5

Using Your Personal Profile to Support Your Business

Create your own Interest list in your business niche and add yourself to the list. Then share the list and watch your numbers go higher.

To see who is in each category, click the Friends link on your Timeline. Then click Followers to see the people who are following you, like you see in Figure 5-5. Notice that some of your followers have turned on the Follow button themselves, and you can follow them back right from here. (Keep in mind that you will see only their Public updates, also.) Or if you mouse over their name, a hover card pops up, and you can request friendship or see whether they have requested friendship from you and you haven't responded yet (which is why they appear in your Followers list).

If you've been put on an Interest list, you see the name of the list and numbers that are hyperlinked to those people by clicking the Followers via Lists link. See Figure 5-6 for a list of several numbers and information to explore.

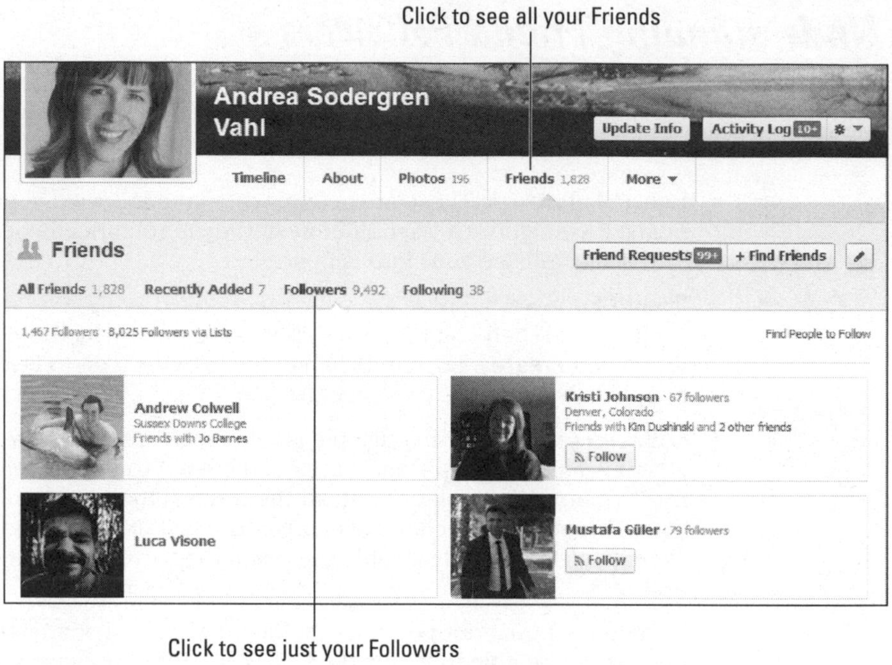

Click to see all your Friends

Figure 5-5:
See who
has fol-
lowed to
your public
updates.

Click to see just your Followers

Figure 5-6:
Explore the
hyperlinked
numbers
for more
information
about the
Interest List.

Adding Public Life Events to Your Personal Profile

This step is very important. Some people call the personal Timeline the ulti-mate résumé because of the wonderful Life Events feature. This is basically the same thing as adding milestones on a business Page except that this interface is really detailed. (We discuss milestones in great detail in Book III.) Life Events can go all the way back to when you were born! Now you can add as many Life Events as you want, in many areas, but in this section, we focus on using Life Events to support your business.

You can add Life Events when things like these happen:

**Book II
Chapter 5**

**Using Your Personal
Profile to Support
Your Business**

+ You get a book deal.

+ You publish an article.

+ You win an award.

+ You gain special recognition from your industry.

+ You launch a new product.

+ Your business reaches a financial milestone.

+ You're featured in a local paper or magazine.

You can add all sorts of things to this list. Focus on adding these life events, and make sure to make them Public. Add your personal experience to each post, in your authentic human voice.

A few don'ts: You can't add things with future dates. Don't make Life Events one big infomercial. And don't post all your Life Events at one time; spread them out over a few weeks.

Here's how to create a Life Event on your personal Timeline:

1. **Go to your personal Timeline.**

2. **In the posting box, click the Life Event tab.**

   You see a set of options: Work & Education, Family & Relationships, Home & Living, Health & Wellness, and Travel & Experiences.

3. **Click the category of Life Event you want to post.**

   Subcategories appear in a submenu, as shown in Figure 5-7.

Figure 5-7:
The Life Event interface is very detailed.

4. **Choose the subcategory that matches what you want to post, or choose Create Your Own.**

   All the subcategories have Create Your Own as an option. If you opt for that, you get to create a custom title for the Life Event. Unless your Life Event matches one of the categories perfectly, choose Create Your Own.

5. **Fill in the fields.**

   Each subcategory has slightly different fields to fill in. Fill in as much information as you can. Make sure you adjust the date fields to be the date of the Life Event.

6. **Upload or choose a photo.**

   Always upload or choose a photo. A photo really makes a Life Event pop on the Timeline.

7. **Make sure that the viewing icon is set to Public.**

   The whole point of this task is to create items that the Public and your Public followers can see on your Timeline. (The Public icon is the globe.)

8. **Click Save.**

   Your Life Event is placed on your personal Timeline on the date you set for it. Go look. Life Events are wonderful to view on a Timeline.

Adjusting Your Timeline for Public Viewing

When you place Life Events that support your business on your personal Timeline, you'll want to see how your Timeline looks to the public. You can view your personal Timeline as though different types of people are viewing it: the Public or a particular Friend. To do that, click the gear icon on your Cover photo and then choose View As from the drop-down menu as shown in Figure 5-8.

At the top of your Profile, you can see a black strip indicating that you're looking at your Timeline as someone from the Public would see it. You can look through your entire Timeline to see what Joe Public sees. If you see anything that you don't want the public to see, go back to your Timeline and change who can see a particular post. For example, if you find a post that you meant just your Friends to see, follow these steps:

1. **Click the X button (at the top of the page in the black strip).**

2. **Find the post whose settings you want to change.**

3. **Click the drop-down arrow next to the globe icon.**

4. **Choose the setting you want (for example, Friends instead of Public).**

**Book II
Chapter 5**

Using Your Personal
Profile to Support
Your Business

Figure 5-8:
The View As option lets you see how your personal Profile looks to the public.

You can view your Timeline as a particular person sees it, so you know if you've shared other posts correctly. Just click the View as a Specific Person link in the black strip and put that person's name in the box. Now you can make sure any posts that you shared just with local friends or just with business lists appear correctly.

Think about your business and how your followers will see your account. Use this system of checking what's public and what's for Friends to clean up your Profile. If you're using your personal Profile to support your business, make sure the Public view does just that. Change the view settings to fit the types of posts you make on Facebook.

Uploading a Cover Photo that Supports Your Business

Facebook doesn't want you to think of your Page's Cover photo as a billboard; it wants you to think of the Cover photo as a view of the spirit or soul of your business. The same idea applies to the Cover photo for your Profile.

Figure 5-9 shows a Profile Cover photo that supports a business, but other sides of Amy Porterfield's life, too.

Figure 5-9: Use a Cover photo that conveys who you are without breaking Facebook's rules.

Book III

Adding the Basics to Your Facebook Page

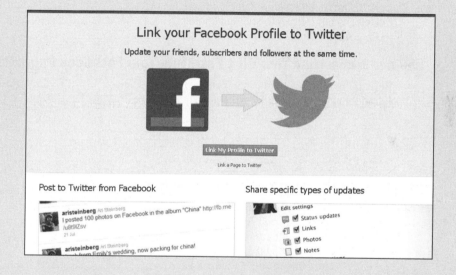

Link your Facebook Profile to Twitter

Update your friends, subscribers and followers at the same time.

Link My Profile to Twitter

Link a Page to Twitter

Post to Twitter from Facebook

aristeinberg Ari Steinberg
I posted 100 photos on Facebook in the album "China" http://fb.me /u8t9IZsv
21 Jul

aristeinberg Ari Steinberg
from Emily's wedding, now packing for china!

Share specific types of updates

Edit settings
☑ Status updates
☑ Links
☑ Photos
☑ Notes

For more on adding to your Facebook Page, go to www.dummies.com/extras/ facebookmarketingaio.

Contents at a Glance

Chapter 1: Posting to Your Page. 177

Posting Updates to Your Timeline via the Publisher 177
Including Attachments...180
Using Facebook Offers..191
Targeting Your Updates by Location and Language 192

Chapter 2: Facebook Apps 101 197

Defining Apps and Understanding Facebook Installed Apps.................197
Adding an App to Your Page 201
Rearranging the Positions of Your Apps 203
Deleting an App from Your Page 204
Customizing the App Title and App Photo...204
Finding Apps in Your Page Dashboard 205

Chapter 3: Importing Your Blog Posts into Your Facebook Page. . . .207

Getting the Address of Your RSS Feed..207
Introducing the Facebook Blog-Import Applications 210
Using the NetworkedBlogs Application...210
Installing Social RSS..218
Using RSS Graffiti 221
Using the dlvr.it Tool 224

Chapter 4: Connecting Your Page to Twitter 229

To Connect or Not to Connect...229
Connecting Facebook and Twitter 230
Using HootSuite to Update Facebook 234
Using Other Posting Applications 237
Adding a Twitter Tab to Your Facebook Page 240

Chapter 5: The Fine Print: Legal and Other Considerations 243

Digesting Legal Considerations...243
Understanding U.S. Regulations on Testimonials and Reviews 245
Meeting Content Compliance for Certain Industries 248

Chapter 1: Posting to Your Page

In This Chapter

✔ **Exploring the best practices for your posts**

✔ **Becoming a pro at attachments**

✔ **Targeting your updates**

The most critical aspect of your Facebook presence is your posts. What you put on your Timeline is the showcase of your business. After a Facebook user likes you, he most likely won't go to your Page very often; typically, a user sees you only as an update in his News Feed. So you have to be interesting, engaging, responsive, useful, and fun. No pressure, right?

You want your posts to establish you as an authority and expert in your field, and this chapter tells you what types of material you can use to accomplish that goal.

Never forget, however, that Facebook is a place where people come to be *social*. It's like a big cocktail party where people are having fun talking, so don't be a wet blanket and talk only about the big sale you're having. You don't want to be that irritating sales guy at the networking event whom everyone avoids — or, worse, "un-likes"!

Helpful tips, useful information, links, and photos can go a long way toward making your Page engaging and popular. To that end, in this chapter, you find out how to post text updates, photos, links, and videos. You also discover how to target your updates to specific members of your community.

Posting Updates to Your Timeline via the Publisher

To post an update to your community, you do so in the *Publisher*, which is located on your Timeline and contains the prompt, What have you been up to? See Figure 1-1.

The function of the Publisher on your Page is very similar to that of the Publisher on your Profile. When you post a status update to your Profile, however, it goes out to the News Feed of all your Friends, whereas an update to the Timeline on your Page goes out to the News Feed of all those who like you. Then your Page's status update shows up in the News Feed, just as a person's status update shows up in the News Feed of Friends.

Status
Photo / Video
Offer, Event +
What have you been up to?

Figure 1-1: The Publisher is where you post information to your Timeline.

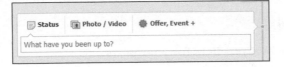

Your update also appears in people's *Tickers* (the scrolling real-time updates on the right side of the home page of your Profile). For more information on the Ticker, see Book II, Chapter 1. Realize that when you post to your Page Timeline, your post shows up in people's News Feeds along with all the other posts of their Friends and Pages they like. Don't refer to previous posts or things on your business Page that people can't see right then. If you want people to come to your Page to see those things, make sure that you tell them to come to your Page. Also make sure that each post can stand alone as a complete thought.

Not every single post on your Page will be seen by every single fan, and not every post actually makes it into your fans' News Feeds. You can actually see how many of your fans potentially saw your post after you post it. Facebook determines whether your post goes into your fans' News Feeds based on its News Feed algorithm. Find out more about the algorithm and getting your posts into the News Feed in Book IV, Chapter 2.

How long to make your post

Facebook extended the length of the status updates to a whopping 63,206 characters! It's almost a small blog post. ***Note:*** After you type around 240 characters (depending on word structure), your post will be cut short, and a See More link appears, as shown in Figure 1-2.

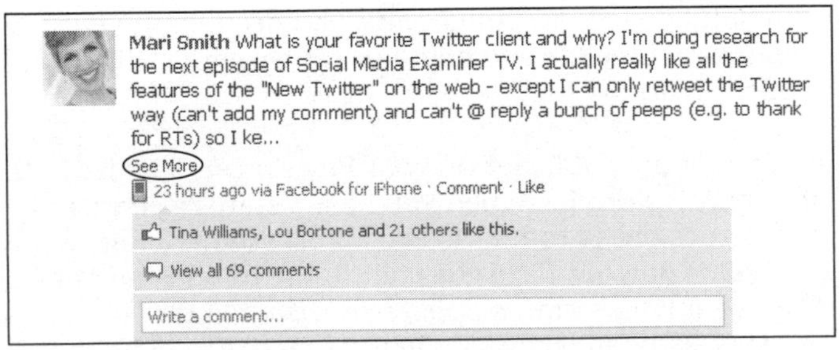
Mari Smith What is your favorite Twitter client and why? I'm doing research for the next episode of Social Media Examiner TV. I actually really like all the features of the "New Twitter" on the web - except I can only retweet the Twitter way (can't add my comment) and can't @ reply a bunch of peeps (e.g. to thank for RTs) so I ke...
See More
23 hours ago via Facebook for iPhone · Comment · Like
Tina Williams, Lou Bortone and 21 others like this.
View all 69 comments
Write a comment...

Figure 1-2: A long status update is truncated in the News Feed, but the whole post is still there.

Keep your post short so that people can easily read it and not miss anything valuable if they don't click the See More link.

How often to post an update

One of the most frequently asked questions is, "How often should I post?" The answer will vary depending on your goals and comfort level. Some people worry about "bothering" their community with too many posts, or they worry that some people will un-like or hide their Page if they post too much. We can assure you that most of your community members won't mind your posts if you're doing them in the right way. That's why it's important to provide value.

Also, many people aren't on Facebook all the time and may not see your posts. Depending on how many Friends a user has or how many Pages a user likes, your post may go through a News Feed fairly quickly.

If you have one person who likes your Page and has ten Friends who post one update per day, and your Page is posting five updates per day, you'll be very visible, occupying one-third of the daily News Feed. But if you have a person who likes your Page and has 500 Friends who post one update per day, your updates will just be one percent of the daily News Feed, and that person may miss your posts.

Bottom line: Don't worry about posting too often. People will miss your updates, and you want to continue to stay visible.

Studies have shown that posting two to five times per day is ideal. If that sounds like too much, at least try to post once daily during the week. Weekends can also be a great time to post — people are checking on Facebook, and there may not be as many other Pages posting on the weekends. But you also need to take a break every once in a while!

What types of material to include

When you go to create a post, think about your community. What do its members need? What's in it for them? Think of yourself as the funnel that guides the best information to your community — and that will be what keeps your community coming back for more. Also realize that you're participating in a conversation. Just as you do at a cocktail party, you want to respond when people comment on your post. Don't just post and run. (And don't post when you've had too many cocktails; you may regret it in the morning!)

Be sure to vary the types of material you post, too. Following are types of posts that you can use to market yourself as an expert, have fun, and plug your business all at the same time without being annoying:

✦ Pictures of a great event you had

✦ Video of behind-the-scenes happenings at your business

**Book III
Chapter 1**

Posting to Your
Page

✦ Questions that engage your audience and allow you to do some market research

✦ Links to blog posts that solve people's problems within your niche

TIP

Don't worry that you're giving information away for free. Your community will appreciate the information and look to you when they need help that they can hire you for.

✦ Controversial news stories within your niche that will spark conversation

✦ Events you're hosting that will benefit your community

✦ Links to resources that are helpful for your niche

Again, this is just a partial list of post types. How do you use these types to market your business? You establish yourself as the go-to person for your market. You notice that these posts aren't all about you and what you're selling, but you're continually popping into the News Feed and reminding your community that you're there. You're branding yourself as an expert in your business.

Including Attachments

You may have noticed icons above the Publisher (refer to Figure 1-1). You use these icons to attach items to your post. The icons are, from left to right, Status, Photo/Video, and Offer, Event +. The plus sign (+) means that additional options for attachments are available when you click that selection, as shown in Figure 1-3.

Figure 1-3: Click the + symbol to see additional types of attachments.

We recommend varying your posts so that you use these attachments frequently. People like multimedia, and your status updates will be more visible when you use these features.

Updating status and posting links

Posting a status update is relatively straightforward, especially if you've been using your Facebook Profile for any length of time. All you do is start entering your text in the Publisher (shown in Figure 1-1) and click Post.

If you'd like to add a link to a website, all you need to do is to copy the website's address (or type it yourself) into the Publisher area. When you post a link, you can use the 63,206 characters of the status box, or Publisher, to introduce the link and entice people to click the story. (There's no need to be quite that verbose; a short introduction or comment is just fine.)

After you add the link to the Publisher, the website is represented as a title and a short description next to a thumbnail image, as shown in Figure 1-4. These items are pulled in from the website itself. You can edit this information by clicking the title or description. You also may have a choice of the thumbnail image to post, or you can click No Thumbnail if the image doesn't match the story.

Figure 1-4: When you add a link, Facebook brings in the description and a picture.

Book III Chapter 1

Posting to Your Page

To add a link with your status update, follow these steps:

1. **Copy the URL from the website you want to put into your post.**

2. **Paste the URL into the Publisher or just type the address into the Publisher.**

   You see the website information, as shown in Figure 1-4.

3. **Adjust the information as necessary by selecting a thumbnail (or No Thumbnail), modifying the description of the site by clicking the description, and modifying the title of the site (by clicking it).**

4. **Add some scintillating text to the Publisher right before the website address.**

   You can add the text after the address, but we recommend placing the text before it.

   This text might be a short description of, or plug for, the site you're linking to. The purpose of the text in this post is to give your community a reason to click the link.

5. **Click the blue Post button to post this status update with your link to your Timeline.**

As mentioned in Step 3, you may be able to choose among several thumbnail images to go with your link. The images are pulled from the site and might include images from advertisements on the website's sidebar, so the images may not match the story. If you can't find an image that matches the link, you can select No Thumbnail.

The title and description are pulled in from the metadata (title and description) on the website. Depending on the site, these items may not even match the story on that site that you're trying to promote. The webmaster of the site has control of the metadata, but you can edit what shows up in your post by clicking the Title and Description before you attach the link.

Here's another thing you can do when posting a link. After you have the link *attached* — meaning that the picture and description are shown as in Figure 1-4 — you can remove the link in the Publisher area. Then the post won't have a clickable link in the text area, but if people want to read the story, they can just click the title, picture, or description that's attached, and they're taken to the website. You may want to use this option if the link is really long (or if it looks messy). All you need to do is to backspace or delete the link before you click Share. If you want to have a highlighted, clickable link in your text area, just leave the link in the Publisher.

You can also add a location to your status updates by clicking the Place icon in the bottom-left corner of the Publisher. When you click this icon, you can add a Facebook Place or Facebook Page name. This can be like your Page "checking in" at a Place to let people know where you are at. We see limited benefit from this feature, but it is available.

A different way to post a link is to post it with a photo. Sometimes posting a photo with a link gets more attention than posting just a link because the photo shows up larger in the News Feed. See the next section, "Attaching photos," to find out how to post photos with a link.

Don't post links only to your own website, though. Vary your content so that you become a funnel of information on the web for your community. So where do you find these interesting links to post? Here are several ways to attract interesting material so that you can share it with your community:

✦ **Google Alerts:** Get e-mail updates of the latest relevant Google results based on keywords in your niche. All you have to do is go to `www.google.com/alerts`, enter keywords you want to monitor, and then you can select how frequently you want to receive them (once per day, once per week, or as it happens).

We also recommend adding the name of your company as a keyword (unless it's a common name) so that you can monitor a blog post or news about your company posted on the web that you need to be aware of.

✦ **Feedly:** Subscribe to other interesting blogs in your niche via an RSS feed, and check in with your blogs each day to find interesting posts. You can also share to your Facebook Page right from Feedly (`http://feedly.com`). You can find other tools to help bring in RSS feeds, but Feedly is a nice choice.

✦ **Alltop:** This site is a gathering of interesting blogs on various topics, arranged by topic and most recent posts (`http://alltop.com`).

✦ **Other Pages in your niche:** Make sure to like or follow a "competitor" Page to see what those folks are doing. It's okay to repost a link if it's an interesting bit of news. You can also add these Pages to a Facebook Interest list on your Profile.

✦ **Twitter:** A lot of interesting links are on Twitter (`www.twitter.com`). Follow the top people in your niche, and when you find something newsworthy, post it to your Page.

Sometimes, a link doesn't post correctly and doesn't pull any metadata or website information in with the link. In that case, you can try to debug the link in the Facebook Developers area before posting. Just go to `http://developers.facebook.com/tools/debug`, paste the link into the Debug field, and click Debug. You get information on why the link may not have been working, but usually, there's nothing you need to do with this information. Just go back to your Facebook Page and try pasting the link into your Publisher again. This works 99 times out of 100!

Attaching photos

People love multimedia, so attaching photos is a great strategy for getting more interaction with your audience and marketing your brand. A photo is more noticeable than just a status update because it takes up more space in the News Feed. Disney Pixar posts a lot of photos of its movies with a little caption to engage. Take a look at Figure 1-5 for an example.

If you're a speaker, a photo of you speaking at an event will market your business in a more exciting way than if you just post an update saying, "Spoke at an event with business owners today." The great thing is that you can "show and tell" — that is, post the status and show the picture.

Figure 1-5:
Disney
Pixar gets
thousands
of likes and
hundreds of
shares on
each photo
posted from
its movies.

Or suppose that your business is a restaurant. You can post pictures of your food, kitchen, busy Friday-night crowd, and so on. The possibilities are endless! Spend some time thinking of all the picture posts you can have about your business.

To attach a photo, just click the Photo/Video icon in the Publisher. Then you have the choice to upload a photo or video, or create a photo album, as shown in Figure 1-6.

Figure 1-6:
You have
two choices
for upload-
ing your
photos.

Status	Photo / Video	Offer, Event +
Upload Photos/Video		Create Photo Album

You can also post a photo as a link from a third-party site, such as Instagram or TwitPic. When you upload a photo to the Publisher as an attachment, however, it's stored on your Photo tab for people to reference easily later. If you share a photo from Flickr as an attachment, it's just a Timeline post that will be harder to get back to and enjoy.

Another tactic is to post a photo or screen shot and then add other interactive things, such as a link to a website and tags for other Pages. Whenever you add a photo, you can always add a tag and a link within your status update that goes with the photo. The benefit of posting your update as a photo is that it appears larger in the News Feed. In Figure 1-7, you see that Mari Smith added the following:

✦ An actual photo from the article she's talking about

✦ The link to the article

✦ A tag for the Page

Read more about tagging other Pages in Book IV, Chapter 2.

Figure 1-7: Add a photo and then include a link and/or tags to other Pages.

You may have multiple photos to post on a certain topic at one time. In that case, you should select the Create Photo Album option (refer to Figure 1-6). When you do, you can select the photos on your computer, and as they upload, you can add more. You can add captions, tag the photos, and select an album cover before you post the photo album. The photo album posts at one time, with multiple photos showing up in the News Feed.

You can upload multiple photos by just adding another photo using the plus symbol, as shown in Figure 1-8, after you've uploaded one photo. In this case, both photos will be in your Timeline Photos album.

Figure 1-8:
Add additional photos to a status update.

As of this writing, you can add unlimited photos by using the + symbol, but only the first three photos will be displayed in the update. If you attach more than three photos to your status update, a note lets people know there are more photos to see.

Attaching video

Video is a powerful tool to help your audience get to know you. When you click the Photo/Video icon in the Publisher, you're given the choice to upload a file from your computer. Facebook will be able to tell right away if it is a photo or video after you select the file (refer to Figure 1-6).

The uploaded video must be shorter than 20 minutes, be smaller than 1024MB, and made by you or your Friends per Facebook terms. Again, you always want to abide by Facebook's Terms and Conditions; otherwise, your Page will be in danger of being shut down.

You can upload video files in many formats, but MP4 format works best. You can find the entire list of supported video formats here:

`www.facebook.com/help/?faq=218673814818907`

After you select the video that you want to upload from your computer and type a comment about the video, click the Post button. Facebook shows your video upload progress as a bar at the bottom of the Publisher, and you're alerted when it's done.

The video processing can be slow; sometimes, it can stall. Files in MP4 format typically work best.

While the video is processing, you can click the Edit Video button to edit some of the details in the screen shown in Figure 1-9.

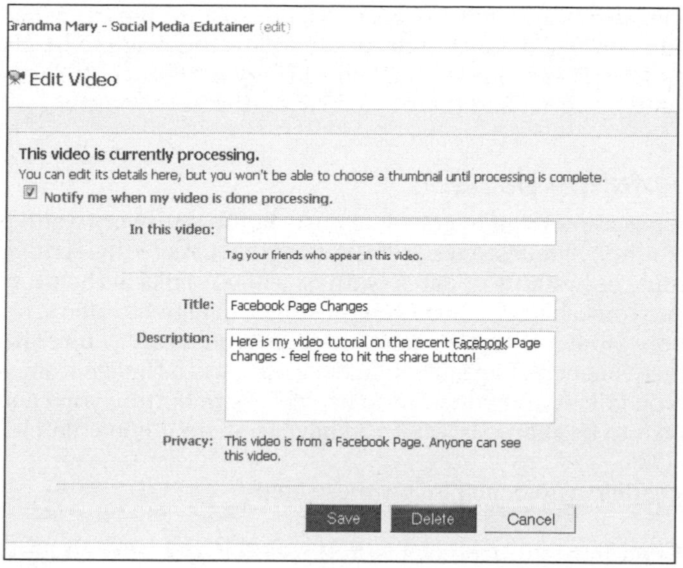

Grandma Mary - Social Media Edutainer (edit)

📹 Edit Video

This video is currently processing.
You can edit its details here, but you won't be able to choose a thumbnail until processing is complete.

☑ Notify me when my video is done processing.

In this video:
> Tag your friends who appear in this video.

Title: Facebook Page Changes

Description: Here is my video tutorial on the recent Facebook Page changes - feel free to hit the share button!

Privacy: This video is from a Facebook Page. Anyone can see this video.

Save   Delete   Cancel

Figure 1-9:
Edit the details of your uploaded video.

Uploaded videos can play right within the Facebook status update and will stay in your Videos area for your community to reference later.

Another advantage to uploading videos directly to Facebook is that when non-likers view your videos on Facebook, they see the Like button for your Facebook Page in the top-left corner of the video screen, as shown in Figure 1-10. This is a great way to make it easy for people to like your Page.

Figure 1-10:
A Like button appears in the corner of your video to let non-likers connect with you easily.

Andrea Sodergren Vahl
Here is Grandma Mary's video on all the Facebook Page changes.

👍 Like Grandma Mary - Social Media Edutainer

Grandma Mary - Social Media Edutainer

0:03 / 6:46

about a minute ago · Like · Comment · Share

You can also post videos by posting a link to a third-party video site, such as YouTube or Vimeo. Most of these sites allow the video to be played within the update. These videos aren't stored on your Facebook Page for people to see later, however, and there's no Like button in the corner.

Scheduling posts

Facebook allows you to schedule posts in the future or to add posts to the past (although milestones are better for that). As of this writing, you can schedule only status updates (with or without links in them), photos, and videos. You can't schedule event postings, questions, offers, or postings of photo albums. You also can't schedule a post that you're sharing from another Facebook Page. If you find a great post or image from another Page that you follow, and you want to use the Share button, you cannot schedule the post to be shared later — you have to share it immediately.

To schedule a post, just follow these steps:

1. **Complete your post just as you would if you were to post it immediately.**

2. **Click the clock symbol in the bottom-left corner of the Publisher, as shown in Figure 1-11.**

    When you click the calendar, the Date drop-down menu appear where you can specify details exactly when you want to have the post scheduled.

Figure 1-11: Click the clock symbol in the bottom-left corner of the Publisher.

3. **Add the date and time that you would like the post to be published.**

4. **Click the blue Schedule button to schedule your post.**

    Your post is scheduled.

To view the post, check your Activity Log, which you access from your Admin panel. Click the Edit Page button, and choose Use Activity Log from the drop-down menu. You see your scheduled posts, as shown in Figure 1-12.

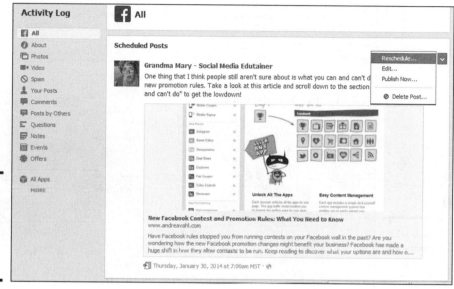

Figure 1-12: View your Activity Log to see your scheduled posts.

From here, you can reschedule, edit, publish, or delete your scheduled posts by mousing over the upper-right corner area of your post and clicking the down arrow that appears, as shown in Figure 1-12.

Adding events

You can also post an event directly from the Publisher. A word of caution, however: Every time you use the Event option to publish, you're creating a brand-new Facebook event.

To create a new event from the Publisher, just click the Offer, Event + icon (note that you may have a different combination for this icon depending on the category of your Page but the one you want includes "Event"). A pop-up window appears; you can create your event in this window.

See Book VI, Chapter 1 for more information on creating and marketing your Facebook event.

Adding milestones

Milestones are big events in your company's history that you want to highlight. Milestones appear slightly different from traditional updates, as shown in *The New York Times'* milestones for 1912 (see Figure 1-13). Milestones are a great way to showcase awards, new products, and other momentous occasions.

Figure 1-13: Milestones from *The New York Times.*

When you publish a milestone, it's placed in the appropriate area of your Timeline. You can add a photo, if you want, or just a status update about what happened at that time. Milestones are great for letting people know more about the history of your business and can be fun for people to discover on your Timeline. They can give people a reason to hang out on your Timeline longer.

People can go to your milestone or periods of time on your Facebook Page by using the months and years chart on the right side of your Timeline. The milestones are individually listed on your About page. Go to any Page and have fun with this feature by jumping around to see the posts at that point in the Page history. Try this with www.facebook.com/cocacola to see the history of Coca-Cola, for example.

To add a milestone to your Page, simply click the Event, Milestone + icon (or the Offer, Event + icon, depending on what you have). In the pop-up window that appears, you can fill in the details of your milestone, as shown in Figure 1-14.

Your milestone is published in your News Feed (which is also a fun way to tell your audience about cool things that are happening). If you have several milestones to add, space the milestones out so that you don't have so many posts at the same time, or select the Hide from News Feed check box so that it posts on your Timeline but doesn't overwhelm your audience.

Social Media Examiner Clubs hit 6000 members!

Yesterday

Come join us in the Social Media Examiner Clubs! Welcome to our community for social media marketers -
6000 strong and growing! http://www.socialmediaexaminer.com/clubs/

Finally, a place you can call home, help out others, make connections and get answers! Free now, free
forever!

Event	Social Media Examiner Clubs hit 6000 membe
Location	⊙ Optional
When	2012 ▾ July ▾ 14 ▾
Story	Come join us in the Social Media Examiner Clubs! Welcome to our community for social media marketers - 6000 strong and growing! http://www.socialmediaexaminer.com/cl
Hide from News Feed	☐

Choose from Photos...

Upload Photo...

🌐 **Save** Cancel

Figure 1-14:
Fill in the
details
of your
milestone.

Using Facebook Offers

Posting a Facebook Offer is also done through the Publisher. A Facebook Offer
is like a coupon that people redeem and then claim either at your place of
business or online. After you post your offer, it goes out into the News Feed,
and your fans can click it to claim it. When they claim it, they add their e-mail
addresses to the form, and the offer is sent to them. The great thing about
offers is that they can be very viral. When someone claims your offer, they can
share your offer posts to their News Feed, and then all that person's Friends
can see it and possibly claim it for themselves, as shown in Figure 1-15.

Andrea Sodergren Vahl shared Panda Express's offer.
10 seconds ago ⊙

Why not?

**Get a FREE single serving of Firecracker
Chicken Breast. Valid only on Fri, January
31**
80,920 people claimed this offer

✉ **Resend Offer**

Like · Comment · Promote · Share

Figure 1-15:
A claimed
offer in the
News Feed.

Facebook Offers are for local businesses and do cost money to run. Find out how to set up the offer and some of the best practices in Book VII, Chapter 1.

Targeting Your Updates by Location and Language

A little-known trick that you can do with the Publisher is to target your updates to certain members of your community. As of this writing, targeting is still being rolled out to all Pages, and you may not yet have access to this feature, but it is scheduled to roll out to all Pages with 100 likes or more. You can target your updates by the following options:

✦ **Gender:** Men or Women

✦ **Relationship Status:** Single, In a Relationship, Engaged, or Married

✦ **Educational Status:** In High School, In College, College Grad

✦ **Interested In:** Men or Women

✦ **Age:** Select a range between 13 and 65

✦ **Location:** Country, Region or State, City

✦ **Language:** Type the language

When you select the targeting, only those likers whom you specify in your target will see your status update in their News Feeds. This can be very helpful when you're posting something where you want a certain demographic to respond or if you have a local event. Say, you have an Event happening in San Francisco: You can update only the people who live near there, meaning that your community members in New York won't see those posts in their News Feeds.

To use this feature, follow these steps after you type your status update:

1. **Click the target icon (to the right of the clock icon) in the Publisher, as shown in Figure 1-16.**

You then see an additional link to Add Targeting.

Figure 1-16:
Click the
Target icon
to enable
the target-
ing options.

2. **Click the Add Targeting link.**

A drop-down menu appears where you can select which options you want to target, as shown in Figure 1-17.

Figure 1-17:
Choose a
specific
audience for
your status
update.

3. **Select a target demographic from the drop-down menu.**

   You see the selection listed as shown in the Target by Gender field in
   Figure 1-17.

4. **Use the drop-down menu next to the demographic to select which part
   of the demographic you want to target.**

   For example, in Figure 1-17, Women is selected.

   If you select Target by Location, a pop-up box appears (as shown in
   Figure 1-18) from which you can select the radio buttons for Country,
   Region or State, or City. You can select many countries to target, many states
   or regions within one country, or many cities within one country. After
   you make all your location selections, click the Choose Locations button.

Figure 1-18:
You may
choose
to target
regionally.

5. **Click the blue Post button after making all your targeting selections
   and writing your post in the** `What have you been up to?` **field.**

   Your post will then go out into the News Feeds of only those targeted fans
   of your Page. The post won't show that it's been targeted, but you will
   be able to see that it's been targeted if you mouse over the world icon on
   the post when it's on your Timeline. You will see the exact demographic
   that you selected in the targeting options listed in a small pop-up.

   In Figure 1-18, notice that the number of people in the targeted demographic are listed in the post. You may want to use the targeting option
   just to see more about your demographics.

Boosting posts

In the Publisher, you have the option to boost a post, which is a way to pay to have that particular post pushed out to more of your fans. You pay a set fee to get your post shown in the News Feeds of more of your likers than would have seen it organically. You can do this as you get ready to post your update or after the fact.

Read more about boosting posts in Book VIII, Chapter 2.

Pinning and highlighting posts

After you publish a post, it's time to have a little fun by highlighting certain posts or by pinning a post to the top of your Timeline for a certain period to draw more attention to it.

When you highlight a post, the post spans the width of your Timeline. Kia Motors does a great job of highlighting a photo, as shown in the post in Figure 1-19.

Figure 1-19: Use highlighted posts to emphasize something on your Timeline.

To highlight a post, you first have to post it; then click the down arrow in the the top-right corner of the post to access the drop-down menu as shown in Figure 1-20. Select Highlight to highlight the post.

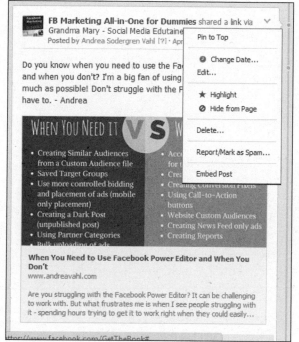

Figure 1-20:
Click the
down arrow
to access
the drop-
down menu.

Note: Highlighting a post doesn't affect how it shows up in the News Feeds of your likers. It affects only how the post is displayed on your Timeline.

Pinning a post to the top of your Timeline can be a great way to draw attention to one of your posts for people who visit your Page. You can pin a post for a total of seven days. Then the post automatically returns to the area of your Timeline where it belongs.

You may decide to pin a promotion to the top of your Page, a question, or a video. Try it to see how it works for you. To pin a post to the top of your Page, just follow these steps on any published post:

1. **Click the down arrow in the top-right corner of the post (refer to Figure 1-20).**

2. **Choose Pin to Top.**

   Your post appears at the top of your Timeline with a small orange flag on it indicating that it's a pinned post. To unpin it, click the down arrow in the top-right corner of the post and then choose Unpin from Top.

Chapter 2: Facebook Apps 101

In This Chapter

✔ **Defining Facebook apps**

✔ **Adding, rearranging, and deleting apps**

✔ **Customizing the app photo and title**

✔ **Exploring the Facebook App dashboard**

*Y*ou may have seen customized tabs or apps on some Facebook business Pages. The apps appear below the Cover photo on the left side column of a Page and can have a wide range of functions. You can use apps to showcase your other social sites, have a storefront, give a coupon, run a contest, and much more! Apps can also help contribute to the branding of your company and make your Facebook Page come alive.

The term *Facebook apps* encompasses a wide range of products. When someone refers to a Facebook app, he can mean everything from Facebook games like FarmVille to Facebook Events and highly customized apps that can be mini-websites within your Facebook Page.

In this chapter, you read about the apps — sometimes referred to as "tabs" — that can appear on your Facebook Page. (We use the terms *apps* and *tabs* interchangeably in this chapter.) You discover the basics about how to install apps and how to move them so that they're featured more prominently. In Book V, we cover Facebook applications in much greater depth and discuss a wide range of specific apps to enhance your Page.

Defining Apps and Understanding Facebook Installed Apps

Facebook has developed four apps that are installed on your Page when you create it:

✦ **Photos:** Organized into Albums, Timeline Photos, and photos posted by fans

✦ **Events:** Upcoming and past events (covered in depth in Book VI)

✦ **Video:** Videos uploaded directly to Facebook

✦ **Notes:** Mini blog posts with photos or other text

Only Photos appears on your Timeline when you start your Facebook Page. The Video and Notes apps are on your Facebook dashboard under Apps.

The apps that Facebook has created can't have custom names or custom Cover images. The Photos tab defaults to the last photo that was uploaded, and the Events tab defaults to a photo of the most recent event or the event that is coming up soonest. Notes and Video show snapshots of the notes and videos that you've uploaded most recently.

If you want any other apps on your Facebook Page, you have to install them. Facebook has created the four basic apps, but any other app has been created by an independent developer or third party. All Pages are capable of displaying 12 Facebook apps. You can have more installed, but only 12 will appear on your Page for your community to view, and Facebook displays only the first 3 apps on the left sidebar when someone navigates to your Page. Although Facebook displays only the first 12, you can see and access all your apps as Admin. Your community can access your apps also by clicking the More button right under your cover photo as shown in Figure 2-1.

It's fun to look at all the ways you can spruce up your Page with apps. Pages are using apps in different ways, and the apps can be very engaging. Look at the interesting examples in Figure 2-1 as shown by accessing the More menu and in Figure 2-2 as shown on the left sidebar.

You can adjust the apps that appear first in the left column, but the About section can't be moved. To see any additional apps, the user needs to either click the More button (as shown in Figure 2-1) or click the arrow next to the apps, as shown in Figure 2-2. Once you click the arrow, you get a pop-up box listing all the apps as shown in Figure 2-3.

Figure 2-1:
Macy's uses an app to list its job openings.

Access apps in the More drop-down menu

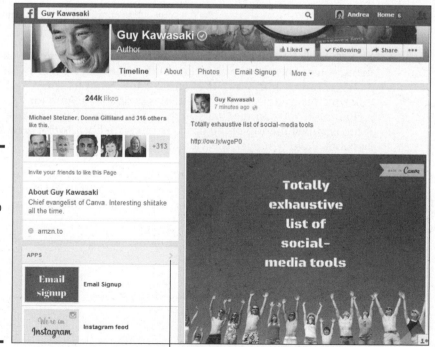

Figure 2-2:
Guy Kawasaki uses an app to capture e-mail addresses and showcase his Instagram feed.

Click the arrow to show all available apps

Figure 2-3:
A pop-up box shows all the available apps.

Use the scroll bar to scroll through all the apps

When you click the photo of the app or select the app name from the More menu, you're taken to the associated tab within your Page. If you click the Macy's is hiring! link shown in Figure 2-1, for example, you're taken into the app, which is a mini-website that allows people to search for jobs, as shown in Figure 2-4. You can see that you're on the Macy's Page because the cover photo is still at the top of the page. To navigate back to the main Macy's Facebook Page, just click the Timeline link.

Some apps that you find may not have been updated recently or may be a bit difficult to work with. All the third-party apps covered in this book work well, but so many apps are out there that it's important to be aware of the potential pitfalls!

Click here to get back to the Page Timeline

Figure 2-4:
An inter-
active
Facebook
tab on
Macy's
Facebook
Page.

Adding an App to Your Page

Installing a new app can be a different process for each app because all but the four Facebook-created apps were developed by third parties. As we discuss each app in this book, we take you through the appropriate steps, but it helps you to have general knowledge of how apps work:

1. **Go to the app you want to install.**

You see in Book V how to find appropriate apps to install. Usually, you install the app from within Facebook, but sometimes you have to navigate to the app's website, configure the app there, and then install it.

2. **Give the app permission to access your information and permission to post to your Page.**

Usually, you must be logged in as your Profile rather than as your Page, as shown in Figure 2-5. This process may make you nervous because you know that you want to add the app to your Page, not your Profile. But rest assured — you'll be able to specify where the app is to appear! You may or may not see this step, depending on the app.

Figure 2-5:
You must
give
permission
for an app
to post to
your Pages
from your
personal
Profile.

3. **Choose the Page where you want to add the app, as shown in Figure 2-6.**

    This process can be a bit different for each app, as you see throughout this book.

Figure 2-6:
You have
the chance
to add the
app to your
Page.

When you complete these steps, the app appears in the Apps area on your Facebook Page.

As we mention earlier in this chapter, you can have more apps installed on your Facebook Page, but only the first 12 will be visible to anyone visiting your Page. As the administrator of a Page, you see *all* your apps. Just remember that your likers can see only the first 12 and only the first 3 apps are visible on the left sidebar. You can shift the positions of the apps as you see the in next section, "Rearranging the Positions of Your Apps."

Also, you can have more apps that are not shown but are installed on your Page. To access those apps, go to the Apps section in your Page Dashboard. See the "Finding Apps in Your Page Dashboard," section, later in this chapter.

Rearranging the Positions of Your Apps

The most visible apps are going to be the ones in the first row, so make them count! Put your best apps in the first row. (Because the Photos app is fixed, you have only three apps to work with in that row.) Then, of course, put any other apps you want to showcase in the next two rows. Many people don't have more than 12 apps, but if you enjoy trying new apps, you can have more than the allotted 12.

Also note that you can't move the Facebook Likes tab below the first three rows of apps to hide it. That tab is visible on every Facebook Page and can't be hidden.

To swap the positions of the apps on your Facebook Page, follow these steps:

1. **Click the More button under your Facebook cover photo.**

   A drop-down menu appears with all the available apps and a Manage Tabs selection.

2. **Select Manage Tabs.**

   A pop-up box appears as shown in Figure 2-7.

3. **Click and hold the app that you want to move and drag it to the appropriate spot to re-order the tabs.**

   You cannot re-order the About section — it always appears first in the left column.

4. **Click Save.**

Figure 2-7:
Manage
your tabs.

Deleting an App from Your Page

When you add an app to your Page, it doesn't have to live there forever. You can delete it completely or just hide it so that it doesn't appear on your Timeline. Go to the Settings at the top of your Page, and select Apps from the sidebar on the left. You can then remove the app from your added apps. The steps on how to do this are in Book V, Chapter 1.

If you have an app that isn't functioning correctly, remove this app so that anyone who's clicking around on your Page doesn't stumble across it.

Customizing the App Title and App Photo

Two of the key parts of the apps you add to your Page are the app title and the app photo. The apps you install have a default title and photo, which usually aren't that interesting. Figure 2-2 shows how customizing app photos can enhance your branding, draw attention to the app, and give your page a professional look.

App titles and photos that have a "call to action" in them are more likely to be noticed. Click Here, Free Report, and Get a Coupon, for example, are all valid and intriguing app titles containing a call to action.

The app photo is 111 pixels (px) x 74 px, which isn't enough space for a very detailed photo. But even having a colored background with some interesting text, as shown in Figure 2-2 earlier in this chapter, is a good strategy.

To change your app title and app photo, follow these steps:

1. **Click the Settings link at the top of your Page.**

   You're taken to your Page dashboard.

2. **Click Apps on the left sidebar.**

   You see all your available apps.

3. **Click the Edit Settings link within the app you want to edit.**

   A pop-up window appears, as shown in Figure 2-8.

Figure 2-8: Change the tab name and the tab image.

Edit Hosted iFrame - Home Icon Settings

Profile

Tab:	Added (remove)
Custom Tab Image:	Change
Custom Tab Name:	Welcome Save
	Leave blank to use the default name.

Okay

4. **Type the Custom Tab Name you want to use and click Save.**

   Only the first 15 characters appear on your Page; then the name is cut off.

5. **Click the Change hyperlink next to Custom Tab Image to change the tab image.**

   You're taken to a new browser window, where you can upload a custom image.

6. **Mouse over the image and click Edit in the upper-right corner of the image.**

   A pop-up window appears, allowing you to choose a file. The image must be 111 px x 74 px (or an even multiple of that ratio); otherwise, it will be resized.

7. **Go to the file you want to upload and click Open.**

   Your image appears in the Image section, as shown in Figure 2-9.

Figure 2-9:
Upload a custom image.

Book III
Chapter 2

Facebook Apps 101

The photo changes, and now you can close the new browser window that was opened and navigate back to your Facebook Page; the other browser window should still be open. To see the change in effect, just refresh your Page in the browser window.

Finding Apps in Your Page Dashboard

As we mention earlier in this chapter, the Photos tab is the only one that appears on your Facebook Page when you first get started. You do have other Facebook apps installed on your Page, though. You just need to know where to look for them. To access all your apps, follow these steps:

1. **Click Settings at the top of your Page.**

   You are taken to your Page Admin Panel.

2. **Select Apps from the left sidebar.**

   You now see all the apps that you've installed on your Page (see Figure 2-10) and you also see the available Facebook apps to install.

Read more about adjusting, deleting, and adding the apps from the Page dashboard in Book V, Chapter 1.

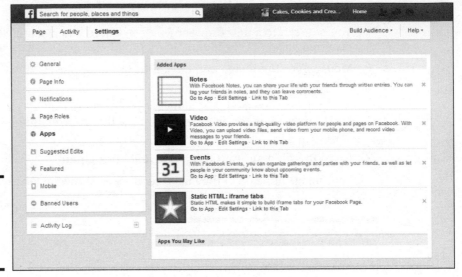

Figure 2-10:
Viewing apps from your Page dashboard.

Chapter 3: Importing Your Blog Posts into Your Facebook Page

In This Chapter

✔ Obtaining the web address of your RSS feed

✔ Deciding which Facebook application to use to import your blog

✔ Installing and configuring the NetworkedBlogs application

✔ Looking at Social RSS

✔ Exploring RSS Graffiti

✔ Using the dlvr.it tool

If you have a blog, the easiest way to add new content on your Facebook Page is to import your blog posts. Easier yet would be getting this job done automatically.

You're in luck because several Facebook applications (and some web-based tools) are available for doing just that. When you post something new on your blog, the application automatically creates a new entry on your Page, which in turn goes out to the News Feeds of people who like you. This automation means one fewer task for you after you post a new blog entry.

In this chapter, we tell you how to use four of the most popular applications for importing blog posts to your Facebook Page. Each application requires your RSS feed's URL, so the chapter starts by telling you how to find that URL.

Importing your blog automatically saves you time and hassle. Luckily, you have lots of choices how. Try one. If it doesn't work for you, you can always stop that application and install a different one.

 We believe that manually is the best way to post your blog posts. You have more control over how the post appears and it doesn't take that long. But we also know that a few time-saving devices are always welcome.

Getting the Address of Your RSS Feed

No matter what blog-import application you decide to use, you need to know the web address, or *URL*, of your blog's RSS feed. *RSS*, which stands for *really simple syndication*, is a standard used on the Internet to pull information from websites in an organized manner. It pulls only the text, leaving all the fancy graphics that appear on your blog behind.

Your RSS feed address is typically something like this: www.*YourWebSite*. com/feed. Depending on how your website is set up, though, this address could be something quite different. If you don't know the address of your RSS feed, check with your web developer. If that's not an option, here's a handy trick for discovering your feed address.

On Internet Explorer

If you're using Internet Explorer, follow these steps to find your RSS feed address:

1. **Go to your website or blog in Internet Explorer.**

Above the website is the orange RSS icon, as shown in Figure 3-1. If the icon is gray, the browser can't find an RSS feed on your site, and you need to contact your web developer (or you may want to try one of the other methods listed here).

Figure 3-1:
The RSS icon appears in orange above your website.

2. **Click the main RSS feed listed (if you see more than one).**

In Figure 3-1, Amy's blog also shows the Comments feed for all the comments posted on her blog. You're taken to the view of the RSS feed, and the address for that feed displays in the browser address window.

On Firefox

If you're using Firefox, follow these steps to find your RSS feed address:

1. **Go to your website or blog in Firefox.**

2. **Click Bookmarks on the menu bar.**

A drop-down menu appears.

3. **Mouse over the Subscribe to This Page option.**

A submenu appears.

4. **Click the main feed.**

The RSS feed opens in a new window, and the address of the feed displays in the browser's address bar.

In HTML code

Another handy trick for finding the RSS feed is looking at the HTML code of the website. You can do this in any browser although the steps may vary, depending on your browser. In this section, we offer the steps for several browsers.

If you're using Firefox

1. Go to the website or blog.

2. Right-click anywhere on the page.

A drop-down menu appears.

3. Choose View Page Source.

A new window opens, showing the HTML code.

If you're using Internet Explorer

1. Go to the website or blog.

2. Click Page on the menu bar.

A drop-down menu appears.

3. Choose View Source.

A new window opens, showing the HTML code.

If you're using Google Chrome

1. Go to the website or blog.

2. Click the menu icon (three bars) in the top-right corner.

A drop-down menu appears.

3. Choose Tools.

A drop-down menu appears.

4. Select View Source.

A new tab opens, showing the HTML code.

If you're using Safari

1. Go to the website or blog.

2. Click the page icon in the top-right corner.

A drop-down menu appears.

3. Choose View Source.

A new window appears, showing the HTML code.

When you've opened the tab or window containing the HTML code in any of the browsers, press Ctrl+F (⌘+F on a Mac) on your keyboard to search for a phrase. Enter **rss** to find the RSS feed address. Using Amy Porterfield's website as an example, you find the following when you search on the term *rss*:

```
<link rel="alternate" type="application/rss+xml" title="Amy Porterfield | Social
    Media Strategy Consultant RSS Feed" href="http://amyporterfield.com/feed/" />
```

The RSS feed address is right after the `href=` term and is `http://amyporterfield.com/feed/`.

Introducing the Facebook Blog-Import Applications

After you have the address of your RSS feed (as we discuss in the previous section), you're ready to begin using one of Facebook's applications to import your blog. But which one? Here's a list of some ways to import your blog into Facebook automatically:

✦ NetworkedBlogs application

✦ Social RSS application

✦ RSS Graffiti

✦ dlvr.it

These applications were developed by third parties (not Facebook). All these applications have some benefits, and deciding which one to use is a matter of preference. As a metric, the number of users can indicate popularity. NetworkedBlogs has more than 100,000 monthly users, Social RSS has more than 10,000, and RSS Graffiti has more than 100,000. dlvr.it doesn't have a use statistic available.

To help you decide which application is right for you, the following sections describe each application, show you how easy it is to set up, what features it has, and what the imported posts look like. All these applications are free although Social RSS has a paid option that provides a higher level of service.

Using the NetworkedBlogs Application

NetworkedBlogs is one of the most popular methods of importing your blog posts into your Page automatically. You import your blog into both your Page and your Profile. After you import your blog, a tab appears on your Page that contains your previous posts for people to reference; see Figure 3-2.

Figure 3-2:
Your blog posts are stored on a tab when you use Networked-Blogs.

Clicking one of these links takes a viewer directly to that blog post. Each post is also posted on your Timeline automatically (if you choose automatic posting) and looks similar to the one shown in Figure 3-3. The first few lines of the blog post, as well as a picture from the post, are pulled in automatically. You can tell where the post came from by the note below it ("via NetworkedBlogs").

Figure 3-3:
See where the post came from.

If you don't have a picture embedded in your post, the NetworkedBlogs application displays a screen shot of your whole blog as the thumbnail picture next to your Timeline post.

Registering your blog on NetworkedBlogs

The NetworkedBlogs application can be a little tricky to navigate, but it has a good frequently asked questions (FAQ) section that can help you through the process. Your first step is to register your blog by following these steps:

1. **Log into Facebook as your personal Profile.**

2. **Go to** `http://www.networkedblogs.com/` **and click Get Started Now.**

    You may have to click through a couple of pages that ask you to follow some initial blogs. You don't have to follow them. Click Next at the bottom of the Page.

3. **Click Allow to allow NetworkedBlogs to access your Facebook profile.**

   Remember that you choose where NetworkedBlogs will publish your content.

4. **Click the Register a Blog link at the top of the page.**

   A new page appears.

5. **Enter the home page of the blog and then click Next.**

   You're taken to a page where you fill in the information about your blog, as shown in Figure 3-4.

Figure 3-4:
Fill in this information for your blog.

The items with asterisks in Figure 3-4 are mandatory; everything else is optional. You can edit any of this information later. Use these tips for filling in this information:

- *Blog Link:* The link to the home page of the blog.
- *Blog Name:* The title of your blog. Keep it short.
- *Tagline:* A little more space to tell people what your blog is about.

- *Feed Link:* The RSS feed link for your blog. (See "Getting the Address of Your RSS Feed," earlier in this chapter.)

- *Topics:* Three keywords that indicate what your blog is about. These keywords can be any keywords that people who use the NetworkedBlogs app might use in searching for blogs that they're interested in.

- *Language:* The language your blog is written in.

- *Description:* A description of your blog. What you enter here shows up in the NetworkedBlogs directory, so make it interesting, and tell people why they'd want to read your blog.

- *Your Email:* For NetworkedBlogs verification. You don't receive e-mail from NetworkedBlogs.

- *Terms of Service:* An agreement that the blog doesn't contain nudity or other adult content.

6. **Click the Next button at the bottom of the screen (refer to Figure 3-4).**

   A new screen asks whether you're the author of the blog for which you just entered information.

7. **Click the Yes button.**

   Another screen appears, which determines the method you want to use to verify that you're the owner of your blog.

8. **Choose a method to verify your ownership of the blog: Ask Friends to Verify You or Install the Widget.**

   You can have your Facebook Friends verify that you own the blog; if you select that option, you can select nine Friends and send the request for verification to them. The problem with this option is that not everyone sees that request in her notifications (people don't always know to look there), so your verification can take a long time. The better option is to use the widget to verify ownership, if you can.

Verifying ownership of your blog

If you select the Ask Friends to Verify You option, a screen listing all your Facebook Friends appears, and you can select who gets a request to verify that you own your blog. After you select the Friends who will verify the ownership of your blog, you're done. You can move to the next section on setting up syndication.

If you choose the widget to verify ownership, you just need to install this widget temporarily until the NetworkedBlogs application verifies that you put the widget on your blog; you get a notification; then you can remove the widget. You may choose to keep the widget to promote the fact that you're part of NetworkedBlogs. If you keep the widget on your website, people can click the Follow This Blog button to follow your blog through the NetworkedBlogs app.

If you install the widget, you're taken to the screen shown in Figure 3-5.

Click here

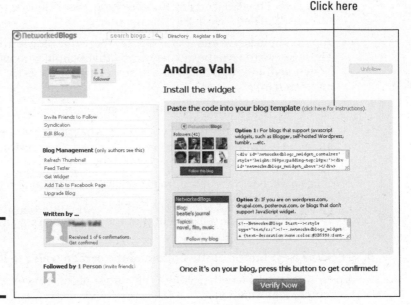

Figure 3-5:
Choose
Option 1 or
Option 2.

Continue by following these steps:

1. **Choose Option 1 if you have a self-hosted WordPress blog or Tumblr or Blogger; choose Option 2 if you have your blog on WordPress.com, Drupal.com, or Posterous.com.**

The code in Option 1 is for sites that allow JavaScript; the code in Option 2 is for sites (such as WordPress.com) that don't allow JavaScript.

A self-hosted blog typically is on a site where you pay for hosting. The WordPress.com, Blogger.com, Drupal.com, and Posterous.com sites will host your blog for free, but they have some limitations.

2. **Highlight the code for the appropriate option and press Ctrl+C (⌘+C on a Mac).**

3. **Click the blue Click Here for Instructions link, shown in Figure 3-5.**

A new window displays instructions for different platforms.

4. **Follow the instructions to install the code.**

5. **Click the blue Verify Now button.**

If you installed the widget correctly, you get a Verification Successful message. You can remove the NetworkedBlogs widget or badge, if you want.

Setting up syndication

Syndication tells NetworkedBlogs where you want your new blog posts to be posted in Facebook (and NetworkedBlogs can automatically tweet your new post, too). Syndication is a great tool to help you automate sending your blog content to Facebook and Twitter.

To set up your syndication, follow these steps:

1. **Click the Blogger Dashboard link in the top-right corner of the NetworkedBlogs application.**

2. **If you're using the application for the first time, click the Grant Permissions button.**

A pop-up window asks you to allow the NetworkedBlogs app to post on your behalf and access your data. This request can look daunting, but the app is reputable.

3. **Click Allow.**

You see your Blogger dashboard.

4. **Click Syndication in the left sidebar.**

You see a drop-down menu with your blog and the places you want to send your post listed.

5. **From the drop-down menu, choose the blog you want to configure.**

6. **Add Facebook targets and/or Twitter targets, as shown in Figure 3-6.**

Book III
Chapter 3

Importing Your Blog
Posts into Your
Facebook Page

Figure 3-6:
Click Add
Facebook
Target to
select your
Facebook
Profile or
Page.

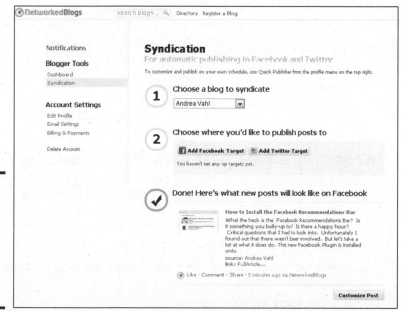

You can also customize the post by clicking the Customize Post button at the bottom of the Syndication page (as in Figure 3-6). You can specify whether to include an image; we highly recommend that you do. You can also choose whether you want to hide the NetworkedBlogs toolbar when people navigate to your post from the NetworkedBlogs link. The toolbar can make it easier for people to share, but the choice is up to you.

If you get stuck, the NetworkedBlogs application has a support page at www. networkedblogs.com/help.

After you successfully configure your NetworkedBlogs application and post a new blog post, the application automatically sends the post to your Page or personal Profile (depending on how it's configured). The post usually appears within a few minutes after you post to your blog, but we've seen it take as long as an hour. Just be patient if you don't see it right away.

If your blog post isn't updated in the NetworkedBlogs application, you have to click a Pull Now button to find any new blog posts on your blog and bring them into the application. To do so, go to the Blogger dashboard, click the name of your blog on the dashboard, and then click the Pull Now button shown in Figure 3-7.

Figure 3-7:
Click Pull
Now if your
blog post
hasn't been
brought into
the applica-
tion auto-
matically.

Reposting a blog post with NetworkedBlogs

You can repost any of your old blog posts by clicking the Quick Publisher link below the post (refer to Figure 3-7). Just follow these easy steps:

1. **Click the Quick Publisher link.**

   A pop-up window appears.

2. **Select the target (where you want to send the blog post) by clicking the Publish To field.**

   You can select multiple targets.

3. **Select the post to send by clicking the Attach a Post from My Blog button.**

   A drop-down menu appears, listing your blog posts, as shown in Figure 3-8.

4. **Choose one from the list and then click the blue Publish button.**

   The post is sent.

Figure 3-8: Select which blog post you want to send to your networks in the Quick Publisher.

 We recommend reposting some of your blog posts from time to time if they're still relevant and helpful to your audience. New people who are coming to your Page won't have seen all the posts when they first came out. Even longtime members of your community may have missed a post or didn't have a chance to read it, so they'll welcome the opportunity to view helpful posts. As long as you use the reposting feature prudently, it's a good thing to do occasionally.

Many people ask whether they should post their business blog to their Profile as well as their Page. Our recommendation is that you should, unless you feel very strongly about "bothering" your Friends and family members. You probably aren't posting to your blog that often, and your Friends and family should know what you're doing in your business. Many referrals can — and should — come from your Friends and family, and seeing a blog post may spark a connection for them to share your post with one of their Friends.

Adding the NetworkedBlogs tab to your Facebook Page

NetworkedBlogs allows you to add a tab to your Facebook Page to display your blog posts, as shown in Figure 3-2. This paid feature costs $9.99 per month or $99 per year. The nice thing is that having a tab with all your blog posts on it gives your Facebook fans easy access to your blog from Facebook without having to go elsewhere.

Book III
Chapter 3

Importing Your Blog
Posts into Your
Facebook Page

Some people decide to use only NetworkedBlogs as a way to import their blog posts onto a Facebook tab, and they don't use NetworkedBlogs to automatically post to their Page. But if that's all you're looking for, you may want to consider another free app that does this, such as Social RSS or TabSite.

 Manually posting your new blog post to the Timeline gives you more control of how the post looks and of the commentary that goes along with the post. Ultimately, you have to weigh the benefit of automation against the benefit of manually posting something that could be a bit more engaging because of the personal touch you add.

If you want to add a blog tab to your Page with NetworkedBlogs, follow these steps:

1. **Go to the Blogger dashboard.**

2. **Find the blog you want to add.**

3. **Select Add Tab to Facebook Page.**

4. **Make payment when asked.**

5. **Keep customizing your tab.**

Installing Social RSS

Another Facebook application that you can use to import your blog posts automatically is Social RSS. Social RSS (part of Social Bakers) is a little easier to set up than NetworkedBlogs is, but the free version may not work for you if you're posting more than three times per week. See "Deciding when to upgrade to paid service," later in this chapter, for more information.

To start using the Social RSS app, follow these steps:

1. **Log in to Facebook as your personal Profile.**

2. **Go to** `http://apps.facebook.com/social-rss`.

    You see information about the Pro version of the app at the top of the Page and Feed Settings below that.

3. **Select the Page you want to send your the RSS feed to from the Your Page drop-down menu.**

4. **Add your RSS address in the Add Your First Feed box, as shown in Figure 3-9.**

    Refer to "Getting the Address of Your RSS Feed," earlier in the chapter, for more information about this address. Notice that you can bring in multiple RSS feeds with this app.

5. **Select the Publish to Wall check box if you want your feed to be posted to your Timeline automatically.**

6. **Select the post thumbnail image you want:**

   • *Image from the RSS Feed:* This is the default, and recommended, choice.

   • *Let Facebook Decide:* The OpenGraph protocol selects the image from your post.

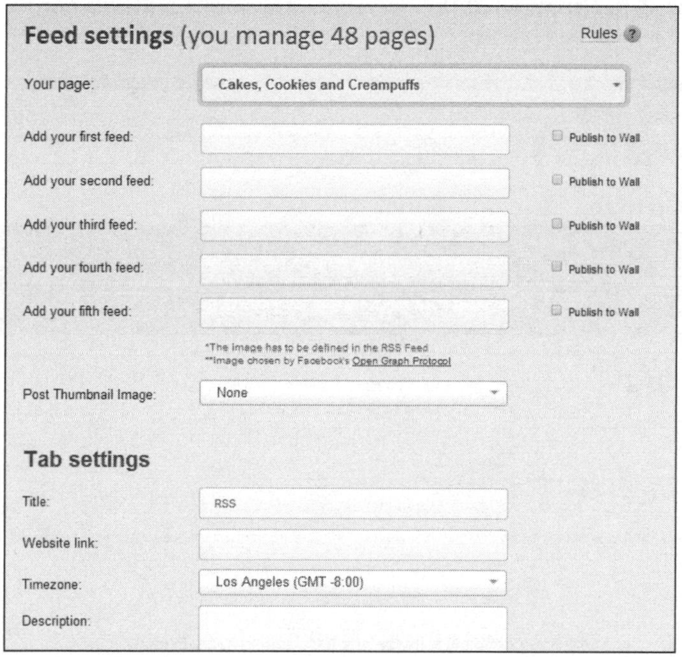

Feed settings (you manage 48 pages)   Rules ⓘ

Your page:	Cakes, Cookies and Creampuffs ▾	
Add your first feed:		☐ Publish to Wall
Add your second feed:		☐ Publish to Wall
Add your third feed:		☐ Publish to Wall
Add your fourth feed:		☐ Publish to Wall
Add your fifth feed:		☐ Publish to Wall

*The image has to be defined in the RSS Feed.
**Image chosen by Facebook's Open Graph Protocol

| Post Thumbnail Image: | None ▾ |

Tab settings

Title:	RSS
Website link:	
Timezone:	Los Angeles (GMT -8:00) ▾
Description:	

Figure 3-9:
Configure
the Social
RSS
application.

7. **Scroll down to and configure the tab settings if you want a tab on your Page for the RSS feeds you have listed.**

   These settings are for the tab that appears on your Page. Here's some information about what to put in each field:

   • *Title:* The title of your app as it appears below the app photo on your Page. If you're pulling in multiple RSS feeds with the Social RSS app, all the feeds appear on the same Page. If you're pulling in just your blog, you can title the app *Blog.* If you have multiple feeds coming in, you may want to call the app *Industry News* (or whatever characterizes those streams best).

   • *Website link:* Your website address for people to click.

   • *Description:* A brief paragraph about your blog or the set of RSS feeds. This description appears at the top of the page of posts.

   • *Timezone:* Your time zone.

8. **Click the Save Settings button at the bottom of the page.**

A pop-up window appears, saying that your feeds have been success-fully updated. The window also promotes the Social RSS app's paid service. The free service lets you import just one post per day; the paid service lets you import new articles each hour. Click the x to close the window.

Figure 3-10 shows what the Social RSS tab looks like on your Page.

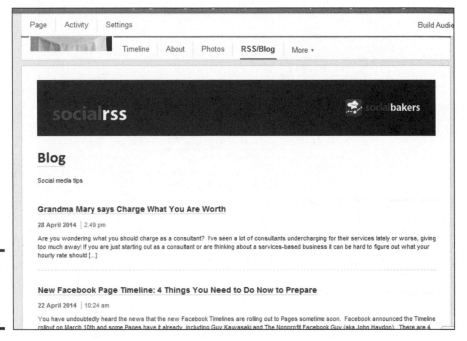

Figure 3-10:
The Social RSS tab on a Page.

Using Social RSS

After you configure Social RSS, it automatically adds your posts to your Page Timeline (if you selected that option) and to your RSS/Blog tab on your Page. You can always edit the settings or add more feeds from other places.

You also can add a feed to your Profile from the Social RSS application. Just choose User Profile Wall from the drop-down menu in the Social RSS configu-ration area.

Beyond that, Social RSS doesn't have too many other features unless you upgrade to the paid service (described next), which gives you some added statistics.

Deciding when to upgrade to paid service

The Social RSS application (`http://apps.facebook.com/social-rss`) offers a paid service ($24 per year, as of this writing) that grants you more posts per hour (up to five per feed per hour, with a maximum of five feeds). By comparison, the free Social RSS currently allows for one post to your Timeline per day. If you're using this application for multiple feeds that post every day, it's not going to work.

If you're using Social RSS to bring in your own blog to Facebook, the free option will probably work just fine because most people aren't blogging more than once per day.

Using RSS Graffiti

Another Facebook application that you can use to post your blog entries automatically on your Facebook Timeline is RSS Graffiti. This app doesn't limit you to importing only blog posts: You can use it to bring in any RSS feed from anywhere, much as you can with Social RSS. You can also use RSS Graffiti to post in Facebook Groups. You can control how many posts per day are pulled in, just in case the RSS feed you enter has more posts than you want to share with your community.

Adding RSS feeds can help you add content to your Page. You may want to use RSS feeds to import industry news or other helpful blogs. You can search some of the RSS-feed directories that are available, but you're better off bringing in a feed from a site that you know, like, and trust.

RSS Graffiti is highly configurable. You can configure the post style, scheduling of updates, and times when the messages are posted. All these features translate into many settings, all of which you can change. Most of the settings can be left at their default values.

One thing that RSS Graffiti doesn't have is a tab that you can add to your Page. It only posts the RSS feed on your Timeline. If you want a place to show your most recent blog posts on your Facebook Page, we recommend using Social RSS or TabSite.

To get started with RSS Graffiti, follow these steps:

1. **Log in to Facebook as your personal Profile.**

2. **Go to** `http://apps.facebook.com/rssgraffiti`.

   If this is the first time using the app you see a pop-up window asking you to allow RSS Graffiti permission to post. Click Allow. You're taken to the RSS Graffiti dashboard.

3. **Click Add New Publishing Plan.**

   A window appears, allowing you to name your publishing plan.

4. **Type a name in the text box and then click Create Publishing Plan.**

   A configuration area appears, as shown in Figure 3-11.

Figure 3-11:
Select the
source (RSS
feed) and
the target
(Page or
Profile).

5. **Click the New Sources button next to Sources.**

   A pop-up window appears, allowing you to add your RSS feed.

6. **Add the address of your RSS feed (refer to "Getting the Address of Your RSS Feed," earlier in this chapter), and click Add Source.**

   A pop-up window appears, allowing you to configure the RSS feed, as shown in Figure 3-12.

   As we mention earlier in this chapter, you can choose many features of RSS Graffiti, but the default settings work well for most people, and you can skip to Step7.

   Or, if you want to customize your settings, you can read a little bit more about what each of the settings means here:

   • *Source Name Override:* Change the name that appears when you post the article or blog post.

   • *Source URL Override:* Override the URL that points to the website. Leave this field blank to use the feed's URL.

   • *Scheduling:* Change the maximum posts per update, and specify whether you want the newest posts to post first.

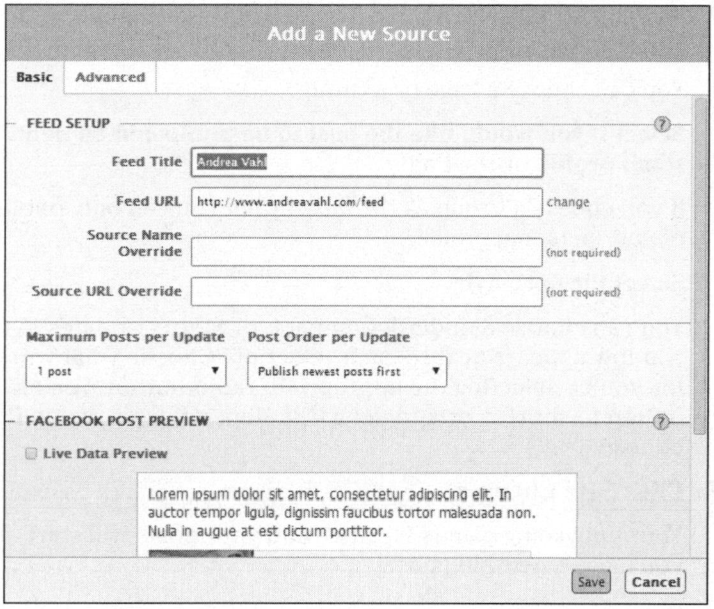

Figure 3-12:
Configure
your
settings.

On the Advanced tab, you can set these options:

- *Format Message:* Add messages to each post, using these options. You may choose to add a static message such as *New Post from My Blog* or something similar.

- *Filtering Options:* Set the date and time after which posts can be published on your Timeline. Older posts won't be published unless you change this option. You can indicate how long a post must be up (in minutes) before it's posted to your Timeline by setting the Publish Delay option. You may want to use this option if you sometimes make minor edits in posts shortly after you publish them. That way, you have a buffer of time before the story is posted to your Facebook Timeline.

7. Click Save after you configure your source RSS feed.

The pop-up window disappears, and you see the name of the feed in the Sources area (refer to Figure 3-11).

8. Click New Target, next to Target.

A pop-up window appears giving you the choice between publishing to Facebook or CoveritLive (an online blogging tool).

9. Select Facebook.

A new pop-up box appears showing the configuration for posting to Facebook including a drop-down menu for where you want to post.

10. **Select your target from the Target drop-down menu in the Target Setup section.**

    You can choose a Page or a Group.

11. **Select if you would like the post to be published on behalf of your personal profile or the Page.**

    If you choose a Group as the target then you can only publish on behalf of your personal profile.

12. **Select the post style.**

    You can choose Standard, Compact, or Status Updates. A preview window appears next to each selection. Choose what works best for you by selecting the appropriate radio button. You also have the option to shorten or append a URL depending on which Post style you choose.

13. **Click Save Changes.**

    Your publishing plan is finished, and your posts will start updating when you make a new blog post.

Be careful about adding just any RSS feed to your Page. After all, you don't control that content, and you may not agree with a post that's brought in.

Using the dlvr.it Tool

dlvr.it is a great tool that you can use to automatically post your blog or any RSS feed to Facebook and Twitter. It's a cinch to set up, and it offers analytics on the posted articles, which is a nice feature for helping you track clicks. You can also use the tool to schedule any post (not just a post from your blog) for later.

Signing up and getting started are easy. Just go to http://dlvr.it and follow these steps:

1. **Click Sign Up.**

   You're given the option of signing up with your Facebook login, your Twitter login, or signing up with your e-mail address. Choose which option works best for you and follow the steps. You may need to grant permissions from Facebook or Twitter and also add your e-mail address depending on which option you choose.

2. **Click the + symbol next to Routes to add a new Route.**

   A dialog box lets you add your source and destination, as shown in Figure 3-13.

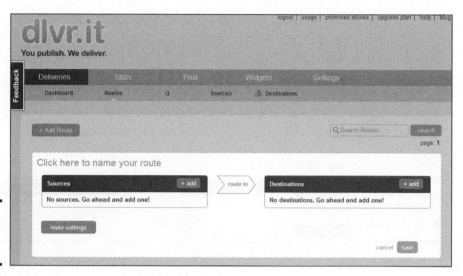

Figure 3-13:
Add your
RSS feed.

3. **Click the +Add button next to Sources.**

   A pop-up box appears where you can select the RSS feed symbol, the Twitter symbol or the e-mail symbol.

4. **Select the RSS feed symbol and then click Add Feed.**

5. **Enter the RSS feed of your blog.**

   Refer to "Getting the Address of Your RSS Feed," earlier in the chapter.

6. **Choose from the drop-down menu to indicate whether you want to post your first item now or the next time a new item is published, or to post all items in the feed.**

7. **Click the Save Source button.**

8. **Select the +Add button next to Destinations.**

   A pop-up box offers different icons for social site options.

9. **Click the Facebook button.**

   The application detects whether you're logged in to Facebook and, if you're not, it prompts you to log in to your account. If this is the first time using the app, you see a number of permission requests to post on your behalf. Click Agree on all of them.

10. **From the drop-down menu, choose the Facebook Page where you want to post your blog.**

11. **Click Continue.**

    You get a message that the *route* (the automated posting from your blog to your Facebook Page), has been added, and you see your new route, as shown in Figure 3-14.

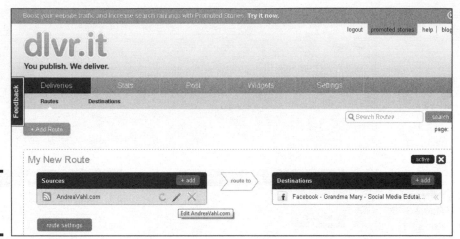

Figure 3-14:
Your dlvr.it
route.

You can add more routes (to Twitter, LinkedIn, or your Facebook personal Profile), if you want, by clicking the +Add Route button.

If you mouse over your Sources or Destinations (as in Figure 3-14), you see a pencil icon; click that icon to see advanced settings. These settings give you much more control of when your blog posts are posted, what text is displayed, what filters you can add to the RSS feed, and more. These settings are beyond the scope of this book, but Figure 3-15 shows you a snapshot of the types of customization that are available.

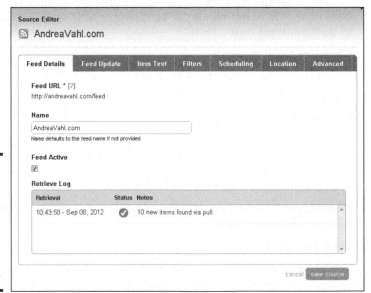

Figure 3-15:
Advanced
settings for
the RSS
feed gives
you many
customiza-
tion options.

Don't worry about duplicating content. Some people ask whether they should post on their blog and then repeat that information on their Facebook Page and on Twitter, and maybe also send a newsletter with the link to the post. Don't worry that people are going to get sick of that post. They most likely see it in only one or two places unless you're posting the same thing over and over. After all, you're trying to get the word out about your blog post, and people need multiple opportunities to read it.

Chapter 4: Connecting Your Page to Twitter

In This Chapter

✔ Connecting to Twitter in various ways

✔ Using HootSuite to manage your accounts

✔ Exploring other posting tools

✔ Adding a Twitter tab to your Facebook Page

*Y*ou likely know what Twitter is and how to use it. You may not have heard of HootSuite and Buffer, though, or know how to use them to your advantage when you coordinate your social networks in tandem with Facebook marketing.

Bottom line: In this chapter, we show you the benefits (and a few considerations) of connecting your Facebook presence with Twitter to complement and diversify your Facebook marketing campaigns. And, yes, we also show literally how to connect these so you can put them to best use.

Some of these third-party applications may not get the same visibility as a traditional post that you put straight on your Timeline. Posts that come into Facebook via Twitter and the other apps mentioned here are sometimes hidden with other posts coming in from the same application, but at this writing, we did not find that to be the case. Watch your News Feed to see how the posts are being shown.

To Connect or Not to Connect

So do you want to tweet everything you post to your Page, post to your Page from Twitter, or update simultaneously? More important, should you? First, consider the implications of linking the two accounts.

Most social media thought leaders agree that posting in both Twitter and Facebook all the time isn't a good idea because your Facebook community is different from your Twitter community; it expects different things. Twitter typically has more quick interactions and conversations, whereas a Facebook community expects fewer updates and more threaded conversations.

Also, if you're participating on other social media sites, we recommend connecting them with your Facebook Page because people on Facebook may not be aware of where to find you on YouTube, Pinterest, Twitter, or LinkedIn. And adding your other accounts can give your users a richer experience through SlideShare presentations and YouTube videos. (Find out more about adding these apps in Book V, Chapter 1.)

To help you coordinate all your social networks, consider using a tool like HootSuite to simplify your life by creating a single dashboard where you can monitor your various social profiles and update from one place. You may also want to consider some of the other posting and scheduling tools mentioned in this chapter to help create a steady stream of good content for your audience.

Connecting Facebook and Twitter

How to connect Twitter and Facebook? Let us count the ways! There are many ways to link your Facebook Page to your tweets. (For those of you who aren't familiar with Twitter, a *tweet* is equivalent to a status update in Facebook, but it's only 140 characters long.) Here are some of the options for connecting Facebook and Twitter, each of which we cover in detail:

✦ **En masse:** Send every post on your Facebook Page to your Twitter account automatically.

✦ **Selectively:** Update Twitter and Facebook simultaneously *or* individually by using a tool like HootSuite, Sprout Social, SocialOomph, or Buffer.

Linking your Facebook Page to Twitter

If you want to send everything that you put on your Facebook Timeline to Twitter, you can do that easily and automatically through Facebook. This isn't a bad thing to do because typically, you're posting to your Facebook Page less frequently than you post to Twitter. Also, the Twitter community accepts more-frequent posts than the Facebook community does.

Just keep in mind that Facebook status updates can be 60,000 characters long — way longer than the 140-character limit of a tweet. In a bit, we'll show you how to handle that limitation.

Sending all your Facebook updates to Twitter can be a good way to connect your community on Twitter to your Facebook Page. Just be mindful that some people don't like the duplication with Twitter and Facebook: If you're going to tweet, just tweet as Twitter was meant to be used, without trying to fit more than the original 140 characters into your tweets.

That said, you must decide what is right for you and your brand. Automation between Facebook and Twitter can be a good thing for the following reasons:

✦ Saves you time

✦ Adds more content to your Twitter feed

✦ Can bring your Twitter community to your Facebook Page

To make the connection, log in to your Facebook Profile. (Logging in as your Page doesn't work with these steps.) After you're in the application, specify the Page where your tweets will be sent. Just follow these steps:

1. **Go to** www.facebook.com/twitter.

You can open a new window in your browser or just type the URL in your browser window. You see the screen shown in Figure 4-1.

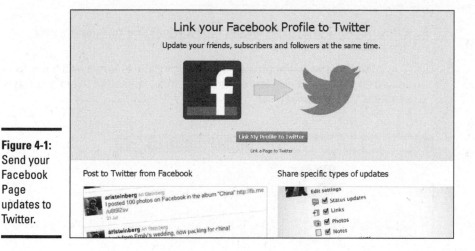

Figure 4-1: Send your Facebook Page updates to Twitter.

2. **Click the Link a Page to Twitter link, located just below the Link My Profile to Twitter button.**

You go to a screen that shows the Pages where you are an Administrator.

3. **Click the Link to Twitter button next to the Page you want to link.**

You go to Twitter to authorize this action; what you see is shown in Figure 4-2. If nothing happens when you click the Link to Twitter button, your pop-up blocker may be blocking the access to the site, and you may need to allow access.

If you're not logged in to your Twitter account, you'll be asked to log in at that time to authorize the postings. But if you are logged into Twitter, make sure you're logged in to the Twitter account that you want to link to that Facebook Page, rather than a different one!

Figure 4-2:
Twitter
requires
that you
authorize
the postings
from your
Page.

4. **Click the Authorize App button to allow posting to your Twitter account.**

You're redirected to Facebook, where your Page is now confirmed to be linked to Twitter, as shown in Figure 4-3. You can select exactly the types of posts you want to tweet.

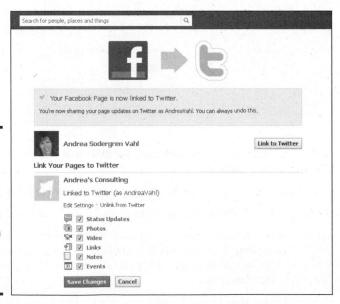

Figure 4-3:
Your
Facebook
Page and
Twitter are
now linked,
and you can
select what
to send to
Twitter.

5. **Clear the check boxes of the items you don't want to send to Twitter.**

6. **Click Save Changes.**

If you ever decide to stop tweeting your Page posts, just go back to www. facebook.com/twitter and click the Unlink from Twitter link to stop the tweeting. You can also use this link to change the settings of what is tweeted out, as shown in Figure 4-3.

Seeing what happens to too-long tweets

As we mention earlier in this chapter, status updates in Facebook are potentially longer than the ones allowed in Twitter. So what happens if you post something in Facebook that's too long to tweet, but you have Facebook and Twitter linked? Well, Facebook automatically cuts off the tweet and posts a link to the actual Facebook update so that someone could click it to read the entire post.

Figure 4-4 shows a too-long tweet that was sent from a Facebook Page.

Figure 4-4: A too-long tweet sent from Facebook.

Someone following the post on Twitter who wants to read the rest of that sentence just clicks the link at the end of the tweet to be taken to the Facebook update, as shown in Figure 4-5.

Figure 4-5: The whole status update is now visible within Facebook.

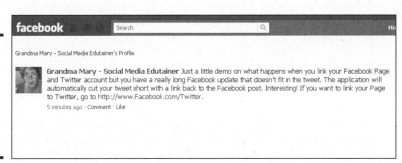

Notice in Figure 4-5 the two links that the person viewing the tweet could click to go to your Facebook Page:

✦ The link preceding the status update that reads Grandma Mary – Social Media Edutainer

✦ The link above the status update — in this example, Grandma Mary – Social Media Edutainer's Profile

If there is a link in your update, the person who clicks the link in Twitter may not get to your Facebook Page to read the rest of the update but instead go directly to the site of the attached link.

Using HootSuite to Update Facebook

HootSuite is a free, web-based app you use to manage multiple social media accounts. Because it's web-based, you can run the application from its website and have access to it from any computer. HootSuite also has a mobile app for your smartphone, which retains all your settings from the web application so that you can post on the go.

HootSuite was initially designed mainly for Twitter, but you can also use it to update multiple other social media platforms at the same time, such as LinkedIn, Facebook, Google+, and Foursquare.

Don't post a lot of Twitter-specific lingo to your Timeline, such as messages with @reply or tweets with hashtags in them. Your Facebook community may not be on Twitter and won't understand all the symbols and messages. And although Facebook does now include the use of hashtags, most Facebook users don't use them in every post, only occasionally.

Walking you through the entire setup of HootSuite is beyond the scope of this book, and the install is pretty intuitive. We just want to show you how you can align your Facebook accounts with this applications and how it works.

HootSuite is a free app, but it does have some nice perks if you upgrade to its paid Pro Plan at $8.99 per month. The Pro Plan includes features such as the ability to adding more than five social media accounts, the ability to have a team member monitor the same social media accounts, and Google Analytics integration.

To start using HootSuite, go to www.hootsuite.com. Enter your name and e-mail address, choose a password, and then click the Create Account button to get started and walk through the configuration steps.

With HootSuite, you can add multiple social profiles. You may have added your profiles during the setup process. But if you didn't, do so now by clicking your picture icon in the top-left corner of the page and then selecting Add a Social Network in the boxes on the lower part of the tab, as shown in Figure 4-6.

A dialog box like the one shown in Figure 4-7 appears; you can add your various social profiles by selecting the sites on the left side of the dialog box, as shown in the figure. With the HootSuite tool, you can update Twitter, Facebook, LinkedIn, Google+, WordPress, Mixi, and Foursquare. You can add your Facebook Profile as well as any Facebook Page that you administer. Having your Profile and Facebook Pages all in one place with HootSuite means that you can do all your updating in one place. You can also see your News Feed and comments within HootSuite.

Figure 4-6:
Add social profiles to HootSuite here.

Click to add multiple social profiles

Figure 4-7:
Configuring your social networks in HootSuite.

Figure 4-8 shows what the HootSuite dashboard looks like. The Compose Message field (top-left corner) is where you enter your status update for Twitter, Facebook, LinkedIn, or some combination of all these websites.

Update these profiles simultaneously

Figure 4-8:
The
HootSuite
dashboard.

Next to the Compose Message field is a series of icons, all indicating the social media profiles that you can update at the same time. In Figure 4-8, left to right, are social media profile pictures with small icons for Twitter, Facebook, Facebook Page (a flag), and LinkedIn. The icons appear in the bottom-right corner of the pictures.

Suppose that you want to post a message and send it to your Facebook Profile, your Facebook Page, Twitter, and LinkedIn at the same time. You could click to select each of those profiles, enter your message, and then click Send Now to update all your profiles simultaneously, as shown in Figure 4-9. Note the Facebook preview link below your post when you check any of your Facebook Profiles. This preview link gives you the ability to customize the photo you attach to the post, just as you can do when you post a link in Facebook directly. Make any adjustments to the post and then click Send Now.

Figure 4-9:
Click the
profiles you
want to
update with
the same
message.

HootSuite can also schedule your status updates. If you're going to be gone for the day or for a vacation, you can schedule a few updates to post to your social profiles when you're gone. HootSweet!

Scheduling updates is good for your business so that you aren't completely out of sight while you're gone. Many businesses even let their community know that they will be gone but will be posting useful content or some of their best past blog posts. This technique is a good practice because your community members will know not to expect immediate return messages if they respond to a posting.

To schedule a post with HootSuite, compose your message just as you would a normal message; select the social media profile(s) to which you want the message to be sent; and then click the calendar icon below the update window, shown in Figure 4-10, to choose the time and date to send the message.

Figure 4-10: Click the calendar icon to schedule your message.

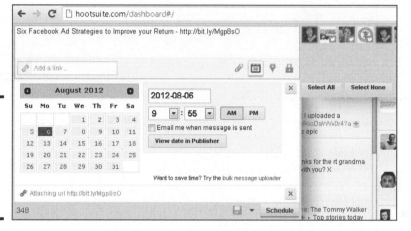

After you have the time and date set, click the Schedule button, which replaces the Send Now button.

Using Other Posting Applications

Many other applications are available that post to your Facebook Profile, your Page, and other social media profiles from one place. In fact, there are so many ways you can post to multiple social media profiles at once, that we can't possibly list them all. All the applications have different features — some include automatic scheduling, some have statistics, and some have bulk uploading.

Understand that this isn't an exhaustive list and that you have to choose which features are most important to you. Some of these applications are free, and others have a monthly fee. Many of them offer a few features for free but more options with a paid subscription.

SocialOomph

This web-based tool (available at www.socialoomph.com) focuses mainly on Twitter, but the paid version lets you update Facebook Profiles and Pages. As of this writing, the paid version is $17.97 every two weeks (a little different than your traditional weekly or monthly billing cycles), but some of the features are quite useful, as shown in Figure 4-11.

For example, you can bulk upload a file of posts and schedule them. Or you can use posts into a set of status queue reservoirs so that you always have posts to draw on when you need them. You can reword the post a bit and post it out again for some of the "evergreen" content on your website.

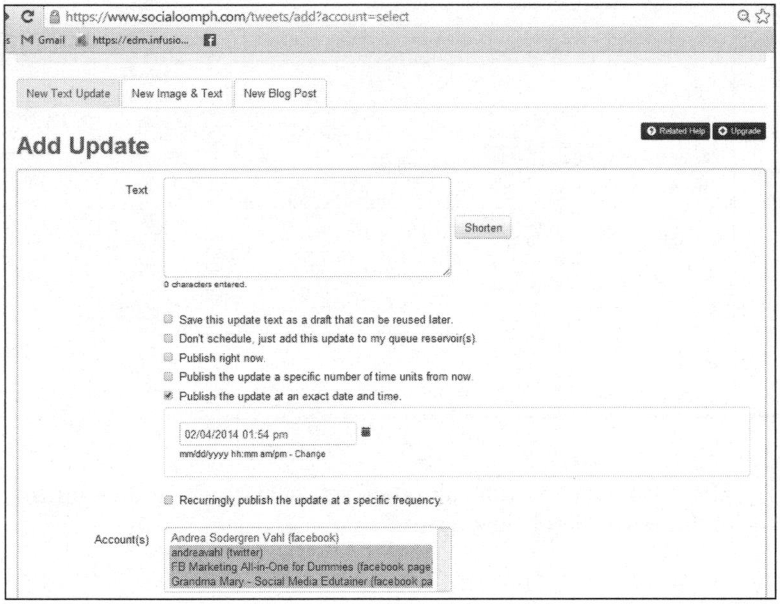

Figure 4-11: Use Social-Ooomph for bulk uploading posts and recycling posts.

Buffer

This tool, available at www.bufferapp.com and shown in Figure 4-12, can schedule your posts to your sites a few different ways. You can either

✦ **Let the application decide when to post based on times that it determines are the optimal times to share content for your audience.** For example, if your audience is more active in the evening, your posts can be sent in the evening.

✦ **Program the times to post the content for each social site.** For example, you can program that you want four tweets per day going out at 7 a.m., 11 a.m., 1 p.m., and 4 p.m. You can also select that you want two

Facebook posts per day: one at 9 a.m. and one at 2 p.m. Now you can "fill your buffer" with content, and the application puts the posts in the appropriate time slots for each social site. You can also program different posting schedules for each day of the week. Pretty slick!

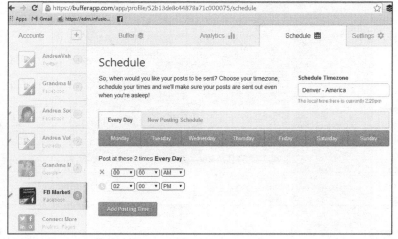

Figure 4-12: Use Buffer to schedule your posts at particular times.

Book III
Chapter 4

Connecting Your Page to Twitter

One other cool feature of Buffer is the available Chrome extension. If you're using Chrome as your web browser, you essentially click one button at the top of the browser to add an item to your Buffer contents. So if you're browsing around the web and you find an interesting article that you know you want to share to your social sites, just click the button, and a pop-up appears to add the content to your Buffer. Okay, it's really *two* clicks, but having a second click ensures that you really want to share the content.

After the Buffer free trial, plans start as low as $8.50 per month.

Sprout Social

This tool, available at `http://sproutsocial.com`, also offers some helpful reporting features that you can use to automatically create shareable reports regarding your social media activity and growth. See Figure 4-13. The reports are especially useful if you're managing someone else's Facebook and/or Twitter accounts so you can easily show what has happened over the last month with their accounts.

You can monitor different "feeds" for content like a Twitter list, RSS feed, or LinkedIn news feed and then share posts from those Feeds. Sprout Social has a free trial and then starts at $39 per month.

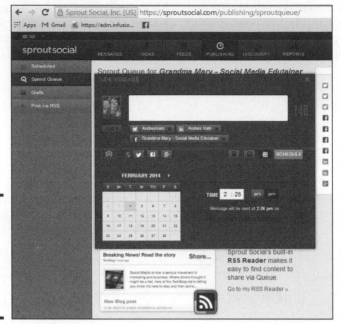

Figure 4-13:
Use Sprout
Social for
scheduling
and posting
as well as
reports.

We've touched on only a small sample of the posting clients that are available. More are being added every day! Some of these clients have analytics that track your followers, keywords, and retweets or give you the ability to schedule your updates in the future. Some have free features; others are available for a subscription price.

Adding a Twitter Tab to Your Facebook Page

Another thing you can do to connect Facebook and Twitter is add a custom tab to your Facebook Page that shows your recent tweets. (We cover adding applications more extensively in Book V.)

Adding an application like this can be a good way to add a little pizzazz to your Page and to let people know about your Twitter profile. You can use a few applications to showcase your tweets, but Woobox is one of the best options — and it's free! Another notable option for adding a Twitter tab is TabSite.

To install the Woobox Twitter application, just go to www.woobox.com, and follow these steps:

1. **Click the green Get Started for Free button.**

If you're not logged in already, you're prompted to log in to your Facebook account.

2. **Log in to Facebook.**

   You may be prompted to allow Woobox to manage your Pages and allow access your profile. If so, click Allow, and you'll go to the Woobox dashboard.

3. **Select Static Tabs at the top of the page.**

   You see a list of all your tabs.

4. **Select Create a New Tab, as shown in Figure 4-14.**

   A drop-down menu appears.

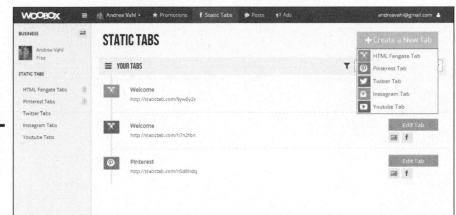

Figure 4-14: Select the Twitter Tab to add to your Page.

Book III Chapter 4

Connecting Your Page to Twitter

5. **Select Twitter Tab.**

   You're taken to a screen to customize the tab, as shown in Figure 4-15.

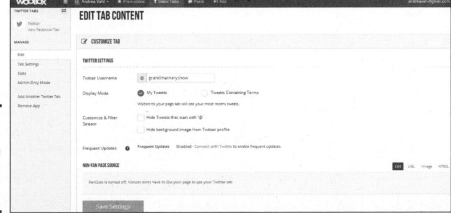

Figure 4-15: Add the features you want on your Twitter tab.

6. **Enter your Twitter username in the box, make any other changes, and then click Save Settings, as shown in Figure 4-15.**

   You don't have to add the @ symbol in the text box. Just add your Twitter username.

   Your Twitter tab is added to your Page. You can view it by clicking View Facebook Tab on the upper left.

You can also see your Twitter tab in your list of apps under the More link below your cover photo on your Page. You may want to switch the order of the applications or include a custom Cover photo. See Book V, Chapter 1, for information on how to do this.

Chapter 5: The Fine Print: Legal and Other Considerations

In This Chapter

✏ **Finding the fine print**

✏ **Complying with the Federal Trade Commission**

✏ **Posting content for regulated industries**

Remember when you signed up for Facebook, and you selected the check box agreeing to Facebook Terms and Policies? You sat down and read all that fine print right then and there before agreeing, right? Surrre, you did. As most of us do, you probably just clicked OK or Agree or whatever you needed to do to get into the site as quickly as possible.

The good news is that the Facebook Terms and Policies are fairly manageable, with no online bullying, no virus uploading, and no general law-breaking. But don't overlook point 1 in the Safety section:

> *You will not send or otherwise post unauthorized commercial communications (such as spam) on Facebook.*

That's vague at best. Allow us to explain a bit better in this chapter, with some guidelines for staying on the right side of Facebook — and U.S. federal law — as you embark on your Facebook marketing endeavors.

Digesting Legal Considerations

The first step in figuring out the legal considerations is finding them! The main site for the Facebook Terms and Policies is `www.facebook.com/policies`. Within this page, you can find links to many other lists of terms and policies, such as Ads and Sponsored Stories, Pages, Promotions, and Platform Policies (for Developers).

Facebook does monitor these Terms and Policies although not always thoroughly, because after all, it can't be everywhere at once. And yes, Facebook will indeed disable your account if you violate these terms.

We've frequently seen enforcement against spam. You may (or may not) know, however, that you can send messages to people who aren't your Friends. This ability is helpful sometimes, say when you need to get a private message to someone who likes your Page but who isn't a personal Facebook Friend. The problem with sending messages to people who aren't your Friends on Facebook is that you don't know "how much" is "too much." Facebook doesn't specify how many messages you can send without getting banned. Typically, you aren't going to be sending many messages to people you aren't Friends with, so you should be riding on the right side of Facebook law.

If you go to the Profiles of people you aren't Friends with, you see a Message button if they've allowed people who aren't their Friends to message them. If you click the button, you can send a message even though you aren't Friends with that person. In Figure 5-1, you see a profile of someone named Molly, and you can see that we're not Friends with Molly. We can't see some of her personal information — but we can send her a message.

Figure 5-1: Send a private message from your personal account.

If you send a message to too many people you don't know, though — especially if the message contains a link to a website — you'll get a warning from Facebook. If you continue sending messages like this, your account will be disabled. Not good. So the message (ha!) here is that you *can* send messages to people you don't know — just don't send too many simultaneously. We recommend sending ten or fewer messages a week to people you don't know if you need to contact people you aren't Friends with on Facebook.

Another important aspect of sending messages to people you don't know is that your message typically ends up in the Other folder of the Facebook Messages area. Most people don't check this folder regularly, if at all. Facebook sometimes gives you the option to pay $1 to get the message into the main Inbox, but not with every message.

You can't send any Facebook messages actively as your Facebook Page. You can respond to Facebook messages that come into your Page only if you have the Message button activated. (See Book II, Chapter 3 for more information on the Message button.) You can send Facebook messages only through your personal Profile, in any case — to Friends or non-Friends.

Pages have also been shut down for violating the Promotions Policies. So, if you're going to run a contest or sweepstakes, or have some type of promotion on your Facebook Page, make sure you read through the Promotion Policies. The one that gets violated the most is the first one listed in the Promotions section: Promotions on Facebook must be administered within apps on Facebook.com, either on a Canvas Page or a Page app. See Book VI for more information on running a Facebook contest the right way.

You are also responsible for following the applicable local laws for running a contest in your geographic region. Consult with a lawyer if you have questions about running your promotion or contest.

The Facebook Advertising Guidelines are fairly extensive, and we recommend reviewing them before you run an ad (www.facebook.com/ad_guidelines.php). Although you won't violate any laws and your Page won't be shut down if you go against these guidelines, you will save yourself some time by starting your ad the right way.

Understanding U.S. Regulations on Testimonials and Reviews

Businesses often use their Facebook Pages to sell their own products or possibly to market other people's products and get a commission on the sale of those products. Using testimonials and reviews can help sales because people like to see *social proof* of a product: That is, if one person likes it or gets good results, maybe you will, too. Testimonials and reviews are good marketing tools. But you do need to be aware of some of the Federal Trade Commission (FTC) regulations concerning reviews and testimonials if you intend to use them in your marketing efforts. The FTC's job is to protect consumers from fraudulent business practices and general marketing sliminess.

In October 2009, the FTC released updated guidelines for how advertisers are allowed to show testimonials and reviews. You can find the regulations here:

```
http://www.ftc.gov/sites/default/files/attachments/press-releases/ftc-
    publishes-final-guides-governing-endorsements-testimonials/
    091005revisedendorsementguides.pdf
```

This document gives examples that can help you decide how to phrase any testimonials or advertisements you may put on your website or on social media.

One of the big unknowns in all these regulations is how they'll be enforced. The FTC can't monitor every Facebook Page, website, and e-mail sent out, of course. But as with every rule, law, or terms set forth by a governing body, it's best to try to comply from the beginning. All it takes is one disgruntled customer to bring infractions to light. You don't want to end up with some hefty fines from the FTC.

A fine mess to not get yourself into

The FTC fine is rumored to be $11,000 per infraction, but Richard Cleland, assistant director of the agency's Division of Advertising Practices, said this: "That $11,000 fine is not true. Worst-case scenario, someone receives a warning, refuses to comply, followed by a serious product defect; we would institute a proceeding with a cease-and-desist order and mandate compliance with the law. To the extent that I have seen and heard, people are not objecting to the disclosure requirements but to the fear of penalty if they inadvertently make a mistake." Richard goes on to say that there is no penalty for a first infraction, which is good news. That tempers the fear a bit, but as we mention in this section, you should follow the FTC guidelines from the beginning to avoid any issues.

The first change that may affect you is the disclosure of material connections between you and a company whose product you're promoting. If you're familiar with affiliate marketing, this change can affect what you might post on your Page. In *affiliate marketing*, a business compensates someone for sales brought in by that person's marketing efforts. The person promoting the company's products is typically compensated with a percentage of each sale, like a commission. Many companies, including Amazon, have affiliate programs to encourage sales through this independent sales force.

But the FTC guidelines, noted here, state that you need to disclose a material connection between you and a business that may compensate you for promoting its product:

255.1 Consumer endorsements

(d) Advertisers are subject to liability for false or unsubstantiated statements made through endorsements, or for failing to disclose material connections between themselves and their endorsers. Endorsers also may be liable for statements made in the course of their endorsements.

Many people comply with this regulation by stating that the link is an "affiliate link" when they promote a product or program. This practice is compliant with the FTC guideline. An example is shown in Figure 5-2.

Here's another way to be compliant: Post an explanation of the product being promoted, as well as a link to a site where someone could buy the product, and make a statement such as, "This is an affiliate link, but I don't promote anything I don't believe in wholeheartedly." (Grandma Mary states her case in her own unique way in Figure 5-2.)

Figure 5-2:
Promoting affiliate links to products.

Your audience will understand that sometimes you bring them products that fit their needs, much as you do your own products. As long as you aren't continually selling to them, they don't mind. Some people disclose that a link they're posting isn't an affiliate link, so that it's clear that they aren't making any money by promoting this product.

Many people "endorse" a product with which they're affiliated. Be careful what you say about a product as you post about it.

255.2 Consumer endorsements

(b) An advertisement containing an endorsement relating the experience of one or more consumers on a central or key attribute of the product or service will likely be interpreted as representing the endorser's experience is representative of what consumers will generally achieve with the advertised product or service in actual, albeit variable, conditions of use. Therefore, an advertiser should possess and rely upon adequate substantiation for this representation. If the advertiser does not have substantiation that the endorser's experience is representative of what consumers will generally achieve, the advertisement should clearly and conspicuously disclose the generally expected performance in the depicted circumstances, and the advertiser must possess and rely on adequate substantiation for that representation.

This means that you need to be careful about making claims relating to your product. If you have a weight-loss or health product, you can no longer say something like this: "Tim lost 100 pounds in his first 2 weeks with our product. Results not typical." Even if this claim were true, the FTC would like a clearer representation of expectations for your product. The reasoning is that consumers tend to ignore the "Results not typical" warning, and the FTC's job is to protect consumers. A good addition to the preceding statement would be something like this: "Typically, our clients lose an average of *x* pounds over *x* time."

Meeting Content Compliance for Certain Industries

Certain industries have more regulations than others regarding what they can share online. Some industries follow specific regulations outlined by law, and other companies follow self-created policies relating to social media and online activities.

If you're in one of the following industries, you have some form of guidelines relating to online activity:

✦ **Finance (investments, mortgage lending, banking, and so on):** Any financial institution needs to be cautious about what information it shares. Financial institutions are expected to keep records of customer communications, which could include online social media communications, and they need to be concerned about sensitive customer-confidentiality issues when interacting with clients.

✦ **Insurance:** Insurance agents are allowed to give advice only to people in the state in which they're licensed. This can pose a problem on a Page used by people from other states because you can restrict who likes your page by country, but not by state. If you're an insurance agent, make sure that your posts avoid giving straight insurance advice.

✦ **Public companies:** Publicly traded companies need to be cautious about making any forward-looking statements. The Regulations Fair Disclosure policy, introduced in 2000, states that all publicly traded companies must release information to investors and the public at the same time. If this policy isn't followed, insider-trading or selective-disclosure charges could be filed.

✦ **Pharmaceuticals:** Pharmaceutical companies need to worry about claims being made online and also about outlining adverse effects of their products. This restriction could include any statements made within the company's Facebook community itself.

✦ **Health care:** Health care industries have to be careful about patient confidentiality, which includes the fact that a patient/doctor relationship exists. They also have to beware of giving medical advice. Figure 5-3 shows a Page of Dr. Karen Becker, who is a veterinarian. Her About page clearly states that she can't give out advice. We recommend that you make a similar statement or include a link to your disclaimer on your website.

Figure 5-3:
In your
About area,
say outright
if you can't
give specific
advice.

If you're in one of these industries, you're probably aware of regulations and guidelines already set forth by the governing bodies related to your industry. This section is just a gentle reminder to be aware of your Facebook posts, tweets, and comments on the web.

Bottom line: You can still have a Facebook Page to connect to your community, but you may have to keep your posts slightly more social. You can post about things you are doing in the community and things that are happening in the office, ask fun questions, and do other things to promote your business in a general way.

Book IV

Building, Engaging, Retaining, and Selling to Your Community

Contents at a Glance

Chapter 1: Building Visibility for Your Page .253

Inviting Your Existing Customers and Connections to Your Page............................254
Sharing Your Page with Your Friends on Facebook 263
Adding Photos to Attract People to Your Page..269

Chapter 2: Engaging and Retaining Your Community 277

Creating Posts and Updates That Engage Your Readers..278
Creating and Participating in Conversations with Your Audience 287
Keeping the Conversation Civil...290

Chapter 3: Using Like Links and Buttons 295

Comparing the Like Button and Like Link...295
Answering Common Questions...296
Placing the Like Button Code..302
Generating the Code for a Like Button 303

Chapter 4: Expanding Your E-Commerce Products and Services 307

Understanding Facebook e-Commerce...308
Using the Featured Apps Space for Your Store...308
Using PayPal to Accept Payment 310
Finding e-Commerce Apps That Fit Your Needs..311
Installing a Facebook e-Commerce App..314
Creating a Link to Your Website Store on Your Page...315
Using Other Apps to Create a Custom Link for Your Storefront..............................315
Posting Facebook Offers 317

Chapter 5: Building Visibility for Your Timeline 319

Inviting People to Follow Instead of Friend 320
Connecting Your Timeline to Your Offline World...320
Creating a Cover Photo Strategy...321
Making Photo Albums Public...322
Using Life Events to Support Your Business 325
Adjusting and Adding Apps...326

Chapter 1: Building Visibility for Your Page

In This Chapter

✔ Letting everyone know where to find you on Facebook

✔ Sharing and suggesting your Page with your existing customers and connections

✔ Sharing photos to attract people to your Page

*I*n Books II and III, we explain how to design a functional Facebook Page. In this minibook, you find some practical ways to increase the visibility for your Page by letting people know where you're located on Facebook and learning how to share and suggest your Page to Friends.

Imagine that you open a new storefront. You want to send out notifications to everyone on your lists, both existing and potential customers, so they can find you. You need to do the same for your Facebook Page.

Some of your existing customers and connections are already on Facebook, but some (depending on your customer demographics) are not. At the ready are Facebook's built-in systems for attracting people to your Page and some time-tested offline strategies to bring people not on Facebook to your Page.

 A Facebook business Page is completely public, which means that anyone can view it regardless of whether he has a Profile on Facebook. People without Profiles won't be able to like, comment on, or share anything on your Page, but they can view all your posts and photos.

When you open the doors to your new Facebook location, you'll be stepping into a new type of marketing — one based on conversation, content, value, and sharing. The next few pages contain ideas you can use right away to add Facebook to your existing company materials and website, as well as some basic techniques using the Facebook Photo Album that are sure to attract people to your Page.

Inviting Your Existing Customers and Connections to Your Page

Think of your Facebook Page as a new bricks-and-mortar space. It has an address and is open 24/7. You just moved in, and it's time to let people know about it. The point is to build a bit of a buzz about your new place so people will like the Page and share it with their Friends.

Some businesses create a Page launch day to make a big splash with their entry on Facebook. Others go slowly and build their presence on Facebook over time. Pick the way that suits you and your business, but make sure you do all the following (that apply) to invite your existing customers and connections.

You might be able to get your vanity URL right after you create your new business Page, or you might need to have at least 25 people like your Page to be eligible for a vanity URL. Plan ahead, and if you need to, get your 25 people right away so you can use a more elegant Facebook address (such as www. facebook.com/SociallyCongruent) on your hard-copy materials. See Book II, Chapter 1 for how to secure a vanity URL.

A vanity URL docsn't contain numbers like this:

```
http://www.facebook.com/Pages/manage/?act=40641063#!/Pages/
    Socially-Congruent/147368801953769?ref=ts
```

Changing your hold message

If your business has a phone on-hold system, update it and add your Facebook address. Here are several great (made-up) examples:

Thank you for calling. We're so sorry you have to wait. Waiting makes me cranky, but if you are at your computer, why don't you go to facebook. com/johnhaydon.digitalmarketing and check out all the latest tips on using Facebook for your business.

Thank you for calling. If you are listening to this hold message, maybe we are out brewing some tea! If you're like many of our customers — you have Facebook up and running — find Planetary Teas and see what's steeping there.

While you're holding, you might as well go over to my Facebook Page. Yes, I'm on Facebook. In fact, you might find a discount or two over there that might come in handy when I pick up your call! Go to facebook.com/johnhaydon. digitalmarketing.

Adding your Page address to your e-mail signature

Most businesses want to add their Page name to their e-mail signature right away. You don't have to have your vanity URL yet to do this because you can hyperlink a long URL to simple text. In case you don't have a signature yet, we show you how to fix that, too.

Follow the instructions for the e-mail client you use to create an e-mail signature that promotes your Page.

Microsoft Outlook 2007

If you use Microsoft Outlook 2007, follow these instructions. Other versions of Outlook will be similar, but it's always good to check Outlook's tutorials on how to modify your e-mail signature.

1. **Open Outlook and sign in to your account.**

2. **Choose Tools⇨Options.**

3. **On the Options dialog box that appears, click the Mail Format tab.**

4. **Click the Signatures button.**

   Doing so pulls up the Signatures and Stationery dialog box. Make sure that you're on the E-mail Signature tab, as shown in Figure 1-1.

5. **Either select an existing signature to edit or click New to create a new signature, as shown in Figure 1-1.**

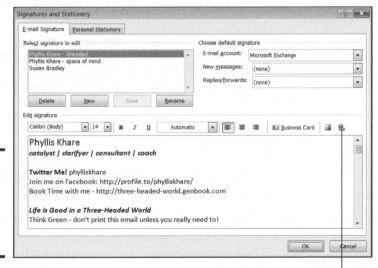

Figure 1-1: Edit an existing signature or create a new one.

Click to add a URL to your signature

- *Editing an existing signature:* Select the existing signature, enter your new text, select it, and click the Hyperlink icon, as noted in Figure 1-1. This pulls up the Insert Hyperlink dialog box. Type your Facebook Page URL in the address field and then click OK.

- *Adding a new signature:* Click the New button, and a dialog box opens where you can give this new signature a name. Name it and click OK. Then design your signature in the editing box. Again, to add a hyperlink to your Facebook Page name, type the name of the Page, select it, click the Hyperlink icon, and add the URL in the Address field.

6. **Click OK.**

When you create a new e-mail message, your existing signature autopopulates in the new e-mail. To change the e-mail signature from within the message, click the Insert tab in the new e-mail window, select Signatures from the Ribbon, and click the name of the new signature. Outlook replaces the signature in the new e-mail message with the one you choose.

Gmail

If you use Gmail, you design your signature a little differently than you do in Yahoo! and Outlook. The good news is that you can add an image to your signature; however, you can't upload it from your computer. You need to host images "in the cloud," which means using a service such as Flickr, or even Facebook, to store the images online.

1. **Open Gmail and sign in to your account.**

2. **Click the Options icon (it looks like a gear) in the top-right corner of the page.**

   Note: The Gmail Options link may look different, depending on which browser, and which version of that browser, you're using. The link may be labeled Settings.

   The Settings page appears and defaults to the General tab.

3. **Find the Signature section (about halfway down the page), and select the e-mail address to which you want to add the Facebook address.**

   If you have only one Gmail address, you won't see a drop-down menu.

   You can have as many signatures as you have Gmail addresses.

4. **Design your signature with your name and contact info.**

5. **Enter the name of your Facebook Page, select it, and click the Hyperlink icon.**

6. **Type or paste your Facebook Page URL in the Web Address field.**

   If you type the URL in your signature (for example, *https://www.facebook. com/GrandmaMaryShow* instead of *Grandma Mary Show*), the URL information is autopopulated when you click the hyperlink icon.

7. **Click OK.**

8. **(Optional) Add an image (a photo or logo image) to your signature:**

   a. *Click the Image icon (the one with the land-and-sky image).*

   b. *In the Add an Image dialog box that opens, enter the image's URL.*

   This is what makes Gmail's signature program different from the others. You can't just upload an image from your computer. The image has to exist somewhere online. Gmail will connect to that address online and pull it into the signature each time you send an e-mail.

   If the image you want to use exists only on your computer's hard drive, you can upload it to your Facebook album or to an image site such as Flickr. After you upload it, right-click it (Control-click on a Mac) and then choose Copy Image URL (or Copy Link Address or Copy Image Location) from the menu that appears.

   c. *Paste the URL in the Add an Image dialog box, shown in Figure 1-2.*

   A preview of the image is there for you to check.

   d. *Click OK.*

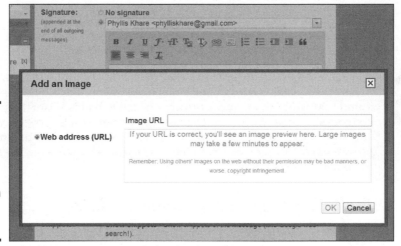

Figure 1-2: Add the image URL, and it loads automatically in each e-mail you send.

REMEMBER

All images online have an address or URL. You can use any image on your website, or any image hosted on Facebook or photo-hosting sites (such as Flickr).

WARNING!

Using other people's images could be an infringement of copyright. Use only those images for which you have permission to use.

9. **Click Save Changes at the bottom of the page.**

Figure 1-3 shows a full signature example, including an image, created with Gmail.

Figure 1-3:
Signatures
with added
links and an
image.

You can add some simple text to your signature with the link spelled out (not hyperlinked), as follows:

You might Like Us on Facebook, too.
`http://facebook.com/`*yourcompanyname*

Do you hang out on Facebook? Come say hi at
`http://facebook.com/`*yourcompanyname*

You can also use an Internet browser extension or application to create a signature that contains a Facebook icon linked to your Page. The best one we've found that works in all major browser-based e-mail is WiseStamp. When you go to `www.wisestamp.com`, the site figures out which browser you're using and shows you the correct download link. Then just follow the instructions provided. When your e-mail recipients click the Facebook icon, they go straight to your Facebook Page.

Including your new Facebook address on hard copy mailings

Some businesses dedicate a hard copy mailing to their customers to tell them about their new Facebook Page. You can include the announcement in a regular mailing or create a special one, but if your customers read what you send them in the mail (postcards, brochures, newsletters), you need to make the announcement in that medium, too.

Many companies are now including in all their hard copy mailings a small social connection area that shows their online connections, including their website address, YouTube channel, Twitter username, LinkedIn company page address, and more.

Updating your letterhead and stationery

You need to have your vanity URL before you update your letterhead. As we discuss earlier in this chapter, you may need 25 people to like your Page to be eligible to get one. Then you can add an elegant URL, like `www.facebook.com/SociallyCongruent`, to your stationery, as shown in Figure 1-4.

Figure 1-4:
A Facebook address can be added to any letterhead design.

Including a Facebook icon on your web page

Web pages now commonly feature a Facebook icon. In fact, a website without one seems to be missing something. You eventually want to integrate everything Facebook has to offer with your website. See Book VII (on advanced marketing) for everything Facebook offers. For now, a simple first step is to connect your website to Facebook.

Putting a linked Facebook icon on your website or blog is very easy. All you need are your Facebook Page URL address and an image of the icon you want to use. You can even do this before you secure your vanity URL. You can have a graphic designer create an icon image for you or use an existing one, as shown in Figure 1-5.

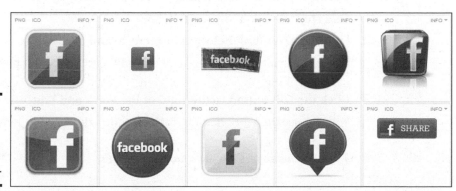

Figure 1-5:
Standard Facebook icon images you can use.

A great source of Facebook icon images is Iconfinder (`www.iconfinder.com`). Enter **Facebook** in the search bar and then select the icon you prefer. The drop-down menu gives you three options: No License Filtering, For Commercial Use, and No Link Back. We suggest opting for No Link Back because it's the simplest to use.

After you select the appropriate category, find an icon that blends well with your website. Select it and then select the size you need. If you don't know what size you need, download all the sizes and save them to your computer. Then you need to send these images to your webmaster to place on your website or do the job yourself.

If you're using a WordPress, Joomla!, or Drupal template for your website, you may find that Facebook icons are built into the template offerings, and all you need to do is add your Facebook Page address to activate the icon on your website. Many plug-ins for those systems allow you to add a Facebook icon and link it to your Page. You need to explore your website-creation system and see whether this feature is available.

If you're using an HTML system to create your website, you can create your own linked image and then upload the new HTML page with the new icon (with the link code) to your server. If that last sentence made no sense to you, you need to talk to your webmaster or website designer.

Linking to your Page from your Profile

If your Page is a service that you offer, go back to your Facebook Profile and add a little bit to your About tab about your new Page's location. If your business is something that you want to keep completely separate from your Profile on Facebook, you can skip these steps. Book II, Chapter 2 covers how to edit your About tab.

To link to your business Page from your Profile, follow these steps:

1. **Click your name in the top-right corner of any page on Facebook.**

   This step takes you to your Timeline.

2. **Find the About link below your picture, and click it.**

   You go to an interface where you can edit all the bits and pieces of your personal account.

3. **Click the Edit button to the right of the Work and Education heading.**

   You can use the Work and Education section to add your new Page address.

4. **Type the name of your new business Page.**

5. **When you see the Page come up in the suggestions, click it to add it to your Work section.**

   Fill in your position and any other important information (address and so on).

6. **Click the Add Job button.**

7. **Click the Done Editing button.**

Figure 1-6 shows how the editing space looks on the Timeline.

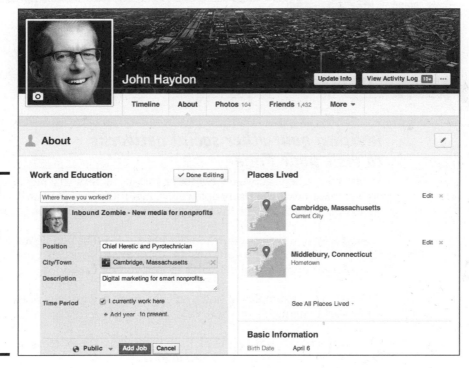

Figure 1-6: This screen is where you add your business Page location on your personal Timeline.

Make sure that the viewing option is set to Public so that people will be able to see your Page linked and be able to click through to it. You can change the icon by clicking the drop-down arrow while you're in Editing view and selecting the world icon (Public).

Another creative idea is to put your business Page URL on your Profile's Cover photo. You have to do a little photo editing, but the result will help move people over to your Page. Or you can put your website address on the image, as in Figure 1-7.

Figure 1-7:
Modify your personal Cover image to show people where you want them to find you.

Inviting your other social networks to visit your Page

Maybe you've been active on Twitter or various niche social media sites, and now you want to invite the people you've met there to visit your Page. You can get people to click the link to check you out, but you want them to like you, too.

A good way to develop a flow to your Page — so that people are asking questions or commenting on your posts — is to invite your most engaged members of your other social networks to join you on Facebook.

Here are some examples of how you can connect your Facebook Page with other social media:

✦ **Twitter:** Add your Facebook Page link to any Direct Messages you already have going out to new followers.

✦ **LinkedIn:** Add your Facebook link to any message you send, and make sure that it's listed on your Profile.

✦ **YouTube:** Add your link to any YouTube channel in the info section and to the first line of each video's description section. You can also use the LinkedTube service (www.linkedtube.com) to create a clickable link right on the video itself.

Every social media system has a place to add links; be sure to go to each one you already use and add your new Facebook Page address.

After you add the link to your Page on your other networks, you can start to invite people to your Page through your regular posts and updates. One of the attractive things about a Facebook Page is that you can have a longer conversation than the 140-character limit in Twitter, so your Twitter followers might enjoy a longer conversation with you on Facebook.

On a regular basis, create a post that links back to your Page on all your other social networks. You can also post the direct links to any photo or album you've created. See the upcoming section, "Sharing your albums and photos." This is a nice way to invite people to see your Page and (ideally) stick around and like it.

Growing your Page manually or buying automatic fans

The debate between growing your Page manually and buying automatic fans is a controversial subject. As much as we'd like to take the middle ground on this, we recommend that you grow your Page organically. It's always better to have people on your Page who are real, engaged fans of your product or service rather than to pay companies for any "Get fans fast!" services you hear about or see online.

Think creatively about contests, games, applications, and other forms of Page building rather than buying your way into Facebook fame. See Books V–VIII for those strategies.

Sharing Your Page with Your Friends on Facebook

You have several ways to invite your Friends to like your Page:

+ As a Page administrator, you can use the Invite Friends link in your Admin panel.

+ As an admin, you can invite your e-mail contacts to like your Page.

+ You and everyone else can share the Page. Sharing a Page puts the invitation in the sharee's Notifications.

If you don't want any of your Friends to be invited to be connected to this Page, you can skip inviting and sharing.

Still, you may want to go through the steps to share your Page because these steps are the same ones you'll want your supporters to duplicate to show your Page to their Friends. Understanding how sharing works allows you to craft the best message to solicit your Friends' help in expanding your reach.

There are countless other ways to bring people other than your Facebook Friends to your Page, but these ways are built into Facebook's own system and can be used effectively to create momentum toward an engaged community for your business. After you have a few friendly faces who have liked your Page, you can start to use some of the advanced marketing ideas in Books V through VIII.

Inviting Facebook Friends to your Page

Only the Page admins can use the Invite Friends feature. Everyone else needs to use the Share feature.

As an admin, to invite your personal Facebook Friends to your business Page, follow these steps:

1. **Go to your Page, and look above the Admin panel.**

2. **Choose Build Audience⇨Invite Friends, as shown in Figure 1-8.**

A dialog box appears.

Figure 1-8: The Build Audience drop-down menu.

3. **Search for and select your Friends.**

You have several ways to do this:

- From the Search All Friends drop-down menu, choose Recent Interactions, a geographic location, membership in a shared group, or members of your Friends lists (see Figure 1-9).

- Type a person's name.

- Click a person's Profile image to select that person.

4. **After you select everyone you want to invite, click Submit.**

The invitation will be sent.

If a person has already been invited to like the Page, it will say "invited" with a check mark to the right of their name.

You know your Friends. Don't overdo inviting because getting an invitation week after week for the same Page, either through Suggesting or Sharing or posting, can be really irritating. To find other ways to attract your Friends to your Page, keep reading this book!

Friends lists are created in your Profile. You can't create any business Page lists. One time when a Friends list is important for your Page is when you're asking your Friends to like your Page by using the Share or Invite link.

As of this writing, you don't get a chance to add a personal message to a Friends invitation. Your Friends can ignore the message, click the link that takes them to your Page and click the Like button there, or click the Like link in the notification.

Sharing your Page

The other main way to invite your Friends to your new Page is this:

1. **Choose Build Audience⇨Share Page, as shown in Figure 1-10.**

A dialog box opens.

A window is automatically fills with some of the information from your Page's Info section. The items included are defined by the type of business category you choose, as we discuss in Book II, Chapter 1. If you filled in your Info fields fully, you see a description of your business, including your Page's Profile image, all ready to send.

2. **(Optional) Add a comment in the status box above the invitation.**

Anyone sending a Share invitation can edit the title and the information by clicking in those fields and typing something new.

3. **Choose where to post it: your Timeline, on a Friend's Timeline, in a group, on your business Page, or in a private message.**

If you're posting to your own Timeline, you can also change who can see the Share post by opening the Post Privacy Setting drop-down menu (see Figure 1-11) and deciding whether everyone, just Friends, or others can see it. You have several choices, and you can also select Custom and then set who can and who can't see this invitation.

You should post an invitation to your Friends in many ways — on and off Facebook — to have them connect to your new Page.

Figure 1-10: Invite Friends to like your Page.

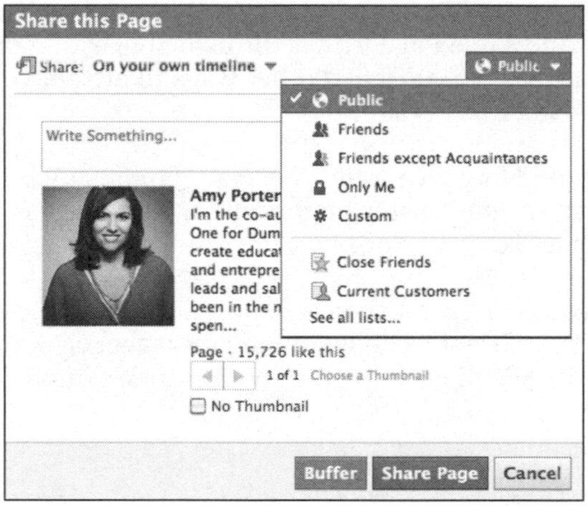

Figure 1-11: Set who gets to see your Share Page message.

The next few figures show examples of what the Share invitation will look like, depending on which business category you chose for your Page.

Figure 1-12 shows someone who chose Product/Service. It populates the invitation only with the Company Overview text from the Basic Information page. Look how much information can be sent!

Figure 1-12:
Only the
Company
Overview is
used in the
invitation
from a
Product/
Service type
of Page.

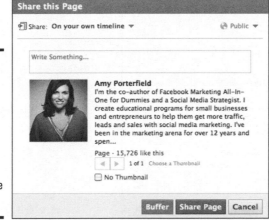

In Figure 1-13, the category is Public Figure, which populates the invitation only with the Personal Information from the Basic Information page.

Figure 1-13:
The
Personal
Information
field is
used in the
invitation
for Public
Figures.

Figure 1-14 shows what is pulled up for a Page with the category Musician/ Band. It populates the invitation only with the Biography part of the Basic Information page. If you don't put anything in the Biography field, the invitation pulls information from the Members field.

You may need to experiment with where you place text on your Basic Information page so that your Share Page invitation contains the text you want other people to see.

Figure 1-14:
The
Biography
section
might be
used for a
musician.

Figure 1-15 highlights a TV show. The invitation populates only with the Plot Outline text of the Info link, as shown in.

Figure 1-15:
The Plot
Outline
information
is used
in the
invitation
if the Page
type is TV
show.

The people who end up sharing your Page this way usually don't know that they can edit the Title and Information fields. They don't know they have control of the information that populates the invitation, so you can see why it's important to have the right category and to fill in the Basic Information section fully.

Sending requests to promote your Page

It's perfectly okay to privately message some of your closest Friends and business partners to ask them to share your Page with their Friends on Facebook. You can call them on the phone (imagine that!), e-mail your new Facebook address link to them, give them a handwritten invitation over drinks (it's been done), or use the built-in instant messaging (chat) system that Facebook offers. If your Friends like using the chat system, you can have a nice little conversation with them about your new Page.

You can see which Friends are online by clicking the Chat menu in the bottom-right corner of any Facebook Page. A green dot appears next to a Friend who is online and available to chat, and a phone icon appears next to a Friend who has her phone connected to her Facebook account.

If you click someone with the phone icon, the regular chat message box opens up, but the message is delivered to the phone. On Profiles and anywhere else on the site, clicking a chat icon starts a conversation with that person.

To send a chat message, simply type your message and then press Enter/Return.

Finding and thanking your key enthusiasts

Acknowledging the people who spread the word about your Page is always a good idea. You can offer an incentive or reward for their efforts.

The trick is figuring out who is helping you out! Currently, the only way is to ask. So take the bull by the horns, pop the question in the form of a Page update, (such as "Who has shared this Page today?"), and offer discount coupons or codes as rewards.

We've seen many creative ways of thanking enthusiastic supporters. The folks behind one Page we know offer free, live training to anyone that evening if they can get their like count above a certain number. If they can add 50 new likers to their Page by 5 p.m., everyone is invited to free training to create a custom video tab (see Book V, Chapter 2 on creating custom tabs)! This strategy has been very effective for this business.

Adding Photos to Attract People to Your Page

No matter whether you have a physical product or are in a service industry, photos sell and attract. You have many ways to use photos to invite people to your Page and to keep them actively engaged.

Collect many high-quality photos of your product, or shots of your service, or anything that relates to your Page's focus. Continue to collect these photos, and make sure to post them on a regular basis.

Read the information in this section to develop a marketing strategy using photos in Facebook.

Creating a marketing strategy with your Cover photo

The Timeline format features a large Cover photo, which we talk about in Book II, Chapter 2. Here, you need to think about how to really use this large image to your business advantage.

As we discuss further in Book II, Chapter 2, Facebook is very clear about not having this image turn into an ad or a billboard. Facebook wants to keep it kind of an artistic experience, which can be a challenge for some businesses. Here are some ideas to jump-start your creativity:

✦ **Highlight your fans.** Mari Smith does an excellent job of executing this marketing idea. You can see her images through time where she highlights a single fan or all her fans. You can go directly to her Cover photo album here: `http://on.fb.me/MariCoverPhotos`.

✦ **Show happy customers.** If you have images that convey satisfaction with your product or service, there's no better way to use the Cover photo space. A nice example is `www.facebook.com/CrustPizzeria`. If the happy faces are not currently Crust Pizzeria's Cover photo, click Photos and then click Cover Photos to see the Cover photos that show the happy customers.

✦ **Issue a call to action.** This strategy is a fine line to tread, but it can be done. Take a look at Amy's Cover photos for a few good examples here: `http://on.fb.me/AmyCoverPhotos`. You can't use the words "Click Here" or "Go to This Website," but you can put the title and date of an upcoming webinar on the image, as Amy has done.

Creating a marketing strategy with photo albums

Consider your business before you click the photo-upload link. Think about what would be interesting to people who already know you and what would be interesting to those who have never heard of you. Use the photo system in Facebook to its fullest, keeping in mind best practices for your niche or industry.

Take a moment to think of some really interesting Photo Album names that would promote your business. You always have the Album called Profile Pictures and Cover Photos, which will always contain all the photos you use for your Profile image and Cover images, but you can name every other album that you create.

If you're selling a physical product, for example, create an album called Happy Customers, and upload shots of happy customers using your product. Create an album called Found in Chicago for photos of your product on the shelves of a store in Chicago. You could use this idea in a contest; see more in Book VI on making Facebook come alive with events and contests.

If you're selling a service, create an album called Here I Am, *Doing It* (replace *Doing It* with your service), and upload photos of your staff doing their work, or showing you providing a session of your service. How about creating an album called Award-Winning for photos of your awards and achievements?

Your business might use humor to attract a strong group of fans: that is, likers. If you think that putting up a picture of your dog and labeling him the Acting CEO works for your customer base, go ahead and have fun with it! The people who really like your Page will most likely share these photos, so make them relevant to your business. They can be funny — and goodness knows, we all could use a laugh.

Uploading photos to your Facebook Page

Uploading photos to your Facebook Page involves the same process as uploading to your Profile except that you start from your Page.

Uploading photos to Facebook is a snap. Here's how:

1. **Log in to your personal Facebook account and go to your Page.**

2. **Click the Photos app box below your Cover photo.**

3. **On the new page that appears, click the +Add Photos button on the top-right side of the page.**

   Yet another new page appears.

4. **In the dialog box that appears, browse your computer for and select the photos you want to upload.**

   You can select multiple images by Ctrl-clicking on a PC or ⌘-clicking on a Mac.

5. **While your photos upload, fill in a name for your album (use the strategies described in the preceding section), the location, and the quality.**

6. **Add a description.**

   This step is very important because this text stays with the photo no matter where it's viewed. Try to incorporate your full website address or full Facebook Page address. These addresses will be hyperlinked and clickable.

   Include the `http://` part of your URL, your product name, or contact info in the caption field to make the link clickable, like the one shown in Figure 1-16.

7. **When the photos are loaded, click the Post Photos button.**

   The album of photos appears on your Page's Timeline.

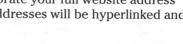

Figure 1-16:
Adding an
http:// link
is a vital
marketing
step.

You also want to designate a photo to be the album cover, which you do by following these steps:

1. **On your Page, click the Photo app and select the album you want to work with.**

    You can set the cover only for albums you've created. You can't set a Cover photo for the Cover photos album or Profile pictures.

2. **Click Edit.**

    All the images in the album are in view.

3. **Hover over the image you want to designate as the Cover.**

4. **When a small drop-down arrow appears in the top-right corner of the image, click it and choose Make Album Cover.**

5. **Click Done.**

Use Adobe Photoshop or other photo-editing software to create beautifully designed photos that will become your album covers. Upload these photos and select them as the Cover, and you create something very clear and easy to select when viewing and sharing.

If you already have a photo album created and want to add more to that particular album, follow these steps:

1. **Log in to your Profile and click your Page's name in the left sidebar.**

    You're taken to your business Page.

2. **Click the Photos app box below your Cover photo.**

3. **On the new page that appears, click the album to which you want to add photos.**

   The album's thumbnail images appear.

4. **Click the Add Photos button in the top-right corner of the Page.**

5. **In the dialog box that appears, browse your computer for the photos you want to upload.**

6. **Follow Steps 5–8 in the steps list at the beginning of the "Uploading photos to your Facebook Page" section.**

7. **Follow the steps in the preceding list to designate a Cover photo.**

Sharing your albums and photos

The marketing strategy behind sharing your albums and photos is something that you need to sit down and design. Maybe every Friday you send out a new album or every Tuesday, you post an image of your products that you found around town or in another city.

You can also share this album or individual pictures again, after publishing, from two places:

+ **Your business Page Timeline:** If you see your album or photo on the Page Timeline, you can click the Share link below the photo, as shown in Figure 1-17.

   You can put a call to action in the Message field when you share, asking people to share the album with their Friends.

+ **The album itself:** The second way is to go through the album, which we show you in the next set of steps.

Figure 1-17:
You can click the Share link below the photo album posted on your Timeline.

Boulder Book Signing
By Grandma Mary – Social Media Edutainer (Albums) · Updated about 9 months ago

Like · Share

To share an album (or individual pictures) after publishing, follow these steps:

1. **Go to your Page and select the Photos app box.**

2. **Select the album you want to share.**

3. **Click the Share link below the images.**

4. **Choose where to share the album by clicking the drop-down arrow shown in Figure 1-18:**

   - On Your Own (personal) Timeline

   - On a Friend's Timeline

   - In a Group

   - On Your Page

   - In a Private Message

   If you share in a private message, the link to the photo or album will go to the recipient's Messages section. You can also send the album to folks outside the Facebook platform by using an e-mail address, but they will need to join Facebook to see the picture(s). See the following section for more details.

5. **Select a viewing option: Public, Friends, Friends Except Acquaintances, Only Me, or any of your personal lists.**

6. **Click the Share Album button.**

Click to choose where to share the album

Click to choose a viewing option

Figure 1-18:
You can
share your
photo album
in several
ways.

Sharing with people other than your personal Friends on Facebook

You can send any photo or album directly to anyone other than your personal Facebook Friends by following the steps in the preceding section — except this time, instead of selecting to send it to your own Timeline, choose In a Private Message from the drop-down menu and type an e-mail address rather than a Facebook name. Facebook sends an e-mail with a link to the photo. *Note:* If the person you send it to is on Facebook, he'll be able to view it. If he doesn't have a Facebook account, the link will take him to a Page with the message that he can't view the photo unless he joins Facebook.

You also have a direct URL to each album that you can send to anyone, and those people will be able to view it. Or you can post anywhere online. To find this direct URL, follow these steps:

1. **Go to your Page and select the Photos app box.**
2. **Select the photo that you want to share.**
3. **Make sure that you're viewing the photo (it will be in a lightbox setting).**
4. **Copy the URL of the image from the browser bar.**
5. **Paste the URL in an e-mail message.**
6. **Send the e-mail.**

   If the person to whom you sent the URL to doesn't have a Facebook account, she can view the photo anyway as long as you have viewing set to Public. An invitation to join Facebook will be there, too.

Chapter 2: Engaging and Retaining Your Community

In This Chapter

✔ **Engaging people to keep them coming back to your Page**

✔ **Understanding and making the most of the News Feed**

✔ **Learning the art of responding to comments**

✔ **Banning and removing people and comments as a last resort**

*E*ngagement is the Holy Grail for Facebook Pages. To engage your target audience, you need to be clear about your purpose and branding, and let your own personality (or your brand's) shine through.

Best practices dictate that you can post almost anything to your Page as long as you adhere to the express purpose of having conversations with current and potential customers. *Remember:* Facebook is a friend network where conversations are the whole point.

If your Page is about DIY tips, for example, ask fans for their favorite DIY hack to create more closet space. By contrast, posting a video of your favorite *American Idol* contestant might confuse people. What's the connection between DIY tips and *American Idol?*

In Book II, Chapter 3, we explain how to use the regular posting features, status updates, video posts, audio, events, and other aspects of posting. In this chapter, we explore how to use those features to engage your community even further.

Specifically, we tell you how to use questions, milestones, and images to create conversations on your Page. We also explain why you need to understand Facebook's News Feed algorithm (how it affects who sees what on your Page) and how to create posts that will give you more views and engagement.

We explain the difference between what your visitors see when your Page has Highlights selected and how that changes when they select Posts by Others, Posts by Page, or Friend Activity, and how that all ties into Admin settings for your Timeline. Finally, we show you how to remove unpleasant guests from your Page.

Creating Posts and Updates That Engage Your Readers

Facebook has millions of Pages, but the majority are still trying to figure out how to attract an audience, authentically engage the people who might like them, and increase revenue. Many brands, on the other hand, have well more than 1 million likers and have figured out the best ways to engage their particular base so that a viral effect starts and they recruit even more people to their brand or cause.

How do they do it? They use these strategies (most of which we explain in the following sections):

✦ **Use Facebook-approved contests.** We cover contests in detail in Book VI.

✦ **Share the best.** Share your best videos, tutorials, resources, and quotations.

✦ **Ask questions.** Use both types of questions (see "Asking questions," later in this chapter) to see which works best for you. Encourage conversation by responding to all questions with an answer and another question.

✦ **Give attention where it's due.** Recognize fans with "shout outs" in updates.

✦ **Give away things.** Give coupons, discount codes, e-books, and other stuff related to your business. Make giveaways a regular activity to encourage return visits.

✦ **Acknowledge people.** Reward your community through activities such as Fan Friday, charity support, and random acts of thanking.

✦ **Respond quickly.** People are impressed when an actual human responds to a customer question or comment.

✦ **Post on a schedule.** After you discover the formats that your audience responds to most favorably, post in those formats on a regular schedule. Doing so sets the stage for the conversations.

Some types of posts resonate with your audience better than others. In the beginning, you might try a variety to see which ones work the best.

As of this writing, more than 1 billion active Facebook users access Facebook through their mobile phones (and devices). Make sure to view your Facebook Page through your device so that you can see what those people see. View it with the direct browser link at http://m.facebook.com and through iPhone and Android applications.

Consider these three scenarios and ask these questions:

✦ How do I get visitors to not only view my Page after they initially like it, but also return regularly?

✦ Do visitors *need* to return to my Page (for example, after posting a customer service question to follow up on your reply)?

✦ Can I send everything I want visitors to see in a post?

Asking questions

Asking questions or inviting your audience's opinion on something instantly creates a personal connection. People like to tell you their opinion on subjects that are dear to them. Your most enthusiastic likers have an opinion about your brand, marketing message, or community involvement (or lack thereof). Asking them to express those opinions can open the door to lots of conversation and involvement. To ask a question, simply post a status.

Here are some engaging ways to ask a question:

✦ Find a topical news story that connects to your business, and ask what people think about it. Post the question with a link to the news story for a bigger response.

✦ Pose a question you get from your potential customers, and ask your enthusiasts how they would answer it.

✦ Use fill-in-the-blank questions. The Life is Good Facebook Page (`www.facebook.com/Lifeisgood`), for example, asked this fill-in-the-blank question: "A positive life lesson I'd like to share is XX." There were more than 1,300 comments and more than 500 likes in just a few days!

✦ Ask a question with a one-word answer. Don't ask your audience to write a detailed evaluation of something. Some of the most popular fill-in-the-blank questions require just a one or two word response: "Chocolate — Dark or Milk?"

Giving away something

To extend the idea of asking questions, combine asking and giving: for example, "Who wants a coupon?"

The prospect of receiving discounts is always one of the top two reasons for consumers to like a brand on Facebook, so asking the question "Who wants a coupon?" usually gets a good response. We discuss creating coupons for your Page in Book VI, Chapter 2.

Measure and note your audience demographics. Note whether your readers prefer coupons or contests. (If you don't know, ask them!) Pay attention to what kinds of status updates they respond to and then do more of what's working. Think "incentive" all the time. You know what motivates *you* to seek something out. Analyzing your own behavior can lead to insights about what may work on your Facebook business Page.

Promoting your fans and enthusiasts

Nothing in marketing is more powerful than word-of-mouth promotion. We all know that.

So how do you find and encourage people to open their mouths and speak favorably on your behalf?

First, acknowledge them. You know how it feels when you've been acknowledged for something you've done. You can give that feeling to someone else on your Page in a variety of ways:

✦ Ask your fans whether they've volunteered for any charities or donated to one. Then challenge your fans to match that good will, or write a blog post about the charity and mention your fan by name.

✦ Publicly thank, by name, the people who are sharing your posts with others. ***Remember:*** Pages can't tag Facebook users unless they've commented on the post you're tagging them in.

✦ Have your Page be a place for fans to share what they do by dedicating a day to those posts. If your Page is dedicated to sustainability, be a forum for fans to share their best resources. Have a Resource Wednesday, a Sharing Saturday, or whatever suits your Page.

Many Pages use a Fan Page Friday concept, similar to Follow Friday on Twitter. Figure 2-1 shows how that looks on Boom Social with Kim Garst Page (`www.facebook.com/kimgarstboomsocial`).

Tagging key players in updates

How do people know you've thanked them on your Page? If they happen to see your status update come through their News Feeds, they'll see their names. But what if they don't catch your update in the News Feed?

If you tag them by using the @ symbol, they see the post on their personal Timelines and get notifications that they've been tagged in a post by you. This works for your Friends and Pages that you like.

Figure 2-1:
Fan Page
Friday is a
time-tested
strategy for
developing
your Page.

Keep these things in mind:

✦ If you're posting as the Page, you can't tag Friends or individuals in the main status update (but you can tag other Pages).

✦ If you're posting as yourself, you can tag Friends, individuals, or Pages.

If you have a lot of fans who are also Facebook friends, tagging them in page updates can be quite effective.

To tag a Friend or Page in a post, follow these steps:

1. **Type the @ symbol in the Status Update box on your Page and then start typing the name of the Friend or Page you want to tag.**

   Make sure not to put a space between the @ and the name you type; see how @Am appears in Figure 2-2.

   A list of all your Friends and Pages with that name appears.

2. **Click the correct name or Page name.**

   The name you click appears in the status-update box, hyperlinked to that person's Profile or Page.

3. **Finish the message.**

4. **Click Post.**

   The person or Page sees your message on her Timeline and notifications.

Figure 2-2:
Use the
@ symbol
to put a
hyperlinked
Page name
in the status
update.

Status	Photo / Video	Event, Milestone +

Great post from @Am

Amy Porterfield
Product/Service

Amazon
260,000 monthly users · App

Mejores Amigos
1,200,000 monthly users · App

Using public posts to thank people

Key players are your cheerleaders and enthusiasts. On Facebook, these key players can influence hundreds of people with their comments. Most of us take our friends' recommendations more seriously than those of strangers' we found searching online. After you establish who *your* key players are, thank them and encourage them to interact even more.

Through your Insights dashboard, you might find that women age 25–34 are your highest viewing demographic. Thank the members of that age group, too, by providing something valuable to them generally. For example, you might create a post that provides a link to something they value, such as discount codes for diapers, as a way to thank them for being part of your Page.

Consider your audience scenario

Most of the 1 billion-plus people on Facebook go through a process that looks a little like this: They log in and see the News Feed (the one that Facebook aggregates for them, which might not include your Page posts). Next, they scan the top 15 or so posts and maybe click through or comment on a few posts. They may watch a video of two. They quickly go to their favorite game, look at the clock, and realize the enormous amount of time that they just spent online!

Another scenario for a smaller percentage of people looks like this: They log in, and they know how to click the Sort link to see either Top Stories or see more Recent Stories. They scan through the Ticker commenting, liking, and sharing posts with their Friends. They notice the ads on the side and ask, "How did I get targeted for this one?" as they hide the ad, and request that Facebook no longer shows ads from that particular brand.

Another scenario, one that 20- to 35-year-olds tend to fit, looks like this: They don't need to log in because they never log out; they check Facebook via their phones pretty much all day. They filter their view to see only status updates, and that's all they view — period.

If you find through your Insights dashboard that a huge number of people from California visit your Page, say hi to them and thank them. You could say, "Hi to all the people in California who have liked this Page! Post a picture of you outside on your favorite hiking trail with our Brand Z hiking shoes!"

You can find a textbook case of using questions on the NFL Page (`http://facebook.com/NFL`). Just scroll through the posts to see the mix of videos, polls, questions, discounts, and giveaways. Most importantly, note the number of people who liked the post; also note the number of comments generated by that post. Check out their use of call to action via tagging in Figure 2-3.

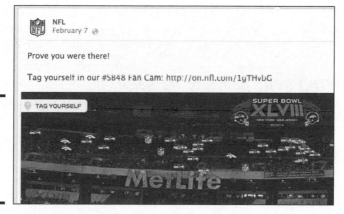

Figure 2-3: A variety of posts engage the fans of the NFL Page.

Creating a posting schedule

One aspect of engaging readers is how often you post. Good social media consultants tell you to post at the rate your audience expects. Say, every Friday you post a coupon code or Facebook Offer (review Offers in Book III), a clue to a treasure hunt contest, or a free training ticket. When you continue a pattern like this, people will start to remember and look for your posts on those days.

Your audience's expectations for your rate of posting depends on what you post. If you post breaking news in your field, for example, your audience depends on you to give that information as it becomes available. This can make for frequent posting.

Even different news Pages handle posting frequency in other ways:

✦ **iPhone Life magazine** (`www.facebook.com/iphonelifemagazine`), an online and hard copy magazine for iPhone enthusiasts, posts three to eight times per day.

✦ **GeekBeatTV** (www.facebook.com/geekbeattv), a channel of the well-known Internet TV Station Revision3, posts once or twice per day with lots of comments.

✦ **NPR** (www.facebook.com/NPR) posts as often as hourly.

Here are some examples of how often small businesses with a local reach post:

✦ **Noah's Ark Animal Foundation** (www.facebook.com/NoahsArkIowa) finds loving homes for stray and neglected dogs and cats. It posts adoption photos or videos once daily to help boost adoption. It sponsors Meow Mondays, Woof Wednesdays, and Foster Fridays. In between, it posts news about its dog park project.

✦ **Finnywick's** (www.facebook.com/Finnywicks), a toy store, posts only once per week and highlights a new toy that just arrived.

Targeting your posts to be seen

To know how to send your posts, you need to understand how Facebook decides where to post them. Your posts can show up in one of four areas:

✦ **Top Stories feed:** Aggregates the most interesting content (from Pages and Friends) based on a News Feed algorithm.

✦ **Most Recent feed:** Shows you the posts of your Friends and Pages you've liked and have conversations with on a regular basis in chronological order.

✦ **Ticker:** Appears to the right of the News Feed, and is where Facebook puts *activity stories* — actions such as someone liking a Page, subscribing to a Profile, commenting on a photo, and so on. Personally, we find the Ticker to be full of wonderful things, as you can see in Figure 2-4.

Posts could also show up in any custom list someone has created through a Profile.

Figure 2-4:
The Ticker shows activity stories to a wider audience.

Facebook's own research says that 95 percent of users view only the Top Stories feed. From our experience, we can tell you that most people don't know that Facebook's News Feed algorithm decides which posts will show up in Top Stories.

Try to educate your fans to click the name of your Page when they see it in the News Feed and then hover over the Like button to make sure that Get Notifications is selected (as shown in Figure 2-5).

Figure 2-5:
Let your fans know to select Show in News Feed.

In the Facebook iPad app, you also see a drop-down menu where you can further filter what you see: only posts by Pages, only posts with links, only posts with photos, only status updates, or any custom Friend lists.

What does this mean for your Page? First and foremost, you need to understand the News Feed algorithm so that you can deliver your updates in the best way for your likers to (potentially) see them. You also need to educate your fans about how they can adjust what they see in their News Feed by clicking the Sort arrow and changing it from Top Stories to Most Recent.

Understanding the News Feed Algorithm

You want more than anything for your Page to have high visibility and to show up in people's Top Stories feeds. A Page with high interaction ends up in the Top Stories feed, which means that more people will see your posts.

The algorithm that Facebook uses to determine the visibility of a Page post is based on four factors:

✦ **Affinity:** How often two people interact on Facebook. Affinity scores increase the more often you (or your Page) and a person exchange messages, Timeline posts, comments, and links. The more often a person who likes your Page posts, the better the affinity exists between your Page and that person, and the more likely your Page posts are to show up in that person's Top Stories feed.

✦ **Weight:** How many comments and likes a post gets. Weight value increases the more comments, likes, and other variables a post has, based on what Facebook is weighing at the moment. Places, video, and photos seem to have the most weight.

✦ **Decay:** How old the post is. Decay weakens the News Feed algorithm automatically as your post grows older in the Timeline; as time increases, value decreases.

✦ **Negative Feedback:** Facebook users can mark any update in their News Feed as being spammy, offensive, or simply unwanted. An increase in negative feedback hurts that posts ability to appear in more News Feeds.

Like and make a comment for each post made on your Page to engage conversation. You can comment as yourself (if you've selected that option) or as the Page. Commenting as both is good unless it just feels unnatural to you. One action — commenting — will help increase the Weight value.

If one of your likers clicks the Share link for one of your posts and likes it, too, the shared post has a better chance at showing up in the Top Stories feeds of his Friends (those who have the highest affinity scores with the sharer).

Using News Feed optimization strategies

We don't explain the nitty-gritty details of the News Feed algorithm (what's the point?), but we can explain a few strategies to help increase reach for your posts.

Here are a few proven News Feed optimization strategies:

✦ Encourage people to like your posts. Ask them directly, as in "Like this post to show your support for XX."

✦ If you have a Facebook Places Page, consider merging it with your regular Facebook business Page to increase the weight, or relevance, of what is posted. Before you do that, please see Book II, Chapter 1.

✦ Be sure to post photos, videos, and use Facebook Questions on a regular basis because they have more weight. Even better is having your likers post their photos to your Page's Timeline.

✦ Post when your audience will see the posts. Are they looking at Facebook daily or only on the weekend? Post when they're online and looking. (Find out in Book IX how to determine when your fans are seeing your posts.)

✦ Ask your closest Friends and key players to make comments on your Page as much as possible, and return the favor to start the conversation rolling and help shy people feel safer about commenting.

Following these easy strategies will help boost your News Feed algorithm and help deposit your posts in your likers' Top Stories feeds. It may also be helpful to educate your Friends and likers about how this system works. Many people have asked why they don't see posts from certain Pages and people. The News Feed algorithm is the reason.

Creating and Participating in Conversations with Your Audience

Creating and participating in conversations is why we're on Facebook. Having an authentic conversation that involves and motivates people feels good and draws more people to the conversation. All the writers of this book have found new and wonderful people through personal conversations on Facebook.

When you can converse with someone about a customer service issue or tell someone through a post how happy you are with that person's product, and he responds to you quickly and respectfully, a bond is created that will bring you back to that business. The business is counting on this reaction, and that's why so much attention is being given to the art of conversation in Facebook.

Optimize the settings for posts to your Timeline

When you create your Page (see Book II, Chapter 1), you make the decision to have the posts on the Timeline be just your own or open for posting by the public, as well. Most Page creators select the Everyone options to encourage conversation — anyone can post something. If you don't select those options, people can comment only to something already posted by the Page.

After you start to have conversations with people on your Page, you can modify those original settings. To review and possibly change those settings, follow these steps:

1. **Go to your Page and open the Admin panel at the top.**

2. **Click Edit Page.**

3. **Choose Edit Settings from the drop-down menu.**

4. **On the resulting page, select Posting Ability, Post Visibility, and Tagging Ability selections, as shown in see Figure 2-6.**

5. **Click Save Changes.**

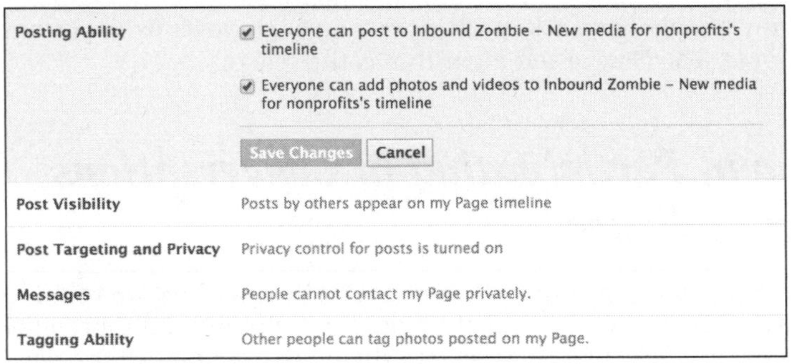

Figure 2-6:
Modify your Timeline posting options.

Understanding the different views people see on your Page

It would be a wonderful thing if we all saw the same thing on a Facebook Page, but because of the toggle views (Highlights, Posts by Page, Posts by Others), we don't.

By understanding all the different views a person can have on *your* Page, you'll be more educated about how to generate and participate in conversation with them. Figure 2-7 shows where people can toggle the view of a Page from Highlights to Posts by Page, or to Posts by Others.

Figure 2-7:
Toggle the view of a Facebook Page Timeline.

Facebook defaults the Page view to Highlights, which are determined by Facebook. Highlights are collections of posts that have the most interaction, posts that you've highlighted, and photos. The viewer can choose Posts by Page to see posts in chronological order.

If you prefer that people see your posts in chronological order, explain to them how to toggle the link at the top of the Timeline to Posts by Page. Some Pages occasionally create a post to remind people how to toggle the view. Here's some suggested text to use for that post:

> *You can view the posts on this Page in chronological order by clicking Highlights (right below the Timeline Cover photo) and choosing Posts by Page.*

If you let other people post on your Page's Timeline, you can toggle the view to see only those posts by selecting Posts by Others.

Being responsive and allowing conversation

Regardless of whether your fans select the Timeline view to be Highlights or Posts by Page, you still need to comment, ask questions, be responsive, and generally be available to the people who like your Page.

The best way to be aware when people interact with your Page is to monitor your Notifications section in your Admin panel and the Posts by Others view (or box).

You get perks with a conversational, friendly Facebook Page:

✦ You can nurture a community of people whom they can run ideas by or test new products on via giveaways. By having a friendly, responsive Page, you can realize many opportunities for testing and expanding your business.

✦ You get to direct the conversation but also should be open to the conversation going in a different direction from what you anticipated. More than anything, people on Facebook are looking for a community of like-minded people.

If you have a controversial subject on your Page, you gain respect by behaving like an adult when you need to be responsive. Allow the conversation to flow, but also moderate, remove, or report users and Pages if things get out of hand.

Keeping the Conversation Civil

Most of the time, the conversation on Facebook is fun and enjoyable. Occasionally, however, someone posts things on your Page that aren't congruent with your business — spam or rude, derogatory statements.

We hope that you never need to remove or ban someone from your Page, but you have a responsibility, as the admin of your Page, to keep the conversation going in a positive direction and in line with what your Page is all about.

Know the four types of posts to your Page and also how you can delete, hide, or report them:

✦ **To remove a post that *you* posted:** Click the hidden pencil icon to the right of the post and then choose Delete or Hide from Page.

✦ **To remove a post from your Page in which your Page was tagged:** Click the pencil icon and then choose Hide or Report/Mark as Spam. You can't delete this type of post, though, because it was created by someone else. The best you can do is to hide it from people who visit your Page or report it.

✦ **To remove a post that was posted directly on your Page (not tagged):** Click the X and then choose Hidden from Page, Delete, or Report/Mark as spam.

✦ **To delete a comment:** Hover over the comment, click the X that shows up on the right, and choose an option: Delete, Hide Post, or Report as Abuse.

After you delete a post, you can't undo the action, so be sure that you really want to delete it before you click the Delete button. The person who created the post isn't notified that the post was removed. The only way that person will know that it was deleted is if she comes back to your Page to look for it and can't find it.

Note: Deleting a post doesn't ban the poster from posting again.

Reporting a poster

Deleting or hiding a post is one thing; using Report/Mark as Spam takes it up a notch. This process is for posts that cross the line into spam, abuse, or use of violent words.

Anyone can create a new Facebook account, like your Page, and again post inappropriate comments. Be vigilant about bad apples.

We describe two ways to ban a user or a Page from posting to your Page. If you have a few likers, the first way is really easy to use. If millions of people have liked your Page, the second way is the only way to go.

Banning someone when you have a small following

If you have only a few likers and want to ban someone or another Page from your Page, go to your Page, and follow these steps:

1. **Open the Admin panel and click the See All link in the New Likes box.**

   A dialog box appears with a list of all the users who have liked your Page (see Figure 2-8).

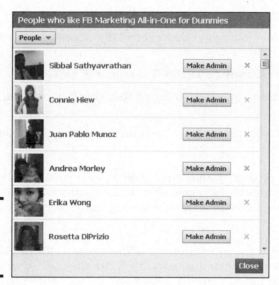

People who like FB Marketing All-in-One for Dummies

People ▼

| | | Make Admin | × |
Sibbal Sathyavrathan | | Make Admin | × |
Connie Hiew | | Make Admin | × |
Juan Pablo Munoz | | Make Admin | × |
Andrea Morley | | Make Admin | × |
Erika Wong | | Make Admin | × |
Rosetta DiPrizio | | Make Admin | × |

Close

Figure 2-8: Find the name of the offender.

2. **Click the X to the right of the user you want to ban.**

   A dialog box opens.

3. **Select the Ban Permanently check box.**

4. **Click OK.**

   Now this person or Page can't re-like your Page and post again unless he creates a new account with a different name.

Banning someone when you have a large following

The other way to ban a person or another Page from your Page — especially if a large number of people like your Page — is to ban her directly from an offending post that she made. Follow these steps:

1. **Put your cursor on the right side of the offending post and click the X.**

   A drop-down menu appears, with the six options shown in Figure 2-9: Default (Allowed), Highlighted on Page, Allowed on Page, Hidden from Page, Delete, and Report/Mark as Spam.

2. **To ban someone from your Page, select the Report/Mark as Spam option.**

   You will see a confirmation in the Timeline with two links.

3. **Select the option you want: Undo, or Ban This Person from Posting Publicly.**

   If you make a mistake, click the Undo link right away. You can't undo a banning later.

Sometimes a post crosses the line and becomes what you consider abusive. Facebook defines "abusive" as spam or scam; hate speech or personal attacks; violence or harmful behavior; or nudity, pornography, or sexually explicit content.

If you need to report a post as abusive, follow the steps for deleting a single post, choose Report/Mark as Spam, and then ban the user. After you submit the post, Facebook investigates the report and decides whether it needs to ban the user or the Page from Facebook.

Remembering that users can block your posts too

Just as you can block or ban users from posting on your Page, users can turn the tables on you by blocking your posts from their News Feeds or reporting your Page!

Not too long ago, Facebook rolled out a new feature that enables fans of your Page to hide your posts from their view (without un-Liking your Page). When someone sees your post in his News Feed, a hover card pops up; he can then hover over the liked button in the bottom-right corner and deselect Show in News Feed. This action effectively removes your posts from his view unless he visits your Page directly.

Deselecting Show in News Feed keeps the user as a liker of your Page but leaves your posts out of his News Feed completely. You can find out how many people (but not specific names) have hidden your Page's posts in your Insights dashboard. Find a complete description of the Insights dashboard in Book IX, Chapter 2.

Last, but certainly not least, anyone can go to your Page and report it. When you click the drop-down menu to the right of the Message or Like button on any Page, you see options that let you unlike the Page or report it (see Figure 2-10). If users report your Page, Facebook investigates you and your Page for any violations.

Figure 2-10:
Report a
Facebook
business
Page.

Chapter 3: Using Like Links and Buttons

In This Chapter

✔ Understanding the Facebook Like link and button

✔ Seeing the implications of using the Like button code outside Facebook

✔ Discovering how to create a simple Like button code for your website

This chapter explains both the Like *link* and the Like *button* and how to use them to engage your audience on Facebook and outside the Facebook environment. Find a fuller discussion of the enormous implication of using this Facebook integration tool in Book VII, Chapter 2.

Comparing the Like Button and Like Link

You can see the Like interface on Facebook itself in two ways. One way is as a link, which appears at the bottom of posts on Facebook. See Figure 3-1 for an example of a simple link on a Facebook post. The other way is as a button, as shown in Figure 3-2; buttons appear at the top of a Facebook Page.

If you've spent any time on Facebook — or on the Internet, for that matter — you'll have run across a Like link and Like button in many places.

Here are a few places where you'll find them:

✦ As a link at the bottom of each post in your Facebook News Feed

✦ As a link on the bottom of each comment from any post in your News Feed

✦ As a link on Facebook Ads

✦ As a button at the top of any Page you haven't liked yet

✦ As a button on blog posts outside Facebook

✦ As a button on a Facebook box on websites outside Facebook

The Like *link* is generated automatically for you in Facebook posts and comments. The Like *button* is also automatically generated on your Facebook business Page; you also can add a Like button to any website to which you can add HTML code. The Facebook Like button installed on your website allows people to share content from that site with their Friends back on Facebook.

Noland Hoshino
36 Reasons to life in Seattle (or Washington State)

36 Reasons Seattle Wins At Life
36 Reasons Seattle Not Only Won The Super Bowl, But Also Wins At Life
Between the Super Bowl, Macklemore's Grammy win, and the ever-increasing popularity of recreational marijuana use, Seattle is pretty

Like · Comment · Share · 37 minutes ago via The Huffington Post ·

Figure 3-1:
The Like link.

Like link

Inbound Zombie – New media for nonprofits
16,880 likes · 239 talking about this

Update Page Info Like Follow

Figure 3-2:
The Like button.

Like button

Answering Common Questions

If you're new to the Facebook environment, you might not know what happens when Like buttons and links are clicked. What will your fans experience when they click the Like button at the top of your Facebook Page or your website's Facebook Like widget? We also try to help you understand what happens when fans click any Like link on your Page posts or any ads you create.

Facebook marketing doesn't work fully unless you have a group of people who are connected via liking your Page. All the fun stuff you can do on Facebook for marketing really depends on this liking aspect. Without liking, none of those social-sharing advantages can fully come into play.

You can make liking your Facebook Page easy by placing the Facebook Like button in as many places as possible.

Here are some common questions you might have (and the answers):

Q. What happens when someone clicks the Like link on one of my Page posts?

A. As shown in Figure 3-3, a Like link will always be there when you post on your Page.

Figure 3-3:
There are many reasons to click the Like link on a post.

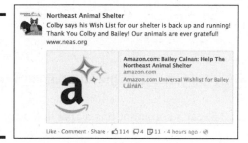

When people click the Like link on a post on your Page, engagement on your Page increases, thereby increasing overall reach for your Page throughout Facebook.

Each time someone clicks the Like link on a post, the post has a better ranking from Facebook. See our explanation of Facebook's Newsfeed Algorithm in Book IV, Chapter 2

If several people like the post, Facebook tallies the number of likes and puts that number next to a thumbs-up icon on your post, as well as wherever the post shows up on a fan's News Feed. If someone clicks the thumbs-up icon, the comments open; if the thumbs-up icon is clicked again, a box displays the names of the other people who liked the post.

When you view your Page as the admin and select the Notifications check box in the Admin panel, you see who has liked a post on your Page. Click the See All link to see all the notifications for the past week.

You can also scroll through the posts on your Page, click the numerical notation, and like any Pages (as your Page) by clicking the Like button next to their names. (*Note:* If you've already liked a Page, there won't be a Like button.)

The notification of the like also shows up in the Ticker, which is great because that expands the reach of the like. People may notice it and click through to your Page, or they may click the Like button for your Page right there through the Ticker. See Figure 3-4.

Figure 3-4: People can click Like in the Ticker.

Like button

Ticker

Q. What happens when someone clicks the Like link on a comment on one of my Page posts?

A. As shown in Figure 3-5, each comment has a Like link, too.

Figure 3-5: Liking a comment that someone posts on your Page acknowledges that you read it.

Again, clicking the Like link for a comment adds to the engagement on your Page, and that's exactly you want! Your like acknowledges that you've read the comment. That person gets a Facebook notification (which he can find by clicking his Notification icon) in his personal account that you liked the comment.

Q. What happens when someone clicks the Like button at the top of any Facebook Page?

A. As shown in Figure 3-6, the Like button at the top of a Page tells you that you haven't liked the Page yet. This Like button is one of the most important on Facebook. It's the button you want people to click!

Like button

Figure 3-6:
This is the
Like button
you want
people to
click.

After users click the Like button at the top of your Page, several things happen:

✦ Your Page appears in the Activity section of the users' personal Timelines.

✦ A notification goes on users' Timelines that they liked your Page (unless they modified their privacy settings to disallow those types of postings on their Timelines).

✦ The users potentially see your posts in their News Feeds. (This big topic is discussed more thoroughly in Chapter 2 of this minibook.) And a notification that you liked the Page shows up in the Ticker, as we note earlier.

✦ You can target your ads to users who have liked your Page.

✦ You can also tell Facebook fans that they can get notifications from your Page to make sure that they don't miss any posts, as opposed to depending upon Facebook News Feed to display the post or not.

When a person likes your Page, they join your community. Each person who joins your community is a *connection* (in Facebook-speak). Your connections consist of the people with whom you'll have conversations and who'll be spreading the word about you, your product, or your brand.

Those people are connected to your Page through the act of liking it. You have gained permission, by their liking of your Page, to communicate with them through your posts. Now your posts will hopefully find their way into their News Feeds, and you'll be able to target any ads to all your likers or subsets of them — a very good thing.

**Book IV
Chapter 3**

**Using Like Links
and Buttons**

Anyone can like a post, comment on a post, and share a post without having liked the Page. You absolutely want people to like your Page because of the benefits we list earlier; the door is open for anyone to engage with your Page without liking it first.

Q. What happens when someone clicks the Like link on my Facebook Ad?

A. As shown in Figure 3-7, a Facebook Ad can have a Like link or no link at all. If no link appears below the ad, the ad is notifying users of an event, or it links to a site outside Facebook through the hyperlinked title of the ad.

This ad doesn't have a link

Figure 3-7:
Some Facebook ads have a Like link; some don't.

Ad with a Like link

When a user clicks the Like link on an ad, that user immediately becomes a liker of the Page that the ad is representing. In other words, an ad's Like link is the same thing as the Like button on the top of a Page. Clicking the link on the ad and clicking the Like button on a Page do the same thing.

The added benefit of having a Like link on an ad is in having the opportunity to explore the analytics of who liked the ad and draw some conclusions about the community you're developing. We delve into ad analytics in Book VIII.

Q. What happens when someone clicks the Like button on my individual website or blog posts?

A. The blog post shown in Figure 3-8 has a Like button so that readers can show their support of the post.

You can set up the Like button on your blog post to allow users to post a comment to Facebook without leaving your blog. You can install a similar button by inserting code on your website, or using a Like button plug-in in WordPress. For more on this, read the section later in this chapter called "Placing the Like Button Code."

Figure 3-8: Don't make users leave your blog to post comments to Facebook.

When someone clicks a Like button on a blog post, she's liking the post, not the Page (or the website). When a user clicks a Like button on your website or blog, a short summary of the content — a *story* — is posted to her Facebook Timeline along with a link back to the content on your site. The user can have the story post on someone else's Timeline, to one of her groups, or as a private message. The story also appears in the News Feed, with the potential to be seen by all the user's Friends.

Sometimes a website owner changes the text on this button to read *Recommend,* but it does the same thing (as we note earlier) if it reads *Like.* You can also modify the code to allow someone to post a comment as he likes the post (refer to Figure 3-8).

Depending on which code you use (more about that in Book VII, Chapter 2), users cannot only like your post (and have that notification show up in their News Feeds), but make a comment that will show up on Facebook, all without leaving your website.

Q. What happens when someone clicks the Like button on a Facebook Like box on my web page?

A. Figure 3-9 shows a Like box. If you include a Like box on your web page or blog (discussed in Book VII, Chapter 2), your website or blog page has a direct link to your Facebook business Page. This means that when a user clicks a Like button on your Page inside the Facebook Like box, a connection is made between your Facebook Page and the user. Clicking that Like button in the Like box is the same as clicking the Like button at the top of your Facebook Page.

Figure 3-9:
Clicking the Like button in a Facebook Like box (widget) on your website is like clicking the Like button on your Facebook Page.

Your Facebook Page now appears in the Activity section of the user's Profile Timeline, and the user sees your posts in her News Feed. Your Facebook Page will show up in the same places that Facebook Pages show up around Facebook (such as through a search), and you can target your ads to those people who clicked that Like button. When a Facebook user clicks Like in a Like box on a website, she becomes a fan of that Facebook page, just as if she liked the page directly on Facebook.

Placing the Like Button Code

The Like *link* is generated automatically for you in Facebook posts, comments, and ads, and on your Facebook business Page.

You can place the Like *button* on pages outside Facebook by generating HTML code and then inserting it into your website's code so that it's part of every blog post you make, as shown in Figure 3-10.

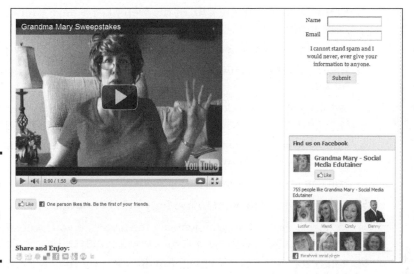

Figure 3-10:
This is
how a Like
button looks
on a blog
post.

If talking code accelerates your Geek Meter to the Overwhelm level, take a minute to read the very simple instructions in the following section to see whether you can figure them out. If not, talk to your webmaster; have him generate the code and place it for you.

 If you have a WordPress blog or website, plug-ins are available that do the same thing as this Facebook generator. An easy one to use is the Facebook Like Button Plugin for WordPress, available at

`http://wordpress.org/extend/plugins/fblikebutton`.

All the steps to install this widget in WordPress are in Book VII, Chapter 2.

Generating the Code for a Like Button

The following steps create code for a Like button. We're not going to go into the deeper development of code with Open Graph tags, which would provide you additional analytic data from liking activity. In fact, we're going to go through only what Facebook calls Step One:

1. **Go to** `http://developers.facebook.com/docs/reference/plugins/like`.

This is the page that generates the code for your Like button.

2. **In the form, enter the URL of the web page where users will like your posts.**

   Type your website's complete URL, including the `http://` part.

3. **Decide whether you want to include a Send button with your Like button.**

   We suggest that you include a Send button so that users have the ability to send a private message to their friends about your content.

4. **Choose your layout style from the drop-down menu: Standard, Button Count, and Box Count.**

   You can click each one to see a preview.

5. **Set the width you want to use for your Like button.**

   Choose a width that complements the layout of your website or blog. The default size, 450 pixels (px), works for most sites.

6. **Select the Show Faces check box if you want to show the Profile images of the people who like your post.**

   The faces show up on the standard button style only and appear next to the button. Having the faces of visitors' Facebook Friends on a blog post helps build social trust and encourages them to like something if they see that their Friends have already liked it. *Note:* Users see only the faces of their Friends, not of everyone who liked the post.

7. **From the drop-down menu, choose Like or Recommend.**

   "Like" is more widely recognized by Facebook users.

8. **Choose the color scheme for your button from the drop-down menu.**

9. **Choose the font for your button from the drop-down menu.**

10. **Click Get Code.**

    A dialog box pop ups, displaying two code boxes.

11. **Choose iFrames code or XFBML code.**

    eXtensible Facebook Markup Language (XFBML) code is more versatile, but you need to know how to use the JavaScript SDK. XFBML code lets you resize the button height dynamically (and, with a bit of code tweaking, to know in real time when someone clicks the Like button). XFBML creates a comment box to allow people to add a comment to the like. You may have seen on other blogs that when you click the Like button, a little text field opens that gives you a chance to type a comment (refer to Figure 3-8).

Modifying code takes a little expertise. If you enjoy working with code and are a do-it-yourself kind of person, Facebook has some support and training for you here:

`http://developers.facebook.com/docs/reference/javascript/`

If you aren't concerned about the deeper analytics of tracking and just want people to like and share your posts on Facebook, set up the code from the preceding steps and copy either the XFBML or iFrames code that's generated.

12. **Copy the code you want.**

Now you can place the code on your website or give the code to your webmaster to place on your site.

**Book IV
Chapter 3**

**Using Like Links
and Buttons**

Chapter 4: Expanding Your E-Commerce Products and Services

In This Chapter

⮮ **Creating a storefront on your Facebook**

⮮ **Exploring e-commerce app options**

⮮ **Installing third-party e-commerce apps on your Page**

⮮ **Using Facebook offers to drive engagement**

*N*othing says "engagement" like shopping. By providing your loyal enthusiasts a way to buy your products and in the same stroke share the news of their purchase with their Friends on Facebook, you could start momentum toward brand awareness with the potential of increased revenue. And as you know, that's one of the main reasons to have a Facebook Page in the first place! It all comes back to social proof.

Social authority means you have a reputation for being the expert on the subject of your business on social media platforms. *Social proof* (or *social trust*) happens when people try your products or services because they see their own Friends and connections liking your products and services.

In terms of Facebook, social trust is built when people see that their Friends have essentially said, "I like this." Imagine this scenario from your customers' perspectives. If they look at one of your hats for sale on your regular website, and you have Facebook's Open Graph application programming interface (API) implemented, or they click your Facebook Page shopping link, and right next to the Add to Cart button, they see thumbnail images of four of their Facebook Friends who already bought the hat, it brings social proof (trust and authority) and better customer engagement to your store. (And hopefully, it creates another sale for you!)

Here's a comment that we read on a shopping site on Facebook:

> *I like that I can still chat with my Facebook Friends while shopping in the same window. Easy way to get their input on my potential buys!*

This kind of social proof and real-time interaction leads to sales, which is why the largest corporations in the world are now on Facebook. In this chapter, we explore the world of social shopping and all the ways you can add your e-commerce to the Facebook environment.

Understanding Facebook e-Commerce

You should consider using your Facebook Page as an e-commerce store because

✦ Facebook is becoming *the* hub of all kinds of activity, including shopping.

✦ Free shopping applications make it easy for anyone to have an online storefront or store.

✦ Users engage more when you offer discounts, coupons, or other exclusive deals as Facebook shopping incentives.

Potential customers on Facebook like to stay on Facebook. They might see in their News Feeds that one of their Friends has liked your Page and then go explore what you have to offer. Keep in mind that people may spend more money if it's easy to stay and shop on your Facebook Page or right there in the News Feed!

Facebook offers four types of shopping interfaces:

✦ **Storefront:** The storefront appears in an app on your Page (those boxes below your Cover photo) and is a place to browse products. When visitors click the Buy button, they're whisked away from Facebook to the company's website store to complete their purchases.

✦ **Store:** This is a fully functioning store where shoppers can browse goods and purchase them without leaving the Facebook environment.

✦ **News Feed Store:** This is where the store is in a News Feed post.

✦ **Offers:** This built-in Facebook function allows you to create an offer (discount or code) that people can claim and then use at your store or on your site. It's a great feature by itself, and it complements other e-commerce solutions. As of this writing, offers are available only after your Page has more than 400 likes. You can find the Help section for offers here: `https://www.facebook.com/help/offers`.

Using the Featured Apps Space for Your Store

Facebook gives you three of the four featured app spaces on a Page, and you can use all of them for your e-commerce. If you have several types of products, you can use each app for each different product type. Your consultation services can be one of the apps, your e-books are another, and the third contains all your affiliate products.

Using apps for your e-commerce has both pros and cons.

Pros:

✦ You can replicate, or pull in through an RSS feed, an entire page from your e-commerce website. (You can use Heyo, covered later in this chapter, for this purpose.)

✦ You can create a call to action on the app image, such as *Buy Tea HERE!* or *Free tea with every order!* (You can change the image and the hyperlink for each app.)

✦ You can create an entire sales page using your own HTML code and direct people to your e-commerce site. (You can use the Static HTML app by Involver for this. For more on Involver, check out `http://www.oracle.com/us/solutions/social/involver/index.html`.)

Cons:

✦ As of this writing, if you copy the URL from the app page and post it in the News Feed, you can't see it from the mobile app. Still, many third-party apps are beginning to offer smart URLs that redirect on mobile.

✦ Generally, people don't visit a Page, preferring instead to scan their News Feeds. (You do this yourself, don't you?)

In the following sections, we offer strategies that help kick the cons and turn lemons (mobile view of custom apps) into lemonade (more clicks).

Posting product images

Regardless of whether you use custom apps for your e-commerce, post the images of your products. That way, you bypass the mobile problem. All images are viewable in the current official mobile Facebook app. In the descriptions of the images, remember to include the `http://` link to the website where visitors can purchase the products.

Facebook gives you lots of character space in an image description but shows only the first 400 characters before the See More link. (We tested this limit and made it to 6,000 characters with no end in sight.)

Keep these tips in mind when posting pictures:

✦ If you create an album with your products, you can also send the link to the album to your e-mail lists and other off-Facebook promotions.

Make sure that any text on the image takes up less than 20 percent of the total area. This way, you can use the image for a Facebook ad if you need to.

✦ Upload images of your ads and design them to fit the size limitations of the app.

Posting off-Facebook URLs

Because these featured app spaces don't show up in a mobile app, you can always post the URL of your e-commerce site in a regular post. The people viewing this post from a mobile app will be directed to your e-commerce site through a browser. As long as your e-commerce site looks great on a mobile device, you're good to go.

If your e-commerce is hosted on your own website, make sure it has a responsive design so that your site visitors can see an interface set up for mobile viewing. Interfaces configured in this way are quite smart, and can tell when a visitor is viewing from the site on a computer or a mobile phone and then show the appropriate view.

Posting an offer

We talk about using the built-in Facebook offers in Book II, Chapter 1, and in Book IX. We also discuss the topic briefly at the end of this chapter as a reminder of what wonderful features offers are. Facebook offers show up in News Feeds and are completely accessible through mobile phones.

Using offers is a good marketing tactic because people generally prefer to scan through their News Feeds instead of clicking ads or going to your Page.

Using PayPal to Accept Payment

Before you choose and install a storefront e-commerce app, you may need to create a PayPal account for your business. Most apps use PayPal for payment.

Using PayPal has these main benefits:

+ Many of your users already have PayPal accounts.
+ Those who don't have a PayPal account can use a credit card with the PayPal interface.
+ You don't need to open a bank merchant account to start collecting payments.

Setting up a PayPal account is quick and easy, but verifying the bank account that you associate with PayPal can take several days. After you have your PayPal account set up and verified, you can start installing and connecting any third-party shopping application, which we discuss in the very next section.

If you need help setting up a PayPal account, go to www.paypal.com and click the Business tab.

Finding e-Commerce Apps That Fit Your Needs

You can integrate many storefront applications into your Facebook business Page. In this section, we show you how to find these apps and choose the one that's right for your business.

Many of the hundreds of Internet shopping sites (such as eBay and Etsy) have realized that they need to integrate their sellers' stores with Facebook to stay current in the space where potential customers are already spending their time and money.

You can add your e-commerce products and services to your Facebook Page in many ways. The few we present in this section can get you started. The only limit is your imagination.

 Here's an important thing to think about when choosing the best shopping interface for your business: Are your customers looking for and buying products on Facebook using an iPhone or iPad? Many storefront apps use Adobe Flash, but as of this writing, Apple doesn't support Flash on any of its iOS devices, so many businesses use apps that post directly to the Facebook News Feed instead of to a custom app page.

 If you're a retailer or are considering promoting a product or service, check with the e-commerce system you're currently using to see whether that system already has a Facebook integration application.

Storenvy

Storenvy (www.storenvy.com) is a storefront application. It has a marketplace of independently owned stores. You can open an online store for free, and the Storenvy Facebook app lets you put an interface on your Facebook Page. When people click to buy your products, they go to your page on the Storenvy site.

 A storefront app opens on your Page (boxes under your Cover photo) so users can check out your products. When they click Buy, users leave Facebook and are taken to your company's website store to finish buying.

The app requires no setup fees, no monthly fees, no listing fees, and no transaction fees. You can have an unlimited amount of products, display up to five images per product, and fully customize your store. See Figure 4-1 for an example of a Storenvy e-commerce interface on Facebook.

Book IV
Chapter 4

Expanding Your E-Commerce Products and Services

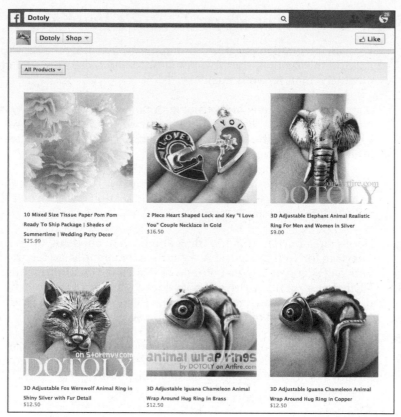

Figure 4-1:
A Storenvy
e-commerce
interface on
Facebook.

Ecwid

Ecwid (www.ecwid.com) is a shopping cart that seamlessly integrates with your existing website. You can also be added to your various social media sites, including Facebook.

If a customer leaves your Ecwid store on your Facebook Page without purchasing the items in his cart, those items remain in his cart. The next time he goes to purchase something anywhere on Facebook (using that same Ecwid app on someone else's Page), those items will still be in the cart, queued up for purchase. See Figure 4-2 for an example of an Ecwid e-commerce interface on Facebook.

ShopTab

ShopTab (`www.shoptab.net`) is a storefront application that's easy to set up. To use ShopTab, upload your products to the ShopTab website and then add the ShopTab application to your Facebook Page.

This application doesn't have a free version, but it does have a free trial.

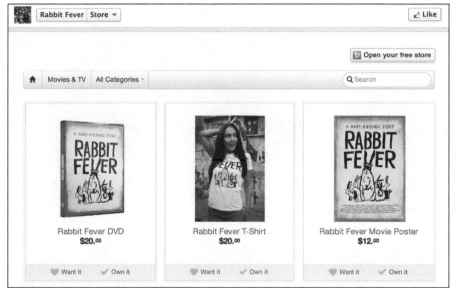

Figure 4-2: An Ecwid e-commerce interface on Facebook.

Etsy

Thousands of artists and crafters who are listed with Etsy (`www.etsy.com`) have Facebook Pages. Etsy has designed a way for users to post directly to the Facebook Page News Feed from the Etsy page. This method keeps products in the News Feed instead of on a stand-alone app page. This is a good thing because most people view just the News Feed, and with the higher number of customers using mobile devices to purchase products, the News Feed is the best place to showcase items.

See Figure 4-3 for an example of an Etsy e-commerce interface on Facebook. Notice, though, that this process doesn't place a Share link on the post. Someone would need to click through to the product to Share the item on Facebook.

**Book IV
Chapter 4**

**Expanding Your
E-Commerce
Products and
Services**

Installing a Facebook e-Commerce App

All Facebook third-party app companies make it really easy to install an app on your Facebook Page. When you decide on the app you want, the app will provide step-by-step instructions for the installation process.

You still need to adjust the hyperlink text below the app box and the app cover image, and those instructions are fully explained in Book II. If you're installing a storefront application (one that allows visitors to browse your products but requires them to complete the purchase at another website), go to the website for that application and enter the products you want to sell in your store. Then your product information will be fed to the Facebook app link.

If you're installing a complete store application, you can load product information right there on Facebook or on the application's website. Then your customers can view product information and purchase those products on Facebook.

If you're using a News Feed store, follow the instructions to create those great News Feed store posts.

Creating a Link to Your Website Store on Your Page

With a Facebook Page, you have many opportunities to link back to your existing e-commerce website without installing an application. You can

+ Create status updates with the specific URL of any products you mention.

+ Upload promotional videos with links back to your website's store.

+ Highlight your store URL on your Page's Info tab.

+ Include your store's link in your business Page's Profile image description (not on the image itself).

+ Use any of the other strategies that we discuss in Books II and III.

A very good way to connect an e-commerce site to Facebook, however, is to create a storefront link that takes you back to your regular website e-commerce Page, and we discuss that in the next section.

You can link to your My Etsy e-commerce page, eBay page, Amazon e-store, Tinypay.me pages, or any site where you sell your products. Just remember that many of these sites offer their own Facebook apps, and creating a storefront link with their official applications might look (and perform) better than just a link back to your website's storefront.

Using Other Apps to Create a Custom Link for Your Storefront

You can use several applications to create a custom app box on your Page that will link to your e-commerce website. The following aren't considered to be shopping applications; they offer ways to create custom links for your Page that can be used for anything, including links to your e-commerce web pages.

ShortStack

ShortStack (www.shortstack.com) is priced from free to $300 per month depending on the number of fans your Page has. You can create custom apps for Facebook Pages, websites, and mobile. The platform contains 35 widgets and applications where users can integrate fan gates, photo contests, sweepstakes, RSS feeds, Twitter, YouTube, and MailChimp newsletter signups. You can even edit the CSS for your tabs and see previews of how it will look along the way.

**Book IV
Chapter 4**

**Expanding Your
E-Commerce
Products and
Services**

TabSite

TabSite (www.tabsite.com) is a Facebook and web promotion tool priced from free to $30 per month for use on one Facebook Page and domain. (See Figure 4-4.) Larger companies and social media managers can choose agency plans. There's a free version of TabSite, or you can try other plans free for 14 days. They also have mobile options. TabSite offers photo and Instagram contests, YouTube channels, and coupon deal offers.

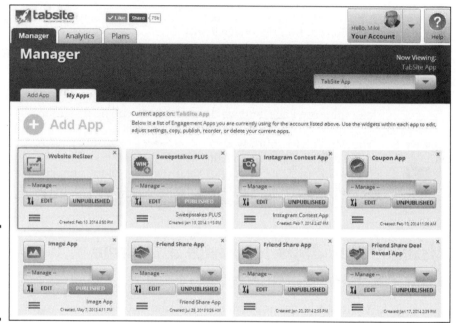

Figure 4-4:
The editing interface for a TabSite tab.

Heyo

Heyo (https://heyo.com) is a great interface that we're very excited about. It led the way with drag-and-drop applications onto a canvas. You don't have to know any kind of code to create a beautiful custom e-commerce storefront. The interface was built with noncoders in mind. Heyo comes in a free version as well as several paid versions.

BandPage

BandPage (www.bandpage.com) is an option to consider if you have a band or are a musician. This app offers a fully customizable storefront link for your music. BandPage connects your SoundCloud e-commerce site to this link for easy purchasing.

Posting Facebook Offers

We're taking a moment here to explore using Facebook offers because this feature is great for e-commerce, especially if your business is local. We discuss local business Page types fully in Book II, Chapter 1 and offers in great detail in Book VII, Chapter 1.

If your business has store hours, a physical address, and more than 400 Facebook Likes, you can create an offer for your Page.

Here's a summary of the great features that offers bring to your business:

✦ Offers reach more people who have liked your Page than regular posts do.

✦ Offers have a three-day life span without your having to repost.

✦ Claimed offers are another level of engagement that build loyalty because fans need to either bring the offer into your place of business or present it to you at time of payment.

✦ Offers are essentially free News Feed ads.

We show you how to create and post an offer in Book VII, Chapter 1.

Consider pinning the offer to the top of the Timeline for visitors to see right away. You can also use Promotions to get the offer in front of more people or run a Sponsored Story ad, all of which we discuss in Book VII, Chapter 1.

**Book IV
Chapter 4**

Expanding Your
E-Commerce
Products and
Services

Chapter 5: Building Visibility for Your Timeline

In This Chapter

↙ Getting people to follow to your posts

↙ Directing the offline world to your Timeline

↙ Using a Timeline Cover image that supports your business

↙ Using Public photo albums and milestones to spread the word about your business

↙ Supporting your business by posting life events on your Timeline

↙ Highlighting your business by rearranging apps

Can you count how many things have changed with Facebook in the past two – three years? Some of the most important changes happened with personal Timelines.

The biggest change for Facebook users was the introduction to Timeline, a completely redesigned Timeline that allows users to share stories and organize them by time (birth all the way to present).

Beside the transition to Timeline, Facebook opened the door for public figures to be able to post to followers with their public updates. This is big. We introduce this topic in Book II.

In this chapter, we look at a few specific things you can do with building, engaging, retaining, and selling to your community by using your Timeline.

If you made the decision to turn on your Follow button (see Book II, Chapter 5), you can do specific things to encourage people to follow your Timeline instead of asking them to be your Friend. All those things we discuss in Book II — about connecting your offline world to your business Page — come into play when you focus on your Timeline.

The most important thing to remember when using your Timeline to support your business is to make sure the public posts and public images reflect your personality. Facebook is a friend network where people interact with people first, brands second. Posting content that reflects your personality will be much more interesting to followers than promotional messages about your business.

Because Timelines have Cover photos too, you can develop a way to support your business with some specific shots woven between your more personal photos. We discuss how to make a photo album Public and how the visitors will see your Timeline. Make sure that to read Book II, Chapter 4 for basic setup information.

Inviting People to Follow Instead of Friend

In Book II, Chapter 4, we discuss how to modify your settings so that only Friends of Friends can ask to be your Friend; everyone else will see only the Follow button. Having a Follow button on your Timeline is a passive way to get people to follow to your public posts instead of requesting to be your Friend. What about some active ways? Here are a few ideas to try:

✦ **Change your wording.** When you're at events, instead of saying "Friend me on Facebook," say "Follow me on Facebook."

✦ **Educate your audience.** Explain why being a Follower is a good thing — your public posts are what people want to read anyway.

✦ **Ignore Friend requests.** People who ask to be Friends are automatically Followers. Ignore their Friend requests, and they'll still see your Public posts.

At some point, you may find a lot of people following your Timeline. This may mean that you're being "suggested" by Facebook. You can see the whole list of people who have their Follow button turned on here

www.facebook.com/subscriptions/suggestions

Occasionally, you see suggested people in the right column of your own News Feed.

Connecting Your Timeline to Your Offline World

Chapter 1 of this minibook includes a section on connecting your business Page to your offline world. That content can be applied to your personal Timeline. Reread that section, but replace *business Page* with *Timeline*. Also consider these highlights:

✦ **Change your phone hold message.** Say, "Follow me on Facebook."

✦ **Add your personal URL to your e-mail signature.** All the how-to's are in Chapter 1 of this minibook. Just change the URL you use to the your Timeline URL, and you're good to go.

✦ **Include your Timeline URL on hard copy mailings.** If you have fliers, posters, hard copy newsletters, and the like, include your Timeline URL, and include the sentence "Follow me on Facebook."

✦ **Update your letterhead and stationery.** As in the preceding item, use your Timeline URL.

✦ **Modify your website's Facebook icon.** On your website, use your Timeline URL as the link to the Facebook icon. If you have text with your icon, use *Follow* instead of *Friend.*

The most important point is this: If you're using your Timeline to support your business, make sure that you let people know about the Follow button located on your Timeline! Don't assume that they understand it or know how it works; just make it easy for them to click it and see your public updates.

Creating a Cover Photo Strategy

In Chapter 1 of this minibook, we talk about creating a strategy using the Cover photo on your business Page. The same strategy can be applied here, except that the nature of the images can be a little more personal. Here's a link to some fine examples to help you design your own: www.amyporterfield. com/2012/06/facebook-timeline-covers

To create a Timeline Cover photo that will support your business, remember these points:

✦ **Include your face in the image.** Faces are much more interesting than the best logos, and authentic action shots are very interesting to people on Facebook. Images work better than almost any other type of posts, so use this knowledge to rock the Cover photo.

✦ **Reference your business in the image.** You can have your storefront on the image, a shot of the inside of your store, or an image of you holding one of your products. All these images are perfectly okay to use as a Cover photo.

✦ **Happy customer faces need model releases (so have them handy).** Not many people realize this, but if you're taking pictures of someone else, it would be prudent to have a *model release,* which is a form that the person being photographed signs, saying that he knows his image will appear on Facebook.

✦ **Don't include any calls to action.** Think artistically about your image. Make it charming, attractive, and informative. You can't have text on the image that says *Try our hot dogs! 10% off your next order!*

You can see a nice way of presenting your life in Figure 5-1. For example, Mari Smith is dressed professionally as she does when she speaks at various conferences.

Figure 5-1:
Create a
Timeline
cover to
span your
personal
and public
lives.

What are some strategies you can use to have your personal Timeline support your business?

✦ **Do you have business events? Or does your business sponsor events?**
Both types of event provide opportunities to take photos that you can use as a Cover photo strategy. You can change out the image as the event progresses, or take a shot that shows your happy face and the event sponsors' logos in the background.

✦ **Do you have new products? Are you intimately involved with the development of new products?** An image of you working on a product would be a perfect Cover photo for a Timeline.

✦ **Do you travel with your business?** A shot of you at an event or on the beach after the event are good ways to promote without promoting. Great airplane shots of the clouds or the food you're eating in a restaurant in Singapore, with a description of where you are and what you're doing, are excellent uses of the Cover photo. Most people put these types of photos in an album, but consider them for the Cover photo, too.

Making Photo Albums Public

Think about the images you have that show you doing something in your business, such as holding a product or shaking someone's hand. You also may have images of the outside of your store, the inside of your store, one of your products, or a crowd of people at your last event. We could go on and on.

When you have a collection of these types of photos, you can create an album and upload the photos to it. Then you have a URL you can share that will take people right to the album. Because you're making this folder Public, anyone, whether or not he or she has a Facebook account, will be able to view the photos.

Making a new Public album

Here's how to create a Public album from scratch. Go to your Timeline and follow these steps:

1. **In the Update Status box, click the Add Photos/Video option.**
2. **Click the Create Photo Album option.**

   A window opens to select photos on your computer.
3. **Select the images on your computer that you want to upload.**
4. **Click Open to start the upload process.**
5. **Type a name for the album. Enter a location and date, if appropriate.**

   See Figure 5-2.

Album name   Click to designate when these photos were taken

Enter location here

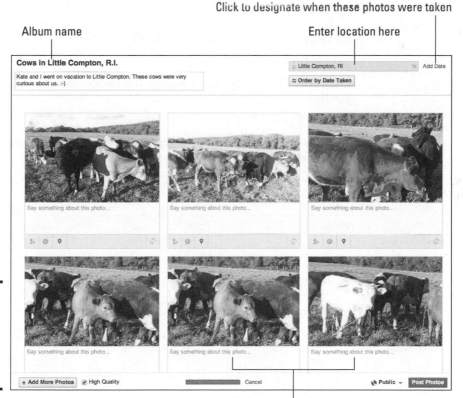

Figure 5-2: Give the new Public album a name and description.

Descriptions tell a story about the photo

6. **Fill in the description for each photo as fully as you can.**

    Always include an `http://` link to direct people to your website, product page, or your Facebook business Page, if it's relevant to the image.

    A drop-down menu appears in the bottom-right corner of the page; see Figure 5-3.

7. **At the very bottom of your album, select Public for the privacy setting (as shown in Figure 5-2).**

8. **Click Post Photos (as shown in Figure 5-2).**

    This step publishes the whole album at one time as a Public post. Every Public Follow and personal Friend will be able to see this album.

Making an existing album Public

If you already have an album that you're using for these types of public photos, follow these steps:

1. **Go to your Timeline, and click the Photos tab.**

    See Figure 5-3.

2. **Click the Album tab and then click the photo album you want to make public.**

    See Figure 5-4.

3. **Just under the name of the album, you will see a privacy drop-down menu represented by an icon (as shown in Figure 5-3).**

    The privacy setting for your album with automatically be saved.

Figure 5-3:
You can make any existing album public.

Click for the privacy drop-down menu

Figure 5-4:
You can share any photo album with your friends or on a Page you manage.

Using Life Events to Support Your Business

We discuss how to use milestones for your business Page in Books II and III. You can use *life events* (which are the same things as milestones, only with a different name) in your Timeline to support your business, too.

Think about all the milestones you have for your business and then put a personal spin on them for life events in your Timeline. You need to use a few little tweaks to use this business-supporting process in your personal Timeline. Regardless of whether you have a business Page, you can add these types of life events to support your business.

On a business Page, when you select a milestone, you can immediately name the event. In a Timeline, though, you have several categories to choose from to create a life event: Work & Education, Family & Relationships, Home & Living, Health & Wellness, and Travel & Experiences. Each category has several options, always including Other. Choosing Other enables you to name your life event whatever you want.

Using life events to support your business is actually pretty simple:

1. **Take a business event.**
2. **Make it personal by choosing the Work & Education category.**
3. **Select Other Life Event.**
4. **Type a name in the Event text box.**

Table 5-1 shows a couple examples. These life events can support your business in a completely appropriate way in your Timeline.

Table 5-1   Presenting Business Milestones as Personal Life Events

Business Page Milestone	Equivalent Personal Life Event Name	Accompanying Images	Other Tips
Opened business	Opened My First Business	You cutting the ribbon, opening the door, and so on	Write in first person. Share your personal feelings.
Article in national magazine	Honored to Be Featured in This Cool Magazine	The article or the magazine's front cover next to your smiling face	Write in first person. Share a bit of the interview process.

Adjusting and Adding Apps

Timeline apps don't have the functionality of business Page apps, but you can still use apps to support your business. On a personal Timeline, apps appear below the About section in the left-hand column. You can't move Friends and Photos.

Moving apps

To change the order of app placements, follow these steps:

1. **Click the pencil icon to the right of the apps.**

2. **Click Manage Sections.**

   A pop-up window appears where you can rearrange the order of apps (as shown in Figure 5-5).

3. **Once you've rearranged your apps, click Save.**

Choosing apps

Think about the types of apps that would support your business. You can peruse the available ones here: www.facebook.com/about/timeline/apps.

Here are a few that we recommend:

✦ **Pinterest:** To create an app for Pinterest, you have to start on Pinterest itself. Go to your Pinterest settings and connect your Pinterest account to your Timeline.

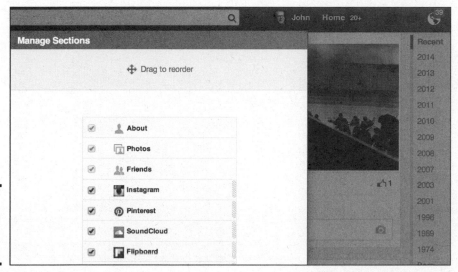

Figure 5-5:
Rearranging
the order of
apps.

✦ **Spotify and/or SoundCloud:** If your business is in the music field, consider using Spotify to showcase your likes and SoundCloud to showcase your own music. Again, start with a personal account with Spotify or SoundCloud, and connect it to your Timeline.

✦ **RunKeeper or Map My Fitness:** If your business is in the fitness field, consider using one of these popular apps to showcase your own workouts.

✦ **TripAdvisor:** Do you travel for your business? Add this app to let people know where you are and what you're doing or where you want to go.

In all cases, make sure that you set the Posts on Your Behalf option (see Figure 5-6) to Everyone for widest impact.

Figure 5-6:
Set the
Posts on
Your Behalf
option to
Everyone.

Change to Everyone

Book V
Understanding Facebook Applications

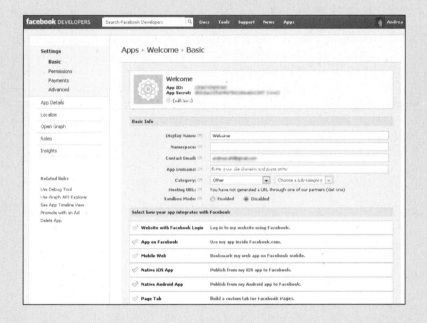

For more on Facebook Page management, go to www.dummies.com/extras/
facebookmarketingaio.

Contents at a Glance

Chapter 1: Customizing Your Page with Facebook Apps 331

Understanding How Facebook Users Make Use of Apps...331
Introducing Apps Developed by Facebook 332
Finding and Adding Apps to Your Page..335
Deleting Apps from Your Page..337
Using Apps for Marketing 337

Chapter 2: Using iFrame Apps to Create Custom Tabs. 343

Looking at Tabs 344
Defining iFrames 345
Outlining the Options...346
Exploring the Facebook Developers Site..348
Becoming a Verified Facebook Developer 349
Creating an iFrame Application...351
Using Third-Party Applications 356

Chapter 1: Customizing Your Page with Facebook Apps

In This Chapter

✔ Grasping the importance of Facebook apps

✔ Discovering Facebook-developed and other installed apps

✔ Adding and deleting apps

✔ Exploring ways to use apps for marketing

*U*sing an *application* (app) is how you can expand the way Facebook interacts with your audience. iPhones and other mobile phones have educated most people about what an app is. "There's an app for that" has been a well-known phrase for years. Thousands of apps can be used on mobile phones, and developers have built hundreds of applications for use in Facebook.

We need to make a distinction between the apps we discuss in this chapter and "social," or Open Graph, apps for your Profile (such as Spotify, Netflix, and Foodily).

If you need a true Introduction to Apps 101 and how apps work with your personal Facebook account, see Book III, Chapter 2. The apps in this chapter make your business Page more interesting and functional. Social apps connect through personal accounts, and activity through those apps shows up on people's News Feeds and Tickers.

And you, as a business owner, can develop an app. That subject is a big one, which we expand on in Chapter 2 of this minibook. For now, we focus on business Page apps.

Understanding How Facebook Users Make Use of Apps

The App Center hosts more than 1,000 apps that are geared to personal accounts, and more than 100,000 apps not listed in the App Center are available for your Facebook business Page. Apps are the engine that drives the Facebook experience.

There seem to be three camps of Facebook application users:

✦ Those who are there for personal conversations and ignore or block many applications

✦ Those who are there to enjoy the applications and play games

✦ Business owners looking for ways to drive eyeballs to their Pages by using appropriately targeted applications

You're free to place as many existing apps on your Page as you want, or create custom apps.

If you view Facebook on an iPad, iPhone, or iPod touch, check whether your apps use Adobe Flash; if so, you won't be able to view the content on those devices. Keep this fact in mind while you build your Page. Test all the apps you install on your Page on all platforms: iOS, Android, web browser, and so on.

Introducing Apps Developed by Facebook

Facebook Page apps are what make your Page unique and interesting. If all the content that you present on your Page is Timeline, Info, and Photos, it looks as though you haven't put any attention into presenting your business. On the other hand, you want to be very discerning about which types of apps you put on your Page. Having too many bells and whistles isn't charming, either!

Exploring the App Center apps

Facebook has developed a space called App Center (www.facebook.com/appcenter). If you're interested mostly in apps that function on your business Page, App Center isn't the place to look. When you click App Center, you see a drop-down menu on the left-hand side:

✔ **All:** Obviously, this tab is where you can see all the apps.

✔ **Web:** This tab lists apps that you can connect to your Profile that will work and be functional if they're interfacing with a computer.

✔ **iOS:** This app lists all iPhone, iPod Touch, and iPad apps.

✔ **Android:** This tabs lists all Android apps.

✔ **Mobile Web:** Go here to find apps that work with the mobile Facebook app.

Then you see several filters, including: Games, Entertainment, Facebook, Lifestyle, Music, News, Photos & Videos, Sports, Travel & Local, and Utilities. You also see the Requests link. If a number appears next to it, someone has requested that you use the app with him. (Birthday calendar, anyone?)

You can find apps developed by Facebook itself as well as by third-party developers. The ones developed by Facebook are Photos, Events, and Video. These apps are really easy to activate on your Page, as we show you in this chapter. We like to call them "ready-to-go" apps because you don't need to go outside your Page to find them.

Some people are confused about the difference between the apps we recommend installing on your business Page and the apps listed in the App Center, which is where you find apps for your Profile. We describe the App Center in the nearby sidebar, and you may want to connect a few personal sites to your business Page to support your particular type of business. Pinterest, Foursquare, TripAdvisor, and ReverbNation come to mind. You can connect these to your business Page using a third-party app, or visit the site itself for Facebook connect details.

The apps that are in App Center generally are connected to your Profile. If you have your Subscription button turned on, and one of these apps supports your business, you can enjoy it through App Center. As a new Page owner, you already have a few ready-to-go apps in play, as we mention earlier. You find them by following these steps:

1. **On your Page, click Settings at the top of your Facebook Page.**

2. **Click Apps in the left-hand sidebar.**

   The screen shows you all the apps that are currently available to be installed on your Page, as shown in Figure 1-1.

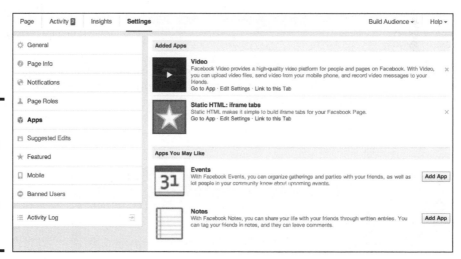

Figure 1-1: The list of apps added to your Page. Edit Settings to install them on your Page.

3. **Click the Apps link to see which apps are ready to be installed on your new Page.**

A new Brand or Products Page with Product/Services as its main category, for example, has these apps available:

- Events
- Notes
- Video

Each app has one, two, or sometimes three links below it: Go to App, Edit Settings, and Link to This Tab, as shown in Figure 1-2. We describe the links in this list:

✦ **Link to This Tab:** Click this link, and a dialog box opens, displaying the direct URL to that particular place on your Page (as shown below). So, for example, if you want to provide visitors a direct URL to your Static HTML tab, you can look for the Static HTML application, click the Link to This Tab link, and then copy and paste the URL in a message to send someone directly to that place on your Page.

Figure 1-2: Each app has a permalink.

✦ **Edit Settings:** For apps that have been added to your page, click this link, and a dialog box appears, offering you the option of adding the app to or removing the app from the application group. For Facebook-built apps, you can't change the text of the link, but you can for custom apps, as shown in Figure 1-3.

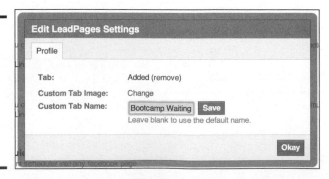

Figure 1-3: Click Edit Settings to add or remove an app tab, or to customize certain aspects.

✦ **Go to App:** Click this link to go directly to the editing page for that app or to a page where you can set options for the app. For example, if you click the Go to App link for the Events app, you go directly to the page where you can start creating an Event, as shown in Figure 1-4.

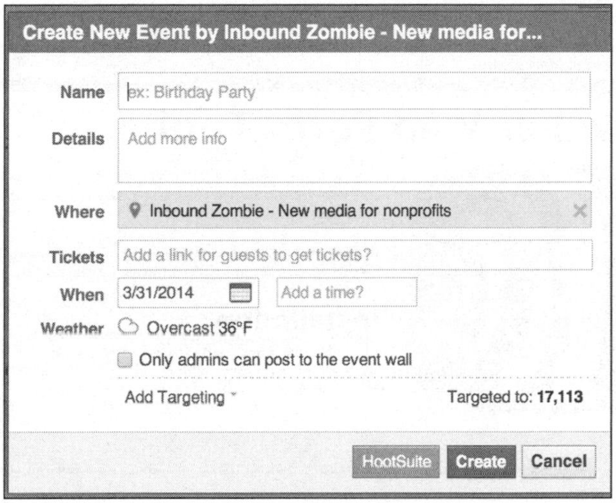

Figure 1-4:
Click Go
to App to
view the
creation/
customiza-
tion page for
that app.

> **Create New Event by Inbound Zombie - New media for...**
>
> | | |
> |---|---|
> | Name | ex: Birthday Party |
> | Details | Add more info |
> | Where | ⚲ Inbound Zombie - New media for nonprofits ✕ |
> | Tickets | Add a link for guests to get tickets? |
> | When | 3/31/2014 🗓 Add a time? |
> | Weather | ☁ Overcast 36°F |
>
> ☐ Only admins can post to the event wall
>
> Add Targeting ▾   Targeted to: **17,113**
>
> HootSuite   **Create**   Cancel

You should go through all the apps already listed on your Page's Apps dashboard and decide whether you want to have them on your Page.

Pages come with the Photos app on the Page Timeline. After someone (or you) clicks the Like button for the Page, you will have another app box called Likes. If you want any more of the apps that are available for your Page, click the Add App button to the right of the application (as shown in Figure 1-1). This process is described fully in Book II, Chapter 3.

Finding and Adding Apps to Your Page

The Facebook App Center is where you find apps for your Profile. If you want to use business apps on your Page, find them somewhere other than the App Center.

If you've seen or know about an app that you want to install on your page, follow these steps:

1. **In the search box in the top-left corner, enter the name of the app you want to install on your Page.**

The search function brings up everything that has the name you're searching for: Pages, Apps, people, and so on. Make sure that you find the one that's in the Apps category.

2. **Click the application name.**

   You're taken to the application's Page. Depending on the app, you may see a page with just the one application or a page with all the apps available.

3. **Click the Add App to Page button, as shown in Figure 1-5.**

Figure 1-5:
Find the
Page that
you want
to add the
application
to and click
the Add
App to Page
button.

4. **You may be asked to give the app more info for authorization.**

5. **Go to your Page, and click the More drop-down menu under your cover image, and click Manage Apps.**

6. **A popup window appears that allows you to reorder your apps (as shown in Figure 1-6).**

   Reorder the apps to suit your preference by dragging them up or down in the list.

7. **To edit the name of your app, click Add or Remove Tabs (as shown in Figure 1-6).**

   Once you click Manage Apps, you will go to the place in the settings part of your page for apps (see Figure 1-1 earlier in the chapter).

8. **Edit the name of your app link by clicking the Edit Settings button.**

   Facebook still calls this link a tab.

9. **Click Save.**

   A new browser tab opens, and you can browse your computer for and click the image you want to use. You can upload a custom image for the tab box.

At this point Facebook will no display mobile third-party apps on iOS or Android devices. When using a third-party app, make sure you're using a mobile-friendly URL to direct traffic to that.

Figure 1-6:
Manage
and change
the order of
your apps.

Deleting Apps from Your Page

Sometimes you have an app that just doesn't click with your audience. If that's the case, don't worry: Applications are very easy to remove from your Page.

To remove the app from your Page, follow these steps:

1. **On your Page, click Settings at the top of your page.**

2. **In the left hand sidebar on the next page, click Apps.**

   You will then be able to see all of the apps associated with your page (refer to Figure 1-1).

3. **Click the X icon next to the app you want to remove.**

   The app no longer appears on your Timeline.

Using Apps for Marketing

In Book II, Chapter 2, we discuss which type of apps truly support a business. Think about your business and figure out the best use for these featured spaces. Many businesses use them for these three things:

✦ **E-mail capture:** This is a vital process for businesses.

✦ **Webinar sign-up:** Use the sales page information for this type of app, or add upcoming event information. (Your company is a sponsor for a community event, for example.)

✦ **E-commerce:** You can re-create your off-Facebook e-commerce website pages for viewing right on Facebook.

In this section, we highlight a few apps that we like to suggest to Page owners.

Contact forms and e-mail forms

You may already have an e-mail capture system set up on your website. Maybe you give something away in exchange for an e-mail address. Many e-mail systems such as AWeber.com have a Facebook app that you can access right from your accounts with those systems.

Check with the e-mail list system you're using to see whether it provides an easy way to add your e-mail capture form to your Facebook Page. If you're using systems such as MailChimp, ConstantContact, or iContact, you can use the way they provide, or just copy the form code and paste it in an iFrame or Static HTML app, re-creating the same thing you have on your website. The trick is using an app where you can paste this HTML or iFrame code.

Here are a few apps you can use for e-mail capture if you don't use the provider's app:

✦ **Heyo:** The trial account (at `http://heyo.com`) allows you to completely design one app box. You can add images and all sorts of Like and Share buttons, and there's a space where you can paste the HTML code from your e-mail service. You can use this app as a fan gate, too.

✦ **Woobox:** Sign up at `http://woobox.com` to try the HTML fan gate app, and use your e-mail capture HTML.

✦ **Contact Tab:** This particular contact app (available at `https://apps.facebook.com/contacttab`) contains a place to display all your social accounts, company information, a map to your business (Bing or Google), and a header image.

✦ **Contact Form:** You can use the free version (available at `https://www.facebook.com/contact.form`) or upgrade to the paid version if you'd like to add a custom footer and get other little perks. You can see a nice use of this app at `https://www.facebook.com/contact.form/app_141149985924076`.

Discussion board apps

Facebook retired its own Discussion app a while ago, but some businesses still want to have some sort of forum or discussion board available to their communities.

Here are two apps to explore if you need this type of app:

✦ **SocialAppsHQ:** The free account (available at `http://socialappshq.com`) allows you to add a discussion app to your Page Timeline. This company also has several really interesting apps to explore.

✦ **Forum for Pages:** This free app (at apps.facebook.com/forumforpages) has ads in the left column; the paid version doesn't. The user interface is very clean and large.

Video apps

Almost every app company that we suggest in this chapter has an app for adding your YouTube videos to your Page. Generally, you add the username of your (or anyone else's) YouTube channel, and the app pulls the videos to your Facebook Page. Some apps allow you to select a particular playlist instead of pulling in the entire channel.

If you use Vimeo for your videos, we have an app for you, too. Check out Tabfusion in the bulleted list.

We don't recommend using the built-in Facebook app Video for two reasons: Facebook might retire it at some point (and you could lose your videos), and other apps look better on a Facebook Page. If you upload videos directly to Facebook, they automatically go in the app box called Video.

Here are a couple of companies that have good YouTube apps:

✦ **YouTube App:** One of its free apps (at `https://www.facebook.com/youtubetabapp`) is the YouTube app.

✦ **Tabfusion:** Tabfusion has three video apps: one for YouTube, for Vimeo, and for Blip.tv. This app (at `http://tabfusion.com/applications.php`) charges for its services, so you need to consider that fact before choosing to use those apps. See `http://tabfusion.com/pricing.php`.

Finding apps with Involver

One way to find really good apps for your business Pages is to use Involver (`www.involver.com/applications`). Involver has many apps that are quite relevant to a Facebook business Page, including an RSS feed, the YouTube channel, Photo Gallery, and File Sharing (which is a great way for authors to give away chapter previews or book teaser copy). An app of note is Scribd. You upload a PDF file to `www.scribd.com`, and then it's automatically available on the app for viewing, sharing, downloading, e-mailing, and more — all from your Facebook Page.

If your business uses video as a marketing device, try to find the best interface by testing and looking at samples to find the right fit. You can always hide or delete an app and try something else.

Pinterest apps

You can't pin items from Facebook to Pinterest, but you can pull in your pins and boards from Pinterest through an app to post on your personal account or your business Page.

Our favorite app for Pinterest is Woobox (`http://woobox.com/pinterest`). You can see an example of how it looks on Facebook at `https://www.facebook.com/TheSocialClassroom/app_305927716147259`. The interface for configuring this app is very easy to understand and use, as you can see in Figure 1-7.

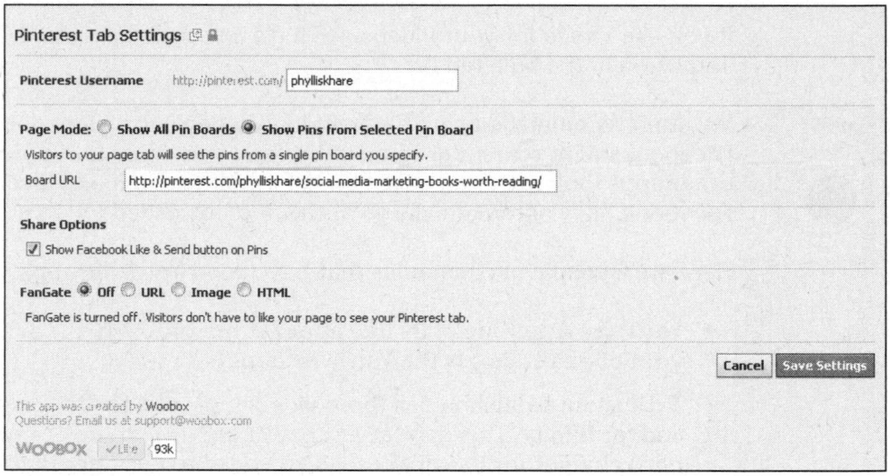

Pinterest Tab Settings

Pinterest Username http://pinterest.com/ phylliskhare

Page Mode: ○ Show All Pin Boards ● **Show Pins from Selected Pin Board**
Visitors to your page tab will see the pins from a single pin board you specify.
Board URL http://pinterest.com/phylliskhare/social-media-marketing-books-worth-reading/

Share Options
☑ Show Facebook Like & Send button on Pins

FanGate ● Off ○ URL ○ Image ○ HTML
FanGate is turned off. Visitors don't have to like your page to see your Pinterest tab.

Cancel   Save Settings

This app was created by **Woobox**
Questions? Email us at support@woobox.com

WOOBOX ✓ Like 93k

Figure 1-7: Setting up the Woobox Pinterest app is easy.

Google+

The Google Plus Tab for Pages app (`https://www.facebook.com/googleplustopages`) is extremely easy to use. The app pulls in all your Google+ posts and puts them on a tab on Facebook, as you can see in Figure 1-8. Any visitor can click the +1 (Google+'s equivalent to liking) next to any post.

Social RSS

The Social RSS (`https://apps.facebook.com/social-rss`) app allows you to add your blog or any RSS feed to your Page. It can be really handy if you want to pull in specific posts from all over the Internet, not just your blog. If you want to post your tweets to your Timeline, for example, you can add your Twitter RSS feed to this app. This app is also discussed in Book III, Chapter 3.

Your existing business services

Many of the services that you may already be using outside the Facebook environment have apps, including these:

✔ Eventbrite: `www.eventbrite.com`

✔ MailChimp: `http://mailchimp.com`

✔ SurveyMonkey: `www.surveymonkey.com`

✔ PayPal: `http://paypal.com`

Go to these websites, and look for any Facebook integration. Some of these services have actual Facebook apps; others give you code to place in an app like Static HTML, which creates a nice link on your Page. See Book V, Chapter 2 to find out how to use Static HTML.

Figure 1-8: People can +1 your Google+ posts right on Facebook.

Click the +1 to like

Other apps

Here are a few more apps you might want to explore for your personal account, with the Subscribe button turned on (see Book II, Chapter 1), or your business Page.

✦ **Goodreads** (`https://apps.facebook.com/good_reads`) is an app for your personal account. The app corresponds to the Goodreads website (`www.goodreads.com`). You can add your own books and those that you'd like to recommend to others. The dedicated link creates a nice Timeline view of the books you want to discuss or share. This particular app is best for your Profile if you have the Subscribe button turned on.

✦ **Band Profile** (`www.facebook.com/rn.mybandapp`) currently has more than 8 million active users on Facebook! This app, powered by ReverbNation (`www.reverbnation.com`), creates a link called Band Profile and pulls info from your account at ReverbNation. People can join your fan list or mailing list, share and play your music, watch your music videos, see where your next show will be, and see your fans. In other words, it's a complete site for your music on your Facebook Page.

✦ **Tinychat** (`http://apps.facebook.com/tinychat`) has been a popular tool for Twitter users for a few years. Its Facebook app allows you to open a video chat within your Facebook Page and host discussions. You can send notifications to your personal friends or e-mail them a link they can use to connect. From a marketing perspective, consider using this app to create a weekly event in which you chat with your customers or clients, or an impromptu chat when something topical that relates to your business comes up. Currently, this app is best for a personal account with the Subscribe button turned on.

✦ **Zillow real estate apps** (`www.zillow.com/webtools/facebook-apps`) is a nice collection of apps you can use to add Listings, Reviews, Local Info, and a Contacts tab.

✦ **Livestream** (`https://apps.facebook.com/livestream`) is a live-video app that's used by some very active social media marketers and by Facebook itself for its live events. If using video appeals to you and your business, check out a fuller use of the Livestream app in Book VIII.

As we mention early in this chapter, you should choose the apps that are most appropriate for your business. Also, don't overload your fans with needless clutter on your Page. Choose wisely. See Book I, Chapter 2 to review creating a marketing plan.

Facebook mobile app

Facebook has an app for your mobile phone. The interface is optimized for mobile phone viewing, which means that you'll find pluses and minuses about viewing Facebook business Pages through the mobile Facebook app. When using the mobile Facebook app on an Android or iOS device, for example, and you go to a business Page through a link in the News Feed, you see only two tabs: Timeline and Photos.

All the apps that you've added, along with any custom-designed links you may have built for your Page, are unavailable for viewing on a mobile phone (currently). Take a good look at your demographics. Are your visitors viewing your Page only on mobile phones? If so, keep that fact in mind as you build your Page. You may need fewer apps and more posts to your Timeline.

Chapter 2: Using iFrame Apps to Create Custom Tabs

In This Chapter

✔ Reviewing custom tabs

✔ Defining iFrames

✔ Touring the Facebook Developers site

✔ Creating your own iFrame application

✔ Letting someone build your iFrame application

✔ Using third-party applications to create your custom tab

Do you have a vision for a special tab on your Facebook Page and haven't been able to find an app that did exactly what you wanted? Maybe you want a certain function or a layout that you haven't been able to find? Then it's time to create your own custom tab! Luckily, plenty of options are available to help you create exactly what you need.

You can also have a *fan gate* tab on your Page, which means that people must become fans before they can see the content. This tab is also known as a *reveal tab* where the initial graphic tells people that they must click Like before they can see what's below the image. These kinds of tabs are great at helping convert your visitors to fans because these tabs usually offer something good in exchange.

These custom tabs are sometimes called iFrame apps because they use an iFrame to pull in your designed content. In this chapter, you discover what iFrames are, how to create your own iFrame application, and how to add it to your Page. We also introduce third-party applications that make creating a custom tab easy if you aren't comfortable coding your own iFrame (or don't have the resources to do so).

We cover the Facebook Developers site in depth in this chapter, but it's not for the timid. Feel free to skip that section and go to the middle of the chapter, where we list some resources for hiring someone to write the code for you. Or move on to later in the chapter, where we cover simple third-party applications.

Looking at Tabs

Tabs on Facebook can be highly customized, with branding and links that highlight a company. These custom tabs usually have

✦ A strong call to action (such as *Like our Page!*)

✦ Some fun and practical links (such as a video message, a newsletter sign-up link, or coupons for fans)

The world is your oyster! Using a custom tab within your Facebook Page can further enhance your brand and make your Facebook Page stand out. Figures 2-1 through 2-3 show some examples of custom tabs.

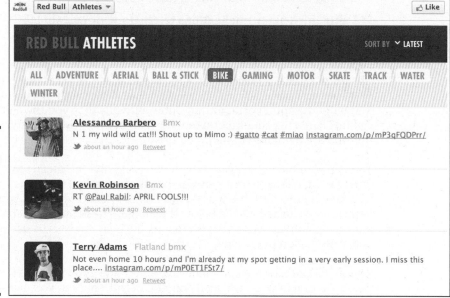

Figure 2-1: Red Bull has a tab that posts the most recent tweets by its athletes that can be filtered by sport.

Distant past

If you've been on Facebook for a long time, you may remember when custom tabs were allowed to be default landing tabs, so that someone who hadn't liked your Page still got a customized message. This feature is no longer available, but with some ingenuity and some attractive tab Cover images, you can attract people to your tabs and engage them. See Book III, Chapter 2 for more information about changing your tab Cover photos.

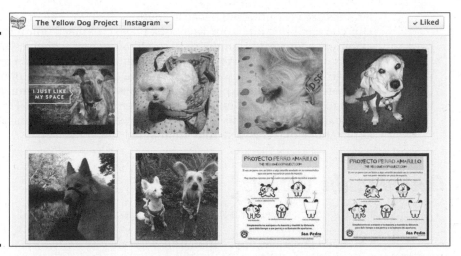

Figure 2-2:
The Yellow
Dog Project
has a tab
the pulls in
the latest
pictures
from
Instagram
that are
tagged with
#yellowdog-
project.

Figure 2-3:
ShortStack
uses a
reveal tab
to entice
people to
click Like
first.

Defining iFrames

iFrame — short for Inline Frame — is an HTML document embedded inside
another HTML document on a website. An iFrame pulls the content from
one website into another. So in the context of Facebook, an iFrame pulls the
content of another website into an area on your Facebook Page.

iFrames are very powerful because anything that you can create on a website you can bring into your Facebook Page, creating a unique and rich experience for your community. To use iFrames on Facebook, you need to have a place on the web to put your content. By this, we mean that you need to have a server or host website where you can upload your photos, files, or whatever you'll be displaying on your custom tab. If you don't have a place to which you can upload your content, skip to "Using Third-Party Applications," later in this chapter, where we introduce several third-party applications that can host your content for you.

Outlining the Options

For Facebook Pages, you have three choices:

✦ Build an iFrame application from scratch.

✦ Hire someone to build the application for you.

✦ Use a third-party application.

The following sections explain some of the considerations involved with each option.

Building an iFrame application

Building an application sounds daunting, but the process can be broken down into several easy steps. We walk you through the specifics a little later in the chapter, but for now, here's an overview of the steps for building an iFrames application:

1. Become a verified Facebook Developer.

This simple process requires a mobile phone (that can receive text messages) or a credit card (for verification purposes only).

2. Design the content for your Facebook app.

Typically, this content is designed with HTML, JavaScript, and/or CSS.

3. Upload the content for your Facebook app to your website.

You may need to use an FTP (File Transfer Protocol) program to upload the HTML document and necessary images to your server.

4. Configure your Facebook application.

You configure your application in the Developer area of Facebook.

5. Install the application on your Page.

Outlining the Options **347**

Book V
Chapter 2

Using iFrame Apps
to Create Custom
Tabs

When you create and install your own iFrames application, it shows up below your Cover photo with your other tabs.

You need your own Secure Sockets Layer (SSL) certificate on your website to host your uploaded content for your Facebook app. SSL, which allows information on the website to be securely encrypted, is typically used when processing payments on a website. Facebook requires that any app have the content hosted by a secure server. An SSL certificate isn't too expensive; typically, it costs around $50.

If you don't have an SSL certificate, Facebook provides free hosting through a partnership with Heroku. You can read more about this partnership at `http://developers.facebook.com/blog/post/558/`.

Although building your own application can be challenging, it has some advantages, as follows:

✦ You have complete control of your application (no extra references to third-party applications).

✦ Developing your own application is free (unless you hire someone to help you do the development). Many third-party applications cost money.

✦ You don't have to worry about something happening to the third-party application where you have your content stored. (For example, something goes wrong in the third-party application, or it goes out of business, and then your custom tab may not work properly.)

Hiring someone to build the application for you

If you aren't savvy about HTML and are trying to do something fairly complicated (such as embedding videos or an opt-in form), you may want to hire an app developer to do the work.

To find an app developer

✦ Check within your own network first. You may be surprised to find that some of the website developers you may know can easily create an app for you, depending on your needs. Try doing a search on LinkedIn for Facebook app developers among your connections.

✦ Look at sites such as `www.elance.com` and `www.odesk.com`, which have a huge supply of freelancers who can help you out. Many of these developers have references and examples of their past work available. You can post your requirements, and the freelancers can bid on the project. You choose the freelancer who's the best fit for your needs.

Using a third-party application

Third-party applications are created by another company (that is, a company other than Facebook) to simplify creating custom content on Facebook. The idea is that you can use a third-party application to create your Page and then add the app to your Facebook Page. You don't need to code anything, and you don't have to upload files to your website.

Many of these apps have a drag-and-drop design interface to make designing your app a snap. Be aware that many apps are available, and more are being developed every day. Do your homework before you settle on one app, though, because there may be something new tomorrow that's a better fit for your needs.

Here are some of the applications that you can use to create a custom tab. We discuss these applications later in the chapter.

+ **Heyo:** www.heyo.com

+ **AgoraPulse:** www.agorapulse.com

+ **ShortStack:** www.shortstack.com

+ **Static HTML:** iFrame Tabs: www.facebook.com/apps/application. php?id=190322544333196

+ **TabSite:** www.tabsite.com

Third-party applications are developed by independent people or companies not connected with Facebook, and these applications may or may not work well.

Occasionally, you'll come across some applications that are developed but then aren't updated, or you'll find that some applications don't work well from the start. If you're at all concerned about a particular application, we suggest visiting the website of the company that developed the app and noting which other companies are using the app. Many times, a website has links to the Facebook Pages using the company's applications so you can see the apps in action and get an idea of how they work as well as gauge the applications' popularity. All the apps that we cover in this chapter work very well; we just want to remind you to use caution when discovering new apps that may be available.

Exploring the Facebook Developers Site

The Facebook Developers site is where you begin your journey of creating your own application. To get to the site, log in to Facebook as your Profile and then go to www.facebook.com/developers. The Facebook Developers home page offers links to several areas of the developers platform: Build for Websites, Build for Mobile, and Build Apps on Facebook. You can also link to the blog, the App Center, and other sites, as shown in Figure 2-4.

Figure 2-4:
The
Facebook
Developers
site.

Here are some of the elements of the Facebook Developers site that you can access from the top navigation menu:

✦ **Docs:** Click this link to find information about creating code for the Facebook plug-ins, creating applications, and so on.

✦ **Apps:** Navigate to the apps you've created here.

✦ **Products:** Facebook's resources for building apps.

✦ **Tools:** Access debugger tools, the JavaScript Test Console, and more. You won't need most of these tools for a simple Facebook app.

✦ **Support:** Get information about bugs, technical Q&A, and more.

Becoming a Verified Facebook Developer

Applications can be malicious and often created to spread spam messages and viruses. To combat developers of these types of applications, Facebook requires some method of developer tracking.

To become a verified Facebook Developer, you need to verify that you're a real person by providing a mobile phone number (that can receive text messages) or a credit card number.

The verification process (and the pop-up boxes you see) can vary from person to person depending on when the user joined Facebook. Some people were required to verify their account with a mobile phone number when they joined Facebook; others weren't. Also, if you've never set up an application before, your app creation might fail, as shown in Figure 2-5. So if you see the App Creation Failed message when creating your app (in the upcoming "Creating an iFrame Application" section), come back to the steps that follow to verify your account.

Figure 2-5:
You might
need to
verify your
account to
become a
Facebook
Developer.

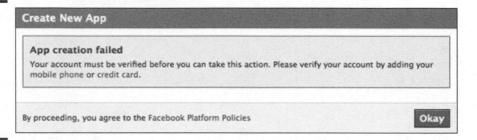

Verifying with a mobile phone number

If you want to verify your account with a mobile phone number, follow these steps:

1. **Click the Mobile Phone link (refer to Figure 2-5).**

A pop-up window appears, asking for your country code and cellphone number.

2. **Select your country code and cellphone number.**

3. **Click the Continue button.**

You receive a text message with a string of letters or numbers, which is your confirmation code. On your computer, you see a box for your confirmation code.

4. **Enter the confirmation code and click Confirm.**

You're now a verified Facebook Developer, and you can create an iFrame application.

The mobile phone verification process may not work well outside the United States. People have reported having trouble receiving the text message, so if you're outside the United States, you may want to use the credit card option.

Creating an iFrame Application **351**

Book V
Chapter 2

Using iFrame Apps
to Create Custom
Tabs

Verifying with a credit card

If you don't have a phone that can receive text messages, you need to verify your account by adding your credit card. Here's how:

1. **Click the Credit Card link (refer to Figure 2-5).**

   You're taken to a new window, and Facebook asks you to reenter your Facebook password.

2. **Reenter your password and click the Continue button.**

3. **Type your credit card information in the text box.**

4. **Click the Save button.**

5. **Click the Send button.**

You're now a verified Facebook Developer, and you can create an iFrame application.

Creating an iFrame Application

So you decided to try your hand at creating your own iFrame application. Excellent! Although creating an iFrame app isn't terribly difficult if you're familiar with basic CSS and HTML code, you need to have a few things ready before you begin.

First, you need to create the web page on which you'll be displaying in the iFrame. Creating a web page is beyond the scope of this book, but you need to create a page 810 pixels (px) wide to fit into the Facebook iFrame space.

The possibilities for your web page are literally endless. You can have a simple design with just an image or something more elaborate, such as a mini store. Here are some possibilities:

✦ A single image (very easy to code)

✦ Several images fitted together that allow for links

✦ Embedded video

✦ An opt-in box for your newsletter with additional photos, video, or both

✦ Photos or video combined with Facebook comments so that people can interact with your Page

If you create a web page wider than 810 px, it won't fit into the space on your Facebook Page and will have scroll bars on the bottom.

Making the iFrame app

After you have your web page created and you've become a verified Facebook Developer, you're ready to create your iFrame app. Log in to your Profile, and follow these steps:

1. **Go to** www.facebook.com/developers.

2. **Click the Create New App under the App menu.**

   The Create New App dialog box appears, as shown in Figure 2-6.

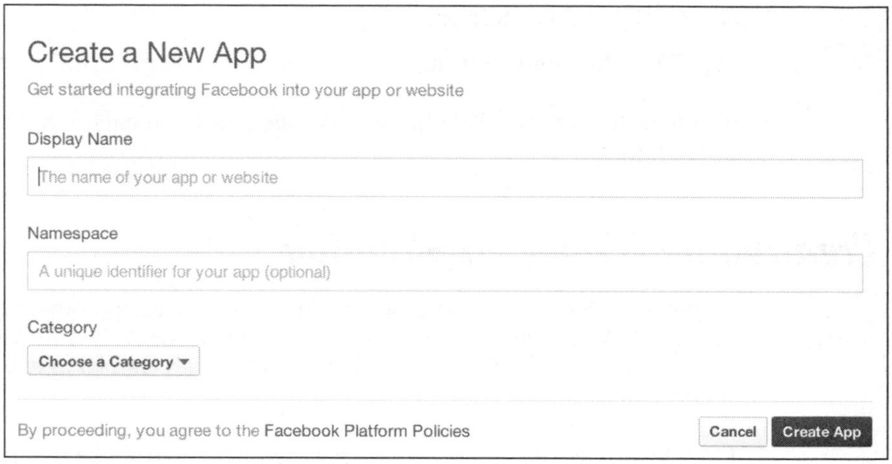

Create a New App

Get started integrating Facebook into your app or website

Display Name

The name of your app or website

Namespace

A unique identifier for your app (optional)

Category

Choose a Category ▼

By proceeding, you agree to the Facebook Platform Policies   Cancel   Create App

---

Figure 2-6:
Name your app.

3. **Type the name of your app in the Display Name text box.**

   The name you enter will appear on the tab of your Page.

4. **(Optional) Add a Namespace for your app.**

   This is a unique identifier for your app.

5. **Click the Continue button.**

   You're taken to the Security Check Page. At this point, you might see the App Creation Failed message, and you must complete the verification process with your mobile phone or credit card. Refer to the earlier section, "Becoming a Verified Facebook Developer," if necessary.

6. **Type the security-check text in the text box.**

7. **Click the Submit button.**

   You're taken to the application's Settings page, as shown in Figure 2-7, landing on the Basic tab.

John Haydon's blog ▾	Basic	Advanced	Migrations
◉ Dashboard	App ID		App Secret
⚙ Settings	434921403260846		●●●●●●●●	Show
★ Status & Review	Display Name		Namespace
🐷 App Details	John Haydon's blog		
👤 Roles	App Domains		Contact Email
♣ Open Graph	johnhaydon.com ✕		Johnscotthaydon@gmail.com
	Website		✕
⚠ Alerts	Site URL		
📕 Localize	http://johnhaydon.com		
💳 Payments	Mobile Site URL		
	URL of your mobile site		

Figure 2-7:
Edit your
application.

TIP

Many of the fields on this page are for games or other Facebook applications designed to be used by many Facebook users; they're optional for someone developing a custom tab with iFrames. For the purposes of an iFrame custom tab, you have to fill out only the information on the Basic tab. We explain which fields you need to worry about and which ones you can skip.

8. **Fill out the information for your application as follows:**

- *Display Name:* The name of your application that is displayed to users. This entry is the title of the tab and is populated with the name you provide in Step 2.

- *Namespace:* The Canvas Page URL name, which must be unique. The Canvas Page is the unique name of your URL for the application on Facebook and is in the form `https://apps.facebook.com/Your_App_Namespace`. (***Note:*** This setting is optional for Page tabs.)

- *Contact Email:* Primary e-mail address for communication related to your application. This field should be populated by your Facebook login e-mail address, but you can change the address if needed.

- *App Domain:* The URL of the website where you'll have the application. (***Note:*** This setting is optional for Page tabs.)

- *Category:* The category that best fits your application (optional and directed toward other apps).

- *Hosting URL:* The URL address given to you by Facebook's partner Heroku if you're using its hosting option.

- *Sandbox Mode:* If enabled, only app developers can use and see your app. Switch to Enabled if you want to keep your app private while you develop it. There's no need to make a custom tab private because it won't be installed on your Page.

Then select how your app will integrate with Facebook. Each option requires you to enter additional information when you click the check mark next to it. The options are

- *Website with Facebook Login:* You want to allow people to log in to your website using Facebook.

- *App on Facebook:* You want to build an app on Facebook.com.

- *Mobile Web:* You have a mobile web app.

- *Native iOS App:* You have a native iOS app.

- *Native Android App:* You have a native Android app.

- *Page Tab:* You want to build a custom tab for Facebook Pages.

9. **Click the check mark next to the Page Tab option.**

You see the fields shown in Figure 2-8.

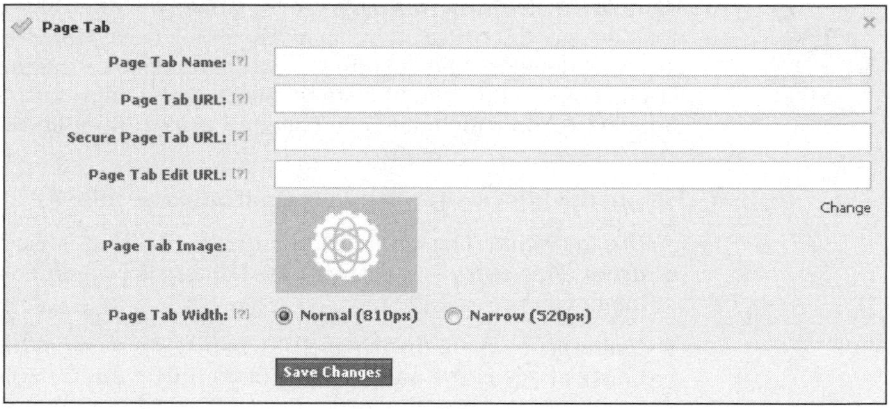

Figure 2-8:
The Page
Tab fields.

Here are the descriptions of these fields:

- *Page Tab Name:* This field is the title of the tab and is populated from the Display Name entry. If it isn't autopopulated, enter the text used in the Display Name field.

- *Page Tab URL:* Facebook pulls content for your tab from this URL. This URL is the full path to the web page that you want to have displayed on your Facebook Welcome Page.

- *Secure Page Tab URL:* The content of your tab needs to be hosted on a secure website that has an SSL certificate. The URL starts with `https` to indicate that it's secure and is in the form `https://www.`*yourwebsitename*`.com/folder/index.html`. If you're using the Heroku option, enter the URL you received from Heroku.

- *Page Tab Edit URL:* This URL is given to Page Admins to edit or customize the Page Tab app. This setting is optional.

- *Page Tab Image:* You have the opportunity to upload your image for your app Cover photo.

- *Page Tab Width:* You can choose a Normal width of 810 px or a Narrow width of 520 px centered on the tab.

10. **Click the Save Changes button.**

The Page Tab is created. If you click the Apps link at the top of the page, you see all your apps listed, as shown in Figure 2-9. The app is available to you to edit at any time. Your next step is to navigate to the App Profile Page, where you can install this app on your Facebook Page, as we explain in the next section.

Figure 2-9:
Your iFrame
Page Tab
has been
created.

Installing the iFrame application on your Facebook Page

After you create your iFrame app, you need to install it on your Facebook Page. You can complete the steps in the preceding section, or you can go to the Developer page at `https://developers.facebook.com/apps`, select your app in the Recently Viewed section of the left sidebar, and then click the Edit App button in the top-right corner (see Figure 2-9).

To add the application to your Facebook Page, find your 15-digit app ID/API key at the top of the App page and then follow these steps:

1. **Type the following URL in your browser window, using your app ID and replacing *YOUR_APP_ID* with the 15-digit app ID/API key:**

   ```
   https://facebook.com/add.
   php?api_key=YOUR_APP_ID&pages=1.
   ```

   You're taken to the site where you add your app to your Page, as shown in Figure 2-10.

2. **From the Add This Application To drop-down menu (see Figure 2-10), choose the Page where you want to add your app.**

3. **Click the Add *App Name* button.**

Figure 2-10: Select the Page where you want to add your app.

Now your iFrame app is added as a custom tab to your Page. You can navigate to your page and change the position of your tab just as you would any tab.

Using Third-Party Applications

If you're not an experienced HTML coder and don't want to mess around with creating an iFrame app, there's still hope! Several third-party applications exist to make installing an iFrame app easier.

Many third-party applications host your content for you, which means that you don't need to have your own web host or server. (We go deeper into these applications and their capabilities later in this section.) Many apps give you the option of uploading an image or HTML code. If you're good at coding a web page, you can use this space to create a mini web page, and the code is hosted by the app. If you're using HTML to code a mini web page, you have to host the images that you're putting on the Page.

Many of these applications allow you to have *fan-only* content. (Some call this content the *reveal tab* or *fan gating*.) This feature allows you to have one image on top of some hidden content, and visitors can't see the hidden content until they click Like (refer to Figure 2-3). If they like your Page already, the hidden content is available to them at any time.

Here's what you need before using a third-party application:

✦ **Custom image:** This image can be in any picture format, and it must be a maximum 810 px wide. There's no limit to the height, but if you want the image to appear "above the fold" on computer screens, don't make it higher (taller) than 500 px. Many apps also have a 520 px option that centers the image on the tab.

You can create a custom tab that shows only this image. Or you can add fan-only content, which requires another image with the same dimensions or HTML code that displays a web page hidden below the image.

✦ **HTML code:** You can use this code to display a mini web page. You can use the HTML code alone or use that code below a custom image for fan-only content.

You can tell what application was used to create a custom Page by the icons below the tab Cover photos. If you see a star that matches the icon on the Static HTML: iFrame Tabs Page, for example, the Page owner used this app to create the Page. This information is useful sometimes if you're spying on the competition to see what they're doing.

Setup of the apps is left to the user, but you can see a bit about the back end of the apps and their capabilities.

Heyo

Heyo has a drag-and-drop design process that makes it very easy to add different elements to your custom tab without knowing how to code HTML. Because of the flexibility and configurability of Heyo, we don't cover all the steps here. Heyo has some nice video tutorials on its website. Free and paid options are available; you can find out more at `https://heyo.com`. Figure 2-11 shows an example of a custom tab created with Heyo.

In the dashboard area of Heyo, you can select different widgets to add to your custom tab, add a background, or use a template to get started. The Heyo dashboard is shown in Figure 2-12. When you have the custom tab in show-worthy condition, you can publish that tab to your Page.

Figure 2-11:
A custom
tab created
with the
Heyo
application.

Static HTML for Pages

Involver's application is called Static HTML for Pages, and the best place to access it is www.involver.com/applications. You can display an image on your custom tab or write HTML code to display something more complex.

Involver has also developed several Facebook applications, such as YouTube and Twitter apps that you can read more about in Book III, Chapter 4.

Involver allows you to use two of its applications for free; after that, you're charged a monthly fee to use any additional applications. If you're using two of Involver's existing applications, you may want to choose one of the other iFrame applications for your custom tab.

Figure 2-12:
The Heyo
dashboard.

To install the Static HTML for Pages app, log in to Facebook as your personal Profile and then follow these steps:

1. **Go to** www.involver.com/applications **and scroll down to the Static HTML app.**

2. **Click the Free Install button.**

   A pop-up window appears, listing the Pages you manage. Choose which Page to install the app.

3. **Click the Add to Static HTML for Pages button next to the Page where you want to install this app.**

   You see a place where you get information about the app and select the visibility (who can see the app).

4. **Choose Everyone from the drop-down menu in the bottom-left corner (if it isn't selected already).**

5. **Click Go to App.**

   You see the permissions page.

6. **Click Allow.**

   You're taken to a page where you enter your company name and phone number and accept the terms of service.

7. **Enter your company name and phone number, check the box next to the Terms of Service link, and click Save Changes.**

   You're taken to a page where you can enter your HTML or select an image to display (see Figure 2-13).

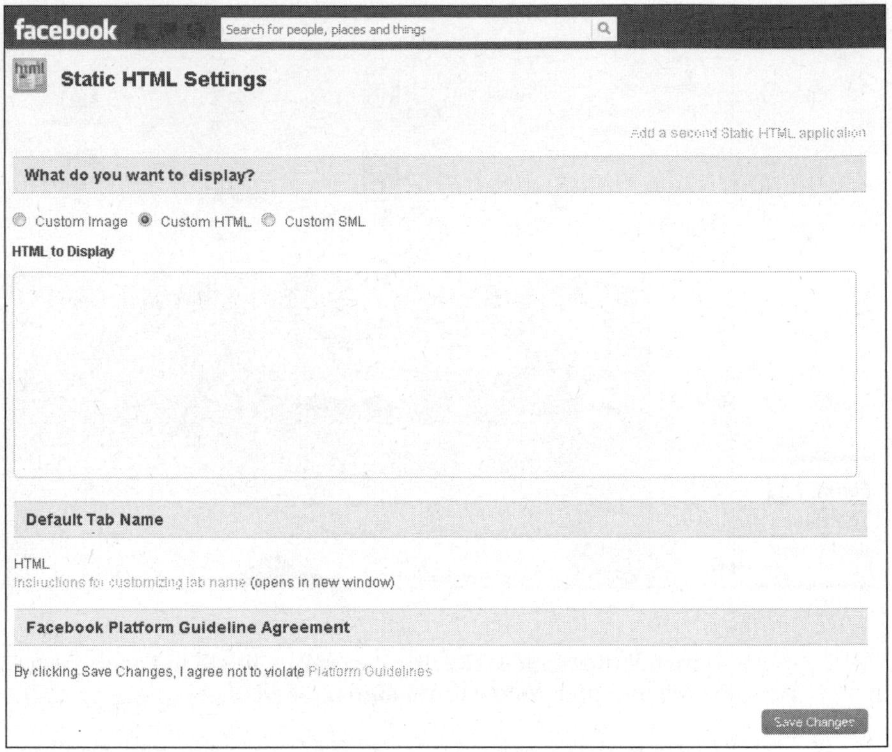

Figure 2-13: Configure Static HTML for Pages.

8. **Select the radio button next to the type of information you want to display:**

   • *Custom Image:* A browser box appears, and you can browse your computer files to enter the image file.

   • *Custom HTML:* A box appears, allowing you to enter your HTML code.

   • *Custom SML: SML* stands for *Social Markup Language* and requires a license from Involver to use. You can find out more at www. involver.com/sml.

9. **Click Save Changes.**

   You see your images uploaded in a preview box. You're finished and can click Return to Facebook Page in the top-right corner to verify that your custom tab is working properly.

ShortStack

ShortStack is a drag-and-drop custom tab editor that offers various widgets that you can add to your tab, as shown in Figure 2-14. With the widgets, you can add photos, text, forms, products, HTML code, and many more features. The widgets stack on top of one another, but templates divide the space into segments that you can edit separately. ShortStack also has a sweepstakes app that you can design yourself.

Figure 2-14:
ShortStack
has widgets
that you can
add to your
custom tab.

ShortStack has a free plan for pages with fewer than 2,000 likes; the prices go up incrementally, depending on how many fans you have. The nice thing about a free option is that you can try your hand at the design tool before committing to purchase it.

To get started, go to www.shortstackapp.com, and click the Register Now link, or click the Login with Facebook button to link the app to your Facebook Profile.

Static HTML: iFrame Tabs

With the Static HTML: iFrame Tabs application, you can create fan-only content. This application allows you to upload an image directly (if you have a $29-per-month paid plan), or you can use HTML code to reference an image to display. You can have multiple Static HTML tabs on your page for free if you don't need to have the images hosted.

To use this application, go to http://apps.facebook.com/static_html_plus. Alternatively, you can usually find it by searching for the title of the app in the search bar of Facebook; you should see it in the drop-down list of search results. You'll know that you've found the correct app if you see a star icon on the application Page. (With all the similar application names, it helps to know what you're looking for!) You must use HTML coding for this app, but the good news is that the app is free. Also, you can have multiple tabs on your Page with this app for free.

When you're on the Static HTML: iFrame Tabs application Page, follow these steps to install the app on your business Page:

1. **Click the blue Add Static HTML to a Page button.**

You're taken to a screen with a drop-down menu that allows you to choose the Page where you want to add the app.

2. **Choose the Page from the Add Page Tab drop-down menu, as shown in Figure 2-15.**

With your Page selected, click here

Add Page Tab

Select the Facebook Pages to add Static HTML: iframe tabs to:

Epic Change ▾

Add Page Tab   Cancel

Choose the Page that you want to add the app to

3. **When you have your Page selected, click the Static HTML: iFrame Tabs link.**

You're now taken to your Facebook Page.

4. **Click the Welcome tab with the star icon below your Cover photo.**

You see the editor page for the app, as shown in Figure 2-16.

View tab in Facebook ▸   Done editing tab ✖

Content   Fangate   Analytics   Settings   ❓ Support   Save & Publish   🔍 Preview tab

⭐ Static HTML   See more apps   Choose an HTML template

index.html

You only need to use this index.html box to host your code, style.css
and script.js are for if you prefer to organize your code further.   Upload image...

5. **Enter your HTML content and the optional fan-only HTML content.**

6. **Click the Preview tab in the top-right corner.**

   You're taken to another window, where you have to view your tab as a fan, view your tab as a nonfan, or go back to the editor.

7. **Click the View Your Tab as a Public and Fans link to make sure that the tab looks right if you are using the Fans-Only content option.**

8. **Click the Edit Tab button to get back into the editor page.**

9. **Click the Save and Publish button in the top-right corner.**

   You've set up your custom tab!

TabSite

TabSite is another iFrame application that you can use to create multiple subpages within one page. TabSite is very versatile, offering a variety of paid plans and a free plan that includes ads (not recommended). When you look at the pricing, note the Bronze plan, which features two tabs and no ads for $5 per month.

TabSite also has several engagement apps available, allowing you to give people deals on your products for sharing the link to your app or pinning the app in Pinterest, or to give a group deal to a certain number of people.

Figure 2-17 shows the design area of TabSite, where you can add widgets or use a template to get started. You can have multiple tabs within the custom tab so that you create a mini website within the page. We don't cover all the steps for installing the app, but you can get started by clicking the Sign Up Free! button at www.tabsite.com.

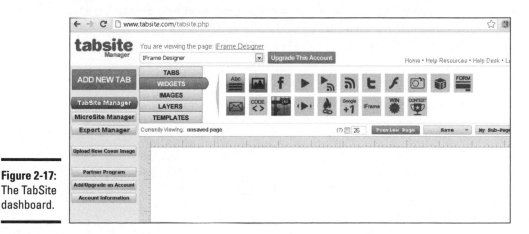

Figure 2-17: The TabSite dashboard.

FanPageEngine

FanPageEngine has some great templates that you can customize to give your tab a professional look. It also has photo and video contest apps, as well as a Deals app, as shown in Figure 2-18. Pricing starts at $27 per month for one Facebook Page.

Figure 2-18:
FanPage
Engine
has video
tutorials
and contest
apps.

FanPageEngine also has great videos that help you see exactly how to set up its apps. To watch some of the setup videos and to get started, go to www.fanpageengine.com, and scroll down to click the Choose Your Plan Now button.

Book VI

Making Facebook Come Alive with Events and Contests

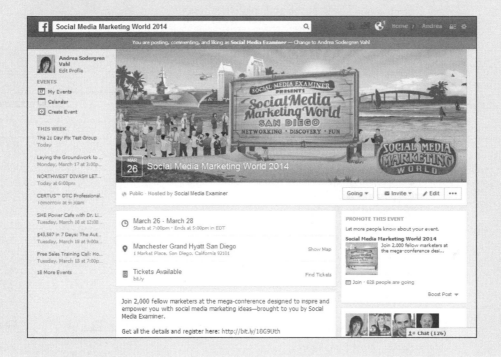

Contents at a Glance

Chapter 1: Creating Facebook Events..........................367

Getting Started with Facebook Events...367
Showing Your Facebook Events in Different Places..........................369
Uncovering Limitations of Facebook Events......................................380
Promoting an Event 381

Chapter 2: Building Excitement with a Contest 389

Thinking about Running a Contest? 389
Deciding What You Want from a Contest 391
Choosing a Contest Type 393
Understanding Facebook and Legal Restrictions 397
Defining Success 398

Chapter 3: Running a Timeline Contest 401

Preparing for Your Timeline Contest...401
Administering Your Timeline Contest..408
Promoting Your Timeline Contest..411
Selecting a Lucky Winner 412

Chapter 4: Using Third-Party Contest Applications...............417

Finding a Contest Application...417
Comparing Contest Applications on the Web.....................................418
Getting to Know the Contest Applications..420
Delivering the Prizes 422
Budgeting for an App 422
Designing Your Contest with the TabSite Application 423
Using the Heyo Application for Your Sweepstakes 431
Using the Woobox Sweepstakes Application......................................433
Using the Offerpop Application 439
Adjusting the App's Photo 443

Chapter 5: Promoting Your Contest and Analyzing the Results 447

Setting Up a Blog Tour 447
Promoting Your Contest on Your Blog or Website.............................449
Using Facebook Open Graph to Allow Entries Anywhere on the Web..................451
Using Social Media to Promote Your Contest.....................................452
Using Facebook to Promote an External Contest...............................455
Analyzing Your Contest Results...456
Adjusting Your Strategy Based on Analytics 459
Planning Future Contests 461

Chapter 1: Creating Facebook Events

In This Chapter

✔ **Creating an event: the basics**

✔ **Working around Page event limitations**

✔ **Sharing your event with your community**

*U*sing the Facebook Events feature can create a lot of buzz around an event, your store, an online event, or even a product or book launch. Facebook Events show up on people's Timelines and within their Events area, and are even searchable by anyone on Facebook. Add to the mix the fact that any time a Friend interacts with your event, that person's Friends all see something in their News Feeds about the event, which gives it a lot of free publicity courtesy of Facebook.

If you've been on Facebook for very long, you've probably received an event invitation yourself, so you may be familiar with Facebook Events. If not, don't worry; in this chapter, you see how to set up an event, the best practices for getting the word out about your event, and tips on using events with your Page.

Getting Started with Facebook Events

Facebook Events can be a powerful way to get your event noticed and shared within the Facebook community. But just as with any marketing activity in Facebook, you need to be mindful of the balance between sharing your event and spamming people with unwanted posts about it.

Because Facebook Events show up in multiple places within Facebook, they are more visible than just Timeline posts. Facebook makes it easy to have Friends invite other Friends to events, and if an event is public, anyone who has a Facebook account can RSVP. Figure 1-1 shows a fundraising event.

Don't make your event public if your event is at your home. Random strangers have shown up to events that were posted on Facebook publicly and then vandalized the homes.

Facebook Events can be beneficial for many types of events:

✦ Charity events

✦ Book tours

✦ Virtual webinars

✦ Open houses

✦ Big sales at your store

When you create a Facebook Event on your Page, you won't be able to invite your fans directly; see the section "Uncovering Limitations of Facebook Events," later in this chapter. However, other people can invite guests if they RSVP to your event. Note that after you "Join" or respond Maybe to the event, you can invite your friends. News of a Facebook Event can spread through Friends inviting other Friends.

Figure 1-1:
A fundraising event.

Social Media Examiner has done a great job of promoting its virtual webinars and live conferences through Facebook Events. (Figure 1-2 shows an example.) It uses the Event page actively to answer questions about the event and give new information about the event.

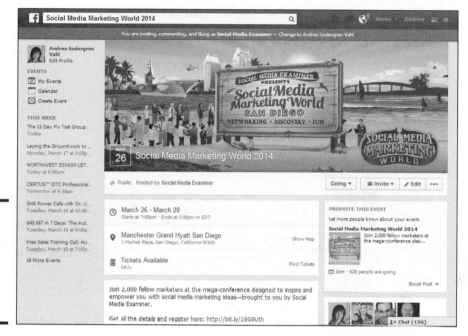

Book VI
Chapter 1

Creating Facebook
Events

Figure 1-2:
Social
Media
Marketing
World had
over 2,000
attendees.

You can create Facebook Events through your Profile, and you can create them through your business Page (or Page; we use those terms interchangeably). Depending on the type of event you're promoting, we recommend creating an event through your Facebook Page because it's better for your branding and complies with Facebook's terms that disallow you from using your Profile for your own commercial gain. There are some limitations involved with creating events on your Page, and we cover the best ways to get around those limitations later in this chapter, in "Uncovering Limitations of Facebook Events."

Showing Your Facebook Events in Different Places

Facebook Events are potentially seen in five places, which is why you want to create them. You give your connections five ways to find out about your event, as follows:

✦ The right sidebar of the home page lists the next upcoming event.

✦ The Events link on the left sidebar of the home page shows a link to all the current events you've created or are invited to.

✦ When an event is created, it appears in the News Feeds and tickers of all your Friends (if you create the event on your Profile) or in the News Feeds and tickers of all your likers. Facebook Events created by a Page are always public. Facebook Events created by personal Profiles can be visible only to invitees or certain personal lists.

✦ When people are invited to an event, they get a notification in their notifications area.

✦ When people are invited to an event, they get an e-mail about the event (if they have e-mail notifications enabled).

On the right sidebar of your home page, you see the most current event coming up, as shown in Figure 1-3. You may have to expand the events to see all the ones coming up, as shown.

Figure 1-3: Events appear on the home page.

Having the events listed on the home page of Facebook makes them very visible to potential customers, which is a perfect reason to create events for your business. The events listed are happening now or coming up next, so this area is good for reminding people of near-future events — just not as effective for events further in the future.

You also find a link to all your events on the left sidebar of your home page. When you click that link, all the events you've been invited to appear on the Events page, as shown in Figure 1-4.

You can see your events two ways, and you get to choose the way:

✦ **List form:** See Figure 1-4. This is the default view.

✦ **Calendar form:** See Figure 1-5.

To open Calendar view, click the Calendar button in the top-left corner, near the Events heading.

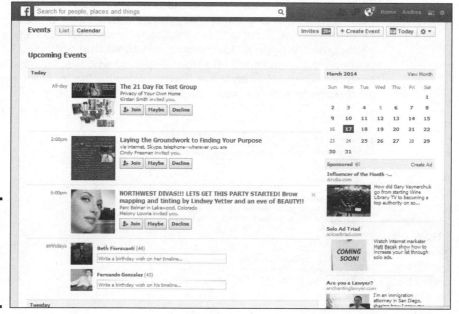

Figure 1-4:
All your events on the Events page (in List view).

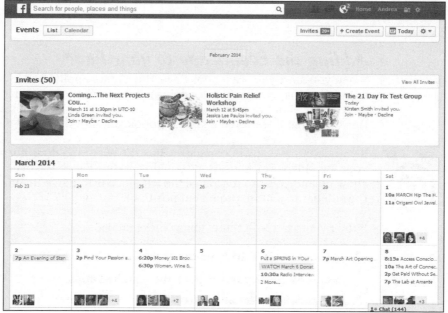

Figure 1-5:
See your events in Calendar view.

When you get invited to an event, it also shows up in your notifications area (see Figure 1-6). This is another way that your event gets increased visibility. Everyone you invited or who is attending receives notifications when you change something about the event or post about the event. (See SummerToast's post notification in Figure 1-6.) The only people who won't see the notifications are those who weren't invited or have declined the invite. These postings can be great reminders and can give your event increased visibility.

Figure 1-6: You're notified about posts regarding events you're invited to.

Adding the Events app to your Page

When you start your Facebook Page, the Events application is available although it may not be immediately visible under the More link just below your cover photo as shown in Figure 1-7. Events is a Facebook application (meaning that it was created by Facebook, and not by a third party).

If you don't have any upcoming events, the event tab does not show up in your left sidebar of Apps. Once you do create a Facebook Event, the tab does show up and you can rearrange the left sidebar to move the tab higher up the sidebar to a more prominent position.

If the Events tab isn't there, follow these steps:

1. **Click Manage Tabs from the More menu.**

   You see a pop-up box with all the installed apps.

2. **Select Add or Remove Tabs.**

   You are taken to the Page dashboard, displaying all the current apps and the available apps you can add as shown in Figure 1-8.

3. **Select Add App next to the Events app, as shown in Figure 1-8.**

   The Events app is added to your tabs.

Book VI
Chapter 1

Creating Facebook
Events

Figure 1-7:
Look for the
Events tab
under the
More menu.

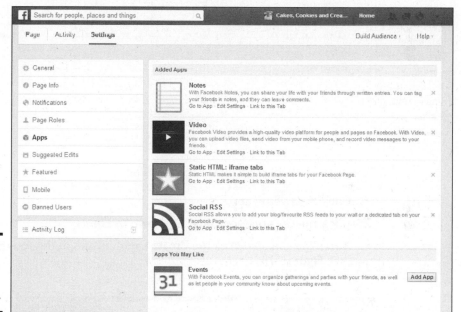

Figure 1-8:
Add the
Events App
to your tabs.

Once you create an event, the event shows in the left sidebar as an
upcoming event. But you may want to position the tab higher up the page
so that it is more visible to visitors. To swap the Events app with one of
the other apps:

1. **Click the More menu under the cover photo.**

A drop-down menu appears.

2. **Select Manage Tabs.**

A pop-up box appears; see Figure 1-9.

3. Click and hold on the Events tab and drag it up to a higher position.

The About Tab cannot be moved. See Book III, Chapter 2 for more information about adding apps to your Page.

4. Click Save.

Figure 1-9:
Swap app
positions
to make
sure that
the Events
app is more
visible.

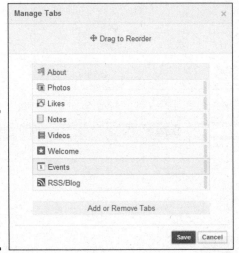

To create an event from your Facebook Page:

1. Click the Events app.

2. Click the Create Event link, as shown in Figure 1-10.

Note: You can also click the Create Event button in the top-right corner (see Figure 1-10).

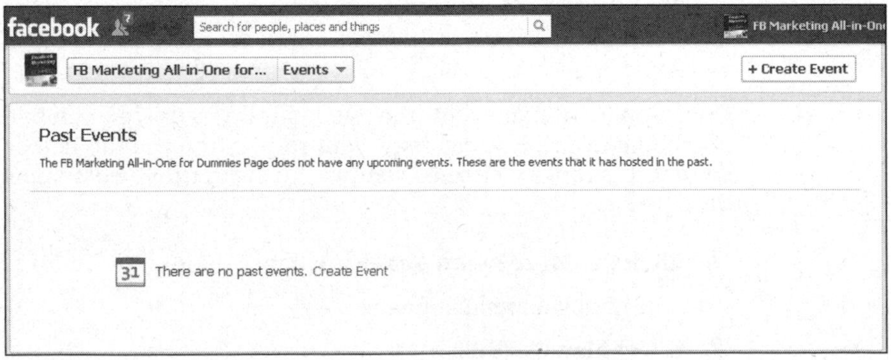

Figure 1-10:
Click the
Create
Event link to
start creat-
ing your
event.

You can also create an event from the Publisher directly on your Timeline. See Book III, Chapter 1 for more information about using the Publisher to create an event.

Entering the event details

When you're creating an event, you have to enter details. See Figure 1-11.

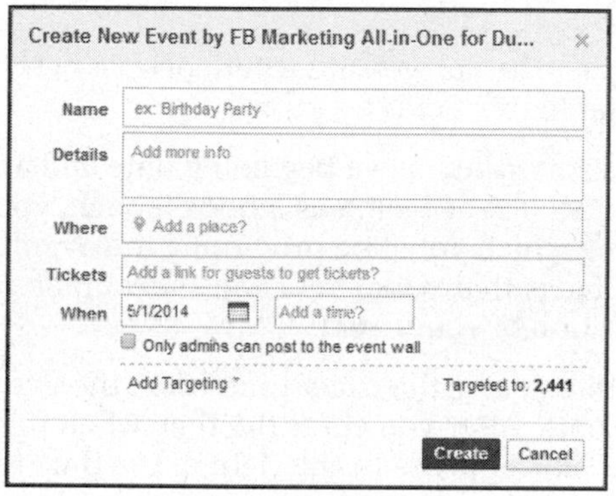

> **Create New Event by FB Marketing All-in-One for Du...** ✕
>
> **Name** | ex: Birthday Party
> **Details** | Add more info
> **Where** | ⚲ Add a place?
> **Tickets** | Add a link for guests to get tickets?
> **When** | 5/1/2014 📅 | Add a time?
> ☐ Only admins can post to the event wall
> -
> Add Targeting ˅ | Targeted to: **2,441**
>
> [Create] [Cancel]

Figure 1-11:
Enter event
details here.

You can't start working on an event and save it as a "draft" and then publish it later. So before you start, make sure that you have all the details ready! As soon as you click the Create button, the event will be published. (You can make changes, however, which we discuss in the later section, "Editing your event.")

Enter your event details in the following fields:

+ **Name:** The event name will show up in people's calendars, their notifications, and posts about the event, so make the name compelling and descriptive.

+ **Details:** Write a description about the event, what you plan to do, why someone should attend, and so on. Put the main information in the first seven lines because that's what people see. After seven lines, users have to click the See More link to see the rest of the description.

  As of this writing, Facebook doesn't offer a way for attendees to pay to register for events. If your event requires paid registration, you need to send attendees to another site where you can accept payments (such as Eventbrite); put the link to this site in the first part of your description. You can have a very long description in the Details field, and giving people as much information as possible here is a good idea.

+ **Where:** Fill in this field with a description of where the event is to be held. The information in the Where field also shows up if you post a link to this event or share this event, so make sure that you provide the name of the venue and a description.

If the event is going to be held at a place that has a Facebook Page, or if the place has been categorized as a Facebook Place, you can start typing the place's name and link to it. That way, people will be able to see more information about the place within your event. If you start typing the address of your event, the Place or Page may come up in the field that's tied to that address, and you can select the Facebook Place or Page.

If you're holding an online or virtual event, you can add more description to market it, such as "In your pajamas at home" or "An online exclusive event."

✦ **Tickets:** If you have an external website where people need to register or buy tickets, enter that in this field.

✦ **When:** For typical events, you have a beginning time and an end time. If you're promoting an occurrence such as a book launch, you can specify a range of time during which you'll be promoting the event. The benefit of using a range of time is that your event will show up on people's sidebars for the duration of your event.

To enter a range of time, enter the exact time when the event begins, rather than just the date. After you enter the time when the event begins, an End Time? link appears to the right of the time field; click that link to enter the end time for your event.

✦ **Only Admins Can Post to the Event Wall:** By default, this check box is deselected. If you don't allow attendees to post on the Event page (also called the Event Wall), they can't ask questions, communicate about the event, or connect with other people — all things that you want them to do! Disable this feature by selecting this check box.

✦ **Add Targeting:** You can select some targeting based on Gender, Relationship status, Educational status, Interested In, Age, Location, or Language so that the initial post about the Event is only shown to those people. In general, we recommend not restricting the post because it's better to have it be seen by as many people as possible.

Click the Create button when you've filled out all the fields. You are taken into the Event where you can add a photo as shown in Figure 1-12.

Your event will be immediately posted to your Page Timeline, so we recommend adding a photo right away. You can't add a photo until you create the event, though. You can immediately hide the event if you aren't ready to announce it to the world, but your event shows up on your Events tab.

Even if you don't have a specific picture to go with the event, find one on the web (making sure that you have the appropriate permissions or that the picture is royalty free), or use one of your previous photos you have uploaded to Facebook. You want a picture to go with your event to make your display more visibly interesting. See Figure 1-13.

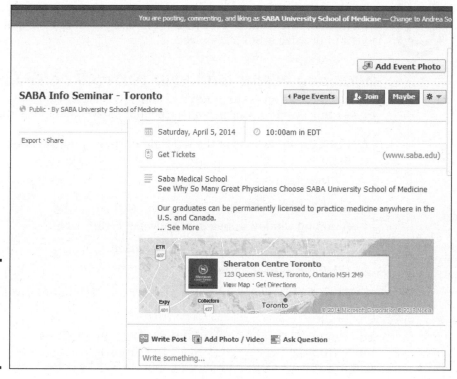

Figure 1-12: Add an Event photo right after creating the Event.

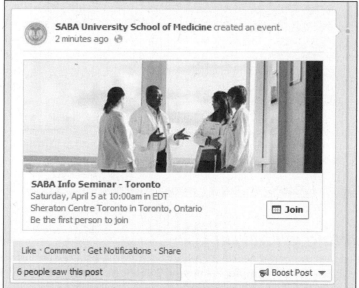

Figure 1-13: Your Event is posted to your Timeline.

If you're hosting a large event, design a picture or image specifically for it. You'll have more branding for your event and get a better response. The best Event photo size is 801 x 250 pixels.

Synching events with your personal calendar

After you create an event or RSVP to someone else's event, you can easily export this event to your personal calendar so you don't miss the event.

1. **Click the three dots in the top-right corner of the Facebook Event page.**

   A drop-down menu appears.

2. **Choose Export Event.**

   A pop-up window appears, as shown in Figure 1-14.

3. **Select the Save to Calendar radio button.**

4. **Click the Export button.**

   The event is downloaded as an ICS (`.ics`) calendar file, which works with Outlook.

You can turn off notifications for the event from the three dot's drop-down menu (top-right corner) if needed. The three dots appear only after you confirm you are Going (by clicking Join) or Maybe going to the event.

Figure 1-14:
Choose where to export the Facebook Event.

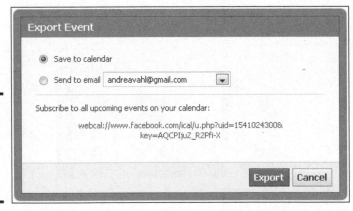

Editing your event

In case you need to make a change to your event after you create it, editing the event is very simple. From your Facebook Page, follow these steps:

1. **Click the Events tab below your Cover photo.**

   You see your events listed, as shown in Figure 1-15.

Figure 1-15:
Your events
are listed
when you
click the
Events tab.

**Book VI
Chapter 1**

**Creating Facebook
Events**

2. **Click the title of the event you want to edit.**

   You're taken to the Event details area.

3. **Click the Edit button under the event photo, as shown in Figure 1-16.**

4. **Edit any of the event details just as though you were creating the event.**

5. **Click the Save button after you make your changes.**

Figure 1-16:
Click the
Edit button
under the
Event photo.

Canceling your event

Canceling a Facebook Event is easy. Of course, you can edit the Event information if you need to, as we discuss in the preceding section. If you accidentally create multiple events or need to cancel an event, however, follow these steps:

1. **Go to your event by clicking the Events tab below your Cover photo.**

2. **Click the title of the event.**

You're taken to the Event details area.

3. **Click Edit.**

4. **Select Cancel Event in lower-left corner of the pop-up box that appears (see Figure 1-17).**

A warning asks whether you're sure you want to cancel.

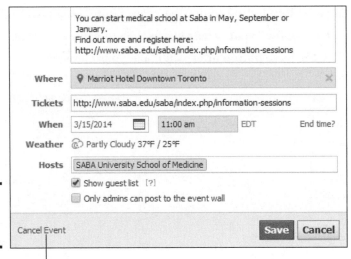

Figure 1-17:
Cancel an
Event here.

Click here to cancel

5. **Click the blue Yes button.**

Your event is canceled. As the warning reads, the cancellation can't be undone, and you'll no longer be able to see the event. Invited guests receive a notification that the event has been canceled.

Uncovering Limitations of Facebook Events

Creating a Facebook Event on your Facebook Page is different from creating the event on your Facebook Profile in two main ways:

✦ **When you create an event via your Page, you can't directly invite your fans to your event.** You can log in as your Profile, join the event, and then invite your personal friends to it. You may have some friends who overlap as fans of your Page and it can be helpful to invite them. When you create an event on your Profile, you can select the guests whom you want to invite from your list of Facebook Friends. These people receive a notification that you've invited them to your event; they also get an e-mail notification if they have that feature enabled. But because Facebook Pages can't invite their fans, you have to get the word out about your event by posting it to your Timeline and encouraging others to invite their Friends from within the event itself.

A business Page can't invite its fans to an event because the guest list could be public information. Facebook does watch out for privacy concerns at times!

✦ **When you create the Event via your Page, you can't send Facebook e-mails to the people who will be attending the event.** Facebook e-mails are very visible and helpful when you need to let people know about a major change. Any activity within the event will still show up in a user's notifications area (unless they declined), which is also visible.

Even though you have these limitations when you create an event on your Page, we still recommend that you use your Page for any business activities. Facebook Events can still be beneficial ways to promote your event to your community.

Promoting an Event

After you create your Facebook Event, promote it. Make your promotion fun and exciting; post a few teaser announcements to let your community know to be watching your Page. Something like "Big news coming tomorrow about something you won't want to miss" can work well to create some buzz before you post the actual event.

Remind people about your event often, just in case they missed the post in their News Feeds. Having said that, there's a line between getting the word out about your event and overpromoting it. To avoid crossing this line, make sure that you still have plenty of value in your other posts. Also, don't just post your event over and over, or people will unlike or hide your Page! A good general rule is to have no more than ten percent of your posts promotional.

Inviting your community to your event

Because you can't invite your community via a standard Facebook invitation, try these main ways to get the word out about your event:

✦ Post your event to your Timeline as a link.

✦ Tag your event in a Timeline post.

✦ Post updates.

You may also think about running a Facebook ad campaign that targets your audience or using Facebook Promoted Posts. See Book VIII for more information on advertising.

Vary your posts and keep them fun.

Notifying your Page community of your event

Your event was posted to your Timeline when you created it, but you should repost your event regularly. Some people will have missed the initial post, and others may need to be reminded to RSVP to your event.

To continue getting the word out about your event, share the event as a link on your Page at least once or twice per week. Include the link your updates — just click the Link button in your update and paste the link.

Each Facebook Event has its own unique URL, just like any other website. You can find the link to the event this way:

1. **Click the Event tab on your Facebook Page.**

2. **Select the event.**

   See Figure 1-18. The picture for your event is the one posted next to the event.

Copy this URL

Figure 1-18: Copy the Event's link, and paste it into a post on your Page.

When you post your event as a link, it's easy to share with other people. If the event link is in the News Feed, people can click Share to see a pop-up window that lets them fill out their own invitation to the event, as shown in Figure 1-19. In the status part of your post, ask people to click the Share button and spread the word about your event.

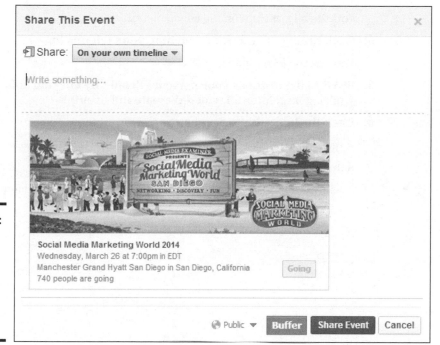

Figure 1-19: Encourage people to Share to post your event to their News Feeds.

Find ways to vary your posts about your event. Give away a promotional item, feature a particular vendor or sponsor of your event, or add something new to the event to give you a reason to make a new announcement about it.

Inviting Friends to the event

After you create your event, you can invite your Friends. If you don't have any Friends who are also fans of your page or who are interested in your business, this might be a step you don't need to take.

If you have some overlap between your Friends and fans, though, take some time to invite your Friends:

1. **Click the down arrow in the upper-right corner. Select your Profile from the drop-down menu under Use Facebook As.**

You have to be logged in as your Profile rather than your Page to invite your Friends.

2. **Go to your Facebook Page but remain logged in as your Profile.**

You can do this by typing the URL of your Facebook Page in your browser window or selecting your Facebook Page name from the left sidebar of your personal Profile home Page under the Pages heading.

3. **Click the Events tab on the left sidebar our under the More menu under the cover photo.**

You see all your upcoming events listed.

4. **Click the event you will be inviting your Friends to.**

You see the Event page.

5. **RSVP to the event as your personal Profile by clicking Join (assuming you're going; after all, you did create the event).**

6. **Click the Invite button under the Event photo.**

A drop-down menu appears.

7. **Select Choose Friends.**

A window shows a list of your Friends, as you can see in Figure 1-20.

Figure 1-20: Select the Friends you want to invite to your event.

8. **Select the Friends you want to invite and click the blue Send button.**

You see a message that your Friends have been invited and that you're done. Your Friends receive a notification that you invited them, and the event will appear in their Events area. If your Friends have already RSVP'd to the event, they will be grayed out.

There is no Select All button when inviting your Friends to an event; you have to individually select the check boxes next to your Friends' Profile pictures. You can also filter your Friends by using the Search by Name drop-down menu (refer to Figure 1-20). You can then display all the Friends from one of your Facebook Lists to make selecting them easier. This works well if you have created a Facebook List just for your business contacts.

Asking attendees to share the event

The people who are attending the event can be your best advocates for spreading the word, but you may need to educate people about how to share the event and invite their Friends.

Anyone can share an event, regardless of whether that person has RSVP'd or has even been formally invited. However, you can invite your Friends only to an event that you have RSVP'd for. Even if you declined the invitation, you can still invite your Friends to the event.

Your invitees have three ways to share:

✦ Click the Share link in the post when the event has been shared as a link as described earlier.

✦ Paste the direct link to the event as shown in Figure 1-18 into their Facebook status area.

✦ After people have RSVP'd to the event, they can invite their Friends to the event using the Invite button that appears in the upper-right corner of the Event page (refer to Figure 1-21) in the same way you invited your Friends. The person must have responded to the event by clicking the Join, Maybe, or Decline button of an event before she can invite Friends.

The fewer steps you ask users to take, the better. Telling people to share the post by clicking the Share link is the easiest way; don't make the process too hard! You may need to educate your connections about how to share this event:

✦ When you post your event in a Timeline post, include a call to action such as "Feel free to share this event with your Friends by clicking the Share link below this post."

✦ E-mail people, asking them to help promote your event by going to your Facebook Event URL and clicking the Share link in the bottom-left corner.

✦ If you want to tell someone how to Invite their Friends to the event, share your event as a Link, tell people to click the event (if they've already RSVP'd), and then click the Invite Friends button to invite their Friends directly.

Figure 1-21:
Click the
Invite button
in the upper-
right section
of the event
and select
Share Event.

Encouraging interaction within your Facebook Event

Your Facebook Event contains its own page on which people can post messages about the event. Here's what you should do on that page:

✦ **Respond ASAP.** If people are posting about the event, make sure that you're responding and connecting. People may have questions about the event, and you want to answer those questions as quickly as possible. Other people likely have the same questions, and the sooner you address any issues that arise, the better for your business.

✦ **Post evidence.** If your event is recurring, post some pictures of past events to show people how much fun or well attended the past events were. You may also want to post pictures of past events on your Page Timeline and then tag the events.

✦ **Enlist friends' help.** Ask some of your close friends who are coming to the event to post on the event's Timeline to get buzz going, as well as to provide *social proof* — when you can see your Friends or other people giving good feedback about something, you're more likely to respond favorably to it or to give it a try.

The Event postings aren't sent to the News Feeds of people attending the event, but they're visible on the Facebook Event page. People you've invited also get a notification when someone posts to the Timeline of the event, which can be a good reminder to RSVP.

Making a Facebook Ad for your event

Another way to promote your event is to run a Facebook Ad. Putting together such an ad is fairly easy, and it doesn't have to cost a lot of money. Advertising your event can be an effective tool for reaching your target demographic and connecting to new people on Facebook.

When you create a Facebook Ad for an event, people can RSVP easily by clicking the Join link in the ad.

Find out how to set up a Facebook Ad for an event in Book VIII, Chapter 2.

Sharing your Facebook Event outside Facebook

Part of your promotion strategy should be to share your event on other sites as well. When you drive traffic to the Facebook Event, you also increase exposure to your Facebook Page.

When you send the link to your event, just copy and paste the URL (refer to Figure 1-18). Here are some places to share your event:

✦ **Blog or website:** If you have a blog, post a blog entry when your event is announced. If you have a professional logo, place it on the sidebar of your blog or website, with a clickable link that goes back to the Facebook Event.

✦ **E-mail subscribers:** Send an update about your event to your subscribers. If they're not on Facebook, they won't be able to RSVP there, but they will be able to view the event. Give them an alternative way to RSVP if they're not on Facebook.

✦ **Twitter, LinkedIn, and other social media:** If you're on Twitter, tweet the link to your event at least a couple times a week after you announce your event. This can depend on how much you post on Twitter. You want your promotional tweets to stay under ten percent of your total tweets. Also send a message to your LinkedIn connections and to any other social or professional networks you belong to, if appropriate. If your event is local, for example, make sure that you're inviting only local people from your LinkedIn network, and if certain colleagues have a completely different business focus from the topic of your event, don't invite them.

Chapter 2: Building Excitement with a Contest

In This Chapter

✔ Choosing a type of contest

✔ Outlining the details of your contest

✔ Setting targets for success

People love when a Facebook Page lets them know about special offers and promotions. For that reason, we recommend running a contest on your Facebook Page. A contest also gives people a reason to connect with you, makes your Page more fun, and attracts more people to your brand and your site.

So what will your contest look like? You have a lot of options to consider when setting up your contest. In this chapter, we explore how to design your contest, set your targets, and make sure that you're riding on the right side of Facebook law.

Later in the chapter, we clarify the differences between contests and sweepstakes. In a nutshell, a true *contest* has some type of vote to choose the winner (or you choose the winner through judging), and a *sweepstakes* has the winner chosen at random. Throughout this and the next two chapters, we use the term *contest* more collectively to refer to both contests and sweepstakes. To muddy the waters, Facebook refers to contests and sweepstakes as *promotions*. We combine all the terms into one and call them *contests*. Whatever the term, your winning strategy lies in this minibook's next three chapters.

Thinking about Running a Contest?

All different types of businesses can benefit from Facebook contests. The benefits include

✦ **Grow your Facebook community.** Draw attention to your business. If you want more people to join your Facebook community, make liking your Page a requirement for entry. You can run a Timeline contest where all people have to do is like or comment on a certain post on your Page. A Timeline contest is great for boosting engagement with your community, but it won't be as good for adding subscribers to your e-mail list.

Contest disadvantages

Running a contest has some disadvantages:

✔ **Investment of time:** Good promotion can take a lot of time, possibly taking time away from your core business. Plan your contest when you won't be caught trying to do too much at once.

✔ **Investment of money:** Your contest may cost money to run; the prize also may cost money. If you don't receive the benefits you were hoping for, such as a large group of new likers, giving out that prize can feel painful.

✔ **Possible community dissatisfaction:** Some people just don't like contests. If judging is involved, people may get angry if they feel that the judging wasn't done properly, and this situation can create some bad buzz around your brand. Others don't like contests that involve voting because it can cause continual updates of people begging for votes.

One way to combat potential community dissatisfaction may be to think of a special gift for everyone who enters. That gift doesn't have to cost much money. It could be a special e-book or discount given only to contest entrants. Even just a personal note thanking people for entering and for their participation can go a long way to fostering good feelings about your contest.

You can also think about retaining some of the judging rights so that your contest winner isn't based on votes alone. Retaining some of the judging rights also gives you some control over the best candidate when the voting is close.

✦ **Increase brand awareness.** You can also have entrants check in to your Facebook Place to get extra entries in your contest, which can drive awareness of your business location. Checking in can't be the only way entrants enter your contest, however. (For more about Facebook's contest rules, see the "Understanding Facebook and legal restrictions" section, later in this chapter.)

Drawing attention to a product or service that you offer is a way to market it. If you're a consultant, for example, you can offer a consulting package that people may not know about. If you're a florist, you could offer a Fresh Flowers for a Month package to get your community thinking about treating themselves to flowers every week.

✦ **Add subscribers to your newsletter.** It's the same as getting a list of people who are interested in your product or service (which you get when people enter your contest).

Let contest entrants know that they will be added to your e-mail list when they enter (and make sure that they have a way to unsubscribe to comply with spam rules).

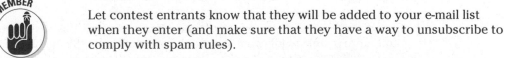

Your prize doesn't have to be expensive or lavish. It just has to be something that your community wants. (A Facebook Page called Chocolate for Breakfast gave away a premium-chocolate prize pack and received more than 700 entries in one week!) You might also receive a glowing recommendation and referrals from the winner of your contest.

Your contest is part of your marketing budget. A well-run and well-publicized contest can be much more effective than a print ad for increasing awareness and engagement.

Deciding What You Want from a Contest

How you design your contest can have a big impact on its success. Ask yourself these questions:

✦ **What type of contest will I run?** It can be a sweepstakes in which the winner is drawn at random or a contest in which people vote for the winner. Will I choose the Timeline contest or use an application? The nice thing about third-party applications is that they handle entries, voting, rule posting, and winner selection within Facebook guidelines. The applications make it easy to run a professional, well-designed contest. Chapter 4 in this minibook explains third-party applications.

Structure your contest to align with your goal.

✦ **How long will it run?** The contest type determines how long you should run it. If it requires voting, how long will the voting period be? Will you have a judging period to narrow the entrants and then allow people to vote on the ones you selected? How much time are you willing and able to promote the contest? For example, if you're running the contest for a month, you need to promote it heavily for a month.

Keep these time frames in mind:

- *Photo or video is required to enter:* One month

- *Sweepstakes:* One to two weeks

- *Timeline contest:* Maybe three or four days — one week, tops

✦ **What will be the requirements for entry?** Will you have users upload a photo or video, comment on your post, send a short essay about why they should win, like your Page as part of the requirements, or just enter their name and e-mail address? The possibilities are endless. If you make the contest too difficult, you may not get as many entrants. Make the contest fun, and you'll have a better chance of having people spread the word about it.

✦ **Should I design the contest application myself?** You have more control over how your contest works if you design it yourself but you will have to code your contest on a separate website and then use an iFrame application to bring the website onto a tab on your Facebook Page. (See Book V, Chapter 2 for more information about creating applications.)

✦ **Will I pick a random winner or have a contest that is judged?** If you intend to have people upload content, it can be more entertaining to have the winner picked by a community vote. This method gives people a reason to come back and check on the progress of their picks.

✦ **Will I ask people to invite their Friends to enter?** You can do this informally in your posts about the contests saying "Feel free to share this with your friends" or you can use an contest app that rewards people for inviting their friends to share with extra entries.

✦ **Will I have an option to sign up for your newsletter?** You can let people know that they will automatically be signed up for your newsletter when they enter (with the contest apps only) or you can give them the option to opt-in to your newsletter by checking a box to receive it. Some apps have this capability and some don't.

✦ **How will I run the contest according to Facebook's contest and promotional rules?** The easiest way is to do a Timeline contest but there are some advantages to running your contest through a third-party application, which we cover in Chapter 4 of this minibook.

Facebook has strict rules about contests. If you don't follow the rules, you're in danger of having your Page shut down. For more information, see the section "Understanding Facebook and legal restrictions," later in this chapter.

✦ **What will the prize be?** Although it helps to have a big budget so you offer something like a trip to London (as offered by Ultimate Women's Expo in Figure 2-1), you can still offer something valuable to your community even if you own a small business. Spend some time considering the prize, and maybe even poll your audience members to see what they'd like.

Some people who enter your sweepstakes are interested only in the prize, not in your company. If you can connect the prize with your business, you have a better chance of connecting with the right audience.

Polling your audience for ideas

Sometimes, you may not be sure what prize you want to offer or what would get the most response from your community. The best way to overcome this obstacle is to ask your users. You can create a poll or survey easily at sites like SurveyMonkey (www.surveymonkey.com) and Zoomerang (www.zoomerang.com). You can use the Question tool in the Facebook Publisher to create a poll for your Page. Ask, "What prize would you like to receive if I held a Facebook contest?" and then add prize options that people can vote on. See Book III, Chapter 1 for more about creating a poll for your Page.

You may be deciding among two or three prizes, and involving your audience in the decision builds more about for the prize and also builds more buzz around the contest. If you don't have any ideas, your audience can help suggest things, but you may not get a consensus.

Figure 2-1:
Ultimate
Women's
Expo offers
an entic-
ing prize
to contest
entrants.

Choosing a Contest Type

You can run two main types of contests:

✦ A contest on your Timeline where people can enter by doing a variety of things: commenting on a post, liking a post, uploading a photo to your Timeline. See Figure 2-2.

✦ A contest that is administered through an app. Typically, the app gathers e-mail addresses.

Each types of contests could also be administered as a

✦ *True contest,* in which there's some vote to choose the winner (or you choose the winner through judging). For example, the contest using an App could have a voting component if people were uploading a video or a photo, and the Timeline contest could also have a voting component if the community was Liking the comments of the entrants.

✦ *Sweepstakes,* in which the winner is chosen at random. Sweepstakes are prevalent on Facebook. The barrier to entry is low because to access the entry form, people typically just have to enter their name and e-mail address, and/or like the Page. Some third-party applications, such as Offerpop or Tabsite, can assist you in choosing a random winner.

Figure 2-2:
Timeline
contests
can be
entered
by liking
a post or
commenting.

Typically, Timeline contests are better for engaging your current community, and contests using an App are better for growing your community and your e-mail list which is better to ensure future sales from the entrants.

Table 2-1 offers some considerations for choosing a contest.

Table 2-1	Choosing a Contest Type	
Contest Type	*What It's Good For*	*Example*
Timeline Contest	Timeline contests are typically more interactive because they require people to enter with a comment or photo but then also vote for their favorite choice. The voting can increase the traffic to the post because people ask their friends to vote for them.	Have your community judge the entries by liking the comments submitted in the post or the photos that are uploaded to your Timeline by the entrants. Hold a "Caption This Photo" contest where people enter their captions under the photo and the one with the most Likes wins.

Contest Type	What It's Good For	Example
Timeline Sweepstakes	A Timeline sweepstakes is where people comment on a post, like a post, or do something like upload a photo to your Facebook Page, and then a winner is chosen at random from all the entries. The challenge can be choosing a random winner from the entries but there are tools that can help. Learn more in Chapter 3 of this minibook.	Post a photo that announces the contest and the prize. The contest photo might have a "Comment and Win" text or something similar so it's obvious what you want them to do.
Contest with an Application	A contest increases your community involvement by having users vote and may drive more of the entrants' Friends to your Page. Plus the Application organizes the entries into a nice format for people to vote easily. If the entry requirements are too complicated, however, you may not get the turnout you hope for.	Have people write a short statement about why they want the prize. A coaching professional judged the entries herself and picked the winner of a free registration to the prize: a retreat. Just remember that you have to use the contest application as the place where people will upload their pictures, enter their essays, and actually enter your contest. Have entrants upload pictures for your community to judge. Realtor.com, for example, ran a holiday-lights picture contest that involved having people upload pictures of their houses decorated with holiday lights. The Facebook community voted on the pictures, and the winner won a $100 gift card.

(continued)

Book VI
Chapter 2

Building Excitement with a Contest

Table 2-1 *(continued)*

Contest Type	What It's Good For	Example
Sweepstakes with an Application	A sweepstakes is better than a contest for growing your Facebook community or e-mail list. In a typical sweepstakes run using Applications, entrants provide their names and e-mail addresses, and possibly like the Page, to access the entry form, and these things are very easy for most people to do. Because of the ease of entry, you may get more participation than a contest application but possibly not as many people sharing word about the contest with their Friends.	Use a Facebook app to collect e-mail entries. Create an image to use within the app that shows the prize and tells people to enter to win.

If you're running a Timeline contest, your contest will be a little more visible to friends of the entrants if you require a comment for entry. When someone comments on a photo, it's more likely to show up in the News Feed. You can get creative with what type of comment you require: a caption to a photo, a name of someone they would share the prize with, or a favorite dish at your restaurant.

Before you put your contest out there, make sure that you have everything in place to kick it off with a bang. As a reminder here's what you need to have in place first:

✦ Decide what type of contest to run

✦ Decide on your prize

✦ Decide how long to run the contest

✦ Make sure you understand the legal restrictions

✦ Get any graphics or images you may need for the contest

✦ Schedule your promotion

✦ Make your measurements

You may be spending money on the contest application, and you want to make sure that you're getting the maximum benefit. You also want to make sure that the contest is well thought out so that you don't get negative results.

Even if you require people to like your page to enter, they also have to officially enter within your contest application or according to the guidelines in your Timeline contest.

Understanding Facebook and Legal Restrictions

You should definitely understand Facebook's promotion guidelines before starting your contest. You may see other people violating the terms, but Facebook can remove materials relating to the promotion or even disable an offender's Page or account, so it pays to follow the rules.

As of this writing, you can find the entire list of Facebook's Promotion rules in section E under point III here:

```
www.facebook.com/page_guidelines.php
```

You can run a contest or sweepstakes on your Facebook Page Timeline or through an application.

One of the more confusing points for businesses is that Timelines can't be used to administer promotions. This means that you can't do any of the following things:

+ Make it a requirement that people "Share this post" to enter.

+ Have people upload a photo to their Timeline to be entered in a contest.

+ Have people share a post on their friend's Timeline to enter.

+ Automatically enter in a drawing anyone who likes your Page. (You can have liking a Page be a condition of entry, but it can't be the only way that people can enter the contest.)

You can suggest that people share the contest with their friends but that cannot be a requirement for entering. You also must include a copy of the official rules either within the application itself or you can link to the official contest rules on an external site such as your website.

Here are some legal restrictions that you need to be aware of:

+ The promotion can't be open to anyone under the age of 18. Facebook does allow people under the age of 18 on its site, however (minimum age of 13).

+ If you set up a sweepstakes, that contest can't be open to people in Belgium, Norway, Sweden, or India.

+ You can't award as prizes or promote the following items: gambling, tobacco, firearms, prescription drugs, and gasoline.

Again, the nice thing about the third-party applications such as the ones mentioned in Chapter 3 of this minibook is that they're set up to follow Facebook's guidelines.

Defining Success

The first thing you should consider when running a contest is your goal. Are you looking for more people in your Facebook community, more subscribers to your newsletter, or more brand awareness? If you begin with the goal in mind, the pieces fall into place.

Before you start your contest, make sure that you know what you're aiming for so that later, you'll know whether you were successful. How many entries, new web hits, and/or mentions of your brand are you hoping for? If you fall short of your goals, you can analyze what you could have changed in the promotion or execution of your contest. We cover the analysis in Chapter 5 of this minibook.

Setting targets

How do you set reasonable targets for entries to your contest? Setting targets can be a bit of a challenge if you've never hosted a contest before. You may look at your first contest as a training ground for future contests — and yes, it's a good idea to do multiple contests.

Of course one of the main targets is a high number of entries. More entries mean more involvement, more excitement, and more awareness about your contest. And if you are using an app for your contest, then it also means more e-mail addresses. Win-win-win!

The number of entries depends on several factors:

✦ **Size of your Facebook community:** If you're starting your contest with 25 people who like your Page, a target of 12 entries from your Facebook Page may be reasonable.

✦ **Size of your e-mail list:** If you have an e-mail list of 500 addresses and an e-mail open rate of 50 percent, you might estimate that of those who open your e-mail, 10 percent will enter, representing 25 entries from your e-mail list. You only know your open rate if your e-mail provider reports that information.

✦ **Other social-media lists (Twitter, LinkedIn, forums, and so on):** You also want to promote your contest on Twitter, LinkedIn, and other places that you frequent online, but the entry rate from these sites may be lower still. You probably can estimate that one percent of your Twitter following and your LinkedIn connections will enter, depending on how engaged you are with these connections.

✦ **Website hits:** If you have your contest listed prominently on your website, you can estimate that some of your website visitors will enter your contest. Entries may be fairly low — possibly around 0.5 percent of your website traffic.

✦ **Size of the prize:** You get a higher opt-in for a bigger prize.

✦ **Length of the contest:** The longer the contest goes, the more time people have to opt in, but don't make the contest run for so long so that people get tired of hearing about it.

- One month is a good time frame if photos, videos, or essays are required.

- One to two weeks is good for sweepstakes.

- Set three to four days for a Timeline contest.

✦ **Other promotional efforts:** These efforts could involve guest posting on another blog to promote your contest, advertising your contest, or distributing flyers about your contest in your local community.

You may want to set a conservative goal of a five percent opt-in for your e-mail and Facebook community, and smaller percentages for other places that you participate on the web. Then take a look at that number and see whether it's a worthwhile number for the money and the time you'll be spending.

Goodwill and buzz are hard to measure and hard to put a price on.

Setting your plan

After you set your targets, set your promotion and marketing plan for your contest. Make sure to get the word out on all channels to engage your audience. Here are places to market your contest:

✦ **Facebook Page:** Obviously, you'll be posting about the contest on your Facebook Page because it's easy for your community members to enter on Facebook. Make sure you provide the URL to the contest App tab on your Facebook Page so that people can easily click over to enter. Remember that people are seeing your updates in their News Feeds and without the URL, they won't know where to enter.

✦ **Blog or website:** If you have a blog, make sure that you have a blog entry ready to go when your contest kicks off. If you have a website, make sure that you have a link or banner that visitors can click to enter the contest.

✦ **E-mail subscribers:** To get buzz about your contest going, start with your current customers. Let them know how they can enter, and ask them to spread the word.

✦ **Twitter and other social media:** If you're on Twitter, make sure that you tweet the link to your contest daily. Send a message to your LinkedIn connections, if appropriate.

✦ **Facebook Ads:** Facebook Ads (see an example in Figure 2-3) are natural places to get people to enter your contest. You can target your demographic in the setup of the ad and send users directly to the link on your Facebook Page that has the entry form to your contest. Or you can boost the post (you boost the post by using the Boost button on the post and pay to have it pushed into the News Feed) that has the Timeline Contest.

Figure 2-3:
Ad for winning a shopping spree.

Win $1,000 at GoLite   ✕

Win a $1,000 shopping spree at the GoLite Holiday Outlets stores in Denver.

You also need to know how you will measure your success. If you are running a Timeline contest, you should keep track of how many entries you get over time, but that is a manual process. One nice thing about third-party Facebook applications is that they do extensive analytics of the entries. The analytics the applications provide vary from app to app. Figure 2-4 shows an example of what these analytics can look like.

Figure 2-4:
A partial snapshot of the analytics on Woobox.

DIRECT AND VIRAL RESULTS BY SOURCE						
SOURCE	DIRECT			VIRAL		
	VISITORS	LIKES	ENTRANTS	VISITORS	LIKES	ENTRANTS
tab	31	4	4	61	0	0
direct	274	102	81	383	0	0

We discuss analyzing your contest results in Chapter 5 of this minibook. Make sure that you have Google Analytics on your site so that you're tracking clicks to your contest entry form. To learn more about Google Analytics and how to install it, go to http://www.google.com/analytics/.

When your plan is in place, you're ready to set up your contest, which we cover in Chapter 3 of this minibook for Timeline Contests and Chapter 4 of this minibook for Contests with Applications.

Keep it fun and exciting so that your community will help spread the word about your contest and make it go viral.

Chapter 3: Running a Timeline Contest

In This Chapter

↳ **Deciding on the parameters of your Timeline contest**

↳ **Administering your Timeline contest**

↳ **Choosing a winner at random**

The easiest way to run a Facebook contest is to run one on your Page Timeline. But don't let the quick setup fool you! Planning is required for your contest to get the results you want. You also have to know the rules of Timeline contests so that you set it up correctly.

A Timeline contest is basically a post that you put on your Page that can be as simple as "Like this post to be entered to win" or as involved as "Upload a photo to our Timeline, get your friends to vote for you by liking your photo, and the photo with the most Likes wins." A Timeline contest takes place on your Timeline, and people do things such as liking a post, commenting on a post, or posting on your Timeline in order to enter.

Timeline contests are great way to get your community participating on your Facebook Page — and they're free to run — but you also want to have a goal in mind, such as bringing awareness to a product or service. Think about the follow up to the contest as well so you can make the most out of your time and effort.

In this chapter, we look at how to structure and set up a Timeline contest and best practices to running them.

Preparing for Your Timeline Contest

After you decide that a Timeline contest is the type of contest for you, spend a little time to think about the following:

✦ When will contest start?

✦ Where will I post the rules of my contest?

✦ How will I monitor my contest?

✦ How will I choose a winner?

✦ What if a tie occurs?

✦ How will I get in touch with the winner?

✦ How long will your contest be?

In this chapter, you learn how to make these decisions for your Timeline contest.

Most important of all: Do you understand Facebook's contest rules?

Understanding the rules

In Chapter 2 of this minibook, we cover some of the Promotion Terms set up by Facebook, but we want to break these down further so that you understand what you can and cannot do with Facebook Timeline Contests.

Businesses can

✦ Require people to like a post and/or comment on a post to be entered

✦ Require that someone post something directly on your Timeline to enter (could be a text post or a photo)

✦ Use Like as a voting method (either liking a post or photo on your Timeline)

✦ Require that someone message your page to enter

✦ Announce the winner of the contest on your page

✦ Require that to win the prize, entrants come back to your page to see who has won the contest

✦ Use a Like button plug-in on a website as a voting mechanism

✦ Use an app plug-in to post an entry to your contest directly on your page

Businesses can't

✦ Require that people share a post or photo to be entered

✦ Require someone to post something on their own Timeline or a friend's Timeline to enter

✦ Require people to tag themselves in a photo to either vote or enter

✦ Have anyone who likes your page be entered to win (contest does not take place on the Timeline)

The biggest mistake currently being made with Facebook Timeline contests by businesses is telling people, "Share this post to be entered." That is a big no-no, and your entire Page is in danger of being shut down without warning if you violate Facebook's terms. But other than that, there are a myriad options available to you with a Timeline contest.

Keep current with Promotions rules because they do change. Before you get started with your contest, check the link for Facebook Page Terms at www.facebook.com/page_guidelines.php.

Assembling the parts

After you review the rules, get a few items in place. You need these basic components:

✦ A photo to post to your Timeline that promotes the contest

✦ A location for your contest rules

✦ Text to announce the contest

✦ Your Facebook Page settings optimized

Photo to post

The ideal photo has text and is eye-catching. Whenever someone shares your contest (and you hope they do), the photo and text travel.

You can create an image that announces the prize in the text, as shown in Figure 3-1.

Figure 3-1: Create a photo that announces your contest.

If you're doing a "Caption this photo" contest, make sure the photo is fun and inspires a lot of different possible captions, like the one in Figure 3-2. Make sure you are following copyright rules around sharing photos and that you have the appropriate permissions to use that photo if it is submitted by someone in your community.

Figure 3-2:
This fun image is perfect for a caption contest.

Don't create an image with a lot of text, or you won't be able to promote the post or boost the post with a Facebook ad. Facebook ads are restricted to a maximum of 20 percent text overlay on the photo.

If you want to test out how much text is in your image according to Facebook's advertising guidelines, they have a Grid Tool where you can upload your photo. Facebook uses a grid system where any image is marked with five columns and five rows and you are allowed a maximum amount of text showing in any five of the squares. To test your image, go to `https://www.facebook.com/ads/tools/text_overlay` and follow these steps:

1. **Click the Choose File button.**

    A popup box appears with your files.

2. **Navigate to the image you want to use for the Timeline contest.**

3. **Select Open.**

   Your photo appears with the 5 x 5 grid system as shown in Figure 3-3.

4. **Click on any box that has text in it.**

   A box that is clicked appears in red. If you are able to click more than five boxes that have text (as shown in Figure 3-3), your image has too much text and can't be advertised with a Boost Post or Promoted Post on Facebook. You may need to consider changing the size and position of your text on your image or not use Facebook Ads for this contest.

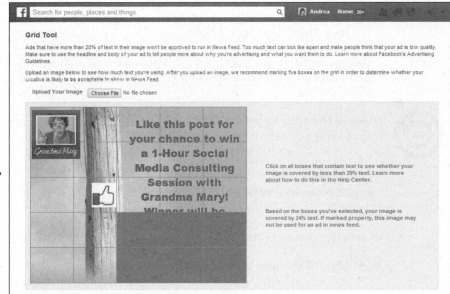

Figure 3-3:
You can test how much text your image has with the Grid Tool.

Once you have determined how much text is in your image, you can just close the window or navigate to another website if needed.

Learn more about Facebook advertising in Book VII.

Location for contest rules

Because you don't want to bog down your post with all your contest rules, put them where you can easily reference them. You have some options:

✦ Put the rules on a separate page on your website and then link to that page, as shown in the first comment on Figure 3-2.

✦ Create a Facebook Note whose URL you can post. See Book III to learn how to create a Facebook Note. You can then post the URL to the Facebook Note in the comments of the announcement of the Facebook contest so that people can reference the official rules.

State these important points in the rules:

✦ "This contest is, in no way, sponsored, endorsed, administered by, or associated with Facebook."

✦ "By entering the contest, the entrant agrees to a complete release of Facebook by each entrant or participant."

This is also known as *Indemnification and Limitation of Liability*. It basically means that people can't sue Facebook because of this contest.

✦ "Winner must claim prize within (a limited time) of notification."

You select how long you want to give the winner to claim the prize. This allows you the ability to safely choose another winner. If one week is too long, three days is sufficient.

Make sure you review Facebook's Promotion terms found under III E to understand Facebook's requirements for contests: `https://www.facebook.com/page_guidelines.php`.

One of the advantages of using an application to run a contest is that the apps typically have a built-in location within the app itself for your rules.

Text to post

Spend some time carefully crafting the text you will use to announce the contest.

Consider these points:

✦ **Should you add hashtags?** Adding hashtags, such as `#Contest` or `#Win`, can help your contest gain visibility, but you may attract the type of people who just enter contests because they constantly monitor these hashtags. If you have a local business, these hashtags may not attract your ideal customer to your business. If you're a larger brand with a wider audience, these types of hashtags could be a good thing. You may also consider adding a keyword from your niche as a hashtag. Spend some time researching the hashtags you may consider before adding them to the proposed text.

✦ **How readable is it?** Ask someone else to take a look at what you've written. If they can't understand it easily, rewrite it.

✦ **How clear is it?** Make sure your instructions are clear. In steps, spell out exactly what people need to do, as shown in Figure 3-1.

The clearer you can make your instructions, the easier it will be for people to enter. Don't make them follow too many steps to enter.

Optimal page settings

Before you start your contest, make sure you have the correct settings selected on your Facebook Page.

✦ **Posting Ability:** This setting depends on your contest.

  • If people must upload photos or videos to your page, choose Anyone Can Add Photos and Videos to My Page Timeline.

  • If people must make a text post, choose Anyone Can Post to My Page Timeline.

✦ **Post Visibility:** Set to "Allow posts by other people on my Page Timeline" as shown in Figure 3-4 if you're doing a Timeline contest where people post to your Timeline. If you aren't requiring that people post directly to your Timeline, this setting can be set however you want it.

✦ **Messages:** Set it as people can Contact my Page privately. While you're running the contest, we recommend allowing people to contact your Page privately if they have a question or concern or if they have been notified as the winner.

Book VI
Chapter 3

Running a Timeline
Contest

Posting Ability

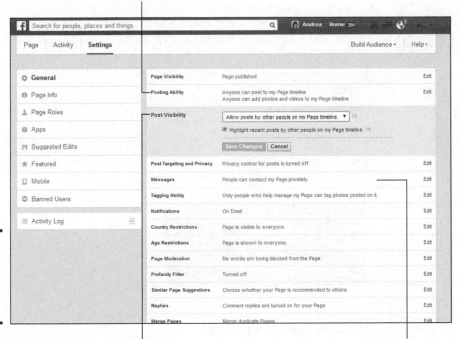

Figure 3-4:
Make sure your page settings are optimized.

Post Visibility

Messages

Do not set the Country Restrictions or Age Restrictions settings, even if you're limiting your contest to a certain age or country. Restricting access to your Page in this way makes it unable to be seen unless you're logged into Facebook, which can hurt your promotional efforts.

Administering Your Timeline Contest

With all the pieces in place, it's time to post your contest. Posting the information itself doesn't take much time, obviously, but you should be aware of a few things when you are continuing your promotion.

Editing your post

If you post your contest and see an error early on, edit your post by clicking the down arrow in the upper-right corner of the post.

Even if you edit the text, anyone can access the previous text (even after you edit). *Don't change the rules of the contest.* Make sure you're just correcting a mistake or clarifying if someone has a question about the contest and you want to edit the text to clarify.

Consider pinning your post to the top of your Timeline to make it more visible and accessible to new visitors. Click the down arrow in the upper-right corner of the post and choose Pin to Top, as shown in Figure 3-5.

Figure 3-5: If you have errors, edit your post.

Sharing your contest

Sharing your Timeline contest again with your community can be a little tricky. If you share the photo to promote the contest again, you will most likely get people entering on that new post by commenting on the shared post. Figure 3-6 shows how this can happen in their shared post where they received 62 new entries on the new post.

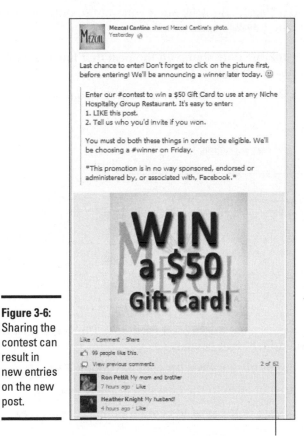

Figure 3-6:
Sharing the contest can result in new entries on the new post.

New contest entries on the shared post

Now you have to decide how you will handle those entries. Will you count those as well? If so, how will you process them all?

Contest Capture has an Export system where you can export the Likes and comments of the individual posts. Learn more in the "Selecting a Winner" section of this chapter. If you have multiple shared posts, you can export all of the Likes and comments from each of them to help choose the winner from one big list. You can find Contest Capture at http://contestcapture.com/.

A better way to share your post could be to share the specific link to the original post without a preview of the details of the contest.

We discuss posting to your Page in Book III, but if you want to only share the link to your contest, use the following steps:

1. **On your Timeline, click the date stamp on the post that has the contest announcement, as shown in Figure 3-7.**

   Your post opens in a window with the URL of the individual post in the browser window.

Click the date stamp

Figure 3-7:
Click the post's date stamp (shown here as Yesterday).

2. **Copy the URL of the post from the browser window. Close the post by clicking the X in the upper-right corner.**

3. **Paste the URL into the publisher area on your Facebook Page.**

   The image and text are pulled in to the post in a preview window.

4. **Add text at the beginning of the post to remind people to enter, as shown in Figure 3-8.**

   The text might say something like, "Don't forget to enter the special Caption this Photo contest for your chance to win a seat in my Facebook Advertising Secrets course! Go here to see the photo and submit your caption: *insert URL of original Timeline contest photo.*"

5. **Click the X in the upper-right corner of the preview.**

   The photo preview and previous contest are removed.

6. **Click the blue Post button.**

   Now people won't be tempted to enter a new comment as an entry. They can't see the photo, and the previous post will have told them that they have to click the link to enter.

Figure 3-8:
Add your text to tell people to enter at the previous post.

Click to close preview

Promoting Your Timeline Contest

In Chapter 5 of this minibook, we talk more about the promotion of contests, but we want to highlight the main way you may be promoting your Timeline contest: with a Facebook Ad. You can also learn more about Facebook Advertising in Book VII.

One of the easiest ways to use Facebook advertising for your Timeline contest is by boosting the post. We suggest boosting the post only to the people who like your Page and their friends, as shown in Figure 3-9. The typical goal of a Timeline contest is to re-engage your current fans, so you want the post to be shown to them.

You can find out more about all the nuances of options in Book VII.

After you post the contest:

1. **Click Boost Post (in the lower-right corner of the post), as shown in Figure 3-9.**

2. **Set your budget for the boost post.**

3. **Click the blue Boost Post button to complete your order.**

Your post will most likely be boosted for a couple days. If you want to stop the advertisement, you can come back to the post and discontinue the ad by selecting the same button.

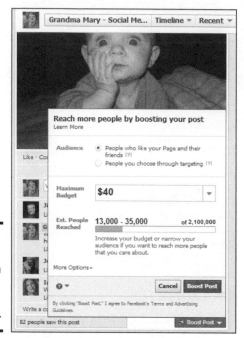

Figure 3-9:
Boost your
post to push
it into the
News Feed
of your fans.

If you have too much text (more than 20 percent) in the photo of your post, your ad won't be approved, and you cannot boost it. Keep this in mind when creating your contest photo. Review the steps to determine how much text is in your photo earlier in this chapter and use Facebook's Grid Tool found here: `https://www.facebook.com/ads/tools/text_overlay`.

Selecting a Lucky Winner

If your contest involves voting, selecting the winner is most likely easy. The only challenge is when you have a tie vote, and hopefully you added provisions for what to do in that case. But what if your contest is supposed to have a random winner (a *sweepstakes*)? A few tools can help.

Exporting data with Contest Capture

Contest Capture is a free tool that exports the Likes and comments from any post on your Timeline into a CSV file. From there, you can use a random number generator to pick a line number on your CSV file. That would be the winner.

This tool is good if you have multiple posts where people have entered. You can merge the CSV files to create one single list to choose the winner from.

To download to Contest Capture, follow these steps:

1. **Go to** www.contestcapture.com.

2. **Click the blue Connect Now button.**

   If you're not logged in to Facebook, you're prompted to log in and you also have to allow them permission to access your Facebook account.

3. **Select the Page of your contest from the drop-down menu.**

   The Pages for which you're admin are listed in the menu.

4. **Select the contest post from the drop-down menu.**

   All your posts from the last month are listed.

5. **Click the blue Download CSV button, as shown in Figure 3-10.**

   Your CSV file downloads to where files you download are sent (often a folder labeled Downloads).

6. **Open the file that you downloaded from Contest Capture, and it will typically open in an Excel spreadsheet.**

   Take note of how many entries you have by how many rows of names there are in the spreadsheet.

7. **Visit a random number generator tool, and use it to select a number between 1 and the maximum number of entries you have.**

   Here are some suggestions:

   * www.random.org
   * www.randomnumbergenerator.com

8. **Select the winner of the contest by using the number generated from the random number generator tool.**

   The winner is located in the row of the random number.

Book VI
Chapter 3

Running a Timeline Contest

Figure 3-10: Use Contest Capture to download people who have liked or commented on your post.

Export Likes and Comments

Select a page ☞ Select a post ☞ Get a CSV export, FREE

Pages: | Grandma Mary - Social Media Edutainer ▼ |

Posts: | 3/14 Let's have some fun! Caption this photo in the comment ▼ |

Download CSV

Using Woobox to pick a winner

Woobox also has an easy-to-use Timeline contest winner picker. The application is free and all you need to do is to create an account.

Woobox also has a lot of other great Facebook applications that can enhance your Page, including one that runs contests that require an e-mail address to enter (as we mention in Chapter 4 of this minibook).

To use the Woobox Timeline contest winner picker, follow these steps:

1. **Go to** `http://www.woobox.com`.

2. **Click the green Try it Free button.**

If you've never connected with Woobox, you're taken to Facebook where you are prompted to log in if you aren't already. Then you're prompted to allow the Woobox app to connect to your Facebook profile.

3. **Click Okay.**

You return to the Woobox site.

You need to connect apps to your profile to access your Pages.

4. **Click Posts on the upper menu to get to the recent posts from your Page.**

You may need to select the correct Page from the drop-down menu on the upper left.

5. **Click the green Pick Winner button next to the appropriate post; see Figure 3-11.**

You are taken to a page where you can choose whether people can enter by liking or by commenting on the post.

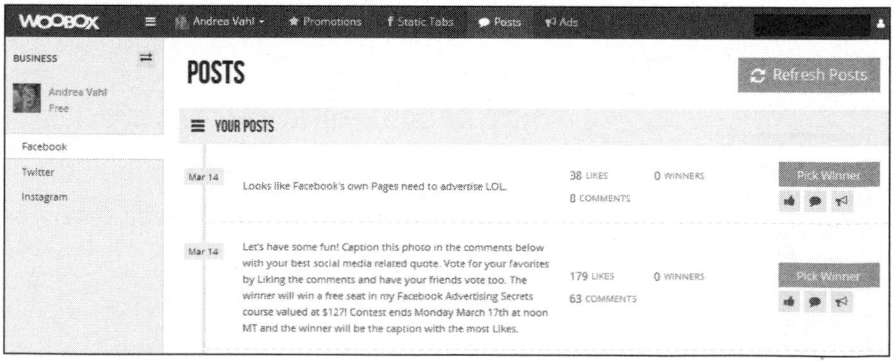

Figure 3-11: Pick a winner for your Timeline contest.

6. **Select the criteria for the winner: Liking the post, commenting on the post, or either.**

   If you select commenting on the post, you can restrict people from only being eligible for one comment that they have made rather than counting each separate comment as one entry thus giving them extra chances to win.

7. **Click the green Pick a Winner button.**

   Your winner is displayed in the Winners area.

Chapter 4: Using Third-Party Contest Applications

In This Chapter

✔ Browsing contest applications

✔ Selecting the right application for you

✔ Setting up the application within your Page

If you want to use your contest as a lead generator, use a third-party contest application. Turning Facebook Fans into e-mail subscribers is the best way to get the most out of using Facebook. Facebook could go away tomorrow (although we are sure it won't), and you would still be able to reach your community through e-mail.

Facebook contest app are designed to work within Facebook's contest guidelines, so they make getting started a snap. They give your contest a professional look, and in many cases have features with which you can analyze your results.

Like with other Facebook applications, you have to go through a few steps to add a contest application to your Page, and most of these applications aren't free. But, they're very affordable and also offer a lot of features to help you facilitate a well-run contest.

In this chapter, we look at how to find those often-elusive third-party applications, set them up, and notify the winners and deliver your prizes.

Finding a Contest Application

Finding contest applications in Facebook can be challenging. The Facebook Graph search function for these apps doesn't always find all the apps that are available, and more contest applications are being added as we write.

It can also be challenging to figure out how to add contest applications to your Facebook Page. In most cases, we recommend going directly to the website of the third-party application for directions on adding the app to your Page.

Four of the applications that we cover in this chapter — TabSite, Heyo, Woobox, and Offerpop — are *self-service* applications, which means that you can set them up from start to finish on your own. The steps for setting them up appear later in this chapter. The other self-service contest applications are also fairly straightforward to set up. Some contest applications require you to contact the vendor to get pricing and other information, and typically are better for large campaigns.

Each application has its pluses and minuses, so opt for the one that fits your needs. If you're running a large campaign, get quotes, look at the third-party application's past performance, and ask for referrals. Whichever third-party application you use, be ready with all your other promotional efforts, and take some time to analyze your results. We cover both of these aspects of your contest in detail in Chapter 5 of this minibook.

Comparing Contest Applications on the Web

Here are some of the current third-party Facebook contest developers:

✦ **TabSite** (www.tabsite.com) offers a contest option (photo, video, or essay) and a sweepstakes option. TabSite also offers a 14-day trial (which could mean that your first contest is free if you time it right) and templates to make setting up your contest easy. Pricing is $29.95 – $79.95 per month depending on your plan.

A *contest* involves some type of voting or judging. A *sweepstakes* selects the winner at random from all the entries. See Chapter 2 of this minibook for more details on contests and sweepstakes.

✦ **Heyo** (www.heyo.com) has templates you can use or a very easy drag-and-drop builder for more custom designs. Heyo offers only sweepstakes-style contests but has other interesting templates you can use for custom tabs. Pricing is from $25–$125 per month depending on your plan.

✦ **Woobox** (www.woobox.com) has a lot of different apps (such as Pinterest and YouTube) for your Facebook Page. Some are free, and some are for-fee. The sweepstakes app isn't free, but you can unlock all the paid apps for one monthly fee. The pricing is based on how many people like your Page and runs from $1–$249 per month.

✦ **Offerpop** (www.offerpop.com) has a suite of 19 Facebook and Twitter applications to help engage your audience that are easy to use and customize. Offerpop is free for Pages with fewer than 100 Likes. You can have per campaign pricing or pricing for all of the applications and the pricing runs from $16–$808 per month.

✦ **Votigo** (at www.votigo.com) offers a self-service contest option. To use its custom contest application, visit the Votigo website for prices and details.

✦ **Antavo** (www.antavo.com) has a number of easy-to-install sweepstakes and contest templates and a free trial to get you started. Pricing runs from $25–$125 per month.

✦ **Strutta** (www.strutta.com) has a very nice photo, video, and text contest application that you can set up yourself. It is a little more expensive that some of the other apps, but the photo and video contests are very well done. Pricing is $249 for the Turnkey solution and $399 for the Designer solution.

✦ **ShortStack** (www.shortstack.com) has a drag-and-drop sweepstakes form that you can set up yourself for a customized look. ShortStack is free for Pages with fewer than 2,000 Likes but has some limitations for the free plan. Pricing is based on the number of Likes you have on your Page and runs from $25–$300 per month.

✦ **Easypromos** (www.easypromosapp.com) has a very inexpensive basic version ($15 per promotion) to help you get started with contests or sweepstakes. If you need more features, you can use the premium version ($100 per promotion).

✦ **Pagemodo** (www.pagemodo.com) has some great basic templates to help you get started with contests and sweepstakes at a very reasonable monthly fee. Pricing runs from $6.25–$33.25 per month.

✦ **TabFoundry** (www.tabfoundry.com) has a totally free sweepstakes or contest application for a single Page. If you have multiple Pages you are running sweepstakes or contests on then there is a fee based on the number of Pages ranging from $14–$54 per month.

Because so many contest apps are available, we can't address all the steps for setting up the apps. And there are many more contest apps than we can even list here. Also, if you're using a custom app, the company that offers the app can help you get started. In fact, if you run into trouble with any of the apps, most companies have a very good help department for troubleshooting your problem.

Many of these sites have examples of contests that companies have administered or video tutorials. These tutorials are helpful for showing how the contest applications work and can be good places to start when you're deciding which application to use.

Getting to Know the Contest Applications

In this section, we cover some of the contest applications that you can install and set up yourself: TabSite, Heyo, Woobox, and Offerpop. We don't cover some of the other apps that you can set up yourself because some of them have more variables as you design your contest.

All four of these applications also include a *fan gate feature* where you can display an image telling a visitor to like the Page in order to get access to your contest. After a visitor likes the Page, the contest entry form is revealed. This is a great option if you want to ensure that only fans of your Page enter your contest.

Being able to access your contest application via a mobile device is critical. All these applications have a mobile-ready link that you can share to promote your contest.

Exploring TabSite

TabSite, just like many of these apps, has a number of different custom tabs you can create including the contest and sweepstakes apps. TabSite even help with picking a winner for a Timeline contest. Figure 4-1 shows the TabSite Manager area, where you create your contest.

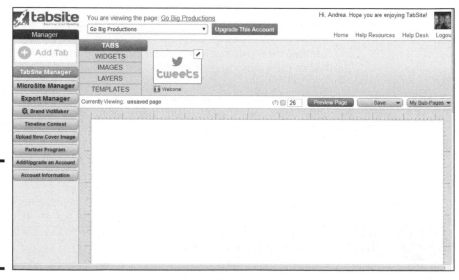

Figure 4-1: Use the TabSite Manager to create your contest.

To create your contest, you add Apps — which are basically the different types of things you can have on your custom tab and includes sweepstakes, essay contests, or even things like a Twitter feed, or an Instagram feed — to the design area.

TabSite has some free options, but the contest and sweepstakes are available only with the Gold plan, which costs $19 per month after your free 14-day trial.

Looking at Heyo

Heyo is another popular custom Facebook application that you can use for a lot more than just sweepstakes. The templates are easy to use and offer a countdown to the drawing so people are motivated to enter. See a countdown example in Figure 4-2.

Although you can't require a Share to be eligible to win the contest (see the preceding chapter for more on that), we recommend making it easy to share the contest.

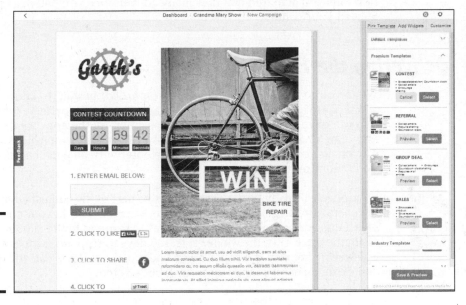

Figure 4-2: Create a countdown with Heyo.

Heyo has a free 7-day trial and then is priced starting at $25 per month. You can purchase have additional templates for $50 per month.

Investigating Woobox

Woobox has a monthly subscription fee that allows you to access all its applications, which are based on the number of fans you have. As of this writing, it offers these free apps: Pinterest, Twitter, Instagram, Pick a Winner (for Timeline Contests), and Static HTML Fangate Tab. You can use the Static HTML Fangate Tab application to create custom tabs (which we cover in more depth in Book V, Chapter 2).

Woobox also offers Sweepstakes, Photo Contests, Polls, Rewards, Instant Wins, and Group Deals apps; you can access these apps for $1 per month for 100 fans or less, $15 per month for 1,000 fans or less, $29 per month for 20,000 fans or less, and then up from there. Woobox has some nice features, such as giving people extra entries in the contest if they get a friend to enter (which is still within Facebook's terms because it is not a requirement for entry).

Understanding Offerpop

Offerpop also has many apps that you can access with a monthly subscription. A nice feature is that you can pay by the campaign or pay a monthly subscription fee if you want ongoing access to all the apps. If you have fewer than 100 fans, your campaign is free. Offerpop charges according to how many fans you have. Offerpop reveals good statistics, such as how many new fans you acquired and how many conversions you had from people who viewed your contest.

Delivering the Prizes

When you're exploring contest apps, you probably want to know how the winners are selected and notified. Because you're collecting e-mail entries, you will have the e-mail address of the winner. All the apps we describe mentioned have a way to randomly draw the winner from within the app. The challenge can be that some people enter with an e-mail address they don't monitor frequently.

Your prize will likely be the most expensive part of the contest campaign — and in general, the bigger the prize, the better the response. In your contest rules, give a time frame in which the winner has to respond to the announcement and claim the prize. Give the winner at least 3 days to respond, with a maximum of one week. That way, the contest won't be too old, and you can still generate some excitement if a new winner must be selected.

If you have to mail the prize to the winner, make sure that you mention in your rules that you need a street mailing address. State that if you can't contact the winner to get a deliverable address, a new winner will be selected.

Budgeting for an App

You can see exactly how much the campaign will cost as you set up your parameters. You can pay for the campaign up front, so there shouldn't be any danger of going over your budget after you commit to the contest. The apps we mention in this chapter charge a monthly fee. Many of the apps are very affordable and well worth the $20 – $50 per month fees.

Heed these tips to get the most for your app money:

✦ Whenever you begin your contest, you start your monthly subscription.

✦ With some apps, you can design the contest before you actually have to start your subscription.

✦ For apps that require you to pay before you start the design, have all the pieces ready before you start your subscription: images, text, and promotional plan.

✦ Turn off your subscription when you're done with your campaign.

Designing Your Contest with the TabSite Application

Like with other Facebook applications mentioned in this book, you design your contest or sweepstakes on the TabSite website and then install it onto your Facebook Page. You can save your progress and come back into the design process later, but you do have to start your free trial or pay for your monthly subscription (if you've used up your free trial) to begin the design process.

Because there are so many options with the Contest section of TabSite, we leave that section to you to explore and cover only sweepstakes setup in this section. TabSite has an excellent step-by-step contest tutorial in its Help section.

Signing up for TabSite

If you haven't completed a free trial with TabSite before, sign up by going to www.tabsite.com and clicking Free Trial in the upper-right corner. Then follow these steps:

1. **Click the Sign Up link.**

You can use an e-mail address to sign in or use Facebook to sign in. Once you sign in you see a place to choose your plan.

2. **Pick the appropriate plan for your needs and click the Try Free button if you have not already used the free trial. Otherwise click the Buy Now button.**

You are taken to a page to add your billing information.

3. **Enter your billing information, select the check box to agree to the terms, and select Purchase Now.**

You do have to enter your billing information because the monthly plan begins as soon as the trial is over, so you do need to remember to change your plan if needed.

You are taken to the Manager area to set up your contest.

Creating a sweepstakes with TabSite

As soon as you complete your signup and you into TabSite, a pop-up box asks you to choose a tab type, as shown in Figure 4-3.

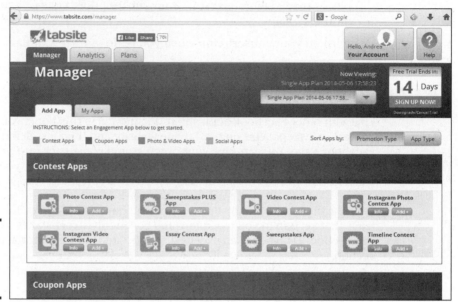

Figure 4-3: Start your sweep-stakes here.

Setting up bare bones

In this example we cover setting up the Sweepstakes Plus option. You can click the Info button on the other options to get more information about each of your choices. To start designing your sweepstakes, follow these steps:

1. **Click the Add button in the Sweepstakes Plus box.**

   You are taken to the design area for the Sweepstakes Plus app, as shown in Figure 4-4.

   The Sweepstakes Plus option is a good choice because it gives people an extra entry for sharing which is a good incentive to help spread the word about your sweepstakes.

2. **Enter a name in the Sweepstakes Name field.**

   This name is for your tracking purposes only and is not seen by others.

3. **Select the start date and end date for your sweepstakes and set the time zone you are in.**

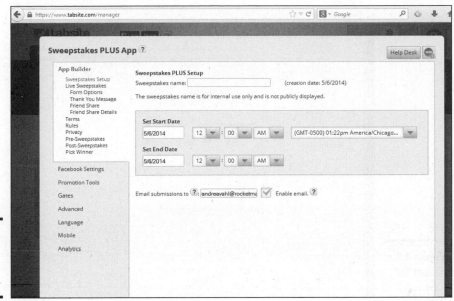

Figure 4-4:
Build your
sweep-
stakes here.

4. **Confirm that your e-mail is correct, and keep the box checked next to "Enable email" if you would like each submission e-mailed to you.**

   The e-mails entries are stored by TabSite automatically and you can download them in a file later so we suggest unchecking this box so you don't get flooded with e-mail notifications.

5. **Click the Live Sweepstakes link on the left sidebar to enter the information about the sweepstakes requirements.**

   You are taken to a screen as shown in Figure 4-5.

6. **Select the type of layout you want on your sweepstakes tab by checking the radio button next to the Sweepstakes Layout and also keep the boxes checked near Text Area and Image if you want both text and image.**

   You can also rearrange the boxes by dragging them and dropping them into place as shown in Figure 4-5. If you use an image only without text, make sure it has text that describes the prize and more about the sweepstakes.

   This section is the most important part of your sweepstakes because it entices people to enter. Having an image of the prize is good. Very clear text is how you let visitors know what they might win.

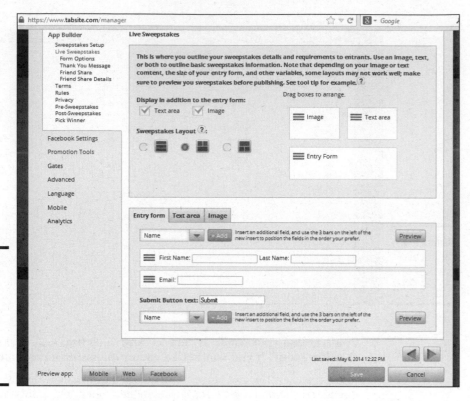

Figure 4-5:
Select the
layout,
and enter
the details
about the
sweep-
stakes.

7. **Customize the Entry form if desired.**

   - **Insert an additional field.** By default First Name, Last Name, and Email are used on the entry form.

   - **Edit the length of the fields.** Mouse over the sections hosting the available fields to show the pencil icon and then click on the pencil to access the length of the fields.

   - **Edit the text of the Submit button.** If you want to change the language of the button, edit the Submit button text field. Other options might be "Enter Now" or you could get creative and say something like "I'm In!"

8. **Click the Text tab to edit the Text area of the sweepstakes tab.**

   You can change the size of the font, the justification of the text, or change the text area into an HTML editor by clicking the Source button.

9. **Click the Image tab to upload an image for your sweepstakes tab.**

   The recommended size for the layout with the larger image is 810 pixels by 610 pixels but you can use different sized images. You can also set the image alignment to Left, Center, or Right.

10. **Click Save.**

The basics of your sweepstakes is now set up, but you should customize the other elements such as Terms, Rules, and other parts of the App Builder section which is covered next.

Customizing Terms and Rules

You have set up the basics of the sweepstakes but you should go into the other sections of the TabSite app so that you can customize the sweepstakes to your needs. You may want to keep most of the default settings but you should definitely customize the Terms and the Rules of the sweepstakes to include your specifics. You can click on the ? symbol next to any of the settings to find out more about that setting. Refer to Figure 4-5 to see the sections listed on the left sidebar.

✦ **Form Options:** On by default are the two check boxes in this section, Entrant must agree to Terms, and Add a newsletter check box. These are two good options to keep checked so that your liability is limited and so that people opt into your e-mail newsletter list. *Note:* Allowing entrants to opt in to your newsletter may reduce them marking your message as spam in the future.

✦ **Thank You Message:** Keep the default message of "Thank you for Entering" or enter your own message. You can also add an image here that people will see with your thank you message, or you can select that they see only the image after entering.

✦ **Friend Share:** This section allows you to customize the message that tells the entrants that they can get extra entries by sharing with their friends. An example would be "Get extra entries by sharing this sweepstakes with your friends."

✦ **Friend Share Details:** This section allows you to customize the message that will be shared with friends when someone who has entered shares your sweepstakes. You can include a 90 pixels (px) x 90 px image of the prize (or an image that captures the essence of the promotion).

✦ **Terms:** TabSite has a good template of terms, but you must customize it according to your own contest. Add things like how many times they can enter, what entries are valid, when the drawing will be, and review the conditions that TabSite has set up in the template.

✦ **Rules:** Again, TabSite has a good template of rules, but you must customize it according to your own contest.

✦ **Privacy:** Make sure you let people know that their e-mail addresses will not be sold but also make sure that they know that you will announce the winner on your Page (if you plan on doing that) and other privacy concerns.

✦ **Pre-Sweepstakes:** If you would like something on the tab before the sweepstakes starts, enter that in this section. Otherwise, uncheck the boxes. You can add a Text message, an Image, and include a Countdown timer to the start of your sweepstakes.

✦ **Post-Sweepstakes:** If you would like to have a text message or an image displayed after your sweepstakes has ended, enter that information in this section.

✦ **Pick a Winner:** This is where you will go to choose a winner from the names and e-mails that have entered.

Facebook Settings and Promotion Tools

The Facebook Settings option and Promotion Tools allow you to connect the sweepstakes app to your Facebook Page and your blog as well as help you schedule promotion about your sweepstakes.

To connect your TabSite sweepstakes with your Page, follow these steps:

1. **Click Facebook Settings as shown in Figure 4-6.**

2. **Click Connect with Facebook.**

   You are prompted to log in if you aren't already. Then you may be asked to give TabSite permission to access your profile if you haven't already. Click Okay to the prompts and a popup box appears showing your Facebook Pages.

Figure 4-6: Use the Facebook Settings section to connect your sweepstakes with your Facebook Page.

3. **Select the Facebook Page where you want to add the sweepstakes.**

4. **Change the Tab Name to something more meaningful for your sweep-stakes by typing the Tab Name into the box.**

5. **Upload a custom tab cover by dragging and dropping the image into the Tab Logo area or select Click to Browse to find the image on your computer and upload it.**

   You can also leave the default Win! Tab logo or browse the TabSite library of tab cover images.

6. **Click Save at the bottom of the Facebook Settings section.**

While you have selected the Facebook Settings you want, your sweepstakes is still Unpublished and does not appear on your Facebook Page until you officially Publish it which is shown later in this section after we cover some of the optional settings.

Choosing optional settings and viewing Analytics

Some of the settings you run into aren't things you have to do. In that case, consider whether you want to get more detailed or leave things as is.

✦ **Promotional Tools.** To set up your Promotion tools, click the Promotion Tools link on the left sidebar. You then see the options as shown in Figure 4-7. Customizing the tools here are optional but they allow you to control the text when people to share your sweepstakes. Add a Title and Description to the social sharing options since this will be what is posted on the social sites. Also add your own Tweet text to entice people to enter the contest when they see the Tweet.

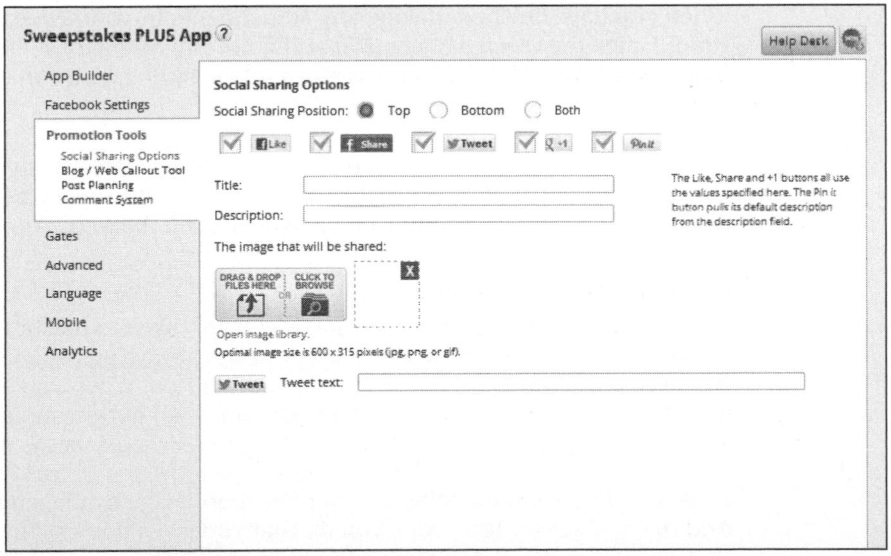

Figure 4-7: Customize your Promotion Tools.

✦ **Gates.** Add a Like Gate image by clicking on the Gates link on the left sidebar. The optimal image size is 810 x 810 pixels and ideally should be of the prize, and have an arrow pointing to the upper-right corner of the image (where the Like button is). It should have some text that tells people to Like the Page first.

A *like gate* requires folks to Like your page before they see can the entry form. It's a good way to make sure you are getting new Fans. If they already Like your Page, they're taken straight to the entry form.

✦ **Advanced.** The Advanced section allows you to add a header image (not necessary if you've already added images), change the style (which includes the link color, text color, or background color), or customize the CSS of the app.

✦ **Language.** You can change the language of the Header Links, Friend Share, or Friend Share box. You can put the exact text that appears in each of these places.

✦ **Mobile.** The Mobile section allows you to specify if you want to use the mobile version of the contest on mobile devices (recommended and set to yes by default). And you can specify if you want to use the Like Gate on mobile devices. This is your preference — while it can be a good thing to get the Like, the mobile device can be harder to use and could result in people not entering your sweepstakes from their mobile device.

✦ **Analytics.** Come back to this area when your sweepstakes is live so that you can get more information about the entries to your sweepstakes. From here you can see Views (from the website, mobile, Facebook, or microsite), Entries, Shares, Likes, and you can Pick a Winner at the end of the sweepstakes.

Save and preview your

When you have finished making any adjustments to your sweepstakes, you should click the green Save button at the bottom of the form. If you can't continue all the edits you need to make in one sitting, you can click Save, exit the app, and come back later.

You can also click the Preview buttons at the bottom of the form as you go along to see how it will look so that you can make adjustments as needed. You can preview how it will look on a mobile device, on the web, or on Facebook.

Publish your sweepstakes

Once you have saved your sweepstakes you are taken to the TabSite Manager area where your sweepstakes is listed. You can always go back in and Edit the sweepstakes settings by clicking the Edit button. When you are ready to publish your sweepstakes, click the Unpublished button and pop-up box appears as shown in Figure 4-8 stating that your sweepstakes is now live.

You can add the sweepstakes to your Facebook Page by clicking the green Add to Fan Page button. Once you do that you see a pop-up box confirming that the sweepstakes has been added to your Page.

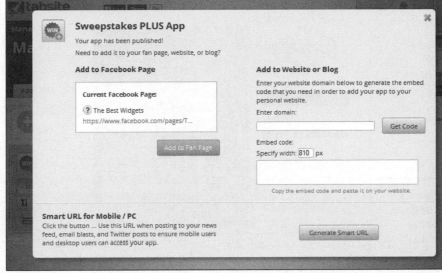

Figure 4-8:
Publish your
TabSite
sweep-
stakes and
add it to
your Page.

Using the Heyo Application for Your Sweepstakes

The Heyo sweepstakes template tool is very easy to use and set up. You can also create your own look with its drag-and-drop tool. If you're just getting started with contests, the templates might be exactly what you need to avoid getting overwhelmed with the setup.

To use Heyo, follow these steps:

1. **Go to** https://heyo.com.

2. **Enter your name, e-mail, and password into the form.**

3. **Click the Try for Free button.**

   You may be prompted to login to Facebook if you aren't already.

4. **Click Contest Templates in the upper-right corner.**

   You see several types of templates in the drop-down selections.

5. **Click Select next to the Sweepstakes option.**

   You have a template for your sweepstakes, as shown in Figure 4-9. If you click any of the selections in the template, you can edit them by clicking the Enter Email Below section.

6. **(Optional) Customize the entire template by clicking the sections and adding text and photos or swapping widgets for something on the right.**

Figure 4-9:
The Heyo sweepstakes template.

For example, you can add your own logo by clicking the Garth's logo shown in Figure 4-9. When you click the logo, the area on the right shows a button where you can upload your own logo. At the very minimum you should customize the images shown so that they reflect your sweepstakes. The recommended logo image size is 192 x 132 pixels and the recommended main image size is 443 x 581 pixels.

7. **(Optional) Click the Enter Email Below area to connect a MailChimp, Constant Contact, or Aweber account.**

   If you use MailChimp, Constant Contact, or Aweber account for your e-mail provider, you can connect it to automatically import the entries into your contest. Once you click the Enter E-mail Below box, the options appear in the right sidebar, and you can select your e-mail service and complete the connection.

8. **Click the Save & Preview button.**

   If you can't see the button at the bottom right of the sidebar, click the gray area just outside your contest template to go back to the widgets.

9. **Choose where to publish it: Facebook, Mobile, and Web are options.**

   See Figure 4-10. You can also edit the thumbnail image and tab name at this point.

   Make sure you actually select which Facebook Page to publish it to before you click the Publish button (next step).

10. **Click Publish.**

    Your sweepstakes is live, and anyone can view it.

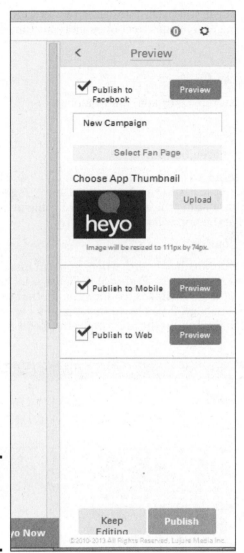

**Book VI
Chapter 4**

Using Third-
Party Contest
Applications

Figure 4-10:
Publish
your Heyo
sweep-
stakes.

Using the Woobox Sweepstakes Application

Woobox has some useful sweepstakes features. The application is easy to
set up and has a fan-only graphics page built in, or you can create one yourself to customize your campaign. Woobox has plans that range from $1 per
month for less than 100 Likes up to $249 per month to use for greater than
100,000 Likes, and you unlock all the apps available with your subscription.

You can give people extra chances to win if they share your sweepstakes
with their Facebook Friends, which can give people an incentive to spread
the news about your sweepstakes. One downside of using Woobox is that

you don't have much space in the Description area to talk about your sweepstakes, but you can use custom images to convey more information about your sweepstakes.

Signing up for Woobox

To get started using the sweepstakes app, follow along:

1. **Go to** www.woobox.com.

2. **Click the green Try It Free button.**

   You're taken to Facebook to connect the app. You may have to switch to your personal Profile or log in to Facebook if you aren't logged in. Again, don't worry about authorizing the app from your Profile because you get to choose which Page the app will be connected to.

3. **Click the blue Okay button.**

   You're taken to the Woobox dashboard, where you can manage your free Woobox apps and your paid apps, as shown in Figure 4-11. From this dashboard, you can add sweepstakes, coupons, and other products to any of the Pages you manage. If you leave the app, you can always log back in and click Manage next to the app you want to edit or manage.

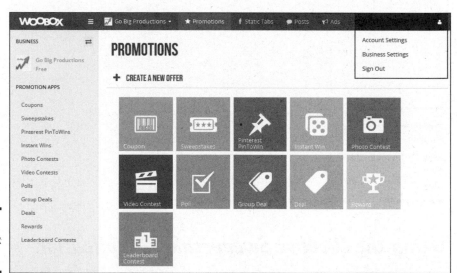

Figure 4-11: The Woobox dashboard.

Adding a sweepstakes

To add a sweepstakes to the Woobox app, follow these steps:

1. **Click the teal Sweepstakes icon.**

   Or click the Sweepstakes link on the left sidebar of the Woobox dashboard; refer to Figure 4-11. You're taken to the page shown in Figure 4-12.

ADD SWEEPSTAKES

☑ GENERAL SETTINGS

Title ❓
Max length: 100

Description ❓
Max length: 400

Restrictions ❓
Max length: 100

Fan-Gate ❓ ⊙ Off   ○ On

Fan-gate is turned off. Users are not required to Like your Facebook page. You can require users to Like one of your pages as a gate for a promotion in Multiple Likes.

Entry Settings ❓

Start Date   End Date
📅 2014-03-17 ⏱ 09:21:52 PT   📅 2014-04-16 ⏱ 09:21:52 PT

☐ Only allow users to enter once per Email Address

☐ Award 1 bonus entries per Facebook friend that enters after entrant.

☐ Automatically post Opengraph Enter action to user's Facebook Timeline

2. **Add your sweepstakes details; refer to Figure 4-12.**

   The following list details more information about each of the fields on that page (not all fields are shown in the figure):

   - *Title:* Your sweepstakes title can have 100 characters maximum.

   - *Description:* You have up to 400 characters to describe your offer.

   - *Restrictions:* You may want to specify whether the rules call for one entry per person or one entry per person per day. You only have 100 characters here.

   - *Fan-Gate:* This option lets you allow people to enter your contest only after they like your Page, which is a good way to increase your Likes. If you have a branded image, you can use it to tell people to click Like to enter. To enable this option, toggle the radio button to On. Customize the image after you save the changes to this section.

   - *Start Date and End Date:* Enter the start and end dates of your sweepstakes. Typically a sweepstakes is best run for between 1 to 2 weeks but it could be longer depending on the size of the prize.

   - *Only Allow Users to Enter Once Per:* Use the drop-down menu to restrict the contest to one entry per user (verified by e-mail address), one entry per day per user, one entry per Facebook Profile, or one entry per day per Facebook Profile by making a choice from the drop-down menu.

- *Award Bonus Entries:* You can reward people for sharing your contest by permitting extra entries for sharing. In the text box, enter the number of extra entries people will receive for sharing your contest. From the drop-down menu, choose how you want to keep track of those entries: by Facebook Friend who enters, or by user who clicks the Entrants Shared link. Leave the text field set to 0 if you don't want to give out any extra entries.

  You can get more entries if you ask users to share the offer on Facebook.

- *Automatically Post Opengraph Enter action to User's Facebook Timeline:* This option posts a story on the user's Timeline, saying that he entered the contest, but the user must authorize the app to do so, which may decrease the entries you receive. This option is not selected by default.

- *Users Must Be at Least:* Enter how old users must be to access your contest. The default is age 13.

  If you set the access age for the contest above age 13, people will have to be logged in to Facebook to even see your contest. You're better off restricting the age in the rules.

- *Users Must Follow on Twitter:* Select this check box if you want to require entrants to follow you on Twitter before they can enter. You must enter your Twitter username in the Business Settings to use this function.

- *Users Must Share Offer Link on Twitter:* Select this check box if you want to require entrants to share the offer ink on Twitter before they can enter. If you're running the contest primarily on Facebook, this may not be a good idea because not everyone has a Twitter account.

- *Award Bonus Entries if User Sends a Tweet:* Select this check box and enter how many bonus entries you would like to award for people tweeting about the contest. Or, leave this option unchecked if you don't want to award bonus entries for this action.

- *Admin Only Mode:* This is enabled by default until you purchase a plan is purchased. After you buy a plan, you can publish your contest by clearing this check box and clicking Save Changes (next step).

3. **Click the Save Changes button at the bottom of the page.**

Customize your sweepstakes

After you click the Save Changes button, you have access to more customization. From the left sidebar, you can go to all these sections individually, as shown in Figure 4-13.

We can't go through each of these sections here, but check out the Customize Content selection shown in Figure 4-13. This is where you can add a special image or text to your Facebook Fan-Gate page.

✦ Select **Image** to upload a custom like gate image.

✦ Select **HTML** if you want to do your own coding for your Fan-Gate page.

✦ Leave it at **Default** to have the default Woobox image telling people to click Like.

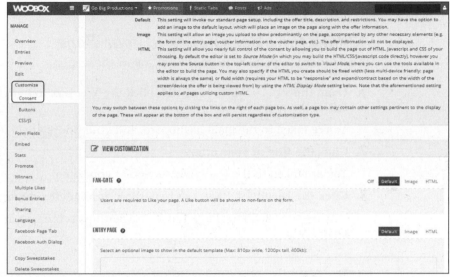

**Book VI
Chapter 4**

Using Third-
Party Contest
Applications

Figure 4-13:
Customize
your sweep-
stakes
and add a
Fan-Gate
image.

You can click the ? icons to get more information about the actions you need to complete or the available settings.

Choosing a payment plan

After you have your sweepstakes saved, you need to pay for a plan to enable the sweepstakes. Follow these steps:

1. **Click the Upgrade hyperlink at the bottom of the Sweepstakes form.**

   Some Woobox options are free, but you have to pay for the Sweepstakes plan.

   You're taken to the outline of the plans. Most people need to select the Pro plan, which is the minimum required for a sweepstakes. If you have fewer than 100 fans, you can use the Starter Plan.

2. **Select your plan.**

   A set of fields appear.

3. **Enter your payment method and select Purchase Account Level.**

   You're billed automatically for the monthly plan, so if you're running a short contest, remember to stop your monthly plan when you're done.

Without taking your sweepstakes out of Admin Only Mode, the sweepstakes will not be published. That's what you do next.

4. **Click the Woobox logo in the upper-left corner of the page.**

5. **Click the Sweepstakes title.**

6. **Click the Activate button next to the Admin Only section in the upper-right corner.**

Adding the sweepstakes to your Page

To add the sweepstakes to your Page, follow these steps:

1. **From the** www.woobox.com **site, click the Woobox logo in the upper-left of the page.**

   You're taken to the main dashboard, and your offers are listed.

2. **Click the title of your offer.**

   You are taken to the Overview section of your offer.

3. **Click the Facebook Page Tab hyperlink on the left sidebar.**

   You see the Facebook Page Tab & App Settings screen, as shown in Figure 4-14.

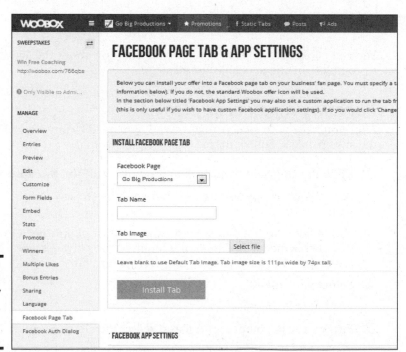

Figure 4-14: Title the tab, and add a custom tab image.

4. **From the drop-down menu, select the Facebook Page that gets the sweepstakes.**

5. **Enter a tab name for your sweepstakes.**

6. **Upload a tab image for your sweepstakes or leave the default image.**

7. **Click the Install Tab button.**

   Your sweepstakes is installed on your Page, and you can change the position of the app by following the steps at the end of this chapter.

To alert your Facebook community to your sweepstakes, you can

✦ Share the link to the Sweepstakes tab and let people know to enter there.

✦ Copy the mobile-ready link in the upper-left of the sweepstakes dashboard area and post that as a link in your Facebook status update.

In the sweepstakes dashboard (which you access by clicking on the sweepstakes name from the main Woobox dashboard), you can track the entries and views, and see how many people are sharing the sweepstakes with their friends by clicking on the Stats selection on the left sidebar.

Using the Offerpop Application

Offerpop is a very easy application to use. Because it has so many promotional tools, you may want to choose the monthly subscription plan, which is very reasonable. You get one trial campaign for up to 14 days. It's worth trying!

Signing up for Offerpop

To get started, follow these steps:

1. **Go to** www.offerpop.com.

2. **Click the orange Try It Free button.**

   A pop-up window asks whether you want to select Facebook or Twitter as your platform.

3. **Select Facebook.**

   Another pop-up window prompts you to log in to Facebook if you aren't already logged in and requests authorization of the app.

4. **Click the Okay button to allow Offerpop access your account.**

   You are taken to a page to set up your Offerpop account.

5. **Enter the required information (see Figure 4-15).**

   You can select the Page on which you want to run your promotion now, or you can add that information later.

Figure 4-15:
Fill out your
company
information.

6. **When you're done, click the Continue button.**

   You're taken to the terms page.

7. **Click Accept.**

   You see the main dashboard (shown in Figure 4-16), where you can add Pages, start campaigns, and access the other apps. You can get more information about any of the campaigns by mousing over the ? icon next to the name of the campaign. If you're looking to add a sweepstakes to your Page, the Offerpop sweepstakes app is titled Sign Up.

Publishing a sweepstakes

To publish a sweepstakes, follow these steps:

1. **Click the Sign Up option in the list on the left side of the dashboard (refer to Figure 4-16).**

   You may be taken to a page that asks you if you want to be a beta tester for their new app. Click continue so you can continue on with your sweepstakes and you're taken to a Customize page that displays a filled-in example.

Book VI
Chapter 4

Using Third-
Party Contest
Applications

Figure 4-16:
Start
campaigns
from this
page.

2. **Replace the sample information with your campaign information:**

- *Facebook Page:* From the drop-down list, choose the Page on which you want the campaign to appear (see Figure 4-17). If you don't see the correct page, go back to the dashboard (refer to Figure 4-16) and click Add Page.

- *Headline:* The headline appears at the top of your sweepstakes app, as well as in the News Feed when people enter or share the contest. Make it brief, eye-catching, and engaging.

- *Banner:* This image appears at the top of your sweepstakes app but replaces the headline. We recommend that the image you use says something about the contest itself.

- *Instructions:* Use this area to say more about the contest and how to win. This area supports HTML if you want to use HTML tags to format your instructions.

- *Custom Form:* Specify the fields in which people need to enter information. The less information you require, the easier it is for people to enter your contest. However, if you need to mail something to entrants, it's a good idea to require an address. You can also let people select a check box to get on your e-mail list. If you're going to add entrants to your newsletter list, you must have them opt in and state that they want to be on your e-mail list.

Home ❯ Sign Up

To run campaigns with Offerpop, you must follow Facebook's Promotion Guidelines. Questions? Ask your Offerpop rep, or your Facebook rep.

❶ Create your campaign

Facebook Page: Grandma Mary - Social Media Edutainer

Fan-gating: ☐ Must "Like" you to participate

Sign up page

Headline: Sign up for a chance to win a trip to NYC!

Banner: *optional*

Change image | Delete

810px wide, recommended height: 300px

Instructions: *optional*
As a special thanks to our awesome fans, sign up here and you'll be entered to win a trip to NYC on us! We're picking three winners at the end of this month!

Custom form: Select and customize fields for the sign up form
- ☑ Email ☑ Required Field
- ☑ First name ☑ Required Field
- ☑ Last name ☑ Required Field
- ☐ Name ☐ Required field

copyright © 2014 offerpop | terms | privacy | cookie preferences

Figure 4-17: Fill in your contest information.

- *Include CAPTCHA:* You can require participants to fill out a CAPTCHA before they can be entered. This could reduce spam entries but is most likely not necessary unless you have a very valuable prize. A CAPTCHA is typically a series of hard-to-read letters and/or numbers that prevents programs from automatically entering information. It can be frustrating if the CAPTCHA is very difficult to read for the user.

- *Facebook Profile:* You can require participants to share Facebook identities with you. This can help in the future to get a list of Facebook profiles who entered your contest. You can then use Facebook ads to create a custom audience and advertise directly to those people.

- *Submission Limit:* From the drop-down menu, you can set that people can only enter once, once per day, or once per 24 hours. The default is Unlimited.

- *Fine Print:* (Optional) Add additional rules or regulations in the Fine Print text area.

- *After Sign Up:* You can add a custom text message thanking people for entering your sweepstakes.

- *Campaign Ends:* Select the time and date when you'll stop taking entries. Again, a sweepstakes is ideally between 1 to 2 weeks but could be longer for a larger prize.

- *Advanced Options:* You can work with the Facebook API, show the signup count, and other advanced options.

3. **From the drop-down menu, click Fan View, Non-Fan View, and After Sign Up.**

   Take a look at those views, both on desktop and mobile, to see how your sweepstakes entry looks with those settings.

4. **Click Save Draft or Publish Now, depending on whether you're ready for your sweepstakes to go live.**

   When you click Publish Now, you're taken to a confirmation page, as shown in Figure 4-18.

Book VI Chapter 4

Using Third-Party Contest Applications

Figure 4-18:
Confirm
your Page.

> **offerpop**
> FACEBOOK PLATFORM
>
> Confirm the Facebook Page you want to publish to
> ◉ The Social Classroom with Phyllis Khare | Education
>
> **Page App Name** click here to publish to a canvas page or iframe
> Win Social Media Manag
>
> [Publish now] or Do this later

5. **Confirm your Page, and name your tab appropriately.**

6. **Click the red Publish Now button.**

   You can also click the Do This Later link if you aren't ready to publish it yet. Your campaign is saved and can be accessed from your Offerpop dashboard.

   You're taken back to the Offerpop dashboard, where you get confirmation that your campaign has been published (if you clicked the Publish Now button).

Adjusting the App's Photo

The following steps apply to photos for any of the contests we outline in this chapter.

Editing the position of the app

Only the first two apps are very visible to your fans. Ideally, place the sweepstakes app in the top two apps to be more visible.

To edit the position of an app, follow these steps:

1. **Click the More menu just below the Page cover photo.**

A drop-down menu appears.

2. **Select Manage Tabs.**

A pop-up box appears as shown in Figure 4-19.

3. **Click on the name of the sweepstakes and drag the mouse up to the first or second position below About.**

You can't change the About location, it must be first. Put the sweepstakes or contest app in the first position below About for maximum exposure.

Editing the cover photo and title of an app

You may want to change the title of the sweepstakes or contest if you didn't do that already within the sweepstakes or contest app dashboard. Or maybe you didn't get a chance to upload a new tab cover photo. To edit the title or cover photo for the app, follow these steps:

1. **Click the Settings link in the upper-left corner of your Facebook Page.**

2. **Choose Apps from the left sidebar.**

All of the Apps you have installed are displayed.

3. **Edit the Title of the tab by typing in the new title in the Custom Tab Name field and click Save.**

4. **Click Change next to Custom Tab Image.**

   You're taken to a Page where you can select a new tab image, as shown in Figure 4-20.

Book VI Chapter 4

Using Third-Party Contest Applications

Figure 4-20: Replace the picture with an eye-catching image.

5. **Click Change to select an image from your computer.**

   A pop-up window appears.

6. **Select the file you want to use.**

7. **Click the Open button to add your selected image as the Tab Image.**

   The image is changed.

Chapter 5: Promoting Your Contest and Analyzing the Results

In This Chapter

✔ Using a blog tour to drive traffic to a contest

✔ Publicizing a contest on a website or blog

✔ Allowing entries from anywhere on the web

✔ Promoting a contest with Twitter, LinkedIn, and YouTube

✔ Handling external contests

✔ Watching the numbers

✔ Making changes based on the numbers

✔ Strategizing for future contests

*Y*our contest is set up, and the prizes are ready. Now comes the fun part: getting those entries! The success of your contest comes when you can drive more traffic to your entry site. In Chapter 2, we discuss different things to help promote your contest, in Chapter 3 we talk about Timeline contests, but we go a little more in-depth in this chapter.

Later in the chapter, we show you how to a look at your contest results, what they mean, and how you can improve them next time.

Setting Up a Blog Tour

A *blog tour* — where you guest post or are featured or interviewed on a variety of different blogs in your niche — is a fantastic way to get exposure to a whole new audience, but it does take some planning and legwork. One way to kick off a blog tour is to contact bloggers and ask whether you can write a guest post or whether they can post about your contest. This technique is more appropriate if you're running a longer contest that may include voting or a larger prize. The benefit to doing this is that you get exposure with their audience, who may not know you but because the blog is in your niche, would be interested in winning the prize you are offering.

Some blogs are *single-voice* blogs, meaning that only the original author writes posts, and the blog doesn't have guest posts. Other blogs welcome guest posters because they give the blogger a short respite from pumping out content. Figuring out which type of blog you're approaching isn't difficult. Just take a look through the posts and look at the author bylines. If the posts never show a guest poster or an author bio for someone other than the blog owner, you can safely assume that it's a single-voice blog.

A single-voice blog may not be as interested in having a guest post by someone else because the blog owner does all the posting. But they may be interested in interviewing you. Knowing which type of blog it is can help you craft your pitch whether you offer an interview or a guest post.

When you contact bloggers to ask about promoting your contest, either through a guest post by you or by mentioning it themselves, contact them at least a month in advance so that they have plenty of time to respond.

In the following ways, you can find blogs that are a good fit for your message:

✦ **Research blogs to contact, and have a list of blogs that would be a good fit for your message.**

You can also start with bloggers you know and have relationships with. Often, these bloggers are very receptive to a guest post. A good guideline is to approach bloggers who have complementary businesses with yours and aren't direct competitors. If you have a graphic design business and are giving away your services, for example, you may want to look at blogs about business or marketing.

✦ **Perform keyword-based blog searches on the following sites:**

• *Technorati:* http://technorati.com

• *Google Blogs:* http://blogsearch.google.com

• *Alltop:* http://alltop.com

✦ **Get to know the styles of bloggers.**

Make a short list (or a long one, if you're ambitious) of the bloggers you want to approach about a guest post. Poke around on their blogs, and get to know the styles of the bloggers. You might even comment on some posts before approaching the bloggers.

✦ **Prepare an introductory e-mail about what you'd like to post about, and describe how it can help the bloggers' audiences.**

Try to offer valuable content that can help the bloggers' readers, in addition to getting those readers to sign up for your contest. Because everyone loves a contest, most bloggers will be receptive to having you encourage contest entries.

✦ **Schedule your blog tour so that it coincides with the time when your contest is live, and you can promote your guest posts properly.**

✦ **Create the content for the blog tour. Get your guest post to the bloggers with ample time for them to review it and suggest any changes.**

✦ **When the guest post is live, make sure that you're doing all you can to promote it.**

You want to help bring traffic to the blog, as well as to promote your content and encourage contest entries. Tweet about the guest post, post it to your Facebook Page, update your status in LinkedIn, and send it to your e-mail list if appropriate.

**Book VI
Chapter 5**

Promoting Your
Contest and
Analyzing the
Results

Promoting Your Contest on Your Blog or Website

You should also have your own blog post about the contest. You may want the post to be simply an announcement, or you can have some valuable content to go with the contest announcement.

If you're running the contest on Facebook, make sure that you link back to the Page where people can enter the contest. You can find that URL by clicking the contest or sweepstakes app link below your Page's Cover photo. It will look something like this:

```
www.facebook.com/GrandmaMaryShow?v=app_28134323652
```

You may also want to post a permanent banner or widget advertising your contest on the sidebar of your website so when your blog entry is no longer visible, you're still letting visitors know about your contest. Figure 5-1 shows an Ann Taylor contest for a $1,000 gift card. The link at the bottom of each page on the website took users directly to Facebook, where they could enter the contest.

Golfsmith used a banner ad across the top of its website pages, advertising its Golf Oasis sweepstakes (see Figure 5-2).

Figure 5-1:
This site uses a banner at the bottom of each page that's link to its Facebook contest.

Figure 5-2:
This site uses a banner at the top of its website linked to its Facebook contest.

Adding your contest information to your blog isn't too difficult; all it takes is adding a widget to your sidebar of your blog with an image that links to your contest. The TabSite application, for example (see Chapter 4 of this mini-book), has an easy way you can create an embeddable image. If you created your contest with TabSite, log in to your account, go to the TabSite Manager of one of your promotions, and then scroll down to Blog/Web Callout Tool. You get some code, as shown in Figure 5-3.

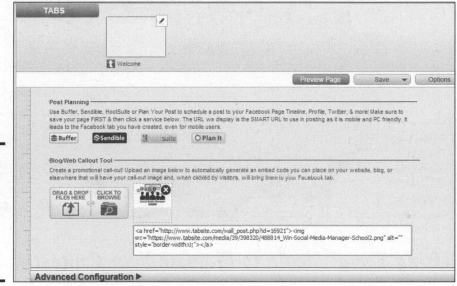

Book VI Chapter 5

Promoting Your Contest and Analyzing the Results

Figure 5-3: Use the TabSite Blog/Web callout tool to create a link to the contest.

Just copy that embeddable code in the box and paste it onto the text section of a page on your blog or into a sidebar widget. If you aren't familiar with installing code, you may need your web designer to help you.

Using Facebook Open Graph to Allow Entries Anywhere on the Web

You can use the Open Graph protocol (http://ogp.me/), which is a Facebook tool that integrates websites into Facebook, to allow entries directly on your website. By letting people log in via Facebook, you make it easier for them to enter and share your contest with others. Figure 5-4 shows how Blowfish Shoes used Open Graph to let people enter its Shoe A Day giveaway: You can log in with Facebook to enter. Find out more about using Open Graph on the Facebook Developer site at

https://developers.facebook.com/docs/opengraph

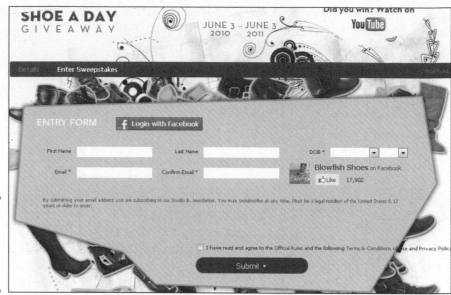

Figure 5-4:
This site
used Open
Graph for its
entry form.

Using Social Media to Promote Your Contest

Using social media can be critical for getting the word out about your contest. You should post about your event on your Facebook Page, of course, but how much should you emphasize it? Well, you don't want to be obnoxious, but you do want to get the word out.

Your promotion levels can vary, depending on your comfort zone, but we suggest at least two to three times per week. Vary your posts, and make them light and fun:

✦ *Have you heard we are having a contest?*

✦ *Thanks to everyone who has entered already. Make sure that you get your entry in!*

Ask other people to promote your contest. Contact some of your Facebook Friends who would have the right audience, or ask people to share the link with others so that those others can enter.

Make sure that you use an eye-catching graphic as the app cover photo for your contest. (See Chapter 4 of this minibook for more information on changing your app cover photo.) Figure 5-5 shows how Macy's highlighted its VIP Trip to Vegas contest with a custom graphic.

**Book VI
Chapter 5**

Promoting Your
Contest and
Analyzing the
Results

Figure 5-5:
Use the
cover photo
on the app
to draw
attention
to your
contest.

Twitter

If you're using Twitter, follow these tips:

✦ Tweet about your contest frequently.

✦ Tweet about it at different times of the day.

✦ Ask for retweets.

✦ Contact some of your Twitter friends directly in case they don't see the tweet.

Twitter also has hashtags that you can use to reach people who are tracking contests to enter. Use hashtags like #contest, #sweepstakes, #win, and #prize. Some tweets use lots of those hashtags, as shown in Figure 5-6.

Figure 5-6:
MyCoupons.
com used
hashtags to
promote its
Facebook
contest.

Without getting too deep into Twitter, some people are monitoring certain hashtags to find tweets about that subject. You can search on the hashtag and see all the tweets with that hashtag in it. So you may get people entering your contests who are serial contest enterers and not really interested in your product. Still, you may be able to connect with these people through your posts on your Facebook Page and turn them into customers.

LinkedIn

LinkedIn can also be a good place to promote a contest, and here's how:

✦ **Update your status** so that when your connections log in to LinkedIn, they can see it in their LinkedIn Updates area, as shown in Figure 5-7.

✦ **Create a LinkedIn event** announcing your contest. Invite your connections to the event, and direct them to your Facebook Page to enter the contest.

✦ **Send out an e-mail to your LinkedIn connections,** inviting them to enter your contest.

Figure 5-7:
Update
your status
in LinkedIn
with your
contest.

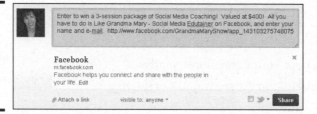

 Be careful about some of these strategies, though. Some people don't appreciate getting e-mails of this type and feel that they constitute spam. It's a fine line, and your comfort level should determine how you promote your contest. If you spam too many groups or e-mail too many people with your announcement on LinkedIn who report you, you may get a warning from LinkedIn that they will shut down your account.

YouTube

Another way to promote your contest is to make a YouTube video. You can show off the prize in the video or talk about what you'll be providing. If you're providing some type of coaching, using a video can be very beneficial so that people can get to know you a little and see your style.

Robeson Design Studios used a YouTube video to promote a Facebook contest giving away beds, as shown in Figure 5-8. They utilized their existing YouTube subscribers to get the word out about the contest.

 The benefit of having a video on YouTube is that you can then embed it in a Facebook Page using a Facebook YouTube app (or just post the link to the video several times) or embed it on your blog so that people can find it in multiple places. You never know how someone will stumble across your contest, and the more places on the web you can advertise it, the better.

Book VI
Chapter 5

Promoting Your
Contest and
Analyzing the
Results

Figure 5-8:
A YouTube
video is a
great way to
promote a
contest.

Using Facebook to Promote an External Contest

You can use your Facebook Page to promote a contest hosted on your website.
But make sure that you still look at the Facebook Promotion Guidelines, con-
tained in Section E of Facebook's Page Guidelines:

```
www.facebook.com/page_guidelines.php
```

Facebook has general guidelines about when you can even mention a contest or sweepstakes on the Facebook platform, and you want to make sure
that your contest adheres to those guidelines.

When you're promoting a contest on your website, try these ideas:

✦ Post the entry link frequently on your Facebook Page.

✦ Ask your community members to share the link with their Friends.

✦ Incorporate Facebook Connect and Open Graph into your contest site so that people can share and like your contest entry form. That technique ensures that the contest enters the Facebook arena and gets more exposure. (Read about Open Graph earlier in this chapter.)

Analyzing Your Contest Results

Tracking your results is critical in any marketing effort, and you can easily see what you've gained when you have all your contest entries. Analyzing the real effect on your business may not be possible until later, though. For example, say you got a lot of entries. Did you eventually get customers and business, though? Have a plan in place to track later business and see where it came from.

If you're running a Timeline contest, you can track your results based on the Facebook Insights with how much engagement your post received. Tracking direct sales from that post may be more difficult unless you were linking to more information on the product you were giving away with a trackable link.

Also, we encourage you to have some type of e-mail subscriber list that your entrants can sign up for in addition to just liking your Page. Contrary to some rumors, e-mail isn't dead and can be an effective way to reach your customers with new offers. Again, with Timeline contests, you don't get the e-mail address unless you do something in your post to ask for it.

Using analytics within third-party contest applications

Third-party sweepstakes and contest applications can make tracking and analyzing the effectiveness of your contest simple. When you use TabSite, Heyo, Offerpop, and Woobox (covered in Chapter 4 of this minibook), you have built-in analytics. Woobox, for example, provides details about the entries and shares, as well as traffic stats, as shown in Figure 5-9. Offerpop, TabSite, and Heyo track slightly different metrics, as you can see in the Offerpop report in Figure 5-10.

Figure 5-9:
Woobox
traffic stats.

**Book VI
Chapter 5**

Promoting Your
Contest and
Analyzing the
Results

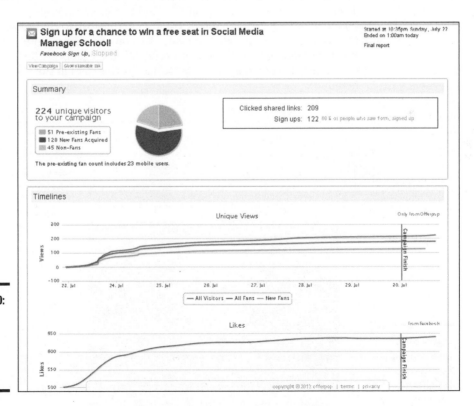

Figure 5-10:
Offerpop
tracks
slightly
different
metrics.

Monitoring community growth and tracking Facebook Insights

Make sure that you're tracking your new Likes on your Page and comparing them with the contest or sweepstakes entries. The newest Liker will be at the top of the list. Unfortunately, you have no easy way to download your list of Likers, so if someone who liked your Page a long time ago enters your contest, finding that person will be difficult.

Keep these guidelines in mind, depending on what kind of contest you're running:

✦ **Try a fan gate feature.** If you're using the TabSite, Heyo, Offerpop, or Woobox sweepstakes application, you have the option of creating the contest as a fan-only application. This means that a visitor to your Facebook Page can't enter the contest unless he clicks Like — a "fan gate" feature. If you set up your contest this way, you won't have to track whether the person who entered your contest also clicked Like.

✦ **Try a Timeline contest or Agorapulse** (www.agorapulse.com). In a Timeline contest, someone can like and comment on your post without Liking your Page, which makes you do a little work to determine whether the winner was a Fan. With AgoraPulse, you can search your Fans by name. If you're running a Timeline contest, watch the Facebook Insights on the post itself, as shown in Figure 5-11 (access this data in the Posts section of Insights).

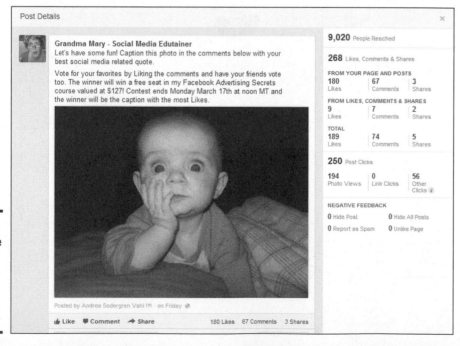

Figure 5-11: Dive into the Facebook Insights to see how your post was shared.

Souplantation & Sweet Tomatoes

Souplantation & Sweet Tomatoes has a history of good Facebook contests and promotions. In 2010, the company had a very successful "pucker face" contest in which people submitted photos of themselves after eating a lemon. Sweet Tomatoes ran this promotion to coincide with some of the lemon dishes it was featuring. The winner of the contest won 20 meal passes. Having a photo contest is a fun way to involve your audience, and the prize doesn't have to cost a lot of money. The contest was so successful that the company ran it again in 2011.

Sweet Tomatoes also ran a Refer a Friend contest, in which people were entered to win ten free meals when they referred Friends to the contest. After someone enters the contest, they have the choice of publishing something about it to their Timeline, as well as personally inviting their Friends.

These touches in your contest can really help spread the word. Then everyone can see some of the positive feedback the winner receives when the winner's name is posted. You can space your contests close together so that your fans are excited to sign up for another round of the contest.

**Book VI
Chapter 5**

Promoting Your
Contest and
Analyzing the
Results

✦ **Track your Facebook Insights before and after the contest.** This applies no matter what kind of contest you're running. That way, you can see how your contest affected the interaction on your Page. We tracked Facebook Insights the month before and after we ran a contest on a Page, and we saw that the comments and Likes to the posts more than doubled, as did the new Likes for the Page. See Book IX, Chapter 2 for more information about Facebook Insights.

Watch the trends of new comments and engagement on your Page. With luck, you'll have an influx of new people who are interested in your brand and decide to connect with you on Facebook.

Adjusting Your Strategy Based on Analytics

Analytics are key in helping you determine where your strategy is working and where to shift your focus. Running multiple contests over the course of the year can help you assess what works best as you try new things.

Watch the entries over the course of your contest and see how your promotional efforts are going with each new tactic. For example, say you find that the entries and views go significantly down over weekend or at times you aren't promoting enough. You may want to try changing that situation in the next contest and see whether you can connect with more people who are on the web on the weekend, looking for fun things to do — such as entering contests.

Assuming you run more than one contest, compare analytics from them to see what improved (or declined) in the other contests. In one case, we ran a second contest not long after a first contest, and although it didn't get as many entries as the first (mostly because we didn't promote the second contest quite as heavily), it did get a higher entry rate through Facebook, which showed that more people were paying attention the second time. The community members also might have seen the testimonials of previous winners and wanted to make sure that they entered the second contest.

If you spent any money on advertising, analyze how effective that investment was. Would it have made more sense to do a different type of contest, or spent more or less money on advertising? With a $40 budget, we had a lot of engagement on the post but only 39 entries (which were comments in this Timeline contest), as shown in Figure 5-12. However, two sales resulted from the contest for the product itself, proving that running the contest was worthwhile.

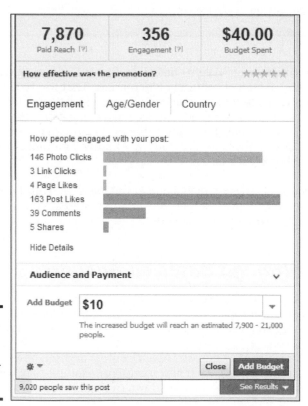

Figure 5-12: Analyze the effectiveness of your advertising.

Planning Future Contests

After you have your first contest under your belt, start mapping out your contest schedule. After you've run one contest, you can see the benefits for your Facebook community, such as added members and more interaction. Maybe you want to run only one more contest, or perhaps three or four per year.

Whatever you do, though, running multiple contests is a good idea, for several reasons:

Book VI Chapter 5

Promoting Your Contest and Analyzing the Results

+ You give the people who entered before a second chance to win.

+ You encourage your community to watch your Page because people like contests.

+ It's easy to have others promote your contests because people like to win things.

+ You can showcase some of your services and products as giveaways, which then encourages people to buy them.

+ Contests are fun!

Plan your contests strategically so that you can promote them adequately. Don't have so many contests so that your community gets contest fatigue, however.

Mapping out your contests for the year

To prevent contest fatigue and to allow room on your calendar for promotion of your contests, make sure to schedule all your contests for the year.

Cold Stone Creamery and Papa John's Pizza

Cold Stone Creamery had a Gold Cone Contest, in which people suggested new flavors. The winners traveled to the company's headquarters in Arizona to perfect the winning flavors.

More than 4,000 people entered the contest, and the Cold Stone Creamery Facebook Page saw about 66,000 new Likes over an 8 week period.

Papa John's Pizza saw a similar success when it ran a Specialty Pizza Challenge contest in 2010 and received more 12,000 entries. Papa John's had a live stream to announce the three winners (chosen from the ten semifinalists) and got a lot of buzz from the event.

How many contests you have and how far apart you space them can depend on

✦ **The duration of the contests:** If you're running month-long contests, for example, you may want to have a buffer of a couple of months between them so you can focus on other parts of your business. That schedule would allow four contests per year.

✦ **The type of contest:** Are the contests the same, or are you giving away a different prize each week? Exodus Travels in the United Kingdom gave away a trip a month to each of the seven continents, for example, so its contest lasted for 7 months.

Watching for successful contest ideas

If you're planning multiple contests, you should be watching other contests running on Facebook for ideas for your contests.

It may not be easy to tell how successful a contest is, but you can watch for some clues:

✦ If the business is promoting the contest on Twitter, you can search for tweets about it to see whether many people are tweeting about the contest.

✦ If the company has a YouTube video of the contest, you can see how many views the video gets.

✦ And if you're really paying attention, you can track the new Likes on the company's Facebook Page each day because the Likes may correlate with contest entries.

You have several ways to search for contests that are running on Facebook:

✦ Search the #contest or #sweepstakes hashtags on Facebook.

✦ Many contest apps have examples or case studies on their websites or on their Facebook Pages updates.

✦ Watch the Facebook Ads area to see who is advertising contests.

✦ Use the Facebook Search feature to see who is posting about contests.

✦ Use Twitter search to search for tweets about contests.

We discuss each of these methods in depth in the following sections.

Search the #contest or #sweepstakes hashtags on Facebook

You can find people on Facebook talking about contests or sweepstakes by entering **#contest** or **#sweepstakes** in the search bar at the top of your Facebook page.

When you enter those terms, there may be other related terms that appear, but the one with the word *hashtag* under the entry is the one you want to match.

Your search results in posts that are made publicly on Facebook. If someone is posting with privacy setting other than public, those results are not included. The actual term with the hashtag may or may not be in the actual post itself, as shown in Figure 5-13, where Martha Stewart's post does not actually contain the word with the hashtag.

Viewing examples of contests on app Pages

The Votigo website (www.votigo.com) has a Case Studies section of successful contests that have run through its platform; see Figure 5-14. Choose Case Studies from the Clients drop-down menu at the top of the page. Some contests and some sweepstakes are featured. These aren't current promotions but show previous promotions that have been successful for Votigo clients.

Book VI
Chapter 5

Promoting Your
Contest and
Analyzing the
Results

Figure 5-13: Use the terms in the search bar to find posts about contests or sweepstakes.

Figure 5-14: Peruse contest and sweepstakes Case Studies on the Votigo site.

You can also watch the Facebook Pages of the contests and sweepstakes apps because they may post examples of contests that are currently running using their app, as shown in the Heyo post in Figure 5-15.

Figure 5-15: Watch for contests posts on Facebook Pages of the apps.

Keeping an eye on the Facebook Ad Board

Watch Facebook Ads because it often advertises contests. The easiest place to see all the current Ads at one time is the Facebook Ad Board (`www.facebook.com/ads/adboard`). The Ad Board shows all the Ads being served to your Profile demographic at that time, so check back at different times and possibly have people with different demographics checking in.

Finding contest information on Twitter

You can use Twitter search, at `https://twitter.com/search-home`, to find people who are tweeting about Facebook contests, as shown in Figure 5-16. You can use keywords like **enter, contest,** and **Facebook,** or hashtags like `#contest`, `#win`, and `#facebook` to see who's tweeting about contests.

Book VI
Chapter 5

Promoting Your
Contest and
Analyzing the
Results

Figure 5-16: Find people who are tweeting about Facebook contests.

Book VII
Facebook Advertising

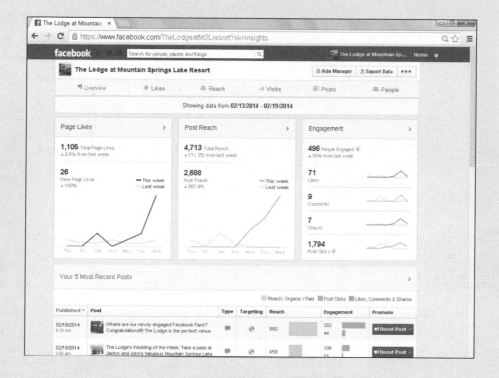

Contents at a Glance

Chapter 1: Advertising in Facebook 469

Introducing Facebook Advertising...469
Grasping the Anatomy of Facebook Ads 475
Defining Types of Ads 479
Identifying Your Goals 484
Making Your Initial Decisions 490

Chapter 2: Creating a Facebook Ad.............................493

Getting Started with the Ads Create Tool 493
Identifying Your Internal or External Ad Objectives 496
Making an Ad Work...502
Targeting Your Audience 508
Setting Up Your Account and Campaign Page 514
Crossing the Finish Line..518

Chapter 3: Exploring Power Editor 521

Deciding Whether Power Editor Is for You..521
Enabling Power Editor..522
Navigating Power Editor..524
Campaigning in Power Editor 526
Using Power Editor to Create and Promote Posts 534
Pinpointing Your Ideal Audience...538
Optimizing Ad Bids in Power Editor 547
Optimizing Ads for Ideal Placement 549
Tracking Conversions...550

Chapter 4: Testing, Measuring, and Modifying Your Ad 553

Understanding the Ads Manager...553
Adding a User to Your Facebook Ads Account..................................559
Changing Your Attack Plan..562
Trying Out Split-Testing...562
Viewing Facebook Reports 567

Chapter 1: Advertising in Facebook

In This Chapter

✔ Attracting new clients with Facebook advertising

✔ Understanding how advertising works on Facebook

✔ Developing ad campaigns to meet your goals and objectives

✔ Setting your budget and time frame

According to *Business Insider,* Facebook posted almost $7 billion in advertising revenue in 2013. And, in a rebuff to its many critics, Facebook's mobile advertising revenue started outpacing its web-based revenue in fourth quarter 2013, with mobile advertising accounting for 53 percent of advertising receipts. That gave Facebook its first-ever quarter with more than $1 billion in mobile ad revenue. (For more information on using Facebook's mobile advertising, see Book VIII, Chapter 4.)

By any measure, that's a lot of money, so it shouldn't surprise anyone that Facebook makes an effort to keep that revenue stream a-flowin'. Clearly, Facebook has a vested interest in making the ads an easy and pleasant experience for both the marketer and the Facebook community.

In this chapter, you find out how to make strategic and tactical advertising decisions that produce the results you want. You discover how to set your marketing goals and objectives, allocate a budget, and set your time frame.

In Chapter 2 of this minibook, you learn the mechanics of using the Ads Create tool to set up a campaign, write and target an ad, and start running it. Chapter 3 deals with the Power Editor for more complex campaigns. By the time Chapter 4 of this minibook comes around, you'll be ready to hone your advertising skills by setting up ad testing, measuring your test results with the Ads Manager tool, and modifying your campaign if needed. Hang on — it's going to be fun!

Introducing Facebook Advertising

Placing ads on Facebook provides one of the most targeted advertising opportunities on the Internet today. You decide exactly which Facebook users will see your ad. Your choices include (but are not limited to) age, gender, education, location, language, interests, relationship status, and keywords in your targets' Profiles. You can even choose to advertise only to people who have a birthday within a specific week. When you can narrow your target audience to that granular level, you can be pretty sure that whoever clicks your ad is a prospective customer.

Within Facebook Ads, you can advertise an external URL (directing people out of Facebook to your website), or you can advertise something internal to Facebook, such as your Page, an event, a post, or an application.

Understanding auction bidding

Facebook uses an auction-based system, in which you bid on how much you're willing to pay for each action. (By *action* here, we mean each time someone clicks your ad or each time Facebook places your ad in front of 1,000 people.)

There are two different bidding processes for advertising: One process is for advertising by clicks you receive, and the other is advertising by the number of times your ad appears (impressions).

Before we dive deeper into Facebook Ads, we want to introduce the terminology.

+ **Cost per click (CPC):** Cost per click is a model in which you pay for an ad only when someone clicks on your ad, whether it appears in the right-side column of a Facebook Page or within someone's News Feed. This works particularly well when you want to direct people to your website or other external URL.

+ **Cost per impressions (CPM):** You pay based on how many thousands of people see your ad — a measurement known as *impressions,* or *CPM.* (CPM stands for cost per thousand. Okay, really, it stands for cost per mille; *mille* means one-thousand in French.) You may find this option works better for branding purposes, or when you're trying to direct people to someplace within your own Facebook presence. Facebook optimizes the delivery of your ads to target the people most likely to help you reach your stated objective, such as Likes or joining an Event.

Facebook Ads competes on more than price. Facebook will show the ads that it determines are the most likely to be successful — that is, the ads that will give Facebook the most revenue!

The actual amount needed to "win" a bid fluctuates constantly. That's partly because Facebook continually evaluates ad performance and partly because the pool of competing ads is always changing.

You can make your ad more competitive by raising your bid. Facebook will only charge the amount necessary to win the auction even if that amount is less than your maximum bid. Therefore, you have nothing to lose by entering your true maximum bid.

You'll never be charged more than the maximum cost per click you set. And you'll never be charged more than your daily or lifetime budget for your ads, regardless of the option you choose.

Setting a flat fee to promote a post

Facebook's Promoted posts are a special type of internal advertising. Instead of paying by click or by thousands of impressions, you pay a flat fee to have Facebook to push a post directly into the News Feeds of your fans.

You will be able to set a lifetime budget that lasts for the time frame you set for your Promoted post campaign. Charges, which are incurred by impression, will be deducted from your budget.

Why would you want to pay to advertise your Page Post? Facebook enables you to reach out to other Facebook users who might not have another means of discovering your company's expertise, product, event, application, or service. You may also want to target Friends of your existing fans to show social proof (that is, your Friend likes me, so you should, too). Or you may want to push an important sales message or update into the News Feeds of your community for people who may not see your updates otherwise.

We discuss Promoted posts (sometimes called Promoted Page posts) in more detail later in this chapter.

Paying a premium price

Premium ads are reserved for clients with a budget of $30,000 or more per month. (Wouldn't that be nice?) They may appear on the Logout Page, which offers the largest creative format to drive video views or direct response traffic, or on the home page. Ads within the Mobile News Feed, Desktop News Feed, or Right Column on the Homepage offer the greatest visibility. After all, they appear on the most visited Pages of Facebook.

Targeting your ads strategically

Facebook gives you multiple options for targeting your ads to Facebook users. By far the most common method is demographically, but you can also target by interest areas, by geographic region, by keywords that people use in their Profiles, and/or by how they have behaved on Facebook in the past (target users who are most apt to like something).

Compare Facebook's methods for targeting to the search term-matching method used for most Google AdWords or ads in Yahoo!/Bing. (Google does offer a demographic option, but it's not as accurate as Facebook's.)

When you place ads on these search-engine platforms, you select and bid on certain keywords that might be entered by searchers. If your business is car insurance, for example, you could opt for "car insurance," "car insurance quotes," or "auto insurance" as keywords.

By comparison, on Facebook you select the demographics or other characteristics of the audience you want to view your ad. People with those characteristics may or may not be searching for what you offer. Suppose that you determine that your ideal customer for car insurance is a 35-year-old male college graduate who lives within 25 miles of your city. You can easily enter those target demographics when you set up your advertising; only people who meet those criteria see your ad.

Targeting by demographics

Since the search term approach isn't relevant to Facebook, knowing your target demographic is critical. You may have some general thoughts about whom you're trying to reach in terms of your marketing efforts, but we recommend going through your customer list (or a small sample, if your list is large) and charting the following attributes to start:

+ Age
+ Gender
+ Location

Using Facebook Insights to obtain basic demographics

If you don't already have a customer list with demographic data, use your own Facebook presence to glean demographic information. From your Facebook Page, take a look at Insights — Facebook's statistics area, which shows your community's demographics, including gender, age, and location. Here are the steps to get to that information.

1. **Log in and navigate to the Admin panel by clicking on the page name beneath the heading "Pages" in the left-side navigation.**

2. **On the Admin panel, click the See Insights button in the top right.**

3. **On the Insights page, choose the People tab at the far right in the first row of navigation, as shown in Figure 1-1.**

4. **Choose whether you want the demographics for Your Fans (people who liked your Page), People Reached, People Engaged, or Check-Ins in the second row of navigation.**

   For basic demographic information, you probably want either Your Fans or People Reached.

   For example, Figure 1-1 shows detailed information about the demographics of Your Fans, broken down by gender, age, location, and language for a specific Facebook Page. Now you can apply this information to decide which demographic segments to target in your ad campaigns.

   We cover Facebook Insights in more detail in Book IX, Chapter 2.

Figure 1-1:
View Page demographics here.

You need to decide not only the target demographic for your ad, but also what to advertise. Match the content of your ad to what's likely to appeal to your target demographic. For instance, a sporting goods company might have one ad for younger people who are interested in extreme sports and another for an older demographic interested in Pilates or yoga.

Targeting with additional parameters in Facebook

To get a bit closer to your target audience, try selecting Precise Interests and/ or Broad Categories when you set up your ad campaign, as we explain in the next chapter. In addition, users may have entered specific words within their Profiles on their About page, or in their Timelines. Perhaps they indicate they like volleyball or horror movies, or that they liked The Beatles' Facebook Page.

If you use the Power Editor (see Chapter 3 of this minibook), you will find other options for identifying your audience based on external activities, such as people who have visited new car websites.

Figure 1-2 shows an About page with text within the user's Work and Education section that might be used as keywords. See the interest areas listed under the More drop-down menu.

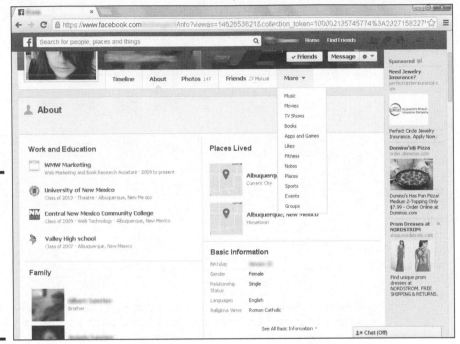

Figure 1-2: The About section of a Profile includes text that might be designated for targeting.

When you create a Facebook ad, as we show you how to do in Chapter 2 of this minibook, you can enter the demographics, Likes, Interests, and keywords in the Audience section. Figure 1-3 shows the Audience section of the Facebook Ad Creation Tool. You can see how many choices you have. Fortunately, Facebook displays a dial to estimate the size of the potential target audience based on the selections you make.

Be careful not to narrow your audience too much when using Precise Interests or keywords from Profiles. Different people may use different keywords in their Profiles or may not select all their Precise Interests. You might exclude many potential customers. Watch the size of the potential audience on the dial; remember that only a small fraction of that audience will actually take an action.

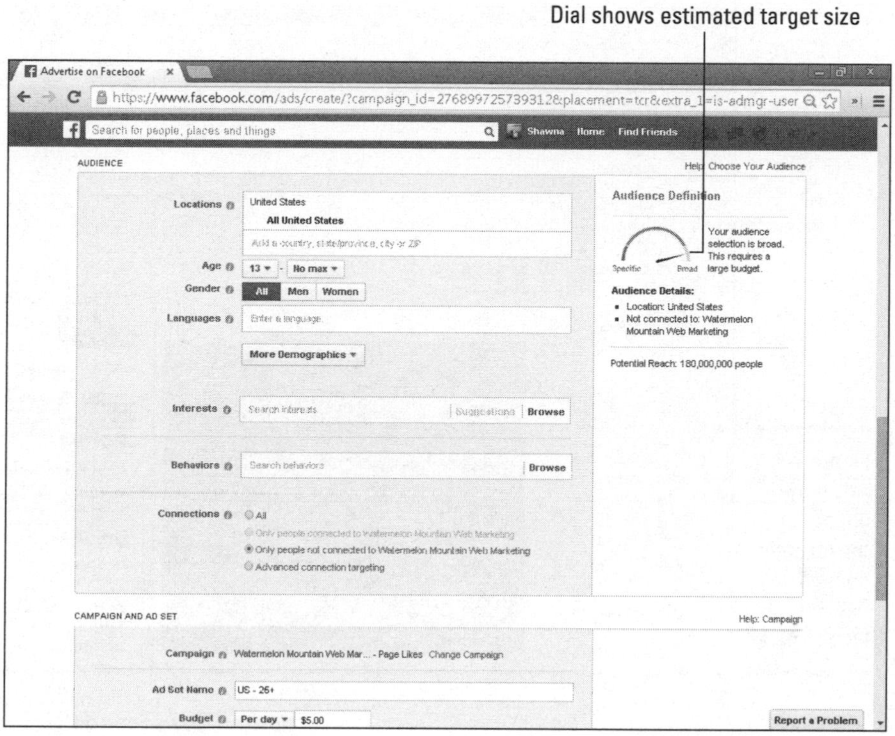

Dial shows estimated target size

Figure 1-3:
Target your
Facebook
ads by
choosing
demo-
graphic
details in
the Ads
Create tool.

Grasping the Anatomy of Facebook Ads

You've probably seen Facebook ads in the far-right column of a Facebook
Page below the Sponsored heading, in your News Feed, or on your Facebook
home page or log-out page. (If you haven't, check out Figure 1-4.) Depending
on the type of ad, you can choose where your ad will appear.

As many as seven ads may appear in that column at one time, depending on
where you are within Facebook. They may appear on any page of Facebook
or search results.

You can't choose whether your ad will receive the top, middle, or bottom position, but the bid you place for the ad and how many clicks your ad receives
affect the placement. Facebook uses its own algorithm to choose which ad to
display based on multiple factors, including the historical performance of a
particular ad at a particular bid price.

If you're advertising something internal to Facebook, and you optimize your
ad to show it to people who are most likely to engage with it somehow,
Facebook does the bidding for you.

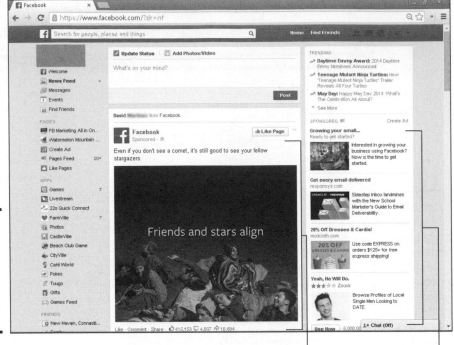

Figure 1-4:
Ads may appear in the far-right column or within a News Feed.

News Feed ad   Right column ads

Ads placed within the News Feed usually have a more eye-catching graphic component than those in the right column. Again, Facebook uses complex algorithms to decide whose News Feeds will display your ad.

According to Nanigan's Performance Marketing Insider, ads in Facebook News Feeds have a much higher click-through rate than ads in the right column, but a lower return on investment (ROI). For more information, see `http://prfm.us.nan`. Consider showing ads in both places, depending on your objectives. You'll have to test for yourself!

Advertising by objective

Recently, Facebook simplified its advertising products, especially for small business users. It reduced the number of ad types and improved consistency in the look and feel of ads. Facebook streamlined the process of purchasing ads by focusing on specific marketing objectives.

As you see in the next chapter, your process starts with the question, "What's Your Advertising Objective?" Facebook offers these choices:

✦ Clicks to Website

✦ Website Conversions

+ Page Post Engagement
+ Page Likes
+ App Installs
+ App Engagement
+ In-store Offer Claims
+ Event Responses

Facebook will recommend an appropriate type of ad and pricing strategy based on your choice of objective. However, you can always choose to test a different strategy if you want. In Chapter 4 of this minibook, you learn how to judge the performance of your ads against your objective and how to compare results based on your bidding choice.

Promoting posts

Promoted posts may appear in either the News Feed or the right column. A "Sponsored" notice appears just below the post in a News Feed. Posts appear higher up in the feed so the audience will be more likely to see them. As with any other post, users can interact by liking or commenting on the posts.

Advertising on Facebook versus other platforms

Facebook Ads works a little differently than Google AdWords, Yahoo!/Bing, or LinkedIn pay-per-click (PPC) ads, or even banner (display) ads. (If you aren't familiar with banner ads, don't worry; we go into a little more detail on that topic in a bit.)

While the ads look superficially similar, the click-through rate (CTR) on Facebook's right-side column ads is usually lower than the CTR on PPC search engine advertising that appears in the right-hand column of search results pages.

There are obvious explanations for this difference. Not only is the social audience larger and less specific than the search audience, but the social audience may not be actively searching for what you're advertising. (That's bad.) But if people do click your advertisement, you know that they're your target demographic. (That's good.)

Banner ads are graphic ads placed on targeted, third-party websites or blogs that you believe your customers will visit. These ads may appear at the top, bottom, sides, or be embedded within the text on a web page. Sample banner ads are shown in Figure 1-5.

When people click a banner ad, they're taken to a specific page on your web site, called a *landing page.* More highly trafficked ad publishing sites charge a higher rate to host banner ads. Banner ads are typically purchased directly from the publisher of a site or are placed on multiple websites when you purchase them through an advertising network. Google is one of many such advertising networks.

Banner ad

Figure 1-5:
Banner ads appear on web pages or blogs.

As with Facebook, Google and Yahoo!/Bing ads work on an auction system. You place a bid for ad space (either for search engine ads or banner ads), essentially letting the search engines know how much you're willing to pay per click or per 1,000 impressions. With search engine ads, you may pay less for your ad when there's less competition; however, if you bid too low, your ad may appear on page 3 or later of search results, which few people ever actually see.

The cost per click (CPC) on search engines can range from 10 cents to a few dollars, depending on how competitive the market for search terms is. In many cases, the CPC on Facebook is significantly less — but so is the return.

Comparing CTR and conversion rates

The *click-through rate* (CTR) — the percentage of visitors to a site who have clicked on a specific ad — typically runs around 0.10 percent for banner ads averaged across the Internet, roughly the same as the CTR on all types of Facebook ads combined at 0.11 percent.

Let's look at the fine print. Prior to the development of News Feed ads, Facebook's stamp ads — the ones that appear in the right column with a small graphic — used to receive a CTR between 0.04 percent and 0.40 percent. That's much lower than Google's typical 1.5 percent CTR on its PPC search ads, and even lower than Google's 0.2 percent to 0.45 percent CTR on its display ads.

According to AdSpringer (`blog.adspringr.com/battle-ctr-conversion-facebook-news-feed-ads-vs-stamp-ads`), Facebook's CTR rose dramatically after October 2013, when Facebook introduced large format graphic ads within the News Feed. CTR on these ads shot up to a remarkable 1.5 percent to 6 percent.

This doesn't mean that you've found advertising's Holy Grail! Alas, News Feed ads linked to outside sites appear to have a lower conversion rate than Google search ads. (*Conversion rate* is the percentage of visitors who take the desired action, such as making a purchase.) As a result, your return on investment (ROI) may plummet. One option is to use Facebook's Lookalike Audience feature in the Power Editor, which we discuss in the next chapter.

Defining Types of Ads

Facebook allows you to create many types of ads. Different types of ads may appear in News Feeds, in the right column, or in mobile environments. Facebook offers the following ad types:

**Book VII
Chapter 1**

Advertising in Facebook

+ Pages
+ Events
+ External websites
+ Applications
+ Individual posts in the News Feed

For more detail on ad types, see `https://fbcdn-dragon-a.akamaihd.net/hphotos-ak-prn1/t39.2365/851593_514339305349474_836951008_n.jpg`.

Readers who formerly used Facebook's Sponsored Stories know that they are no longer available. But one of their best features — social engagement — is now available on *all* eligible ads. Whether you advertise an external site, or something internal to Facebook, people can respond to your ad without actually leaving the ad by clicking Like, Join, Comment, or Share as indicated. When someone clicks one of these options, you'll be charged for a click.

For example, when people click the Like button in the ad shown in Figure 1-6 on the left, they automatically like the website URL listed in the ad. Similarly, people can RSVP to an event by clicking Join, as shown in Figure 1-6 on the right.

Figure 1-6:
Sample
right-hand
column ads
with social
context.

The social engagement component of Facebook Ads may make it easier to get the outcome you're looking for, because people don't have to click through to another page to take an action. If you have powerful ad copy that makes people want to connect with you, you lessen the chance that they'll forget to like you or take another action after they click your ad.

You don't need to do anything special to create ads that promote part of your Facebook presence. Facebook automatically creates a layout like those in Figure 1-6 when you indicate that you're advertising a Facebook Page, group, or Event. Read more about how to create ads in Chapter 2 of this minibook.

Facebook tracks these clicks and much more in the statistical reporting section of the Ads Manager, which is shown in Figure 1-7. In-depth statistical analysis of your ad performance is covered in Chapter 4 of this minibook.

Looking at Promoted posts in more detail

Promoted posts push a post into more of your fans' News Feeds. You can create them directly from the Facebook Timeline on your Page. This type of ad involves no targeting or bidding. Facebook has made it clear that not all posts on a Page are seen by all the people who like a Page. At the Facebook Marketing Conference in February 2012, Facebook stated that on average, each post is seen by 16 percent of a Page's fans. Over the span of a week or a month, you may reach more than 16 percent of your fans with all your posts collectively, but not everyone will see *every* post.

Figure 1-7:
The
Facebook
Ads
Manager
provides a
wealth of
statistical
information.

The reach for many posts is low because people are connected to a lot of Friends and may like many Pages. It simply isn't possible to show all the updates from all their Friends in someone's News Feed.

Facebook uses complicated algorithms to determine whether a specific person is shown a post. (See Book IV, Chapter 2, for more information on these algorithms.)

If your fans haven't interacted with your posts for a while, they may stop seeing your posts in their News Feeds. Oh, no! Engaging content is the best way to solve this problem for free. Make sure that your fans are watching for your posts, and make sure that you're posting fun things to keep the Likes and comments rolling in for each post.

If this doesn't work, however, you may need to spend a few advertising dollars to give your Page a lift with a Promoted post. The Promoted post appears in the News Feeds of more of your fans and their Friends, and/or to people you choose through targeting.

Facebook offers a shortcut, called Boost Post, for promoting a post. You can choose to boost any post directly from your Timeline, without bothering to use the Ads Create tool. Except for the fact that a boosted post can appear only in a News Feed (not in the right-hand column), a boosted post works exactly the same as a promoted post. For more about boosted posts, see `facebook.com/business/promoted-posts`.

You also may want to consider which posts are best to promote. Certainly, Facebook Offers (discussed in Book III, Chapter 1) are leading candidates for this advertising solution. Other good options are fun posts that get a lot of interaction; occasional sales messages that you don't want people to miss; and intriguing photos that interest your audience and boost interaction. Or you may want to watch the interaction a previous post receives and then decide to promote it after the fact to reach more fans with a post that is already a winner.

Structuring ad campaigns strategically

In the Facebook Ads Manager, you arrange your ads into campaigns. A *campaign* is a group of similar ads.

For example, if you're advertising your Facebook Page, your goal is to get people to like your Page. If you run an ad and get 30 clicks, but only 15 people like your Page from those clicks, your conversion rate is 50 percent. If you change the copy of your ad, and 30 people click your ad and 20 people like your Page, your conversion rate is 66 percent. The second ad converts better and gets you more for your money. Facebook automatically optimizes ads within an ad set to display the best performing ones.

The Ads Manager is where you can see all your campaigns in one place and access your reports and settings. We discuss the Ads Manager in Chapter 4 of this minibook.

You may want to create a separate campaign for different products, services, goals, or marketing objective. You can set daily budgets for your whole campaign, ad sets, and/or for each individual ad. You can run a single ad, but it's placed under a campaign heading and ad set that you choose. Create a new campaign when you're advertising

+ A particular product

+ A particular product in a region or country

+ An event

+ Your Page

You may want to run two identical ads — one using the CPC model and one using CPM — to see which gives you a better ROI.

Typically, you want to run some test campaigns with small budgets first to find out which ad performs best. Lest you think that this testing will break your bank, you can set a daily budget so that the ad stops running automatically when it reaches your limit. After you know which ads are performing best, you can run them for longer periods with bigger budgets.

Knowing what you can't advertise

Facebook has guidelines about what you can and can't advertise. It reviews each ad for appropriate language, content, and formatting. If your ad doesn't comply with the guidelines, Facebook *will* reject it. Some of the items that you can't advertise include

✦ **Work-at-home sites that promise easy money for little or no investment**

✦ **Multilevel marketing opportunities, such as Mary Kay and Avon**

✦ **Software that contains spyware or malware**

✦ **Sites that have *domain forwarding*, in which the listed URL forwards to another website**

   Even if your site is innocently forwarding the domain, many places that have domain forwarding may be doing so for shady reasons.

✦ **Landing pages that have a pop-up window**

   Having a pop-up window may be an innocent way to get subscribers to your e-mail list, but many people don't like pop-up windows, and sometimes, they can't even close them.

The obvious items are prohibited or highly restricted:

✦ Tobacco

✦ Gambling

✦ Pornography

Facebook heavily restricts the language that can be used in ads for certain products or that are targeted at certain demographic groups. See the Facebook Advertising Guidelines at www.facebook.com/ad_guidelines.php if you're advertising any of the following items, among others:

✦ Adult products

✦ Dating sites

✦ Alcoholic beverages

✦ Drugs and tobacco

✦ Gambling and lotteries

✦ Pharmaceuticals and supplements

✦ Weapons and explosives

✦ Subscription services (such as ringtones)

Identifying Your Goals

Before you start spending money, have a goal in mind. What does a success-ful ad campaign look like? Attracting 50 more Likes? Selling 25 more widgets? Having ten people sign up for your newsletter? Getting ten comments on a post? Whatever goal you decide on, write it down, and come up with a way to track your progress.

Review your baseline values before you start advertising. For instance, look at your website analytics to check how much site traffic Facebook currently generates for you. How many sales come from those leads? With that infor-mation in hand, you can assess whether paid advertising makes sense and how much you should spend.

Gaining connections

Advertising your Page is one of the best things you can do with Facebook Ads. You know that the people who click your ad are in your target market and enjoy Facebook. Connecting with new people on your Page allows them to get to know you and your company.

Before you begin your advertising, collect more baseline data on how your Facebook Page performs currently. The Insights feature makes it easy.

Note these measurements:

✦ How many new Likes for your Page do you get per week, on average?

✦ To what extent are your current fans making the extra effort to interact with you — likes, comments, shares, and so forth? This statistic is indi-cated by the Engagement numbers.

✦ Do you find a difference in the demographics of Reach versus the demo-graphics of Likes, Comments, or Shares? (We discuss how to view demo-graphics in the earlier section, "Targeting by demographics.")

We talk more about Insights in Book IX, Chapter 2, but here's an overview of how to access your baseline performance data:

1. **Log in to Facebook as your Page admin.**

2. **Click the See Insights button in the top right of your Admin panel.**

   The Insights Overview area opens, which has some nice graphs. As shown in Figure 1-8, you can see tabs for Overview, Likes, Reach, Visits, Posts, and People. We cover Insights in more detail in Book IX, Chapter 2.

- *Overview:* This tab provides a summary where you see all the critical information about your Page. Click the section header for more details about each category, including statistics on posts, user interaction, and what you spent to promote your posts.

- *Likes:* Number of unique people who have liked your Page. You can compare the number of new Page Likes in the current period with the number acquired during the previous week, month, or quarter. Use this to keep track of the growth of your Facebook Page and whether your Likes come from free traffic or ads.

- *Reach:* Number of unique people who have seen any of your Page posts from either free traffic or paid ads and how they have interacted with your posts. Compare this with Total Reach, which tallies how many unique viewers have seen any component of your Facebook presence, including ads. By looking at activity of your Page overall, you can assess whether efforts to increase user interaction have worked. The chart in Figure 1-8 compares Post Reach in the past week with Post Reach in the prior week.

- *Visits:* Shows which parts of your Facebook presence that people visit the most (tabs, Timeline, Profile) and what actions they have taken. This is somewhat like the old "Engagement" section, but more detailed. It now includes information about which sites have referred traffic to your Facebook presence. Use that information to decide where to place content and where to promote your page to increase Likes.

- *Posts:* Lots of details, such as when people visit your Facebook Page, which posts work best, and what you've spent to promote your posts. Drop-down arrows let you segment results by audience characteristics or actions taken. Use this information to refine your content to increase interactive and decrease negative responses.

- *People:* Demographic information about the people who have visited, liked, or otherwise interacted with your Page. Use this tab to see how successful you are in reaching your target market and whether the demographics match up. If not, you might want to revisit your targeting and other marketing assumptions.

3. **To download your data, click the Export Data button in the top-right corner of the page. Refer to Figure 1-8.**

   A query window appears, where you can set the date range, data type, (Page or Post), and file format you prefer: a Microsoft Excel spreadsheet or a comma-separated values (`.csv`) file.

Click here to download file

Tabs

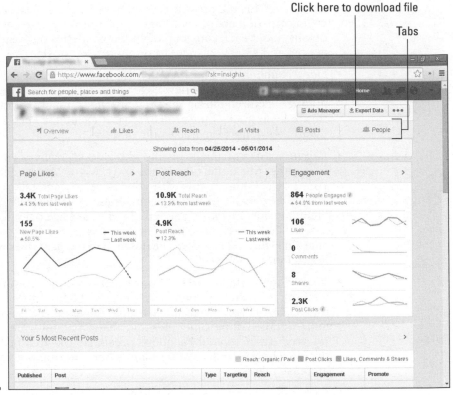

Figure 1-8:
The Insights
area
displays
trend
lines for
how many
people are
engaging
with your
posts.

4. For strategic advertising analysis, select Page Level Data, a file format, and the date range.

You can download any date range, but there is a limit of 500 posts at a time. See Figure 1-9.

5. Click the Download button.

With these settings, you can get the data to graph how many Likes you're getting per week, how many Likes and Comments you receive on your posts, and your demographics.

Write down all these baseline measurements or save them in a file so that you can compare them with your Insights after you run the campaign. Make sure you're reaching people on Facebook who will interact with and be part of your community.

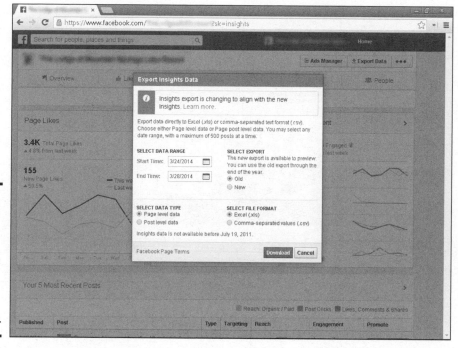

Figure 1-9:
The Export function enables you to manipulate your data in a spreadsheet.

If your current Facebook community isn't too large, see whether you can determine how many of your fans are already customers and how much money they've spent with you. With that information in hand, you'll have a more accurate picture of the effect that your Facebook community has on your bottom line. That's not to say that having a community isn't of value in itself, but you're running a business, after all, and your advertising dollars — and advertising labor hours — need to be well spent.

If (and only if) you have selected Page Likes as your advertising objective, you can send new visitors who click on your ad to a special Welcome tab rather than to your Timeline. You set this up in the Ads Create tool (see the next chapter). Click the Advanced Options drop-down list under the Text and Links section and select Landing View. On the following drop-down list, choose which tab or app you want to establish as the landing page. (See Book VI to learn more about adding tabs to your Page.)

A special tab should tell more about your business and give users a compelling reason to join your community. Figure 1-10 shows the REI Trail Mix tab, which tells visitors to click the Like button, shows the store locator, and offers some special blog posts with expert advice and information about the company.

Store locator   Link to information   Call to action: Like this page

Figure 1-10:
REI has
a call to
action to
Like its Page
and gives
information
about the
company.

Acquiring leads

Acquiring leads for your business with Facebook Ads could be your goal. Maybe you'd like your potential leads to sign up for your newsletter, a free half-hour consultation, or a free quote. In this case, you've probably set up your ad so that clicking it sends users to a website outside Facebook. When you do this, make sure that the landing page correlates directly with the Facebook ad.

You may want to have a special landing page on your website that clearly relates to your call to action. If you send visitors to your general website, they may not see the link to request your newsletter, or they may be distracted by all the other nice things on your website and forget to request a quote.

The landing page is part of your website; just make sure that the response to the call to action in the ad is very clear.

Figure 1-11 shows an example of a good landing page. The only thing users can do on this page is click the Try It For Free! button (people always like free) or give the company a call. There's no menu to start clicking, and there are no distracting ads on the page.

Figure 1-11: This landing page keeps the focus on the call to action (Try It For Free).

If your goal is simply to drive awareness of your brand rather than acquire leads, you may want to have your phone number or store address in the ad so that someone doesn't necessarily have to click to contact you. If you're having a grand opening or open house, put as many key details as you can fit in the 90 characters you have available in the body of the ad. See Chapter 2 of this minibook for more information on creating your ad.

Reconnecting with your community

By using Facebook ad features, such as Promoted posts, you can reconnect with your current community and gain interaction from dormant fans. As we mention earlier in the chapter, and as you can see at the bottom of each of your Page posts, only a portion of your community sees any specific post. Once you drop out of someone's News Feed, it's very difficult to get back into that News Feed organically. Advertising is a good way to reconnect with that person.

If your goal is to reconnect with an existing community, choose to target *only* those people who have previously liked your Page. Go to the Connections area of the Create Your Audience section in the Ads Create tool to accomplish this. You can also use a Promoted post to push a post directly into the News Feeds of existing Likes, who otherwise may not see it. (The Connections area offers other options, such as reaching out only to new users.)

Making Your Initial Decisions

Map out your strategy before you start. You need to decide how long to run your ad, how much to spend, and how often to change things. Read the case study in the nearby sidebar for a story about how one business makes successful Facebook advertising decisions.

Allocating a budget

Allocate a budget and time for the initial testing, as well as the longer-term Facebook ad. You don't want to spend money week after week on an ad that isn't converting as well as it could be. Your initial testing budget should be, at most, one-tenth of your entire ad budget. Run each variation of your ad for a short time. Even after just 20 clicks, you can start to see whether one is outperforming another significantly.

When allocating a budget, knowing what your clicks are worth to your bottom line is critical. How your product is priced and how many conversions you need to be profitable are factors to consider when you set your budget. Think of it this way: If you need 100 people to visit your site before you get a sale, and each sale of your product earns you a net profit of $20, it doesn't make sense to spend more than 20 cents per click.

Rotating your ad

Plan on rotating your ad every couple of days to keep things fresh, especially if you're advertising to a small demographic.

Again, this strategy isn't a "set it and forget it" campaign. Ideally, after you finish your testing, you'll have zeroed in on several ads that perform well. You can manually schedule one of those ads to run for a few days; and then schedule a different ad to run for the next few days. A bit of a nuisance, but it increases viewer attention.

If you aren't getting as many clicks as you'd like, try adjusting your demographics to a slightly wider range by

✦ Adding more keywords

✦ Expanding the age range, adding more cities

✦ Increasing the geographical range

Setting a time frame

How long should you run your ads? This question is intimately tied to your budget and how effectively your ad is converting. Make sure to allocate time to do your testing. Testing may take a few weeks, depending on how many campaigns you're testing and how many ad variations you have.

You can also target day and hour when your ads start and stop, along with many other variables. You can find more about these options in Chapter 2 of this minibook.

Allow time for your ads to be approved. Ads are reviewed manually at Facebook, and approval can take anywhere from several hours to a full day. After the ad is approved, it starts running automatically. The ad approval process is covered in Chapter 2 of this minibook.

Outfitting Facebook ads for success

Seagull Outfitters (seagulloutfitters.com) offers self-guided wilderness canoe fishing trips into Minnesota's Boundary Waters Canoe Area and Ontario's Quetico Provincial Park. It also rents cabins on both Seagull and Saganaga Lakes on the end of the Gunflint Trail, 54 miles northwest of Grand Marais, MN. Owner Debbie Mark, who has run Seagull Outfitters for 28 years, markets regionally, nationally, and internationally to vacationers who want to spend time in the wilderness.

The company created a Facebook account several years before it started using Facebook paid advertising in June 2013. "We realized that social media has changed the world and we wanted to get involved," Mark explains.

From a strategic point of view, Seagull uses Facebook advertising primarily to direct the large number of users on Facebook to its website, where viewers can find more information or make reservations for camping, canoeing, or cabin rentals. At the same time, the company has steadily increased its following on its Facebook Page (https://www.facebook.com/pages/Seagull-Canoe-Outfitters/62547922591, shown in the following figure) through Likes — almost 1,500 in March 2014! — and shares.

Tactically, Mark varies Seagull's Facebook ad targeting and messages by region, income level, special interest, and/or keywords. The company runs right column and News Feed ads, but hasn't bothered with Promoted posts. You can see examples of ads that the company created for Facebook in the figure.

Mark's approach has been very successful. "Facebook ads have put us in front of Facebook users seeking what we offer. It has engaged them on our Facebook Page, [and] it has increased our customer base, our online presence, and conversion rates," she says.

She and her staff spend 30–60 minutes per day posting updates, creating ads, and viewing/analyzing results in Ad Manager. Mark is enthusiastic about the analytics in Ads Manager. "It is very interesting data!" In addition, she uses Google Analytics to view results on web activity generated by Facebook. To publicize its Facebook presence, Seagull places Facebook icons on the website and in its newsletters.

Mark offers straightforward, no-nonsense advice: "Business owners should know the market they want to reach better than anyone. Be creative, trust yourself. Create ads, fine-tune them, and learn from them. Facebook advertising is a cost-effective method of reaching potential customers." As she insists, with just a hint of impatience, "Social media is here to stay. Educate yourself."

(continued)

(continued)

Courtesy of Seagull Canoe Outfitters.

Courtesy of Seagull Canoe Outfitters.

Chapter 2: Creating a Facebook Ad

In This Chapter

✔ **Using the Ads Create tool**

✔ **Setting your advertising parameters**

✔ **Creating a successful ad**

✔ **Getting your campaign up and running**

This chapter is all about the mechanics of Facebook's Ads Create tool. You learn how to establish your marketing objectives, set up a campaign, write and schedule a good ad, designate your bids, and target your audience, all using this tool.

In the first chapter of this minibook, we talk about strategy and tactics; in the last chapter of this minibook, we talk about measurement using Facebook's companion tool, the Ads Manager. If you're ready to delve into the details of what happens in between, this is the chapter for you.

The advertising process requires the use of two tools: the Ads Create tool (to develop your ads) and the Ads Manager tool (to save, store, and review the results of your efforts).

The Facebook Ads help section (www.facebook.com/help/42528408416 3299) is one of the most complete areas within Facebook Help. You can find step-by-step instructions for setting up your ad, case studies, and a glossary. Also, whenever you see a question mark (?) or lowercase "i" in a circle next to a term or box, hover over it to get an explanation.

Getting Started with the Ads Create Tool

As we mention in Chapter 1 of this minibook, advertising is now organized by objective. Facebook prompts you to build an ad to help you meet your objective. Later, you can see how well your ads meet your objective by using the Ads Manager tool, which we describe in Chapter 4 of this minibook.

When you're ready to create an ad, whether for your Facebook Page or to an external website, your first step is to navigate to the Ads Create tool. There are multiple ways to do this, as shown in Figure 2-1.

1. **Log in and go to your News Feed.**

2. **Click on the Create Ad link in the left navigation or any ad in the right column with that link visible.**

To get to the same place, you can also select Create Ads from the drop-down menu in the far right of the top navigation or type **facebook.com/ads/create** in the address bar at any time.

All these methods take you to the Objectives screen, shown in Figure 2-2.

Choose Create Ads

Create Ad link in navigation pane   Click here for drop-down menu

Figure 2-1: Click on any of the Create Ad options in your account, or enter facebook. com/ads/ create in the address bar.

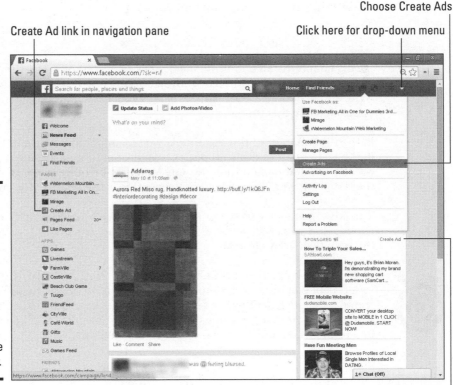

Create Ad link in an ad

Courtesy of Watermelon Mountain Web Marketing (WatermelonWeb.com).

For ongoing inspiration and news about changes to the advertising interface, like the Facebook Marketing Page (`facebook.com/marketing`) to receive regular updates.

3. **Select an objective:**

- *Page Post Engagement:* Promote your Page posts.

- *Page Likes:* Get Page Likes to grow your audience and build your brand.

- *Clicks to Website:* Get people to visit your website.

- *Website Conversions:* Promote specific conversions for your website.

  You'll need a conversion pixel for your website before you can create this type of ad. This Facebook-supplied snippet of code, which your developer can insert on your website, tracks when a user has completed a desired action — like buying something!

- *App Installs:* Get people to install your mobile or desktop app.

- *App Engagement:* Get people to use your desktop app.

- *Event Responses:* Increase attendance at your event.

- *Offer Claims:* Create offers for people to redeem in your online or bricks-and-mortar store.

  The options are explained in the following sections.

Click for help

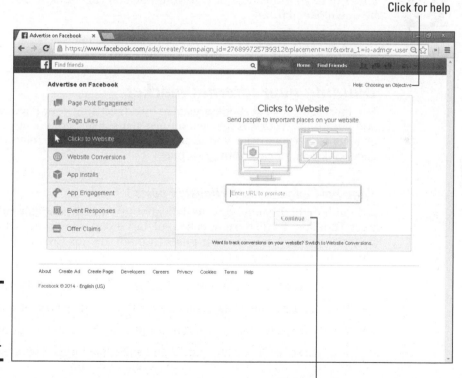

Figure 2-2:
Select your
objective
from the list.

Click to continue

Courtesy of Watermelon Mountain Web Marketing (WatermelonWeb.com).

If you have a question about any objective, hover over the objective or click the link for Help: Choosing an Objective.

Identifying Your Internal or External Ad Objectives

Of the various types of ads available on Facebook, most are used to

✦ Build up your Facebook presence

✦ Increase engagement

✦ Find new prospects

✦ Enhance customer loyalty

Only two — Clicks to Website and Website Conversions — are designed to drive people to web pages outside Facebook. We talk about the internal uses first.

You can always build your Facebook presence in the real world, too. Take advantage of Facebook table tents and stickers to remind customers to check in to your business or Like your Page on Facebook. These items can be downloaded from

```
https://fbcdn-dragon-a.akamaihd.net/hphotos-ak-prn1/t39.2365/851579_376385309150
    392_137721597_n.pdf
```

Building your internal market

You increase your Facebook presence by advertising your Page, your posts, and your apps. Your ads may encourage visits, likes, comments, shares, or installs. In every case, you're attracting new visitors or reinforcing your Facebook relationship with prior ones.

Page post engagement (Boosted posts)

In Chapter 1 of the minibook, we talk about boosting posts directly from your Timeline. That shortcut is helpful, but if you want more options and better targeting, promote your posts through the Ads Create tool. The benefits of using the "long way" include

✦ Promoted posts can appear in the right column as well as News Feeds.

✦ The targeting can be as detailed as with any other type of advertising.

✦ You can set the start and end dates of your Promoted Page post.

✦ You can set both a daily budget and a lifetime budget, whereas a post boosted from a Timeline has only a one-day duration.

✦ You can choose cost per click (CPC) or cost per impressions (CPM) bidding through the Ads Create tool, instead of flat-rate bidding starting at $5. (Read all about CPC and CPC in Chapter 1 of this minibook.)

At least 50 people must like your Page before you can boost a post from your Timeline, but that restriction doesn't apply to Promoted posts developed using the Ads Create tool.

After you select the Page Post Engagement option, you'll see the screen shown in Figure 2-3. Go through the options, which we explain in more detail. The trickiest thing is to estimate a budget for boosting your post because the cost depends on multiple variables, including the geographical location of your target market and the size of your reach.

If you click the phrase Boost Post beneath the desired post on your Page, Facebook provides the potential reach for the spending level you enter. You can fiddle with the spending level until you're satisfied with the reach.

Page Post Ads Specs

Page post photo ad

Text: 90 characters

Image ratio: 1:1

Recommended image size: 1200 x 1200 pixels (px)

Page post text ad

Text: 90 characters

Page post video ad

Text: 90 characters

Image ratio: 16:9

Recommended thumbnail size: 1200 x 675 px

Max video size, length: 1GB, 20 min

Page post link ad

Text: 90 characters

Link title: 25 characters

Image ratio: 1.91:1

Recommended image size: 1200 x 627 px

You can toggle between previews of the Right Column and News Feed versions of your ad by clicking the tabs above the Ad Preview area. Or, you can remove a placement by clicking Remove.

Page Likes

Ads to increase Page Likes can appear in either the News Feed or the right-hand column. You can take viewers to a tab or an app, not just to your Timeline.

Click the Page Likes objective (refer to Figure 2-2) and follow the same steps as for the Page Post ads.

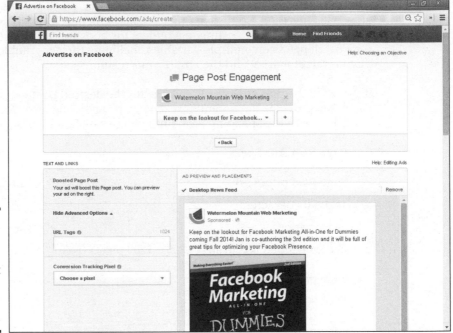

Figure 2-3:
Creating a
Page Post
Engagement
ad with the
Ads Create
tool.

To choose a particular landing page, open the Show Advanced Options box in the bottom-left corner of the Text and Links section. From the Landing View drop-down menu that appears, choose the tab or app where you want people to go.

People can sign up to like your Page right from your ad. Take advantage of this to increase Likes; the fewer extra clicks, the better.

Page Like Ad Specs

Text: 90 characters

Image ratio: 2.7:1

Recommended image size: 1200 x 444 px

Event Response

Planning a book signing? A webinar? An equipment demonstration at your store? Use Event Response ads to increase attendance at any type of special occasion. Event Response ads can be placed in the right column.

As with Likes, people can sign up to join an event right from your ad! Always take advantage of this option. The easier you make it for viewers, the better the results.

Event Responses Specs

Text: 90 characters

Event title: 25 characters

Image ratio: 1.39:1

Recommended image size: 1200 x 444 px

Offer Claims

Make people an offer in a Facebook ad that they can't refuse! These ads promote offers that you've created in your Timeline, or you can create the offer via the Ads Create tool. We discuss offers in greater detail in Book VII, Chapter 1, and Book VIII, Chapter 1.

Because offers can be promoted either by boosting a post directly from the offer or through the Ads Create tool, you have several options to introduce your existing Likes and their Friends to special promotions, discounts, coupons, and other time-limited opportunities. Users redeem your offer either on your website or in your store.

If you create Offer Claims ads using the Ads Create tool, they appear in the News Feed and right column.

Offer Claims Ad Specs

Text: 90 characters

Offer Title: 25 characters

Image ratio: 1.91:1

Recommended image size: 1200 x 627 px

Minimum required image size: 470 x 245 px

At least 50 people must like your Page before you can create an offer, even in the Ads Create tool.

Building your outside market

You can use two types of ads to drive traffic to your website, outside the confines of Facebook itself. Whether you choose the objective of driving traffic for content purposes (Clicks to Website) or to encourage sales, downloads, or user registration (Website Conversions), advertising can be a cost-effective way to target your particular market segment within the vast Facebook user base.

Clicks to Website

Certainly, one of the most valuable ways to use Facebook advertising is to drive the huge Facebook audience to your website. Click to Website ads can appear in the News Feed, the right column, or mobile environments. If you also create both News Feed and right-column ads, they use the same landing page that you select.

Choose the option to show social activity (Like, Share, Comment) with your Clicks to Website ads so people can respond without actually clicking through. Should they do so, these options will be counted as clicks. There is an option to turn social activity on or off in the Edit Text and Links area of the Ads Create tool.

Make sure your landing page (the destination URL for a click) meets Facebook guidelines. You can find more information at

```
https://www.facebook.com/ad_guidelines.php
https://www.facebook.com/help/www/196334053757640
```

Clicks to Website Ad Specs

Title: 25 characters

Text: 90 characters

Image ratio: 1.39:1

Recommended image size: 100 x 72 px

Note: Offsite URLs that are not connected to a Facebook Page default to this ad type.

Website Conversions

Perhaps the most complex of Facebook ad types, Website Conversions ads are tied to users taking a specific action (conversion) on your website itself, such as making a purchase, filling out an inquiry form, downloading a white paper, signing up for an account, or subscribing to an e-newsletter.

To keep tracks of conversions on your website that result from your Facebook ads, Facebook will ask you to create a *conversion tracking pixel,* which is simply a snippet of code that your developer (recommended!) or you (not recommended!) insert on your website.

Inserting a conversion pixel can be done in three ways:

✦ When you select the Website Conversions objective, you're prompted with a Create Tracking Pixel link in the Ads Create tool, if you don't already have one.

✦ Go to the Ads Manager tool (www.facebook.com/ads/manage/home), click the Conversion Tracking link in the left column, and follow the directions.

✦ Go to the Power Editor (www.facebook.com/ads/manage/powereditor), select the Conversion Tracking link from the Manage Ads drop-down list in the top-left corner, and follow the directions. We discuss the Power Editor in greater detail in Chapter 3 of this minibook.

Choose the type of conversion that best fits your needs (checkouts, leads, registrations, key page view, adds to cart, or whatever other website conversion matters to you). You will see reports on conversion events sorted by type in the Ads Manager.

You can now use conversion pixels not only on website conversions, but also on ads with Clicks to Website or Page Post Engagement objectives. This makes sense only if you are later asking people to link from your post or from another web page to complete an action on your site.

After you create the conversion tracking pixel, e-mail the snippet of JavaScript to your developer to place between the <head> and </head> tags on the web page where the conversion occurs. (You always have access to the conversion tracking pixel, so don't worry if you don't copy and e-mail it right away.) For more help, send your programmer to

www.facebook.com/help/373979379354234?sr=2&sid=0J34GkYsKFiBa
BoYN

Be sure your developer puts only one tag on each conversion page. Otherwise, the statistics on conversions may not be reported correctly. Consequently, you won't be able to assess the efficacy of your ads.

You can always retrieve the code for the conversion pixel or create another one for use on another site the same way you created the initial one. To e-mail an existing conversion pixel to another developer, find the Conversion Tracking tab in your Ads Manager. Hover over the name of the pixel you want from the drop-down list, and click the e-mail icon. Insert the e-mail address and click Send Pixel.

Web Conversion Ad Specs

Title: 25 characters

Text: 90 characters

Image ratio: 1.39:1

Recommended image size: 100 x 72 px

Note: Offsite URLs that are not connected to a Facebook Page default to this ad type.

App Installs

These ads get people to install your mobile or desktop app. When a user clicks your ad and accepts the permission prompt for your ad, an "install" is counted. This way, you can measure the success of your ad based on installs. Mobile ads work similarly, but have different technical requirements.

App Engagement

App Engagement ads are similar to App Installs, but they are designed to encourage people to go one step further and actually use your desktop app. For example, a restaurant could target existing users of its table reservation app by writing an ad with a call to action to Reserve Now for a special wine tasting. When users click the ad, they are sent straight to the table reservation app to book the wine tasting. The process is similar to a website conversion, but for your app instead of your website.

Making an Ad Work

After you select an objective and click the Continue button (refer to Figure 2-2), you'll come to the main portion of the Ads Create tool, with five sections whose options are already preset to what's available for your objective. You'll need to scroll through and set the parameters for each of these sections before your can finish your ad.

Selecting images

Images are required in all Facebook ads except for Page Post Engagement. Facebook makes specific suggestions for the size of the images based on where they will appear and the type of ads. You can choose images from Page photos or prior ads, or upload new ones.

Because Facebook lets you select up to six images per ad at no extra cost, you can quickly test which image best helps you attain your objective. Facebook automatically optimizes your ads to show the most successful of the images. If you provide multiple images, Facebook will automatically create multiple ads for you under one campaign.

Here are some points to remember:

✦ Images that appear in News Feeds should not contain more than 20 percent text within the image.

✦ In general, the best size image to upload is 1200 x 627 px, with a 600 px minimum width for News Feeds; more specific recommendations may appear for some ads.

Selecting images

Facebook offers solid tips for when you're choosing ad images:

✔ Use a simple, eye-catching image that is related to your ad text.

✔ Use an image that is bright, even when viewed at a small size.

✔ Use an image that is the right size. (You can find the sizes in this chapter.)

✦ Facebook will choose an initial image for your ad based on your objective. For instance, for the Web Click objective, it will grab an image from your website. If you have an internal Facebook objective, Facebook will find an image from your Page or Event. To get rid of this image, simply click the X in the top right of the picture. Then locate and upload an image or images you prefer.

✦ If you upload an image that's too small, some ads won't run at all; in other cases the ad will run but the image will appear in the old "postage stamp" format of 100 x 100 px.

✦ To specify an image, select one of the buttons located below the six image boxes shown in Figure 2-4 to opt for

• *Upload Images:* Follow the standard prompt from the pop-up box to upload an image from your hard drive or other device. Click Open in the bottom right of the pop-up box to preview the image.

• *Browse Library:* Select image(s) from prior ads, page images, or your website.

• *Find Images:* Look for free stock photos via Shutterstock. Such a deal! *Note:* These images are licensed only for use within Facebook.

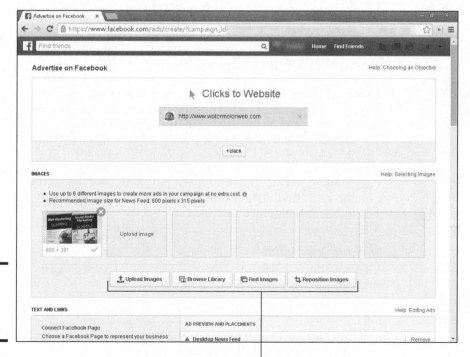

Figure 2-4:
Select
images for
your ad.

Choose your image with these buttons

- *Reposition Images:* Follow the prompt to reposition the image you have uploaded. Repositioning isn't quite what it sounds like. Facebook tries to auto-fit images into the space available, but sometimes you might prefer a smaller image with more graphic pizzazz. Deselect the Auto-Fit check box in the lower-right corner of the image preview.

You'll be charged only once for the budget even if you create multiple ads under one campaign.

Editing text and links

As you edit the text and links for your ad, you'll see your ad take shape in the Ad Preview area on the right side of the screen, as shown in Figure 2-5.

The exact steps in the Text and Links section vary by objective, but Facebook walks you through it.

Connecting to your Facebook Page

When you're in the Edit Text and Links area for ads that are building your outside market (Clicks to Website or Website Conversions), you see an option to connect your ad to your Facebook Page. If you do that, your ad will link to your site, but the ad will appear to be coming from your Facebook Page. You can see this in the Ad Preview section of Figure 2-5, where the Facebook reference appears above the ad and the link to your website appears below it. It's kind of a twofer.

Facebook will automatically try to pair your ad with one of the Facebook Pages you administer based on the URL. If Facebook goofed, simply click the arrow next to the page showing in the box, and select the correct one from the drop-down menu that appears. Click the + sign to confirm.

You also have an option to turn off News Feed ads below the Connect Facebook Page field. News Feed ads have a much higher CTR (but lower conversion rate) than right-column ads. This is a strategic marketing decision, not to be taken lightly.

Writing a headline

The headline appears above the picture. You have to make it interesting *and* concise. Here are the parameters:

✦ You get 25 characters.

✦ You can use capital letters at the beginning of each word, but the body of the ad doesn't allow excessive capitalization.

If you're advertising a website, include your business name or other key information in the headline.

Choose your Facebook Page here

Desktop News Feed tab

Ad Preview area

Figure 2-5:
The Text and Links section for the Clicks to Website objective, with a preview on the right side.

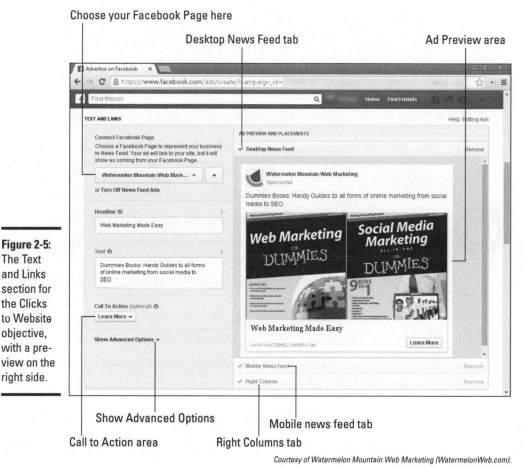

Show Advanced Options

Call to Action area

Mobile news feed tab

Right Columns tab

Check out the following examples of 25-or-fewer-character headlines to see why they're effective:

Do Zombies Worry You? (Poses a question)

Free Green Chile Samples (Offers something for free)

Put an End to Mess (Solves a problem)

Don't Miss 30% Off Sale (Sends out a call to action)

You can't put a headline or text with Page Post Engagement ads. By default, the headline will be your Page name and the text will be the content of the post that you want to promote.

To see many more examples of what other people are currently advertising and perhaps get ideas for headlines, take a look at Facebook's Ad Board at www.facebook.com/ads/adboard.

The Ad Board consists of all the current ads that could be shown to the user who is currently logged in. So when advertisers set up their ads to be shown only to women ages 45–55, if you're a woman in that age range, you can see that ad in the Ad Board area. You may have even seen some of them already in the sidebar of your personal Profile, but by using the Ad Board, you can see the ads all in one place, as shown in Figure 2-6.

Crafting your message

You have 90 characters to work with in the text of your ad, so make them count! There's nothing like an ad to prove the maxim that "less is more." It may take a bit of practice, but you'll soon become an expert. The best advice, especially for right-column ads, is to keep your text direct and simple.

✦ Consider the keywords you want in the ad to attract attention.

✦ Emphasize the benefit that your offer provides to your ad's readers. What problem do you solve for the customer?

✦ Start your text with a question or two. It engages the reader and gives him something to relate to.

✦ Follow a question by identifying the benefit that will solve the problem:

  • *Are you always short on time? Have someone else do your house cleaning!*

  • *Would you like to earn your degree? You can in just six months with our online program.*

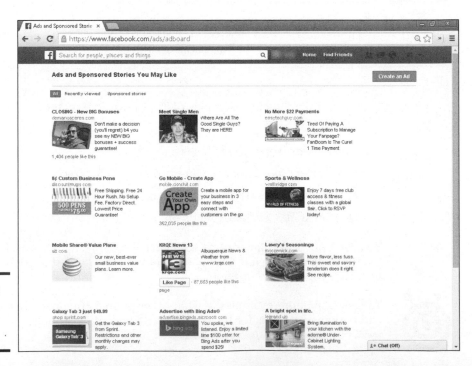

Figure 2-6:
The
Facebook
Ad Board.

Take a look at the sample ads in Figure 2-7 for examples of good ad copy.

Figure 2-7:
Examples of
compelling
ads.

Whole Foods Market
Strut your
Thanksgiving cooking
style! Take our quiz for
a chance to win a Gift
Card!
Like Page · 1,433,756 people like this
page

Nothing Bundt Cakes
Win A Year Of Cake.
Share your favorite family
photo for a chance to win
free Nothing Bundt Cakes
for a year!
Like Page · 136,382 people like this page

Angie's List "A" Rated
motherroadplumbing.com
Plumbing, Heating,
Cooling. 2012 Super
Service of the Year Award
Winners (505)933-9665
Like Page · 121 people like this page

Writing calls to action

If you select one of the external marketing objectives (Clicks to Website or
Website Conversions), you're prompted to select an optional Call to Action
button within the Text and Links section of the Ads Create tool (refer to
Figure 2-5). Choose the action you want people to take from the list that
Facebook suggests:

+ No Button (this option is not to show a button)

+ Shop Now

+ Book Now

+ Learn More

+ Sign Up

+ Download

The options aren't available unless you have chosen Connect Facebook Page
(the first step under the Text and Links section in the Ads Create tool). After
you choose your Call to Action button, it appears in the preview section, but
only for News Feed ads.

+ If you don't use one of Facebook's optional buttons, include a strong call
to action at the *end* of the body text.

+ Tell your audience what to do and what benefit they get for taking that
action. These are all good calls to action:

  • *Find the best shoes.*

  • *Access your free financial report.*

  • *Get your free quote.*

+ Make sure that your landing page always matches the call to action in
the ad. If you ask viewers to sign up for a newsletter, direct them to the
web page where they can easily do so.

If you make the process the least bit inconvenient or confusing, you'll lose
ad responders in a flash.

Specifying advanced options

Advanced options are located in the bottom-left corner of the Text and Links section of the Ads Create tool; refer to Figure 2-5. When you click the drop-down arrow, a list of options appears. The options available vary depending on the objective you chose.

Find explanations and what options appear with what objectives in the following minitable.

If you chose Clicks to Website or Website Conversions, you must insert your destination URL.

Option	For Objective(s)	What It Is
News Feed Link Description	Clicks to Website or Website Conversions	Indicate the benefits of visiting your site.
Entering URL Tags	Page Post Engagement or Offer Claims	Hand off this coding-related task to your developer.
Landing View	Page Likes	Choose which tabs or apps on your Page that people will land on when they click your ad.
Turning on a Conversion Tracking Pixel	Website Conversions, Clicks to Website, or Page Post Engagement	Select the conversion pixel you want. If you haven't created one, you may not see one; if you've done this multiple times, you may see several.

Targeting Your Audience

Unlike the previous section for Edit Text and Links, audience targeting options are the same for all objectives. Your options are listed in the Audience section of the Ads Create tool, as shown in Figure 2-8.

Locations

Select the geographic region(s) where you want your ad displayed. You can choose one or more countries, states, cities, or zip codes. Targeting by cities is available in only some countries; zip code targeting is only for the United States.

Demographics

Knowing the physical, behavioral, psychographic, and interest characteristics of your target audience is a classic component of marketing. Because

Facebook garners this information directly from its users, some people consider it to be an accurate depiction of the Facebook population.

People don't always tell the truth, or the whole truth, about themselves when they create their Facebook Profiles. If your ads don't perform as expected with your demographic profile, sprinkle your data liberally with salt. Note that in some cases, the data selection may not be based on what people have entered into their Profiles, but on data from various third-party sources. Such data is often aggregated according to zip codes or by other forms of data mining.

Your choices follow:

✦ **Age:** The choices are for minimum age (set to 13 as default) and maximum age, which is optional. Select the range that's appropriate for your ad. Since not everyone indicates his age, the only way to reach everyone is to leave the maximum age blank.

✦ **Gender:** The default is All. However, you may want to target to only one gender choice for certain products or services. Not everyone specifies gender on Facebook, so the only way to reach everyone is All. (Users can now select LGBT categories within their Profiles, but that option doesn't exist within the Ads Create tool at this time.)

✦ **Languages:** A drop-down menu appears as you begin typing; choose the language you want. As long as the language you want is common to the location you specified, you can leave this blank. However, if you're trying to reach American expatriates in France, or speakers of Arabic in the United States, specify the language.

✦ **More Demographics:** Click the arrow to display these additional options, broken down by categories:

✦ **Relationship**

• *Interested In:* Use this option only if you want your ad shown to people who are interested in a specific gender for friendship, dating, a relationship, or networking. The choices are All, Men, Women, Men and Women, and Unspecified. Many people leave this blank, so select All to reach the broadest audience.

• *Relationship Status:* Choose All unless you want your ad shown only to people with a specific relationship or marital status. Again, because many people leave this blank, you must select All to reach everyone.

✦ **Education**

• *Education Level:* Target users by their highest achieved education. Note that marketers consider education to be a rough indicator of household income — the higher the education, the higher the income.

• *Fields of Study:* Target ads by Facebook users' field of study or school major.

- *Schools:* Target users by the school they attend.

- *Undergrad Years:* Target users by their college years.

✦ **Work**

- *Employers:* Target your ads based on where people work. You probably want to leave this field empty; relatively few ads are targeted to people who work only for a specific company.

- *Job Titles:* Use the job title people provide in their Facebook Profiles to target your ads. If you fill out this field, your ad is visible *only* to people who have entered the title or titles specified. Otherwise, leave this field blank.

- *Industries:* Use the industry choice people enter in their Facebook Profiles to target your ads. If you fill out this field, your ad is visible *only* to people who work in the industries specified. Otherwise, leave this field blank.

- *Office Type:* Target your ads according the type of office people work in (corporate, small office, home office). If you select this field, your ad will be visible *only* to people who work in the type of office specified. Otherwise, leave this field blank.

- *Net Worth:* This field is available for selection only when your ads are restricted to the United States. You can target your ads based on income ranges supplied by a third party. If you fill out this field, your ad is visible *only* to people with the specified levels of net worth. Otherwise, leave this field blank. This field is often used by financial industry professionals, retirement advisors, and investment counselors.

✦ **Home**

- *Home Type:* This field is available for selection only when your ads are restricted to the United States. You can target your ads based on home type supplied by a third party. If your ad is directed at all home types, leave this field blank.

- *Home Ownership:* This field is available for selection only when your ads are restricted to the United States. You can target your ads based on home ownership data supplied by a third party. This field may be useful to companies that market home repairs, home maintenance equipment, or services that are more likely to be purchased by homeowners than renters. If this doesn't apply to your product or service, leave this field blank.

- *Home Value:* This field is available for selection only when your ads are restricted to the United States. You can target your ads based on home value data supplied by a third party. If you fill out this field, your ad is visible *only* to people with home values in the range(s) shown. Otherwise, leave this field blank.

- *Household Composition:* This field is available for selection only when your ads are restricted to the United States. If you fill out this field, your ad is visible *only* to people with the household composition shown. Otherwise, leave this field blank.

✦ **Ethnic Affinity:** This field is available for selection only when your ads are restricted to the United States. If you fill out this field, your ad is visible *only* to people who have indicated an interest in, or affinity with, a certain ethnic group. It does not necessarily mean that someone is actually of that ethnicity. The ethnic options are currently limited. Unless you want your ad shown only to people with a specified ethnic affinity, leave this field blank.

✦ **Generation:** This field is available for selection only when your ads are restricted to the United States. If you fill out this field, your ad is visible *only* to people in a specific generation. Currently, the only subset available is Baby Boomers. Unless you want your ad shown only to people who are Baby Boomers, leave this field blank. Of course, you can also reach this market segment using the Age filter.

✦ **Parents**

- *All Parents:* In most cases, choose All. Because many people leave this field blank, that's the only way you can reach all parents.

- *Moms:* You can really tell who's subjected to a barrage of advertising when you see a group broken down into seven segments! This field is available for selection only when your ads are restricted to the United States. Unless you know whether you want only moms with a specific interest or lifestyle (Green moms? Trendy moms?), just select All Moms. Of course, you can also reach all moms with the Parents filter — but then you have dads, too.

✦ **Politics (U.S.):** This field is available for selection only when your ads are restricted to the United States. Different subsets represent data from Facebook self-identified fields or third-party sources. Select this field to have your ad shown only to people with certain political affiliations. You can only reach everyone by selecting All. Otherwise, leave this field blank. (This field was probably requested by political campaign consultants!)

✦ **Life Events:** Target your ads according to which of the dozen or so life events that people have indicated on their Facebook Profiles. If you select this field, your ad is visible *only* to people who are experiencing that life event. Otherwise, leave this field blank. If you are interested in life cycle marketing, this might be a useful filter for you.

**Book VII
Chapter 2**

**Creating a
Facebook Ad**

REMEMBER

Watch the Dial and Potential Reach number as you make your Audience selections. The more narrowly you target your audience, the smaller your reach. However, one of the advantages of Facebook advertising is that its user base is so large that you can filter your target audience significantly and still reach hundreds of thousands of prospects.

Interests

Given the size of the Facebook user base, there are likely to be hundreds of thousands of people — if not millions — with almost any interest you can imagine! The Interests filter follows the More Demographics options on the Audience section of the Ads Create tool.

There are benefits to spending the time it takes to target your ad to your specific audience. It is apt to perform better and continue running successfully when the people who see it are the ones most likely to be interested in what you have to offer. Niche targeting like this helps you personalize your ad copy and images.

You can always target multiple groups of people by creating different versions of your ad.

1. **Click the Browse button to the right of the Interests text field, as shown in Figure 2-8.**

   A drop-down menu opens, showing primary categories.

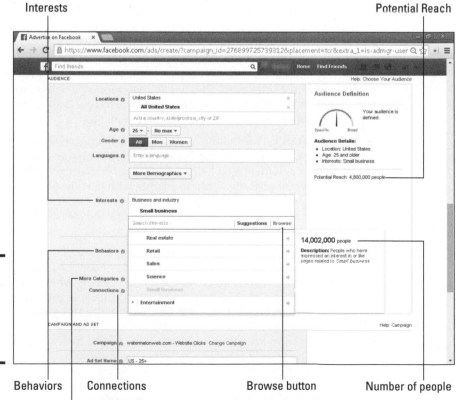

Interests   Potential Reach

Figure 2-8:
The
Audience
section of
the Ads
Create tool.

Behaviors   Connections   Browse button   Number of people

More Categories

2. **Choose a category or type a keyword in the Interests field to reach a more targeted audience.**

If you type a keyword, the list shows appropriate categories.

3. **Click the + sign to the right to add people in this area to your target audience.**

After you select the interest you want, it appears in the Interests field.

Note the box to the right of the Interests field in Figure 2-8. It shows the approximate number of people in the pool as you drill down. If your ad isn't performing well, the target audience may be too small. You may want to add interests, or "retreat" to the next highest level.

Behaviors

An option to select Behavior filters follows the Interests section, as shown in Figure 2-9. This filter works particularly well if you prefer a behavioral marketing approach. Some of this information has been self-reported by Facebook users, but much of it comes from third-party databases. The pop-up box to the right of your choices indicates whether a particular data category is available for only U.S. audiences.

Potential Reach

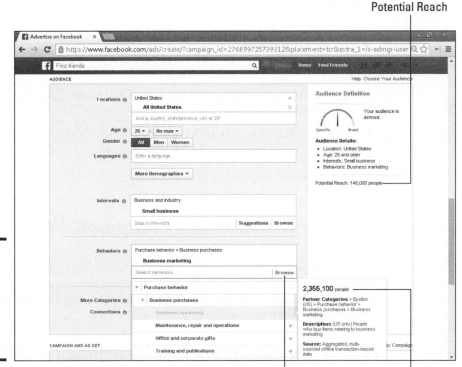

Figure 2-9:
The Behaviors filter option within the Audience section.

Browse button   Number of people

Follow the same steps as with Interests section. Click the Browse button and select as many categories and subcategories as you like. Click the + sign to add people to your target audience.

More Categories

Choices in More Categories, the section below Behaviors in Figure 2-9, are currently fairly limited, but Facebook may expand them at any time.

This section allows you to filter for any Facebook or Partner (third-party data source) Categories. Right now, the only available option is Facebook Mobile Subscribers under Facebook Categories. In some cases, data may only be available for the U.S. user base.

Connections

This option lets you limit your ad so that it displays only to those who already have some kind of connection to your Page, app, or event, such as people who have already liked or shared it. The options you see vary by the objective you select.

To see these options listed, you must have already connected your ad to a Page, app, or event. (Review this step under the Text and Links section in the Ads Create tool.)

If you have not yet connected to a Page, select the radio button for Advanced Connection Targeting to see options with fields for you to enter your Page, app, or event name. Your maximum choice fields are:

✦ All (widest choice: people either connected to the specified Page or not connected)

✦ Only people connected to the specified Page (in any way)

✦ Only people not connected to the specified Page

✦ People whose friends are connected to the specified Page, app, or event

Setting Up Your Account and Campaign Page

After you write your ad and name your campaign, you're ready to set up your advertising account with Facebook, as shown in Figure 2-10. You see different options in this section when you set up your first campaign than you see subsequently. In fact, even the title will change to "Campaign and Ad Set" after you have created your ad account.

Filling Out the Account and Campaign section

At this point in the setup, you're getting near the end — honest! The following directions apply if you're setting up a new campaign. If you've already set up campaigns (whether they're running or not), slightly different options will appear. In particular, the Account Settings section is visible only the first time around.

Renaming your campaign

Facebook auto-generates a name for your campaign; see Figure 2-10. To change it, follow these steps:

1. **Click Change Campaign.**

A pop-up window appears with an editable text field where you can enter the name of your choice.

2. **Click in the field and type the new name.**

Try to be descriptive.

3. **Click Save to keep the new name.**

Campaign

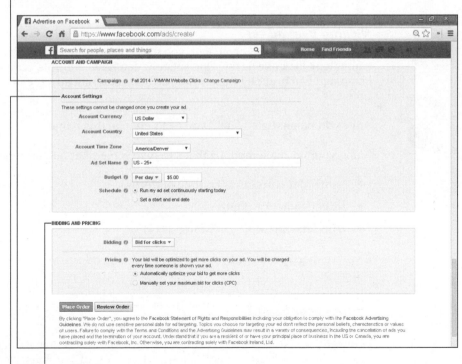

Figure 2-10: The Account and Campaign section of the Ads Create tool as it appears the first time you set up an account.

Bidding and Pricing

Account Settings

You may already have an ad campaign and want to use your new ad in it. If so, follow these steps:

1. **Click the Change Campaign link next to the campaign name.**

   A pop-up menu appears.

2. **Select the campaign you want.**

3. **Click Save to add your ad to that campaign.**

   A campaign can contain multiple ads or sets of ads.

Establishing account settings

After you specify the Account Currency, Account Country, and Account Time Zone settings in your ad, you can't change those settings. These choices apply to all your ads, ad sets, and campaigns going forward.

As a user, you can have only one account unless another account holder gives you permission to manage her ad campaigns as well. See Chapter 4 of this minibook to see how to add other administrators to an advertising account.

Naming your ad set

After naming your ad campaign, you name your suite of ads. As we discuss, campaigns look like a tree. One account can have multiple campaigns, one campaign can branch into multiple ad sets, and one ad set can contain multiple ads.

After you name the ad suite, you can't change this name.

Name your ad set something that's easy to remember and understand, such as

✦ Name of the product (knitting patterns)

✦ Target audience (knitters)

✦ When the ads will run (winter 2014)

If you're merely adding a new ad to an existing ad set, you can keep the same name.

Setting your budget

Don't confuse your budget with your bids! Your *daily budget* is the maximum you want to spend per day; your lifetime budget is the maximum amount you want to spend during the entire time this ad (or ad set) runs. Neither has anything to do with the maximum bid for each click or impression, or the total for the entire campaign, which is composed of multiple ad sets or ads.

Don't obsess over the budget numbers. You can change them anytime within the Ads Manager tool, as we discuss in Chapter 4 of this minibook. Facebook never charges you more than the total of the daily budgets you establish for your active ad sets.

1. **From the Budget menu in Account Settings, select Per Day or Lifetime Budget.**

2. **In the field, enter a dollar amount.**

   - *If you chose Per Day in Step 1:* Enter the maximum amount you want to spend each day.

   - *If you chose Lifetime in Step 1:* Enter the maximum spending limit for the entire run of the ad set.

You have more control if you set a daily limit unless you're trying to cram a lot of impressions into a very short window. You might expect your Lifetime budget to last for a month, but Facebook may spend it all within a week or less! For the best of both worlds, calculate your Lifetime budget for your ad set. Divide that by the number of days the ads will run to get your Per Day budget. Then your ads run evenly throughout your schedule without exceeding your overall budget. If you don't set an end date, your Lifetime budget may be expended quickly, based on the bidding and pricing options you select, as we explain in the next section.

CPM campaigns are more likely to be set by Lifetime expenditure, especially if they're being used for branding over a long time period. Per Day makes more sense for CPC and external objectives.

Establishing a schedule

You have only two choices: Run your campaign continuously from now until the money runs out, or specify a start and end date.

Completing the Bidding and Pricing section

The bidding options that appear in this section will depend on what objective you selected and the bidding method you choose.

Choosing your bid option

As we discuss in Chapter 1 of this minibook, you can choose to bid by clicks, impressions, or objective. (In that arrangement, a cost per impression is debited against the flat budget you establish for your objective.) Your choice determines your ultimate cost and who sees your ad. Here's the section where the rubber meets the road.

When you expand the bidding drop-down, you see bidding options that vary depending on the objective that you chose. CPC and CPM bidding is available for all objectives.

**Book VII
Chapter 2**

**Creating a
Facebook Ad**

For certain internal objectives, the third (and default) option is a bid per impression according to objective. What you see depends on the objective you select. For example, if you choose Page Likes for your objective, Bid for Page Likes is the third choice; if you choose Event Response for your objective, Bid for Event Responses is the third choice.

You're charged every time people see your ad, regardless of whether they take the internal action you're promoting.

Answering the pricing question

At the very bottom of the Account and Campaign screen are two options:

✦ **Automatic:** Facebook optimizes your bid to help you reach your objective. That is, your ad is shown at the price (up to your daily limit) at which it performs the best.

✦ **Manual:** You're in control of your maximum bid, whether CPM or CPC. If you want to force your ads to rotate without incurring additional cost, select Manual settings. If you put them in different ad sets, they run congruently and incur additional costs.

Even if Facebook optimizes your bid to best achieve your objective, it does not guarantee a specific number of clicks or impressions.

The Automatic ad choice may result in the display converging very quickly on your objective with only one ad showing. If you need the variety, or want to assess the results for yourself over time, start out with Manual bidding. You can always switch to Automatic later.

Crossing the Finish Line

The final steps are to review your order, place it, and set up a payment method. After choosing all your account settings, click the green Review Order button (refer to Figure 2-10). You'll see the dialog box shown in Figure 2-11.

Placing your order

After you review your order, follow these steps:

1. **Click the blue Place Order button located at the bottom of the Review Your Order pop-up window.**

2. **Select a payment option: credit card or PayPal.**

3. **Enter the required information.**

   Facebook uses this information for all future advertising unless you change or remove it in your Account Settings.

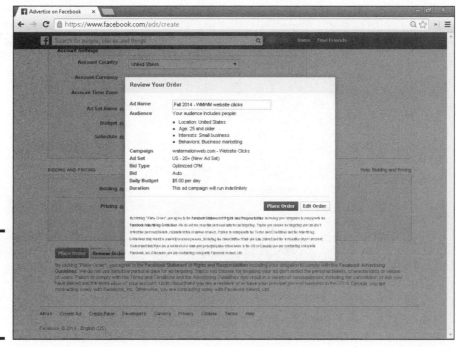

Figure 2-11:
Review
your order
carefully
before
placing it.

After your order is placed, you're directed to the Ads Manager screen shown in Figure 2-12. The Ads Manager is a dashboard for managing your ads and your campaign and to review results. We talk about the Ads Manager in greater detail in Chapter 4 of this minibook.

Facebook predetermines a daily spending limit when you first open your account. Your limit increases after Facebook successfully receives payments from your charge card or PayPal. If you need to spend more than $1,500 a day or want your limit to increase faster, fill out the Daily Spend Limit Increase Request Form at

`https://www.facebook.com/help/contact/168771979839539`

Getting your ads approved

Alas, Facebook is not a great source for instant gratification. Your ad is eligible to start running only after Facebook reviews and approves it. This process usually takes less than 12 hours.

If you have a time-sensitive ad, set it up early so there's time for approval. Either schedule it to start at a certain time, or pause the approved ad through the Ads Manager until you're ready let it run. Slide the status bar from On to Off for your ad, ad set, or campaign. For more about the Ads Manager, see Chapter 4 of this minibook.

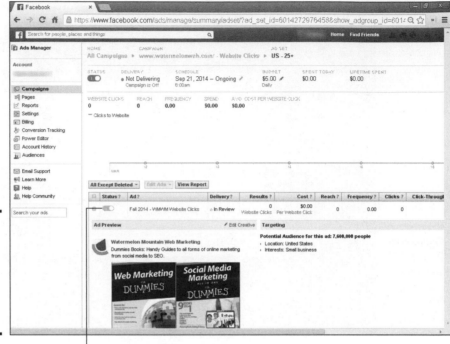

Figure 2-12:
After you place your order, you see the Ads Manager screen.

Status

Facebook reviews ads through both manual and automated reports. If it receives negative feedback, it not only receives fewer impressions, but it may be removed or may not run at all.

Generally, Facebook suggests changes to bring your ad into conformance with its rules or to improve your ad targeting.

Chapter 3: Exploring Power Editor

In This Chapter

✔ **Understanding when to use Power Editor**

✔ **Creating and managing multiple ads and campaigns**

✔ **Taking advantage of scheduling tools for Promoted posts**

✔ **Using Power Editor features to reach known customers or prospects**

✔ **Optimizing your campaign bidding for special actions**

*P*ower Editor makes it easy to create, edit, and manage accounts and campaigns in bulk. It also contains some advanced target marketing tools that enable you to pinpoint your ideal audience for Facebook advertising.

Now that Facebook has moved many capabilities formerly limited to Power Editor — such as mobile ads and conversion pixels — into the regular Ads Create tool (see Chapter 2 of this minibook) or Ads Manager (see Chapter 4), there are only two primary reasons for using Power Editor.

First, if you're an advanced Facebook Ads *power user* — that is, you create a lot of Facebook ads with a large budget, or need to segment target audiences at a very detailed level — you may want to use Power Editor to manage multiple campaign variations from one access point.

Second, if you work for an ad agency with many clients who advertise on Facebook, Power Editor is an efficient tool for administering client accounts and campaigns from one convenient dashboard.

In this chapter, we detail the steps required to create and manage multiple accounts, campaigns, ad sets, and ads through Power Editor, and explore advanced tools to pinpoint customers and prospects within your target market.

Deciding Whether Power Editor Is for You

Because Power Editor was developed to enhance advertisers' ability to bulk manage multiple ads, ad sets, campaigns, or accounts, it offers specific features for this purpose:

✦ Mass editing of campaign settings, bids, budgets, audience targeting, and flight dates

✦ Easy modifications to creative elements

✦ Specialized targeting tools to narrow ad placements to an audience of known customers and prospects or to audiences that are similar to them

✦ Monitoring advertising statistics and making modifications to improve performance within the tool itself

✦ Uploading and downloading data to or from Excel or other spreadsheet applications

You can manage up to 25 accounts at one time in Power Editor. If you are an agency managing multiple clients, rest assured that each account will retain its own access credentials, permissions, billing, preferences, and other characteristics.

Become familiar with the Ads Create tool first. Unless you have a large Facebook advertising budget and the staff time to delve deeply into analytics for multiple campaigns, you will probably find that the Ads Create tool is more than adequate for managing your Facebook advertising. Power Editor is intended for experienced users who find the Ads Create tool too limited for managing complex campaigns or multiple accounts.

Enabling Power Editor

Start by logging in as an admin and accessing Power Editor at www.facebook.com/ads/manage/powereditor. Alternatively, click Power Editor in the left sidebar of the Ads Manager (refer to Figure 4-2 in Chapter 4 of this minibook).

As soon as you do that, the Download Facebook Ad Accounts pop-up window appears (see Figure 3-1). If you have already downloaded one or more accounts into Power Editor, those account numbers will appear in the drop-down account field (to the right of the words Power Editor) in the dark blue row at the top of the main Power Editor screen.

The Power Editor runs only under the Google Chrome browser. If you don't already have it, download and install Chrome first from:

www.google.com/intl/en/chrome/browser

Once you see the pop-up window in Figure 3-1, follow these steps:

1. **Select the account you want to download to Power Editor.**

There are several methods for choosing:

• *Choose your accounts by name or number.* Use the Ad Accounts tab at the top of the pop-up window to display a list of your accounts. (This view is shown in Figure 3-1.) Check the one(s) you want to download.

• *Choose by Page ID.* Click the Pages tab at the top of the pop-up. The pop-up window changes to reveal a field to enter a Page ID number.

Already downloaded accounts   Upload Changes button   Tabs

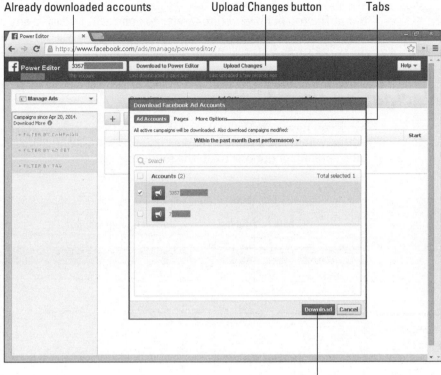

Figure 3-1:
Start by
choosing ad
account(s)
to download
into Power
Editor.

Download button

**Book VII
Chapter 3**

**Exploring Power
Editor**

- *Search by account ID or name.* Click the More Options tab. The pop-up window will change to reveal a field to enter an account ID number, as well as options to search for accounts or download deleted campaigns or ads.

2. **For the first and third options, you will see a note and a drop-down list where you can add inactive campaigns to Power Editor.**

   From the drop-down list, you can select the campaigns from within the past 1, 3, 6, or 13 months, or *from the start of time.* The default is *from the start of time,* which produces the most data.

   The 13-month choice is often quite valuable, since it allows you to compare ad performance to the same time frame in the prior year. This takes into account how seasonal or other cyclical factors may affect advertising. For instance, you would expect ads for school supplies to perform better from August through September, at the start of school, than during the rest of the year.

3. **Click the Download button in the lower-right corner of the pop-up window.**

   Depending on how many ads, campaigns, and accounts you've run in the past, downloading may take a while. When the download completes, you're ready to use Power Editor.

You must always click the Upload Changes button, located in the blue tool-bar at the top of Power Editor (refer to Figure 3-1), to save any new items or edits from Power Editor to the Ads Manager. Otherwise, the changes you make in Power Editor won't be implemented.

Navigating Power Editor

After you have completed downloading, you are ready to start using Power Editor, which has a rather complex layout, as shown in Figure 3-2. You have interdependent options to do the following:

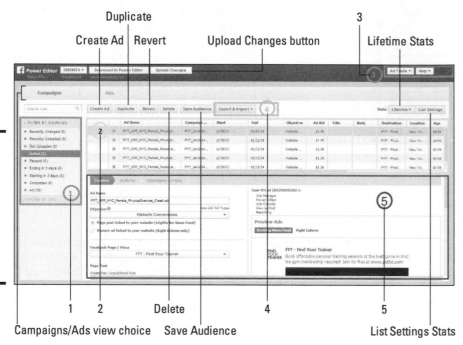

Figure 3-2:
The main screen for Power Editor as it appears when viewing by Ads.

✦ Click the tabs in the top row to toggle among the choices to view information organized by Campaigns, Ad Sets, or Ads.

✦ **Left Pane (Block Number 1 in Figure 3-2):** Allows you to filter results by campaigns, ad sets, or tags. Click the + sign next to each filter to reveal your list of options. The selections that appear vary according to the filter you choose.

✦ **List view (Block Number 2 in Figure 3-2):** The table displayed varies depending on your choice of view in the top row of data. You will see relevant columns of data for each respective row within the account you selected. These pre-set columns change according to your choice of view.

✦ **Work Space (Block Number 3 in Figure 3-2):** This displays editable fields for campaigns, ad sets, or ads, depending on which view you select. If you select multiple ads, ad sets, or campaigns, you can make similar changes to all of them at once.

✦ **Manage Ads drop-down menu (see Figure 3-8 later in this chapter):** This menu will be discussed later in this chapter.

To select multiple ads, ad sets, or campaigns at the same time in List view (Block Number 2), hold down the Shift key while you click rows in sequence. Hold down the Ctrl/⌘ key to select rows that are separated.

After you select Campaigns, Ad Sets, or Ads view, you see a row of additional icons and buttons above the List view. The buttons available depend on your choice of view. These options may include:

✦ **Create:** Creates a new ad, ad set, or campaign, depending on which view you're in.

✦ **Duplicate:** Makes an identical copy of a selected row or set of rows in the List view and appends a version number. It works for any view.

✦ **Revert:** Undoes any changes made to a selected ad, ad set, or campaign since it was downloaded to Power Editor — that is, as long as the changes have not yet been uploaded to the Ad Manager.

✦ **Delete:** Removes selected row(s) for an ad, ad set, or campaign from Power Editor.

✦ **Export & Import:** Transfers information to and from spreadsheets. Works for any view.

✦ **Save Audience (for the Ads view only):** Creates and saves a Profile for a target audience to use in other ads or campaigns. We discuss saving targeted audiences later in this chapter.

✦ **Tags (for Campaigns view only):** Tags are used to label, identify, and organize similarly themed or timed campaigns (for example, *Christmas, running shoes, white sales*). You can assign as many or as few tags as you like to a campaign. For convenience, you can use the Filter by Tag option in the left pane of Power Editor to display similarly tagged campaigns together.

View Campaigns

✦ **View Campaigns (for Ad Sets view only):** View Campaigns in which specified Ad Sets appear.

View Ad Sets

✦ **View Ad Sets (for Campaigns and Ads views only):** View Ad Sets included in a specified campaign or to which specified ads belong.

View Ads

✦ **View Ads (for Campaigns and Ad Sets views only):** View ad(s) included in specified Campaigns or Ad Sets.

◆ **Stats (for Ad Sets and Ads views only):** Allows you to select the time frame to display performance statistics for ads or ad sets. The menu defaults to Lifetime, but you can choose Last 7 Days, Yesterday, Today, or Custom.

◆ **List Settings (for Ad Sets and Ads views only):** Lets you select the performance metrics you want to review for your ads or ad sets.

At some point, you simply have to get your hands dirty. Try things out. Experiment with the various display choices to see which one is best for your needs. The more you use Power Editor, the more comfortable with it you will become.

Campaigning in Power Editor

Whatever you can do in Ads Create, you can do in Power Editor. Rather than jumping back and forth between the two, you may find it more convenient to create or edit campaigns, ad sets, or ads directly within Power Editor while you are actively using it to manage or review multiple campaigns.

To create a campaign in Power Editor, follow these steps:

1. **Choose Campaigns➪Create Campaign + icon.**

The Create Campaign pop-up window appears, as shown in Figure 3-3.

2. **Complete the details in the Create Campaign pop-up: Name, Buying Type (Auction or Fixed Price), and Objective.**

The objectives are the same as in the Ads Create tool (see Chapter 2 of this minibook), except that Power Editor further distinguishes between desktop and mobile app installs and engagement. See Chapter 1 of this minibook for a discussion of auction versus fixed-price bids.

3. **Click the Create button in the lower-right corner of the pop-up.**

Your new campaign now appears within the Campaign list view.

4. **Click the Upload Changes button in the top row of the main Power Editor screen.**

This uploads your changes to the Ads Manager. If you refresh or return to your Power Editor screen, your new campaign will now appear in the left pane under Filter By Campaign when you click the arrow next to the sub-tabs for Recently Changed or All.

The Upload Changes button changes from gray to green if you've created or edited campaigns, ad sets, or ads in the Power Editor workspace that you haven't uploaded yet.

Creates a new ad, ad set, or campaign

Campaigns tab   Click to upload your changes

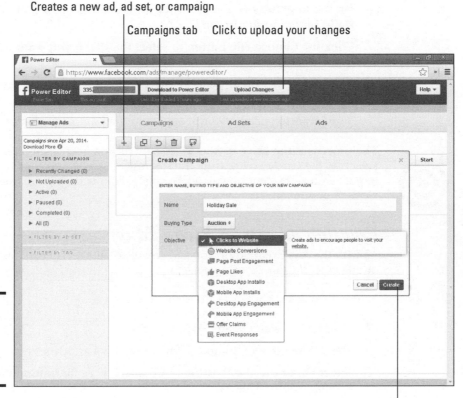

Figure 3-3:
Creating a
campaign
in Power
Editor.

Click to create your new campaign

Creating and importing a campaign from Excel

To import a campaign from a spreadsheet, you must download a template to Excel or an equivalent program, create your campaign, and then upload it. Follow these steps:

1. **Under Campaigns, click the Export & Import icon above the list view.**

2. **From the drop-down menu that appears, select Download Template.**

3. **Save the template, which will be in .xltx format, to your hard drive.**

   Use this template to create your campaign.

4. **Save your file as a tab-separated text file. If you are using Excel, you may need to export your file to Unicode Text.**

5. **Back in Power Editor, click the Export & Import icon, and select Import Ads in Bulk from the drop-down menu that appears.**

6. **On the Bulk Import pop-up window that shows up, select the File radio button under Import.**

7. **Click the Choose File button to select the file(s) you want to import into Power Editor.**

8. **Be sure to click the Upload Changes button at the top of the Power Editor screen to save your campaign to the Ads Manager.**

   Your imported campaign will appear in the Campaigns list view.

The process is the same to import Ad Sets or Ads from a spreadsheet. First, select Ad Sets or Ads view from the top row of tabs. Then click the Export & Import icon and select Download Template. Follow the rest of the steps previously mentioned.

Creating ad sets in Power Editor

As with the Ads Create tool, you can create ad sets for an existing campaign or after creating a new campaign.

To create an ad set in Power Editor, follow along:

1. **Choose Ad Sets⇨Create Ad Set + icon.**

   The Create Ad Set pop-up shown in Figure 3-4 appears.

2. **Select either the Use Existing or Create New radio button under Choose a Campaign for This Ad.**

   If you choose the first button, a drop-down list appears listing your existing campaigns, as seen in Figure 3-4. If you choose the second button, the pop-up expands to display the same Buying and Objective options that appear under Creating a New Campaign.

Take advantage of one of the few time-savers in Facebook! Since you can create a campaign directly from the Create Ad Set or Create Ad pop-ups, you can bypass the separate step of setting up a new campaign.

3. **Name your new Ad Set.**

4. **Click the Create button in the bottom-right corner of the pop-up.**

5. **Fill out the additional budget and scheduling fields in the workspace (see Figure 3-5).**

   Complete these fields just as you would in the Ads Create tool. (See Chapter 2 of this minibook.)

6. **Click the Upload Changes button to save your changes to the Ads Manager.**

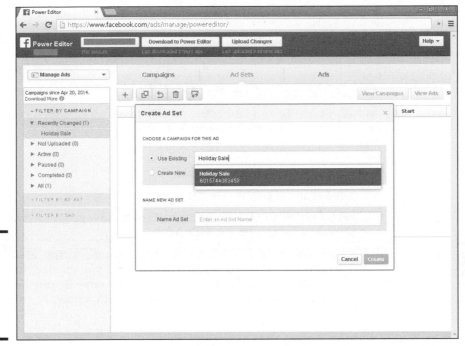

Figure 3-4:
Creating a new Ad Set within Power Editor.

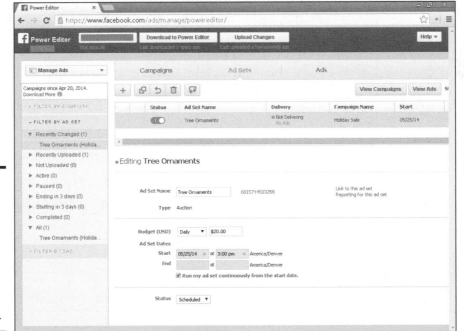

Figure 3-5:
Fill in the budget and scheduling details for your new Ad Set in the Power Editor workspace.

You must always click the Upload Changes button in the top row of the Power Editor screen to save any new or changed content from the Power Editor to the Ads Manager. If you don't do that, your ads won't run, and you won't see any performance results.

Creating an ad in Power Editor

As with Campaigns and Ad Sets, you can create an ad directly from Power Editor without jumping back and forth to the Ads Create tool. Follow these steps:

1. **Choose Ads⇨Create Ad + icon.**

   The Create Ad pop-up shown in Figure 3-6 appears.

2. **Select either the Use Existing or Create New radio button under Choose a Campaign for This Ad.**

   If you choose the first button, a drop-down menu appears listing your existing campaigns, as seen in Figure 3-6. If you choose the second button, the pop-up expands to display the same Buying and Objective options that appear under Creating a New Campaign, as discussed previously.

Figure 3-6:
Creating a new Ad within Power Editor.

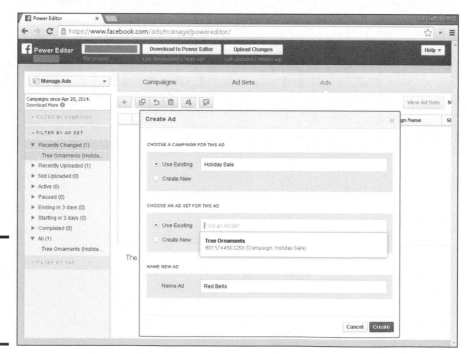

3. **Select either the Use Existing or Create New radio button under Choose an Ad Set for This Ad.**

   If you choose the first button, a drop-down menu appears listing your existing ad sets. If you choose the second button, you'll be asked to enter a name for your new Ad Set.

4. **Below the Name New Ad header, enter the name of your ad.**

5. **Click the Create button in the bottom-right corner of the pop-up.**

   Your ad will be added to the list under the Ads view in Power Editor.

6. **Fill out the additional fields in the workspace (as displayed in Figure 3-7), just as you would in the Ads Create tool.**

   The workspace has tabs for Creative, Audience, and Optimization & Pricing. (See Chapter 2 of this minibook for more details.)

7. **Click the Upload Changes button to save your changes to the Ads Manager.**

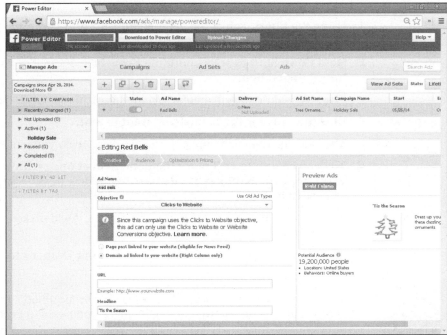

Figure 3-7: Fill in the details for your new ad in the Power Editor workspace.

Modifying existing campaigns, ad sets, or ads

You can modify some of the settings for existing campaigns, ad sets, or ads in a manner similar to creating them. Again, you can choose to do this directly in Power Editor, return to the Ads Create tool, or work from a spreadsheet. You can make different changes at different levels:

+ At the campaign level, you can edit only the name and the objective, as long as ads aren't already running.

+ At the Ad Set level, you can edit the name, budget, start and end dates, and status.

+ For ads, you can edit the creative, audience, optimization, and pricing sections.

Don't try to switch objectives at the campaign level if ads are already running. It's better to create a new campaign with a new objective.

Choose which view you want: Campaigns, Ad Sets, or Ads. Then follow these steps:

1. **Using the filters, select the campaign(s), ad set(s), or ad(s) you want to edit from the left pane.**

2. **Hold down Shift to select multiple items in sequence or the Ctrl/⌘ key for separated items.**

   The selected items will appear grouped together in the list view.

3. **Click the row for the item(s) you want to edit.**

   The selected item will appear in the workspace so you can edit it.

4. **You can choose to edit more than one item at once within the list view. Press the Shift key for items in sequence, or the Ctrl/⌘ key for separated items.**

   When you change one item in the workspace, it will make the same change for all the other rows you selected.

5. **Click the Upload Changes button to save your changes to the Ads Manager.**

Visit your Ads Manager after uploading new or modified campaigns, ad sets, or ads to confirm that all the changes you made in Power Editor appear properly.

Editing Campaigns, Ad Sets, and Ads with Excel

If you have exported your campaigns to Excel as we discuss in the previous section, you can copy and paste to and from your spreadsheet to make changes.

Start by selecting the campaign you want in the left sidebar. Then follow these steps:

1. **From your choice of view, select one or multiple campaigns, ad sets, or ads to edit.**

2. **Press Ctrl+C/⌘+C.**

3. **Open your corresponding Excel spreadsheet and select a cell.**

4. **Press Ctrl+V/⌘+V in Excel.**

   All your campaigns or ads will appear, with headers for each column. You can edit all the fields of your ads and campaigns in Excel except Ad ID, Campaign ID, and Image Hash.

5. **Make your edits.**

6. **Select all the rows in your Excel table, including headers.**

7. **Press Ctrl+C/⌘+C.**

8. **Go back to Power Editor and select a campaign, ad set, or campaign to receive your changes.**

9. **Press Ctrl+V/⌘+V.**

You can also use the Import Ads in Bulk function to import individual images or a zip file of multiple images. This is especially useful if you want to keep the copy for a string of ads but refresh them with new, eye-catching art.

Managing multiple items with the Manage Ads drop-down

Busy advertising managers, marketing directors, and account executives may want to take advantage of features available from the Manage Ads drop-down menu, which appears above the Filters section in the left pane.

These tools, which are shown in Figure 3-8, offer easy access to features and components that affect or are accessed by multiple advertising campaigns. The options include:

✦ **Audiences:** Lists all the custom audiences you've created. (We discuss this topic later.)

✦ **Campaign Dashboard:** Displays active and recently completed campaigns.

✦ **Image Library:** Shows all images you've uploaded for use in ads.

✦ **Conversion Tracking:** Lists all the conversion pixels you've created. (We discuss this topic later.)

✦ **Reporting:** Returns you to the Ads Manager Report section.

✦ **Billing:** Returns you to the Ads Manager Billing section.

✦ **Account Settings:** Returns you to the Ads Manager Ad Account Settings section.

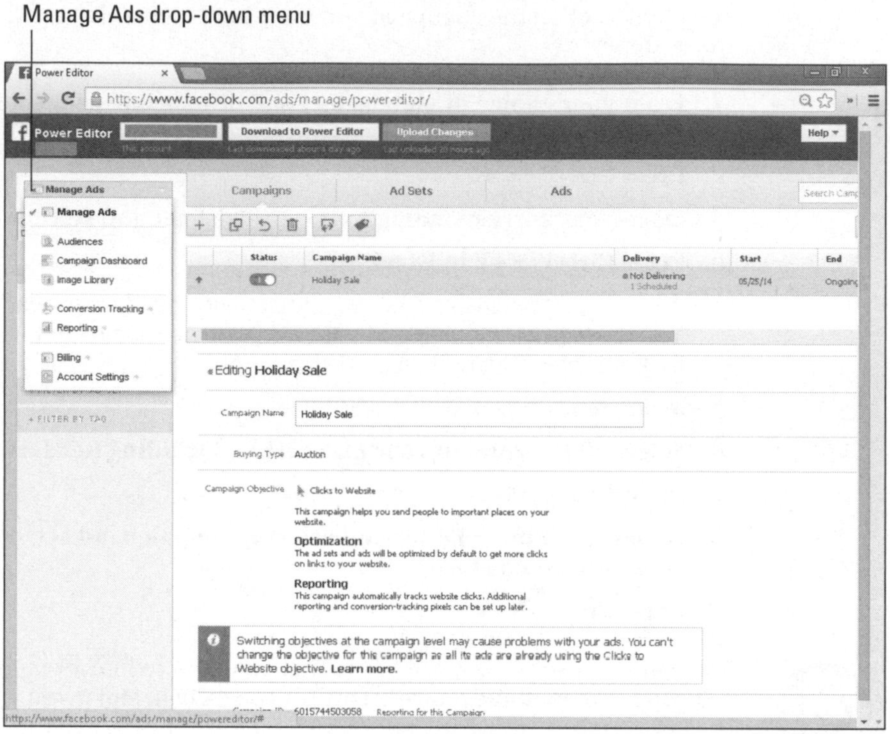

Manage Ads drop-down menu

Figure 3-8:
The options in the Manage Ads drop-down menu access elements applicable to or used by multiple campaigns.

Using Power Editor to Create and Promote Posts

Just as you can create and promote a post via the Ads Create tool, you can create and promote a post in Power Editor.

There's a subtle difference between posts created in the two places: In the Ads Create tool, posts publish immediately to your Page and will show up in the News Feeds of your fans and their Friends. With Power Editor, you have an option to create and promote a post without publishing it to the Timeline on your Page.

Huh? This feature may sound a bit arcane, but it has real-world marketing benefits. Specifically, it means you can test different versions of posts to see which version will be the most successful without having multiple variations appear on your Page and confuse your viewers. Or you can promote various versions of a post as an ad in News Feeds to different selected audiences.

Power Editor also allows you to schedule the publication of posts in advance, which is very convenient for management purposes. Scheduled posts will appear on your Page like regular posts at the time you specify.

You can create Link, Photo, Video, Status, or Offer posts in Power Editor.

Creating a post in Power Editor

To create a status post, link post, photo post, or a video post from Power Editor, follow these steps:

1. **Select Manage Pages from the drop-down field for Account number in the upper-left corner of the main Power Editor page.**

See Figure 3-9.

2. **Select the Page you want to manage from the left-side column.**

A list of posts for that Page will appear.

3. **Click the Create Post button on the left side of the top row of buttons.**

A pop-up called Create Unpublished Page Post will appear, as shown in Figure 3-10.

**Book VII
Chapter 3**

Exploring Power Editor

Manage Pages
drop-down menu   Publish Post button

Create Post button   Create Ad button

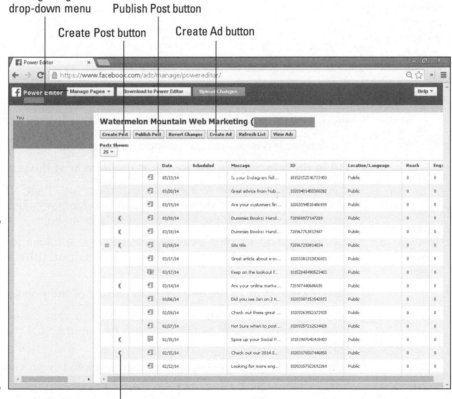

Figure 3-9:
A list of
posts in
Power
Editor;
posts with
a crescent-
moon
symbol are
unpublished.

Indicates unpublished status

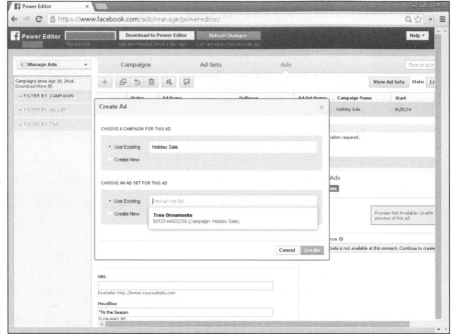

Figure 3-10:
Use the
Create
Unpublished
Page Post
pop-up to
develop
variations
on posts.

4. **On the top row of the pop-up, select the type of post to create: Link, Photo, Video, Status, or Offer.**

   We discuss types of posts in Chapter 1 of this minibook.

5. **Fill in the information for your post on the rest of the pop-up.**

   If you select the option to publish the post on your Page, the pop-up window will expand to show targeting options for language and location. Alternatively, you can publish the post only as an ad.

   If your post will also run as an ad, the language and location choices must match the Audience selection in Power Editor. Otherwise, your ad won't run.

6. **Click Create Post in the bottom-right corner of the pop-up.**

   This post isn't published yet; it will be added to your list of posts with a crescent-moon symbol, which indicates its unpublished status. Refer to Figure 3-9.

7. **After creating your post, select it for publication from your list of unpublished posts.**

8. **Click the Publish Post button.**

   It's in the top row of the workspace. A small pop-up will appear.

9. **To publish the post immediately, select the Publish Now radio button in the pop-up window; then click the Publish button.**

   To publish a post that will appear in the future, select the Schedule a Time to Publish radio button, fill in the desired date and time, and click the Publish button.

10. **Click the green Upload Changes button.**

   Your post(s) should appear on your Page or be scheduled to appear.

If you use your post only as an ad (without publishing it on your Page), it won't get organic distribution in News Feeds, which means that it won't be seen by Friends of Friends. This is a strategic marketing choice. If you are comparing several versions of a post to see which gets the best response, you would publish them only as ads, not on your Page. Once the results indicate the best performing post, you can change the distribution to include publication on your Page.

Promoting a post from Power Editor

You have an option in Power Editor to manage your posts that's not available with other post-creation methods. You can create an ad from your post, as we discuss in Chapter 2 of this minibook, without actually publishing it on your Timeline.

Such promoted post ads can appear on both desktop and mobile environments. This option allows you to see which version of a post is most worth promoting with paid advertising.

When Promoted posts appear as ads in a News Feed or in the right-hand column, viewers can still like or comment on them.

To create a Promoted post, follow these steps:

1. **Select the Manage Pages option from the drop-down menu in the top row of the main Power Editor page.**

2. **In the left column, select the Page for which you want to promote a post.**

   A list of posts appears.

3. **Select the post you want to promote.**

   It will be highlighted.

4. **Click the Create Ad button.**

   The Create Ad button is in the top row above the list of posts (refer to Figure 3-9). A pop-up appears.

5. **On the small pop-ups that appear, select the existing Campaign and Ad Set you want the ad created in.**

   Alternatively, you can create a new campaign or ad set.

6. **Fill in the Promoted post details located in the workspace for Creative, Audience, and Optimization & Pricing.**

7. **Click Upload Changes to save your Promoted Post to the Ads Manager.**

   As with any other ad, your Promoted post won't run until Facebook approves it. You'll be notified when that happens.

Pinpointing Your Ideal Audience

Everything in marketing is about reaching your ideal target audience. Your advertising dollars are best spent talking to people who match your model for leads or customers, when you're trying to do any of the following:

+ Reach people just when they are ready to purchase.
+ Stay "top of mind" with existing customers.
+ Build brand identity.
+ Reach new prospects.
+ Encourage identified prospects to learn more about your business.

In addition to the powerful audience tools available in the Ads Create tool (refer to Chapter 2 of this minibook), Power Editor offers several additional methods for targeting your audience to meet your marketing needs: Facebook and Partner Categories, Custom Audiences, Lookalike Audiences, and Saved Target Groups. We look at each of these in turn.

Pinpoint marketing works well for large companies with multiple, large target audiences and the financial resources to reach them. However, even if you have a limited budget — meaning, you can afford only a few clicks — targeting may be worth the effort, especially if the average purchase price is large and you have the staff and time to analyze results and continuously refine your advertising.

Reaching your ideal audience with Facebook and Partner Categories

Facebook Categories and Partner Categories are available in the Audience targeting section of Power Editor.

Facebook Categories define your audience based on what information users have included on their Profiles or actions they've taken on Facebook.

Partner Categories, like the Behaviors section in the Ads Create tool, enable you to target the audience for your Facebook ads based on activities users engage in away from Facebook, either elsewhere online or in the real world. For instance, if you sell home furnishings or painting services, you might want to target people who just bought a house. If you sell childcare services or baby clothes, you might want to find someone who is expecting or has adopted a baby. The target audiences defined in the Partner Categories are created by matching Facebook user Profiles with outside data provided by third-party sources.

These targeting methods are best used to identify new prospects whose Profiles match known prospects, reach people just when they are ready to purchase, or build brand identity. If you try to over-specify your audience, Facebook will prompt you to broaden your categories to produce a larger pool of potential viewers.

Selecting Facebook and Partner Categories

Follow these steps to select Facebook or Partner Categories, as shown in Figure 3-11.

1. **Select the Ads view in the top row of the Power Editor.**

2. **Select an ad that you want to target with either (or both) of these methods.**

3. **Select the Audiences tab in the Power Editor workspace.**

4. **Scroll down in the Audience section and click on either the Facebook Categories or the Partner Categories section as shown in Figure 3-11.**

   They're below the Categories heading.

5. **If you choose Facebook Categories, you select one or more options from a list of Custom Categories. Choices may vary among ad accounts based on which sorts Facebook thinks might apply.**

   In Figure 3-11, the options shown are Hispanics, Online Spenders, Online Spenders Active, Online Spenders Engaged, and Technology Late Adopters.

6. **If you chose Partner Categories, click the right-pointing arrow to view detailed subsections for Acxiom or Datalogix.**

   They're the data-mining companies that provide this information to Facebook.

7. **Scroll through the subsections (such as demographics, lifestyle, politics, and work), and click an arrow to reveal additional details.**

   Dive into each category that interests you until you see items without an arrow to the left; these are the classifications that you can select.

   A clicked category is pinned right below the gray Categories heading. You can pick as many classifications as you want; if you change your mind, click the X to the right of the pinned item.

8. **Click the Information icon (the lower case "i" in a circle) to the right of a classification.**

    You get details on the number and description of members of a classification.

Partner Categories offer data only on U.S. users at this time.

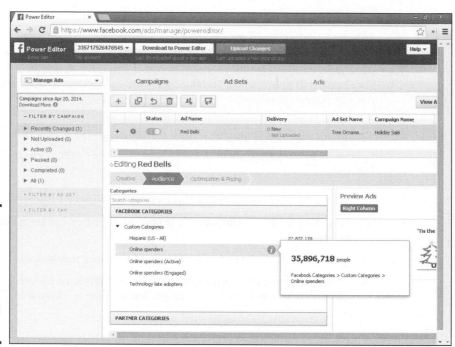

Figure 3-11: Selecting a Facebook Category in the Audience tab of the ad workspace.

It can be a bit tricky to determine whether Facebook or Partner Categories are a good fit for your needs. Try split-testing, as we discuss in Chapter 4 of this minibook. Use the same ad with different categories for at least a week. Then look at the metrics in the List View of Power Editor or visit the Ads Manager for a full report. Adjust your selections as needed.

Reaching existing customers and prospects with Custom Audiences

The Custom Audiences method allows you to target an ad to your existing customers or known prospects who also happen to have Facebook accounts. After you create a list, Facebook will use e-mail addresses, phone numbers, Facebook user IDs, app user IDs, or mobile advertiser IDs to match people on your list to people with active Facebook pages. You can create a Custom Audience using either the Ads Create tool or Power Editor.

To have meaningful reach, your Custom Audience should end up with at least 1,000 people; you'll need more than that on your original list because not all your users will have Facebook accounts. Consequently, this technique is particularly useful for companies that have been in business long enough to acquire enough names. If you have a new business, you may find other targeting techniques more helpful, unless you have permission to use a list from a third party.

Use the Custom Audiences technique to stay "top of mind" with existing customers, encourage repeat purchases, maintain business relationships, or encourage identified prospects to learn more about your business.

You may want to select subsets of current customers or prospects by

+ Product or service area

+ Subscribers to your e-newsletter

+ Members of your loyalty program

+ People who have downloaded a white paper

+ Current or lapsed users who registered on your website

For example, you could target current customers who haven't already liked your Facebook Page to do so. You can micro-target individuals to whom you want to send a highly targeted message as long as they have Facebook accounts.

**Book VII
Chapter 3**

Creating custom lists

After you select a list, Facebook will match your data against its list of active users. This process is *hashing*. If there is no match, the e-mail address or other content is dropped from the list. Facebook will then build a new Audience in your account that consists of the resulting matches. The Facebook version will identify your target market only by Facebook IDs.

Both hashing and encryption make information more secure. Encrypted files can be decrypted to reveal the original content. Hashing creates a "fingerprint" that can't be decrypted. Facebook claims that it can find your ideal audiences without compromising your data.

If you plan to create a custom audience from a data file, identify an existing data source in advance or get a list ready by creating a CSV or TXT file in Excel. The file should be a single column of data without a heading. You can use e-mail addresses, phone numbers, Facebook user IDs, or app user IDs. Use only one.

Exploring Power Editor

To create a custom audience, follow these steps:

1. **Choose Audiences from the Manage Ads drop-down menu located in the top-left corner of Power Editor.**

2. **Choose Create Audience⇨Custom Audience.**

   Create Audience is in the top-left corner of the main Audiences screen, as shown in Figure 3-12. A pop-up appears.

3. **Select the type of list you intend to use:**

   - *Data File Custom Audience*
   - *MailChimp Custom Audience*
   - *Custom Audience from Your Mobile App*
   - *Custom Audience from Your Website*

4. **Follow the steps in the pop-up for each option.**

   You create your custom audience.

Create Audience drop-down menu

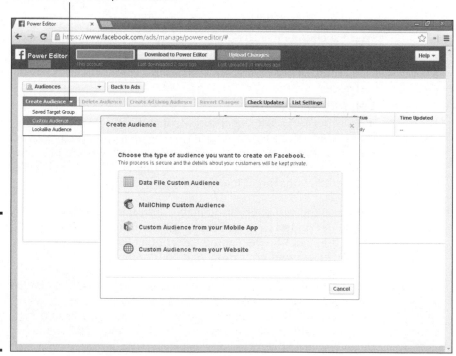

Figure 3-12: Choose a list type to create a Custom Audience in Power Editor.

5. **Click the Create button.**

   It may take half an hour or more for your Custom Audience to upload to Facebook. You'll be notified when it's done. Your Custom Audience will appear under the Type column in the ad List view, as shown in Figure 3-13.

6. **In the ad workspace, choose Create Ad Using Audience.**

7. **Follow the standard steps to create or edit an ad as we describe earlier.**

8. **In the ad workspace, click the Audience tab. Scroll down until you see Custom Audiences.**

   The custom audience you created may be selected in this field, or you can enter the name of the custom audience you want to use.

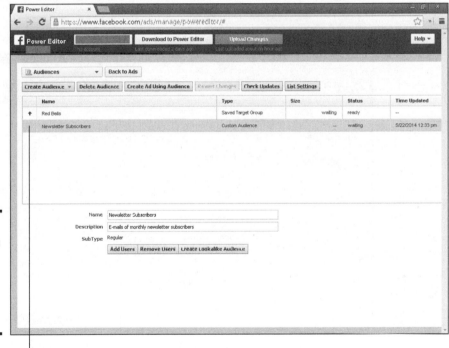

Figure 3-13: Your custom list will appear in the List view for Audiences.

Your Custom Audience appears here

Discovering similar users with Lookalike Audiences

Lookalike Audiences is a variation on Custom Audiences. It lets you reach additional, new people with Facebook accounts who behave similarly to the people in your Custom Audience list. Facebook says it will compare your list with conversion tracking records and outside data sources to identify Facebook users who match yours in terms of fan acquisition, site registration, off-Facebook purchases, coupon claims, and/or brand awareness.

Discovering similar users with Lookalike Audiences

Use Lookalike Audiences to acquire new prospects. None of the people on your Custom Audience list will be included in a Lookalike Audience.

To create a Lookalike Audience, follow these steps:

1. **Create your Custom Audience as described in the preceding section.**

2. **From the Manage Ads drop-down menu in the top-left corner of Power Editor, choose Audiences.**

   The main Audience page appears.

3. **From the Create Audience drop-down menu, select Lookalike Audience.**

   The Create Lookalike Audience pop-up shown in Figure 3-14 appears.

Custom Audience drop-down menu

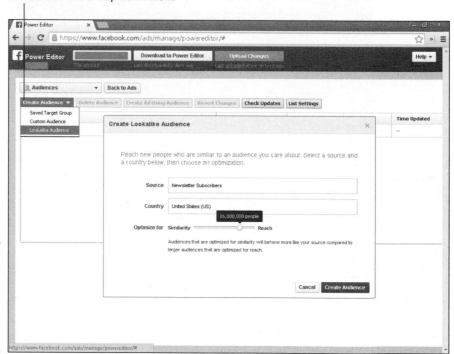

Figure 3-14: Creating a Lookalike Audience in Power Editor.

4. **Click in the Source field in the pop-up window.**

   A drop-down list with available sources appears.

5. **Choose one of the custom audiences, conversion pixel results, or Facebook Pages on the list.**

   Alternatively, you can begin typing your selection; a narrower list of choices appears as you type.

6. **Click in the Country field.**

   A drop-down list of available countries appears. Alternatively, you can begin typing your choice and a drop-down list with narrowed down choices will appear.

7. **Move the Optimize For slider bar toward either Similarity or Reach.**

   The closer you move the slider toward Similarity, the more like your source the Lookalike Audience will behave. The closer you move the slider toward Reach, the larger the audience, but the less similar it will be.

8. **Click the Create Audience button in the bottom-right corner of the pop-up window.**

   Facebook may take a day or more to create your Lookalike Audience. Facebook will notify you when the Lookalike Audience is ready.

A Lookalike Audience can include people from only one country, even if your Custom Audience has people from several countries. To identify residents of multiple countries, create several Lookalike Audience profiles from the same Custom Audience list, one for each nation.

If you receive a message that "You need an audience that includes at least 100 people," you won't be able to create a Lookalike Audience from the Custom Audience you selected. Try selecting Greater Reach in the preceding Step 6 to see if that helps you reach the minimum 100 number.

Saving time with saved target groups

To save time when creating new ads or campaigns aimed at an existing audience, try using a Saved Target Group. Available only in Power Editor, this option allows you to reuse any targeted profile you have already created, except for a Custom Audience.

To create a saved target group, follow these steps:

1. **Select Audiences from the Manage Ads menu.**

2. **From the Create Audience menu, choose Saved Target Group.**

   Options to customize your saved target group appear in the workspace below the list view of audiences, as shown in Figure 3-15.

3. **Complete the relevant fields for your new saved target group.**

   You may enter a name, custom audience to include or exclude, location, age range, gender, languages, more demographics, interests, behaviors, and categories (Facebook and Partner). You can now select this saved target group when creating an ad.

Your saved target group appears here

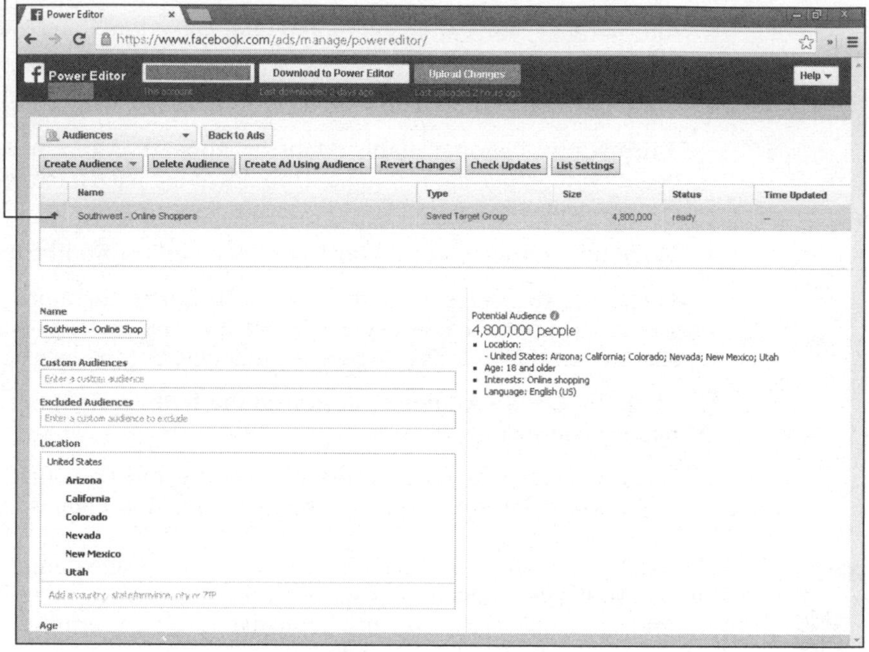

Figure 3-15:
Choose a
list type
to create
a Custom
Audience
in Power
Editor.

To use a group, follow these steps:

1. **Select the Audience tab in the Ad workspace.**

2. **Select Use Existing Targeting Group.**

   A pop-up appears at the top of the page.

3. **Choose the saved target group you want and click OK; see Figure 3-16.**

   Alternatively, you can create a saved target group from the audience you define while creating an ad, ad set, or campaign in the workspace. Establish the profile for your target market using the Audience tab in the workspace as usual.

4. **To save the profile for later use, click the Save Audience icon (the small icon with people in Figure 3-2) that appears in the row of icons above the List View section.**

   This creates a new Saved Target Group.

The option to use a Saved Target Group doesn't work for Custom Audiences. To re-use a specific Custom Audience, simply select it when you pick an audience.

Select Target Audience pop-up window

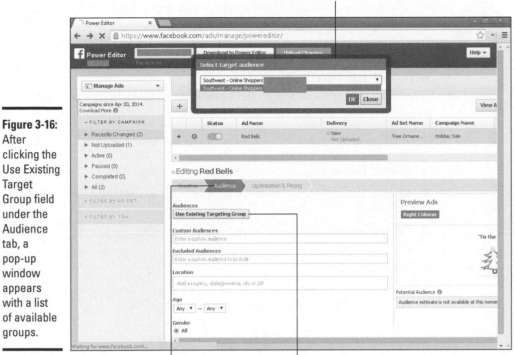

Figure 3-16:
After clicking the Use Existing Target Group field under the Audience tab, a pop-up window appears with a list of available groups.

Audience tab   Use Existing Targeting Group button

Optimizing Ad Bids in Power Editor

Power Editor lets you choose the standard options for bidding, as we discuss in Chapters 1 and 2 of this minibook.

Review the bidding choices and when to use them:

✦ **CPC (cost per click):** Best for getting people to click on your ad; distributed evenly across all active ads

✦ **CPM (cost per 1,000 impressions):** Best for branding and getting people to view your ad; distributed evenly across all active ads

✦ **oCPM (optimized CPM):** Best for showing your ad to people who are most likely to take an action, such as liking a Page or clicking a link to your website

If you're not sure what to bid under the option you want, choose the Default Bid, which appears in a list that expands below the bid type you select. (See Figure 3-17.) Facebook will set the maximum bid to show your ad to the most audiences.

Setting up manual bids

If you're targeting a specific audience or want to use a higher bid than the default, use the option to set up bids manually.

The manual setting also lets you further decide whether to optimize for

✦ **Clicks:** Encourages more people to click on your ad

✦ **Reach:** Shows your ad to more people who are different from your target audience

✦ **Social:** Shows your ad to more people through their Friends

   For example, when someone likes your ad, more of his Friends will see the same ad.

✦ **Actions:** Optimizes for people taking Facebook actions on your ad, including likes, comments, shares, and app installs

Specifying a type of action for optimized CPM

It's simple to select or edit an action option from the preceding bulleted list for use with a specific ad. Follow these steps:

1. **In Power Editor, choose Ads View.**

2. **Select an existing ad from the List view.**

   Or create a new ad by clicking the + symbol button in the top row.

3. **Choose the tab for Optimization & Pricing in the ad workspace.**

4. **Select the Optimized CPM radio button.**

5. **Choose Manually Set Up Bids, as shown in Figure 3-17.**

6. **Enter a maximum bid value for your choice of Clicks, Reach, Social, or Actions.**

   Each field can have a different maximum bid.

7. **Proceed as you would with any other ad, ad set, or campaign as we describe in the preceding sections of this chapter and in Chapter 2 of this minibook.**

8. **As always, click the Upload Changes button to save your work to the Ads Manager.**

Optimization & Pricing tab

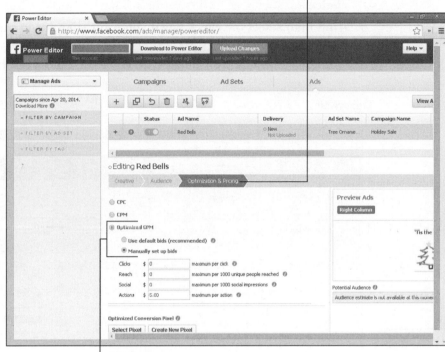

Figure 3-17:
You can
accept
default bids
or set bids
manually for
each type of
bidding.

**Book VII
Chapter 3**

**Exploring Power
Editor**

Make your selections here

Optimizing Ads for Ideal Placement

Power Editor offers one more advantage over the Ads Create tool described in Chapter 2 of this minibook: It gives you greater control over ad placement.

Use the results that appear in List view or in the Ads Manager to determine which placements provide the best bang for your buck. (See Chapter 4 of this minibook.) Revise your placement settings accordingly.

Within Power Editor, you target the appearance of your ads through ad placement radio buttons.

1. **From Power Editor, create or select the ad you want to run in a specific placement.**

2. **Click the Creative tab in the ad workspace, as shown in Figure 3-18.**

3. **Scroll down to Placements and select the radio button you want.**

4. **Under Mobile Devices, select the radio button for your target device choice.**

5. **(Optional) Select the check box if you want your ads to show only when someone is using a Wi-Fi connection.**

   For more information on mobile marketing, see Book VIII, Chapter 4.

Creative tab

Figure 3-18:
Choose
placement
options for
your ad
in Power
Editor.

Mobile devices options

Placement options

Tracking Conversions

Conversion tracking is the be-all and end-all of advertising. It allows you to see which of your advertising efforts really produce results after people view your ad. It is the Holy Grail for measuring return on investment (ROI), but it can measure only online actions.

To track conversions that happen on your website, access the Conversion Tracking dashboard in any of three ways:

✦ Select Conversion Tracking from the Manage Ads drop-down in Power Editor.

✦ Go to the Ads view in Power Editor. Select the Creative tab and scroll down to the subhead Conversion Tracking Pixels.

✦ Select Conversion Tracking from the left pane in the Ads Manager (www. facebook.com/ads/manage).

Whichever way you get there, the process is the same. Click Create New Pixel. In the pop-up window, name the pixel and select its purpose from the list. After you click Create Pixel in the pop-up, Facebook generates a snippet of code for you to save and e-mail to your programmer, who will place it on appropriate pages of your website.

Generally, the code goes on a "Thank You" or "Confirmation" page. We discuss conversion pixels in greater depth in Chapter 2 of this minibook.

Chapter 4: Testing, Measuring, and Modifying Your Ad

In This Chapter

✔ **Becoming familiar with the Ads Manager**

✔ **Exploring split testing**

✔ **Making sense of the reports**

Testing, measuring, and modifying your ad are among the most important things you can do to ensure that you're getting the most for your dollar. Unfortunately, testing is one of the most overlooked aspects of the Facebook advertising experience because it can be overwhelming.

Because of the many variables to test and tweak, you may feel daunted at first. If you approach your Facebook ad campaign systematically, though, you can come away with an ad that has a high click-through rate (CTR) at a low cost.

In this chapter, you begin by familiarizing yourself with the Ads Manager, where all your ad campaigns are displayed. Then you discover how to begin your split testing, view the Facebook Ads reports, and optimize your campaign. Use the Ads Manager to assess performance whether you have set up your ads using the Ads Create tool described in Chapter 2 of this minibook, or using Power Editor described in Chapter 3.

Now it's time to ratchet up your Facebook advertising expertise!

Statistics in the Ads Manager are strictly for assessing the performance of your paid Facebook advertising. For statistics about your Page visits and visitor demographics, use Facebook Insights, which we discuss in Book IX, Chapter 2.

Understanding the Ads Manager

The Ads Manager acts as your Facebook Ads dashboard, whether you're a small business with one campaign or a large company using Power Editor to establish and maintain multiple campaigns.

You can do the following in Ads Manager, which is especially helpful if you need to save/export or deliver reports on a scheduled basis to your supervisor or client:

✦ Customize reports to select the data you want.

✦ Specify date ranges.

✦ Reorganize columns for display.

You must click Upload Changes when you finish using Power Editor. This simultaneously saves your changes in Power Editor and uploads them to the Ads Manager. Double-check the Ads Manager after uploading to confirm that your campaign changes are there.

If you haven't already created an ad on Facebook, read Book VII, Chapters 1 and 2. Ads Manager is easier to understand **after** you have created at least one ad. To get to the Ads Manager after you've created an ad, do this:

1. **Log in to Facebook as the administrator.**

2. **Click the arrow on the far right at the top and choose Manage Ads from the drop-down menu, as shown in Figure 4-1.**

Click the arrow

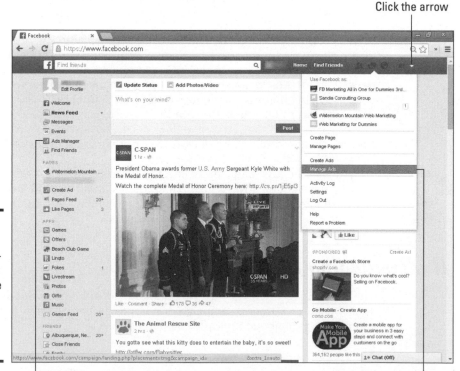

Figure 4-1: If you've already created an ad, it's available in the left column of the Ads Manager.

Ads Manager   Choose Manage Ads

You see an overall picture of each campaign, the campaign status, and how much you're spending; see Figure 4-2. From the Ads Manager, you can delve further into each campaign to obtain detailed statistics.

Review all your campaigns here

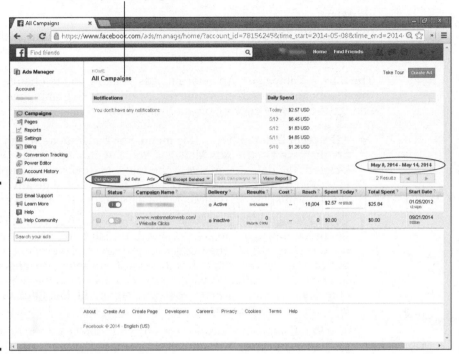

Figure 4-2: The Ads Manager dashboard shows an overview of all your Facebook ad campaigns.

Book VII
Chapter 4

Testing, Measuring, and Modifying Your Ad

You can also reach this dashboard by clicking the Ads Manager link on the left sidebar of the Facebook home page or your Profile. This appears only if you have already created an ad.

Or go to www.facebook.com/ads/manage, which is the easiest and most reliable method.

The following sections break down the parts of the Ads Manager dashboard.

Notifications and Daily Spend

At the top of the screen, you see these two main areas:

✦ **Notifications** include updates, such as when a campaign has been created or whether an ad was approved or declined.

✦ **Daily Spend** is a running total of how much you've spent for each of the past five days for all your campaigns combined. For more details by campaign, look at the table below the columns for Cost per Click, Spent Today, and Total Spent. These amounts will adjust for the time frame you specify by clicking in the date field above the table.

Menus

Below the Notifications and Daily Spend areas are three tabs and three buttons (refer to Figure 4-2).

The tabs — Campaigns, Ad Sets, and Ads — allow you to change the view on the dashboard. The screen automatically defaults to Campaigns, but you can change the view by clicking on another option.

✦ **All Except Deleted:** From this menu, you can choose which campaigns are displayed in the Ads Manager. You can choose to view All Except Deleted (the default), Active, Scheduled, In Review, Not Approved, Inactive, Not Delivering, or Deleted. When you change any of the selections, the display on the Ads Manager changes to reflect your selection.

✦ **Edit Campaigns/Ad Sets/Ads:** This feature may be useful if you have multiple campaigns, ad sets, or ads, but wish to rename, turn on, turn off, delete, or modify the budget for just one or several of them. This button is grayed out (not clickable) until you select the check box next to one or more rows. When you select a check box, the button display changes to show how many rows you are modifying. Click this button to edit the titles or budgets of individual campaigns, ad sets, or ads.

The Edit Campaigns button varies by your choice on the first tab. If you choose Campaigns, it reads Edit Campaigns. If you choose Ad Sets, it reads Edit Ad Sets, and so forth.

✦ **View Report:** Click this button to get your overall advertising report, which shows in-depth statistics from all your campaigns in one place. We cover this report later in this chapter.

Categories

Just below the buttons is a table with several columns, as follows:

✦ **Status:** The slide button on a row turns your campaign/ad sets/ads on and off. Items are on when the status is blue and off when they are grey.

✦ **Name of Campaign/Ad Sets or Ads:** This column lists all the items in the selected category.

A campaign consists of a group of one or more ad sets. An ad set consists of one or more ads.

Deleted ads can never be restarted. It's safer to simply make your ads "inactive" in case you want to run them again. Holiday or seasonal ads are examples of when deactivation makes sense.

+ **Delivery:** This indicates whether each campaign/ad set/ad is active or inactive.

+ **Results:** The number of actions related to your objective that viewers took after viewing your ad, such as the number of clicks, likes, or conversions.

+ **Cost:** This shows the average paid for each action (result) related to your objective.

+ **Reach:** This shows the total number of people who saw your ads (impressions).

+ **Spent Today:** This displays the cost incurred since midnight of the current day.

+ **Total Spent:** This column lists the total amount you've spent on each campaign during the selected time period. For more detailed information on transactions within that time period, use the Billing link in the left pane (refer to Figure 4-2).

You'll never be charged more than the Budget setting amount, but you may pay less.

+ **Start Date:** This shows the start date of a campaign if it's already running, or the date when it is scheduled to begin.

+ **End Date:** This shows the end date of the campaign. You may choose to run a campaign for a specific length of time or stop the campaign manually. You can always change a scheduled end date by visiting an individual campaign.

You don't have to worry if you hit an end date and forgot about it. The item will stop running as planned and won't incur any more charges. To resume running the ended item, click the pencil icon that appears when you hover over the field to edit end dates (or future start dates) at any time.

Performance results for Boost Post ads, which are created from your Timeline, not through the Ads Create tool or Power Editor, also appear in the Ads Manager. A Boost Post is simply a shortcut for creating an ad that publicizes a particular post. Boost Posts work the same way as if you created an ad using the Page Post Engagement objective in the Ads Create tool. Performance results also appear in the Posts of Page Insights (see Book IX, Chapter 2) soon after you boost a Page post. For more on Boosting Posts, please see Chapters 1 and 2 of this minibook.

We recommend renaming the title of a Promoted post campaign to something more meaningful. The Ads Manager also shows statistics for Promoted posts, which encourage engagement. The campaign name defaults to a long name with a link to the Promoted post. To edit the name, hover over the title field and click the pencil icon.

Left sidebar

The left sidebar of the Ads Manager contains several additional links that let you navigate to different areas.

Most of these links are directly related to Facebook Ads, but you can also access your Pages and Facebook Page Insights from the sidebar. Here's the scoop on each of the sidebar items:

✦ **Campaigns:** All your campaigns on the right side of the screen.

✦ **Pages:** A list of all the Facebook Pages you administer, including Page likes and post Insights.

✦ **Reports:** Covered later in this chapter in more detail.

✦ **Settings:** Where you can change your Facebook Ads account information, add advertising account roles so that other users can access your Facebook Ads account or reports, and change the notifications you receive. We cover this area in more depth shortly.

✦ **Billing:** Where you can change your billing method and track how much you spend each month. View details on transactions, set a spending limit, or manage your payment method.

✦ **Conversion Tracking:** Lists all the Conversion Tracking Pixels created to track activities on your website completed by someone who has clicked one of your ads. Recorded conversion events are reflected in the Pixel Status column.

✦ **Power Editor:** Creates and manages multiple campaigns and accounts in bulk. For more about Power Editor and how to enable it, see Chapter 3 in this minibook.

✦ **Account History:** Review all changes to your account over time. You will see a table showing the details of each change and the date and time it was made in reverse chronological order. New changes may take up to 15 minutes to appear.

✦ **Audiences:** Defined target markets for specific ads or campaigns. When you click this link, you'll see a screen with a Create Audience button. Facebook prompts you through the process of creating and saving an Audience with a series of pop-up windows. We talk more about custom audiences later in this chapter. You can also add or remove people from a defined audience.

Here, Facebook will also help you identify potential prospects by matching its e-mail addresses to ones you already have through a third-party service provider, such as MailChimp. Or you can upload your own files of e-mail addresses (in CSV format). Facebook will then create a custom audience for you. We talk more about audiences later in this chapter.

✦ **Email Support:** Ask Facebook tech support questions about your Facebook Ads from here. You can choose from several categories: Advertising Options, Managing Ads and Campaigns, Help with Managing Your Account, Paying for an Ad, Pending or Disapproved Ads, or Managing Pages. If you don't have a Facebook ad currently running, you won't see this link.

✦ **Learn More:** View success stories and find out more about how to use Facebook for business through helpful tutorials.

✦ **Help:** The Facebook Ads help (FAQ) section.

✦ **Help Community:** A message board where Facebook members can post questions and get help from other users.

✦ **Search Your Ads box:** Where you search your ads or campaigns. The search includes ad titles or campaign names but *doesn't* include the text of the ad.

Adding a User to Your Facebook Ads Account

You can add users to your Facebook Ads account to give others access to the ad campaigns at two levels:

✦ **Ad Account Advertiser:** Use this level of access for people who should be able to view and edit ads, and set up new ads using your previously specified payment method.

✦ **Ad Account Analyst:** Use this level of access for people who should only be allowed to view reports on ad performance. This permission is just for advertising access. Book I, Chapter 2, tells you how to add an administrator to your Page.

To add a user, follow these steps:

1. **Log in to your Facebook account.**

You see your Profile.

2. **Go to** www.facebook.com/ads/manage.

Ads Manager opens.

3. **Click the Settings link on the left sidebar (refer to Figure 4-2).**

You may have to reenter your Facebook password. Then you see the Settings area for Facebook Ads.

4. **Scroll down to the Ad Account Roles section, and click the + Add a User button in the upper-right corner.**

A pop-up window appears, as shown in Figure 4-3. In this window, you can add a user and select the access the user has to your Facebook Ads.

Settings   Ad Account Advertiser drop-down menu   Add a User button

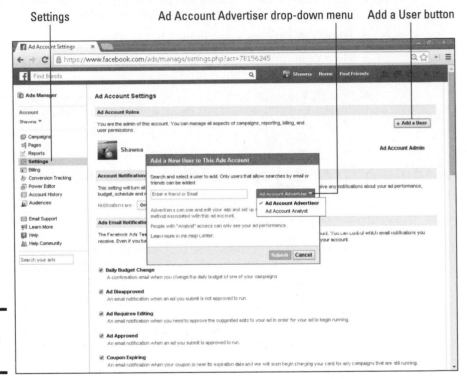

Figure 4-3:
Click Add a
User.

5. **Type the name or e-mail address of the user you want to add.**

When you start typing, a list of your Facebook Friends appears; then you can choose the name of person you want to add from the list.

You must already be Friends with someone on Facebook to add him as a user on your account. If the user has set the privacy level on his e-mail address to public, you can enter the address associated with his account without being Friends.

6. **Choose Ad Account Advertiser or Ad Account Analyst from the drop-down menu in the pop-up in Figure 4-3.**

7. **Click Submit.**

The person you're adding appears in the list of users under Ad Account roles.

Copying an ad

The easiest way to conduct split testing is to take advantage of the Ads Manager to copy an existing ad and then change the copy, image, targeting, website, or bidding.

To copy an ad as a time-saver, follow these steps:

1. **Click Campaigns in the left sidebar.**

2. **Click on the Ads tab located above the table to show a list of your ads.**

3. **Click on the name of the ad you want to create a copy of. A preview of that ad will appear after a few seconds.**

4. **Click Create a Similar Ad below the ad preview; see the following figure.**

   You come to a page titled Create a Similar Ad. It looks like the Ads Create tool, but the fields will be pre-filled with the content and settings of the original ad. As you go through the process, you can change any fields you wish, including the name of the ad, if appropriate.

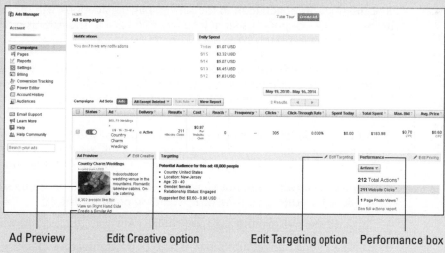

Ad Preview   Edit Creative option   Edit Targeting option   Performance box

Create a Similar Ad link

**Book VII
Chapter 4**

**Testing, Measuring,
and Modifying
Your Ad**

5. **When you're ready, click the Review Order or Place Order button at the bottom.**

In addition to its use in split-testing, the copying technique is helpful when you want to re-create a similar ad for another year or season, or to keep everything the same except for a product name.

Changing Your Attack Plan

It's helpful to test several variations of any type of Facebook ad to find out which one performs best. Ads that are performing well have a higher number of clicks and are rewarded by Facebook with lower costs. Look at the ad metrics on the Ads screen, or check the mini-summary of performance for a specific ad to the right of the preview, as shown in the sidebar "Copying an ad."

Always assess your success against the goal you chose when you set up the ad. If your goal was conversions, don't count as successful those ads that result in a high CTR but no conversions. Make sure that you're watching the right stats; the data can be tricky!

If you aren't happy with your results, try one of the following changes for a week or so and then re-assess your results.

To edit any of these parameters, use the buttons in the Ads Manager or click the relevant pencil icon in the Ads Manager. Facebook will prompt you through a series of pop-ups similar to what you see in the Ads Create tool, which we detail in Chapter 2.

✦ If your ads aren't showing often, try editing your bid price. (Facebook will suggest a bidding range.) It's your responsibility to adjust your bid amount and bid type according to the results you want and what your budget allows.

✦ Adjust the target audience definition so your ad will be seen by people who are most likely to take the action you want. We discuss defining the target audience later in this chapter and in Chapter 2 of this minibook.

✦ If your ad shows often, but viewers aren't taking actions such as clicks or likes, try editing your ad or the landing point for the ad.

✦ Turn off low-performing ads to optimize your spending, if appropriate.

✦ Increase your budget and bids on high-performing ads so more people see those.

If you revise an ad, Facebook still reviews it before allowing it to run. Review may take up to 24 hours during the week and longer on weekends.

Trying Out Split-Testing

Why guess? Split-testing, which is sometimes called A/B testing or multivariate testing, is a systematic approach to determining how various factors affect the success of your ad campaigns. The three primary components of an ad — copy, image, and targeting — are all appropriate for testing. Split-testing is time-consuming, so save it for your important campaigns and allow enough time to assess results. You don't change each and every variable for each campaign that you run. Change one thing at a time and keep the other variables the same. If you're comparing two ads, try to run them with similar bids and at similar times of the day and days of the week. Plan your work systematically.

You might try these split-test scenarios:

✦ Select two different titles, but keep the body copy, image, and targeting the same.

✦ Keep the copy the same, but change the image.

✦ Run an ad one week with one call to action, run a similar ad the next week but with a different call to action, and then compare the two.

You should have at least 50 clicks and run the ads for at least one week for a sound comparison.

You don't need the same number of clicks to compare two ads because many of the variables (such as the bid price and market) can be different. You can use a relative number to compare the ads, such as click-through rate (CTR) or click per thousand (CPM), because these rates are percentages, not absolute numbers.

Before you start split-testing, do a little preparation.

1. Create a new ad.

2. Run the ad for at least a week to gather statistics.

3. Analyze the results of the ad in the Ads Manager to see the results. Pay particular attention to CTR, demographics, and actions taken, all of which we discuss in Chapter 2 of this minibook.

4. Decide which variables to split-test. There are no absolute numbers or guidelines. Use your marketing experience and instinct to determine which variables make sense in your situation.

5. Repeat.

The easiest way to do split-testing is to copy all the information from a previous ad to a new ad. That way, you can tweak the one thing you want to change and keep everything else the same. Follow the directions in the nearby sidebar "Copying an ad."

Split-testing your ad title and text

Let's look first at a split-testing approach for ad copy. The copy of two or more tested ads should include a slightly different ad title or body text. Make one or more copies of your original ad. You may find it helpful to give the various versions a number or some other differentiator — for example, *holiday ad title 1, holiday ad title 2.* Click the pencil icon next to the Edit Creative option shown in the sidebar "Copying an ad" earlier in this chapter and follow the directions in the sidebar to edit the copies.

✦ **Ad title:** Try two or more different titles to see which one encourages more clicks or conversions depending on your objective.

✦ **Body text:** Test different wording and calls to action, just like people used to do in the old-fashioned days of classified ads.

Run the different versions simultaneously for at least a week to collect enough data to be statistically significant. You may want to run your original ad again as well.

✦ Keep the ad that works better in terms of achieving your objective and make the other(s) inactive.

Do your split-testing on copies you make of your ad. Always make sure to keep the original as well.

Figure 4-4 shows two titles that were split-tested. One title is "Country Charm Weddings," and the other is "A Rustic Theme Wedding." The image and body text are exactly the same. Sometimes you won't know exactly why a certain title or copy performs better — and that is why you split-test.

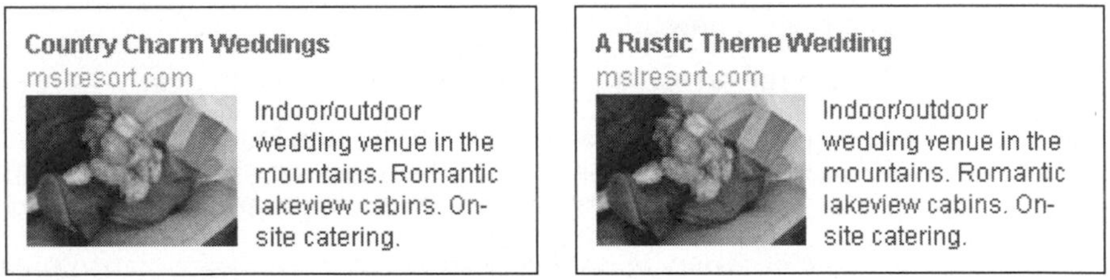

Figure 4-4:
Split-testing
for ad titles.
These ads
are identical
except for
the titles.

Country Charm Weddings
mslresort.com
Indoor/outdoor wedding venue in the mountains. Romantic lakeview cabins. On-site catering.

A Rustic Theme Wedding
mslresort.com
Indoor/outdoor wedding venue in the mountains. Romantic lakeview cabins. On-site catering.

To get ideas for different copy, take a look at the Facebook Ad Board at www.facebook.com/ads/adboard. (You may have to enter your password to see this page.) These ads are currently running on Facebook and use demographics matching your Profile. They may or may not be successful ads, but they can give you an idea of what ads are running now.

Split-testing your ad images

Your ad image is very important for catching people's eyes. As with testing copy, start by making at least one copy of your original ad and giving the new copies slightly different names. Click the pencil icon next to the Edit Creative option shown in the sidebar "Copying an ad" and follow the directions in the sidebar to edit the copies.

+ Try using your logo and a picture of your product.

+ Try using two different images (as shown in Figure 4-5).

+ Run the different versions simultaneously for at least a week to collect enough data to be statistically significant. You may want to run your original ad again as well.

+ Keep the ad that works the best when it comes to achieving your objective and make the other(s) inactive.

If you're advertising something within Facebook, use a version of an image appears on your Facebook Page. Then, when someone goes to your event, Page, tab, or group, the image is consistent.

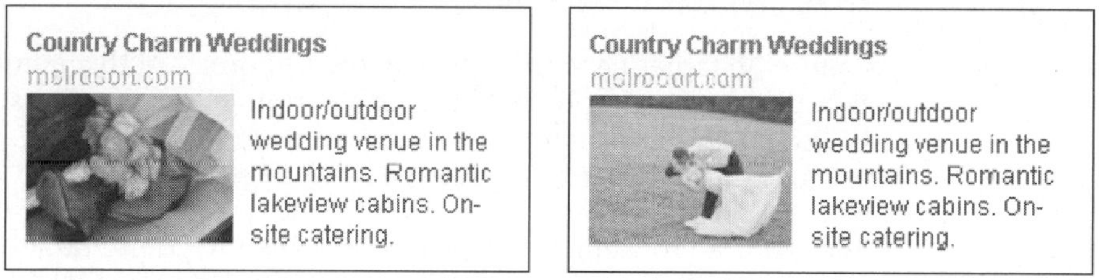

Country Charm Weddings
molrocort.com

Indoor/outdoor wedding venue in the mountains. Romantic lakeview cabins. On-site catering.

Country Charm Weddings
molrocort.com

Indoor/outdoor wedding venue in the mountains. Romantic lakeview cabins. On-site catering.

Figure 4-5:
Split-testing
ad images.

**Book VII
Chapter 4**

Testing, Measuring, and Modifying Your Ad

Keep these guidelines in mind when creating images:

+ **Keep it simple.** Make sure the picture is clear and not too intricate.

+ **Mind your pixels.** Facebook recommends uploading images with dimensions of 1200 x 627 pixels (px), with a minimum width of 600 px for News Feed appearances. Facebook automatically resizes images of other dimensions.

+ **Forego Flash.** Facebook does not support animated or Flash images.

    For more information on ad images, read Chapter 2 in this minibook.

    If you change more than one variable, you won't know which change produced the difference.

Split-testing your targeting

After you run an ad, you can take a look at the clicks and break them down by demographics. That data is listed in the Responder Demographics report, which we discuss later in this chapter.

As with testing copy, start by making at least one copy of your original ad and giving the new copies slightly different names to indicate that you are using different audiences. This time, however, click the pencil icon next to the Edit Targeting option shown in the sidebar "Copying an ad," not the content of the ads.

You may want to try split-testing your targeting this way:

✦ Try the same ad, using different Interests in the split test.

✦ Try the same ad with different selections within Behaviors.

For example, assume you have Women's Clothing under Interests and Luxury brand apparel under Behaviors (Purchase behavior⇨Clothing⇨Women's). If you want a broader audience, split-test by removing the Luxury brand apparel selection under Behaviors. Run your original ad and the copy for a week to see whether the performance improves.

If you want a narrower audience, you could change the Interests area on the identical ad from Women's Clothing to Women's Dresses. Again, run the two versions of the ads simultaneously.

For more on targeting your audience, see Chapter 2 of this minibook. If you're getting a higher response from a certain age range, consider testing with the under-performing age ranges removed from your target audience. See if focusing on the responsive age ranges results in a better CTR.

Adjust your ad rotation to keep your ads fresh. If you're targeting a narrow range of people, those people will potentially see a specific ad multiple times, and the ad loses effectiveness. However, if you need name recognition and branding, we recommend keeping the image the same.

To change the targeting for an existing ad, take the following steps. The same steps apply if you want to change the targeting for an existing campaign or ad set as a whole.

1. **Go to the Ad Manager (**www.facebook.com/ads/manage**).**

You will be on the Campaigns page automatically.

2. **Click the Ads (or Campaigns or Ad Sets) tab located above the table.**

3. **Click the ad name for the ad that you want to edit.**

The page will expand and a preview of your ad will appear.

4. **Click the pencil icon next to the Edit Targeting tab to the right of Ad Preview.**

See the sidebar "Copying an ad" earlier in this chapter.

5. **You'll see all the targeting options that appear in the Audience section of the Ads Create tool.**

Refer to Chapter 2 of this minibook for a list of the targeting options.

6. **When you're satisfied, click Save in the bottom-right corner of the pop-up to update the targeting.**

Testing your landing page

If you're advertising a website outside Facebook, make sure that your website is optimized for what you're advertising. If you'd like someone to sign up for your newsletter, send that viewer to a web page that shows the benefits of the newsletter, a box for her to enter her name and e-mail, and not much else. If you're advertising a sale, send those viewers to the web page where you talk about the sale. Don't make the user hunt through your website to find the relevant content.

That said, you can also split-test your landing pages. Design two similar pages to see which one gets better results when you send traffic to it. In this case, you want to keep the actual ad copy the same within Facebook so that you can really measure the difference.

Split-testing landing pages doesn't have to be too hard. If you created a page about your product along the lines of www.yourwebsite.com/productname, create another page on your site such as www.yourwebsite.com/productname2. The two pages should be identical except for the different copy, layout, or images you want to test. Send traffic to each of these pages with your Facebook ad. Have an analytics program installed on your website to measure the traffic, and watch when people are purchasing your product from one landing page or the other landing page. Google Analytics (www.google.com/analytics) is a perfect tool to help measure the traffic on your website. For more information on analytics in general, see Book IX, Chapter 1. For more on Google Analytics, see Book IX, Chapter 3.

Viewing Facebook Reports

Facebook Reports is the area in the Ads Manager where you find critical performance data on all your ads, such as impressions, clicks, actions, actual CPC, and more.

You can access the reports in several ways:

1. **Log in as an admin and click the drop-down arrow in the top-right corner of the Facebook toolbar. Choose Manage Ads from the menu.**

2. **Alternatively, log in and navigate to** facebook.com/ads/manage.

3. **Either way, click the Reports link in the left pane, as shown in Figure 4-6.**

You're taken to the Ad Reports area, where you start by selecting the type of report you want. You can then customize your report with the *Edit Columns* and *Add Filters* buttons; specify its date range; and save, share, export, or schedule your report to run automatically.

Facebook completely reorganized its report presentation in Spring 2014. You can review current or previous data in the former report format by clicking the Old Reports link in the left navigation, shown in Figure 4-6. You can retrieve previously scheduled reports using the Old Scheduled Reports link directly below it.

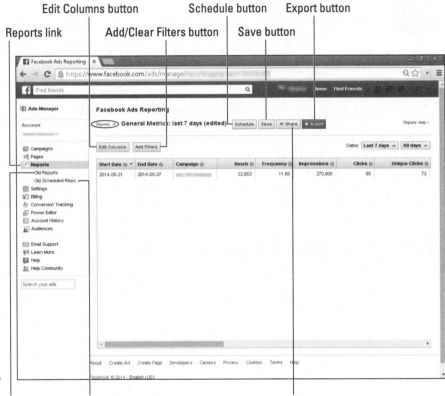

Figure 4-6: Use the Reports link in the left pane to view the performance records for your ads.

Setting up your report

First, you must decide what type of report you want. When you click the drop-down arrow next to the word Reports in the top row of the Facebook Ads Reporting screen, you will see four choices. Select one from this list:

✦ **Manage Scheduled and Recent Reports:** Schedule reports or view recently created ones.

✦ **General Metrics:** The most flexible and extensive data report, this one is the most commonly used.

✦ **Website Conversion:** View results only for ads with a website conversion objective, such as a sale, registration, or download.

✦ **Placement Based Metrics:** View ad performance results sorted by where ads appeared: right column, News Feed, or mobile environment.

Setting dates

To the far right of the second row of the Reporting screen, you see two Date drop-down menus: Last 7 Days and All Days. In the first drop-down menu, select the date range to be included in the report, ranging from Today to the Last 3 Months, or Custom. If you choose the Custom option, additional fields appear to set the start and end dates of your reporting period.

In the All Days drop-down menu, you choose how may days should be summarized in each row of the report: 1, 2, 7, or all days. For a detailed breakdown by the day, you would select 1 Day (for example, a one-day ad blitz for a flash sale); for a summary of an entire, lengthy campaign, select All Days.

Scheduling reports

There are several other buttons on the top row that you may want to select *after* your report has been created. The row of buttons at the top lets you schedule a report to run at a regular interval and have it sent to you and others. To schedule a report:

1. **Click the Schedule button shown in Figure 4-6.**

2. **On the pop-up window that appears (see Figure 4-7), name your report.**

3. **For Frequency, choose Daily, Weekly, or Monthly.**

4. **Choose a start date.**

5. **In the Subscriber Emails field, type or paste e-mail addresses for people who should receive the report, separated by a comma.**

6. **Select either Active or Paused from the Status drop-down menu.**

   Active means that Facebook will run and distribute your report on the selected schedule; *Paused* stops the process.

7. **Click the blue Schedule button located in the bottom-right corner of the pop-up.**

Only people with permissions will be able to access a report that you e-mail them. To set permissions, click on Settings in the left pane of the Ads Manager. Reenter your password when asked. Scroll down to Ad Account Roles and then click + Add a User.

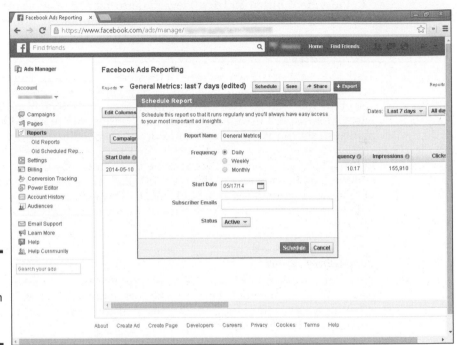

Figure 4-7:
Schedule a report to run as often as you'd like.

Saving a report file

Click the Save button (refer to Figure 4-6). In the pop-up that appears, name your file and click Save in the pop-up to keep the file in your Ads Manager record for future reference.

Sharing a report

When you click the Share button (refer to Figure 4-6), the pop-up that appears will contain a long link that you can copy and paste into an e-mail. You will also have the option to shorten the link, which makes it easier to use.

Exporting CSV or XLS files

Exporting a report file enables you to analyze the data in your report more fully, graph the numbers, or compare two campaigns side by side. To do this, you must *export* (send) your report as an XLS (Excel) or a CSV (Comma

Separated Values) file, depending on the file format your spreadsheet program requires. Follow these steps:

1. **Set up your report exactly as you want it. Save it for security purposes.**

2. **Click the blue Export button (refer to Figure 4-6).**

3. **On the drop-down menu that appears, choose Export Report (.xls) or Export Report (.csv).**

   Your report will automatically download to your computer.

Decoding column headings for General Metrics

If you haven't run ads before on Google or other web platforms, some of the columns in the Ads Manager may as well be hieroglyphics. The specific columns that appear will vary based the report and customization you have selected.

The following definitions cover the default columns for the commonly used General Metrics data aggregation report, which appears in Figure 4-6. (For more terminology, review Chapter 2 of this minibook.) The fields are listed in the order they appear, from left to right. Not all these fields are visible in the figure.

+ **Reach:** The number of different individuals who saw your ads. Reach is different from Impressions, which counts the number of times your ad has displayed. If the same person sees your ad five times, Reach counts that person only once; Impressions counts five times.

+ **Frequency:** The average number of times each person saw your ad. This is the Impressions divided by the Reach.

+ **Impressions:** The total number of times your ads have appeared on Facebook, whether in the right column, News Feed, or in a mobile format.

+ **Clicks:** The actual number of clicks on the ad. If you're promoting a Page, an event, or an app, this metric includes new page Likes, event joins, app installs, and similar actions.

+ **Unique Clicks:** The number of clicks received from different people. This data is helpful for knowing whether the same person happened to see your ad twice and clicked it both times — the second click is not a unique click.

+ **CTR (click-through rate):** How many times your ad was clicked, divided by the number of times your ad was shown on Facebook (Impressions). This ratio of Clicks to Impressions is expressed as a percentage.

+ **Unique CTR:** Unique Clicks divided by Reach (unique viewers). It's best to have your Unique CTR come close to your CTR, but there's nothing you can do to control who clicks your ad.

✦ **Spend:** The amount you spend during the date range you chose for the report.

✦ **CPM (cost per thousand impressions):** The cost for each 1,000 impressions. This is a standard metric for all types of advertising, from billboards and TV to online banners and Google search ads. It is calculated by dividing the total amount spent by the number of impressions received in thousands. Even if you didn't bid with the CPM model when you placed your ad, Facebook Reports calculates it for your reference. CPM not only enables you to compare how ad campaigns with different bidding models perform on Facebook, but also how Facebook advertising compares to ads placed in any other online or offline format.

✦ **Cost per 1000 People Reached:** The average cost for your ad to reach 1,000 unique Facebook users.

✦ **CPC (cost per click):** Simple arithmetic! The total amount spent divided by the number of clicks an ad received yields an average CPC. This number is calculated even if you didn't bid on the CPC model, making it possible for you to compare Facebook performance under different bidding scenarios, or to compare Facebook costs versus other online advertising.

✦ **Actions:** The number of actions (such as liking a page, downloading an app, or making a comment) taken by people on your ad, Page, app, or event after someone saw your ad. Actions, which are now included in the social content, are counted even if viewers didn't actually click your ad. They are calculated within 24 hours of viewing an ad or 28 days after clicking it, unless you specify other parameters under the Actions metric in the Edit Columns pop-up, as described later.

✦ **People Taking Action:** The number of unique users who took an action such as liking your page or making a comment. If the same person takes more than one action, she or he counts as one unique user for this metric.

✦ **Page Likes:** The number of people who like your Page within 24 hours of viewing your ad, or within 28 days of clicking on an ad. (As with Actions, you specify other time parameters under the Actions metric in the Edit Columns pop-up, as described later.) This number can be beneficial because you can see when you have generated awareness that leads to a Like with up to a month of advertising exposure. People will often view an ad multiple times before they take an action.

Customizing your report with Columns and Filters

Facebook collects an unbelievable amount of data! To help you organize the data into meaningful information, Facebook offers dozens of ways to customize which information gets reported and on what level — account, campaign, ad set, or individual ad.

The primary tools for customization are the Edit Columns and Add/Clear Filters buttons, which appear at the top of the Reports section. (Refer to Figure 4-6.) Use these options to prioritize the information that you present in your report, or to set up different report profiles for different purposes.

TIP

You may need to configure more than one report for different needs. Product managers or marketing directors may want demographic information at the ad set level; the VP of marketing may want more budget detail; the advertising folks may want performance data at the level of individual ads.

When you click the Edit Columns button, the complicated pop-up shown in Figure 4-8 appears. It contains three interlocking segments: Column Sets, Dimensions, and Metrics.

Column Sets   Dimensions

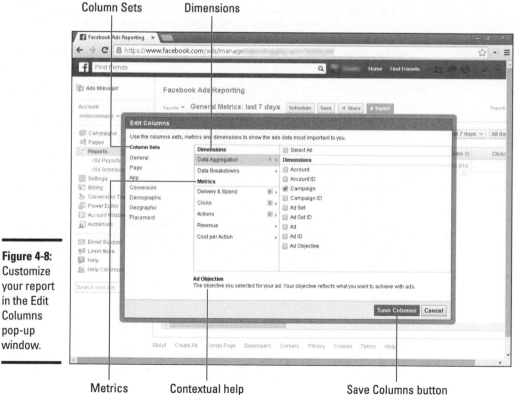

Metrics   Contextual help   Save Columns button

Figure 4-8: Customize your report in the Edit Columns pop-up window.

As you click different options in the Column Sets list on the left, the numbers to the right of some of the Dimensions and Metrics may change simultaneously, as may the default check boxes in the column on the right. The selected check boxes are the actual column names that appear in the report. If you override the default settings, your customized columns will appear in the report.

For a change, Facebook provides meaningful help where you need it. As you hover over any item in the Dimensions or Metrics section, a definition of the item appears at the bottom of the pop-up window. If you try to select an inappropriate parameter or omit a required field, Facebook displays a prompt at the top of the pop-up.

Selecting a Column Set

The far-left column in the pop-up window displays seven basic pre-configured sets of column displays. As you click on each one, the numbers next to items listed in the center section of the window may change accordingly. You will have an opportunity to further customize your report by modifying those sections, as we explain later. The seven basic sets are:

✦ **General:** This broad-based column set includes reach, frequency, impressions, amount spent, CPM, CPC, clicks, CTR, and actions. This is probably the most often-used report. We define these and other common reporting terms in the earlier "Decoding column headings for General Metrics" section; most of these terms are also defined in Chapter 2 of this minibook.

✦ **Page:** This set offers columns related to Page likes, Page engagement, offer claims, and cost per Page likes. For contest and claim information, see Book VI, Chapter 2. This Column Set is often used when conducting an internal Facebook campaign to increase Likes or engagement.

✦ **App:** A suite of columns related to app installations, app engagement, mobile app installs, and cost per mobile app installs. See Book III, Chapter 2, for more about apps in general. See Book V for more specific app information.

✦ **Conversion:** The set displays columns related to conversions, checkouts, registrations, cost per website conversions, cost per checkout, and cost per registration. This column set makes the most sense with the website conversion objective.

✦ **Demographic:** Configures report columns to show ad performance broken down by age and gender.

✦ **Geographic:** Configures report columns to show ad performance broken down by country.

✦ **Placement:** Configures report columns to show ad performance broken down by where an ad appeared: right column, News Feed, or mobile.

Start with the Facebook default settings for Edit Columns. Then play around with the configuration until you get the results that make the most sense for your marketing goals, advertising objectives, budget, and the amount of time it's worth spending on analysis.

A business with $1 million annual budget for Facebook advertising — and the staff to go with it — can afford to spend hours and hours analyzing data. For a small business spending only several hundred dollars a month, a huge level of effort simply isn't worth it. Facebook's default settings should suffice.

Remember to click the Save Columns button in the bottom right of the pop-up for each different report configuration you want to test or keep. Give your different configurations descriptive names so you can compare them later.

Defining Dimensions

Once you choose a column set, you can view (and change) additional details about the report configuration. Start with the top-center section of the pop-up. No matter which column set you choose, beneath the label Dimensions you see two rows: Data Aggregation and Data Breakdown. Click the right-pointing arrow to the right of each row to see available choices. As you select the various boxes, the numbers next to the arrows may change.

At least one choice under Data Aggregation is required. Here you choose whether to display your reports at the account, campaign, ad set, and/or ad level. You may select more than one box, but you must select at least one. The default is Campaign level for the General column set, but may vary with other selections.

Review the Data Breakdown row if you also want your report to provide an alternative view of performance by one of six audience demographics: age, gender, age and gender, country, placement, or destination. You can select none or one of these radio buttons. The default is None for the General column set, but may vary with other selections.

Measuring Metrics

Below Dimensions in the center section, you will see five subsets of Metrics that are listed regardless of your choice of column set. However, the number of default items that appears to the right of the metric varies according to your selection.

1. Delivery & Spend
2. Clicks
3. Actions
4. Revenue
5. Cost per Action

As with Dimensions, each of these subsets has a right-pointing arrow. Click the arrow to see the potential list of parameters associated with that metric. See Figure 4-9.

These are check boxes, so you can select all, none, or as many parameters as you want. Once you have saved your choices using the button at the bottom of the pop-up, these parameters become the column labels that appear in your customized report (refer to Figure 4-6).

TIP

To return to the default settings, just click again on the item you chose under Column Sets.

Figure 4-9:
The list of potential columns in a report varies according to the metrics you choose. This shows the column available for the Clicks metric under the General Column Sets list.

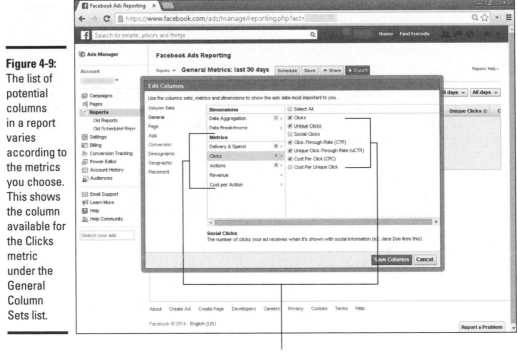

Column Metrics

REMEMBER

You can include as many columns as you want in a report, but the report will display only the data included in the date range and filters (discussed later) that you specify.

Adding filters

If you have been using Facebook advertising for a while, or if you run multiple campaigns, you may find that you want to pull out only specific campaigns, ad sets, or ads for a report. This is easily accomplished by clicking the Add Filters button (refer to Figure 4-6).

As shown in Figure 4-10, another row of options appears above the performance report. Follow these steps to filter your report to display only the results you want.

1. **Click the drop-down arrow next to Campaign Name.**

2. **Select Campaign Name, Ad Set Name, or Ad Name.**

3. **From the drop-down list to the right of Contains, choose either Contains or Is.**

4. **If you selected Is, enter the actual name of the campaign, ad set, or ad in the text field to the right. If you selected Contains, enter at least one keyword that appears in the name.**

Enter search criteria here   Add Filters/Clear Filters button

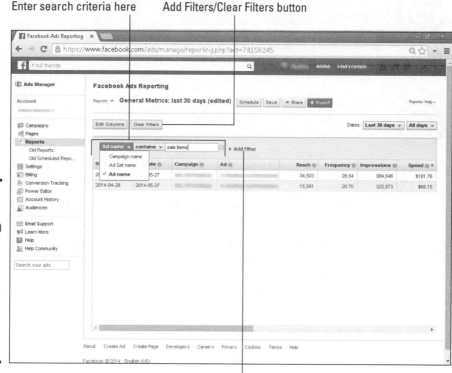

Figure 4-10:
The Add
Filters dialog
box lets
you decide
what level
of reporting
you want:
campaign,
ad sets, or
ads.

Click the + Add Filter link when you're ready to search

5. **Click + Add Filter. Any items that match the search criterion you chose in Step 4 will appear in the table below. Click the item that you want to see.**

6. **To add more campaigns to your filter, simply repeat the process. Start by typing another campaign name into the text field.**

7. **If you want to filter the results of a specific campaign by ad or ad set, repeat the process with the additional fields that will appear to the right. If you are done, just ignore them.**

8. **Once you have added a filter, the Add Filters button changes to Clear Filters. To remove all filters, click that button. To remove just one of several filters, click the small X box next to the text field.**

Viewing Old Reports

Use the Old Reports link in the left pane (refer to Figure 4-6) to view campaign results in the former reporting format. The prior format can be used to present current data, as well as data collected from the past.

Running reports in the old format is easier, but you have fewer ways to customize your report.

You are not required to use the new format for current or future data, or to reconfigure your reports from the past with the new interface. Facebook has *not* indicated that it intends to "retire" the old report format in the future.

Even if you switch to the new Reporting format, save your prior reports for comparison. They offer a wealth of historical performance data that may be useful for the future.

When you click on the Old Reports link, the pop-up window shown in Figure 4-11 will present fields to configure the report. Follow these steps:

1. **Choose one of five types of reports from the Report Type drop-down menu:**

   • **Advertising Performance** provides similar information to the new reporting format.

   • **Responder Demographics** provides critical demographic data about the users who actually view and click on your ads; use this information to optimize your targeting.

   • **Actions by Impression Time** is the number of actions sorted by impression time, which is defined as the time between a user's viewing of an ad and clicking the action: for example, a day, a week, or a month.

   • **Inline Interactions reports** deal only with engagement on Page post ads, with action metrics such as Likes, photos viewed, and videos played that occurred as a result of your ads.

   • **News Feed reports** show metrics for ads that appeared in New Feeds, distinct from the metrics for ads that appear in the right column; they include impressions, clicks, CTR, and average position.

2. **Under the Summarize By drop-down menu, choose Account, Ad Set, or Ad.**

3. **If you chose Ad Set or Ad, an additional Filter By drop-down menu allows you to select No Filter, or to filter by ad or ad set as appropriate.**

4. **From the Time Summary drop-down menu, select Monthly, Weekly, Daily, Custom, or Lifetime. News Feed reports only offer the first three choices.**

5. **For all choices except Lifetime, set the Date Range for starting and ending dates.**

6. **In the Format drop-down menu, select Webpage (.html), Excel (.xls) or Multilanguage Excel (.csv).**

7. **Check whether to include deleted Ads/Ad Sets.**

8. **Click the Generate Report button.**

**Book VII
Chapter 4**

Testing, Measuring, and Modifying Your Ad

Figure 4-11:
The configu-
ration
pop-up
for a daily
advertising
performance
report sum-
marized
by ad sets
in the old
report
format.

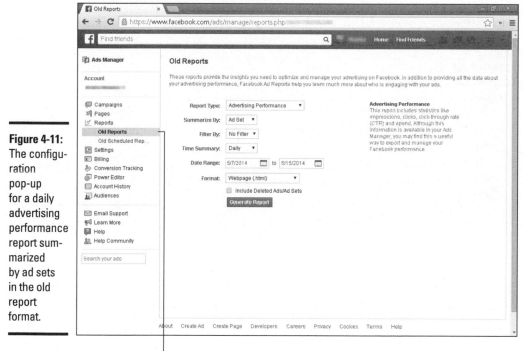

Old Reports link

The two most helpful reports in the old format are Advertising Performance (see Figure 4-12) and Responder Demographics.

Export Report button

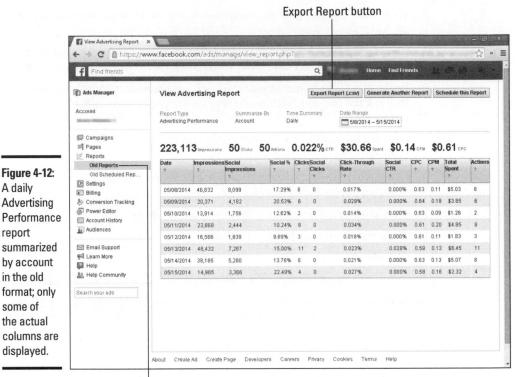

Figure 4-12:
A daily
Advertising
Performance
report
summarized
by account
in the old
format; only
some of
the actual
columns are
displayed.

Old Reports link

You can export a file from the old report format by clicking the Export Report (.csv) button above the table (refer to Figure 4-12).

Book VIII

Advanced Facebook Marketing Tactics

Contents at a Glance

Chapter 1: An Introduction to Advanced Facebook Marketing 583

Remembering the Nine Core Facebook Marketing Rules.........................584
Creating a Facebook Experience 585
Building Social Proof with Facebook Ads 587
Experimenting with Custom Apps...588
Targeting Your Audience with Custom Lists..589
Creating Interests Lists to Focus on the People Who Matter
    Most to Your Business..592
Using Facebook Offers for Your Local or Online Business 595
Expanding Your Page's Exposure 601
Engaging with Likes...601
Getting Viral Exposure 602

Chapter 2: Marketing with Facebook Social Plug-ins 607

Understanding Facebook's Social Plug-ins..607
Choosing the Right Facebook Plug-ins for Your Business.....................610
Finding and Installing Open Source Facebook Plug-ins 629

Chapter 3: Discovering Live Video on Facebook 633

Understanding the Benefits of Live Video...633
Choosing Your Streaming Application..635
Streaming from Your Facebook Page with the Livestream Application 637
Streaming with Google Hangouts on Air with 22Social 644
Creating Buzz about Your Live Video..647

Chapter 4: Using Facebook for Mobile Marketing. 653

Understanding the Rapid Growth of the Mobile World..........................653
Optimizing Your Facebook Presence for Users on the Move.................656
Taking Advantage of Facebook Mobile Ads..662
Measuring Your Mobile Success..668

Chapter 1: An Introduction to Advanced Facebook Marketing

In This Chapter

✔ **Refreshing your knowledge of core marketing principles**

✔ **Examining advanced marketing techniques**

✔ **Targeting market segments with list options**

✔ **Making a Facebook offer they can't refuse**

✔ **Using new Facebook features for viral exposure**

Facebook Pages have become essential parts of many businesses' marketing strategies, but how can you find ways to stand out from the competition? You have a lot to consider as you go about developing a successful Facebook Page. However, the rewards of brand exposure, loyalty from people who like your Page, and increased revenue are well worth your time and effort. To fast-track your success, consider including some advanced strategies in your Facebook plan.

After you create your Page, optimize it with the essential strategies, such as posting great content regularly, and then build some momentum with your base by engaging with people who have liked it. When you have your basic strategies locked in, explore some advanced Facebook marketing strategies. Advanced strategies take more time and effort than basic marketing efforts, but they produce much bigger returns.

You don't have to reinvent the wheel when it comes to Facebook strategies. Instead, take a look at other thriving Facebook business Pages and apply the same success strategies to your own Page. After you give a new strategy enough time to gain momentum, analyze your progress. If what you're doing is working, keep doing it! After a while, if you're not happy enough with the results of your efforts, change direction and try a new tactic. (You won't know if you don't try!)

In this chapter, we give you a quick refresher on the core rules of Facebook marketing; then we take a look at some advanced marketing strategies that can take your Facebook Page from good to great.

Remembering the Nine Core Facebook Marketing Rules

Before you consider experimenting with a few advanced Facebook marketing strategies, make sure that your Facebook marketing foundation is solid. Consider nine core rules when you create your marketing plan. Following these rules will ensure that you stay on track and focus on the most important marketing elements as you increase your Page engagement and number of Likes — and ultimately turn your Likes into new customers.

Although we also mention these core Facebook rules in Book I, Chapter 2, here's a synopsis:

✦ **Give your Page a human touch.** Communicate with your Likes as though you were talking to your friends. Let your personality come through in each post.

✦ **Create fresh content.** Always make sure that your content educates, entertains, and empowers your Likes to keep them engaged and coming back for more.

✦ **Cultivate engagement with two-way dialog.** People love to talk about themselves, so craft your posts and questions around them to get them talking.

✦ **Create consistent calls to action.** To get your Likes to take action, consider offering discounts and specials or asking them to sign up for your newsletter so that you can actively communicate with them on a consistent basis.

✦ **Make word-of-mouth advocacy easy.** Make it easy for your Likes to talk about you by asking them to share your content, getting them to engage in contests, and making the experiences on your Page about them — rather than about you.

✦ **Encourage conversations.** Enhance the experience your Likes enjoy by creating a community that encourages them to interact with one another.

✦ **Focus on smart branding.** Treat your Facebook Page as a mini version of your own website. The key is to create a Page that sparks familiarity with your brand when your existing customers visit your Page.

✦ **Be deliberate, and manage expectations.** Always stay focused on why you want to have a presence on Facebook. When you understand the "why," your actions are deliberate and have purpose, and your Likes clearly understand what your Page has to offer.

✦ **Monitor, measure, and track.** Make sure that you have surefire methods in place that enable you to consistently track your Facebook marketing progress.

Creating a Facebook Experience

Many businesses just getting started on Facebook worry that they'll be lost in the Facebook abyss. Sure, big brands such as Coca-Cola and Southwest Airlines stand out easily. But what about small and midsize companies? Many of our clients wonder whether they even have a chance.

Here's the great news: There's hope for your Page, no matter how small your company may be! You don't have to be a major brand to gain exposure and build relationships with your clients and customers on Facebook.

One way to stand out from the masses is to create *Facebook experiences* — experiences you execute on your Facebook Page that are unique to your brand and of great value to your Likes. No matter how big or small, these experiences can be extremely powerful.

For example, Braxton's Animal Works (`www.facebook.com/BraxtonsAW`) offers a "Caption This Photo" competition every week, as shown in Figure 1-1. These contests are a huge hit! For more about Braxton's successful Facebook marketing, see its case study in Book IX, Chapter 2.

Figure 1-1:
This weekly photo caption contest encourages visitors to participate and then revisit the page the following week to see the winners.

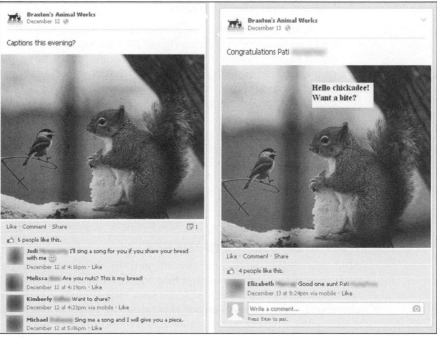

Courtesy of Braxton's Animal Works.

Planning the experience

If you like the concept of an experience and want to create something unique to your brand and your mission, these four steps get you started in the right direction:

1. Decide on the overall vibe you want to create with your experience.

   Do you want to add value? Perhaps you're looking to entertain. Is your desired outcome to educate, create excitement among your Likes, or all the above? Determine the kind of experience that will resonate with your base.

2. Get clear on what your company does best.

   What's your company known for? What does it do best? What do your clients tell you when they're singing your praises? Use this insight to fuel your ideas about unique experiences.

   When you're brainstorming, think of experiences you can do multiple times. An experience that you can execute consistently is the key to building momentum with your Facebook community. After you create your list of ideas, choose the experience that your audience will embrace most fully — and one that your team will enjoy delivering!

3. Map out your execution plan.

   You want to document the process of your experience. For a photo contest like Braxton's (refer to Figure 1-1), for instance, you might collect a set of several dozen photos in advance and carefully track the number of responses for each and the percent of viewers who participate. Over time, you'd develop a sense of which images draw the largest audience and the largest participation rate.

4. Commit to your plan.

   For some people, this is the toughest step! When you decide on your signature experience, it's crucial that you deliver. If you say that you intend to do something once a week, do it. If you don't follow through, you could lose trust with your Likes, and that's something you don't want to mess with!

Optimizing the experience

After you create your experience, begin to think about how you might repurpose the content or information that comes from it. If audio is involved, perhaps you can create a podcast. Or if your experience involves video, think about using that video in an opt-in strategy for anyone who might have missed it that week. This could be a great way to build up your list.

You can also take the content from your experience and post it in new ways weeks later for those who may have missed it. Doing so allows you to continually post great content. Repurposing the content or elements of your experience creates multiple touch points throughout your marketing strategy.

Signature experiences and other out-of-the-box ideas are vital to keeping your Facebook community engaged and enthusiastic about your brand. The key is to find something that you can duplicate and build on over time.

Building Social Proof with Facebook Ads

Before most people make a buying decision, they want to know that their choice is smart. To get reassurance, they look to their friends for advice and recommendations. With the rise of social networks, word-of-mouth recommendations are essential for businesses in their efforts to gain popularity and expand the ranks of their clientele. Studies show that when it comes to buying decisions, people trust friends' recommendations more than they do the actual brand. Facebook now capitalizes on this behavior by including social information, such as "Likes" right within your ads.

This approach takes word-of-mouth recommendations from Friends and promotes them as an integral part of Facebook Ads (see Figure 1-2). The ad now demonstrates social proof!

Figure 1-2:
Example of an ad including social information — in this case, the number of Likes.

Likes displayed

The term *social proof* refers to the psychological phenomenon of people being motivated to do things that they see other people doing. Interactions on social media sites, such as Facebook, have increased the influence and reach of social proof because now it's much easier to instantly see what your friends are doing at any time.

The inclusion of social information reassures viewers that other people have taken action, essentially offering a testimonial, "I bought this!" or "I just ordered the best burger ever at Rocket Burgers!" These viral, instant recommendations may make the 2014 version of Facebook Ads much more powerful than the former version of Facebook Ads. The word-of-mouth add-on is a powerful tool to entice new users to check out your Facebook Page and your business; it may be enough to justify the expense of paid Facebook advertising, as discussed in Book VII.

**Book VIII
Chapter 1**

An Introduction to Advanced Facebook Marketing

Experimenting with Custom Apps

Book III, Chapter 2, explores custom apps. In many ways, custom apps (also known as *custom pages* or *tabs*) are the most important piece to your Facebook marketing strategy.

You can create multiple pages inside your Facebook Page. One powerful advanced strategy is to create a custom page to promote special products or events. Custom pages can give your product or event extra promotion and give it the push it needs to get even greater exposure.

If you have a physical event coming up, you might consider creating a custom page with a video from past events to showcase the experience. Then you can include the Facebook Comments feature from the social plug-in options to encourage people to talk about the event. This strategy showcases your event via your video, and the Comments section on the tab gets people talking.

Or you can use a custom app to encourage Likes, as the Atlanta History Center does in Figure 1-3, using the TabSite app (www.tabsite.com) from Digital Hill. Users must click the Like button at the top of the page in the first image to gain access to information about Swan House Capitol Tours on the lower image. (The Swan House at the History Center was one of the Georgia set locations used in the movie *The Hunger Games: Catching Fire*.)

If TabSite doesn't appeal to you, consider Woobox as an alternative app for creating custom tabs as part of a Like campaign, as described in Book IX, Chapter 2.

Viewers have to click here to see more

Figure 1-3: Viewers click the Like button on the custom page to see the information page below.

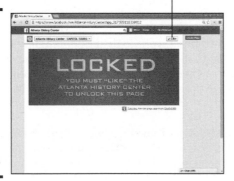 

Courtesy of Atlanta History Center.

Targeting Your Audience with Custom Lists

As we discuss in Book II, Chapter 4, you can use your Profile (when appropriate) for business networking. Keeping up with all your Facebook Friends on your Profile can get a bit tricky. If you're anything like us, you have a mix of family members, friends, acquaintances, potential clients, current clients, and even a few complete strangers as Facebook Friends on your Profile. At times, that volume makes it difficult to decide what you want to share with everyone on your Facebook Timeline.

The good news is that Facebook created a way to segment your Facebook Friends into special lists: smart and custom. The benefit of both types of lists is that they allow you to share your posts with smaller groups of people.

✦ *Smart lists* — which Facebook creates for you — stay up to date based on Profile info your Friends have in common with you, such as family, the city where you live, workplaces, or schools. Although Facebook creates these lists automatically, you can edit them at any time. To access your smart lists, look on the left sidebar of your Facebook Profile home page for the Lists section. Depending on the info in your Profile, you might see smart lists of your relatives, Facebook Friends in your town, and Facebook Friends you went to school with.

✦ *Custom lists* are what you create as a way to selectively group certain people you've added as Friends. Click More next to Friends (see Figure 1-4) to see your custom lists. The name of your custom list and its members are visible only to you. If you send a post to a custom list, those on the list can see whom else that post was sent to, but they won't see the name of your list. For example, if you name a list Prospects I Plan to Land as Big-Money Clients, the people on that list won't see what you called it — so get as creative as you like!

A benefit of using both smart lists and custom lists is that they allow you to share your posts with smaller groups of people. If you just had a family reunion and took a bunch of photos, for example, you may choose to share those photos only with those in your Family smart list. Overall, these lists allow you to intelligently choose whom you talk to and what you want to share with them.

Whenever you want to share something with a specific list, you can use the drop-down audience selector in the status update box and pick one of your lists. (For more info on the audience selector, see Book I, Chapter 1.)

**Book VIII
Chapter 1**

An Introduction to
Advanced Facebook
Marketing

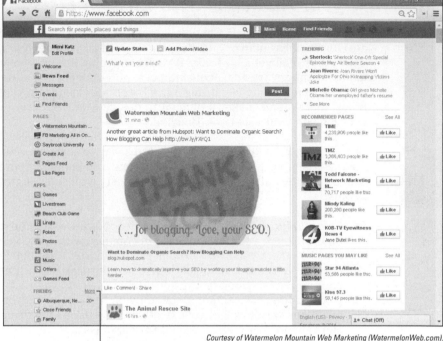

Figure 1-4:
To access
Custom
lists, click
More next
to Friends
in the left
sidebar
of your
Facebook
Profile page.

Click to see Custom lists

Courtesy of Watermelon Mountain Web Marketing (WatermelonWeb.com).

So how does all this relate to your Facebook marketing strategy? We allude to it a bit when we jokingly mention the list Prospects I Plan to Land as Big-Money Clients earlier in this section. Because you likely have potential clients and customers mixed with your Facebook Friends via your Profile, custom lists are a great way to segment your personal friends from current and potential customers. You can communicate with them on a regular basis from your Profile. You can create multiple lists — depending on how you want to communicate with different groups — and then post information, photos, videos, and promotions that you know each group will find valuable. When you laser-focus your communication with custom lists, your marketing messages will pack a bigger punch, and get you even better results.

Creating your custom lists

Here's how you set up a custom list:

1. **Point your browser to** www.facebook.com **and log in to your account.**

   By default, you land on your home page.

2. **In the left column, hover your mouse over the word Friends.**

3. **When the word More appears, click it.**

4. **Click Create List (top-right corner of your screen).**

   A pop-up window appears, prompting you to name your list.

5. **Type a name for your list.**

   The name of your list will be visible only to you — not anyone else on Facebook, including those you add to the list.

6. **In the Members box, below the List Name box, type in the names of the people you want to add to your new list, as shown in Figure 1-5.**

   Each time you begin to type a new name, a drop-down list appears with potential Friends to add. You will want to know the names of the Friends you want to add in advance, so you can type them in at this time.

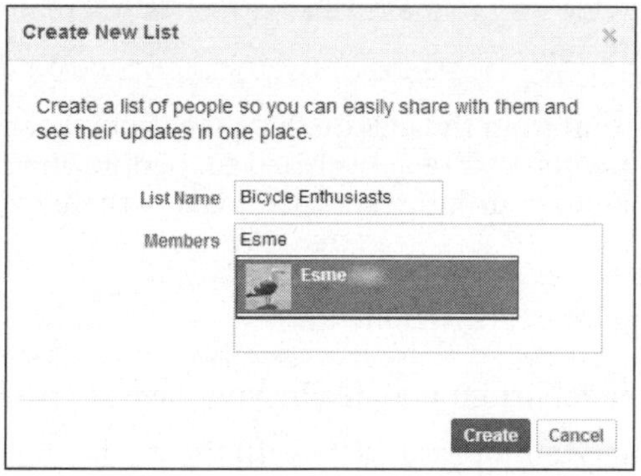

Figure 1-5:
Adding members to a new custom list.

> **Create New List**   ×
>
> Create a list of people so you can easily share with them and see their updates in one place.
>
> List Name   Bicycle Enthusiasts
>
> Members   Esme
>   Esme
>
>   Create   Cancel

Courtesy of Watermelon Mountain Web Marketing (WatermelonWeb.com).

Adding custom lists to your Favorites

Custom lists come in handy when you're posting, but you can also use them to filter which posts you see in your News Feed stream. To see only the updates from people in a specific list, you just click that list; Facebook filters your posts on your News Feed page to show you only status updates from the people in the specific list.

To make things even easier for you, you can add custom lists to your Favorites. The Favorites section appears in the top-left column on your home page as a way to quickly access the links you use most. To add a list to your Favorites, follow these steps:

1. **Log in to your Facebook account.**

   By default, you land on your home page.

2. **In the left column, hover your mouse over your custom list.**

   A little blue pencil (the icon Facebook uses to indicate an edit opportunity) appears to the left of the list name.

3. **Click the blue pencil.**

   A drop-down menu appears, with the option to add this list to Favorites.

4. **Click Add to Favorites.**

Creating Interests Lists to Focus on the People Who Matter Most to Your Business

Because of the sheer number of people on Facebook (more than one billion!), it's easy to get overwhelmed by all the information users are posting. One smart strategy for staying focused is to customize your News Feed to ensure that you see only the Facebook posts that matter most to you and the success of your business. One way to make this happen is to create Interests lists, as shown in Figure 1-6

Interests lists are different from the custom lists mentioned earlier in this chapter: You can add people you're subscribed to, people you're Friends with, and Pages you like to your Interests lists, making them even more useful and interesting.

Advantages of creating Interests lists include

✦ Not missing out on important updates by your favorite people and Pages

✦ The ability to share your Interests lists with the world

✦ The convenience of adding yourself or your Page to your own Interests list so that when others subscribe to it, they subscribe to your updates as well

To see what Interests lists look like, go to `www.facebook.com/addlist` and check out the Add Interests section.

Alternatively, you can go to your Facebook home page; in the left navigation pane, you see Interests listed near the bottom, below Groups. You may have to click the More link to get specific Interests lists to appear.

To create your own Interests list or subscribe to popular ones created by other Facebook users, click Add Interests, as shown in Figure 1-7. As you can see from the first few suggested Interests lists, the popularity of Interests lists can be great. Some have more than 75,000 subscribers!

To set up an Interests list, follow these steps:

1. **Point your browser to** `www.facebook.com/addlist` **and log in to your account if necessary.**

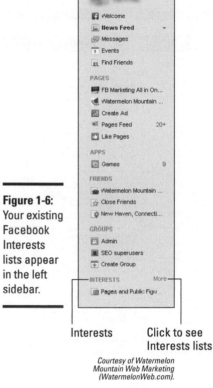

Figure 1-6:
Your existing
Facebook
Interests
lists appear
in the left
sidebar.

Interests   Click to see
                Interests lists

Courtesy of Watermelon
Mountain Web Marketing
(WatermelonWeb.com).

2. **Click the +Create List button.**

   The window that pops up allows you to search Pages you like, people you subscribe to, and Friends. You can also browse people and Pages by category.

3. **Click to select the Pages, Subscriptions, or Friends you want to add to your list.**

4. **Click Next when you finish adding people and Pages.**

5. **Type a name for your list.**

6. **Choose whether you want your list to be seen publicly, by Friends, or only by you.**

7. **Click Done.**

   You're taken to that list immediately, and you see the latest updates by the people and Pages you added.

Add Interests

Figure 1-7:
Facebook offers suggestions for your Interests lists.

Courtesy of Watermelon Mountain Web Marketing (WatermelonWeb.com).

This feature works only with Profile pages, not from business Pages.

To edit your new Interests listlist, click the Manage List drop-down menu near the top-right corner of the page. There, you see the options to rename your list, edit your list (including the option to add or remove people and Pages), choose update types, set notification settings, or delete the list.

To access your list, find the Interests section in your left sidebar. Your newly created or subscribed-to lists are displayed here, but you may have to click More to find them. If you'd like to get easier access to your list, hover over the list name, click the pencil icon when it appears, and select Add to Favorites. Now your Interests list will be below your Favorites near the top of your left sidebar.

You can add a Profile or Page to your Interests lists (or create new lists) when viewing a person's Profile or Page by clicking the settings icon (gear) under the Profile's or Page's Timeline Cover photo. In the drop-down menu, you see Add to Interests lists, as shown in Figure 1-8.

Figure 1-8:
From a
Profile or a
Page, you
can add
people to
an Interests
list.

Add to Interest List   Gear icon

*Courtesy of Mountain Springs Lake Resort &
Lodge (MSLresort.com).*

Using Facebook Offers for Your Local or Online Business

A Facebook offer (as shown in Figure 1-9) is like a coupon that people claim on Facebook, and then either bring in to your place of business or go online to redeem. When you create and promote your offer, it goes out into News Feeds, and your Likes can click to claim it.

You can use Facebook Offers to create a deal of the day, a promotional coupon, or another incentive to encourage people who like your page to shop your online store or a store at their location.

Fifty people must like your Page before you can create an offer.

Tempting offers can go viral quickly. When people claim your offer, their acceptance posts to their News Feeds for all their Friends to see; if those Friends in turn view and accept the offer, then the Friends of Friends will learn about the offer, and so on.

Figure 1-9:
Example of
a Facebook
offer from
Mountain
Springs
Lake Resort.

Courtesy of Mountain Springs Lake Resort & Lodge (MSLresort.com).

**Book VIII
Chapter 1**

**An Introduction to
Advanced Facebook
Marketing**

Creating and promoting a Facebook offer

This is a two-part process. First you create the Facebook offer. Then you market it (optional) with a Promoted post to your Likes and indirectly to their Friends. (For more information on Promoted Posts, see Book VII, Chapter 2.)

Facebook offers are straightforward to set up, either when you are logged into your Page, or from the Ads Create tool (described in detail in Book VII, Chapter 2).

Here's how to do it from your Page. (We show you how to start this process from the Ads Create tool later.)

1. **Log in as the Admin and select the Page you want from the left navigation. Click the Offer, Event + icon that appears in the lower-left section of your Timeline, as shown in Figure 1-10.**

   A drop-down menu appears.

2. **Click Offer.**

   The Create Offer pop-up window (as shown in Figure 1-11) lets you enter the details of your offer.

Figure 1-10:
The Facebook Offer option appears after clicking the Offer, Event + button on your Page.

Click here to get started

Click to enter your details

Courtesy of Mountain Springs Lake Resort & Lodge (MSLresort.com).

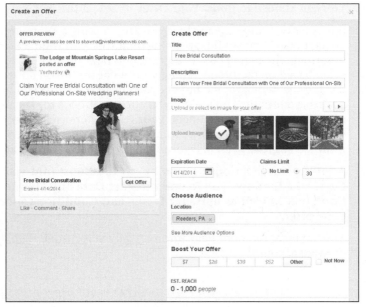

Figure 1-11:
The Create
Offer
pop-up.

3. **Write a title for your offer in the first box.**

   You have only 25 characters, so make the headline compelling and succinct.

4. **Write a Description for your offer in the box below the Title.**

   You have 90 characters to state a concise and tempting benefit.

5. **Add a photo by clicking the Upload Image link.**

   A list of files from your computer appears, so you can upload your image choice in the standard manner. The recommended image size is 1200 x 627 pixels, so be sure that your image is large enough.

6. **Set the expiration date for your offer by clicking on the calendar. Select the date you want your offer to end.**

7. **Under Claims Limit, click No Limit or constrain the number available by entering the number of offers you are willing to honor.**

8. **Within the Location text field, begin typing the geographic location that you wish to target.**

   A drop-down menu will appear with choices. You can choose more than one location.

9. **Click See More Audience Options to target your audience by gender and age.**

   You also have the option to select four to ten interest areas.

10. **You can choose to Boost Your Offer or select the Not Now box.**

Boosting your offer means that you are creating a Promoted post, which costs money! You set the spending limit that you want. Facebook will determine the actual cost of a Promoted post on a CPM (cost per mile) scale based on factors including your location (if you chose to include it), and the demographic targets you chose. The cost will be charged against your limit. The budget you choose applies for the duration of the offer. If you set a larger budget, your reach increases. Select Not Now if you do not wish to create a Promoted post. You can always do this later from the Page, as seen in Figure 1-12, or from the Ads Create tool.

11. **Another More Options section below the Boost (not visible in Figure 1-12) allows you to enter a Start Date and Online Redemption Link, as well as optional Terms and Conditions specific to your offer.**

The Payment Account field automatically selects and displays your existing account.

Figure 1-12:
You always have the option to boost your offer from your Page at a later time.

Courtesy of Mountain Springs Lake Resort & Lodge (MSLresort.com).

Promote your post with Boost Post

12. **Review the Preview of your Offer, which appears in the upper-left corner of the Create Offer pane.**

    It shows the offer as it will appear on your Timeline.

13. **Click the Create Offer button in the bottom-right corner of the Create Offer Pane when you are satisfied.**

    Your offer will run immediately.

14. **You will receive an e-mail copy of the redemption information that Facebook will send out whenever someone claims an offer, as shown in Figure 1-13.**

    You can't customize this e-mail, which generally tells people to bring the offer into your storefront or to go to your website to redeem it.

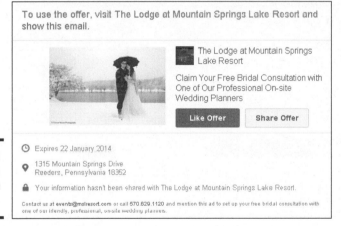

Figure 1-13: Redemption info sent via e-mail.

Creating and promoting offers from the Ads Create tool

As an alternative, you can create an offer and promote it from the Ads Create tool following these steps:

1. **Log in and navigate to** `www.facebook.com/ads/create`. **Click the Offer Claims button at the bottom of the left column.**

2. **To create a new offer, click the + sign in the right pane, as shown in Figure 1-14.**

3. **Complete the fields in the series of three pop-up windows that appear.**

    The fields are similar to those that appear when you create an offer starting with your Page. Follow through these step by step.

4. **Click the Post Offer button when you are done.**

    Your offer starts to run immediately.

5. **To promote this or other offers, return to the Ads Create tool at** www. facebook.com/ads/create. **Click Offer Claims in the left pane and select your offer from the drop-down list in the right pane, as seen in Figure 1-14.**

6. **Click the Continue button.**

   The next screen provides options for promoting this post. (See Book VII, Chapter 2, for more details.)

7. **When you're finished, select the Review Order or Place Order button.**

   Choices may depend on whether or not you have already selected a payment method. After you're done here, you'll be directed to the Ads Manager tool to view reports (see Book VII, Chapter 4).

Figure 1-14: You can create and promote an offer using the Ads Create tool.

Click here first   Select an offer from the drop-down list   Click to create a new offer

Courtesy of Mountain Springs Lake Resort & Lodge (www.MSLresort.com).

When your offer has been published, you can see how many people have claimed your offer, but not who claimed it.

The overall strategy of creating a Facebook offer and using a Promoted post to market that offer is a great way to introduce your Facebook Likes to your special promotions, discounts, and coupons. If you have a local business and are looking to gain even more foot traffic for your business, you definitely want to test this strategy!

Expanding Your Page's Exposure

The way to get seen on Facebook is to create multiple reasons for people to engage with your Page. Try these tips to increase the chances that your Page will be seen often:

✦ Set up your vanity URL for your Facebook Page. See Book II, Chapter 3.

✦ Create a Timeline Cover image that's the maximum size available to give your Page a professional, well-branded look and feel. See Book II, Chapter 2.

✦ Create a custom page that makes the incentive available only after someone likes your page (refer to Figure 1-3). This strategy encourages new viewers to like your site to obtain the reward.

✦ Add a Facebook app to your Page. Consider one that will increase activity and encourage more users to visit your page. See Book V, Chapter 1.

✦ Run a Facebook Ad campaign for 30 days. See Book VII, Chapter 1.

✦ Create a special promotion in an ad (see Book VII, Chapter 2), test out Facebook Offers by creating a coupon and post about it on your Page.

✦ Embed a social plug-in on your website to drive up the number of Likes on your Page. See Book VIII, Chapter 2.

Engaging with Likes

Communicating with your people who like your page helps keep them engaged — and coming back. Here are a few ways to keep the lines of communication wide open:

✦ Create a Facebook experience to execute on your business Page. Think of what your Likes want most from you, and deliver it as a Facebook experience. See "Creating a Facebook Experience," earlier in this chapter.

✦ Ask more questions. The more you make things about people who visit your page and less about you, the more your base of Likes will flourish. Mix up your questions so you have some related to your business and industry, some that get people thinking in new ways, and some that entertain and keep things light. See Book IV, Chapter 2.

✦ Set up notifications to get continuous alerts when your people post on your Page. See Book II, Chapter 3.

✦ If you're having an event online or offline, consider setting up a special custom app to promote the event. (For extra credit, embed a video and a Comments plug-in.) See Book III, Chapter 2.

✦ Turn your Facebook Page into a lead generator by adding a name and e-mail box to your Facebook Page. This box will help you capture the e-mail addresses of your Facebook Likes. See Book II, Chapter 2.

Getting Viral Exposure

Going viral isn't so great in the offline world, but it's the best of all possible worlds online. Here are a few ways to position your Page to get lots of viral exposure:

✦ Connect your other social media accounts, such as Twitter and LinkedIn, to your Facebook Page to ensure that your posts are getting even better reach and exposure. See Book III, Chapter 4.

✦ Stream a live video on your Facebook Page by using the Livestream application (www.livestream.com). Live activity will create a buzz! See Book VIII, Chapter 3.

✦ Create an event by using the Events feature on your Facebook Page. See Book VI, Chapter 1.

✦ Pull your blog into your Facebook Page by using the Networked Blogs app. When you publish a blog, it automatically gets pulled onto your Facebook Timeline and into the News Feeds of your Likes. See Book III, Chapter 3.

✦ Run a contest on your Page, and offer an enticing giveaway to help spread the buzz. Try the Wildfire or Offerpop app for contest support. See Book VI, Chapter 2.

Reaching a new audience with hashtags

Hashtags in Facebook, which can be seen in Figure 1-15, are similar to hashtags in Twitter: a way for people to find posts about the same topic. Facebook rolled out hashtags, which are especially valuable for trending topics, in June 2013.

Before using a hashtag for your post, search Facebook for other posts using your desired tag to ensure the content posted for that hashtag is relevant and appropriate. Enter # followed by your search term into the search bar at the top of the page (#Marketing, for example) and press Enter/Return. The results will display recent posts that include that hashtag.

After you confirm which hashtag you want, simply include it somewhere in your post. Facebook, like Twitter, will turn the hashtag into a link to that search term.

For instance, if you write a Facebook post about social media, use or add #socialmedia to your post. Then, when someone searches for #socialmedia, your post will show up along with all other posts on the topic that appeared within the past few weeks or so. Unfortunately, there isn't a way to filter the results for the most recent.

Hashtags are expected to increase reach because a publicly shared post would be seen not just by your friends or people who like your page, but by everyone searching for #socialmedia or other specified tag.

Current studies show that hashtags increase reach on Twitter, but not on Facebook; in some cases, they may have a negative effect on Facebook viral exposure. Edgerank, a Facebook analytics company, hypothesizes that this may be left over from hashtags being used in mainly promotional posts.

Figure 1-15: Hashtags make it easy for searchers to find recent, related posts on a particular topic.

Courtesy of Lincoln College.

Hashtags

Watching the future: Autoplay video ads in News Feeds

In December 2013, Facebook cautiously began testing autoplay video ads in News Feeds. The videos begin playing as viewers scroll through the News Feed on their own Pages. Viewers will hear the videos, which are available on desktops or on mobile devices connected to Wi-Fi, only if they tap them. Facebook claims that it has "seen a more than 10% increase in people watching, liking, sharing and commenting on [autoplay] videos."

Initially, Facebook opened this option only to select marketers willing to pay $1–$2.5 million dollars for a 15-second video. Facebook has positioned this premium option to attract big brands with deep pockets that wish to "increase awareness and attention over a short period of time. . . . From launching new products to shifting brand sentiment, this video format is ideal for marketers who are looking to make a large-scale impact," Facebook claims. If past experience is a guide, eventually Facebook will make this option available to smaller advertisers at a more accessible price. Stay tuned!

Autoplay videos too rich for your blood? You can always embed either streaming or archived videos in your own or your friends' Timeline and/or News Feeds. See Chapter 3 of this minibook for more information.

Follow your prospects through third-party retargeting services

Facebook Retargeting with FBX (Facebook Exchange) is a third-party, cookie-based technique that displays ads on Facebook related to a user's web-browsing activity outside of Facebook. Similar to retargeting services available through Google AdWords or other online advertising agencies, Facebook Retargeting reaches only users who have already visited your website.

If someone browses your website without completing a purchase or another desired action, the retargeting service places a *cookie* (a piece of identifying code) on his or her computer. When those visitors then log into Facebook, they may see an ad for your company or product in the right column of their Facebook Page (as in Figure 1-16) or in their News Feed.

Facebook Exchange is currently limited to desktop ads; retargeting ads aren't visible on Facebook's mobile site. Facebook allows marketers to purchase retargeting ads through Custom Audiences in the Facebook Power Editor. For more information about the Power Editor, please see Book VII, Chapter 3.

To use retargeting ads, you must select a Facebook Preferred Marketing Developer like those listed here. Follow the directions on the marketing developer's website.

- ✦ **AdRoll:** www.adroll.com
- ✦ **Quantcast:** www.quantcast.com/advertise/
- ✦ **Perfect Audience:** www.perfectaudience.com
- ✦ **Adobe Social:** http://www.adobe.com/solutions/social-marketing.html

You'll find more options for Facebook Preferred Marketing Developers, who have the capability of placing cookies on other people's websites, at www.facebook-pmdcenter.com/category/fbx.

Prices and ad placement vary depending on which third-party marketing service you choose. However, all these services use a bidding system in which you set the highest price you're willing to pay per click (PPC) or per impression (CPM). If your bid is high enough, your ad will appear on Facebook Pages seen by users who have already visited your website, as shown in Figure 1-16.

Figure 1-16:
Retargeting ads, like this one from Modcloth, look like other Facebook ads. Users may not realize they've been "followed" to Facebook.

Retargeted ad

Courtesy of Watermelon Mountain Web Marketing (WatermelonWeb.com).

Chapter 2: Marketing with Facebook Social Plug-ins

In This Chapter

🖙 Exploiting the value of social plug-ins

🖙 Integrating Facebook with your website or blog

🖙 Using social plug-ins as part of a marketing program

🖙 Integrating third-party plug-ins with your website

People used to search the web solo. Today, users look at what their friends are doing, and they take their friends' activities and recommendations into consideration. Social plug-ins allow you to connect your website with your Facebook presence, which makes it easier for visitors to your site to spread information about your business to their friends.

Facebook offers about a dozen social plug-ins, some of which are very similar. You'll want to use only a few at a time. We discuss each social plug-in separately so you can make an appropriate selection. We also suggest several open-source, third-party, Facebook-friendly plug-ins that seamlessly integrate Facebook with your website. Overall, this chapter can help you decide which social plug-ins are right for your business and how to use them in your overall marketing program.

Understanding Facebook's Social Plug-ins

Social plug-ins connect your website with Facebook users without users having to leave your site. With Facebook social plug-ins, you get the advantage of Facebook while keeping control of your content and brand. Considering the large number of people on Facebook today, social plug-ins can be extremely powerful tools. Plug-ins have many benefits — perhaps one of the most important being their capability to encourage your website visitors to spend more time on your site.

Because Facebook's plug-ins tie into the analytical analysis available at Facebook Insights (see Book IX), you can sometimes get demographic details about your website visitors not easily found elsewhere.

Explaining how plug-ins work

The plug-ins appear as buttons and boxes on websites, and their content comes directly from Facebook activity. If you have a social plug-in on your website, when your visitors are logged in to Facebook, they can interact with their Facebook Friends directly from your website. Specifically, they can share their experiences on your site with their Friends, and they can see their Friends' Facebook activity (such as what their Friends have liked, shared, recommended, and posted) via the plug-in on your website.

Technically speaking, social plug-ins work by placing an iFrame from Facebook on your site. If the iFrame recognizes site visitors who have already logged into Facebook, it will show their personalized content within the plug-in. If visitors haven't logged into Facebook, the plug-ins display your content instead.

Here's an example of how social plug-ins work. Suppose you click a link that you received in an e-mail and land on a website that includes a Like button. If you have already logged into *and* if any of your Facebook Friends clicked that button, you see some of their names or Profile images (depending on how the site owner configured the button). Seeing that your Friends have interacted with the site makes you more likely to explore the site's content and possibly share it with your own social networks. The Like button plug-in lets this activity take place directly on your website rather than going through Facebook, which is exactly what marketers want. Read on to find out why.

Does reading code make you cross-eyed? We recommend leaving the installation of plug-ins to your developer. In most cases, she can integrate plug-ins with your site by inserting just a few lines of HTML provided by Facebook or a third-party source. For more details, point your developer to one of these URLs:

✦ `https://developers.facebook.com/docs/web/gettingstarted`

✦ `https://developers.facebook.com/docs/plugins`

✦ `https://developers.facebook.com/docs/plugins/checklist`

✦ `www.facebook.com/help/203587239679209`

Maximizing the value of Facebook plug-ins

Why do you want to integrate your website with Facebook by using social plug-ins? Easy answer: You gain viral visibility. You increase your exposure when you create more opportunities for users to consume your content on your website or blog. Also, by showing how multiple users are interacting with your content every day (ideally), the plug-ins create social proof and increase the credibility of your content.

The term "social proof" refers to the psychological phenomenon of people being motivated to do things that they see other people doing. Although marketers have used social proof as a fundamental principle for many years, the popularity and growth of social media has strengthened its influence and reach.

Social plug-ins enhance the social proof strategy because they highlight the friends and acquaintances of the people you're directly trying to influence. In many ways, social proof acts as a "foot in the door" strategy because it takes viewers' initial interest and quickly turns that interest into acceptance. The acceptance happens when they see their peers' interactions with the information they are currently consuming. The familiarity builds trust.

Social proof is crucial in creating a successful Facebook marketing plan. The goal is to show your visitors what their peers are talking about, liking, and posting — and in turn, your new visitors will naturally match those behaviors.

The key is to create multiple opportunities for your users to see their Friends interacting with your website. This activity increases traffic to your site and encourages site engagement overall. Social plug-ins aid in this marketing endeavor.

Never underestimate the power of a call to action! It always helps to include text that reminds site visitors to like or share your web page or to leave a comment.

One example of a website that uses social plug-ins successfully is Stay N' Alive (www.staynalive.com). Site owner Jesse Stay has implemented several different social plug-ins: the Like Button with comment and a Recommendations feed (see Figure 2-1). (We discuss all in detail later in this chapter.) The Recommendations feed is optimally placed in the right column of the home page for high-traffic viewing. The Recommendations feed is extremely active since Stay often posts content to his Facebook Page and blog that other people recommend. Those recommendations appear in this feed.

Like buttons with counter

Figure 2-1:
This website
uses two
social
plug-ins.

Drop-down comment box

Recommendations feed

Choosing the Right Facebook Plug-ins for Your Business

You have many options — maybe too many! — when it comes to social plug-ins for your website. We separate options into Facebook's own social plug-ins and open-source plug-ins (from third-party developers, which we discuss later in this chapter). Each Facebook plug-in has a specific function with unique benefits and features. The Login tool isn't a true plug-in, but it works like one, so we include it here.

The most common buttons are at the top of this list. The others may help you achieve particular marketing goals on specific sites.

✦ Like button

✦ Like box

✦ Share button

+ Login tool
+ Recommendations feed
+ Recommendations bar
+ Activity feed
+ Comments
+ Embedded posts
+ Follow button
+ Send button
+ Facepile

You can use just one, or you can combine multiple plug-ins based on your overall marketing goals. For most sites, two or three plugs-ins are plenty. Too many options may confuse your visitors and complicate your analytics. Understanding the function and distinctive features of each plug-in can help you decide which works best for your site.

Increasing site traffic with the Like Button plug-in

The Like Button plug-in allows anyone who's signed in to Facebook to like the content on your web page, such as a blog post, video, or product. If a user who is already logged into Facebook clicks a Like button on your website or blog, a short summary of the content — a *story* — with a link back to the content on your site, posts to the Facebook Timeline of that user's Profile and is also sent out into the News Feeds of all the user's Friends, just as if the user had liked something on your Facebook Page itself.

The Like button is a fast, direct way to share Pages. If you display a Share button next to the Like button, people can add a personal message and customize whom they share with. This feature, which results in great viral visibility, drives traffic back to your site. That's why using the Like Button plug-in in multiple places on your site, such as in the header graphic or on each blog post or product detail page, is a good idea.

The top part of Figure 2-2 shows a Like button below a product on AddaRug. com. The image in the middle shows how the results appear in the user's Recent Activity section after she clicks the Like button. The bottom image shows how the Like recommendation appears on the News Feeds of the original user's Friends.

Users will click here

The result of a user clicking the Like button

Figure 2-2:
The viral value of the Like button shows information flowing from the site (top) to user (middle) to user's Friends (bottom).

The Like looks like this on Esme's Friends' News Feeds

Courtesy of netchannel® (top) and Watermelon Mountain Web Marketing (middle and bottom) (WatermelonWeb.com).

Using the Like Button plug-in with the Comments option

When setting up a Like button, you usually have the option of allowing users to leave a comment after they click the button. Comments can be an extremely powerful marketing strategy, because Facebook weighs the comment with the link to the item more heavily than it would to a link alone, giving the post more prominence.

According to Facebook, people always have the option of adding a comment if you use the XFBML (a specific version of Facebook Markup Language) or HTML5 versions of the Like Button plug-in. With the iFrame version of the Like Button plug-in, people can comment only when you use the standard layout.

Figure 2-3 shows an example of the option to leave a comment after clicking the Like button. The top image shows the home page for SliceParlor.com after the user clicked the Like button and entered her comment (Yummy Pizza!) in the Comments box. The middle image shows the comment on the user's Timeline on her Profile. The bottom image displays the comment within the News Feed of the user's Friends.

Using the Like Button plug-in with the Count option

Along with adding the Like Button plug-in, you can display a Like count next to the button, as seen in Figure 2-3 (top), or you can choose just the button itself.

If you opt for a Like count, the number that appears is the total of the number of Likes, shares, comments, and inbox messages containing your web page URL, whether they were generated from a Like button, a Share button, and/or a Send button.

The purpose of adding a Like count is to generate a bandwagon effect that encourages others to get on board. You may want to wait to display the Like button until your website has ten or more Likes. Waiting to display a Like count doesn't make much sense when you're using that option on multiple items in an online catalog or on individual blog posts.

Using the Like Button plug-in with other options

You also see these options: Show Friends' Faces (which reveals the Profile images of friends who have liked the same content) and Include Share Button (which adds a Share button right next to the Like button).

For more information on the Like Button plug-in, see `https://developers.facebook.com/docs/plugins/like-button`.

Clicking Like reveals this

User's comment in her Timeline

Figure 2-3:
A comment left after clicking the Like button flows to the user's Facebook Timeline and then to the Facebook News Feeds of the user's Friends.

The Like looks like this on Esme's Friends' News Feeds

Courtesy of Adam Moffett Design (top) and Watermelon Mountain Web Marketing
(middle and bottom) (WatermelonWeb.com).

Using plug-ins with Open Graph tags

Facebook uses a special protocol called Open Graph to link information from outside Facebook (from your website, for example) with information on the Facebook platform. Open Graph tags are helpful for monitoring marketing efforts and obtaining detailed information about target audiences.

Figure 2-4 shows an auto-generated post on a user's Timeline that Goodreads created using an Open Graph tag. Except for the ranking and personal comment, the content of the post — including the graphic — was provided by Goodreads. The post appears after a logged-in Facebook user reviews a book on the Goodreads site. This post then appears in the News Feeds of the user's Friends. For more information, point your developer to `http://developers.facebook.com/docs/opengraph`.

Figure 2-4: Open Graph makes it easy to share information on Facebook by generating an attractive, custom post (circled) that appears in News Feeds.

Courtesy of Watermelon Mountain Web Marketing (WatermelonWeb.com).

Using a Like Box plug-in to grow your Facebook base

A Like Box plug-in brings attention to your Facebook Page while visitors are on your website and also allows your users to interact with your Page. A Like box attracts new people to your Page, whereas a Like button promotes individual content on your site itself.

Like button best practices

Use these tips to get better click-through rates (CTR) with the Like button:

✔ Choose the Show Friends' Faces option for the Like button.

✔ Let users add comments.

✔ Add the Send or Share button beside the Like button.

✔ Place the Like button at the top and bottom of articles and near visually appealing content, such as videos and graphics.

Specifically, a Like box allows visitors to like your Facebook Page without ever leaving your website or blog, which is something that marketers see as highly advantageous. Use the Like box if you're conducting a campaign to increase the number of Facebook Likes, who will get future Facebook updates. This makes sense only if you're actively using Facebook as a marketing channel.

In addition to allowing people to like your Page with just one click, a Like box lets you display posts from your Facebook Page, encouraging even greater social interaction on your website. If you decide to use a Like box, we suggest that you activate this option because it gives your visitors the opportunity to be exposed to even more of your content. You also have options to include your Facebook Timeline feed, as well as a "Find us on Facebook" header.

In addition, you can include thumbnail images of people who have already liked your Facebook Page.

If site visitors *have not* logged into Facebook, the faces are random viewers who have previously liked your Facebook page. If website visitors *have* logged into Facebook, the images are of *their Friends* who have previously liked your Facebook page. The best place to put a Like box usually is your home page, but you can place it throughout your site.

As you can see in Figure 2-5, Olo Yogurt Studio's Like box includes both a Facebook post and the thumbnail option.

Using a Like button promotes your site or specific content on it, so traffic flows to your website. It is better for generating leads and sales. A Like box, on the other hand, increases your audience on Facebook. Choose one of these two completely different marketing goals.

In theory, you could use a Like box on your home page and a Like button on individual product pages, but we don't recommend it. Your users aren't likely to understand the difference and probably won't take both actions. To them, "Like" is "Like." You can blame Facebook for using terminology that's too much alike!

The Like box

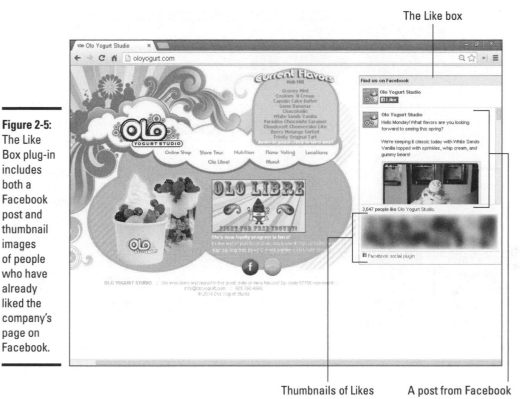

Figure 2-5:
The Like
Box plug-in
includes
both a
Facebook
post and
thumbnail
images
of people
who have
already
liked the
company's
page on
Facebook.

Thumbnails of Likes   A post from Facebook

Courtesy of Olo Yogurt Studio.

TIP

You can adjust the dimensions and number of thumbnail images that show
up in a Like box. That way, you can choose the size that suits your website
design. Generally, the more images that appear, the greater the social proof.

Sharing selectively with the Share Button plug-in

Although you can add a Share button next to your Like button (via the Like
Button plug-in described earlier in this chapter), you can create a separate
Share button using that Facebook plug-in. See Figure 2-6.

Both buttons now allow users to add a message when they click on the button.
However, the Share button lets users specify who will receive the message (on
the users' Timelines, their Friends' Timelines, a group, a page they manage,
or privately). By comparison, the Like button posts the links and optional
messages, on the users' Timelines. This is now visible to everyone who's
allowed to see those Timelines and in their Friends' News Feeds as well. Refer
to Figure 2-3 to see how a message flows from user to user with a Like button.

Figure 2-6:
Facebook recommends using both a Like button and a Share button, as shown on the Cate and Levi website.

Courtesy of Cate and Levi, Inc.

Share button

Like button   Share count

Yes, in theory, you can display both a Like button (with the Share option turned off) and a Share button. However, if you want both functions, we recommend opting for a Like button with the Share option turned on. Otherwise, you risk user confusion and lack of follow-through.

As with Like count (read about that earlier), the Share count option displays the sum of the likes, shares, comments, and stories on Facebook that include your URL, wherever they originally came from.

Finding out more about your visitors with the Login tool

The Facebook Login is ubiquitous. It pops up left, right, and center on an endless stream of websites for good reason. Those site owners hope to capture invaluable demographic information about site visitors that is already stored within their Facebook Profiles.

Basically, the Login tool allows site visitors to sign in to your website via their Facebook accounts. Take a look at Figure 2-7 to see how ModCloth uses this tool on its website. When you install the Facebook Login, you can access all the public Facebook data on your users, such their names, e-mail addresses, interests, Profile pictures, and lists of Friends. This information is valuable to communicate with and market to your Facebook audience.

Installing the Facebook Login tool definitely requires a developer; it isn't for newbies! For more information, point your developer to

✦ https://developers.facebook.com/docs/facebook-login

✦ https://developers.facebook.com/docs/facebook-login/overview

✦ https://developers.facebook.com/docs/facebook-login/checklist

Now you can send these users a private Facebook message or e-mail or post to their Timelines, which in turn will spread the word to their Friends. You can include a link back to your site so they can see new products, receive offers or discounts, enter contests, or participate in focus groups. In other words, the quick, personalized — and supposedly secure — Facebook log-in is easy access to a gold mine's worth of marketing data. (Security these days is in the eye of the beholder. No one can guarantee that data of any type is absolutely secure anymore.)

As a best practice, it's always better to ask permission before posting to the Timeline of someone whose information you have acquired in this way. Visit the FAQ page of ModCloth at www.modcloth.com/help/facebook_faq for an excellent example of how to handle this.

When visitors click the Sign In with Facebook button on your site, they see a notification window asking permission to go forward.

After signing in with Facebook, they are automatically logged into your website whenever they return (as long as they're signed into Facebook as well). If they try to log in to your site and aren't logged into Facebook, they're prompted to log in to Facebook first.

In addition to using the login feature, you can add the Profile images of other users who have clicked the Login button. If the Login with Faces option is activated on your website, visitors initially see only the Login request. After visitors click OK (meaning that they're giving their consent to be logged in to your site via Facebook), their Facebook Profile images appear inside the Login box on your website, along with all their Friends who have also signed in to your website via the Login request. (This group of profiles is also known as a Facepile, which we describe in the following section.)

Sign in with the Login tool   Sign in

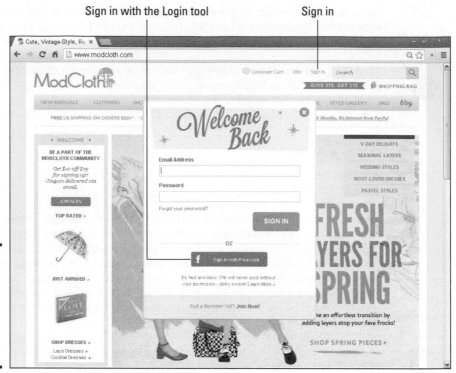

Courtesy of ModCloth, Inc.

Figure 2-7:
ModCloth
uses a
customized
version of
the Log-in
tool.

Using a Recommendations Feed plug-in for social proof

The Recommendations Feed plug-in shows popular content on your website or blog, as well as the number of times that content has been recommended by others.

If someone clicks a Like button attached to an article on your site, that article is considered to be one recommendation. The blog posts, articles, videos, products, or other forms of content that are socially shared the most are listed in the Recommendations feed, though not always in numerical order. (Refer to Figure 2-1 to see this feed in action.)

By acting as an informal crowd-ranking system, Recommendations feeds save new visitors time by spotlighting the most popular content. When a Recommendations feed pulls in content that other users have enjoyed, there's an increased chance that new visitors will interact with your site and, in turn, learn more about your business.

This, of course, leads to a self-fulfilling prophecy: Items at the top of any list always get noticed most. In other words, "Them that has, gets."

Although you can't set a limit on the number of recommendations directly, you can set the width and height of the display, thus limiting the number of recommendations that appear. If you don't have a lot of items or traffic, you may want to skip this option.

Because they summarize what people have found of value in one place, Recommendations feeds make sense for content-heavy sites with many articles, such as news sites or blogs, or e-commerce sites with a large online catalog. Compare this with a Like button, which displays the popularity for an individual item.

Take advantage of a Recommendations feed as a quick (albeit imperfect) guide for content creation. Use Facebook Insights with a Recommendations feed to analyze which articles, products, or posts are the most popular and with whom. You may gain insights about what types of content to add in the future, or which blog authors perform best. As with all forms of marketing, keep doing what works and stop doing what doesn't.

Visitors to your site will see recommendations from anonymous visitors even if they haven't already logged into Facebook. If they are logged in, the content that their Friends have recommended appears at the top of the feed.

Offering smart suggestions with the Recommendations Bar plug-in

A Recommendations bar helps website visitors find items on your website based on what their Friends like and share. As with the Comments option on a Like button, the Recommendations bar publishes a recommended item to a visitor's News Feed and thus also travels to his Friends' News Feeds, giving maximum exposure to your site, products, or articles.

As with a Like counter, low numbers of recommendations on either a Recommendations feed or bar may have an unintended, negative consequence. Visitors may wonder why they should bother viewing anything that few other people think is worth their time.

The Recommendations bar is usually docked to the bottom-right or bottom-left corner of the screen. When a user goes to your website, the Recommendations bar is automatically collapsed, and the user has the option to like your Page. As the user scrolls down your page, the social plug-in actually expands. The expanded view shows users up to five social recommendations of items to view on your site, based on the user's Facebook Friends' activities on your site. See Figure 2-8.

Recommendations Bar plug-in

Figure 2-8:
An
expanded
Recom-
mendations
bar on a
website.

Courtesy of Sound Publishing, Inc.

You can set the number of recommendations that will appear anywhere from 1 to 5. You can also set a limit on the time frame for creation or recommendation of items from 1 to 180 days. As with the Recommendations Feed plug-in, the Recommendations Bar plug-in works best for sites with lots of individual content worthy of ranking.

If you don't have a lot of items, traffic, or Likes, you may want to

✦ Set the number of recommendations low and the number of days high.

✦ Select the Recommendations feed.

✦ Skip recommendations altogether. The Like button may serve this marketing function just fine!

Spotlighting your latest website content with the Activity Feed plug-in

The Activity Feed plug-in allows visitors to see what others rank as the most interesting recent activities that have taken place on any page of your website, even if they aren't logged in to Facebook. It's very similar to the Recommendations Bar plug-in, but it ranks items with the most recent at the top. Visitors can also see the number of times certain content on your website has been recommended by other anonymous visitors.

If a site visitor has logged in to Facebook, he sees only the activity of his Friends. The plug-in gives you the option to include recommendations, meaning that the top half of the Activity Feed box includes activity by the user's Friends, and the bottom half shows recommendations (Likes and shares) from everyone on your site.

We suggest including the recommendations option on your Activity feed. Figure 2-9 shows an Activity Feed plug-in at work.

Activity Feed plug-in

Figure 2-9:
Recent
Activity
box on a
website.

Courtesy of Sound Publishing, Inc.

The Activity Feed plug-in is a great way to guide your visitors to the content that their Friends and peers have already shown interest in. Because people in the same networks tend to enjoy similar content, your new visitors will likely also be interested in the content that their Friends recommended.

You probably wouldn't use the Recommendations Bar and Activity Feed plug-ins at the same time, given that the differences are subtle, and most users won't understand the difference. An Activity feed makes the most sense if you have a large and active base of Likes already. Using a Like button with comments may be more appropriate than an Activity feed for those with fewer than 1,000 Likes.

Optimizing the Comments plug-in

The self-standing Facebook Comments plug-in allows you to add an interactive posting and discussion feature to specific pages on your website. Sometimes this plug-in is used is to allow readers to add comments to a blog site, if your blog doesn't already permit this.

Encouraging your website visitors to leave comments on your site is important because it allows users to share their thoughts and be heard, and also gives them an opportunity to connect with other users of your site. Further, comments act as social proof for your site because the perceived value of your content increases as the number of comments increases.

There is one important difference between the Comment function on the Like Button or Like Box plug-ins and this free-standing Comments plug-in. With this plug-in, users' comments remain visible on website for others to see. Comments made as part of Like button or Like box appear in the user's News Feed but do not remain on the site. You must use the Comments plug-in if you want a trail of comments that provokes ongoing discussion.

With the Facebook Comments plug-in, visitors have a few options: They can leave a comment as their Facebook Profile or as any Page they administer, or they can also choose to have their comments post to their Facebook Timeline (on their Profile or Page, depending whether they posted as their Profile or their Page). When they leave the Post to Facebook check box selected, a story publishes to the News Feeds of their Friends or those who have liked their Page. This option increases the visibility of content on your site, because the story links back to your blog post or website.

What differentiates Facebook Comments from other web- or blog-commenting systems is that the comments are posted on your site as well as on Facebook. This allows Friends and Likes to respond to the discussion by liking or replying to the comment directly in their News Feeds on Facebook or in the comments area of your site.

Comments only post back to users' Facebook pages if they select the Post to Facebook check box within the plug-in.

Also, *threads* (strings of conversations in the comments area) from inside Facebook and from the comments area of your website stay *synchronized,* meaning that no matter where the comment is made for the original content, it always shows up in your Comments box and on Facebook. The conversations are indented, making it easy to identify separate conversations. Also, all the Likes on the comments are synced in both places. The viral exposure from this plug-in is extremely powerful.

The Facebook Comments box also uses social relevance to sequence comments. That means that each user logged in to Facebook sees what Facebook calls "relevant and interesting comments" — comments made by the user's Friends and Friends of Friends, as well as the most liked and active discussions — at the top of the Comments box.

Thus, the comments that Susie would see at the top of a Facebook Comments box would be different from the comments that Sally would see because Susie and Sally have different Friends and connections on Facebook. The experience is personalized for everyone.

You have multiple ways to optimize the comments system on your site:

✦ Enable the Comments plug-in in multiple areas on your website, including specific web pages, articles, photos, and videos. This allows your users to interact with your site in more ways than one.

✦ Respond to your users' comments often and in real time when possible. This allows you to create one-on-one relationships with the visitors to your site.

✦ Encourage users to post comments by asking for their feedback about your article, video, photo, and so on or by asking a question at the end of your post.

If your site doesn't already offer comment functionality, or if you're using a comment system that's getting minimal interaction, consider installing a Comments plug-in. You have great potential for your online exposure to increase as users share their comments on your site.

Embedding Facebook posts on your website

Using the Embedded Posts plug-in on your website is a great way to attract new visitors to your Facebook page, get them to follow or like you, or sign up to attend an event. Site visitors will see the same rich information that appears on Facebook and will be able to follow or like content directly from the embedded image without leaving your website.

First, make sure that the post is public by hovering over the globe icon for the audience selector feature. This will display any attached media as well as the current number of likes, shares, and comments.

You (or your developer) can get the embed code directly from the post itself by clicking the icon in the top right of the post. Choose Embed Post from the drop-down menu, and a dialog box appears with the code to paste into your web page.

Keep the limitations in mind:

✦ You can't customize the size of your post to fit your website layout. What you see on Facebook is what you get.

✦ Long posts will be truncated with a See More option that will display the full post on your site after it's clicked.

If you change or remove an already-embedded post, or change its privacy setting, visitors will see a message on your site that the post is no longer available. That's a real turnoff to users, so be sure to monitor your website often. We recommend keeping track of embedded posts on a spreadsheet. For an example of an embedded post that can appear on a website, look at Figure 2-10.

Attracting a larger audience with the Follow Button plug-in

The Follow Button plug-in allows your website audience to sign up from your website to follow your Facebook Profile and updates. When people subscribe to your Profile with the Follow button, they don't have to become your Facebook Friends to view your public posts. The Follow button effectively increases the reach of your Facebook presence, with very little effort on the user's part.

Figure 2-10: An embedded post on a website.

Because it's not clear how many users understand the difference between liking and following, you might want to stick with only one or the other.

To be clear, there's a Follow button *to your Profile* (discussed in Book II), but this is the Follow Button social plug-in that you add *to your website* to encourage visitors to subscribe to your Facebook Profile. Both elements do the same thing. One is on your Facebook Profile, and the other is on your website.

Comparing a Follow button, a Like box, and Friends

The differences among a Follow button, a Like box, and Friends are subtle but may have implications for your marketing. Using a Like box to like a Facebook page adds it to the list of Likes on a visitor's Timeline. Visitors can unfollow your Facebook Page by hovering over Liked and clearing the Show in News Feed option.

Following a Facebook Page goes a bit further: A visitor will continue to see your public updates in her News Feed without the option of deselecting them. However, if she becomes Friends with you, she can unfollow your posts.

Remember, you should add someone as a Friend only if you know someone personally.

Activating a Follow Button plug-in on your website is strategic marketing. If you're branding yourself, consider activating the Follow button on your Profile as well. We cover this strategy in more detail in Book II.

Sharing super-selectively with the Send Button plug-in

The Send button is very similar to the Like button and may appear next to it on websites and blogs. However, the Send button is used for selective sharing, whereas the Like button has public sharing capabilities.

When a user clicks a Send button next to an article or on a website page, a pop-up window shows a link to the URL of the page the user is viewing, along with a title, an image, and a short description of the link. The user can send the link to specific Facebook Friends, a Facebook group, or a specific e-mail address. The user also has the option to add a personal message.

Optimizing your connections with Facepile

The Facepile feature shows users the Profile images of the Friends of those who have signed in to your website or have liked your Page (refer to Figure 2-5 to see how a Facepile compilation appears on a site). One benefit of this feature is that it doesn't display if the user doesn't have Friends who have signed in to your site.

Don't worry if you don't have a lot of Likes for your site. The Facepile plug-in resizes its height dynamically, so it won't look awkward if only a few Friends are featured in the box.

You have two options for configuring the Facepile plug-in:

✦ **Use the Login tool.** When you include this option (refer to the earlier section), your users can sign in via the Login option; then the faces of their Friends who have already signed in to your site appear in the Facepile box.

✦ **Or not.** If your website has a separate sign-in process not connected to a Facebook Login button, you can install the Facepile box without the Facebook Login tool; then the Facepile box shows those people who sign in to your site via your separate sign-in process.

Following the social proof-appeal strategy, when you have the opportunity to display Friends' faces on your site, do it! People are more likely to look to their Friends for recommendations and suggestions than they are to search independently on the web. Seeing a familiar face on a website can create an instant connection between the visitor, her Friends, and your site. Also, it's easier for your visitors to "know, like, and trust you" when they see that their Friends have already embraced your site.

Comparing Share and Send buttons

Like the Share button, the Send button is Like's companion; you often see the two buttons side by side. The main difference between the Send and Share plug-ins is the private nature of the message. Some users like to customize their messages and choose to whom they're sending a message, whereas others like to share more openly.

The Share plug-in permits posts to the visitors' Timelines and thus may be seen by all their Friends (depending on their privacy settings). Both the Send and Share options allow visitors to add personalized messages to their links.

As we mention earlier in this chapter, the Like count shows the total number of likes, shares, comments, and inbox messages containing a URL that was generated from the Like, Share, or Send button. The three buttons truly work hand in hand to increase your overall exposure through social sharing from those who visit your site.

Warning: At this time, the Send button isn't that widely used. Most users seem content using the more common Share button instead. We don't recommend using Send and Share buttons at the same time. For most marketing purposes, the more people who are exposed to your content (with Share's more visible message), the better.

The Facepile plug-in creates social proof by showing users which of their Facebook Friends have already signed in to a website or liked your Page. Depending on your preferences, you can customize your Facepile box to show just a few Profile images or multiple rows of user images. Figure 2-11 shows the screen for customizing your Facepile display.

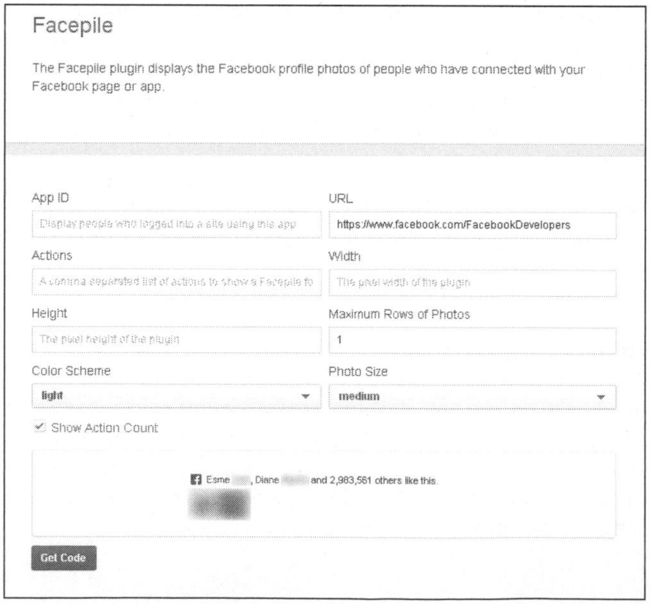

Figure 2-11: You can customize the Facepile display.

The more users your site attracts, the greater the chances that your new visitors will see their Friends' Profile images in your Facepile box. If your site is brand new, you may want to wait a while to build some momentum before you install this plug-in. The plug-in will have greater impact if your users see many of their Friends inside the Facepile box.

Finding and Installing Open Source Facebook Plug-ins

Open source Facebook-friendly plug-ins use Facebook activity but are created by developers outside the Facebook platform. These plug-ins are very similar to the Facebook social plug-ins, but are much easier to install. (No coding!) Open source plug-ins include access to Facebook activity, and some of them also include access to multiple social networks, which can expand your overall online reach. We explore some plug-ins that include multiple social networks in the section "Using Share buttons for multiple social networks," later in this chapter.

If you're considering adding several Facebook-compatible, open source social plug-ins to your website or blog, start with a Like button or Like box and/or a Comment box. You can search the web for something like *third-party Facebook plug-ins* to evaluate your options.

As a refresher, we suggest that you add the Like button to the top or bottom of your home page, and on every blog post or product detail page. This gives your content greater viral visibility and attracts new visitors to your site when it gets posted in the News Feeds of your visitors' Friends.

A Like button or Like box is a great way for a visitor to instantly like your Facebook Page without ever leaving your website. Because the goal is to keep visitors on your site as long as possible, these are extremely useful marketing tools. We also suggest that you choose the option in the Like Box plug-in to show your Facebook Page activity as well. This gives your Facebook content exposure on your website.

Installing a WordPress plug-in

To find Facebook plug-ins on WordPress, please follow the directions in this section. Save yourself the grief, though. This is something that only a developer should try.

1. **Sign into your WordPress account.**

2. **Click the Plugins button in the left pane.**

   You are taken to a page that lists all the plug-ins that you have installed.

3. **Click the Add New button at the top of the page.**

   You are taken to the Install Plugins page.

4. **Enter a search term such as** *Facebook Like*, *Facebook Share*, *Facebook Comments*, **or** *Facebook Recommend* **in the search box.**

   You'll find several plug-in choices with ratings.

5. **Select the plug-in you want to install, and click Install Now underneath the plug-in of your choice.**

   A prompt asks whether you're sure you want to install the plug-in.

6. **Click OK.**

   You're taken to a new page that says your plug-in has installed successfully.

7. **Click Active Plugin.**

   The plug-in is now installed and activated. The plug-in will appear in the list of installed plug-ins.

   All plug-ins have different setting options. To edit your plug-in's settings, go to the bottom of the left navigation pane. The Settings button for your plug-in will either appear in the second tier navigation for Settings, or it will appear directly underneath the Settings button.

Using Share buttons for multiple social networks

Social media Share buttons are great options if you want to combine multiple opportunities for visitors to share your content. These buttons offer your visitors choices about how to share your content with their social networks without ever leaving your site.

 Social sharing buttons link directly to *your visitors' social media sites,* not to your Facebook or other social media page. Always include an icon on your website, like the one in the margin to the left of this paragraph, that links directly to your Facebook Page. Your developer should place this graphic so it will appear on all pages of your website. The developer also should link it directly to your Facebook URL (for example, www.facebook.com/WatermelonWeb).

You have several open source Share Button plug-ins to choose among. Here are two of our favorites:

✦ **Shareaholic:** This company offers a variety of plug-ins that connect your website and blog posts to different social bookmarks and social networks, such as Facebook, Twitter, and LinkedIn. We like the Sexy Bookmarks tool best. With it, your reader can place his cursor on any of the icons to see it pop up on his screen (as you see in Figure 2-12). Then he can click the icon and share your content directly with that social network or bookmarking site.

You can display the number of people who have shared on a specific channel in the upper-right corner for each one.

✦ **DiggDigg from Buffer:** This plug-in provides multiple ways for your visitors to share content from your site or WordPress blog on their social networks. The plug-in has two versions: a static version and one that floats to stay in view as your reader scrolls down the post. You can see this plug-in as it floats to the left of a blog post in Figure 2-13.

Figure 2-12:
The Sexy Bookmarks plug-in shows the shares on each social media channel.

Courtesy of Shareaholic. Get your share buttons at Shareaholic.com.

DiggDigg plug-in   Buffer button

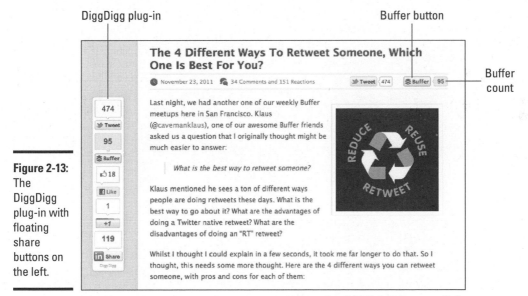

Figure 2-13:
The DiggDigg plug-in with floating share buttons on the left.

Image credit via Social Media Management tool Buffer.

Like Shareaholic, DiggDigg provides social sharing buttons for multiple popular social media channels.

For the general version, visit `https://bufferapp.com/diggdigg`. To access the WordPress option for this plug-in, go to `http://wordpress.org/plugins/digg-digg`.

Chapter 3: Discovering Live Video on Facebook

In This Chapter

✔ Exploring how streaming live video can enhance your business

✔ Choosing a video-streaming application

✔ Setting up a live-streaming application

✔ Marketing your streaming event

Streaming distributes live video of different types of events, from college football games to company announcements. You can use streaming for branding, product introductions, and business seminars, wherever they are. It's also a great way for musicians and all kinds of other artists to connect with their fans. Live video gives you an additional communication platform for your event; adding simultaneous real-time chat boxes can make video events even more interesting.

In this chapter, we first look at what live video can mean to you. Then we discuss some of the most popular live-streaming applications available and show you how to set them up. Finally, we tell you how to use tools to get more exposure for your live events.

Understanding the Benefits of Live Video

Streaming adds a whole new social dimension to any event. Here are the reasons why:

✦ **Audience reactions**: You can see who is participating in the event and gain insight into how well your event is going over with your audience.

✦ **Increased traffic:** The live comments stream drives more traffic to your event or Facebook Page. Viewers post updates to their social networks and bring in more of their friends to watch the event. With a relatively small number of well-connected viewers sharing your content, you don't need to have a huge budget to create a popular event.

✦ **More social engagement:** The most important social addition is the increased engagement you can create for an event because viewers can participate. This is why you want to share your event in the first place, right?

For a glimpse of a social video experience, have a look at Facebook's own official live event Page at `https://live.facebooklive.com`. These live videos are produced by Facebook, not by users.

Attracting viewers with chat

Whether live or archived, videos work best when you use them with chat boxes. Viewer comments naturally encourage others to share their own thoughts.

Combining real-time comments with a live video broadcast also helps grow your audience organically during the event itself. Facebook makes it easy to build a larger, more interactive community around your event by displaying users' chat activity on their friends' News Feeds, which in turn links back to your site.

Some video apps, such as Livestream, have their own chat platform. Or, you can use the Comments plug-in described in Book VIII, Chapter 2.

These real-time chat boxes (also called "live social streams") allow thousands of viewers to interact at the same time. Chat boxes are powerful communication tools when they appear on the Page next to your live video content. Chat boxes may also incorporate Share buttons (see Figure 3-1).

Figure 3-1: Live-streaming video with a chat box and Share button.

Chat box   Share button

Getting closer to customers

Facebook is a social platform — where people come to chat with friends. In this social environment, live streaming is a tool that helps businesses get closer to their audience. With a little planning for both social media and offline promotion, businesses can cultivate interaction, create buzz (see the last section of this chapter), and expand their audience.

Supplementing traditional advertising

Given the size of Facebook and the viral nature of social media, presenting live events through Facebook can give you as much visibility as any traditional media advertising. A live chat box helps you engage a large audience for your real-time video.

You can't always control all aspects of your live-streamed marketing communication. Streaming gives your viewers a platform to share their opinions, exchange ideas with Friends, and read all the comments posted by other viewers. You can't keep other people from speaking their mind in a real-time forum, though you can remove offensive remarks later or set up certain controls before allowing comments from other people to be visible.

For example, you do have some control of what appears in chat boxes if you use the Facebook Comments plug-in or Livestream's chat platform. As an Admin, you can require approval before making comments visible and also blacklist specific words or users. For more information on the Comments plug-in for Facebook, see Chapter 2 of this minibook. For Livestream chat functionality, see http://new.livestream.com/plans.

Choosing Your Streaming Application

You have a few options for streaming video on Facebook, which doesn't offer its own streaming service. In this chapter, we examine two popular applications: Livestream and 22Social. To better understand third-party applications, go to Book V.

✦ **Livestream for Facebook** (http://apps.facebook.com/livestream) supports do-it-yourself video broadcasting and Livestream chat boxes. Livestream offers a free version that links from a Facebook Page tab (as shown in Figure 3-2) to your video hosted on Livestream.com, as shown in Figure 3-3. In most cases, the free version should be all you need to get started. For a modest Basic plan fee of $49 per month, you can get more features. For a hefty monthly fee of $399 for a Premium account, your video will appear directly on your Facebook Page, instead of being hosted by Livestream.

With a free account, events are deleted automatically 30 days after the original broadcast.

✦ **22Social** is an app that offers a variety of Facebook marketing services, including the capability to add a Google Hangouts on Air (it's live video) to your Facebook business Page easily and inexpensively. Other marketing services from 22Social include the simple creation of one-page, custom landing pages, coupons, sweepstakes, surveys, and more, all within Facebook. For more information, see `www.facebook.com/22Social/info`.

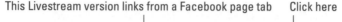

This Livestream version links from a Facebook page tab   Click here

Figure 3-2:
With the free version, users click a tab on a Facebook Page that links to Livestream to watch the video.

Courtesy of Livestream.

Where your hosted video will reside

Figure 3-3:
If you use the free version, viewers actually watch the real-time video on the Livestream site.

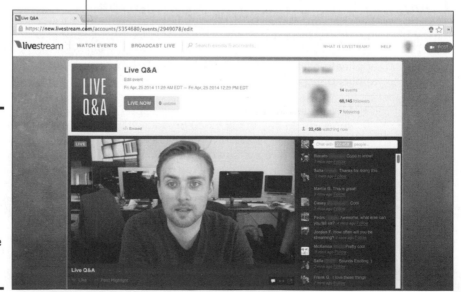

Courtesy of Livestream.

How do you know which application to choose? Your choice depends on what you need to do. See the following minitable.

If Your Business Needs This	*Try This*
To stream live video to your Facebook community (but the video doesn't have to be embedded in your Facebook Page)	Google Hangouts on Air via the 22Social app; free version of Livestream
A robust, professional broadcasting tool and to take full advantage of your Facebook community, without audience size limitations	Paid Livestream application for publishing videos directly on your Facebook Page

Things change rapidly in this field, and other solutions may exist when you read this chapter. Other companies to check out for live video streaming on Facebook are Ustream (`www.ustream.tv`) and Justin.tv (`www.justin.tv`). Look for limited free trials or basic versions with third-party ads; the premium plans may be expensive.

Streaming from Your Facebook Page with the Livestream Application

Are you ready to try a live video event? With Livestream, you can create your own real-time broadcast and have a real-time chat box at the same time.

Livestream doesn't work on your personal Facebook Profile; you must have a Business Page to use this application.

Any public event created with either the free or paid version of Livestream is searchable and promoted on the Livestream.com site.

Depending on your plan, your broadcast will be available by clicking a link via a tab, or directly on your Page.

Creating a Livestream account

For either the free or paid Livestream option to broadcast your own video, you also need a Livestream account. (If you want to broadcast from an existing Livestream account, whether that account is your own or someone else's, you can skip this process.)

To set up a Livestream account, follow these steps:

1. **Go to** `https://secure.livestream.com/myaccount/selectwizard`.

2. **On the screen that asks *What would you like to do?*, click the Broadcast icon.**

3. **At the Livestream Account Center page, enter a name for your channel.**

   Livestream populates the Short Name and Channel Page fields, and instantly lets you know whether the name is available. (If not, choose a new name.) See Figure 3-4.

Figure 3-4:
The
Account
Center
page for
Livestream.

4. **On the same page, click Launch Free Channel or Launch Premium Channel, as shown in Figure 3-5.**

   With the premium channel, you can stream with no advertisements; however, that channel costs $399 per month. If you're okay with ads, choose the free channel.

   You need a Premium or an Enterprise level account from Livestream to embed video on your own page.

5. **Enter your sign-up information.**

6. **Click Sign Up in the bottom-right corner.**

   A Congratulations! screen confirms your sign-up.

Figure 3-5:
The two
channel
launch
options.

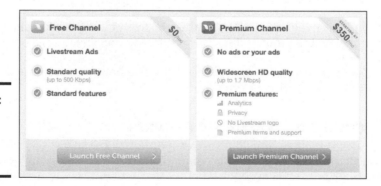

Creating an event in Livestream

Follow these steps to create an event in Livestream:

1. **Go to** www.livestream.com **and click your Profile image in the top right.**

2. **Choose Create Event from the drop-down menu.**

3. **Type your event name in the pop-up window shown in Figure 3-6.**

4. **Click Continue.**

Click here first

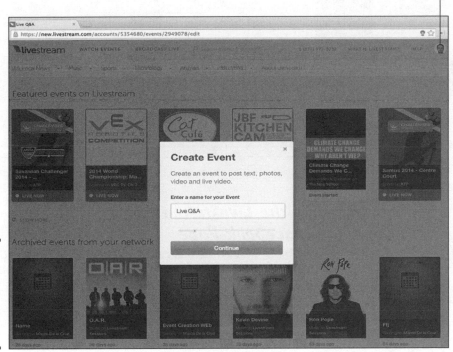

Figure 3-6:
Creating a
Livestream
event and
choosing an
event name.

Courtesy of Livestream.

5. **Choose the event start and end dates and then click Continue.**

6. **(Optional) Upload an onscreen digital poster to advertise your event in JPG, GIF, or PNG format.**

The graphic file can't be any larger than 10MB.

7. **(Optional) Click OK, Let's Go to customize your event.**

You can post text, photos, archived videos, or live videos, or enhance the design, as shown in Figure 3-7. You may want to include your company logo, domain name, and other components to take advantage of this branding opportunity.

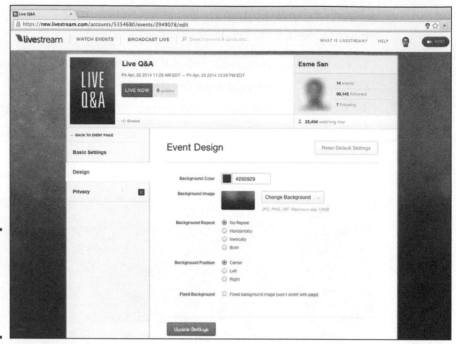

Courtesy of Livestream.

Figure 3-7:
Customizing
the design
of your
Livestream
event.

Installing the Livestream app on your Facebook Page

After you establish a Livestream account and create an event, you're ready to install the Livestream application and add it to a Facebook tab on your Page, as follows:

1. **Log in to your Facebook account.**

2. **Go to** `http://apps.facebook.com/livestream`.

   If you haven't installed the Livestream app, you're prompted to click Connect Facebook to Install.

3. **Livestream requires permission to access your basic information in a permissions box called "Public Profile and Friends List." When you're prompted with permission questions, click OK.**

   For example, Livestream requests to "post to Facebook for you" (shown in Figure 3-8). In the bottom-left corner, you can choose to whom these posts should be visible: Public, Friends of Friends, Friends, Only Me, or Custom.

   For the details of Livestream's Terms and Conditions, visit `www.livestream.com/terms/generalterms`.

Figure 3-8:
The Livestream request to post publicly to your Facebook Page.

4. **Find and click Install for the Page where you intend to use the Livestream application (or click Create New Page).**

   If you already have several Facebook Pages, all are listed below My Pages on Facebook, as shown in Figure 3-9. If you've created only one Page, you see only that Page listed.

   • *If you haven't logged in to Livestream:* Click Login to Livestream on the new screen. When prompted, enter the login credentials you created earlier in this chapter.

   • *If you've logged in to Livestream:* You see the Admin dashboard for your Livestream app. The event we show you how to create earlier in this chapter appears here, along with other events you may have created and other potentially interesting events on Livestream. Click Install next to each event you want to present on a tab, as shown in Figure 3-10.

   Tah-dah! Your event is being promoted on your Page, as Be Inspired Films' video event is promoted on its Facebook Page, as shown at the top of Figure 3-11. The event itself will appear on the Livestream site (see the bottom of Figure 3-11). If you upgrade to a Premium or Enterprise account, your Livestream video will be shown on your Facebook Page itself.

Install button   Create New Page button

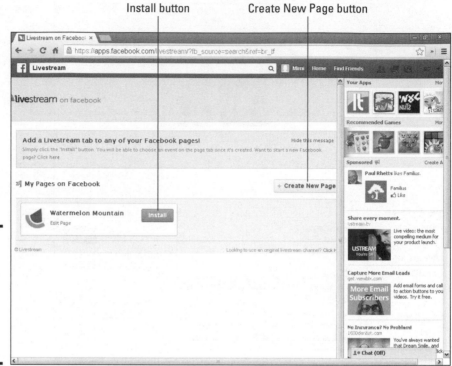

Figure 3-9:
Select the
Page(s)
on which
you wish
to add a
Livestream
tab.

Upcoming events you've created

Click here to present the event on a tab

Figure 3-10:
Select the
event(s)
you want to
display on a
Livestream
tab.

Viewers click this tab

Viewers click this button

Figure 3-11: Clicking the promotional Livestream tab on the company's Facebook Page (top) takes viewers to an event overview (bottom), where they can click the button to watch Be Inspired Films' video.

**Book VIII
Chapter 3**

Discovering Live
Video on Facebook

Streaming with Google Hangouts on Air with 22Social

Hooking up Google Hangouts on Air with the 22Social app is much simpler than it sounds! Google Hangouts lets users stream video in real time. 22Social lets you embed that streaming video on your Facebook page. *Voilà!* Free live video.

You must have a Google+ account (`http://plus.google.com`).

Creating a Google Hangout on Air

We recommend creating your Hangout on Air before installing the 22Social app. That way, you will have the embed code ready to paste in.

1. **Go to** `https://plus.google.com/hangouts` **to create your Hangout on Air.**

2. **Click the Schedule a Hangout on Air button in the top-right corner.**

3. **Give your Hangout on Air a name and description, decide when to start to stream, and choose the audience.**

For the video stream to appear on your Facebook Page without any problems, leave the audience default to Public. That way, Google+ followers who have you in their circles will be able to view the stream as well. Viewers can see any public Hangout on Air on YouTube.

4. **Click the Share button in the bottom left.**

Your YouTube account must be connected.

You are redirected to your Google Hangout on Air Event page.

5. **Get the code to embed your Hangout on your Facebook Page.**

You need this bit of code to insert on the tab that you will create in the next section using the 22Social app.

a. *Find the Details portion of the event page (on the right side of the page).*

b. *Click the Links button.*

c. *Copy the Video Embed code as shown in Figure 3-12 using Ctrl+C as usual.*

For now, keep that code in a safe place by pasting it into a file on your hard drive or on a stick drive.

Installing the 22Social app on your Page

After you have the Google Hangout ready, install the 22Social app on your business Page. Follow these simple steps:

1. **Go to** `http://facebook.com/22social`.

2. **Click the tab below the Cover photo that reads "INSTALL. Get 22s Now."**

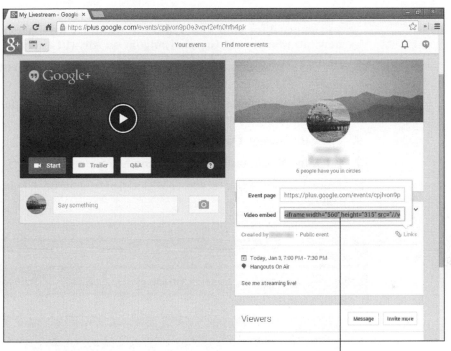

Figure 3-12:
Retrieve and save the embed code from Google +. You will need to place it on your 22Social tab in order to display your Google Hangout on Air on Facebook.

Video embed code

Courtesy of Watermelon Mountain Web Marketing (WatermelonWeb.com).

3. **Click Like to unlock the app.**

   The page reloads with a video about the 22Social product and what it can do for your business.

4. **Click the Install for Free banner below the video.** (You may first have to grant the app permission to access your Facebook information.)

   A new page offers a Pro version, which you can try for 30 days for $2. If you don't want the Pro version, navigate to 22s.com/account, which will then direct you to the 22s dashboard for Facebook. Otherwise, you will be required to sign up for the Pro version.

5. **On the dashboard, click on the green Install Another App button in the top-right corner. You may be prompted to give 22s permission to manage your Pages. Click OK to proceed.**

   The free version is all you need for adding a Google Hangout to Facebook. The Pro version offers many other marketing tools that your small businesses may find useful, but which are not needed for live video streaming.

6. **You will be taken to the 22s Setup Wizard. From the drop-down menu, choose which Page on which to install your Google Hangout, and click Create App.**

7. **Click the orange pencil button to the left of the Facebook Page that you selected for your video tab. You will then see a preview of the new tab where your Google Hangout on Air will appear.**

8. **On the next screen, customize your Page's layout, content, and style on the 22s dashboard.**

   You may want to use a show gate that requires users to like your page before they can view the content on the new tab.

9. **Click the orange Content button.**

10. **Click the Media button beneath the header.**

    A pop-up allows you to add your Google Hangout on Air, as shown in Figure 3-13.

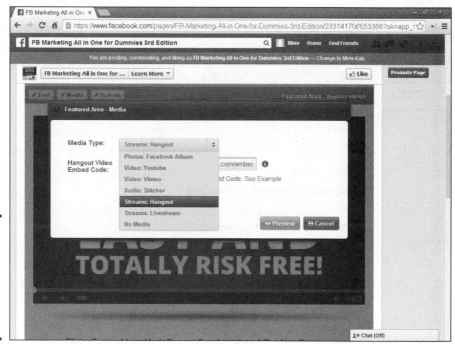

Figure 3-13: Adding your Google Hangout on Air to your 22Social tab.

Courtesy of Watermelon Mountain Web Marketing (WatermelonWeb.com).

11. **Select Streams: Hangout from the Media drop-down menu.**

12. **Enter the Hangout Embed Video Code that you saved in Step 5 into the field below the Media Type drop-down menu.**

13. **Click the green Preview button in the bottom right of the pop-up.**

    The pop-up disappears.

14. **Click the green Save button on your new page/tab.**

Congratulations! You've added your Google Hangout on Air to your Facebook Page. When it's installed, the hangout will be ready to view by clicking the standard play triangle, as shown in Figure 3-14.

Figure 3-14: A Google Hangout on Air ready to play on a Facebook Page using the 22Social app.

Courtesy of Mari Smith International.

Creating Buzz about Your Live Video

After you have your live stream up and ready to run, you want to get people interested in your live-streaming event both in advance *and* during the event. This is where your Facebook marketing skills come into play.

Posting to your Facebook Page in advance

Before your live-streaming event, remember to post an update on your Facebook Page to let your audience know what's coming:

+ Tell them about your live-streaming event.
+ Tell them why they'll find it interesting.
+ Tell them how they'll be able to participate.
+ Ask them to tell their Friends.

You can also create a Facebook event and promote your upcoming event there. To read more about Facebook Events, go to Book VI, Chapter 1.

22Social lets you share the tab featuring your Google Hangout on Air. The Share buttons are at the top of the tab.

Sharing during your event

While your event is going on, be sure to let the audience on your Facebook Page know what's happening live, and give them the link. Different streaming options have different sharing methods.

For instance, Livestream makes it easy for viewers to share your event, by clicking on the Social Sharing option, as shown in Figure 3-15.

During your event, viewers can post comments in the Livestream chat box, which they can then share with their own Friends on Facebook, as we discuss earlier in this chapter.

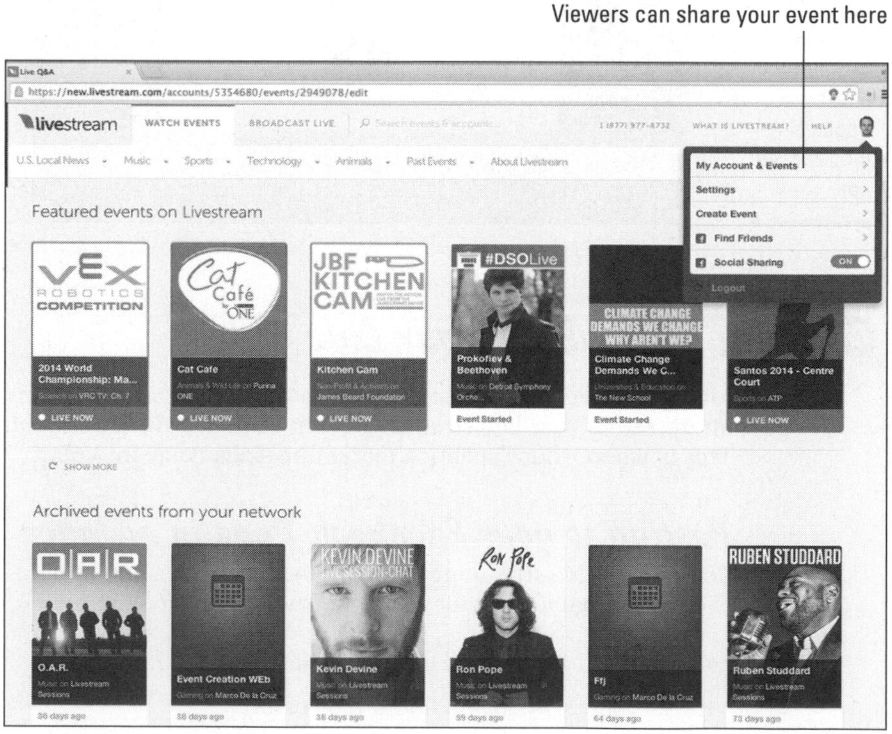

Viewers can share your event here

Figure 3-15: Viewers can use social sharing.

Courtesy of Livestream.

By comparison, if you're using 22Social, the Facebook Comments plug-in is included automatically. For comments to appear on a user's Timeline, the user must select the Post to Facebook check box before creating a comment. Figure 3-16 shows how comments look when using 22Social.

Figure 3-16: A comment posted in response to a Google Hangout on Air with 22Social may also appear on a user's personal Profile or Page.

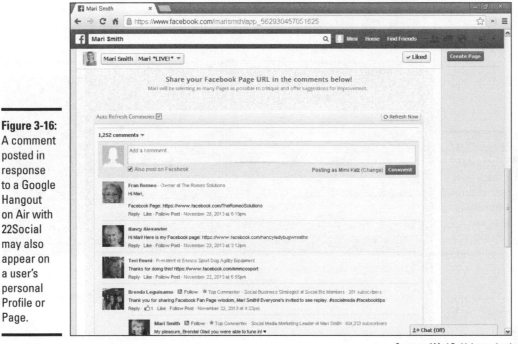

Courtesy of Mari Smith International.

Comments from your viewers give your event extra coverage, and more people are likely to come to see the event while it's going on.

Sharing viewer comments with other social media

It's easy for viewers to share their comments and your event on multiple social media.

Livestream users can quickly share an event via their Share button to Facebook, Twitter, Tumblr, Google+, or e-mail, as shown in Figure 3-17. Depending on the social network, users can personalize a comment or tweet with a link back to the event.

A similar process applies to users who want to share a real-time video event from the 22Social app.

You want to encourage your audience members to use these social buttons often to get the viral exposure necessary to draw a crowd to your video.

Figure 3-17: Users can share your event on multiple social media.

Methods of social sharing

Calls to action are extremely important during a live-streaming event. Remember, the link generated when people use these social buttons sends people back to the live-stream chat box, bringing in more viewers and facilitating even more interaction around your event.

Partnering with other events and organizers

One cool thing about live streaming is that you don't actually need to have your own live-streaming video to chat about it. You can create a live-stream chat to talk about someone else's video content, if you want.

Look for interesting upcoming live-streaming videos on the Livestream new event listings at `http://new.livestream.com/home`. Check out these events to find content that your audience would love to see.

If you create your own videos, find people who have audiences that are interested in your content, and partner with those people. Your video broadcasts will reach wider audiences, and you'll build an interactive community experience around your event.

Keeping Facebook users interested in the stream

As with creating other experiences on Facebook, you'll benefit from a communication plan to promote your live-streaming event. Here are a few key tips to help you maximize your live-streaming experience:

✔ Let people know about your live-streaming event before, during, and after the event.

✔ Reach out to people in different ways and on different communication platforms.

✔ Share the link to your live-streaming event on Facebook, Twitter, and LinkedIn, as well as on your website and blog. Also, e-mail your prospects and clients, and invite them to your live broadcast.

✔ Use a positive, conversational tone in your updates.

As you look for opportunities to bring content publishers and communities together, remember the opportunities that mobile devices offer. It's easy to access Facebook on all mobile devices, and it's also easy to record videos on many of those devices. With so many possibilities, you're sure to see more live-streaming events.

Interested in sharing a non-streaming video? You can always embed a video from YouTube, Vine (`https://vine.co`), or Instagram.

Chapter 4: Using Facebook for Mobile Marketing

In This Chapter

✓ **Understanding the need for mobile visibility**

✓ **Investigating Facebook's mobile presence by the numbers**

✓ **Optimizing posts for Facebook's mobile News Feed**

✓ **Getting your Facebook presence found by mobile searchers**

✓ **Using Facebook mobile ads to draw new customers**

✓ **Measuring your results**

As mobile platforms — tablets and smartphones — become the devices of choice for millions of users, marketers have no choice but to take notice. Among various mobile properties, Facebook now has high visibility for both its mobile applications and its advertising, in spite of its well-publicized early stumbles.

In this chapter, we look at the importance of expanding your Facebook presence into the mobile environment and how that may affect your posting and search strategies, as well as your advertising tactics. We pay particular attention to the value of using Facebook for mobile advertising in a highly competitive environment. In addition to providing directions for implementing your mobile ad campaigns, we look at how to measure the results of your efforts.

Understanding the Rapid Growth of the Mobile World

There is no question that mobile devices — including tablets, smartphones, and cellphones — are becoming more popular than desktop computers. In many parts of the world, there are now more mobile devices than people. Facebook, like many other Internet companies, has profited from this rapid growth in mobile adoption. Figure 4-1 indicates this rate of growth.

Mobile users are particularly active, as shown in Figure 4-2, with lots of smartphone users searching for local information, comparing products, and making purchases.

Regardless of whether you're a Facebook fanatic, as a marketer you can't ignore the mobile environment for your company's website and social media. You need a presence where your prospects and customers are.

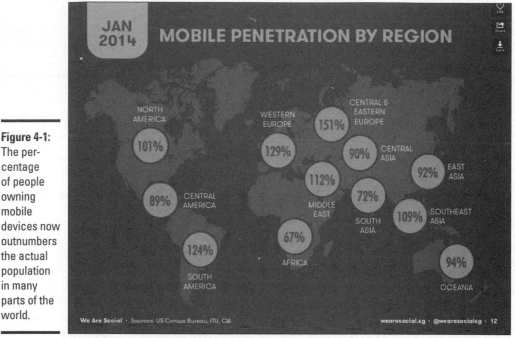

Figure 4-1: The percentage of people owning mobile devices now outnumbers the actual population in many parts of the world.

Courtesy of We Are Social.

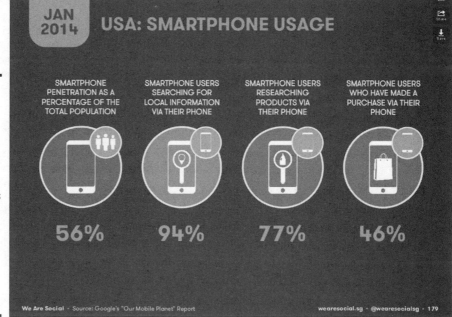

Figure 4-2: High percentages of smartphone owners in the United States use their phones to find information, research products, and make purchases on the go.

Courtesy of We Are Social.

Getting a handle on Facebook's mobile presence

Facebook has almost tied Google properties as the popular mobile destination for smartphone users (see the following figure). By the end of 2013, Facebook reported that 945 million users accessed Facebook each month through a mobile device, with nearly half using only their mobile interface.

Not too surprisingly, as mobile usage has gone up, so have Facebook's revenues from mobile

ads. In the fourth quarter of 2013, Facebook reported that its mobile advertising accounted for 53 percent of its revenue (shown in the following figure).

Facebook also increased its share of the $16.7 million global mobile advertising market to 18 percent, second only to Google's 53 percent share. The following chart compares U.S. mobile ad revenues for multiple publishers.

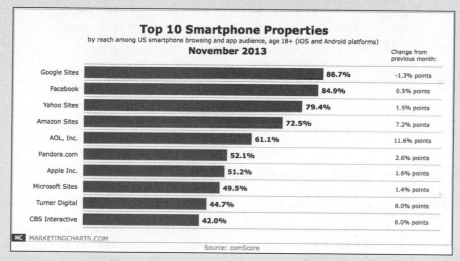

Courtesy of comScore Mobile Matrix.

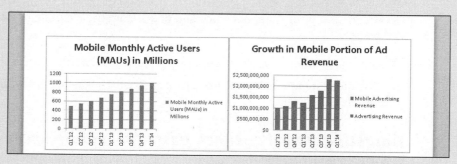

Courtesy of Facebook.

(continued)

(continued)

US Net Mobile Ad Revenues, by Company, 2011-2015 *millions*					
	2011	**2012**	**2013**	**2014**	**2015**
Google	$750.0	$2,171.4	$3,984.4	$6,327.5	$9,293.5
Facebook	-	$390.9	$964.9	$1,510.1	$1,863.0
Pandora	$120.0	$233.2	$372.1	$550.4	$748.6
Twitter	-	$134.9	$266.0	$450.3	$626.7
Apple (iAd)	$38.3	$123.8	$212.9	$376.0	$622.8
Millennial Media	$36.1	$61.3	$94.4	$139.4	$192.2
Other	$533.3	$996.7	$1,395.0	$1,980.3	$2,827.6
Total	**$1,477.6**	**$4,112.3**	**$7,289.6**	**$11,334.0**	**$16,174.4**

Note: includes display (banners and other, rich media and video), search and messaging-based advertising; ad spending on tablets is included; net revenues excluding traffic acquisition cost (TAC); numbers may not add up to total due to rounding
Source: company reports, 2012 & 2013; eMarketer, March 2013

154734   www.eMarketer.com

Courtesy of eMarketer, Inc.

Optimizing Your Facebook Presence for Users on the Move

Assuming that all these facts and figures have convinced you to pay attention to marketing in the mobile environment, what do you need to do? First, optimize your Facebook presence for mobile consumers with a few simple steps.

Users can view your Facebook Page and posts from their mobile devices in two ways:

✦ Using a browser on their smartphone or tablet to reach m.facebook.com

✦ Downloading and using the Facebook app, which is available for all mobile platforms

Adjusting your Facebook posts for mobile users

In any mobile environment, your posts look different from how they appear on a desktop. Photos will be downsized, and long posts may be truncated to fit. The appearance of posts also differs between m.facebook.com and the Facebook app.

The left image in Figure 4-3 (left) shows a News Feed on m.facebook.com (browser version), while the right one shows how a News Feed post appears to someone using the Facebook app.

Pinning special offers or content from your desktop ensures that customers who come to your page on a mobile device will see key information right away. Scrolling is time-consuming on a small screen.

Figure 4-3:
A News Feed post on Facebook's mobile browser site (left) and a News Feed post on the Facebook mobile app (right).

 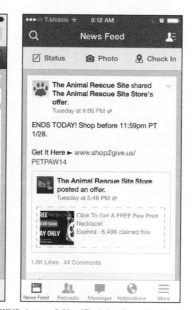

Image provided by WildApricot.com (left) and The Animal Rescue Site (right).

Because of the limited real estate on mobile devices, pin an engaging, visually appealing post or special offer to the top of your Timeline.

Here's how:

1. **Log in to your Facebook account with a desktop computer.**

   The News Feed is the first page you see when you log in.

2. **Under Pages in the left column, click your business Page.**

3. **On your business Page, decide which post you want to pin.**

4. **Hover over the upper-right corner of the desired post, and click the arrow.**

   A drop-down menu opens.

5. **Click Pin to Top, as shown in the left of Figure 4-4.**

   Your page on your mobile site should now refresh with the post you pinned at the top; the pin is indicated by a little ribbon in the upper-right corner of the post, as shown in a mobile display on Figure 4-4 (right side).

Take pity on your mobile users! Less is more when it comes to mobile posts. Keep posts concise and to the point, leaving out unnecessary details. Use graphics when possible — small files, please! — to make your pinned post more visually appealing.

Click here   Indicates pinned post

Figure 4-4:
To enable mobile users to see your post without scrolling, pin your desired marketing post to the top of your Timeline.

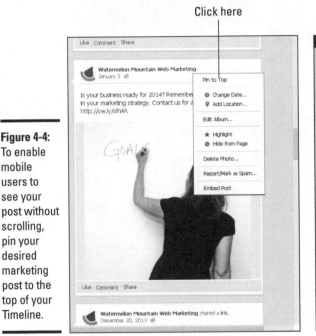

Images courtesy of HubSpot, 2013.

Pinning special offers or content ensures that customers who come to your Page on a mobile device will see key information right away. Scrolling is time-consuming on a small screen.

Adjusting your Facebook Page for mobile madness

The News Feed isn't all that changes. Other parts of your Facebook Page will look different to mobile users, too, depending on whether they use the Facebook app or come in through their mobile browser.

If you don't already have it, download the free Facebook app from `facebook.com/mobile`.

To adjust your Page from the Mobile Browser:

1. **Log in by going to** m.facebook.com.

2. **Log in to the personal account that serves as the admin for your Page with your usual e-mail address and password.**

3. **Tap the three-bar button (sometimes labeled More) in the top-left corner of your screen, as shown in Figure 4-5 (left).**

4. **Under Pages, select the Page you wish to view or edit.**

5. **You will be taken to the Page tab, where you can preview or edit your Page.**

6. **You can also choose the Activity tab (which shows user engagement) or the Insights tab (which shows basic stats for the past 7 days).**

To adjust your Page from the app:

1. **Tap the icon for the app on your mobile device.**

2. **Enter your e-mail and password.**

3. **Click the three-bar More icon located at the bottom-right corner of the screen, as shown in Figure 4-5 (right).**

4. **Under Pages, select the Page you wish to view or edit.**

5. **You will be taken to the Page tab, where you can preview or edit your Page.**

6. **You can also choose the Activity tab (which shows user engagement) or the Insights tab (which shows basic stats for the past 7 days).**

When you preview your page, you *may* see a map of the business location, contact information, reviews and ratings, check-ins, and/or Likes based on the activity of your Friends.

When you first created your Page, you selected a page type such as Local Business or Place, or Company, Organization, or Institution. The details you will see in the mobile preview depend on the type of page you created. For example, there won't be a map for an artist, band, or public figure.

Constant Contact's blog (http://blogs.constantcontact.com/product-blogs/social-media-marketing/facebook-mobile-tips) recommends tagging pictures with your business address as well as encouraging customers to upload photos while they're checked in. The blog is full of other good tips.

**Book VIII
Chapter 4**

Using Facebook for Mobile Marketing

More button

Figure 4-5:
After you
have logged
in, select
the More
function
to make
adjustments
to your
Page.

More button

Check out your Facebook Page on a mobile phone and on a tablet often. How can you improve it?

Getting your Facebook Page found in a mobile search

You're hungry. What's good? Look online. In fact, lots of people use Facebook to find local businesses online. These tips will help:

✦ Keep your contact information up to date, including your business name, address, map location, and operating hours.

✦ Users can tap to call on a mobile phone, so display your phone number prominently.

✦ Choose a category; that's often how users search.

✦ Use a call to action to remind viewers to check in when they visit your Facebook mobile Page.

To make your mobile life as a page admin a little simpler, download the free Page Manager app from the iTunes Store or Google Play Store. With the app, you can review page activity or check mobile analytics directly from your own mobile device.

Using Facebook Nearby

Many mobile Facebook aficionados prefer to use Places Nearby (Facebook's own app for mobile search), as shown in Figure 4-6 (left). Users not only can search for your business name or category, but also see what's around them on a map. Unlike a more neutral search on Google or Yahoo!, Facebook organizes search results by the actions taken by a user's Friends, including ratings, reviews, personal preferences, and check-ins.

When users tap on a business name, they are taken to the business Page, as shown in Figure 4-6 (right).

Figure 4-6: Places Nearby lets people search for businesses near where they are (left); when they click a result, they see that business's Page (right).

Both images courtesy of VentureBeat.

To get to Places Nearby on the app, tap the More button in the bottom-right corner of the screen. Under Favorites, select Nearby. In the browser version, tap the three-bar (More) button in the top-left corner of the screen. Under Favorites, select Nearby Places.

Because the results in Places Nearby may not be the closest by distance as they are in other mobile search engines, you can leapfrog your competitors by having more Facebook user engagement than they do. Encourage visitors to check in on Facebook whenever they're in your store. Use calls to action on the Page itself, on signs, or even considering offering an incentive to check-in. Free cookie, anyone?

It's worth paying attention to your search presence. With your smartphone, you can use major search engines and Facebook Places Nearby to regularly look for your business.

Taking Advantage of Facebook Mobile Ads

Facebook has come a long way, baby, from the early days of scorn for its mobile offerings. As we discuss earlier in this chapter, its mobile site is second only to Google as a mobile destination, and its mobile revenues are growing apace.

From a marketing perspective, it's hard to beat the numbers for Facebook mobile advertising, as shown in Figure 4-7. Facebook mobile ads have a higher click-through rate (CTR) and lower cost per click (CPC) than Facebook Ads on desktops. If you're trying to reach an audience using Facebook, it's important to factor the mobile option into your marketing mix.

Use your precious advertising dollars only in environments that your target market uses. For instance, you might not want to bother with Facebook mobile ads if you're targeting teens, whose attention has shifted to other platforms. As always, keep close tabs on the demographic and interest profiles of your users. You can take advantage of the Facebook and third-party analytics tools described in later in this chapter and in Book IX, Chapters 2 and 3.

Displaying Facebook Ads in mobile News Feeds

Facebook mobile ads appear only in users' News Feeds, unlike desktop ads, which also appear in the right column. As a result, Facebook mobile ads have less competition than in the traditional desktop format, and your ads always gets prime real estate when they do appear. Hence, their better performance.

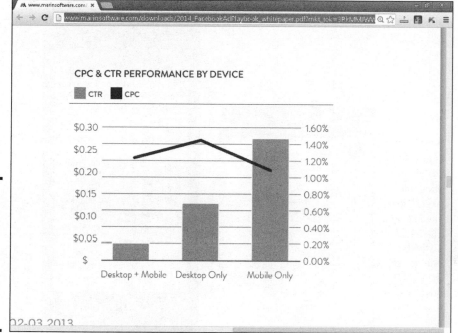

Courtesy of Marin Software.

Figure 4-7:
Facebook's
mobile ads
perform
better than
Facebook
desktop ads
and at a
lower CPC.

Optimize your Promoted Posts and Page Post Ads for mobile users as well.

You can configure all types of ads to display in a mobile environment. You can use standard product ads, event ads, offers, or even ads to promote Likes or Page views. Ads can also promote downloads of a proprietary custom app. For example, a custom app might allow mobile users to order a pizza for pick-up from a specific business right from their smartphones. The left image in Figure 4-8 shows a typical mobile product ad in context, and the right side of Figure 4-8 shows an ad that drives users to install a custom app.

Because apps can be expensive to program and maintain under multiple operating systems, custom apps aren't recommended for most small- to medium-size businesses. Franchise operations are one exception, however. But, all a franchiser may need to do is advertise a custom app developed by the parent company.

**Book VIII
Chapter 4**

Using Facebook for Mobile Marketing

Figure 4-8:
Mobile ads appear in users' News Feeds only. The left is a standard product ad; the right drives users to a custom app.

Displaying Facebook Offers, Likes, and more in mobile News Feeds

Similar to Facebook Offers on a desktop, Offers ads show up in users' mobile News Feeds. Basically, they perform as a coupon that users can claim right from their smartphones or enter as a promo code when buying from your online store. Figure 4-9 on the left shows an offer for Coastal.com within the context of a News Feed on the Facebook app.

Mobile ads aimed to getting viewers to like a page are designed to increase your Like count. As with the equivalent ads on the desktop, these ads have a built-in Like button for one-click action right from the user's mobile feed. A typical Like ad appears in Figure 4-9 on the right side.

Mobile users account for one in three new Page Likes! Don't be shy about asking for a Like.

Similar to Page Post ads on the Facebook desktop, these ads appear can be created as links, photos, text, or video posts, depending on your marketing goals.

Generally, photo, text, or video posts are used to create brand awareness, and Like ads are used to get website *conversions* (sales or leads).

Figure 4-9:
Offers and
Like ads
can appear
in mobile
News
Feeds.

A call to action   Like button in a Newsfeed

Setting up a mobile ad campaign in Facebook

To make it easier to track results, set up a new, separate campaign for your mobile advertising. At the very least, create separate ads for mobile use within your existing campaign.

You create mobile ads in the Ads Create tool the same way you create desktop ads.

1. **Navigate to the Texts and Links sections in the Ads Create tool.**

2. **In the right panel, click the Add button on the Mobile row to display your ad in mobile environments.**

3. **Add the Desktop News Feed and Right Column if you want your ad to appear in either of those places as well; otherwise, leave them off or click Remove. (See Figure 4-10.)**

Review Book VII, Chapter 2, to learn more about creating a mobile ad using the Ads Create tool.

You can also create a mobile ad using the Power Editor (see Book VII, Chapter 3), following a similar process.

Continue through the ad creation process. As with other types of ads, you can select CPC or CPM bidding, or bid by objective within the Bidding and Pricing section of the Ads Create tool.

As of this writing, Facebook mobile ads are cheaper than their desktop counterparts.

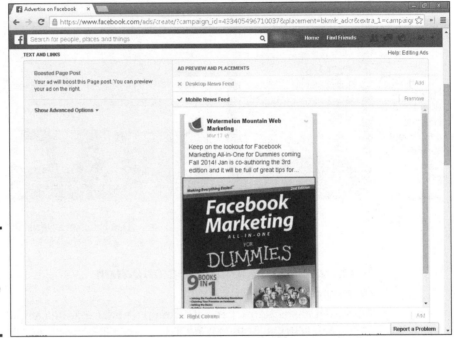

Figure 4-10: Designate the Mobile option in the Ads Create tool.

Courtesy of Watermelon Mountain Web Marketing (WatermelonWeb.com).

Karaoke Heroes sings the praises of mobile ads

Superhero-themed Karaoke Heroes is a one-of-a-kind bar! The only karaoke bar in Connecticut, and the only place with Asian-style, private-room karaoke, Karaoke Heroes draws customers from all over the state as well as Rhode Island and Western Massachusetts.

Facebook became a marketing channel of choice early on. (The Karaoke Heroes Facebook Page appears in the following figure.) According to co-owner Carly Lebwohl, the company started using Facebook Ads as a marketing trial before it even opened in August 2012. "After the trial was successful, we opened the bar." She likes Facebook because it lets her target ads very precisely, it's very user-friendly, and it's easy to see what works with Facebook's web analytics.

Courtesy of Carly & Andy Lebwohl.

"Because there's no minimum spend," she notes, "it's great for a small start-up." Initially, the company just wanted Page Likes, which it hoped would translate into people coming through the door. Now it also uses ads to drive traffic to events and uses both mobile and regular ads.

"We've tried every type of ad Facebook offers," Lebwohl laughs. "We're big on trial and error!" She explains that the ads have become more sophisticated over time. "We use more eye-catching and tailored images and catchy phrases. We've also started targeting more specifically since we've gotten to know our customers better."

Lebwohl tries to sort ad placement by objective, using desktop and mobile ads for branding (see the following figure) and for events. She's found a very high click-through rate (CTR) on mobile ads as well as on promoted posts and sponsored stories. Whenever Karaoke Heroes promotes an event, it uses the Facebook Events link (see the following figure) as a method to RSVP or provide more information to users.

"We developed over 5,000 Facebook Likes in our first year, so our promoted posts are very successful at reaching a big audience," she says. And since its audience is actively interested in Karaoke Heroes content, using promoted posts that appear in fans' News Feeds has been a very productive tactic.

To promote its Facebook presence, the company uses small social media icons (sometimes called chiclets) on its website, www. karaokeheroes.net. Karaoke Heroes has followed the first principle of marketing: Keep doing what works. It does not use any other mobile advertising.

(continued)

(continued)

Lebwohl estimates that she spends 8 hours per week creating ads and content, and an hour per week analyzing results. She has simple advice for other businesses. "Trial and error is the number-one way to figure out what works and what doesn't, and you don't need to spend a lot of money to figure [it] out. You can ramp up the spending once you see where your highest yield is."

Courtesy of Carly & Andy Lebwohl.

Measuring Your Mobile Success

As with any advertising campaign, it's important to measure how well your mobile Facebook Page and mobile ads are doing. You can use Google Analytics to view mobile traffic and conversions on your website, and the Facebook's Ads Manager to measure ad results.

Facebook Insights (discussed in Book IX, Chapter 2) doesn't differentiate traffic from desktop users versus mobile devices. However, you can see whether visitors to your website have arrived as a referral from a Facebook mobile or Facebook desktop source. You must have Google Analytics installed on your website for this to work. Google Analytics is particularly helpful for comparing traffic and conversion results from Facebook to results from other social media or Google AdWords mobile ads.

For more on Google Analytics, check out *Social Media Marketing All-in-One For Dummies* by Jan Zimmerman and Deborah Ng (John Wiley & Sons, Inc.).

Using Google Analytics to track mobile traffic

After you have Google Analytics set up on your website, it takes a few steps to see which platforms best deliver referrals to your site: desktop, mobile, or tablet. For more on using Google Analytics, see Book IX, Chapter 3.

1. **Log in to Google Analytics.**

When you log in, you should automatically be on the Reporting Page. If not, select the tab on the top, as shown in Figure 4-11.

2. **From the Audience section in the left column, choose Mobile⇨Overview.**

3. **The Mobile Overview report opens.**

Reporting tab

Figure 4-11: Use Google Analytics to see which mobile devices deliver Facebook traffic.

Display exact matches for Facebook Advanced Filter

Secondary Dimensions drop-down menu

Navigate to the Mobile Overview report

4. **From the Secondary Dimension drop-down list located below the graph, select Social and then Social Networks.**

5. **To view only Facebook results, use the Advanced Filter option located to the right of the Secondary Dimension field. Choose to display exact matches for the social network Facebook, as shown in Figure 4-11.**

Using Facebook's Ads Manager to measure ad results

For statistics on paid mobile ads, use the Facebook Ads Manager the same way you measure your desktop ad results. For more information, see Book VII, Chapter 4. This is easier than Analytics if you need to view only Facebook mobile results independent of other ad sources.

Either set up a separate campaign for mobile ads, or label your mobile ads with the word *mobile* in the title so you can easily distinguish them.

To see mobile ad results, simply follow these steps:

1. **Log in and go to the Ads Manager (**www/facebook.com/ads/manage**).**

   You're automatically taken to the All Campaigns View.

2. **Click the Ads tab in the main pane.**

3. **Click the View Report button to see the results for each ad by placement.**

Figure 4-12 shows a report in Ads Manager that distinguishes between ads that appeared on desktops versus ads that appeared on mobile devices. You can quickly compare the Reach, Frequency, and Impressions for mobile versus desktop ads to see which platform performs better.

Exporting the data into a spreadsheet and generating a graph may help. No matter what the overall published statistics say, the statistics that matter are the ones for your own business.

There's a sneaky way to measure the results of Offers or Page Promotion posts in Facebook Insights; see Book IX, Chapter 2. If you create an Offer or Page Promotion post using the Power Editor, promote that offer or post only on mobile devices. Under the Posts tab, Facebook Insights will then display how much of the reach for that particular past was paid and how much was organic.

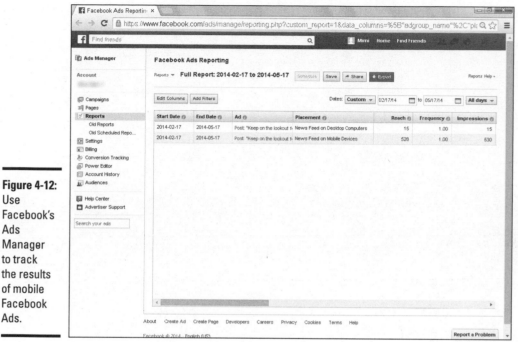

Figure 4-12:
Use
Facebook's
Ads
Manager
to track
the results
of mobile
Facebook
Ads.

Book IX

Measuring, Monitoring, and Analyzing

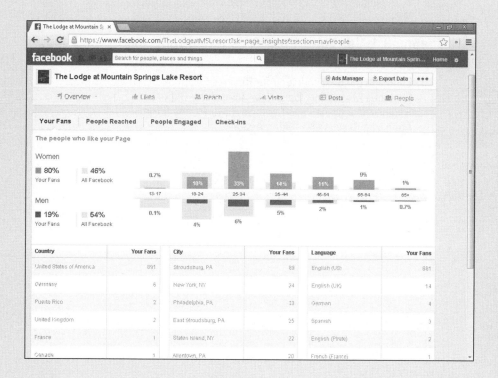

For more on evaluating the performance of posts, go to www.dummies.com/
extras/facebookmarketingaio.

Contents at a Glance

Chapter 1: Setting Realistic Targets to Identify Success 675

Exploring Social Monitoring and Measuring 675
Knowing the Importance of Social Media Monitoring 676
Knowing the Importance of Social Media Measuring 682

Chapter 2: Exploring Facebook Insights 693

Getting Started with Insights 693
Delving into Insights Details: Categories 697
Making Greater Use of Insights 706
Evaluating Activity outside Facebook 710
Making Changes Based on Insights 711

Chapter 3: Using Third-Party Monitoring Tools and Analyzing Results 715

Choosing the Best Tool for Your Business 715
Choosing Monitoring Tools: Your Third-Party Options 717
Finding the Biggest Payoff with Your Monitoring Efforts 728
Analyzing Results and Taking Action 729

Chapter 1: Setting Realistic Targets to Identify Success

In This Chapter

- ✔ Understanding the difference between social monitoring and social measuring
- ✔ Knowing the benefits of real-time engagement
- ✔ Determining the best social metrics for your business
- ✔ Understanding the importance of social media measuring

Gone are the days when businesses could operate behind closed doors. The popularity (or should we say, *massive explosion?*) of social networking has busted open those doors, and there's no turning back.

Your customers are now social customers. They love to share, chat, post, like, and comment — and when they have something important to say (good, bad, or worse), they're quick to share it on their social networks. Their comments run the gamut from the best raves to the worst rants.

This chapter first examines the importance of social monitoring and describes ways that you can take advantage of the social conversations related to your niche and your business. From there, we explore strategies related to social measuring, discussing how you can best measure your prospects' and customers' social activities, and then use this information in your marketing messages to get your fans to take action.

Your customers and prospects are going to be social with or without you, so it behooves you to pay attention, take notes, and get into the conversations at just the right times. This chapter helps you do just that!

Exploring Social Monitoring and Measuring

If you're just dipping your toes into the ever-changing Facebook waters, the idea of taking on social data tracking may be a bit daunting. You may be wondering, "Where do I start?" When you do collect the data, you might ask, "What the heck do I do with it?" We address both of those questions and many more throughout this section.

The purpose of tracking online activity is to identify the overall impact of your efforts. The data that you collect can help you support your customers, promote your brand, and grow your business.

We recommend taking a holistic approach to monitoring and measuring social media activity. That means including all social activity important to you, from Facebook, Twitter, YouTube, or a different social network. All sites that matter to your clients should matter to you.

In addition to listening to your fans, run a reality check to find out whether all your social media marketing efforts are worth your time and effort. Is what you're doing really working? When you're exploring monitoring and measuring strategies, you first want to set your key performance indicators (KPIs). Ask yourself these questions:

- ✦ What do I want to achieve?
- ✦ What does success look like?
- ✦ What are the indicators of my success?
- ✦ By what date will I complete this goal?

Although you'll find some overlap in the data, monitoring and measuring are two different processes. When it comes to taking action, you analyze and use that data differently. This chapter closely examines both processes so you can better understand what overall tracking can do for your business.

Knowing the Importance of Social Media Monitoring

Monitoring is a bit like eavesdropping while pressing your big digital ear against the computer screen. You get to listen to all the chatter about you and your company as well as hear what's being said about your competitors and industry. In this section, we explore what it means to monitor social media activity and what you can do with the data you collect to improve your overall marketing initiatives.

Monitoring involves identifying a set of *keywords* (words or phrases that someone might search on) relevant to your business and brand. Knowing what words your prospects and customers are using online to research your niche or business is paramount to overall marketing success.

After you identify your keywords, you plug them and information about your social media accounts into a monitoring tool. (We review your options for monitoring tools in depth in Chapter 3 of this minibook.) The monitoring tool tracks the communications most important to your niche and business, organizing the data for you in a way that's easy to digest, such as comprehensive charts, tables, and lists. Overall, monitoring allows you to know who's talking about a topic (by means of specific keywords that you identify) and what they're saying about it.

To put a successful social monitoring plan in place, you must understand why monitoring is important to your business and look closely at what you can do with the information you collect.

Seeing why monitoring online conversations is important

Monitoring is all about listening to online conversations with the intent to learn, engage, and support. The benefit of social media monitoring is the opportunity to join the conversations that matter most to your business and its relationships with its fans.

When it's working in your favor, Facebook can function as a word-of-mouth machine, broadcasting every customer rave that hits its airwaves. When you're engaged with your fans and firing on all cylinders, Facebook can be your best friend. At some point, however, all best friends have spats. Sooner or later, someone will use Facebook to tell the world that your product is lacking, your delivery department is slow, or your call-center response time is horrendous. It's bound to happen.

In both cases — that is, in the "singing your praises" scenario and the "lackluster results" scenario — your goal is to be prepared to engage. You want to respond to both types of posts as quickly as possible. And that's why monitoring is a crucial component of your overall social media marketing strategy.

In the case of the raving, happy fans, catching them in the moment only elevates their appreciation for you and their admiration of you. They feel heard and appreciated. See Figure 1-1 for an example of a positive exchange on Facebook.

In the case of the ranting, frustrated customers, keep in mind the two main reasons why responding quickly is crucial:

✦ **You want to take care of your customers.** If someone's upset, you want to genuinely meet his needs and put out the fire quickly.

✦ **You want the rest of your online audience to see that you take care of your customers.** What you say and do for one client or customer directly affects all viewers' perceptions of you, so this situation is your chance to make lemonade out of lemons and shine a good light on yourself.

Situations like these give you the opportunity to protect your brand. One goal of an effective monitoring strategy is to guard your brand's reputation and keep it polished at all times. Also, you can increase your brand's social proof by engaging in these important, in-the-moment, two-way dialogs, which increases fan trust and admiration.

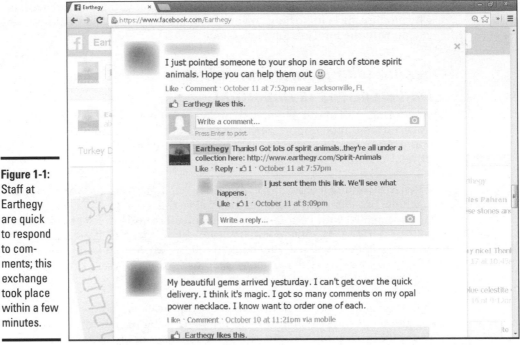

Figure 1-1: Staff at Earthegy are quick to respond to comments; this exchange took place within a few minutes.

Understanding the importance of real-time engagement

Monitoring online conversations is important if you want to stay in the loop about conversations related to your niche and your business. That said, the optimal outcome of social media monitoring is to take full advantage of the opportunity for real-time response. The goal is to get in on the conversations that matter most at just the right time. In this section, we give you a few examples to illustrate just how important real-time response is for your business.

Suppose that you're the owner of an online store that sells wine, and your goal is to increase overall sales. Monitoring for phrases such as *"wine pairing," "the best wine that goes with,"* and *"wine recommendations"* can help you help others.

✦ Knowing when people are talking about your area of specialty gives you an online icebreaker; it allows you to join the conversation at the right time and even do a little consultative selling, where you offer suggestions and advice focused on the products and services you sell.

✦ Because you're monitoring in real time, you're joining the conversation at a time when people are open to suggestions and in need of help. In essence, they're raising a digital hand and saying, "Hey, I need your expertise over here!"

Real-time monitoring is crucial when you want to make an impact online.

To help you grasp the magnitude of real-time monitoring, we want to tell you about a post that was shared on Twitter and Facebook. Tim Ferriss, the best-selling author of *The 4-Hour Workweek* and *The 4-Hour Body* (Harmony), was trying to give a $100,000 donation to St. Jude's Hospital. Not too shabby, right? Although he tried to contact the hospital multiple times, his calls were never returned, so out of frustration, Tim took to the social media airwaves, as shown in Figure 1-2. Imagine that you were St. Jude's Hospital and saw Tim's post online, in real time. You'd be sure to reach out immediately, right?

If a fan posts something negative about you or perhaps asks advice of you, and you delay your response, someone outside your company will likely step in to defuse the situation or offer a better solution. That "someone" just might be your biggest competitor coming to the rescue.

Figure 1-2:
Tim Ferriss posted these time-critical status updates on Facebook and Twitter.

Almost 200 people responded to Tim's post, making suggestions for his donation. (*Note:* St. Jude's did reach out to Tim quickly, and he posted that he was talking with the hospital about his possible donation, as shown in Figure 1-2.) Now do you see why real-time response is so crucial?

Monitoring the right way

Social media monitoring is not just about identifying and responding to your online detractors. To develop a clear picture of what's being discussed online, you should monitor more than just your customers' and prospects' conversations about you. In this section, we take a look at additional ways to use these monitoring strategies to take your marketing initiatives to the next level.

Additional ways to use monitoring strategies include the following:

✦ Follow the conversations of industry thought leaders, your top competitors, and your partners. The goal is to cover all the bases.

✦ Consider monitoring keywords that are associated with products or services that may be complementary to your own. The conversations may give you insights and ideas about possible partnership opportunities or brand extensions.

Monitoring is keyword-based, so choosing the right keywords is crucial. Here are some suggested keywords that you can monitor:

✦ The names of key people in your company

✦ Your company name

✦ All brand names associated with your company

✦ Product names

✦ Names of your services

✦ Your top three competitors' names

✦ Names of industry thought leaders

✦ Names of businesses that you partner with

✦ Competitive product names and services

✦ Industry or niche keywords

Clearly, when it comes to monitoring, you have a lot of information to pull. You can monitor all the public conversations taking place online at any given time. To start off right, you should monitor the communication that's posted on Facebook as status updates, posts where your name or business have been mentioned in a post (also called "@ tagging") or comments, Twitter updates, and comments on blogs.

Identifying your monitoring outcomes

Here are some outcomes of monitoring social activity:

✦ **Check out your competition.** What are they doing online? What do their customers say about them?

✦ **Understand your ideal client.** Find out what she wants and needs, what makes her tick, and what words she uses when talking about your brands and services.

✦ **Participate in conversations.** You want to join the real-time conversations that matter most to your business. When people online are talking about your industry (niche, topics, and so on), you want to get in on those conversations to generate exposure for your company. You can offer advice or just share your thoughts and insights.

✦ **Gather market intelligence.** You want to listen to what people are saying in your industry so that you can create better products and services.

✦ **Manage your reputation.** You want to know what your customers are saying about you. You want to see both good and bad comments in real time so that you can address them quickly.

✦ **Set up a listening portal.** You want to set up a support team to monitor your clients' needs and concerns and to address issues quickly. (We talk in detail about setting up a successful social media team in Book I, Chapter 2.)

Setting up a listening station is the most important piece of social monitoring. While listening,

✦ Observe with the intent to genuinely understand group dynamics and behaviors.

✦ Look out for the influencers and leaders because these people are the ones who can spread the word about your business.

✦ Notice how people interact and pay close attention to the community norms.

✦ Make sure that you understand the rules of engagement before you begin to interact and add value.

To review, here are some of the most important benefits of social monitoring:

✦ You're more responsive to your fans' needs when you can help them in their time of frustration or confusion.

✦ By jumping into online conversations at the right time, you stay relevant and at the top of your fans' minds.

✦ By monitoring regularly, you begin to fully understand your customers.

✦ **Monitoring online communication allows you to hear others sing your praises.** When your fans post compliments, rave reviews, and praise, these communications are great social proof. Take screen shots of these posts to use in your marketing materials.

The term *social proof* refers to the psychological phenomenon of people being motivated to do things that they see other people doing.

✦ **Monitoring allows you to spot trends,** keeping you on the cutting edge of your industry.

✦ **When you understand what your fans are talking about when it comes to your brand,** you can better deliver the features and benefits that your audience is asking for.

Knowing the Importance of Social Media Measuring

Measuring is more statistical than monitoring and occurs over a period of time versus in real time.

In the following sections, we explore how measuring your social activity allows you to evaluate the success of your social media efforts, as well as to better understand the behaviors and habits of your customers and prospects. We also examine what data is best for you to measure, depending on your marketing outcomes. With all the data on the web today, the last thing you want to do is to get bogged down in too much information. When you know what to measure, you can streamline your efforts, saving yourself a lot of time and stress.

Seeing why measuring online activity is important

The benefit of measuring activity that relates to your brand, company, and industry on Facebook and other social networks is to spot trends, behaviors, and reactions early. The goal is to analyze the data quickly and act on it to get your biggest bang for your time and efforts. Constant benchmarking is crucial to ascertaining whether things are working in your favor.

Measuring online activity as it relates to your social networking sites is important because the data allows you to see fairly quickly what's working and what isn't. This valuable data will help you stay on track and continue to move toward your desired results.

For example, say you're a wine seller. When measuring your data, you find that over the past few months, your fans engaged with your content (clicked links, commented, and shared your posts) more often when you posted about wine pairing versus when you posted about the types of grapes used in specific wines. This data helps you determine what content your audience wants to see more of, therefore eventually increasing your overall engagement and reach.

To begin measuring, first identify the keywords that reflect your business and brand. Useful keyword tools for researching and identifying the best search terms for your niche or market include

✦ **Google Keyword Planner**

> https://adwords.google.com/ko/KeywordPlanner/Home

Available through Google AdWords, the Google Keyword Planner is free to use, regardless of whether you spend money on ads. We discuss this tool in greater detail later in this chapter.

✦ **Scribe**

> http://scribecontent.com

Use this tool to evaluate content for search terms and common usage. Its plans start at $97 per month.

✦ **SEM Rush**

> www.semrush.com

This tool stresses competitor keyword research, with plans starting at $69.95 per month. However, limited free results available at www.semrush.com/info/empty/phrase_fullsearch include search volume, cost per click, competition on search terms, and number of search results.

Using Google Keyword Planner

After you enter a word or phrase, Google Keyword Planner suggests other popular keywords or phrases that users search for online, as shown in Figure 1-3. You can research which terms are searched for most and determine the words that best fit your brand.

Next, plug your keywords into a monitoring tool. (Again, we review monitoring tools in depth in Chapter 3 of this minibook.) The monitoring tool scans the Internet; grabs all blog posts, online articles, videos, and so on that contain those keywords; and disseminates the information in different data combinations, building patterns that tell a story about the social activity collected. The tool might tell you the specific keywords that were mentioned on specific social media channels and how many times they were mentioned. This type of data is useful for finding out what people are talking about online and where they're talking.

One of the major benefits of measuring the data is that measurement keeps you accountable. When you see what's working and what's not, you can take action to do more of what's working and tweak what's falling short.

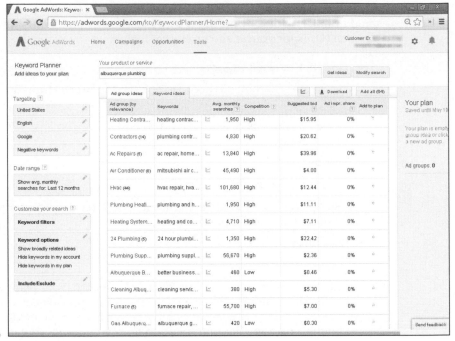

Figure 1-3:
Keyword
suggestions
from Google
Keyword
Planner.

Determining what you should measure for your ROI

When monitoring and measuring, it's important to pay attention to your return on investment (ROI), meaning you want to make sure that your time, efforts, and dollars are delivering real results toward your specific goals and outcomes.

When it comes to tracking and measuring online data, you have numerous options, so it's important to identify the metric indicators that are most important to you.

One of the ultimate benefits (and goals) of monitoring and measuring, after all, is uncovering information that allows you to increase the impact of your social media posts. Tracking the time of day you generate the most activity on your Page, such as clicks and comments, can help you decide the best time of day to post a call to action.

Suppose you own a store for runners, and you're having a special on running shoes for men. By analyzing your data, focusing especially on how many men are engaging with your content, the time of day they're most active on your Page, and what content they're engaging in, you can find out the best time of day to post your promotion and how to craft your post around this data.

By measuring these behaviors at this depth, you can reach more of your targeted audience with each post and turn your fans into loyal, paying customers.

Posting content with blog links

If you post content with links to your blog, for example, track which links get the most clicks from your fans by using a link-tracking tool such as Bitly (`https://bitly.com/`).

A free tool with a premium option, Bitly allows users to shorten, share, and track links (URLs). You copy and paste a long URL into the Bitly portal, and the tool automatically generates a shorter link that you can use on social networks or anywhere else on the web. These shorter links are trackable, meaning that Bitly will tell you how many times that link has been clicked and on what social sites it has been shared, as shown in Figure 1-4. Over time, this data helps you see which content your fans interact with most. For more detail on Bitly, please see Chapter 3 in this minibook.

Figure 1-4:
Click metrics from the free version of the Bitly dashboard.

Courtesy of Bitly.

Increasing comments

If you're looking to increase the comments on your Facebook Page, you may want to use Facebook Insights. Insights is Facebook's built-in analytics dashboard. You can use it to look at trends in the activity on your Page, including how many comments you're getting from your posts. We talk in detail about Facebook Insights in Chapter 2 of this minibook. This tool can paint a picture of what types of posts your fans respond to best — most favorably and most frequently.

Read on for specific ideas about what to measure, based on your business outcomes and goals.

Turning social activity into key metric indicators

When it comes to social media activity, you can track and measure numerous indicators. Here are the most important areas to consider:

✦ Engagement

✦ Brand awareness

✦ Influence

✦ Sentiment

✦ New likes/unsubscribes

✦ Click activity

✦ Financial return

✦ Volume

✦ Demographics

To help you understand how these indicators can support your marketing efforts, we dive a little deeper in the following sections, exploring the benefits of each indicator. To decide which indicators are a good fit for your business, keep your marketing goals in mind as you read the options.

Engagement

Engagement refers to the relevance of the Facebook Page to users and the actions they take when they visit the Page. You can measure engagement by taking a look at the types of activities users engage in, such as becoming a fan, writing on your Timeline, liking or commenting on an update, uploading a photo or video, or mentioning your Page in status updates. You can monitor this information weekly and monthly with Facebook Insights (see Book IX, Chapter 2, for details) and by spending time on your Page on a daily basis.

You can also monitor and measure all the words and phrases that your fans and prospects use when they talk about your brand. Are these words and phrases what you expected? Are they the same words that you're using to explain your programs and services? These words and phrases are key to understanding how people are talking about your business! In addition, when you know the words your fans use online, you can build rapport more quickly because using the same words creates a connection.

Brand awareness

Brand awareness refers to how much your company is talked about on the social web and, even more important, why people are talking about you. It also refers to how recognizable and known your brand is to your ideal audience. Is it in relation to a product announcement, a press release, or some company news you've played a role in? Or did someone write a review or mention your company in a blog post? Regardless of where the awareness comes from, you don't want to be the last one to hear about it.

You may want to add a reference point to your social mention tracking to see how many times your company and products are mentioned along with your competitors and their products during a 30-day period. You tally all the mentions of your business and the mentions of your competitors, and then divide your mentions by the total to arrive at your share of voice. *Share of voice* means that you're sharing this social space with your competitors and monitoring and measuring how often your brand is mentioned compared with theirs. You can access the information you need to monitor share of voice through third-party monitoring tools.

You can monitor your competitors' Pages using Facebook's tool *Pages to Watch.* (For directions, see `facebook.com/help/www/209826452542432`.) Google Alerts (google.com/alerts) for web pages and HootSuite (`http://blog.hootsuite.com/use-hootsuite-social-listening`) and Mention (`https://en.mention.com`) for social media monitoring are also helpful for getting a sense of how your competitors perform, socially speaking. For more details, see Chapter 3 of this minibook.

Influence

Influence refers to how much your company is referenced and respected on Facebook, other social media, and the web in general. If a company whose Facebook Page has 10,000 engaged fans posts a link to your new video on YouTube, and your video goes viral overnight as a result, you'd be able to attribute your success to being discovered on that company's Facebook Page. Then you'd be able to monitor the increase in comments, likes, and shares on one of the social listening tools, such as Netvibes (`www.netvibes.com`), as shown in Figure 1-5.

You'd also want to send a shout-out to the company for helping make your video a success. In the future, when you launch a new video, you'll probably want to add that company to a list of companies to alert.

Sentiment

Sentiment comprises both positive and negative reactions to your brand on Facebook, other social networks, and around the web. Perhaps someone ordered a product from you and was dissatisfied with the color or the overall quality. Perhaps that person went to your Facebook Page and wrote that he'll never order another product from you. But what if your customer service reps were monitoring the Page in real time, and one of them offered to take the product back, refund the customer's money, and send him a new model? You could nip the situation in the bud, not only undoing the negative sentiment, but also turning it around significantly.

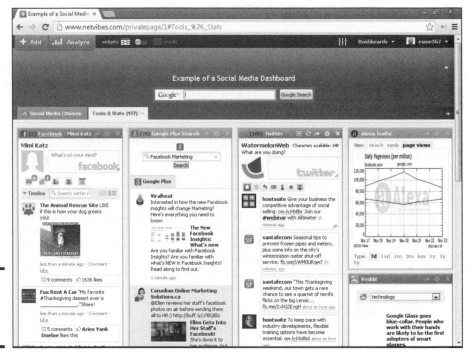

Figure 1-5:
A Netvibes listening station.

Courtesy of Netvibes, a Dassault Systemes Company.

New likes/unsubscribes

You should measure how many new Likes can be attributed to individual updates and your collective activity on Facebook. If people respond favorably by liking your Page, and especially if they respond to a specific update, you can gain a good sense of how your users feel about that type of content. If videos get more attention than other links do, for example, you want to post more videos for your fans.

On the other hand, if users unsubscribe in reaction to a particular update, that situation gives you invaluable information, too. Perhaps users don't want to see that type of content from you, or maybe you've overloaded your users with too many updates. Although ascertaining why you lose one fan here or there may be hard, a major exodus would be very revealing. You can monitor the number of new likers and unsubscribes on Facebook Insights.

Click activity

Click activity refers to the times when a person clicks your Facebook Ad and is taken to your website or a tab on your Facebook Page. We recommend measuring click activity so you'll know how effective your ad campaign is and whether you want to run it again or tweak it the next time around.

You can monitor this type of data by using Facebook Ads reports. (See Book VII, Chapter 4, for more about these reports.) Clicks are also tracked for Page Likes and event RSVPs. You'll want to know whether your event is drawing people in on Facebook; if not, you may need to change the description or the date. Will you have enough interest to run it? You can see information about Likes, comments, and shares in the Facebook Insights reports, as seen in Figure 1-6. (For more on Facebook Insights, see Chapter 2 of this minibook.)

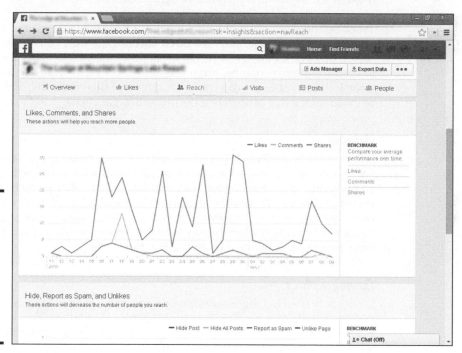

Figure 1-6:
Facebook Insights offers important information on likes, comments, and shares.

Financial return

Financial return is the same as ROI and looks at the efficiency of your efforts in terms of time, resources, and dollars; it compares those efforts with your end results. When examining your financial returns, you want to make sure that your efforts are paying off — meaning they are moving you toward your overall goals.

Asking yourself specific questions related to your goals and marketing outcomes will help you determine whether you're moving toward a financial return. For example, what are you getting in return for the time you spend on your Facebook marketing efforts? Have you increased your number of fans? Sold an online or in-person event via Facebook promotions? Brought more people to your web page and in turn sold them your programs or services? Had people download a white paper or report that, in addition to adding value, promoted a product or service? Brought more people to a special offer through a Facebook-specific promo code?

To see a real financial return on your social media activity, think in terms of conversion. The goal is to convert an interested potential customer to an actual, paying customer. Social media allows you to add value and to create engagement, trust, and affinity with your fans. After you capture your fans' trust, it's time to sell them your programs and services.

Tracking tools can show you how much traffic is generated, what content is of interest to your fans, and how often fans engage with you. To see a financial return on your social media activity, use these metrics to generate activity and to create and sell products, programs, and services for your ideal audience. Google Analytics, as we discuss in Chapter 3 of this minibook, includes tools to evaluate the ROI of social media, including Facebook.

Volume

Volume is how frequently people search for your company in search engines. Facebook Pages come up in search engine results for your company name, so someone who's looking for your website might also decide to check out your Facebook Page. Google Analytics shows which Facebook custom apps on your Page sent traffic to your website, which is all the more reason why you want to make sure to display your URL prominently in the About box of your Facebook Timeline and on the Info tab.

Demographics

Commonly used demographics include age, race, gender, language, location, and household income. Tracking tools such as HootSuite (www.hootsuite.com), which we cover in more detail in Chapter 3 of this minibook, can display a breakdown of Likes by region (as shown in Figure 1-7), while Facebook Insights (see Chapter 2) can display a breakdown by gender, countries, cities, and languages, as shown in Figure 1-8.

You may already know the demographics that are most associated with your products and services, but if you suddenly discover (through monitoring your Facebook Insights reports) that a significantly different group is coming to your Facebook Page, that discovery could not only potentially affect your social media marketing efforts, but also demonstrate that your company is connecting to a different demographic than you realized! You may want to adjust your products and services accordingly.

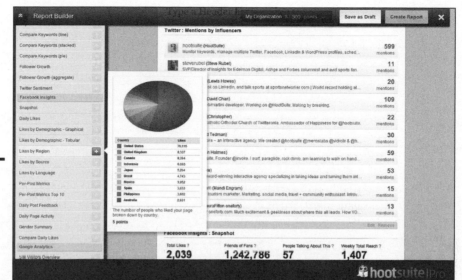

Figure 1-7:
Regional
Facebook
data
generated
by
HootSuite.

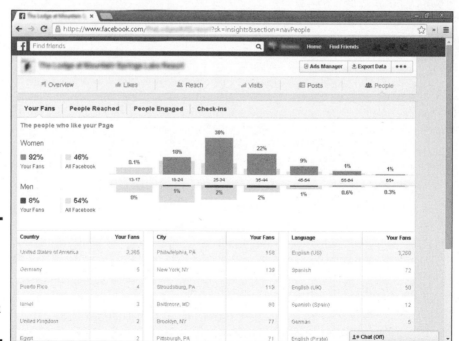

Figure 1-8:
Demo-
graphic
metrics
generated
by Facebook
Insights.

Chapter 2: Exploring Facebook Insights

In This Chapter

✔ Using Insights, the Facebook built-in monitoring tool

✔ Interpreting Insights tracking details

✔ Deciding which data to track

*I*nsights, the built-in Facebook analytics dashboard, helps you look at trends revealed by the activity on your Page. Insights helps you get a feel for who is using your Page and how those users are interacting with it. In this chapter, we dive into the data and explore ways to better understand your Facebook users' behaviors in relation to the content you share.

We look at how to interpret the myriad graphs and charts available in Facebook Insights. Now who doesn't like to do more of the good stuff and less of the bad stuff, right? Don't worry: We've set up this chapter so that exploring the analytical data of your Facebook Page won't be painful, we promise!

The keys are to find out which marketing strategies work and replicate those efforts (and to understand what isn't working so that you can create more productive, meaningful interactions). This chapter focuses on understanding analytical data that Facebook provides; the next chapter focuses on analytical data from third-party sources.

Getting Started with Insights

Think of Insights as your personal road map to Facebook success. That may sound a bit cheesy, but Insights truly can help you navigate your way to a thriving Facebook Page.

At least 30 people must like your Page before the Insights dashboard becomes available for viewing. Ask your friends, family, employees, colleagues, and valued customers to like your Page so you can reach this level quickly.

To understand the true value of your Facebook efforts, you need to know

✦ How many users have been exposed to your posts

✦ How much of your audience is actively responding or interacting with your posts

✦ Which posts are the most popular with your ideal audience

Fortunately, no matter what goals you have for your campaign, you can use the metrics to guide your next steps.

Accessing Insights data

To access Insights, do this:

1. **Log in to Facebook.**

2. **Go to the Admin panel for your Facebook Page.**

3. **Click the See Insights tab to open the entire Insights panel.**

The See Insights tab is near the top-right corner of the Admin panel, as shown in Figure 2-1.

View Insights tab

Figure 2-1:
The Admin panel dashboard with the See Insights tab at top.

Understanding the Overview display

When you're in Insights, click the Overview tab. At the top, you see tabs for five metrics: Likes, Reach, Visits, Posts, and People, as shown in Figure 2-2. Summaries below the tabs have green (positive) or red (negative) arrows and percentages that summarize the difference in values from the previous week.

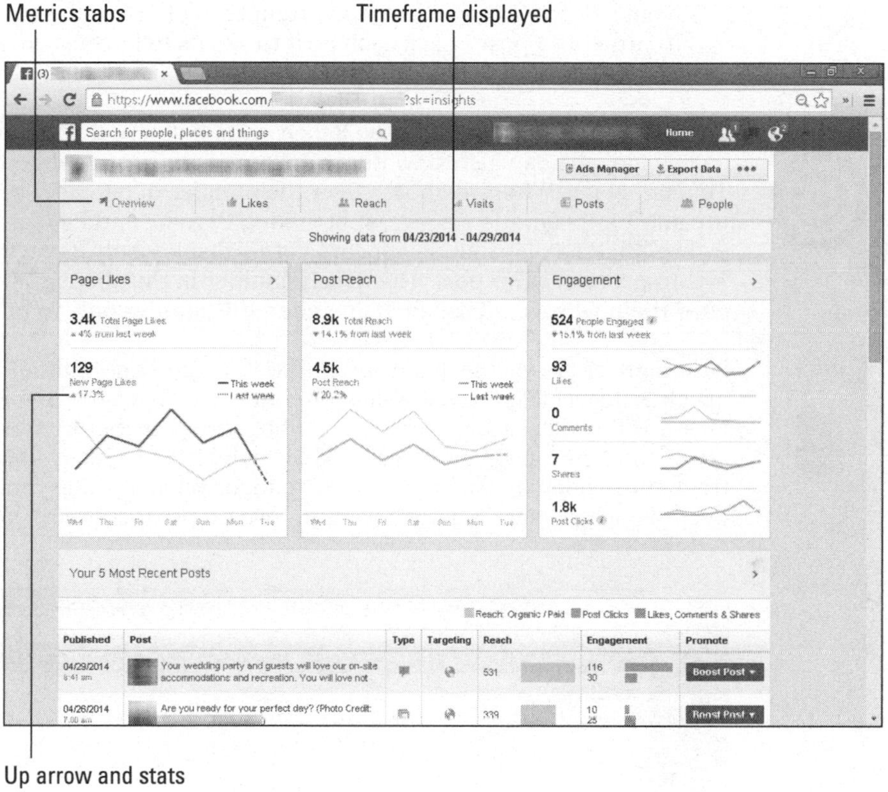

Metrics tabs   Timeframe displayed

Figure 2-2:
Arrows, graphs, and percentages on the Insights Overview compare key metrics to the prior week.

Up arrow and stats

> **TIP**
>
> The Overview page displays metrics for only the past week. The time frame for the data on the Overview display appears directly above the metrics boxes. To select other date ranges, you will need to drill down further into Insights.

To drill down for additional detail, click on the header for Page Likes, Post Reach, or Engagement in the center of the page. On the new page that appears, enter your desired date range for a custom report. You can also click on any metric in the top navigation to enter a date range. Here's a brief explanation of each key section on the Overview display:

✦ **Page Likes:** Shows Total Page Likes and new Page Likes.

✦ **Post Reach:** Shows Total Reach (the number of people who saw *any* activity from your page) and Post Reach (the number of people who saw your posts).

✦ **Engagement:** Shows how many Likes, comments, shares, and clicks your Page posts received.

✦ **Your 5 Most Recent Posts:** This table, located below the three graphs, displays your five most recent posts, the date they were published, a shortened version of the posts themselves, and the types of posts (photo, link, video, and so on). Additional columns are Type (for example, status, image, link), Targeting (public to everyone, or limited to a particular segment), Reach, Engagement, and Promote (a shortcut if you want to pay to promote a post). Click each post to see its full details, including Likes, comments, and shares, as shown in Figure 2-3.

There's an alternative way to see Reach data. If you're the Admin of a business Page, you can also view Reach below each individual post on your Timeline itself. When you hover over the number of people reached, you see the number of unique viewers, split among Organic and Paid, as shown in Figure 2-4. Paid distribution appears in this display only if you used Facebook Ads to promote your post. The Reach number in this display is calculated after the post was published. Remember, this applies only to business Pages!

Four metrics are visible to *anyone* who visits your Page without any access to Insights: Total Likes, People Talking About This, Check-ins, and Friends Who Like this Page. These metrics are meant to show Facebook users how popular, active, and engaging your Page is. That's why it's extremely important to track these numbers and to continue to focus on increasing your fan base and overall engagement. You don't want to turn off prospects with poor results.

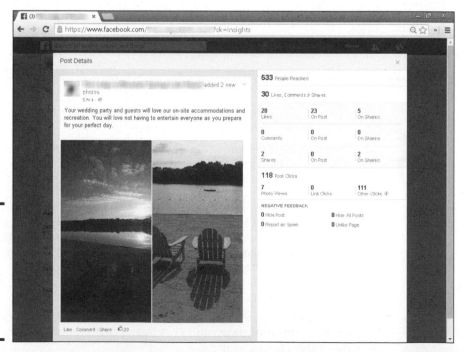

Figure 2-3:
A pop-up window showing the detailed metrics for a specific post.

Figure 2-4:
If you are
an Admin,
you can
see Reach
data for an
individual
post directly
on your
Timeline.

Hover here to see Organic and Paid reach

Using these metrics, you can identify which types of posts are most popular
with your audience and tweak your content strategy to post more of what's
working best.

Delving into Insights Details: Categories

This section reveals what information you can access within the five subcategories of Likes, Reach, Visits, Posts, and People. By diving into each category,
you better understand your fans' demographics and behaviors, who is talking about you, and what those people like most about your Page.

You can select the date range of your choice for Likes, Reach, and Visits at
the top of each respective subcategory page. Click the calendar icon next to
the date range and then select the range you want to analyze.

Tracking your Like activity

The Likes tab provides a good understanding of

+ Your total current Likes

+ A breakdown of Likes versus Unlikes

+ How visitors found your Page

The first set of metrics is total Likes to date with a graph tracking when you received each Like, as shown in the top graph on Figure 2-5.

The second set of metrics, shown at the bottom of Figure 2-5, displays the number of new Paid and Organic Likes compared to the new Unlikes for the past 28 days.

Keep your eye on new Unlikes. If people seem to be unliking your Page at an alarmingly high rate, you need to see whether a specific activity triggered them. Make sure your newer posts match what people Liked in the first place.

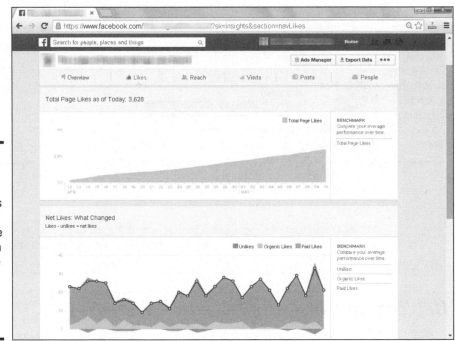

Figure 2-5: The top graph shows Likes for the past 28 days. The lower graph displays the net change between Likes and Unlikes.

The third set of metrics on the Likes tab, Where Your Page Likes Came From (Referrals), tells from where on Facebook or elsewhere on the web that new Likes originally found your Page, as shown in Figure 2-6: The actual list of sources will vary by Page. For instance, you used Paid ads to drive traffic to your Page, Ads may show up as one of these sources.

Did people who liked your Page find it in their News Feed or perhaps in a social plug-in on your website? Did they click the Like button on the ad or on your blog? Did they find you on Facebook's mobile site?

It's valuable to know where your Likes come from because you can identify the best ways to drive desirable traffic to your Facebook page — "desirable" meaning traffic that is apt to turn into Likes.

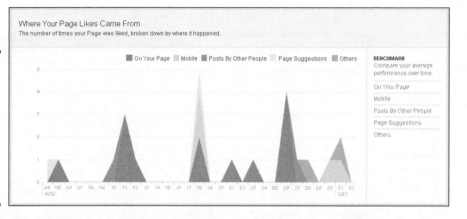

Figure 2-6:
Referral
metrics for
Likes will
help you
evaluate
future
marketing
efforts.

Reach-ing for the Facebook stars

The Reach tab gives you a good understanding of who is actually seeing your content and how you reached them.

✦ **Post Reach** shows both Organic and Paid post reach. Organic Reach includes the total number of unique viewers who saw content from your Page in their News Feeds, on their Tickers, or on your Page.

The more engagement you create on your Page, the more likely you are to get out into the News Feeds and Tickers.

✦ **Likes, Comments, Shares** shows how many people have liked, commented on, or shared your posts. They are shown together, but you can click Likes, Comments, or Shares on the right side of the graph to see these metrics individually, as shown in the bottom of Figure 2-7.

✦ **Hide, Report as Spam, and Unlikes** is a breakdown of negative actions on your page. Because these actions decrease the number of people you can reach, they are important to monitor. Pay particular attention to Report as Spam numbers that spike suddenly. Assuming you've been acting honorably, a spike might indicate that your account has been hacked. Although these metrics are combined on the graph, as shown in the top of Figure 2-8, but you can separate them by clicking each metric to the right of the graph.

✦ **Total Reach** shows the number of unique people who saw any content associated with your Page (including any ads pointing to your Page) in any way.

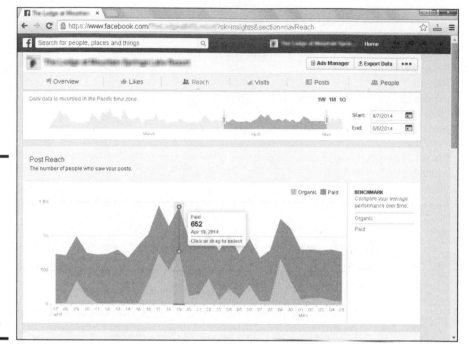

Figure 2-7:
The Post Reach graph distinguishes between paid and unpaid (organic) viewers of your posts.

Figure 2-8:
The numbers for Hide, Report as Spam, and Unlikes are displayed at the top of the Reach page, with Total Reach, segmented by organic and paid sources, displayed below.

Visiting the Visits tab

The Page and Tab Visits graph, on the Visits tab (shown at the top of Figure 2-9), indicates which areas of your Facebook Page (such as Timeline, Photos, or Profile) are viewed the most. These appear together, but you can distinguish them by clicking each area to the right of the graph: The areas shown may vary by Page and over time.

The second graph on this tab is Other Page Activity. This may include Mentions, Posts by other people, check-ins, offer claims, or other activities. The items that appear may vary by Page and over time.

Again, these metrics are summed but can be viewed separately by clicking each metric on the right of the graph. See the bottom of Figure 2-9.

Figure 2-9:
The Page and Tab Visits graph shows how many times people have accessed parts of your Page; the bottom graph displays the number of times users undertook other Page activities.

The final graph (see Figure 2-10), shows External Referrers, which are the top sites from which your Facebook Page receives traffic. Tracking the external sites that send traffic to your Facebook Page tells you about your audience. We discuss referrer sites in more detail later in this chapter, when we look at tracking activity outside Facebook.

Pay attention to the content on the external sites that refer traffic to your Page. This content is likely the content that attracts your ideal audience.

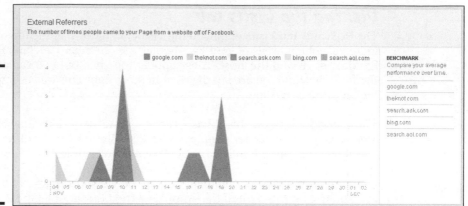

Figure 2-10:
Referrals
from other
sites are
crucial for
successful
Facebook
marketing.

Perusing the Posts tab

The Posts tab conveys a great deal of important information on three sub-tabs: When Your Fans Are Online, Post Types, and Top Posts from Pages to Watch.

The graph at the top of Figure 2-11 — When Your Fans Are Online — shows how many fans are online each day of the week and at what times of the day. This important metric helps you decide when to post and advertise.

Below that, the All Posts Published section offers a table similar to the one on the Overview tab, as shown in the bottom of Figure 2-11. It includes the following:

✦ **Published:** The date and time the post was published.

✦ **Post:** A short preview of the post. If you click the text, you'll see the entire post in a pop-up.

✦ **Type:** Type of post — Photo, Status, Link, or Video.

✦ **Targeting:** Whom the post was shared with, which applies if you chose to share with only a segment of your fans.

✦ **Reach:** The reach by post from both paid and organic sources.

✦ **Engagement:** How many clicks, comments, Likes, and shares each post generated.

✦ **Promote:** A shortcut to promoting a post, which you can do from here, instead of going to the advertising dashboard.

Click to see posts with most reach/engagement

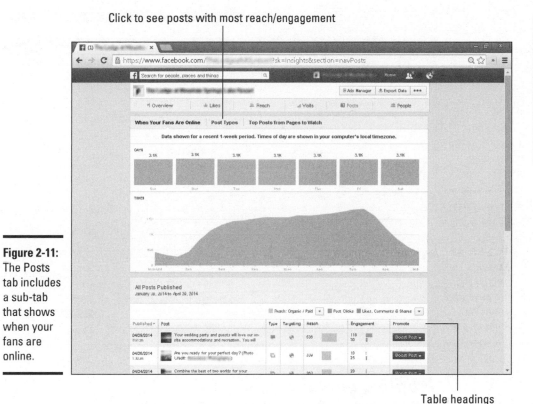

Figure 2-11:
The Posts
tab includes
a sub-tab
that shows
when your
fans are
online.

Table headings

The next sub-tab, Post Types, shows which posts receive the most reach and engagement. The top bar graphs in Figure 2-12 compare the average reach and engagement by type and a graph of All Published Posts appears at the bottom. It lets you know which type of post your fans respond to most. You can see in Figure 2-12 that the Status type of post had the greatest reach and engagement for this company.

The final sub-tab in this section, "Top Posts from Pages to Watch" lists popular recent posts from other Facebook pages that you have decided to "watch." You can search for and select Pages to watch or choose from Pages that Facebook recommends in the Page Manager section. (You must be logged in as an Admin on a Facebook Page to see these recommendations.) This is an easy to way to keep tabs on what your competitors are doing on Facebook.

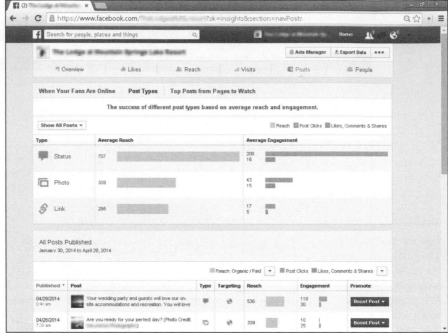

Figure 2-12:
The Post
Types
sub-tab
shows
reach and
engagement
rates by
type of post.

Profiling your People

This tab, shown in Figure 2-13, displays demographic metrics for

✦ **Your Fans** shows data about the people (demographics) who like your Page based on the information they provided in their user Profiles:

  • Gender

  • Age (13-17, 18-24, 25-34, 35-44, 45-54, 55-64, and 65+)

  • Country and city where they live

  • Language setting they selected when they accessed Facebook

✦ **People Reached** provides stats for people who have looked at your posts in the past 28 days (for example, for all the people who visited your page, whether or not they did anything). Similar to the data on the Your Fans tab, this section shows information about age, gender, location, and language.

✦ **People Engaged** provides demographic information for the people who liked, commented on, or shared your posts. (That's how Facebook defines and measures engagement.)

✦ **Check-ins** data can be seen only after 30 people have checked in at your business. After this is unlocked, you can see the demographic information for everyone who has checked in to your business for the previous 28 days.

Check-ins can only be executed by people who have turned on Location Services on their smartphones *and* logged into Facebook mobile. From their News Feeds, users must tap the Check In icon and select their location from a list of nearby places. They can add an optional description of what they're doing — shopping, eating, just messing around — and then tap Post to share their location with their own Friends.

Book IX
Chapter 2

Exploring Facebook Insights

Click tabs for details   People tab

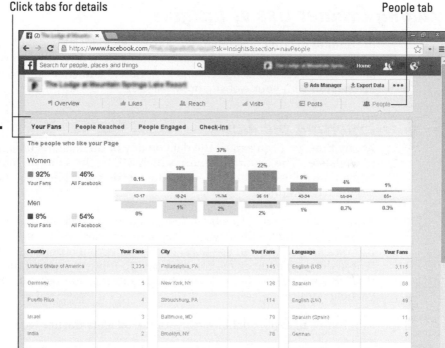

Figure 2-13:
The People tab shows demographic information for your fans (Likes), people reached, people engaged, and check-ins.

Making sense of the numbers

Compare demographic differences between Your Fans, People Reached, and People Engaged to see how successfully you're targeting your most important cohorts — People Engaged and Likes. The closer the match between your Reach demographics and your Engaged or Like demographics, the higher the conversion rate for your overall marketing campaign.

For example, if the demographics of your Reach is broader than that of your likes or engaged users, you might find that modifying your ads or re-targeting your efforts to a narrower set of characteristics will help increase likes or engagement. On the other hand, if your Reach matches your desired group, but people aren't liking or engaging with your page, review and revise your content.

Also consider in detail how the demographics match the target audience you have defined as prospective customers in your marketing plan. In theory, people who like or engage with your page are better-qualified prospects. If the demographics are similar, keep on doing what you're doing. If they differ, dig deeper to see whether your campaigns aren't successful, or if this unexpected population represents a new potential market segment.

Making Greater Use of Insights

In addition to crunching numbers, you can send Insights data to other places for further analysis, using it to make your content as good as possible, taking advantage of results to better target your ideal audience, and to improve interaction with your website or newsletter.

Exporting the data

At any time, you can export the data on any of the Insights tabs to an Excel spreadsheet. The exported report, which will be the same no matter which tab you download from, includes all the metrics from the Insights tabs, but without the graphics.

As they appear within Facebook, Insights data are difficult to sort and manipulate. You're stuck with however Facebook has decided to present the data. By comparison, you can use Excel to create custom reports, compare content in different campaigns, combine data to report for time frames longer than 28 days, or do whatever your bean-counting, number-crunching, analytical heart desires.

Here's how to export data from any of the Insights dashboards:

1. **Click the Export Data button in the top-right corner of the dashboard.**

   The Export Insights Data dialog box appears, as shown in Figure 2-14.

2. **Select a date range.**

3. **Select Export.**

   As always, Facebook is making changes in the export format to match the new version of Insights. You may choose either the New or Old Export format, as shown in Figure 2-14. You can continue to use the old export format through the end of 2014.

4. **Select a data type: Page-Level Data or Post-Level Data.**

   • *Page-level data* is data about your Page.

   • *Post-level data* shows you data on each of your Page posts.

5. **Select the file format required by your spreadsheet software: Excel or CSV (text file with delimiters).**

6. **Click the Download button.**

   This data file goes to your Downloads file or to where downloads are configured to go on your computer. Then you have a very rich file to analyze — meaning that you have a boatload of information to check out! Don't worry, though, because you don't need to analyze all of it.

Not all the data available in the report may be useful, depending on your overall marketing goals. The data you will find most valuable depends on your type of business and the objectives for your Facebook Page. Look at these, though:

✦ Key metrics will be most useful because they tell you a great deal about the activity on your Page.

✦ City is important if you have a bricks-and-mortar business.

Select Export box   Export Data tab

Figure 2-14:
The pop-up for Export Insights Data.

Evaluating the impact of your content

Analyzing Insights involves more than just counting Likes. Data available through Insights helps you analyze the effect of your content, the value of Facebook comments, and how to respond to Unlikes.

From the initial like to every item they share, post, or comment on, your fans reveal a clear pattern that explains what they think about your content. Content is king! If you produce content that your fans enjoy and find valuable, they will keep coming back for more. And that's why evaluating which content gets your users' attention is so important.

Are you on the right track? Or do you need to make adjustments to your content strategy? In the following sections, we explore ways to evaluate your content strategy as it relates to the data you collect from Insights.

Watching your Likes

To begin with, your Facebook content will have very limited impact if no one sees it.

Review how many Total Likes your Page has as least once a month.

Perhaps your Page has a total of 500 people who have liked the Page. You might set goals for increasing the numbers each month. For that, think in more detail about the activities you're doing outside Facebook to bring people to your Page. The upcoming section, "Evaluating Activity outside Facebook" helps you tackle that topic. Book IV, Chapter 2, offers lots of strategies.

You can't influence everything. Replicate, to the best of your ability, what's working. Get rid of what isn't.

Using photos and videos

Facebook users favor photos and videos. If they haven't been a regular part of your content strategy, now may be a good time to explore using it. Coca-Cola, which has the most engaged fans of any worldwide brand, has made it a point to post videos and photos on its Page regularly. Some of its more than 80 million Likes have followed suit by adding their own videos and photos to the Page. This works for smaller businesses, too. Lazypants, in Figure 2-15, encourages people to post their own photos. Or look at Humans of New York (facebook.com/humansofnewyork). This photographer's Page displays marvelous photos to more than 5 million Likes — and sells a book at the same time.

Likes, comments, and unsubscribes — Oh, my!

Insights data are good storytellers, and the stories come from facts, not imagination. The graphs can tell you the days on which your posts received likes, comments, and — heaven forbid — unlikes. What happened on your Page on a day that suffered a lot of unlikes? Which days generated the most likes and comments?

Figure 2-15:
Lazypants
encourages
visitors to
post their
own photos.

Courtesy of Lazypants.

One of the most valuable takeaways from Insights is about Page posts:

✦ Messages you posted

✦ Dates when they were posted

✦ Types of posts

✦ Overall reach

✦ Level of interactions on the People Engaged metric

You built it, but did they come?

If your Page is getting lots of mentions, and people are adding new discussions on your Timeline and uploading videos, your content is inviting. You have the kind of Page that people want to hang out on.

The difference between success and failure may be whether the Page fosters community or is filled only with its own updates. "Why do some Pages and brands attract more users than others?" may be the million-dollar Facebook question, but our hunch is that engaging, informative, and unique content plays a big role.

Ask yourself these questions while you look at the data:

✦ What posts received the largest reach?

✦ How many engaged users did they attract?

✦ How can you explain why some posts are viewed more times than others: Is it the topic? Is it the wording?

Evaluating Activity outside Facebook

When evaluating activity outside Facebook via Insights, monitor one graph on a regular basis: the External Referrers graph on the Visits tab. The number of external referrers can make or break a website. Know which sites generate the most referrals to your Page so that you can think strategically about when and how to promote.

You may have experienced the good fortune of having someone write about your Facebook Page, without any involvement on your part, in a hugely popular blog — and then suddenly have seen a surge in activity on your Page. That outcome would be good fortune (or perhaps a little more like magical thinking).

That said, chances are good that the sites other than Facebook that refer traffic to your Facebook Page have something to do with actions you've taken *outside* Facebook.

What kind of actions are we talking about? We mean things like the following:

✦ Putting social icons on your website and blog

✦ Adding your Facebook URL to your LinkedIn profile

+ Integrating your Twitter and Facebook updates

+ Promoting your Facebook Page URL on other sites where you comment

+ Adding your Facebook Page URL when you write a guest blog post

+ Adding the URL to your e-mail newsletter signature

In other words, promote, promote, promote!

Making Changes Based on Insights

Enough analysis paralysis! After checking out your data in Insights, it's time for action. This brief list has recommendations for fixing common problems that you may have identified from your Insights data. You can read more in the mentioned chapters.

+ **Getting more Likes:** Use an app like Woobox or TabSite (described in Book VI, Chapter 4) to run a campaign designed to get Likes. Use exclusive content or coupons or contests (described in Book VI). For example, the Hungry Hobo (shown in Figure 2-16) gives fans a free sandwich for liking it on Facebook.

+ **Increasing your reach:** The two ways to increase reach are paid and unpaid. (See Book VII, Chapter 1, for more details about paid.)

Figure 2-16:
Rewards
like this one
from Hungry
Hobo can
encourage
Likes.

Courtesy of Sagemark, LTD dba The Hungry Hobo.

✦ **Increasing engagement:** Read more about this topic in Book I, Chapter 1, and Book IV, Chapters 2 and 3.

✦ **Reaching the "wrong" people:** You can segment your Facebook followers to target your posts. (See Book VIII, Chapter 1.) If you're using paid advertising, take a look at the People tab on Insights to see who your audience is and make sure you target those people. Book I, Chapter 2, has more about finding your audience.

Gaining marketing insight from Insights

Braxton's Animal Works, a 75-year-old, pet supply retail store outside Philadelphia, might be a third-generation business, but it's a first-generation Facebook user, as shown in the accompanying figure.

With most of its customers located within 5 to 10 miles of its bricks-and-mortar store, you might think that Facebook would have little success. Not so, claims co-owner Dave Braxton. He began posting to Facebook on an intermittent and irregular basis in 2009 at the recommendation of a friend and social media consultant. It took until 2012, however, for him to start using Insights to refine his approach. Now, he uses Insights data to guide his content and release schedule for optimum visibility.

"By keeping an eye on releases with the best reach and response, we can continue to deliver content in which our customers are interested," he explains. "We've just begun to look at Insights and Facebook advertising to 'reverse engineer' our best in-store customers. By uploading e-mails of our best clients and allowing Facebook to create demographic and psycho-graphic profiles, we can reach out to similar people in our area."

As a veteran of multiple changes to Insights, Braxton appreciates the new, easier-to-navigate layout and dashboard. In particular, he likes being able to sort by the field values so he can compare posts by any value he wants: for example, by reach.

Braxton's primary marketing goal is to drive traffic to the company website, where visitors can find more in-depth product information and current pet-care suggestions. From there, Braxton wants viewers to sign up for the company's e-mail newsletters, which offer coupons and other promotions to encourage customers to visit the store. "We have had success getting people to the website but are still working on a compelling conversion to e-mail," he says.

Braxton's hasn't needed much outside promotion for its Facebook presence. It uses event-based contests and special promotions to gain reach at specific times that are relevant to the retail store, such as its big annual Harvest Fest and a Halloween costume photo contest.

Braxton's takes advantage of in-store promotional opportunities, too, with Facebook signage and a slide show running on its store registers with the Facebook logo and a call to action asking people to like its page. Braxton's also has a Facebook feed on its website with the latest posts and a Like button.

All this success has been achieved at a minimal cost in dollars and labor. Realistically, Braxton notes, he spends less than 4 hours per month on posting and about the same amount of time on strategy, planning, and reviewing analytics. Dave Braxton offers straightforward advice for other Facebook marketers. "Be sensitive to what your best customers and 'promoters' want to see and engage on your Page. Keep it simple, interesting, and above all, *fun.*"

Courtesy of Braxton's Animal Works.

Chapter 3: Using Third-Party Monitoring Tools and Analyzing Results

In This Chapter

✔ Finding the best tool for your business

✔ Reviewing popular third-party monitoring tools

✔ Turning results into your next steps

*I*n the earlier chapters of this minibook, we discuss the power of monitoring and measuring your social activity. In this chapter, we talk about third-party monitoring and measuring tools that can provide additional insight into your Facebook activity and success. After all, you shouldn't take this on alone. The torrent of data at your fingertips just might make your head spin!

The great news is that numerous third-party monitoring tools have been designed to streamline the monitoring process. These tools scan, grab, and organize your data for easy digestion. And here's the great news: Many of these tools are free or inexpensive.

In this chapter, we look at the key factors you should consider when choosing a monitoring tool for your business. In addition, we examine the core features of multiple different third-party monitoring tools to help you make a well-informed decision for your monitoring and measuring needs.

Choosing the Best Tool for Your Business

When you begin to monitor your social media activity, keep it simple and streamlined. Just because a tool might have 20 features doesn't mean that you should try them all from the get-go. To save yourself some frustration and stress, first get comfortable with the tool's basic features and then move forward to the more-advanced features only after you master the basics.

When choosing a monitoring tool, be clear about what's important to you and your team. The price of a tool may be your number-one deciding factor, for example, whereas another company may be more concerned with a tool's reporting features. Your tool preference depends on your business goals and needs. The following sections describe some key factors to consider when researching third-party monitoring tools.

User flexibility

Even if you start by having just one person in your company monitor your social media activity, you may decide to add other people to your tracking strategy. You want to make sure that you're satisfied with the way the tool allows multiple users to interact at any given time. Not all tools are user-friendly in this area.

Ease of setup

After you select a good tool that meets your needs, the most time-consuming task will be setup. After you take care of this step, the rest will be easy — and, in many cases, automatic. Before you get to the automation, however, you must enter all the data you want to measure.

When selecting a tool to fit your needs, make sure to compile all the login details for your social sites, as well as a list of your needs, including the types of filters (demographics, regions, languages, and so on) and all the keywords you want to track. This data, when compiled before you start to search for a tool, can help you determine which tool has the features that best fit your needs.

Ease of use

You must feel comfortable using the user interface, or you'll quickly abandon the tool. User-friendly dashboards are essential. In many ways, deciding on the specifics of the dashboard layout is a personal preference, and you'll benefit from taking a little time to test a few tools before you make a final decision.

Many tools have guided tours that you can explore before signing up. A tour is a great way to get a sense of how you navigate the tool. We discuss tours in the "Training and support" section, later in this chapter.

Ease of reporting

Each tool has a different depth-of-analysis capability, so determine just how much reporting you need. If you want to keep reporting simple, you might decide to track just a few metrics, including weekly click rates, the number of comments on a post, and the number of likes on your Facebook Page. If that's the case, you won't need a tool that promises depth of analysis and extensive reporting templates. Be careful not to pay for what you don't need.

Cost

If you're just starting and aren't confident that your tracking outcomes are on target with your business goals, taking baby steps may be wise. We encourage you to choose a tool that offers a free version and then upgrade to a paid version when you're certain that the tool will work for you. Also, when looking at cost, consider how important your monitoring needs are and how much time you can dedicate to monitoring.

Training and support

Many tools, both free and premium, offer great guided tours to review before you make your decision. Take advantage of these tours.

In addition, before you choose a tool, find out whether the tool comes with training videos to help you get started quickly. Tutorials and training videos that walk you through the features and benefits of the tool are extremely useful, allowing you to get up and running quickly. They also give you a good sense of where to start and what you may want to build up to when you feel more comfortable.

Choosing Monitoring Tools: Your Third-Party Options

After you're clear about the features of a monitoring tool that are most important to you, it's time to get down to business and choose a tool. In this section, we look at just a few of the many third-party tools that are on the market today.

Each of the following tools differs in its approach, metrics, depth of analysis, channels measured, reporting capability, and user interface. If your goal is to keep costs down, you may find that a combination of free tools works best for you. If you're willing to pay a premium, just one tool may be all you need to cover everything you want to do. The key is to identify your tracking needs first and then research which tool, or combination of tools, best meets your needs.

Many of the tools discussed in this section offer multiple levels of membership. When you find a tool that fits your needs, make sure to research it closely to find the level of membership (if applicable) that best fits what you're looking for in features and functionality. Double-check that your tool choices are compatible with Facebook, which changes frequently.

The tools break down this way:

+ **Alerts:** Mention.net, Social Mention, and Hyper Alerts
+ **Analytics:** Google Analytics and Crowdbooster
+ **Sentiment and influence:** Topsy, Sprout Social, and Klout
+ **Other/Management:** Bitly, HootSuite, and AgoraPulse

Bitly

`https://bitly.com`

Bitly is a free tool (with a premium option) that allows users to shorten, share, and track links (URLs). Because Bitly allows you to see how many people from multiple social networks clicked a specific link, it's a valuable asset for Facebook marketing. This capability helps you to determine which of your marketing efforts are most effective. When you copy and paste a long URL into its portal (for example, `http://www.watermelonweb.com/order-books`), Bitly automatically generates a shorter link (for example, `http://bit.ly/1g8EYuC`) that can be used on social networks or anywhere on the web. Bitly also offers the option of custom links (for example, bit.ly/watermelonbooks).

You don't need to set up a free account to shorten a link. You can do that right from Bitly's home page, as shown in Figure 3-1. However, we encourage you to set up a free account so you can view all your links easily in one interface and have easy access to basic link analytics, as shown in Figure 3-2.

Figure 3-1: The Bitly home page allows you to shorten a link without having an account.

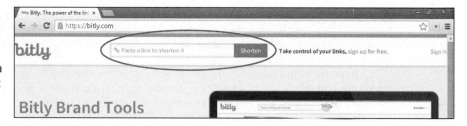

Another perk of creating an account with Bitly is you can view metadata related to click activity for all your links. This tool is useful for tracking where the link has been shared and the geographical regions where your shortened link receives the most activity. Figure 3-2 shows a summary Bitly report for several links. Refer to Figure 1-4 in this minibook for an example of the detailed report provided when you click the View Stats button.

Mention

https://en.mention.com

Mention is an alert service that reports when selected keywords appear on various social media channels. You receive an e-mail when Mention finds your chosen keywords on social networks, news sites, forums, blogs, or any other web page. You can specify whether to receive e-mails daily or weekly, or opt for desktop notifications instantly, every five minutes, or hourly. The free account option offers searches on one term with up to 100 mentions per month, including both Facebook and Twitter posts. The three paid options have higher limits for both terms and mentions.

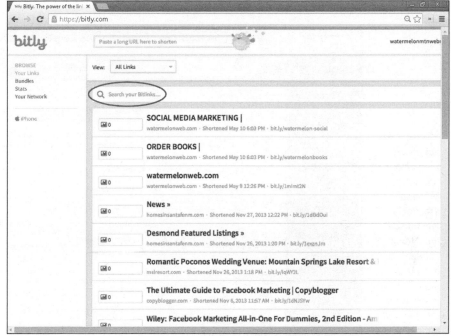

Figure 3-2:
A Bitly summary report on multiple shortened links.

Courtesy of Bitly and Watermelon Mountain Web Marketing (WatermelonWeb.com).

If you opt for the free version, we suggest setting up your alert for your company name. If you want additional searches, for example, on your most popular product or service, or on a competitor's name, you'll need to sign up for a paid account.

You can change your chosen search term whenever you want. This is convenient if you want to monitor the visibility of different events, for example. Figure 3-3 is an example of a report from Mention.

Google Analytics
www.google.com/analytics

Google Analytics is a free tool that provides insights into website traffic and marketing effectiveness, allowing users to see and analyze traffic data, including traffic to your website generated from your Facebook Page and other social media channels.

The number of keyword mentions

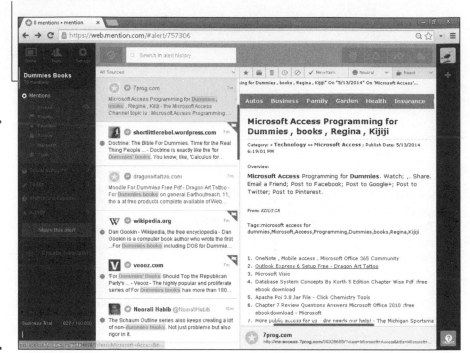

Figure 3-3:
A sample report from Mention lists social mentions in the middle column and shows the full comment in the primary pane on the right.

To set up Google Analytics, your developer will need to copy and paste a few lines of code into every page of your website to start tracking activity on your site.

One of the many great features of this tool is its capability to uncover trends in your visitor activity — meaning that it gives you a visual representation of how your users are interacting with your site over specific periods. This data can help you identify what your visitors are responding to most on your site. A Social section is devoted to your visitors from social networks, including Facebook.

To view this report, follow these steps:

1. **Select the Audience Overview page (in the left column).**

2. **Choose Acquisition⇨Social⇨Overview, as shown in the top of Figure 3-4.**

The bottom of Figure 3-4 shows a Google Analytics Social Value report.

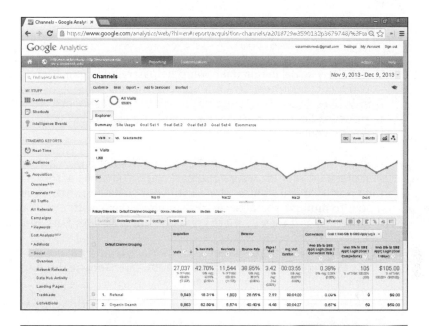

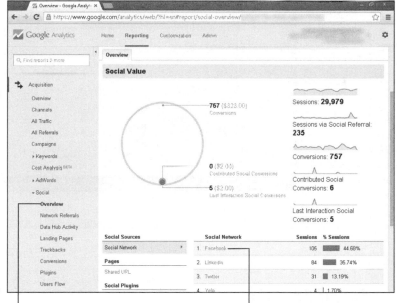

Figure 3-4:
Navigate to the Social section of Google Analytics in the left column to (bottom) view the Social Value report.

Choose Social, then Overview   Facebook

HootSuite

http://hootsuite.com

HootSuite's social media dashboard helps organizations identify and grow social media audiences by creating and tracking campaigns and industry trends in real time. HootSuite has a web-based dashboard, so you don't have to download any software to use it, and you can access your data online from anywhere.

One of the best features of HootSuite is its Hootlet tool, which is a button that you place on your browser's toolbar. When you come across an article or blog post that you want to share with your social networks, you can schedule a post to multiple social networks simultaneously with a click of a button. Hootlet makes it easy to share great content with your fans and customers.

In addition, the multiple-panel user interface makes managing multiple channels easy. Figure 3-5 shows a typical HootSuite statistical report.

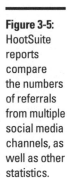

Figure 3-5:
HootSuite reports compare the numbers of referrals from multiple social media channels, as well as other statistics.

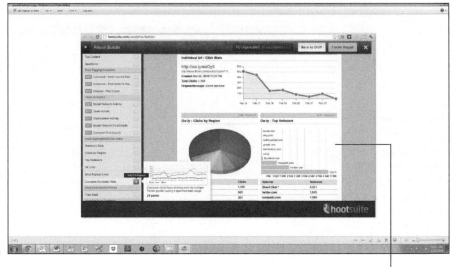

Top Referrers stats

Social Mention

www.socialmention.com

Social Mention is a free alert service that specifically tracks data from more than 100 social media networks. Its real-time social media, search-and-analysis platform allows you to track and measure what people are saying about your company and products on Facebook and other social media properties.

One unique feature of this tool is its analysis service, which reports on the ratio of positive to negative mentions (sentiment), and the number of top keywords, users, and sources. This data is extremely valuable for identifying how people feel about your programs and services.

Figure 3-6 shows a typical Social Mention report. Note that you can select which sources to search for mentions. In the drop-downs, you may also choose to display results by date or source, and by time frame, ranging from the last hour to the last month or anytime.

Unlike the service from Mention, nothing keeps you from entering a competitor's name or any other term in the search field.

Sort by source drop-down menu

Sources   Display results drop-down menu

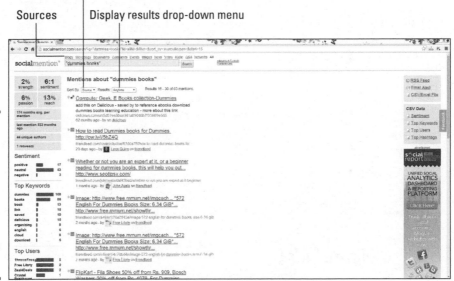

Figure 3-6:
Social
Mention
reports the
appearance
of a search
term on
multiple
social media
channels.

Crowdbooster

`http://crowdbooster.com`

Crowdbooster shows analytics based on your business and social media strategies to help you achieve an effective presence on Twitter and Facebook. This tool measures your follower and fan growth, impressions, total reach, engagement, and other meaningful statistics; then it gives you specific ways to improve each one of these areas. It also gives you insights into your audience and allows you to manage multiple Twitter accounts and Facebook Pages in one location.

The basic Bronze plan, which costs $9 per month (and starts with a 30-day free trial), gives you social media metrics and tailored recommendations, plus weekly account summaries sent via e-mail for one Twitter account and one Facebook Page. To manage more accounts, you can upgrade to the Silver, Gold, or Platinum plans. Figure 3-7 shows a Crowdbooster report.

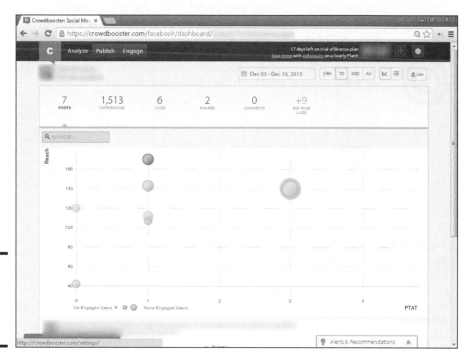

Figure 3-7: A sample Crowdbooster report.

AgoraPulse

http://agorapulse.com

AgoraPulse is an all-in-one Facebook marketing and customer relationship management (CRM) solution that helps small businesses and large brands measure their Facebook return on investment (ROI). Features include a community manager tool kit for managing your Facebook Page, including scheduled publishing, content tagging, and e-mail alerts. It helps you find out more about your fan base and how much your Facebook Likes are worth based on specific information you collect from them.

The beauty of AgoraPulse is it supplies you with easy-to-use tools to collect the data from your fans without being too intrusive or pushy. For example, you can create a contest that offers a giveaway in exchange for some key data you want to collect from your fans, making the contest strategy a win-win for both you and your fans.

You also get access to premium Facebook apps that allow you to add quizzes, sweepstakes, contests, and other functionality to your Facebook Page. Plans start at $29 per month. Figure 3-8 shows one of many AgoraPulse reports.

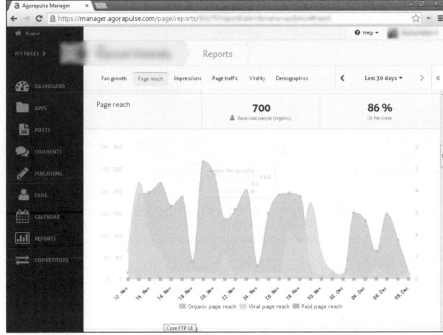

Figure 3-8: An AgoraPulse report on page reach, one of the many reports available.

Hyper Alerts

www.hyperalerts.no

Hyper Alerts is a free tool that allows you to sign up for e-mail alerts whenever someone posts and comments on your Facebook Page. You don't have to be an administrator of a Facebook Page to receive alerts, which makes it a great tool to encourage your fans or employees to use to keep up to date with your latest Facebook activity. It's also a handy tool to monitor your competition. Figure 3-9 shows the Hyper Alerts user interface.

Sprout Social

http://sproutsocial.com

Sprout Social monitors key metrics, discussions, and connections with users, and helps businesses increase brand awareness across demographic groups.

Figure 3-9:
The Hyper
Alerts user
interface.

Two great features of this tool are the engagement and influence scores. These scores are determined by your engagement activity, as well as by your fan growth and interest level over time. The tool

✦ Aggregates average influence and engagement scores of Facebook users

✦ Shows you how your scores compare to the average scores on Facebook

✦ Gives you advice to help you increase your overall scores

Plans start at $39 per month. Figure 3-10 shows a sample Sprout Social report.

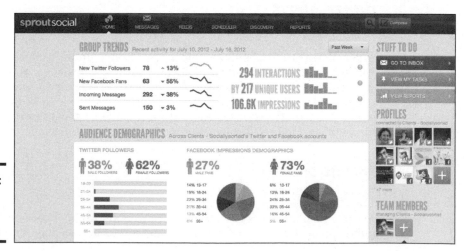

Figure 3-10:
A Sprout
Social
report.

Topsy

http://topsy.com

Topsy is a free, real-time search engine that indexes and ranks search results based on trending conversations that people are having about specific terms, topics, pages, or domains queried.

What makes this search engine different from traditional search tools is that it tracks what people are actually talking about, meaning that you see what people think and feel about the topics being discussed. Understanding the sentiment and the human side of these online conversations gives you better insight to your potential audience. Figure 3-11 shows a typical Topsy report. Note that you can sort results by different time ranges and sources in the left column. As with Social Mention, you can sort on a competitor's name to gather market intelligence.

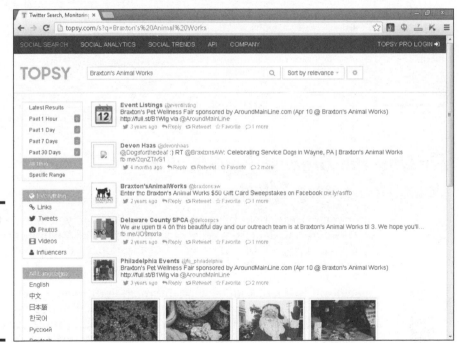

Figure 3-11:
A sample
search
report on
Topsy for
Braxton's
Animal
Works.

Klout

http://klout.com

Klout is a free influence-tracking tool. It gauges the influence level of any social media user on a scale from 1 to 100 by collecting and ranking multiple data points from eight social networks daily (for example, followers, comments, clicks of links, retweets, and so on).

You can use it to identify the influence level of your customers, to see who's most influential in your industry, and to find out where you fall on the influence scale. After you know your own influence score, you can monitor it to see whether it increases or decreases based on your social activity. This tool is a great indicator of which social channels are working for you. Figure 3-12 shows a Klout influence report.

Figure 3-12: A sample Klout influence report.

Courtesy of Watermelon Mountain Web Marketing (WatermelonWeb.com).

Finding the Biggest Payoff with Your Monitoring Efforts

After you're clear about the data you want to collect, you may decide that you need to grab data from Facebook Insights, Social Mention, and HootSuite. Managing multiple tools takes some organization, no doubt, but if combining tools meets your needs, you should do that.

Specifically, Facebook limits what information third-party developers can access and monitor. That limit is why it's important to use the data from Insights if you can't get the data you need from other tools. As you know, however, Facebook Insights monitors only activity related to Facebook. Therefore, research third-party tools to expand your monitoring beyond Facebook, especially to compare the effects of your efforts in a variety of social media outlets.

Your decision on which monitoring tools you use comes down to your tracking goals, resources, time, and money. Only you can determine what's best for your business.

The more actions you can link to the results you obtain from your tracking data, the bigger the payoff. If the data you collect helps you streamline your support team, correct a flaw in your product, ignite a new idea for a partnership, and/or solidify new relationships with potential clients, your tracking strategy can become a vehicle for growing your sales. You can increase the ROI on your time, money, and efforts when you use the data to see real results in your business.

Analyzing Results and Taking Action

One of the ultimate goals of Facebook marketing is to move your fans to action. To do this, you must try different strategies to discover what works best for your team, which is why monitoring and measuring are key to your success. By analyzing this data, you can strategically decide what your next steps should be.

In this section, we explore how to create a plan to take the data that's most crucial to your business and put it into action. In addition, we touch on the importance of eliminating time-wasters and being as flexible as possible so you can change your strategies when challenges arise. In social media marketing, your ability to course-correct quickly is critical to your success!

Building a tracking guide

In Book IX, Chapter 1, we discuss the importance of monitoring and measuring and explain why they're crucial to the success of your social media plan. Here, we show you how to create an overall tracking plan. The key to streamlining your monitoring and measuring process is creating a quick guide for easy reference. The payoff for this extra step is big and worth the time! After you put a plan of action in place (in the form of a tracking guide), the data becomes manageable, and you can more easily understand how to use it to your advantage. The result: Having a growing number of fans and increasing engagement won't feel like work, but will be an enjoyable experience. What a concept!

Creating a monitoring schedule

Inside your company, identify your front-line listening and response teams — specifically, who will monitor the data and who will be assigned to respond to the conversations in real time. These people will be the faces of your company, so choose them wisely! In addition, decide who will analyze the data behind the scenes.

When you're putting your monitoring schedule together, quick response is the goal. Therefore, make sure to cover all bases. What is your plan for nights and weekends, for example? If your company isn't a 24/7 company, one option is an alerting system. Some third-party tools send you a text message when a post has been made. Although you don't want to get messages all the time if you have active accounts, this solution might be a smart one to use when you can't be around a computer. When you're choosing your monitoring tools, be sure to look at alerting features.

In addition, depending on how often you and your team members will evaluate the data, decide how often you should run reports. We suggest starting with just one report per week to track your progress. As you expand your social media activity and start seeing more engagement, you may want to track biweekly. Also, decide which reports to run so that running them becomes an automatic task.

Mapping out a communication plan

When it comes to your communication plan, you have two paths to explore with your team: internal communications and external communications.

First, create an internal path within your company. For your internal path, look at your data and ask, "Who needs to know?" Many small to midsize companies have different departments that follow different metrics.

We suggest that you meet with your teams to clarify what information needs to be sent to specific teams. Consider the following teams when you create your internal communication plan:

+ Sales

+ Marketing

+ Customer service

+ Human resources

+ Research and development

+ Management and executives

In addition to looking at your internal teams, consider how you will be communicating with your customers and fans — your *external path* of communication. As you monitor online conversations, different situations will arise, and you want to be ready for them.

Here are some specific questions to answer:

+ **How quickly will you respond to customer questions, concerns, complaints, and issues?** Responding in real time is ideal, meaning at the time when your fan has posted her questions. However, it's not always realistic to instantly reply to posts on your Facebook Page. You want to determine your response time during work hours and also nonworking hours to ensure the entire team knows what is expected. As a rule, because Facebook is "always on," it would be smart to work out a plan to respond to all inquiries on your Facebook Page within a few hours of the time an inquiry was posted.

✦ **How will you respond to people who post questions about your products or services?** Also decide how you'll respond when someone asks about something related to your area of expertise. Will you offer your support — and, in the process, take advantage of consultative selling, which means you can offer advice and insight while subtly suggesting your own products and services? Plan this strategy so that you're prepared!

✦ **What will you do when a crisis arises?** You need to document this plan, identifying who on your team should be responding and what responses should be used in specific situations. If you sell products on your website, for example, and your site goes down, many frustrated customers may post on social networks that your site isn't working. A crisis plan for this situation may be to designate one person on your team to communicate on your social networks when your company is having challenges with its website. By informing your fans and customers right away, you eliminate the potential of negative chatter before it starts.

✦ **How will you respond to negative and positive posts?** Make it a goal to respond to all comments about you, good or bad. How will you respond to an angry blogger who posts negative feedback about your number-one product, for example? You want to have your plan in place and your team trained.

✦ **How will you respond to posts on your Timeline that aren't aligned with the goals that you've set out for your Facebook community?** It's common, for example, for some fans to post promotional details about their own products and services on your Timeline. These posts tend to clutter the Page and detract from the conversations your fans are having. Define which posts aren't acceptable on your Page and how to address them so that your team will be ready to handle any situation that arises.

Allocating manpower and resources from analysis

After you collect your data consistently, you'll begin to see patterns and areas to tweak for improvement. When you get a clear picture of what you need to do, decide whether additional staff or other resources are needed. As always, focus on the growth of your business. When you're making a decision about taking on more work or changing what you've been doing, weigh the financial, time, and manpower implications against the overall business goal.

Identifying the time-wasters

When considering whether to pursue a particular goal or strategy, ask yourself: Are you doing it because you truly believe that you should or just because everyone else is doing it? With the popularity of social media, taking on a new shiny "social media strategy" just because everyone else is doing it is a common mistake.

We hear all the hype about a tool or a strategy and jump on it, thinking that we'll be left behind if we don't use it. The real question you need to ask is, "Does this make sense for my business?" Stay focused on expanding your business, and take on only the projects that you expect to produce valuable results.

Making adjustments on the fly

Whether you're a new user of social media marketing or have been using it for a while, you're likely to stumble at times. Don't get bogged down by these events: The goal is to fail fast and move on. With a tracking system in place, you can identify issues quickly and rectify them before too much damage is done.

Social media moves fast. The good news is that when you do have challenges, if you respond to them quickly, they're more easily forgotten. Media are always changing, especially Facebook! If you stay in the know and are aware of trends and behaviors early on, you have a huge competitive advantage.

Building on your success

As you continue to build momentum with your social media strategy, pay close attention to your own best practices. Which strategies are working for you on Facebook? Has a pattern emerged regarding the strategies that are working? Your fans are likely to respond well to certain things, while other engagement attempts of yours fall flat. As long as you monitor your success and continue to make adjustments on the fly, some clear best practices will surface over time.

If it ain't broke, don't fix it. When you find a strategy that's producing good results, continue with it and build on it. Add more of what's working, and modify or delete the strategies that aren't showing the results you're after.

Index

Symbols and Numerics

\# (hashtag symbol)
  contest promotion, 453
  contest searches, 462–463
  photo tagging, 345
  posting use, 406
  similar name searches, 602
  Twitter versus Facebook, 603
@ tagging, 680
22Social app
  Google Hangout on Air installation,
    644–647
  Livestream versus, 637
  overview, 636

A

A/B testing
  ad copying, 561, 563
  Ads Manager tweaking, 562
  goal assessment, 562
  image changes, 564–565
  landing page changes, 567
  overview, 562–563
  targeting changes, 555–556
  title/text changes, 563–564
Activity Feed plug-in, 622–623
Activity Log, 143
AddaRug website, 611–612
Admin assignment. *See* Page Admin
Admin panel. *See also* Page Admin
  Activity Log access, 143
  administrative dashboard, 132–133
  apps, 148–149, 198, 200, 204–206
  banned user controls, 143
  Build Audience options, 144
  e-mail contact, importing, 101–102
  Friends invitations, 99–100
  Get More Likes section, 122
  Help section links, 144
  Insights link, 144

  Messages section, 120–121
  New Page Likes section, 128
  overview, 85, 119–120
  Page category changes, 113–114
  Page Tips section, 123
  Pages to Watch section, 123
  Posts/Notifications section, 120
  Publish/Unpublish option, 97
  Share Page option, 102–104
  smartphone setup, 105–106
  Total Page Likes section, 127
administration. *See* Page Admin
AdRoll website, 604
Ads. *See also* Ads Create tool; Power
    Editor; streaming video
  ad sets
    metrics, 524–526
    Power Editor management, 528–530
  ad types, 479–480
  analyzing results
    baseline analysis, 484–488
    Seagull Outfitters example, 491–492
    spreadsheet downloads, 485–486
  approval process, 519–520
  auction bidding system, 470–471, 478,
    517–519
  autoplay video ads, 603–604
  banner ads, 477–478
  budget decisions, 482, 516–519
  campaign decisions, 36–37
  campaign structures, 482
  click tracking, 480–481
  contest promotion, 399
  Event promotions, 387
  external market, 499–502
  Facebook placement algorithms, 475
  goal identification, 484–489
  internal market, 496–499
  landing pages, 477
  Like link effects, 300
  marketing objectives, 476–477
  mobile device optimization, 662–664
  News Feed advantages, 476

Ads *(continued)*
  overview, 469–470
  photos, 404–405
  planning, 490–491
  premium ads, 471
  Promoted posts
    advantages, 480
    Boost Post versus, 481
    location, 477
    options, 482
    overview, 471
  restrictions/prohibitions, 483
  searching for, 465
  target audience research, 32–35
  targeting strategies, 472–474, 491–492
  visibility enhancement, 601
Ads Create tool
  ads, 530–533
  Ads Manager screen, 519
  advertising objective choices, 496
  approval process, 519–520
  audience targeting options
    Behaviors, 513–514
    Connections, 514
    Demographics, 508–511
    Interests, 512–513
    Locations, 508
    More Categories, 514
  campaigns, 528–530, 532–533
  Custom Audiences, 540–543
  external market options, 499–502
  Facebook Account setup, 514–519
  image selection, 502–504
  internal market options, 496–499
  linking websites to Pages, 504
  overview, 493–495
  Place Order screen, 518–519
  Text and Links section, 504–508
Ads Manager
  accessing, 555
  campaigns, 555–557
  Categories area, 556–557
  conversion tracking, 550–551
  data exporting, 670
  Facebook Reports
    accessing, 567–568
    Column editing, 574–576

    date menus, 569
    exporting, 570–571, 580
    Filter buttons, 573, 576–578
    General Metrics data aggregation report,
      571–572
    hover feature, 574
    old reports link, 578–580
    overview, 567–568
    saving/sharing, 570
    scheduling, 569–570
    setup choices, 568–569
  Left sidebar, 558–559
  Menus, 556
  mobile ad metrics area, 670–671
  Notifications and Daily Spend area,
    555–556
  overview, 480–481, 553–555
  Power Editor uploads, 554
  split testing
    ad copying, 561, 563
    image changes, 564–565
    landing page changes, 567
    overview, 562–563
    targeting changes, 555–556
    title/text changes, 563–564
  users, 559–560
advertising. *See* marketing; marketing
      strategies; promotions
age restrictions, 137
AgoraPulse, 348, 458, 724–725
albums
  adding photos, 272–273
  cover photo selection/editing, 272–273
  creating/using, 185–186
  Public
    creating, 323–324
    existing album use, 324–325
    overview, 322
  sharing strategies, 273–275
Alltop website, 183, 448
analytics. *See also* Ads Manager; Insights;
      split testing
  ad sets, 524–526
  adjusting tactics, 732
  AgoraPulse tool, 724–725
  behavior tracking, 684
  Bitly tool, 717–718

blog link tracking, 685
contests
  baseline analysis, 484–488
  re-posting issues, 408–411
  spreadsheet downloads, 485–486
  third-party analytics, 400
  winner selection, 409
conversion tracking, 550–551
Crowdbooster tool, 723–724
feature choices, 715–717
Google Alerts, tracking with, 183
Google Analytics, 400, 669–670, 719–721
Google Keyword Planner, 683–684
HootSuite tool, 722
Hyper Alerts tool, 725
importance of, 682–683
Insights tool, 728
keyword tools, 683–684, 687–690
Klout tool, 727–728
Like Button plug-in, 613
Like link benefits, 300
Likes, 484–486
Mention tool, 718–719
multiple-site use, 728–729
News Feed algorithm, 178
overview, 44, 715, 717
ROI indicators, 684
Share Button plug-in, 618
Social Mention tool, 722–723
social plug-ins, 608
Sprout Social tool, 725–726
Topsy tool, 727
tracking, 729–731
Antavo website, 419
apps (applications). *See also* Facebook
    Developers site; iFrame apps
adding, 148–149
App Center
  overview, 332
  Pages, using with, 333–335
  Profile use of, 333–335
"App Creation Failed" message, 350
app photo editing, 204–205
arranging/managing, 203, 342
custom apps
  "App Creation Failed" message, 350
  installing, 201–202

marketing strategies, 588
mobile devices issues, 96
overview, 94–95
types/locations, 95
deleting, 204, 337
display limitations, 155,
  198, 202
Events, 149–150
Facebook-built
  adding, 93–94
  Events, 197
  name/cover image restrictions, 94
  Notes, 198
  Photos, 197
  title/cover image restrictions, 198
  Video, 198
Featured apps, 155–156, 198, 202
finding/listing, 198, 200,
  205–206, 335
Google+, 340
Interests Page restrictions, 74
Likes tab restrictions, 203
linking from, 200
linking to, 147–148
managing/moving, 373–374
marketing strategies, 337–338
mobile device issues, 336, 342
Notes, 152–154
overview, 147, 197, 331–332
Page dashboard options, 140
Page use
  adding, 87, 93–96
  App Center, limited value of,
    331–335
  arranging/managing, 203
  deleting, 204, 337
  discussion boards, 338–339
  editing, 336–337
  finding/installing, 335–336
  installation/use, 67–68, 87, 93–96,
    201–202
  linking to Profile apps, 334
  marketing strategies, 337–341
  mobile device issues, 336, 442
  overview, 67–68, 147
  Pinterest apps, 340
  Profile app use, 333–334

apps (applications) *(continued)*
  removing, 148–149
  URLs belonging to, 147
  video apps, 339–340
  Photos
    ads, using for, 151
    app photo editing, 204–205
    overview, 150–151
  Pinterest, 340
  Profile use, 331–335
  Promotions requirement, 245
  Social RSS
    display tab, adding, 219–220
    free versus paid service,
      220–221
    installing, 218–220
    overview, 218
    Pages, using with, 340
    posting limitations, 221
    Profile, adding a feed to, 220
    thumbnail image selection, 219
    website, 221
  social versus Page, 331–335
  third-party, 198
  title editing, 204–205
  URLs belonging to, 147
  Video
    formats supported, 155
    limitations of, 154–155
    uploading videos, 155
  video apps
    finding/listing, 339–340
    overview, 339
    testing, 340
    third-party versus Facebook, 339
  visibility enhancement, 601
  website integration, 341
  YouTube apps, 339–340
@ tagging, 680
attachments
  icon descriptions, 180
  multimedia value, 180, 183
Audience Suggestions, Page dashboard
    options, 140
autoplay video ads, 603–604

B

B2B (business-to-business) marketing
  advantages of, 14–15
  buying decisions, 15
  customer acquisition percentage, 14
  personal engagement, 11–12, 15–16, 25
  research reports, 14
B2C (business-to-consumer) marketing
  advantages of, 11–12, 25
  strategies, 12–13, 15–16
badges, 104
Band Profile app, 342
BandPage website, 316
banner ads, 477–478
banning, 143, 291–293
Be Inspired Films, 642–643
Best Friends Animal Society, 38
Bitly tracking tool, 685, 717–718
blocking, 143, 291–293
blog posts
  Admin rights, 151
  app URLs, sharing, 147
  commenting on, 168
  content duplication concerns, 227
  contest promotion, 399
  dlvr.it tool use, 224–226
  Event promotion, 387
  Facebook import options, 210
  Follow button, embedding, 168
  importing, 207, 210, 218
  Like Boxes, 104
  Like button effects, 301
  linking to, 180
  NetworkedBlogs app
    blog registration, 211–213
    display tab, adding, 217–218
    overview, 210–211
    ownership verification, 213–214
    reposting blogs, 216–217
    syndication setup, 215–216
    website, 216
  Notes feature issues, 152, 154
  photos, attaching, 216
  reposting, 216–217

RSS address discovery
  Firefox method, 208–209
  HTML code search, 209–210
  Internet Explorer method, 208
RSS Graffiti app
  content, adding with, 221
  feed import options, 221
  overview, 221
  website, 221
Social RSS app
  display tab, adding, 219–220
  free versus paid service, 220–221
  installing, 218–220
  overview, 218
  posting limitations, 221
  thumbnail image selection, 219
  website, 221
viral exposure opportunities, 602
Boom Social with Kim Garst, 280–281
Booshaka website, 43
Boosting
  Facebook Offers
    promoting from Ads Creation tool, 600
    promoting from Pages, 598–599
  posts
    accessing, 120
    Ads Manager reports, 557
    advantages, 496
    contest promotion, 411–412
    overview, 194
    Promoted posts versus, 481
    spending level choices, 497
    Timeline use, 481
brand awareness, 687
branding
  audience targeting, 27–28
  business versus personal, 67
  contest benefits, 390–391
  Facebook Pages, 38
  News Feed value, 180
Braxton's Animal Works website, 712–713
Buffer button, 104
Buffer tool, 238–239
Build Audience options, Admin panel, 144
business-to-business (B2B) marketing
  advantages of, 14–15
  buying decisions, 15

customer acquisition percentage, 14
  personal engagement, 11–12,
    15–16, 25
  research reports, 14
business-to-consumer (B2C) marketing
  advantages of, 11–12, 25
  strategies, 12–13, 15–16

C

Calendar view (Events), 370–371
calendars
  Event listing, 370–371
  Event synching, 378
  scheduling messages, 236–237
  scheduling posts, 188
Calendars That Work website, 39
call to action
  About section use, 127
  advantages of, 148
  app title/photo editing, 204
  app use, 309
  Cover photo, 270
  custom tab use, 344
  NFL example, 283
  photos/albums, 273
campaigns. *See also* Ads Manager
  Ads Create tool
    budget decisions, 516–518
    management with, 519
    Power Editor versus, 522
    setup choices, 514–516
  Ads Manager overview, 555
  naming, 514–515
  Power Editor management
    ad set management, 528–530
    creating campaigns, 526–527
    Excel imports, 527–528
    modifying/editing campaigns, 532–533
    overview, 521–522
  structuring, 482
Canvas Page, 353
chat boxes
  Admin content control, 635
  Livestream app, 634
  streaming video combination, 634
Chrome browser, 522

click-through rate (CTR)
  conversion rate versus, 478–479
  definition, 478–479
  Facebook versus others, 477
  mobile ads, 662–663
  comma-separated value (CSV) format
  Contest Capture tool, 412–413
  e-mail contacts
    exporting, 558
    importing, 100
  Excel file preparations, 541
  Insight data exports, 485, 706–707
  report file exports
    generating, 570–571
    old report viewing, 578–580
  Timeline importing, 412
Comments plug-in
  benefits, 623
  Like Button comments versus, 623
  optimizing, 624–625
  thread synchronization, 624
  visitor options, 624
Community Pages, 72–73
Company Pages
  creation of, 75
  overview, 75–76
  profile linking, 76
  redirecting visitors, 76
Constant Contact blog, 659
consultants, 47–48
Contact Form app, 338
Contact Tab app, 338
Contest Capture tool
  data exporting, 409, 412
  Timeline contest winner selection,
    412–413
  website, 409
contest promotion
  blog tours
    blog search sites, 448
    finding/contacting bloggers,
      448–449
    guest posting suggestions, 448–449
    overview, 447
    scheduling, 449

external contests, 455–456
  personal blogs, 450–451
  social media advertising
    LinkedIn, 454
    overview, 452
    Twitter, 453
    YouTube videos, 454–455
  Websites
    banners/widgets, 449
    contest links, 449
    examples, 450
    Open Graph use, 451–452
contests. *See also* promotions; third-party
    applications; Timeline contests
  advantages, 389–390
  analyzing results
    AgoraPulse website, 458
    e-mail use, 456
    Facebook Insights use, 458–459
    fan gating, 458
    overview, 456
    strategy adjustments, 459–460
    third-party applications, 456–457
  apps
    administration requirement, 245
    cover photo/title editing, 444–445
    position editing, 443–444
    use of, 391
  consumer endorsement regulations,
    247–248
  design considerations
    entry requirements, 391
    goals/targets, 398–399
    invitation options, 392
    judging/winning options, 392
    length decisions, 391
    planning/promoting, 399–400
    prizes, 390–393
    types, 391–392
  engagement opportunities, 389
  future contest planning
    advantages of, 461
    observing other contests,
      462–464
    scheduling suggestions, 461–462

Legal requirements
  Facebook Promotion rules, 397
  FTC regulations, 245
  sharing restrictions, 397
  third-party app advantages, 392
  Timeline restrictions, 397
metrics, 400
overview, 389
prizes
  audience polling, 392
  brand connection, 390
  Ultimate Women's Expo
    example, 393
referrals/recommendations,
  390–391
searching for
  app Pages use, 463–464
  Facebook Ad Board, 465
  hashtag use, 462–463
  Twitter searches, 465
sweepstakes versus, 389, 393
Timeline
  advantages of, 391–392
  apps versus, 393
  length of contest period, 391
timing of, 128
types
  app-run versus Timeline, 393
  choices/benefits, 394–396
  sweepstakes versus, 393
viral exposure opportunities, 602
winner selection/notification, 422
winners
  response time rules, 422
  selection/notification, 393, 422
conversation
  encouraging/allowing, 289
  monitoring/managing
    banning inappropriate posters,
      291–293
    deleting/hiding, 290
    overview, 290
    reporting, 290–291
conversion pixels
  advanced options selection, 508
  creating, 500

  e-mailing, 501
  inserting, 500–501
conversion rate
  CTR versus, 478–479
  ROI effects, 479
conversion tracking, 550–551
cost per click (CPC)
  mobile ads, 662–663
  overview, 470
  search engines versus Facebook, 478
cost per thousand (CPM), 470
coupons/discounts
  engaging fans with, 279–280
  exclusive offers, 11
  Facebook Offers
    creating from Ads Create tool, 599
    creating from Pages, 596–597
    Likes engagement, 600
    overview, 191–192, 595
    promoting from Ads Creation
      tool, 600
    promoting from Pages, 598–599
  Facebook Page inclusion, 43–44
Cover photo
  connecting with, 87–88
  description, adding, 89–90
  Grandma Mary Show example, 88, 90
  hover card use, 125
  links, adding, 89–90
  logo/product image placement, 87
  Page strategies, 87–89
  Profile choice, 174
  size requirement, 89
  text/hyperlinks addition, 88
  Timeline strategies, 321–322
  upload procedure, 88–89
  website inclusion, 88, 90
CoveritLive, 223
CPC (cost per click)
  mobile ads, 662–663
  overview, 470
  search engines versus Facebook, 478
CPM (cost per thousand), 470
CRM (customer relationship
    management), 724
Crowdbooster website, 723–724

CSS
editing with ShortStack, 315
iFrame app coding, 346, 351
CSV (comma-separated value) format
Contest Capture tool, 412–413
e-mail contacts
exporting, 558
importing, 100
Excel file preparations, 541
Insight data exports, 485, 706–707
report file exports
generating, 570–571
old report viewing, 578–580
Timeline importing, 412
CTR (click-through rate)
conversion rate versus, 478–479
definition, 478–479
Facebook versus others, 477
mobile ads, 662–663
custom apps. *See also* apps; Facebook
Developers site
advantages, 347
app developer, hiring, 347
building process, 346
choices, 346
Facebook integration decisions, 354–355
installing, 355–356
New App dialog box, 352
overview, 343, 345–346
sandbox mode, 353
settings options, 353
ShortStack use, 360–361
social plug-ins, 608
Static HTML for Pages use, 358–360
Static HTML: iFrame Tabs app, 361–363
tabs
marketing strategies, 588
Red Bull example, 344
ShortStack example, 345
suggestions for, 344
Yellow Dog Project example, 345
third-party applications
Heyo, 357–358
overview, 348
Static HTML for Pages, 358–360

visibility enhancement, 601
web page options, 351
widgets, adding, 360–361
custom lists
audience targeting, 589
benefits of, 589–590
existing data use, 541
Favorites listings, 591–592
hashing, 541
new data selection, 542–543
New Feed filtering, 591
overview, 589
setting up, 590–591
smart lists, 589
custom tabs/pages. *See* iFrame apps
customer engagement strategies
fun content, 13
Hubspot example, 21–22
media variety, 12–13
Oreo example, 12
photos, 14
questions, 15–16
Red Bull example, 13
Zappos example, 15–16
customer invitations
automatic fan concerns, 263
card copy mailings, 258
e-mail signatures
Gmail instructions, 256–258
Microsoft Outlook instructions,
255–256
overview, 255
hold messages, 254
letterhead/stationery, 258
Profile links, 260–262
social network invitations, 262–263
web page icons, 259–260
customer relationship management
(CRM), 724
customer service
Livescribe example, 17
online discussion monitoring, 17
real-time advantages, 16–17
virtual service desk, 17

D

demographics
  Ads Create tool use, 508–511
  Ads targeting, 472–473
  Insights metrics, 704–706
  online measuring, 690–691
DiggDigg website (Buffer), 631–632
discussion boards, 338–339
dlvr.it tool
  overview, 224
  setting up/using, 225–226
  signing up options, 224
drop-down menu (Pages)
  finding your own Page, 145
  Help section, 144
  Page toggling, 115–118, 141, 145
Drupal
  blog hosting, 214
  Facebook icon activation, 260

E

Easypromos website, 419
e-commerce store. *See also* hyperlinks
  advantages, 308
  apps
    discussion board, 338–339
    Ecwid shopping cart, 312
    email capture, 338
    Etsy News Feed interface, 313–314
    installing, 314
    iOS issues, 311
    mobile device issues, 342
    overview, 311
    ShopTab interface, 313
    social network, 340
    Storenvy interface, 311–312
    video, 339–340
    website links, 341
  linking to, 315
  offers, 310, 317
  overview, 307–308
  PayPal, 310, 341

  shopping interfaces, 308
  using featured apps spaces, 308–310
Ecwid website, 312
Elance website, 347
e-mail
  capture systems
    Likes addresses, 601
    third-party applications, 338
  contact invitations
    importing contacts, 100–101
    locating, 102
    overview, 100
    provider-specific instructions, 101–102
    restrictions, 100
  contests
    benefits, 390
    promoting, 399
  Event notifications
    advantages of, 369–370
    limitations to, 380–381
    linking to, 385–386
    Share requests, 385
    subscriber updates, 387
Embedded Posts plug-in, 625
engagement. *See also* conversation; News Feed Algorithm; visibility
  album use, 273–274
  apps, using, 198–200
  audience conversations
    key strategies, 40
    monitoring/responding, 289
    overview, 287
    Timeline settings, 287–288
    view toggling, explaining, 288–289
  Booshaka rankings, 43
  commenting/responding, 286, 386
  contests
    judging options, 392
    prize polling, 392
    Timeline advantages, 394
    Timeline contests, 389
  coupons/discounts, 11, 191–192, 279–280
  Follow button use, 63–65
  Like link use, 297–299

engagement *(continued)*
  Likes audience
    ad objectives, 476–477, 487
    ad use, 497–498
    communication ideas, 601
    offers, 499, 595
  metrics, 55, 686
  online monitoring benefits, 677–680
  organic growth versus automatic
      fans, 263
  overview, 42
  personal Profile use, 61–63
  photo use, 183, 269–273, 386
  Places Nearby app, 661–662
  post targets, 284–285
  posting schedules, 283–284
  Promoted posts, 596, 600
  purpose/branding clarity, 277
  questions, 180, 279
  social plug-ins, 609
  strategies that work, 278
  streaming video, 633–634
  TabSite apps, 363
  Timeline contests, 401
  value of, 385
Etsy website, 313–314
Evenbrite website, 341
Events
  advantages of, 369–370
  advertising for, 498–499
  audience targeting, 376
  calendar synching, 378
  canceling, 380
  creating/adding, 189, 369
  detail entering, 375–378
  detail warning, 375
  editing, 378–379
  e-mail notifications, 370
  Event Wall posting, 376
  home page notifications, 369–370
  invitations to
    Page limitations, 368–369, 380–381
    Profile use, 369
  links to, 369
  milestones, 189–191
  News Feed display of, 369
  notifications, 370, 372
  overview, 367
  Page creation limitations, 380–381
  Page versus personal Profile, 369, 380–381
  Pages, creating from, 374, 380–381
  photo additions, 376–377
  photo/image design, 378
  posting, 180
  private posting, 369
  promoting
    attendee Share requests, 385
    Facebook Ads, 387
    Friend invitations, 383–385
    outside Facebook, 387
    restriction workarounds, 381–382
    RSVP reminders, 382
    Share encouragement, 383
    Share links, 385
    Timeline links, 382–383
    Timeline posts, 382
  public event warning, 367
  Publisher, creating from, 179–180, 375
  Publisher, posting from, 189
  Publisher, warning about, 189
  Publisher photo attachments, 189
  scheduling issues, 188
  Timeline posts versus, 367
  types, 368
  viral exposure opportunities, 602
Events app
  finding/listing, 372–373
  managing/moving, 373–374
  overview, 149–150
  Pages, adding to, 197–198, 372
  tabs, adding to, 373
experiences
  optimizing, 586–587
  overview, 585
  planning/creating, 586

F

Facebook
  active followers, number of, 1, 9, 19
  client interactions, 11
  cost of using, 9–10, 14

global market statistics, 19
major brand usage of, 9
privacy options
  accessing/editing, 23–24
  Facebook Pages concealed, 24
  inline audience selector, 22–23
  overview, 22
Profile creation/restrictions, 21
program innovation and change, 1
viral content, 14
Facebook Ad Board, 465
Facebook Ads. *See* Ads
Facebook Developers site
  "App Creation Failed" message, 350
  overview, 348–349
  verification process
    credit card method, 351
    mobile phone number method, 350
    overview, 349–350
  website, 348
Facebook Exchange. *See* FBX
Facebook Preferred Marketing Developers, 604–605
Facebook Reports. *See* Ads Manager
Facebook Reports, Ads Manager
  accessing, 567–568
  Column editing, 574–576
  date menus, 569
  exporting, 570–571, 580
  Filter buttons, 573, 576–578
  General Metrics data aggregation report, 571–572
  hover feature, 574
  old reports link, 578–580
  overview, 567–568
  saving/sharing, 570
  scheduling, 569–570
  setup choices, 568–569
Facepile plug-in
  benefits, 628–629
  Login options, 627
  overview, 627
fan gating
  Heyo site, 338
  overview, 147, 343, 357
  ShortStack example, 345
  ShortStack website, 315

Static HTML: iFrame Tabs app, 363
third-party applications, 420
Woobox trial app, 338
FanPageEngine app, 364
fans. *See also* fan gating
  acknowledgement examples, 12–13
  Fan Page Friday, 280
  promoting, 280
  recognition/awards, 11, 280
  tagging for updates, 280–281
  thanking publicly, 282
Favorites
  apps
    adding, 94
    rearranging, 155
    removing, 156
  custom list additions, 591–592
  profile picture uploads, 84
  See All link, 155
FBX (Facebook Exchange)
  Facebook Preferred Marketing Developers, 604–605
  mobile device limitation, 604
  overview, 604
  pricing systems, 605
Federal Trade Commission (FTC). *See* FTC
Feedly website, 183
File Transfer Protocol (FTP), 346
Follow button
  advantages, 64–65
  advantages/disadvantages, 160
  age limitation, 160
  deciding on use, 161–162
  enabling, 63–64
  Friend versus Public followers, 169
  friends versus followers, 65
  hover card use, 164
  News Feed exposure, 65
  Pages/Profile connections, 60–61
  privacy options, 64
  Profile business postings, 65
  public figure use, 159–162, 319
  settings options, 164–165
  turning on, 159–160, 163
  website, 65

Follow Button plug-in, 625–627
Forum for Pages app, 339
Foursquare website, 234, 333
freelance website, 36
Friend requests, 31
Friends
  Event invitations, 383–385
  Page invitations
    Admin panel interface, 99
    Filter menu use, 99–100
    overview, 264–265
  Page sharing, 265–268
  tagging, 280–281
FTC (Federal Trade Commission)
  advertising guidelines, 245
  affiliate marketing disclosure, 246
  consumer endorsement regulations,
    247–248
  fines/penalties, 246
FTP (File Transfer Protocol), 346

G

gear icon, 130–131
General Metrics data aggregation report,
  571–572
Get More Likes section, Admin
  panel, 122
Get Notifications toggle, 131
global market
  targeting countries, 19
  translation capability, 20
  user acceptance, 19
globe icon, 89
Gmail, e-mail signatures, 256–258
Goodreads app, 341
Google Alerts website, 183, 687
Google Analytics
  contest metrics, 400
  mobile ad metrics, 669–670
  website traffic tracking, 719–721
Google Blogs website, 448
Google calendars, 39
Google Chrome browser, 522
Google Keyword Planner, 683–684

Google+ account
  Hangout on Air account
    22Social app installation, 644–647
    creating, 644
  website, 644
Google+ app, 340
Grandma Mary Show
  Cover photo example, 88, 90
  Like button example, 303
  long tweet linking example, 233
  online store example, 18
  thumbnail image example, 91
Graph Search tool
  filtering strategies, 31–32
  overview, 29–30
  Pages, finding with, 146
  search methods, 30–31
Groups
  advantages of, 72
  Pages, supplementing with, 71
  project collaboration, 71
  Timeline sharing, 81
  types of, 71
  websites about, 72
Guy Kawasaki app example, 199–200

H

hashing, 541
hashtags
  contest promotion, 453
  contest searches, 462–463
  photo tagging, 345
  posting use, 406
  similar name searches, 602
  Twitter versus Facebook, 603
Help section links, Admin panel, 144
Heyo app
  custom tab creation, 348
  e-commerce store links, 316
  e-mail capturing, 338
  fan gating, 338, 357–358
  overview, 421
  RSS feed replication, 309
  sweepstakes creation/setup

app position editing, 443–444
 cover photo/title editing, 444–445
 publishing options, 432–433
 template setup, 431–432
highlighting posts, 194–195
home page
 Event notifications
  advantages/limitations, 370–372
  left versus right sidebars, 369
  list form versus calendar, 370–371
 Tickers notifications, 178
HootSuite
 campaign tracking, 722
 demographics tracking, 690–691
 Hootlet tool, 722
 multiple-site postings, 236
 online monitoring, 687
 overview, 234
 Pro Plan features, 234
 update scheduling, 237
 website, 234
hover card
 ads, using for, 156–157
 creating, 158
 Follow button use, 164
 Like button use, 285
 overview, 156
 using, 90, 125, 148, 156
HTML
 creating Pages, 309
 editing with ShortStack, 315
 e-mail capturing, 95, 338
 Event announcements, 95
 FTP, uploading with, 348
 hiring app developers, 347
 iFrame app coding, 346, 351
 iFrame use of, 345
 Like button creation, 295, 302
 linking to, 260, 334
 RSS feed address, finding in, 209–210
 Static HTML: iFrame Tabs app, 361–362
Hubspot
 business activity generation, 21–22
 Inbound Marketing Research Report, 14
Humans of New York website, 708
Hyper Alerts, 725

Hyper Alerts (e-mail tool), 725
hyperlinks
 apps, linking from, 200
 blog post links, 180
 contest post sharing, 410–411
 contest rules, 405
 Cover photo use, 88
 debugging links, 183
 e-commerce store links
  BandPage, 316
  Heyo, 316
  overview, 315
  ShortStack app, 315
  TabSite, 316
 editing in Publisher, 181–183
 Event promotions, 382–383
 Facebook icon modification, 321
 Info Page listing, 93
 photo use, 182
 photos
  linking from, 271–272
  linking to, 184–185
 Publisher, creating with, 181–183
 resource links, 180
 status updates, adding to, 96, 181
 thumbnail use, 91, 181–182
 video, attaching, 187

I

icons explained, 2–3
ideal audience. *See* target audience
iFrame apps. *See also* apps; Facebook
  Developers site
 advantages, 347
 app developer, hiring, 347
 building process, 346
 choices, 346
 custom apps
  marketing strategies, 588
  Red Bull example, 344
  ShortStack example, 345
  suggestions for, 344
  Yellow Dog Project example, 345
 Facebook integration decisions, 354–355

iFrame apps *(continued)*
  installing, 355–356
  New App dialog box, 352
  overview, 343, 345–346
  sandbox mode, 353
  settings options, 353
  with ShortStack app, 360–361
  social plug-ins, 608
  with Static HTML for Pages, 358–360
  with Static HTML: iFrame Tabs app,
      361–363
  third-party applications
    Heyo, 357–358
    overview, 348
    Static HTML for Pages, 358–360
  visibility enhancement, 601
  web page options, 351
  widgets, adding, 360–361
Inbound Zombie website, 127
Indemnification and Limitation
    of Liability, 406
influence, 687
Info Page
  category changes, 92
  completing, 91–93
  hyperlink listing, 93
  overview, 81
  Places Page creation, 93
  sharing invites, 93
  Start Info/date modifications, 92
Inline Frame. *See* iFrame apps
Insights
  Admin access to, 138–139, 694
  content evaluation
    graph use, 708
    Likes data, 708
    Page posts, 709–710
    photo/video use, 708–709
  correcting deficiencies
    Braxton's Animal Works example,
        712–713
    recommendations, 711–712
  data analysis
    export file information, 707
    Likes, 708
    overview, 708

data exporting, 485, 706–707
External Referrers graph, 710–711
key player evaluations, 282–283
likes requirements, 693
Likes tab
  data analysis, 708
  metrics graphs, 698–699
  overview, 697
online measuring
  click activity reports, 689
  comment statistics, 687
  demographics reports, 690–691
  engagement statistics, 686
overview, 144, 693
Overview tab
  Admin versus viewer displays, 696–697
  date range options, 695
  hover card use, 696
  key sections, 695–696
  metrics comparisons, 705–706
Page activity analysis, 685
People tab
  Check-ins data, 704–705
  demographics metrics, 704
personal Profile versus business
    Page, 67, 161
Posts tab
  All Posts section, 702–703
  Post Types section, 703–704
Reach tab, 699–700
Visits tab, 701–702, 710–711
Interests lists
  adding members, 594–595
  advantages of, 592
  creating, 592–593
  editing, 594
  followers, growing through, 169–170
  home page location, 592
  News Feed filtering, 592
  overview, 131
  Profile versus Pages, 594
  subscribing to, 592
Interests Pages
  claiming/controlling, 74–75
  Company Pages, 75–76
  disadvantages of, 73–74

identifying, 74
overview, 72
Pages (business) Community options
    versus, 72
searching/finding, 74
interfaces, shopping, 308
international markets
targeting countries, 19
translation capability, 20
user acceptance, 19
Involver website
business Page apps, 339
Page creation, 309
SML licensing, 360
Static HTML for Pages app, 358–359

J

Jet Blue, as B2C example
fun content, 13
media variety, 12–13
Joomla!, 260

K

Karaoke Heroes mobile ad example,
    666–668
key performance indicators (KPI), 676
key players. *See* fans
Klout (influence-tracking tool), 727–728
KPI (key performance indicators), 676

L

landing pages
call to action, 488–489
definition, 477
Lazypants website, 708–709
legal considerations
affiliate marketing, 246–247
content compliance, 248–249
contests/sweepstakes, 245, 397
endorsements, 247–248
promotions, 245–246
website, 243

life events
categories, 325–326
overview, 325
lightbox, 151
Like Boxes
Like buttons versus, 616
overview, 104
social plug-in use, 615–616
thumbnail image use, 617
Like button
badges versus social plug-ins, 104
blog post likes, 301
Friends invitations, 265
hover card use, 285
Interest Pages, 74
Like Boxes versus, 616
Like link versus, 295–296
location of, 295
News Feed, effects on, 299
Pages use, 118, 131, 141, 298–300
social plug-in use, 611–614
video use, 154, 187
web page use, 302–305
like gates, 430
Like link
Admin viewing, 297
comment likes, 298
Facebook Ad links, 300
Like button versus, 295–296
location of, 295
Page post likes, 297
Likes
ad use, 497–498
bidding options, 517–518
blog posts, 602
Contest Capture exports, 409, 412
core marketing rules, 584
custom app use, 588
e-mail capturing, 601
experiences and, 585
metrics, 484–486, 571–572, 574
News Feed posts, 489
offers and, 499, 595
Offers claiming, 595
Promoted posts, 596, 600
social proof use, 587

liking
  advertising for, 497–498
  Get More Likes section, Admin panel, 122
  Like Box creation/customization, 104
  links versus buttons, 295–296
  marketing importance, 296
  New Page Likes section, Admin panel, 128
  Page visibility choices, 129
  Personal versus Page Profiles, 118–119
  Total Page Likes section, Admin panel, 127
  Unlike option, 131
LinkedIn, 454
links
  apps, connecting from, 200
  blog posts, 180
  contest post sharing, 410–411
  contest rules, 405
  Cover photo use, 88
  debugging links, 183
  e-commerce store
    BandPage, 316
    Heyo, 316
    overview, 315
    ShortStack app, 315
    TabSite, 316
  editing in Publisher, 181–183
  Event promotions, 382–383
  Facebook icon modification, 321
  Info Page listing, 93
  photo use, 182
  photos
    linking from, 271–272
    linking to, 184–185
  Publisher, creating with, 181–183
  resource, 180
  status updates, adding to, 96, 181
  thumbnail use, 91, 181–182
  video, attaching, 187
List view (Events), 370–371
lists
  custom lists
    adding members, 591
    audience targeting, 589
    benefits, 589–590
    creating, 590–591

existing data use, 541
    Favorites listings, 591–592
    hashing, 541
    interest lists versus, 592
    multiple list management, 590
    new data selection, 542–543
    News Feed filtering, 591
    overview, 589
    smart lists, 589
  Interests lists
    adding members, 594–595
    advantages of, 592
    audience targeting, 589
    creating, 592–593
    custom lists versus, 592
    News Feed filtering, 592
    Profile versus Pages, 594
  smart lists, 589
live social streams, 634
Livescribe, customer service example, 17
Livestream app
  22Social versus, 637
  account setup, 637–638
  Be Inspired Films example, 642–643
  chat boxes, 634
  event creation, 639–640
  Facebook Page installation, 640–643
  overview, 342, 635
  viral exposure opportunities, 602

M

Macy's app example, 199, 201
MailChimp website, 341
Map My Fitness app, 327
Mari Smith website, 127
marketing. *See also* Ads; visibility
  app budgeting suggestions, 422–423
  contest promotion, 399
  core rules for
    branding, 38–39
    calls to action, 43–44
    engagement, 42
    fan-to-fan conversations, 42–43
    fresh content, 39–40

human touch, 40–41
manage expectations, 37–38
monitor/measure/track, 44
overview, 584
word-of-mouth encouragement, 43
cost of using Facebook, 9–10, 14
customer service advantages, 16
Facebook potential, 9
Inbound Marketing Research Report, 14
Insights benefits, 711–713
international markets, 19–20
mobile device revenues, 656
need for online presence, 27
online discussion monitoring, 16–17
overview, 20
Page versus Profile, 20
subscribing versus Facebook Pages, 20
target audience
    attracting/reaching, 1
    identifying/motivating, 10
virtual service desk, 17
marketing strategies. *See also* Pages; target
    audience
administrators
    adding, 49–50
    deleting, 51
    guidelines/rules, 53–54
    overview, 45, 48–49
    Page manager qualifications, 51–52
    role assignments, 49
    social media manager, 52–53
affiliate marketing, 246–247
attraction-based marketing, 167–168
B2B marketing
    advantages of, 14–15
    buying decisions, 15
    customer acquisition percentage, 14
    Inbound Marketing Research Report, 14
    personal engagement, 11, 15–16, 25
    research reports, 14
B2C marketing
    advantages of, 11
    fan acknowledgement, 12
    media variety, 12–13
    personalizing content, 12, 15–16
borrowing from others, 583

branding, 27–28
budget decisions, 36
client interactions
    employee awards, 11
    fan acknowledgement, 11–12
    media variety, 12–13
    personal engagement, 11–12, 15–16, 25
    sales links, 11
contests/sweepstakes, 390–391, 399
custom apps, 588
custom list benefits, 590
e-mail capture systems, 337–338
endorsements, 247–248
experiences, 585–587
Facebook Offers, 190–191
Follow button use, 60–61, 167–168
goals
    Ad campaign decisions, 36–37
    budget considerations, 36
    defining, 35–36
groups, joining, 32
highlighting posts, 194–195
Interests list benefits, 592
Life events, attracting attention with,
    171–172
mobile ads benefits, 662
offers, 310, 600
overview, 35
Pages
    advantages of, 67
    invitations to, 32
photo/album sharing, 273–275
photos, use of, 183–186
pinning posts, 195
Places use, 68–70
posting options, 179–180
promotions
    coupons/discounts, 11
    legal matters, 245
    testimonials, 245–246
Q&A sessions, 11
resource management
    administrators, 45
    consultants/designers/programmers,
    45–48
    in-house versus outsourcing, 46–48

marketing strategies *(continued)*
  sending Friend requests, 31
  social media integration, 45–46
  targeting updates, 192–193
measuring activity. *See* metrics; split
    testing
media variety, 12
Mention (keyword tracking tool), 687,
    718–719
Merante Brothers Market
    (Page example), 86
messages
  enabling, 130, 136
  photo sharing, 275
Messages section, Admin panel, 120–121
metrics. *See also* Ads Manager; Insights;
    split testing
  ad sets, 524–526
  adjusting tactics, 732
  Ads Manager versus Insights, 553
  AgoraPulse tool, 724–725
  behavior tracking, 684
  Bitly tool, 717–718
  blog link tracking, 685
  contests
    baseline analysis, 484–488
    re-posting issues, 408–411
    spreadsheet downloads, 485–486
    third-party analytics, 400
    winner selection, 409
  conversion tracking, 550–551
  Crowdbooster tool, 723–724
  feature choices, 715–717
  Google Alerts, tracking with, 183
  Google Analytics tool, 719–721
  Google Keyword Planner, 683–684
  HootSuite tool, 722
  Hyper Alerts tool, 725
  importance of, 682–683
  Insights tool, 728
  keyword tools, 683–684, 687–690
  Klout tool, 727–728
  Like Button plug-in, 613
  Like link benefits, 300
  Likes, 484–486
  Mention tool, 718–719

multiple-site use, 728–729
News Feed algorithm, 178
overview, 44, 715, 717
ROI indicators, 684
Share Button plug-in, 618
Social Mention tool, 722–723
social plug-ins, 608
Sprout Social tool, 725–726
Topsy tool, 727
tracking, 729–731
Microsoft Outlook, e-mail signatures,
    255–256
milestones
  adding, 98–99
  date adjustments, 98
  first milestone editing, 98
  Friends invitations, 99–100
  naming/dating, 99
  News Feed hiding/unhiding, 99
  overview, 97
  photo uploads, 98, 190–191
  posting to past, 188
mobile devices
  ad campaigns
    creating, 665–666
    desktop cost comparison, 666
    Karaoke Heroes example, 666–668
  App Center filters, 332
  app issues, 336
  contest access, 420
  e-commerce store considerations,
      309–310
  Facebook optimization, 656
  Google Analytics, 669–670
  Google versus Facebook, 655
  metrics, 670–671
  mobile ads
    CTR/CPC rates, 662–663
    desktop ads versus, 662–663
    Like count increases, 664
    News Feed displays, 662–665
    Offers, 664–665
    revenues, 656
  optimizing for
    mobile searches, 660–661
    Page adjustments, 658–660

Places Nearby app, 660–661
post adjustments, 656–658
Page adjustments
app use, 659
Mobile Browser use, 658–659
Page Manager app, 661
search optimization, 660–661
testing/checking, 660–661
Page dashboard setup options, 142
Page viewing simulation, 278
Places Nearby app, 661–662
Places use, 68–69
posting adjustments
browser versus app appearance,
656–657
graphics versus text, 658
pinning versus scrolling, 657
region penetration chart, 654
smartphone setup
Facebook app option, 106
iPhone app, 106, 142
Mobile Email account, 105–106, 142
Mobile Web option, 106, 142
smartphone usage chart, 654
streaming video, 651
Mobile Email account, 105–106
ModCloth website, 620
model release forms, 321
monitoring activity. *See* metrics
multimedia, 180, 183
multivariate testing. *See* split testing

N

Namespace, 353
Nanigan's Performance Marketing
Insider, 476
Netvibes website, 687–688
NetworkedBlogs app
blog registration, 211–213
display tab, adding, 217–218
overview, 210–211
ownership verification, 213–214
photos, attaching, 216
reposting blogs, 216–217

syndication setup, 215–216
website, 216
New Page Likes section, Admin
panel, 128
New York Times website, 127
News Feed
autoplay video ads, 603–604
Boost the Post feature, 120
branding value, 180
business Page use, 116–119
custom list filtering, 591
Etsy storefront interface,
313–314
Event displays, 369
Facebook Offers, 190–191
finding your own Page,
145–146
Follow button exposure,
64–65
Group updates, 71
hiding/unhiding milestones, 99
hover card, 90
hover card use, 90, 125, 148, 156
Interests list viewing, 169, 592
Interests Page restrictions, 74
invitations displayed, 101–102
Like button effects, 299
marketing strategies, 119
milestone use, 190–191
note publishing, 152–153
Page invitations, 178
personal versus Page
Profiles, 115
posting metrics, 178
Profile status versus Timeline updates,
177–178
Public icon selection, 166
social plug-in posts, 615
status update postings, 97
Ticker notifications
business advantages, 66
location, 65
Public comment visibility, 66
viewing from Pages, 66
unfollowing Pages, 131
value-added postings, 179–180

News Feed Algorithm
  determination factors, 286
  optimization strategies, 286–287
  overview, 285–286
News Feed store, 308
NFL Page, question use
    example, 283
notifications
  e-mail versus Facebook, 136
  Event reminders, 386
  Events, 370, 372
  Get Notifications toggle, 131

O

Odesk website, 347
Offerpop app
  free trial, 439
  overview, 422
  setting up, 439–440
  sweepstakes creation/setup
    app position editing, 443–444
    CAPTCHA setup, 442
    cover photo/title editing, 444–445
    customizing, 440–443
    Facebook Profile captures, 442
    saving/publishing, 443
  winner selection/notification, 393, 422
offers
  Ads Create tool
    creating from, 599
    promoting from, 600
  benefits, 595, 600
  e-commerce use, 308
  Likes engagement, 499, 595, 600
  News Feed advantage, 310
  Offer Claim ads, 499
  Offer Event icon, 180, 189–190
  overview, 191–192, 595
  Page postings, 317
  Pages
    creating from, 596–597
    promoting from, 598–599
  Timeline pinning, 317

Olo Yogurt Studio website, 616–617
online measuring
  behavior tracking, 684
  blog link tracking, 685
  Google Keyword Planner, 683–684
  importance of, 682–683
  key indicators
    brand awareness, 687
    click activity, 689
    demographics, 690–691
    engagement, 686
    financial return (ROI), 689–690
    influence, 687
    new likes/unsubscribers, 688
    overview, 686
    sentiment, 687–688
    volume, 690
  keyword tools, 683–685, 687–690
  ROI indicators, 684
online monitoring
  benefits, 681–682
  brand-protection strategies,
    677–678
  goals, 681
  importance of, 677
  keyword identification/use,
    676, 680
  social proof improvement, 677
  third-party tools
    AgoraPulse, 724–725
    Bitly, 717–718
    Crowdbooster, 723–724
    feature choices, 715–717
    Google Analytics, 719–721
    HootSuite, 722
    Hyper Alerts, 725
    Insights versus, 728
    Klout, 727–728
    Mention, 718–719
    multiple-site use, 728–729
    overview, 715, 717
    Social Mention, 722–723
    Sprout Social, 725–726
    Topsy, 727

Open Graph
  social plug-in tags, 615
  social proof provider, 307
  web contest entries, 451–452
  website, 615
opt-in strategies, 43–44
Oreo, as B2C example, 12

p

Page Admin. *See also* Admin panel
  administrative dashboard
    apps controls, 140
    Featured Likes choices, 140–141
    Featured Page Owners, 142
    Mobile section choices, 142
    overview, 132–133
    Page editing, 132–134
    Settings section editing, 135–138
  Admins, definition, 138
  Audience Suggestions options, 140
  contests/sweepstakes, 128
  drop-down menu (gear icon), 130–131
  drop-down menu (three dots), 131
  News Feed, 145
  overview, 115
  Page editing, 132
  Page examination
    About section editing, 127
    About section examples, 127
    apps choices, 125–126
    Cover photo setup, 124–125
    Friends check, 126
    hover card use, 125
    Likes visibility choices, 129
    Message button toggle, 130, 136
    overview, 123–124
    Page data (numbers), 127–128
    Profile image scrutiny, 126
  Page moderation, 137
  Personal versus Page Profiles
    liking business pages, 118–119
    News Feed differences, 115, 119
    posting options, 117–118
    toggling between, 115–118, 141, 145
  roles/privileges assignments, 122, 138–140

vanity URLs, 134
view, differences in, 116–118, 122, 126,
    130, 144
voice changes, 119
Page Manager app, 661
Page Tips section, Admin panel, 123
Page visibility. *See* visibility
Pagemodo website, 419
Pages. *See also* Admin panel; Page Admin;
    posting
  About Page completion, 87
  account types allowed, 66–67
  adding cover photo, 87–90
  adjusting Profile thumnail image, 91–93
  Admin panel interface, 85
  advertising advantages, 67
  apps
    adding, 87, 93–96, 148–149
    arranging/managing, 203
    deleting, 204
    installation/use, 67–68, 87, 93–96,
      201–202
    overview, 147
    removing, 148–149
    URLs belonging to, 147
  Artist/Band/Public Figure, 80
  branding considerations, 38–39
  Brand/Product, 80
  business activity generation
    content delivery, 21
    Hubspot example, 21–22
  business promotion opportunities, 66
  category choices, 79–82
  Cause/Community, 80
  changing, 81–82
  clear vision for, 37–38
  Company Pages, 75–76
  Company/Organization, 80
  completing, 86–87, 87
  content creation
    calendar use, 39–40
    calls to action, 43–44
    coupons/discounts, 43
    dialog engagement, 42
    fan community creation/encouragement,
      42–43

Pages *(continued)*
  highlight people, 40–41
  monitoring/measuring/tracking, 44
  opt-in strategies, 43–44
  overview, 39, 44–45
  word-of-mouth encouragement, 43
  core rules for, 37
  correcting mistakes
    Page category changes, 113–114
    Page deletions, 114
    Page name changes, 114
    Profile deletion, 112–113
    Profile migration, 111–112
    Profile name change, 110–111
  cover photo addition, 87–90
  deleting, 114
  drop-down menu, 131
  e-commerce store integration, 311
  e-mail contact invitations
    importing contacts, 100–101
    locating, 102
    overview, 100
    provider-specific instructions, 101–102
    restrictions, 100
  Entertainment, 80
  Events app, adding, 372–375
  fields completion requirement, 82
  finding own, 145–146
  Groups
    advantages of, 72
    supplementing with, 71
    types of, 71
  Help section links, 144
  hyperlinks
    cover photo addition, 88
    thumbnail use, 91
  Info section completion, 81, 92–93
  Insight analysis, 685
  Interests lists, 594
  invitations to, 32
  linking to, 147–148
  Local, 79
  Merante Brothers Market example, 86
  messaging prohibition, 244
  milestones
    adding, 98–99
    date adjustments, 98

    first milestone editing, 98
    naming/dating, 99
    News Feed hiding/unhiding, 99
    overview, 97
    photo uploads, 98
  milestones, adding, 87
  moderation (spam marking), 137
  name changes, 78, 82, 92, 114
  naming, 77–79, 82
  notifications, 370
  official representative requirement, 83
  overview, 60
  personal engagement, 11–12,
    15–16, 25
  Places
    merging with, 70, 108–109
    overview, 68
    physical address, importance of, 70
  privacy options, 136
  profanity filter, 137
  Profile information sharing, 63
  Profile versus, 21, 594
  Profiles with Following versus, 67
  promoting
    social icons, 710
    URLs, 710–711
  public opening, 83–86
    basic description, 83
    Facebook web address setup
      (optional), 83–84
    Favorites, adding to, 84
    profile picture upload, 84
  Publish/Unpublish option, 85–86, 97
  removing, 137–138
  Report Page (rule-breaking), 131
  Share Page option
    Buffer button, 104
    overview, 102–103
    reviewing/editing, 103–104
  Short Description, 81
  Short Description usage, 81
  social icons
    examples, 491, 667
    finding/adding, 259–260
    multiple links, 630
    value of, 710
    WiseStamp app, 258

status update postings, 96–97
subscribing versus, 20
terms & guidelines website, 60
third-party, 201–202
Timeline sharing, 81
Twitter app, adding to
  overview, 240
  Woobox app installation, 240–242
vanity URL choices, 83–84, 134
visibility controls, 135–136
Woobox app, installing, 240–242
Pages to Watch section, Admin panel, 123
Pages to Watch tool, 687
PayPal
  accepting payments with, 310
  Facebook integration, 341
pay-per-click (PPC), 477
Perfect Audience website, 604
personal accounts. *See* personal Profiles
personal Profiles. *See also* Follow button;
    Page Admin
  attraction-based marketing, 167–168
  business account prohibitions, 63,
    368–369
  business activity allowed, 168
  Cover photo choice, 174
  creating, 380–381
  ease of setup, 60–63
  Event invitations
    creating with, 369
    Page Events versus, 380–381
  fake accounts, 63
  Follow button
    advantages, 64–65
    business postings, 65
    News Feed exposure, 65
    overview, 60–61
    sharing versus, 64
  Life events
    business support with, 171
    creating, 171–172
  linking to Pages, 76
  marketing restrictions, 21, 167
  overview, 60
  Page invitations, 260–261

privacy options
  accessing/editing, 23–24
  Facebook Pages concealed, 24
  inline audience selector, 22–23
  overview, 22
  personal information, 62
public posting
  adjusting Timeline for, 172–173
  default settings, 166–167
  examples, 165–166
thumbnail image, 87, 126
View as option, 172–173
photos. *See also* albums
  album promotion ideas, 270–271
  albums, adding to, 272–273
  blog posts, attaching to, 216
  Cover photo choices, 87–90, 174
  cover photo marketing, 270
  e-commerce store use, 309
  e-mail links, sharing with, 275
  Events
    advertising with, 183
    evidence posting, 386
    posting to, 376–378
  impact of, 708–709
  linking to, 184, 324
  marketing value of, 183–184
  model release forms, 321
  Page Cover strategies, 87–89
  Page uploads
    link inclusion, 271–272
    multiple images, 271
  posting, 179
  Publisher, attaching with, 184
  sharing strategies, 273–275
  status updates versus, 183
  tagging, 136
  Timeline Cover strategies, 321–322
Photos app
  ads, using for, 151
  album thumbnail slideshow, 150–151
  lightbox use, 151
  overview, 150–151
pinning posts, 195
Pinterest apps, 326, 333, 340

Places
  claiming/controlling existing Places
    overview, 69–70
    searching/finding, 106
    selecting/verifying identity, 107–108
  creating for Pages, 69, 93
  merging with Pages, 70, 108–109
  mobile device use, 68–69
  overview, 68
  physical address usage, 70
  status updates, adding to, 182
Places Nearby app, 661–662
plug-ins
  Activity Feed, 622–623
  badges versus, 104
  benefits, 607–609
  Comments
    benefits, 623
    Like Button comments
      versus, 623
    optimizing, 624–625
    thread synchronization, 624
    visitor options, 624
  developer URLs, 608
  Embedded Posts, 625
  Facebook-provided, 610–611
  Facepile
    benefits, 628–629
    Login options, 627
    overview, 627
  Follow Button
    overview, 625–627
    Profiles versus websites, 626
  iFrame connections, 608
  Like Boxes
    benefits, 615–616
    Olo Yogurt Studio example, 616–617
  Like Button
    examples, 614
    options, 613
    overview, 611–612
    Share button versus, 617–618
  Login tool
    benefits, 618–619
    ModCloth example, 620
    permissions, 619

  News Feed posts, 615
  Open Graph tags, 615
  overview, 607–608
  Recommendations Feed
    benefits, 620–621
    example, 622
    location of, 620
    News Feed posts, 620
    overview, 620
    settings options, 622
  Send Button
    overview, 627
    Share Button versus, 628
  Share Button
    overview, 617–618
    Send Button versus, 628
  Stay N' Alive example, 609–610
  third-party plug-ins (open-source)
    advantages of, 629
    DiggDigg (Buffer), 631–632
    Shareaholic, 630–631
    WordPress, 629–630
  visibility, 609
Polldaddy website, 28
Posterous website, 214
posting. *See also* Power Editor
  attachment icons, 180
  Boost the Post feature, 120, 194
  Buffer
    Chrome extension advantages, 239
    scheduling options, 238–239
  engaging/retaining readers, 278
  frequency suggestions, 179
  highlighting, 194–195
  HootSuite, managing with, 234–237
  length suggestions, 178–179
  multimedia value, 180, 183
  News Feed metrics, 178
  overview, 177
  photos
    albums, creating/using, 185–186
    attaching, 184
    linking to, 184–185
    marketing value of, 183–184
    Publisher, attaching with, 184
    status updates versus, 183

pinning, 195
Publisher, updating with, 177–178
responding/following up, 168, 179–180
scheduling options
  HootSuite advantages, 236–237
  Publisher choices, 188–189
SocialOomph, bulk uploading features, 238
spam enforcement, 243–244
status updates
  content, finding, 182–183
  links, adding/editing, 181–182
  location information, 182
  Publisher, creating with, 181
  thumbnail images, 181–182
tagging fans, 280–281
video
  formats supported/recommended, 186
  Like button use, 187
  linking to, 188
  size limitations, 186
  status updates, playing within, 187
Posts/Notifications section, Admin panel, 120
Power Editor
  ad set management, 528–530
  ads
    bulk imports, 532–533
    conversion tracking, 550–551
    creating, 530–531
    Excel editing, 532–533
    modifying, 532
    placement control, 549–550
  Ads Create tool versus, 522, 538, 549
  Campaigns
    creating, 526–527
    Excel imports, 527–528
  exporting/importing, 525
  main screen layout, 524–526
  multiple ad/campaign selection, 525
  multiple ads/campaigns
    managing, 533–534
    selecting, 525
  overview, 521–522
  post management
    Ads Create tool versus Power Editor, 534
    creating, 535–537
    Promoted posts, 537–538

secondary screens, 525–526
setup choices, 522–524
target audience
  Custom Audiences, 540–543
  Facebook/Partners Categories, 538–540
  Lookalike Audiences, 543–545
  Saved Target Groups, 545–547
PPC (pay-per-click), 477
Preferred Marketing Developers, 604–605
privacy options
  age restriction choices, 137
  Follow button settings, 64
  Groups settings, 71–72
  inline audience selector
    accessing/editing selections, 23–24
    options, 23
    overview, 22
  Post Targeting and Privacy setting, 136
  profanity filter options, 137
  Profile versus Pages, 24
profanity filter, 137
Profile Pictures album, 150
Profiles. *See* personal Profiles
project collaboration, Group usage, 71
Promoted posts
  mobile device optimization, 662–664
  overview, 471, 477
  reconnecting with, 489
promotions. *See also* contests; sweepstakes
  app administration requirement, 245
  coupons/discounts, 11
  Events
    attendee Share requests, 385
    Facebook Ads, 387
    Friend invitations, 383–385
    restriction workarounds, 381–382
    RSVP reminders, 382
    Share encouragement, 383
    Share links, 385
    Timeline links, 382–383
    Timeline posts, 382
psychographics
  analysis techniques, 28–29
  definition, 28

public figures
  defining, 160–162
  Follow button use, 159–162
  Timeline use, 319
Publisher
  attachment icons, 180
  Events, creating
    photo attachments, 179, 183
    warning about, 189
  links, adding, 181
  location information, adding, 182
  photos, attaching, 184
  status updates, 181
  targeting updates, 192–193
  Timeline updating, 177–178
  video, attaching, 186–187
Publish/Unpublish option, Admin panel, 97

Q

Q&A sessions, 11
Quantcast website, 604
questions, posting, 180

R

random number generators, 413
really simple syndication (RSS). *See* RSS
Recommendations Feed plug-in
  benefits, 620–621
  example, 622
  location of, 620
  News Feed posts, 620
  overview, 620
  settings options, 622
Red Bull, as B2C example
  custom tab, 344
  fun content, 13
  media variety, 12–13
Remember icon, 2
reports. *See* Ads Manager
reveal tabs. *See also* iFrame apps
  overview, 343, 357
  ShortStack example, 345

ReverbNation app, 333, 342
ROI (return on investment)
  brand recognition metrics, 55
  conversion tracking, 550–551
  defining success, 54–55
  metrics tracking, 55
  online monitoring/measuring
    benefits, 684
  overview, 54
RSS (really simple syndication)
  definition, 207
  dlvr.it tool use, 224
  e-commerce store replication, 309
  Facebook import options, 210
  URL discovery
    Firefox method, 208
    HTML code search, 209–210
    Internet Explorer method, 208
RSS Graffiti app
  overview, 221
  setup/using, 221–224
  website, 221
RSVP
  Friend invitations, 385
  notification reminders, 386
  qualifications, 367
  value of, 368, 378, 385
RunKeeper app, 327

S

sales links, 11
sandbox mode, 353
Scribd app, 339
Scribe keyword tool, 683
searching. *See* Graph Search tool
Secure Sockets Layer (SL) certificate, 347
SEM Rush keyword tool, 683
Send Button plug-in
  overview, 627
  Share Button versus, 628
sentiment, 687–688
Share Button plug-in
  overview, 617–618
  Sends Button versus, 628

share of voice, 687

Share Page option
  Buffer button, 104
  inviting Friends, 265–268
  overview, 102–103
  reviewing/editing, 103–104, 265–268

Share Page option, Admin panel, 102–104

Shareaholic website, 630–631

shopping cart, 312

shopping interfaces, 308

shopping portals
  Grandma Mary Show example, 18
  online store, 18
  storefront, 18

ShopTab website, 313

ShortStack app
  custom tab creation, 348
  custom tab example, 345
  fan gating, 315
  overview, 315
  widgets, adding, 360–361

smart lists, 589

SML (Social Markup Language), 360

social apps, 331

social authority, 307

social icons
  examples, 491, 667
  finding/adding, 259–260
  multiple links, 630
  value of, 710
  WiseStamp app, 258

Social Markup Language (SML), 360

social media
  Buffer tool, 238–239
  contest promotion, 399
  Event notifications, 387
  global acceptance/adoption, 19
  HootSuite app, managing with,
    234–237
  integrating strategies, 45–46
  online measuring
    behavior tracking, 684
    blog link tracking, 685
    Google Keyword Planner, 683–684
    importance of, 682–683

    keyword tools, 683–684, 687–690
    ROI indicators, 684
  online monitoring
    benefits, 681–682
    brand-protection strategies, 677–678
    goals, 681
    importance of, 677
    keyword identification/use, 676, 680
    social proof improvement, 677
  Page invitations from, 262–263
  SocialOomph tool, 238
  Sprout Social tool, 239–240
  viral exposure opportunities, 602

Social Media Examiner
  Event advertising example, 369
  smart branding example, 38

Social Mention (data tracking service),
    722–723

social plug-in
  badge versus, 104
  visibility enhancement, 601

social plug-ins
  Activity Feed, 622–623
  badges versus, 104
  benefits, 607–609
  Comments
    benefits, 623
    Like Button comments versus, 623
    optimizing, 624–625
    thread synchronization, 624
    visitor options, 624
  developer URLs, 608
  Embedded Posts, 625
  Facebook-provided, 610–611
  Facepile
    benefits, 628–629
    Login options, 627
    overview, 627
  Follow Button
    overview, 625–627
    Profiles versus websites, 626
  iFrame connections, 608
  Like Boxes
    benefits, 615–616
    Olo Yogurt Studio example, 616–617

social plug-ins *(continued)*
  Like Button
    examples, 614
    options, 613
    overview, 611–612
    Share button versus, 617–618
  Login tool
    benefits, 618–619
    ModCloth example, 620
    permissions, 619
  News Feed posts, 615
  Open Graph tags, 615
  overview, 607–608
  Recommendations Feed
    benefits, 620–621
    example, 622
    location of, 620
    News Feed posts, 620
    overview, 620
    settings options, 622
  Send Button
    overview, 627
    Share Button versus, 628
  Share Button
    overview, 617–618
    Send Button versus, 628
  Stay N' Alive example, 609–610
  third-party plug-ins (open-source)
    advantages of, 629
    DiggDigg (Buffer), 631–632
    Shareaholic, 630–631
    WordPress, 629–630
  visibility, 609
social proof
  definition, 245, 587
  Event support, 386
  Facepile plug-in, 628–629
  online monitoring benefits, 677
  Recommendations Feed plug-in,
    620–621
  social plug-ins, 609
  value of, 307, 587
Social RSS app
  display tab, adding, 219–220
  free versus paid service, 220–221
  installing, 218–220

  overview, 218
  Pages, using with, 340
  posting limitations, 221
  Profile, adding a feed to, 220
  thumbnail image selection, 219
  website, 221
social trust, 307
SocialAppsHQ app, 339
SocialOomph tool, 238
SoundCloud app, 327
spam
  Activity Log monitoring, 143
  page moderation, 137
spam enforcement, 243–244
split testing
  ad copying, 561, 563
  Ads Manager tweaking, 562
  goal assessment, 562
  image changes, 564–565
  landing page changes, 567
  overview, 562–563
  targeting changes, 555–556
  title/text changes, 563–564
Spotify app, 327
Sprout Social website, 725–726
SL (Secure Sockets Layer)
  certificate, 347
State of Inbound Marketing Research
  Report (2013), 14
Static HTML for Pages app
  configuring, 359–360
  free versus paid service, 358
  installing, 359
  overview, 358
  website, 348
Static HTML: iFrame Tabs app
  fan-only content, 363
  image hosting, 361
  installing, 362–363
statistics. *See also* Ads Manager; Insights;
  split testing
  ad sets, 524–526
  adjusting tactics, 732
  Ads Manager versus Insights, 553
  AgoraPulse tool, 724–725
  behavior tracking, 684

Bitly tool, 717–718
blog link tracking, 685
contests
  baseline analysis, 484–488
  re-posting issues, 408–411
  spreadsheet downloads, 485–486
  third-party analytics, 400
  winner selection, 409
conversion tracking, 550–551
Crowdbooster tool, 723–724
feature choices, 715–717
Google Alerts, tracking with, 183
Google Analytics, 719–721
Google Keyword Planner, 683–684
HootSuite tool, 722
Hyper Alerts tool, 725
importance of, 682–683
Insights tool, 728
keyword tools, 683–684, 687–690
Klout tool, 727–728
Like Button plug-in, 613
Like link benefits, 300
Likes, 484–486
Mention tool, 718–719
multiple-site use, 728–729
News Feed algorithm, 178
overview, 44, 715, 717
ROI indicators, 684
Share Button plug-in, 618
Social Mention tool, 722–723
social plug-ins, 608
Sprout Social tool, 725–726
Topsy tool, 727
tracking, 729–731
status updates
  content, finding, 182–183
  highlighting posts, 194–195
  Publisher, creating with, 181
  targeting options, 192–193
Stay N' Alive website, 609–610
storefront. *See also* hyperlinks
  advantages, 308
  apps
    discussion boards, 338–339
    Ecwid shopping cart, 312
    email capture, 338

    Etsy News Feed interface, 313–314
    installing, 314
    iOS issues, 311
    mobile device issues, 342
    overview, 311
    ShopTab interface, 313
    social network apps, 340
    Storenvy interface, 311–312
    video apps, 339–340
    website links, 341
  interface types, 308
  linking to, 315
  offers, 310, 317
  overview, 307–308
  PayPal use, 310, 341
  using featured apps spaces, 308–310
Storenvy website, 311
streaming video
  22Social app
    Google Hangout on Air creation, 644
    installing, 644–647
    overview, 636
  benefits, 633–635
  chat box combination, 634
  Livestream app
    account setup, 637–638
    Be Inspired Films example,
     642–643
    event creation, 639–640
    Facebook Page installation,
     640–643
    overview, 635
  mobile recording, 651
  overview, 633
  partnering ideas, 650–651
  promoting
    live event sharing options, 648–649
    posting in advance, 647–648
    social media sharing options, 649–650
  visibility, 635
Strutta website, 419
SurveyMonkey website, 28, 341
sweepstakes
  contests versus, 389
  Legal requirements, 245
  overview, 393

T

TabFoundry website, 419
Tabfusion apps, 339
tabs. *See also* Facebook Developers site;
  iFrame apps
  adding, 148–149
  App Center, 332–335
  "App Creation Failed" message, 350
  app photo editing, 204–205
  arranging/managing, 203, 342
  custom apps, 94–96, 201–202,
    350, 588
  deleting, 204, 337
  display limitations, 155, 198, 202
  Events, 149–150
  Facebook-built, 93–94, 197–198
  Featured apps, 155–156, 198, 202
  finding/listing, 198, 200, 205–206, 335
  Google+, 340
  Interests Page restrictions, 74
  Likes tab restrictions, 203
  linking from, 200
  linking to, 147–148
  managing/moving, 373–374
  marketing strategies, 337–338
  mobile device issues, 336, 342
  Notes, 152–154
  Page dashboard options, 140
  Photos, 150–151, 204–205
  Pinterest, 340
  Profile use, 331–335
  Promotions requirement, 245
  third-party, 198
  title editing, 204–205
  URLs belonging to, 147
  Video, 154–155
  video apps, 339–340
  visibility enhancement, 601
  website integration, 341
  YouTube apps, 339–340
TabSite app
  blog posts, 221
  custom tab creation, 348
  overview, 316, 363, 420–421

signup process, 423
sweepstakes creation/setup, 425–431,
  443–445
tagging, allowing/removing, 136
target audience. *See also* marketing;
  marketing strategies; News Feed
  Algorithm
  ad strategies, 472–475
  Ads Create tool options
    Behaviors, 513–514
    Connections, 514
    Demographics, 508–511
    Interests, 512–513
    Locations, 508
  attracting/reaching, 1
  behavior tracking, 684
  blog link tracking, 685
  conversational tone adjustments, 29
  custom lists
    existing data use, 541
    hashing, 541
    new data selection, 542–543
  data tracking, 675–676
  demographic identification
    methods, 28
  educating fans, 285
  engaging/retaining, 277–280
  Event targeting, 376
  Google Keyword Planner, 683–684
  identifying/motivating, 10
  Insights evaluations, 282–283
  Interests lists, 592–595
  keyword tools, 683–684, 687–690
  Lookalike Audiences, 543–545
  mobile ads, 662
  mobile user simulation, 278
  Page invitations, 32
  posting schedules, 283–285
  Power Editor options, 538–541
  psychographics, 28–29
  researching, 28, 32–35
  ROI indicators, 684
  Saved Target Groups, 545–547
  searching within Facebook
    filtering strategies, 31–32
    Graph Search tool, 29–30

methods, 30–31
overview, 29
sending Friend requests, 31
smart lists, 589
social media monitoring
benefits, 681–682
brand-protection strategies,
677–678
goals, 681
importance of, 677
keyword identification/use,
676, 680
real-time engagement, 678–680
Tim Ferriss/St. Jude Hospital
example, 679
targeting updates, 192–193
viewing scenarios, 282
target audience, B2C
marketing, 12
targeting updates
status update use, 192–193
target options, 192
Technical Stuff icon, 3
Technorati website, 448
testing. *See also* metrics; split testing
conversion tracking, 550–551
value of, 553
third-party applications
analytics, 400
app comparisons, 418–419
budgeting suggestions, 422–423
contest advantages
analytics, 400
legal considerations, 391, 394, 406
contest app listing, 418–419
deciding factors for use, 418
engagement advantages, 394
examples/tutorials, 419
fan gating, 420
FanPageEngine, 364
finding/adding, 417
Heyo app
custom tab creation, 348
e-commerce store links, 316
e-mail capturing, 338

fan gating, 338, 357–358
overview, 357–358, 421
RSS feed replication, 309
mobile device access, 420
Offerpop, 422
overview, 348, 417
plug-ins, 629–631
rules/guidelines advantages, 391
self-service apps, 418
ShortStack app
custom tab creation, 348
custom tab example, 345
fan gating, 315
overview, 315
widgets, adding, 360–361
Static HTML for Pages app
configuring, 359–360
free versus paid service, 358
installing, 359
overview, 358
website, 348
Static HTML: iFrame Tabs app
fan-only content, 363
image hosting, 361
installing, 362–363
TabSite app, 221, 316, 348, 363,
420–421
Timeline versus, 393
Woobox, 421–422
third-party monitoring tools
AgoraPulse, 724–725
Bitly, 717–718
Crowdbooster, 723–724
feature choices, 715–717
Google Analytics, 719–721
HootSuite, 722
Hyper Alerts, 725
Insights versus, 728
Klout, 727–728
Mention, 718–719
multiple-site use, 728–729
overview, 715, 717
Social Mention, 722–723
Sprout Social, 725–726
Topsy, 727

threads, 624
thumbnail image
  hyperlink use, 181–182
  Like Box use, 617
  overview, 90
  Publisher, creating with, 181–183
  size requirement, 90
  text/hyperlinks addition, 91
  uploading/editing, 90–91
thumbs-up icon, 297
Ticker notifications
  business advantages, 66
  Events, 369
  likes, 298
  location, 65
  Public comment visibility, 66
  Timeline updating, 177–178
  viewing from Pages, 66
Tim Ferriss (media monitoring
      example), 679
Timeline. *See also* personal Profiles;
      posting
  album use
    creating, 323–324
    existing album use, 324–325
    overview, 322
  apps
    Map My Fitness, 327
    moving, 326
    Pinterest, 326
    RunKeeper, 327
    Spotify/SoundCloud, 327
    TripAdvisor, 327
  business versus personal, 60
  Cover photo strategies, 321–322
  ease of setup, 60–63
  Events
    linking to, 382–383
    posting, 376–377
  follow invitations, 320
  followers, checking, 169
  Group updates, 71
  highlighting posts, 194–195
  inviting Friends, 265–268
  life events, 325–326
  mobile device issues, 442

NetworkedBlogs posting, 210–211
  offline connections to, 320–321
  overview, 319
  Pages sharing, 81
  pinning offers, 317
  pinning posts, 195
  public figure use, 319
  public/personal connection, 319
  Social RSS posting, 220
  status update postings, 96–97
  visibility enhancement, 601
Timeline contests
  Ad promotions
    Boost Post option, 411–412
    photo restrictions, 404–405, 412
  administration
    editing, 408
    links to posts, 410–411
    pinning, 408
    re-posting issues, 408–411
  advantages, 391–392, 401
  analyzing results
    AgoraPulse website, 458
    Facebook Insights use, 458–459
  comments, requiring, 396
  Contest Capture website, 409
  ease of running, 401
  engagement advantages, 389,
      394, 401
  entry requirements, 397
  Google Analytics website, 400
  hashtag use, 406
  Legal requirements/restrictions
    basic rules, 397, 402
    Facebook Promotions website, 403
    "share this post" warning, 402
    third-party app advantages, 391,
        394, 400
  Metrics
    re-posting issues, 408–411
    third-party app advantages, 400
    winner selection, 409
  overview, 401
  page settings
    optimizing, 407
    Restrictions warning, 408

Photos
copyright/permissions issues, 404
Facebook Ads restrictions, 404–405
Grid Tool use, 404–405
selecting, 403–404
text addition, 404–405
Preparation
basic components, 403
planning overview, 401–402
Restrictions settings, 408
Rules
important statements, 406
linking to, 405
location for, 409
third-party app advantages, 391, 394, 406
text suggestions, 406
third-party apps versus, 393
winner selection
Contest Capture tool, 412–413
random number generators, 413
Woobox app, 414–415
Timeline Photos album, 150
Tinychat app, 342
Tip icon, 3
Topsy search engine, 727
Total Page Likes section, Admin panel, 127
tracking activity. *See* analytics
Translation app, 20
TripAdvisor app, 327, 333
tweetpages website, 36
22Social app
Google Hangout on Air installation, 644–647
Livestream versus, 637
overview, 636
Twitter
contest promotion, 453
dlvr.it tool use, 224
hashtags, 453
HootSuite, updating with, 234–237
linking to Facebook, 229–234
long tweet linking, 233–234
NetworkedBlogs posting, 215
tweet length limitations, 232
website, 183
Woobox app for Facebook, 240–242

U

Unlike option, 131
updating. *See* posting
URLs
app addresses, 147
app domain name, 353
Canvas Page name (Namespace), 353
click tracking, 685
contest post sharing, 410–411
hosting address, 353
installing iFrame applications, 355–356
link shortening, 685
Page promotion, 710–711
photo sharing, 275
RSS address discovery, 207–210
username (vanity URL)
adding to Facebook URL, 146
advantages, 134
changing business Page name and, 114
overview, 83–84
page removal issues, 137–138
setting, 134
visibility enhancement, 601

V

video. *See also* streaming video
autoplay video ads, 603–604
formats supported/recommended, 186
impact of, 708
Like button use, 187
linking to, 188
posting, 179
size limitations, 186
status updates, playing within, 187
streaming, 633–634
viral exposure opportunities, 602
viral exposure
definition, 14
hashtag use, 602–603
Livestream app use, 602
photo advantages, 14
social plug-ins, 609
suggestions for, 602

visibility. *See also* engagement
  customer invitations
    automatic fan concerns, 263
    card copy mailings, 258
    e-mail signatures, 255–258
    hold messages, 254
    letterhead/stationery, 258
    Profile links, 260–262
    social network invitations, 262–263
    web page icons, 259–260
  enhancement suggestions, 601
  Friends invitations
    Invite Friends option, 264–265
    overview, 263–264
    Page sharing, 265–268
    promotion requests, 268–269
    thanking/rewarding Friends, 269
  overview, 253
  photos
    album cover photo, 272
    album promotion ideas, 270–271
    cover photo marketing, 270
    Page uploads, 271–273
    sharing strategies, 273–275
  social plug-ins, 609
  streaming video, 633–635
Votigo website, 419

W

Warning! icon, 2
web pages
  blogging tools, 216, 221, 223
  Buffer tool, 238–239
  Click to Website ads, 499–501
  contest promotion, 399
  Event promotion, 387
  Facebook integration, 341
  iFrame app options, 351
  Like button HTML code, 302–305
  Like button use, 302
  linking from Cover photo, 90
  linking to Facebook Pages, 504
  Page promotion, 104
  social icons
    examples, 491, 667
    finding/adding, 259–260

  multiple links, 630
  value of, 710
  WiseStamp app, 258
  status update postings, 96
vanity URL, 83–84
Website Conversion ads, 500–501
websites
  22Social app, 636
  AddaRug, 611–612
  Adobe Social, 604
  AdRoll, 604
  AgoraPulse, 348, 724–725
  Alltop, 183, 448
  Antavo, 419
  Band Profile, 342
  BandPage, 316
  Be Inspired Films, 642–643
  Bitly tracking tool, 685, 687
  Booshaka, 43
  Braxton's Animal Works, 712–713
  Constant Contact, 659
  Contact Form app, 338
  Contact Tab app, 338
  Contest Capture, 409
  Crowdbooster, 723–724
  custom tab creation, 348
  DiggDigg (Buffer), 631–632
  digital calendars, 39
  discussion board apps, 338–339
  Easypromos, 419
  Ecwid, 312
  Elance, 347
  e-mail capture systems, 338
  Etsy, 313–314
  Evenbrite, 341
  Facebook Developers, 348
  Facebook online updates, 5
  Facebook Pages terms & guidelines, 60
  Facebook Promotions rules, 403
  fan rankings, 43
  FanPageEngine, 364
  Feedly, 183
  Follow button, 65
  Forum for Pages, 339
  Goodreads, 341

Google Alerts, 183, 687
Google Analytics, 400, 669–670, 719–721
Google Blogs, 448
Google Chrome browser, 522
Google Keyword Planner, 683–684
Google+ account, 644
Google+ app, 340
Group business usage, 72
Heyo, 309, 316, 338, 348, 357–358
HootSuite, 234, 687, 690–691, 722
Humans of New York, 708
Hyper Alerts, 725
Involver, 309, 339, 358–359
Klout (influence-tracking tool), 727–728
Lazypants, 708–709
legal matters, 243
Like Box customization, 104
Like button HTML code generation,
    302–303
link debugging, 183
Livestream app, 342, 602, 635
MailChimp, 341
Mention (keyword tracking tool), 687
ModCloth, 620
Nanigan's Performance Marketing
    Insider, 476
Netvibes, 687
Odesk, 347
Olo Yogurt Studio, 616–617
online surveys, 28
Open Graph, 615
Pagemodo, 419
Pages to Watch tool, 687
PayPal, 310
Perfect Audience, 604
Pinterest apps, 340
Quantcast, 604
random number generators, 413
ReverbNation, 342
RSS Graffiti app, 221–224
Scribd app, 339
Scribe keyword tool, 683
SEM Rush keyword tool, 683
Shareaholic, 630–631
ShopTab, 313

ShortStack, 315, 348, 360–361, 419
Social Media Examiner, 38, 369
social media profile management, 36
Social Mention, 722–723
Social RSS app, 221, 340
SocialAppsHQ, 339
SocialOomph tool, 238
Sprout Social, 725–726
Static HTML for Pages, 348, 358–360
Static HTML: iFrame Tabs, 361–363
Stay N' Alive, 609–610
Storenvy, 311–312
Strutta, 419
SurveyMonkey, 341
TabFoundry, 419
Tabfusion apps, 339
TabSite, 221, 316
Technorati, 448
Tinychat, 342
Topsy search engine, 727
Twitter, 183
video formats supported, 155
Votigo, 419
WiseStamp app, 258
Woobox app, 240–242, 338, 414–415
WordPress, 632
YouTube app, 339
Zillow, 342
widgets, 360–361
WiseStamp app, 258
Woobox app
    e-mail capturing, 338
    fan gating, 338
    installing, 240–242
    overview, 421–422
    sweepstakes creation/setup, 433–439
    Timeline contest winner selection,
        414–415
    website, 240
WordPress
    blog hosting, 214
    Facebook plug-ins, 303, 629–630
    HootSuite app, updating with, 234
    Like button plug-ins, 301, 303
    website, 632

Y

Yellow Dog Project, 345
YouTube app, 339
YouTube video
  contest promotion, 454–455
  finding apps for, 339–340

Z

Zappos, 15–16
Zillow app, 342

About the Authors

Andrea Vahl is a social media consultant and speaker who works with small- and medium-sized businesses all over the world. She has spoken at events such as Social Media Marketing World, SMX, New Media Expo, as well as spoken about how social media is opening up opportunities for women at the World Islamic Economic Forum in London. She has presented at Stanford University and many corporations including Oracle, Public Service Company of Oklahoma, Camp Bow Wow, and more.

Andrea has also worked closely with Social Media Examiner, one of the top-ranked social media blogs in the world, as their Community Manager for over 2 years. She is a regular contributor to Social Media Examiner as a guest blogger as well as other prominent blogs such as Copyblogger, Hubspot, Jon Loomer, and others. She also regularly writes for the new iBlog Magazine.

Andrea has also been a co-author of the previous two editions of *Facebook Marketing All-in-One For Dummies*. She uses her improv comedy skills to blog as Grandma Mary, Social Media Edutainer. Learning social media is way more fun with Grandma Mary. You can learn more about Andrea and Grandma at www.AndreaVahl.com. In her spare time, Andrea continues to develop her comedic skills by performing stand-up comedy in Denver and Boulder as well as slowly running half marathons and other races.

Andrea can be reached at andrea@andreavahl.com. Your comments, corrections, and suggestions are welcome.

John Haydon is a digital marketing consultant helping nonprofits in the United States and Canada. John is also cofounder of Socialbrite, a cross-industry social media consultancy. He is an instructor at MarketingProfs.com, conducts educational webinars at CharityHowTo.com, and is a regular contributor to The Huffington Post and Social Media Examiner.

John has also presented at New Media Expo, The Nonprofit Technology Conference, 140 Characters Conference, and many other regional conferences. You can read his blog at www.johnhaydon.com/.

Jan Zimmerman has found marketing to be the most creative challenge of owning a business for the more than 30 years she has spent as an entrepreneur. Since 1994, she has owned Sandia Consulting Group and Watermelon Mountain Web Marketing (www.watermelonweb.com) in Albuquerque, New Mexico. (*Sandia* is Spanish for *watermelon.*)

Jan's marketing clients at Watermelon Mountain are a living laboratory for experimenting with the best social media, Facebook, online advertising, and other web marketing techniques for bottom-line success. Her consulting practice, which keeps Jan aware of the real-world issues facing business owners and marketers, provides the basis for her pragmatic marketing advice. Ranging from hospitality and tourism to retail stores, B2B suppliers, trade associations, colleges, and service companies, her clients have unique marketing needs but share similar business challenges.

Throughout her business career, Jan has been a prolific writer. She has written three editions of *Web Marketing For Dummies*, four editions of another book about marketing on the Internet, as well as the books *Doing Business with Government Using EDI* and *Mainstreaming Sustainable Architecture*. She has also co-authored two editions of *Social Media Marketing All-in-One For Dummies*. Her concern about the impact of technological development on women's lives led to her book *Once Upon the Future* and the anthology *The Technological Woman*.

The writer of numerous articles and a frequent speaker on web marketing and social media, Jan has long been fascinated by the intersection of business, technology, and human communication. In her spare time, she crews for a hot air balloon named *Levity* to get her feet off the ground and her head in the clouds.

Jan can be reached at books@watermelonweb.com or 505-344-4230. Your comments, corrections, and suggestions are welcome.

Dedication

To my parents, Marilyn and Carl Sodergren, who taught me everything I know about being social, and to my wonderful family Steve, Devin, and Henry, who so generously supported me through this project and as well as the previous two editions.–*Andrea Vahl*

I dedicate this book to marketers everywhere who are in the middle of the biggest sea change, in marketing history. There's never been a better time to be a marketer, and tools like Facebook are rewriting the rules. I hope that by providing you with straightforward, step-by-step advice, as well as sharing my real-world experience in marketing businesses via Facebook, you'll become better at your craft and thereby take everyone to levels in marketing people have yet to explore. I also hope that you keep your Facebook marketing efforts in perspective, and always put family and friends first!–*John Haydon*

In memory of lost family and friends. Thinking of you brings sunshine.–*Jan Zimmerman*

Authors' Acknowledgments

Andrea Vahl: I want to acknowledge my family and friends who supported me through this incredible journey, Steve, Devin, Henry, my parents and my sister and family, and the wonderful friends I've made online and off. I want to thank my incredibly intelligent co-authors John and Jan — I'm honored to be listed on this book alongside you both.

I also want to thank both of my previous co-authors Phyllis Khare, who is my own social media success story connection — you never know where those connections will take you, and Amy Porterfield who I'm honored to call a friend — love watching your success! Thank you to all my online friends, fans, links, followers, and community! I hope to meet you all someday and am happy to call you friends.

Finally, I also need to profusely thank Amy Fandrei, acquisition editor at Wiley and Mark Enochs, project editor at Wiley, for their support and mentorship throughout this process. Also thank you to copy editor Teresa Artman and technical editor Michelle Krasniak for your work on the moving target we call Facebook. Thank you!

John Haydon: This project couldn't have succeeded without the help and support of many people.

First, I want to express deep appreciation for my family, especially Guthrie and Kate, who support my passion for helping nonprofits make the world an even better place. The time spent away from you can never be replaced. I also want to thank the stellar team at Wiley, including Teresa Artman, for her amazing copyediting; Tonya Cupp, for her careful development of the text; Michelle Krasniak, for her superb technical accuracy; Amy Fandrei, who originally reached out to me and continues to hold my hand through the entire process; and finally Mark Enochs, my project editor, who kept me on track every step of the way. I couldn't imagine working with a better team!

Thanks to scores of bloggers, especially Beth Kanter, Mari Smith, Amy Porterfield, Jon Loomer, and many others who keep me informed about changes at Facebook and what they mean for nonprofits and businesses. Most of all, I want to thank Facebook founder Mark Zuckerberg and his team of young entrepreneurs and software developers for their vision in realizing the most popular online social network on the planet.

Jan Zimmerman: The more books I write, the more I realize how much I depend on others. My contributions to this book couldn't have been completed without my wonderful researchers, Esmeralda Sanchez and Patricia Jephson. Ms. Sanchez, in particular, did an extraordinary job researching numerous modifications in Facebook's advertising interface and reshooting art under tight deadlines to make the book as current and accurate as possible.

They both provided background research and rooted out arcane online facts. They checked hundreds of links and reviewed dozens of sites for screen shots and case studies. They both deserve enormous credit for dealing with the constant changes for which Facebook is infamous. Their patience and tenacity are astounding!

Diane Duncan Martin supplemented their services with her usual persistence obtaining copyright clearances. I owe my staff, also including Shawna Araiza, a great debt for giving me the time to write by working overtime with our clients — not to mention their personal and computer support.

As always, my family, friends, and cats earn extra hugs for their constant support. I'm lucky to have friends who accept that I cannot be there for them as much as they are there for me. The garden, the house, the car, and the cats, alas, are not so forgiving. Special thanks to my clients, who teach me so much and give me the opportunity to practice what I preach.

I'd also like to thank Mark Enochs, project editor at Wiley, for his flexibility and good humor in the face of Facebook challenges, and copy editor Teresa Artman and technical editor Michelle Krasniak for their knowledgeable assistance. Together, they have made this book much better than it started out. My thanks to all the other staff at Wiley — from the art department to legal — who have provided support. If errors remain, they are indubitably mine.

My appreciation also to my agent, Margot Hutchison of Waterside Productions. Margot and her extraordinary family continue to teach us, at http://teamsam.com, lessons about what's truly important in life. If you profit from reading this book, please join me in donating to The Magic Water Project in memory of Sam Hutchison at www.magicwater.org. Thank you in advance, dear readers, for making a contribution "because of Sam."–*Jan Zimmerman*

Publisher's Acknowledgments

Acquisitions Editor: Amy Fandrei

Sr. Project Editor: Mark Enochs

Sr. Copy Editor: Teresa Artman

Editorial Assistant: Claire Johnson

Sr. Editorial Assistant: Cherie Case

Special Help: Tonya Cupp, Debbye Butler

Project Coordinator: Lauren Buroker

Cover Image: Main photo © iStockphoto.com/ Yuri_Arcurs; Laptop Screen © iStockphoto. com/Robert Churchill